ENCYCLOPEDIA OF

◇

SCHOOL ADMINISTRATION & SUPERVISION

◇

Edited by Richard A. Gorton
Gail T. Schneider
James C. Fisher

Phoenix • New York
ORYX PRESS
1988

Copyright © 1988 by
The Oryx Press
2214 North Central at Encanto
Phoenix, Arizona 85004-1483

Published simultaneously in Canada

Library of Congress Cataloging-in-Publication Data

Encyclopedia of school administration and supervision.

  Includes bibliographies and index.
  1. School management and organization—United States—Dictionaries. 2. School supervision—United States—Dictionaries. I. Gorton, Richard A. II. Schneider, Gail T. III. Fisher, James C.
LB2805.E53 1988   371.2'003   87-34959
ISBN 0-89774-232-X

Contents

Preface

The *Encyclopedia of School Administration and Supervision* is intended for administrators, supervisors, school board members, and others responsible for improving school administration and supervision. The primary purpose of this publication is to provide useful, summary information about a wide range of topics that hold implications for or describe some facet of the administration and leadership of the schools.

The topics presented in the *Encyclopedia* were selected on the basis of suggestions from advisory committees of school administrators and supervisors, recommendations from professors of school administration and supervision, a comprehensive review of the literature on school administration and supervision, and the judgments of the coeditors. The two criteria used in making the final selection of a topic for inclusion in the *Encyclopedia* were the following: (a) Was it a topic about which people associated with school administration and supervision would be seeking summary information? and (b) Was it a topic for which a knowledgeable author was available?

Contributors to the *Encyclopedia* were selected on the basis of their knowledge of the subject as demonstrated by their writings or experience. They were instructed to give the reader the most important information about a particular topic and to provide recent references for further study. Furthermore, each contributor was assigned a word limit and was advised to be succinct in composing the article. Contributors were also requested to be clear and concise in their writing and to avoid using jargon or technical language. A model article and guidelines were sent to all contributors to provide information about the desired writing style, topical content, and reference format, although contributors were given wide latitude in defining the nature of their topics.

When manuscripts submitted did not meet the previously mentioned standards, they were returned with suggestions for revision. In most cases this process produced satisfactory results. In a few cases manuscripts were eventually judged to be unacceptable and were not included in the publication.

Although the topics in the *Encyclopedia* are presented in alphabetical order, the reader is encouraged to examine the Guide to Related Topics following the Contributor Profiles. The subheadings used in the Guide and the groupings of the topics under particular subheadings represent somewhat arbitrary decisions. Nevertheless, every effort has been made to place together topics which have some commonality and to identify a subheading which seems to reflect the nature of those topics.

Working with more than 200 contributors on nearly 300 different topics has been a demanding but enriching experience for the coeditors. To those individuals whose manuscripts are included in the *Encyclopedia,* we offer our heartfelt thanks for your cooperation and the quality of your contributions. In addition, we are grateful for the efforts of the Word Processing Center personnel at the University of Wisconsin-Milwaukee, and for the patience and support of our spouses as the coeditors struggled to deal with most of Murphy's Laws. We also appreciate the assistance of Art Stickney, Director of Editorial Development, Tracy Moore, Assistant to the Director, and Carol Hunter and John Wagner, Editors, of Oryx Press.

We believe that, as a result of the excellent cooperation and assistance of many people, the final product—the *Encyclopedia of School Administration and Supervision*—represents a valuable resource for anyone responsible for improving leadership in the schools.

—Richard A. Gorton
Gail T. Schneider
James C. Fisher
Department of Administrative Leadership
University of Wisconsin—Milwaukee

Contributor Profiles

Michael W. Apple is Professor in the Department of Curriculum and Instruction at the University of Wisconsin—Madison. He is author of *Teachers and Texts, Education and Power*, and *Ideology and Curriculum*, all published by Routledge and Kegan Paul. Professor Apple has written over 150 journal articles and book chapters.

Lew Armistead is Director of Public Information for the National Association of Secondary School Principals in Reston, Virginia. He is author of *Building Confidence in Education: A Practical Approach for Principals* and *An Organic Guide to School Public Relations*. Mr. Armistead is currently President of the National School Public Relations Association.

Martha Bagley is Assistant Dean of the School of Education and Assistant Professor of Physical Education at the University of Wisconsin—Milwaukee. She is the author of "Leadership Effectiveness Contingency Model: Implications" in *Administrative Theory and Practice in Physical Education and Athletics*, published by Prentice-Hall, and of "Coaching Athletics: A Tort Just Waiting for a Judgment," *Nolpe School Law Journal*.

H. Prentice Baptiste, Jr. is Professor and Chair of the Educational Leadership and Cultural Studies Department at the University of Houston. He is author of several articles, including "Multicultural Education and Urban Schools from a Sociohistorical Perspective: Internalizing Multiculturalism" and "Internalizing the Concept of Multiculturalism" in *Multicultural Teacher Education: Preparing Educators to Provide Educational Equity*, Vol. I. Professor Baptiste is coeditor of the *Journal of Educational Equity and Leadership*.

Lawrence Barnett is Professor of Administrative Leadership in the School of Education at the University of Wisconsin—Milwaukee. He is author of numerous articles and several books and his area of specialization is organizational theory and planning.

James L. Barth is Professor of Education and Chairman of Secondary Education at Purdue University in West Lafayette, Indiana. He is the author of 100 articles and 13 books, including *Defining the Social Studies* (Bulletin 51), published by the National Council for the Social Studies. Professor Barth has received four Fulbright-Hays Lecture/Research Awards and is current President of the Indiana Council for the Social Studies.

Robert J. Beebe is Associate Professor of Educational Administration at the University of Mississippi. His writing has appeared in the *NASSP Bulletin, ERS Spectrum, The Educational Forum, The Executive Educator, The American School Board Journal*, and *Minority Education*. He is former Director of Personnel for the Williamsburg, Virginia, Public Schools.

Barrie Brent Bennett is Instructional Processes Consultant at the Centre for Education in Edmonton, Alberta. He is the author of several articles related to the training of teachers. Mr. Bennett has developed and implemented staff development programs throughout western Canada, making extensive use of video in the training process.

Diane G. Berreth is Director of Field Services for the Association for Supervision and Curriculum Development in Alexandria, Virginia. Dr. Berreth directs affiliates, policy, and governance efforts for the Association.

Frank Besag is Professor of Cultural Foundations of Education at the University of Wisconsin—Milwaukee. He is author or coauthor of 9 books, including *Foundations of Education: Stasis and Change* and *Statistics for the Helping Professions*. He has authored over 100 articles on numerous topics, including recent publications on integration and on the social history of research. Professor Besag has served as a consultant to the Milwaukee Public Schools, the U.S. Navy, and the Wisconsin Council of Criminal Justice. He is also Vice President of the American Educational Research Association.

C. Robert Blackmon is Emeritus Professor of Education Administration at Louisiana State University and Adjunct Instructor of English for South Florida Community College. He is editor of and contributor to the 4-volume *Selected Papers on Values* and author of *Changing Behaviors and Values: The Educational Administrator in American Society*. He is also coauthor of "Does Academic Achievement Make a Difference in Student Teaching?", *Kappan* and "Principals Think They Can Do What Congress Cannot—Abridge Freedom of the High School Press," *Quill & Scroll*. Professor Blackmon is former Director of the Bureau of Educational Research at Louisiana State University and former Associate Editor of the Decatur (Georgia) *News*.

Rolf K. Blank is Research Director for the State Education Assessment Center of the Council of Chief State School Officers in Washington, D.C. He has published *Survey of Magnet Schools*, a 3-volume report of a 2-year national study of magnet schools for the U.S. Department of Education and "The Role of Principal as Leader: Analysis of Variation on Leadership of Urban High Schools," *Journal of Educational Research*.

William E. Blank is Associate Professor in the Adult and Vocational Education Department at the University of South Florida in Tampa. He is the author of *Handbook for Developing Competency-Based Training Programs*, published by Prentice-Hall, and of "A Statewide System for Competency-Based Instruction," *Journal of Industrial Teacher Education*. Professor Blank has undertaken competency-based consulting assignments in Africa, Canada, the Caribbean, and throughout the U.S.

Peter D. Blauvelt is Director of Security Services for Prince George's County Public Schools in Upper Marlboro, Maryland. He is the author of numerous books and articles, including *Effective Strategies for School Security* and "I'm an Educator Not a Cop" in the National School Safety Center's *School Safety Journal*. Mr. Blauvelt is Chairman of the Board of the National Alliance for Safe Schools and Vice President of the National Association of School Security Directors.

B. Dean Bowles is Professor of Educational Administration at the University of Wisconsin-Madison. Professor Bowles is author of over 25 articles and book chapters on administration, politics, and school-community relations, including "The Power Structure in State Education Politics," *Kappan*. He served as Deputy State Superintendent of Public Instruction in Wisconsin from 1981 to 1986 and as Staff Advisor on Education to the California State Legislature in 1965-1966.

Richard F. Bowman, Jr. is Director of Secondary Education in the Education Department at Moorhead State University in Moorhead, Minnesota. He is author of "A Pac-Man Theory of Motivation: Tactical Implications for Classroom Instruction," *Educational Technology* and "Teaching in Tomorrow's Classrooms," *The Educational Forum*.

Norman J. Boyan is Professor of Education at the University of California, Santa Barbara. The author of 2 books and 40 articles, Professor Boyan edited the *Handbook of Research on Educational Administration*, for which he also wrote "Describing and Explaining Administrator Behavior." Professor Boyan served as Dean of the Graduate School of Education at the University of California, Santa Barbara, from 1969 to 1980.

Paul V. Bredeson is Associate Professor in the Division of Educational Policy Studies at Pennsylvania State University in University Park. He is author of "An Analysis of the Metaphorical Perspectives of School Principals," *Educational Administration Quarterly* and "Perspectives on Schools: Metaphors and Management in Education," *The Journal of Educational Administration*. Professor Bredeson is Executive Director of the Pennsylvania School Study Council.

Edwin M. Bridges is Professor of Education at Stanford University. He has authored or coauthored 3 books and more than 50 articles, including *The Incompetent Teacher*, published by the Falmer Press. Professor Bridges is former Vice President of Division A, AERA.

Wilbur B. Brookover is Professor Emeritus of Urban Affairs Programs at Michigan State University in East Lansing. He is author of over 60 books and articles, including "Can We Make Schools Effective for Minority Students?", *Journal of Negro Education* and "Then and Now Perspectives on Educational Research," *American Behavioral Scientist*. Professor Brookover is a charter member of the American Sociological Association and past President of the Ohio Valley Sociological Society and the Michigan Educational Research Council.

E. Joseph Broussard is Head of the Department of Communication at the University of Southwestern Louisiana in Lafayette. He is author of *Writing and Reporting Broadcast News*, and of 62 scholarly articles and 73 research papers, including 17 on high school journalism and scholastic publications. Professor Broussard is a member of the Journalism Secondary Education Division of the Association of Education in Journalism and Mass Communication.

Lesley H. Browder, Jr. is Professor of Educational Administration at Hofstra University in Hempstead, New York. He has written *Emerging Patterns of Administrative Accountability* and *Developing an Educationally Accountable Program*, both published by McCutchan, as well as *An Administrator's Handbook on Educational Accountability*, published by AASA. Professor Browder is former President of the National Conference of Professors of Educational Administration.

Bernard Brown is a Social Research Analyst at the Administration for Children, Youth and Families of the Department of Health and Human Services in Washington, D.C. He is author of *Found: Long-Term Gains from Early Intervention* and "Head Start: How Research Changed Public Policy," *Young Children*. Dr. Brown is Chairman of the Federal Interagency Panel on Research and Development on Children and Adolescents, and was Federal Project Officer for the Head Start Health Evaluation and the Consortium for Longitudinal Studies. His research areas include stress and self-reliance.

Richard Brown is President of Managing, Inc. in Montgomery, Alabama. He is author of "Preparing Principals for Performance Feedback and Coaching Responsibilities," *Record in Educational Administration and Supervision*; "Principal Leadership Training: The Key to School Improvement," *American Middle School Education*; and "How to Become a One Minute Principal," *NASSP Bulletin*. Mr. Brown is former Chairman of the Department of Educational Leadership at Auburn University and former Vice President of Phi Delta Kappa.

Peter J. Burke is Section Chief of School Improvement for the Wisconsin Department of Public Instruction. He is author of *Teacher Development: Induction, Renewal, Redirection*, published by the Falmer Press, as well as of 28 published articles. Mr. Burke was Acting Director of the Wisconsin North Central Association for 1985.

Lee A. Burress is Professor of English at the University of Wisconsin—Stevens Point. He is author of *The Battle of the Books: Literary Censorship in The Public Schools, 1950-1985; The Students' Right to Know*, with Edward B. Jenkinson; and "Ten Reasons for the Recent Increase in School Censorship Pressures," *Elementary School Guidance and Counseling*. Professor Burress is a former Chair of the Committee Against Censorship of the National Council of Teachers of English.

Craig Buschner is Associate Professor of Physical Education at the University of Southern Mississippi in Hattiesburg. He has written numerous physical education articles, including "Role Conflict for Elementary Classroom Teachers: Teaching Physical Education," *Contemporary Education*. Professor Buschner is Chairperson of the Council on Physical Education for Children (COPEC).

Rolland Callaway is Professor in the Department of Curriculum and Instruction at the University of Wisconsin-Milwaukee.

William B. Castetter is Professor Emeritus of the Graduate School of Education at the University of Pennsylvania. He is author of *The Personnel Function in Educational Administration, Budgeting for Better Schools*, and *Public School Debt Administration*.

James G. Cibulka is Associate Professor in the Department of Administrative Leadership at the University of Wisconsin-Milwaukee. He is author of *Inner-City Private Elementary Schools: A Study*, with Timothy O'Brien and Donald Zewe and "Theories of Education Budgeting: Lessons from the Management of Decline," *Educational Administration Quarterly*. Professor Cibulka is Program Chair for the Associates for Research on Private Education (ARPE).

Delbert K. Clear is Chairperson of the Department of Administrative Leadership at the University of Wisconsin-Milwaukee. He is author of the "Collective Bargaining" chapters in the 1983, 1984, and 1985 *Yearbook of School Law*, published by NOLPE (National Organization on Legal Problems in Education).

Bruce S. Cooper is Associate Professor of Education Administration at Fordham University in New York City. He is author of *The Separation of Church & Child*, with T. Vitullo-Martin, and "The Evolution of Training for School Administrations" chapters with W.L. Boyd in *Approaches to Administrative Training in Education*, edited by J. Murphy & P. Hallinger. Professor Cooper is a member of the editorial review boards of *Education Administration Quarterly* and *Education Evaluation & Policy Analysis*.

Francesco Cordasco is Professor of Education at Montclair State College in Upper Montclair, New Jersey. He is author of *School in the Urban Community, Minorities and the American City,* and *Bilingual Schooling in the United States*. Dr. Cordasco is an urban sociologist who has written widely on urban schools, immigrant children in American schools, the equality of educational opportunity, and bilingual education.

Ray W. Cross is Professor of Education at Corpus Christi State University in Corpus Christi, Texas. He is author of "A University and School District Join Forces for Administration In-Services," *Kappan* and "Down from the Ivory Tower," *Principal*.

Jack A. Culbertson is Adjunct Professor of Educational Administration at Ohio State University in Columbus. He is coeditor of *Microcomputers and Education*, the National Society for the Study of Education 1986 Yearbook, and author of "A Century's Quest for a Knowledge Base" in *The Handbook of Research on Educational Administration*. Professor Culbertson was formerly Executive Director of the University Council for Educational Administration.

John C. Daresh is Assistant Professor of Educational Administration at Ohio State University in Columbus. He is coauthor of *The Renewal and Improvement of Secondary Education: Concepts and Practices*, and author of numerous articles, including "Learning by Doing: Research on the Educational Administration Practicum," *Journal of Educational Administration*.

Larry E. Decker is Associate Professor in the Department of Educational Leadership and Policy Studies at the University of Virginia in Charlottesville. He is author of *Home-School-Community Involvement, The Learning Community*, and "Community Education: Common Sense and Democratic Values," *National Civic Review and Citizen Participation*. During 1987-1988 Dr. Decker is Project Director for a new National Project for State Community Education Planning and Development funded by the C.S. Mott Foundation.

Roger J. De Santi is Associate Professor of Curriculum and Instruction at the University of New Orleans. He is the author of 24 articles and 3 books, including *The De Santi Cloze Reading Inventory*, published by Allyn & Bacon. Dr. De Santi is an active member of several professional reading organizations.

Edward John DeYoung is Principal of Barrington High School in Barrington, Illinois. He is author of "Organizational Patterns in Schools: Impact on Teachers and Students," *NASSP Bulletin* and "A Bridge Across the Grand Canyon—College/High School Articulation," *AWSA Bulletin*.

Robert A. Di Sibio is Professor of Education and Chairman of the Division of Education at D'Youville College in Buffalo, New York. He has published over 25 articles, including "Experienced-Based Learning," *Scholar and Educator* and "Team Teaching—A Certitude," *Education*. Professor Di Sibio received the D'Youville College 1987 Faculty Award and is a member of the Society of Educators and Scholars Advisory Board.

Gordon A. Donaldson, Jr. is Associate Professor of Education at the University of Maine in Orono. He is author of "Sysiphus and School Improvement: Fulfilling the Promise of Excellence," *Educational Leadership*, and "Take Charge! Principals Can Create Their Own Professional Growth," *NASSP Bulletin*. Professor Donaldson is founder and past director of the Maine Principals' Academy National Advisory Board and member of NASSP's PSSAS Committee.

Rita Dunn is Professor in the Division of Administrative and Instructional Leadership, and Director of the Center for the Study of Learning and Teaching Styles at St. John's University in Jamaica, New York. She is coauthor of *Teaching Students to READ Through Their Individual Learning Styles, Teaching Students Through Their Individual Learning Styles*, and *Administrators Guide to New Programs for Faculty Management and Evaluation*. Professor Dunn has been elected to the Hunter College Hall of Fame, ASCD National Board of Directors, and the National Association of Secondary School Principals' Professors of Secondary Education Committee.

R. Warren Eisenhower is Director of Administrative Services for Fairfax Virginia Public Schools. He is author of "Analysis of Virginia's Proposed Bargaining Law for Public Employees," *Association of Educational Negotiators Bulletin*. Mr. Eisenhower is formerly Assistant Superintendent, Personnel, Fairfax County Virginia Schools, and a member of the AASA Employment Relations Advisory Committee.

Edmund T. Emmer is Professor of Educational Psychology at the University of Texas in Austin. He is coauthor of *Classroom Management for Secondary Teachers* and *Classroom Management for Elementary Teachers*, both published by Prentice-Hall, as well as author or coauthor of over 30 articles and book chapters. Professor Emmer is co-chair of the Classroom Management SIG (Special Interest Group) of the American Educational Research Organization.

Donald W. Empey is Deputy Superintendent of Instruction for the Glendale Unified School District in Glendale, California. He is author of "The Greatest Risk: Who Will Teach?", *Elementary School Journal*.

Frederick Enns is Professor Emeritus in the Department of Educational Administration at the University of Alberta in Edmonton. He is author of *The Legal Status of the Canadian Public School Board, The Social Sciences and Educational Administration*, and more than 40 articles. Professor Enns was Associate Dean, Faculty of Education at the University of Alberta (1970-1975), and Acting Dean (1975-1976).

Joyce L. Epstein is Principal Research Scientist and Director of the Effective Middle Schools Program at the Johns Hopkins University Center for Research on Elementary and Middle Schools (CREMS) in Baltimore. She has edited 2 books and authored over 50 articles, including "Parents' Reactions to Teacher Practices of Parent Involvement," *Elementary School Journal*, and "Parent Involvement: What Research Says to Administrators," *Education in Urban Society*. She is active in the American Sociological Association and the American Educational Research Association, and is on the editorial boards and review panels of numerous journals.

David P. Ericson is Associate Professor of Philosophy of Education at UCLA. He is author of "Of Minima and Maxima: The Social Significance of Minimal Competency Testing and the Search for Educational Excellence," *American Journal of Education*; and *Predicting the Behavior of the Educational System*, with T.F. Green and R.H. Seidman; and of 30 other articles.

David A. Erlandson is Professor and Head of the Department of Educational Administration at Texas A&M University in College Station, Texas. He is author or coauthor of 6 articles and 10 books, including *Strengthening School Leadership, Management of Change in Education*, and "Language, Experience, and Administrator Preparation," *Planning and Changing*. Professor Erlandson edited *PSSAS Notes* for the National Association of Secondary School Principals, and is a member of the National Commission on Professional Standards for the Principalship.

John C. Esty, Jr. is President of the National Association of Independent Schools in Boston. He is author of *Choosing a Private School* and of numerous articles appearing in such journals as *The Nation, The College Review Board, The Harvard Educational Review, Business Week*, and *Independent School*. Mr. Esty is a trustee of A Better Chance, Inc., Amherst College, and Emma Willard School in Troy, New York. He is an Adjunct Lecturer at the University of Massachusetts.

Nancy A. Evers is Associate Professor of Educational Administration at the University of Cincinnati. She is author of "Change for School Improvement" in *Children's Success in Schools*; *Developing Interpersonal Competencies in Educational Leadership*, modules for use in preparing individuals for educational leadership positions; and numerous staff development materials on individually guided education. Professor Evers is a consultant on district long-range planning and collaborative decision making and former Head of the Department of Educational Leadership.

Patrick Lawrence Farenga is President of Holt Associates in Boston. He is author of many articles about learning outside of school in *Growing Without Schooling*, of which Mr. Farenga is Managing Editor. Mr. Farenga has also published articles and letters in *Manas, Mothering*, and *New Options*.

Roger Farr is Professor of Education and Director of The Center for Reading and Language Studies at Indiana University in Bloomington. He is author of the *Metropolitan Achievement Test: Reading* (1978, 1986) and is a consultant in measurement and evaluation for Harcourt, Brace, Jovanovich, Inc. Dr. Farr is a former President of the International Reading Association and served for 12 years as coeditor of the *Reading Research Quarterly*.

James E. Ferguson is Executive Director of Secondary Curriculum for the Iowa City Community School District. He is author of over 20 publications, including *Student Council Prospects* and *Student Council Activity Resume Book*, both published by NASSP. Mr. Ferguson has been a presenter at conferences and workshops at state, regional, and national levels.

David M. Fetterman is an administrator and a member of the faculty of the School of Education at Stanford University. He is the author of five books, including *Excellence and Equality: A Qualitatively Different Perspective on Gifted and Talented Education*, published by SUNY Press.

Dale Gene Findley is Professor in the Department of Educational Administration at Indiana State University in Terre Haute. He is coauthor of *The Secondary School Principal: Manager and Supervisor* (Second Edition). Professor Findley is Chairperson of the Committee of Professors of Secondary School Administration and Supervision, a Standing Committee of the National Association of Secondary School Principals.

William A. Firestone is Associate Professor of Administration and Policy at Rutgers University in New Brunswick, New Jersey. He is coauthor of "Using Bureaucratic and Cultural Linkages to Improve Instruction: The Principal's Role," *Educational Administration Quarterly* and "Prescriptions for Effective Elementary Schools Don't Fit Secondary Schools," *Educational Leadership*. Professor Firestone has given workshops on school improvement in the United States and Europe.

James C. Fisher is Assistant Professor of Administrative Leadership at the University of Wisconsin-Milwaukee. He is coeditor of the *Encyclopedia of School Administration and Supervision*, and author of "Older Adult Readers and Nonreaders," *Educational Gerontology*; "The Literacy Level Among Older Adults: Is It a Problem?", *Adult Literacy and Basic Education*; and "Participation in Educational Activities by Active Older Adults," *Adult Education Quarterly*.

Thomas John Flygare is an attorney with Sheehan, Phinney, Bass and Green in Manchester, New Hampshire. He is author of 120 articles in the "De Jure" column of *Kappan*. Mr. Flygare is former Vice Chancellor and General Counsel of the University System of New Hampshire.

Patrick B. Forsyth is Executive Director of the University Council for Educational Administration in Tempe, Arizona. He is author of "Toward a Theory of Professionalization," *Work and Occupations; Effective Supervision*; and "The Predominant Gender Hypothesis: Some Evidence," *Journal of Educational Equity and Leadership*. He is the former Coordinator for the National Commission on Excellence in Educational Administration and the current Chair of the National Graduate Student Research Seminar in Educational Administration.

Nadya A. Fouad is Assistant Professor of Counseling in the Department of Educational Psychology at the University of Wisconsin-Milwaukee. She is coauthor of "Vocational Inventories" in *Handbook of Measurement and Evaluation in Rehabilitation* and "Convergent Validity of the Spanish and English Forms of the Strong-Campbell Interest Inventory for Hispanic Bilingual High School Students," *Journal of Counseling Psychology*, and author of "Construct of Career Maturity in Israel and the U.S.," *Journal of Vocational Behavior*. Professor Fouad is a licensed psychologist with a private practice in career counseling and is a consultant to a number of school districts on career education programs.

Richard G. Fox is Associate Professor in the Department of Exceptional Education at the University of Wisconsin-Milwaukee. He is the author of "Social Skills Training" in *Approaches to Child and Youth Care Work*, and coauthor of "Social Skills Training: Implications for Child and Youth Care Practice," *Journal of Child Care* and "The Generic Team Approach," *Child Care Quarterly*. Professor Fox is a trainer and program consultant in the field of emotional disturbance and child and youth care.

Robert B. Frary is Director of Research and Measurement for the Learning Resources Center at Virginia Tech in Blacksburg, Virginia. He is author of "Elimination of the Guessing Component of Multiple-Choice Test Scores: Effect on Reliability and Validity," *Educational and Psychological Measurement*; "A Simulation Study of Reliability and Validity of Multiple-Choice Test Scores under Six Response-Scoring Modes," *Journal of Educational Statistics*; and "Multiple-Choice Versus Free Response: A Simulation

Study," *Journal of Educational Measurement*. Mr. Frary is author of over 30 journal articles, book chapters, and reviews concerning various aspects of educational measurement.

Hugh W. Fraser is Managing Partner of Fraser Associates in State College, Pennsylvania. He is author or coauthor of several articles on the school principalship, the superintendency, and effective schools, including "Administrative Decision-Making and Quasi Decision-Making: An Empirical Study Using the Protocol Method," *Planning and Changing*. Mr. Fraser is formerly Associate Professor of Education and Executive Director of the Pennsylvania School Study Council at Penn State University.

Robert J. Freeman is Traffic Safety Instructor at Carthage Senior High School in Carthage, Missouri. He is author of "Missouri Survey Reveals Strong Driver Ed Support" and "Beyond the Basics to the Edge of Excellence," both published in the *Journal of Traffic Safety Education*. Mr. Freeman is President-elect of the American Driver and Traffic Safety Education Association and Chairman of the Committee on Excellence in Education and Task Force on Standards of the American Driver and Traffic Safety Education Association.

Marvin J. Fruth is Professor of Educational Administration at the University of Wisconsin-Madison. He is author of *The IGE Principal*; "Organizational Incentives and Secondary School Teaching," *Journal of Research and Development in Education*; and *Commitment to Teaching: Teachers' Responses to Organizational Incentives*. Professor Fruth is Director of Implementation and Staff Development Activities at the Wisconsin R&D Center and Director of Administrator Training Programs dealing with special education, inner city principals, and Native Americans.

Mary Hatwood Futrell has served as President of the National Education Association since 1983, having been elected to an unprecedented third term in 1987. Ms. Futrell taught high school business education in Alexandria, Virginia, where she served as President of the Education Association of Alexandria; she is also a past President of the Virginia Education Association. She was a member of the Task Force on Teaching as a Profession which prepared the report, *A Nation Prepared: Teachers for the 21st Century*.

Eve E. Gagné is Professor at Chicago State University. She is author of many publications, including *School Behavior and School Discipline*; "Educating Delinquents: A Review of Research," *Journal of Special Education*; and "Motivating the Disabled Learner," *Academic Therapy*. Professor Gagné is a member of the American Psychological Association and of the Educational Research Association.

Meredith D. Gall is Professor of Education at the University of Oregon in Eugene. Professor Gall is author of 8 books, 30 articles, and 18 teacher-training films, including *Techniques in the Clinical Supervision of Teachers* (2nd ed.), with Keith Acheson, and *Educational Research: An Introduction* (4th ed.), with W. Borg. Professor Gall is a member of the National Publications Committee of ASCD (Association for Supervision and Curriculum Development) and consulting editor for the *Journal of Educational Research* and the *Journal of Experimental Education*.

Cynthia Elaine Gallant is Supervisor at the Staff Development Academy of the Milwaukee Public Schools. She is author of *Juneau Means Business*, published by the Milwaukee Public Schools, and "Staff Development Teams," presented at the National Staff Development Council Convention in Atlanta in December 1986. Ms. Gallant, as Coordinator and Implementor of Juneau Business High School,

was instrumental in changing the school from a traditional high school to a business high school; she is also past President of the Milwaukee Area Business Education Association.

Arnold M. Gallegos is Dean of the College of Education at Western Michigan University in Kalamazoo. He is author of "The Negative Consequences of Teacher Competency Testing," *Kappan*; "Technology in the Classroom: Another Look," *Educational Technology*; and "The Growing Education Crisis in Developing Countries: Conditions and New Perspectives," *Educational Technology*. Dr. Gallegos is past President of the Teacher Education Council of State Colleges and Universities and a member of the NCATE Board of Examiners.

Walter H. Gmelch is Chairman of the Department of Educational Administration at Washington State University in Pullman. He is author of 36 articles, 6 books and monographs, and several hundred presentations on stress and productivity in public schools, private corporations, and higher education institutions. These publications include *Beyond Stress to Effective Management*; *Coping with Stress*, winner of 1984 Education Press of America Award; and *Productivity Teams: Beyond Quality Circles*.

Richard A. Gorton is Professor of Administrative Leadership and Supervision at the University of Wisconsin-Milwaukee. He is author of *School Administration and Supervision: Leadership Challenges and Opportunities*; *School Leadership and Supervision: Important Concepts, Case Studies, and Simulations*; and "School Personnel Policies" and "Teacher Job Satisfaction" in the *Encyclopedia of Educational Research*. Dr. Gorton has also written over 80 articles on a variety of topics related to educational administration and supervision, has collaborated on a national study of the effective principal, and is a recognized leader in state and national administrator organizations.

Richard Paul Gousha is Professor of Education in the Department of Educational Leadership and Policy Studies at Indiana University. He is author or coauthor of "Where We Are and Where We Are Going in School Administration Preparation in the United States," a paper presented to the American Education Research Association; "Administrators Join Revolution in Professional Standards," *The School Administrator*; and "Shouldn't Effective Administration Involve Effective Teaching?", *Educational Horizon*. Professor Gousha previously served as Dean of the School of Education at Indiana University, as superintendent of the Milwaukee Public Schools, and as Superintendent of Public Instruction with the State of Delaware.

Donn William Gresso is Vice President of the Danforth Foundation in Bridgeton, Missouri. He is coauthor of "A Case Study of the Ridgeway IGE Elementary School," prepared for /I/D/E/A, Kettering Foundation, and author of "The Vital Importance of International Education," published in the St. Louis County *Star Journal*. Mr. Gresso is former Superintendent of Schools in the Pattonville School District, St. Louis County, and former principal and teacher in public schools.

Shirley Ann Griggs is Professor of Counselor Education at St. John's University in Jamaica, New York. She has published approximately 25 articles in such professional journals as *Journal of Counseling & Development, Clearing House, School Counselor Journal,* and *Gifted Child Quarterly*; she is also author of *Counseling Students Through Their Individual Learning Styles*. Professor Griggs is a member of the Editorial Board of the *Journal of Counseling & Development* and of the Media Committee of the American Association for Counseling & Development.

Peter Gronn is Senior Lecturer in Education at Monash University in Clayton, Victoria, Australia. He is author of "Talk as the Work: The Accomplishment of School Administration," *Administrative Science Quarterly*; "Committee Talk: Negotiating 'Personnel Development' at a Training College," *Journal of Management Studies*; and "Choosing a Deputy Head: The Rhetoric and Reality of Administrative Selection," *Australian Journal of Education*. Professor Gronn's research interests include leadership, ethnographic case studies, and psycho-biography.

Susan E. Gruber is Associate Professor and Chairperson of the Department of Exceptional Education at the University of Wisconsin-Milwaukee. She is author or coauthor of *I'm A Lot Like You* (Elementary and Secondary Training Series), published by the University of Wisconsin-Milwaukee; "Multicategorical Programming for Special Needs Students," *Counterpoint*; and *Vocational-Social Follow-Up Study of LD/ED Regular Education Students*, published by the University of Wisconsin-Milwaukee. Professor Gruber is a trainer in cooperative learning for the State of Wisconsin and a member of the Supported Employment Advisory Committee for the Wisconsin Department of Health and Social Services.

Walter G. Hack is Flesher Professor of Educational Administration at Ohio State University. He is author or coauthor of *School Business Administration: A Planning Approach; Economic Dimensions of Public School Finance*; and "Fiscal Accountability: The Challenge of Formulating Responsive Policy," *Perspectives in State School Finance Programs* published by the American Education Finance Association. Professor Hack is consultant to several Boards of Education and a State Department of Education, as well as a member of the Editorial Boards of the *Educational Administration Quarterly* and the *Journal of Education Finance*.

Lenore W. Harmon is Professor in the Educational Psychology Department at the University of Illinois at Urbana-Champaign. She is coeditor of *Counseling Women* and the author of numerous publications, including "Occupational Satisfaction: A Better Criterion?", *Journal of Counseling Psychology* and "Women's Working Patterns Related to Their SVIB Housewife and 'Own Occupational Scores,'" *Journal of Counseling Psychology*. Professor Harmon is past editor of the *Journal of Vocational Behavior* and current editor of the *Journal of Counseling Psychology*.

Ann Weaver Hart is Assistant Professor of Educational Administration at the University of Utah. She is author of "A Career Ladder's Effect on Teacher Career and Work Attitudes," *American Educational Research Journal*; "Career Ladder Reforms," *Teacher Education Quarterly*; and "Preservice Socialization for Teacher Career Ladders," *Journal of Teacher Education*. Professor Hart is an officer of the University of Utah chapter of Phi Delta Kappa.

Harry J. Hartley is Vice President for Finance and Administration and Professor of Educational Leadership at the University of Connecticut in Storrs. He served as Dean of the School of Education and has consulted on public budgeting in 43 states. Professor Hartley is author of 46 articles on resource management and the Prentice-Hall book, *Educational Planning-Programming-Budgeting: A Systems Approach*.

Mel P. Heller is Professor and Chairman of the Department of Educational Leadership and Policy Studies at Loyola University in Chicago. He is author of 2 books and 159 articles and book reviews on leadership, curriculum development, and supervision, including *So Now You're a Principal*, published by the National Association of Secondary School Principals. Professor Heller is a consultant to school districts and professional associations throughout the U.S.

Joseph B. Hellige is Professor of Psychology and Associate Chair of the Department of Psychology at the University of Southern California in Los Angeles. He is author of *Cerebral Hemisphere Asymmetry*, published by Praeger Press, and over 50 articles.

Karl Victor Hertz is Superintendent of the Mequon-Thiensville (Wisconsin) School District. He is author of over 60 articles and coeditor of *Schoolhouse Planning* and *Major Topics of School Business Management* for the Association of School Business Officials. Mr. Hertz was also guest editor and author of the introductory article in the May 1984 NASSP *Bulletin* concerning "Vandalism and School Security."

Fritz Hess is Superintendent of Schools for East Syracuse-Minea Central Schools in New York State. He is editor of *Guidebook for School Administrators*, published by the New York State Council of School Superintendents, and author of "Evolution in Practice," *Educational Administration Quarterly* and "The Socialization of the Assistant Principal from the Perspective of the Local School District," *Education and Urban Society*. Mr. Hess was selected as one of North America's Top 100 School Administrators by *The Executive Educator* in 1984 and is past president of the New York State Council of School District Administrators.

William B. Hinsenkamp is educational researcher in the Department of Educational Research of the Milwaukee Public Schools. He is also staff assistant to the Milwaukee School Board and institutional researcher at the University of Wisconsin-Milwaukee.

John R. Hoyle is Professor of Educational Administration at Texas A&M University in College Station. He is author of *Skills for Successful School Leaders*, published by the American Association of School Administrators; "Programs in Educational Administration and the AASA Guidelines" *Educational Administration Quarterly*; and "The AASA Model for Preparing School Leaders" in *Approaches to Administrative Training*. Professor Hoyle is also author of 50 other articles and book chapters, and past President of the National Council of Professors of Educational Administration.

Irwin A. Hyman is Director of the National Center for the Study of Corporal Punishment and Alternatives in the Schools and Professor of School Psychology at Temple University in Philadelphia. He is coeditor of *Corporal Punishment in American Education* and *School Consultation*, as well as author or coauthor of over 80 articles.

Edward F. Iwanicki is Professor of Educational Leadership at the University of Connecticut. He has numerous publications in the areas of teacher stress/satisfaction and personnel evaluation. His recent book, *Teacher Evaluation for Professional Growth and Accountability*, is being published by Kluwer Academic Press. He serves as Editor of the *Journal of Personnel Evaluation in Education* and has been instrumental in establishing the Connecticut Institute for Teacher Evaluation.

John M. Jenkins is Director of the P.K. Yonge Laboratory School at the University of Florida in Gainesville. He is author of *Instructional Leadership Handbook*, with James Keefe; *Curriculum Development in Nongraded Schools*, with Edward Buffie; and "Teaching to Individual Student Learning Styles," *The Administrator*. Mr. Jenkins is special consultant to the Florida State Department of Education on the Teachers as Advisors Program, and was selected by *Executive Educator* magazine as one of the top 100 executive educators in North America for 1987.

Frances Tegarden Johnson is Administrative Assistant to the Superintendent and the Governing Board for the Sunnyside Unified School District No. 12 in Tucson, Arizona. Mrs. Johnson is currently serving as Southwest Director for the National Association of Educational Office Personnel and is also editor for the third year of the Association's national magazine, *The National Educational Secretary.*

Gladys Styles Johnston is Dean of the College of Education and Professor of Education at Arizona State University in Tempe. She is author or coauthor of *Research and Thought in Administration Theory: Developments in the Field of Educational Administration; School As Conduits: Educational Policy Making During the Reagan Administration*; and "Rule Administration and Hierarchical Influence of the Principal: A Study of Teacher Loyalty to the Principal," *Educational Administrative Quarterly.* Professor Johnston was Chairperson of the Department of Management in the School of Business at Rutgers University.

Beau Fly Jones is Program Director at the North Central Educational Laboratory in Elmhurst, Illinois. He is coauthor of "Enhanced Mastery Learning and Quality of Instruction as Keys to Two-Sigma Results in Schools" and "Guidelines for Instruction—Enriched Mastery Learning to Improve Comprehension," both in *Improving Student Achievement through Mastery Learning Programs.* Mr. Jones is formerly Curriculum Developer in Chicago Public Schools.

Ann P. Kahn is immediate past President of the National Congress of Parents and Teachers. She is author of numerous publications, and has lectured extensively on education-related subjects, having travelled over 200,000 miles in 1987 alone to participate in various meetings and to pursue the importance of parental involvement in education. Ms. Kahn currently serves on the national board and executive committee of the Mathematical Sciences Education Board, an adjunct of the National Research Council.

Roger Kaufman is Professor and Director of the Center for Needs Assessment and Planning at Florida State University in Tallahassee. Dr. Kaufman has authored or coauthored more than 15 books and over 80 journal articles. These publications include *Educational System Planning, Needs Assessment: Concept and Application,* and *Evaluation without Fear.* He has served as President of the National Society for Performance and Instruction (NSPI); as consultant to the U.S. Secretary of Health, Education, and Welfare; and as a member of the Secretary of the Navy's Advisory Board on Education and Training.

Edgar A. Kelley is Professor of Educational Leadership at Western Michigan University in Kalamazoo. He is author or coauthor of numerous articles, reports, and monographs, including the *NASSP School Climate Survey* and *Performance-Based Preparation of Principals,* published by the National Association of Secondary School Principals.

Mary M. Kennedy is Director of the National Center for Research on Teacher Education at Michigan State University in East Lansing. She is author of *Poverty, Achievement, and the Distribution of Compensatory Education Services* and *The Effectiveness of Chapter 1 Services,* both published by the U.S. Government Printing Office. Ms. Kennedy is former Director of the National Assessment of Chapter 1, a Congressionally mandated study which has contributed to the 1987-88 reauthorization of Chapter 2.

Ralph B. Kimbrough is Professor Emeritus in the Department of Educational Leadership at the University of Florida in Gainesville. He is author or coauthor of 7 books, including *Educational Administration: An Introduction* and *Ethics: A Course of Study for Educational Leaders,* as well as of numerous journal articles, chapters in books, and published research reports.

W. Hal Knight is Associate Professor in the Department of Supervision and Administration and Coordinator of the Postsecondary and Private Sector Program at East Tennessee State University in Johnson City. He is author of "Theories of Modern Management" in *Contemporary Business Management*; "Educational Reform and Experiential Education," *Experiential Educator*; and "Leader Behavior and Faculty Perceptions of the Performance of Selected University and College Department Chairpersons," *Journal of Higher Education.* Professor Knight is a member of the Editorial Board of *Mid-Western Educational Researcher* and of the Executive Board of the National Society for Internships and Experiential Education.

Constance K. Knop is Professor of Curriculum and Instruction and teaches French in the ESL Program at the University of Wisconsin-Madison. She is author of 6 books, 11 chapters in books, and 20 articles, including *Basic Techniques for Teaching a Second Language* and "The Supervision of Foreign Language Teachers" in *Learning a Second Language.* Professor Knop is past President of the Wisconsin Association of Foreign Language Teachers.

Herbert Kohl is a writer and educator living in Pt. Arena, California. Mr. Kohl is author of over 20 books and 300 articles and reviews, including *36 Children, The Open Classroom,* and *Growing Minds.*

Richard J. Konet is Assistant Principal of Westfield Senior High School in Westfield, New Jersey. He is author of "Developing a Suicide Intervention Program in Your School," *NASSP Bulletin*; "Suicide Intervention in the Schools—A Model Program," *SAANYS Journal*; and 8 other articles. Mr. Konet has given lectures and workshops throughout New Jersey on how to implement a suicide prevention program in individual schools.

Robert B. Kottkamp is Associate Professor of Administration and Policy Studies at Hofstra University in Hempstead, New York. He is author or coauthor of "Secondary School Climate: A Revision of the OCDQ," *Educational Administration Quarterly*; "Teacher Expectancy Motivation, Open to Closed Climate and Pupil Control Ideology in High Schools," *Journal of Research and Development in Education*; and "Organizational Power in Schools: The Development and Test of an Operational Measure of Etzioni's Power Typology," *Educational and Psychological Research.*

Mark A. Krabbe is Associate Professor of English Education at Miami University in Oxford, Ohio. He is author of "Making Lifelong Readers of Our Students," *Arizona English Bulletin*; "Creative Writing: An Entry into Self," *Delaware English Journal*; and "Self-Directed Learning of the Basic Skills," *Clearing House.* Professor Krabbe is Program Director for Secondary Education at Miami University.

Robert D. Krey is Chairman of the Division of Education at the University of Wisconsin-Superior. He is coauthor of *Supervision of Instruction* and *Interdisciplinary Foundations of Supervision,* as well as author of 21 articles, including "The Effect of Teacher Contracts on Supervision," *Kappan.* Professor Krey is President of the Wisconsin Association for Supervision and Curriculum Development and President of the Wisconsin Association of Colleges for Teacher Education.

William J. Kritek is Associate Dean of the School of Education at the University of Wisconsin-Milwaukee. He is author of "Milwaukee's Project RISE," *Educational Leadership*, and "Lessons from the Literature on Implementation," *Educational Administration Quarterly*. Professor Kritek is Special Assistant to the Chancellor of the University for collaboration with the Milwaukee Public Schools.

William Allan Kritsonis is Editor-in-Chief of the *National Forum of Educational Administration and Supervision Journal*. He is author or coauthor of more than 100 articles and 2 books, including *School Discipline: The Art of Survival*. He has served education as an academic dean, superintendent, principal, and classroom teacher.

John J. Lane is Professor of Educational Administration and Policy Studies at De Paul University in Chicago. He is the coauthor and editor of 5 books and has written numerous papers and articles on different aspects of educational administration. Previously a school principal and the national coordinator for Title V programs at the U.S. Office of Education, he now specializes in the preparation of metropolitan school administrators.

Robert L. Larson is an Associate Professor of Administration and Planning at the University of Vermont. His main research and writing interests relate to school improvement and change processes. He is a presenter on those topics for the AASA's National Academy for School Executives and the NASSP's National Institutes for Secondary School Administrators.

Donna H. Lehr is Associate Professor in the Department of Exceptional Education at the University of Wisconsin-Milwaukee. She is author or coauthor of "Legal Precedents for Students with Severe Handicaps," *Exceptional Children*; "Effects of Opportunities to Practice on Learning among Students with Severe Handicaps," *Education and Training of the Mentally Retarded*; and "Instructional Perspectives on Mainstreaming," *Educational Horizons*. Professor Lehr directed federally funded demonstration programs for students with handicaps.

Daniel U. Levine is Professor of Education at the University of Missouri-Kansas City. He is coauthor of *Society and Education* and *An Introduction to the Foundations of Education*, and editor and contributor of *Improving Student Achievement Through Mastery Learning Programs*.

Alfred Lightfoot is Professor of Education at Loyola Marymount University in Los Angeles. He is author of numerous books and articles, including *Inquiries into the Social Foundations of Education* and *Urban Education in Social Perspective*.

Linda S. Lotto (deceased 1987) was Associate Professor of Administration, Higher and Continuing Education in the Bureau of Educational Research at the University of Illinois in Champaign-Urbana. She was author or coauthor of "Access to Knowledge and High School Vocational Education," *Journal of Vocational Education Research*; "The Unfinished Agenda: Report from the National Commission on Secondary Vocational Education," *Kappan*; and *Basic Skills and Vocational Students*, published by the National Center for Research in Vocational Education.

Patrick D. Lynch is Professor of Educational Administration at Penn State University. He is author or coauthor of "Research on Educational Planning: An International Perspective," *Review of Research in Education* and "Father Versus Mother Custody and Academic Achievement of Eighth Grade Children," *Journal of Research and Development in Education*. Professor Lynch is former Vice President of Division A of AERA, and Consultant for the World Bank and Ministry of Education Project in San Jose, Costa Rica.

Mary Ann Lynn is Professor and Chair of the Department of Educational Administration at Illinois State University in Normal, Illinois. She is Editor of *Planning & Changing*, a quarterly journal; Editor of *NASSP Notes*, a newsletter for professors published by the National Association of Secondary School Principals, and serves as one of 11 District Directors for the North Central Association in Illinois.

James Edward Lyons is Chairman of the Educational Administration Department at the University of North Carolina-Charlotte. He is author of "The Higher Education Role in Staff Development," *National Forum of Educational Administration and Supervision*; "A Study of Career Patterns to the Secondary Principalship and Superintendency," *Clearing House*; and "A Study of Competencies Needed in the Secondary Principalship," *NASSP Bulletin*. Professor Lyons has an active research interest in the principalship, principal effectiveness, and school personnel administration, and has served as a consultant in numerous school districts during the last ten years.

Larry G. Martin is Associate Professor of Adult Education in the Department of Administrative Leadership at the University of Wisconsin-Milwaukee. He is author of *Youthful High School Noncompleters: Enhancing Opportunities for Employment and Education*; "Life-Style Classifications of Adult School Noncompleters," *Adult Education Quarterly*; and "Chapter 8: Stigma: A Social Learning Perspective" in *The Dilemma of Difference: A Multidisciplinary View of Stigma*. Professor Martin is Chair of the Steering Committee of the National Adult Education Research Conference and President of the Milwaukee Council for Adult Learning.

Laura M. W. Martin is Research Scientist at the Bank Street College of Education in New York City. She is author of "Teachers' Adoption of Multimedia Technologies for Science and Mathematics Instruction" and "Preparing Urban Teachers for the Technological Future," both in *Mirrors of Minds: Patterns of Experience in Educational Computing*. Ms. Martin is Research Director of the Mathematics, Science and Technology Teacher Education Project.

Francine Marie Martinez is University Psychologist at the University of Colorado in Boulder. She is author of "A Cross-Cultural Examination of Behavior Intervention Preferences of Teachers, Parents, and Children," her unpublished dissertation. Dr. Martinez is Editor of *SIGUE*, the Newsletter of the Hispanic Special Interest Group of AERA, and Colorado Representative of the National Hispanic Psychological Association.

Eileen McCarthy is Director of Special Education for Rockland County, New York. She is author of many books and articles on people services, including *Research and Field Practices in Special Education Administration* and "Supervision in Special Education" in the *Encyclopedia of Special Education*. Ms. McCarthy is a former professor of Educational Administration at the University of Wisconsin—Madison and President-elect of the Council for Exceptional Children in the Southern Region of New York State.

Martha McCarthy is Professor of Education and Director of the Consortium on Educational Policy Studies at Indiana University. She has authored or coauthored several books, including *Public School Law: Teachers' and Students' Rights, What, Legally, Constitutes an Adequate Education?*, and *A Delicate Balance: Church, State and the Schools*. Professor McCarthy has also written over 100 articles and made numerous presentations regarding various aspects of students' and teachers' rights, church-state relations, equity issues, and characteristics of students and faculty in administrative preparation programs. She has served as President of the National Organization on Legal Problems of Education and the University Council for Educational Administration.

Lloyd E. McCleary is Professor in the Department of Educational Administration at the University of Utah. He is author of 7 books and over 100 articles and papers, including *Educational Administration Today*, "Locating Principals Who Are Leaders: The Assessment Center Concept," *Educational Considerations*; and "Evaluation for the Administrator: The Case for a Course," *Teaching Education*. Professor McCleary is Academic Specialist for the U.S. Department of State and Associate Director of the National Principal Study for the National Association of Secondary School Principals.

Kathleen McCormick is a free-lance writer in Washington, D.C. She is a former Associate Editor of *The American School Board Journal* and *The Executive Educator*. Ms. McCormick also has written about education for *USA Today*, *Changing Times*, and other newspapers and magazines.

Kenneth E. McIntyre is Professor Emeritus of Educational Administration at the University of Texas, Austin. He is author or coauthor of "What Research Says to the Assistant Principal Concerning Teacher Evaluation: Helping Teachers to Improve," *NASSP AP Special*; *In-Service Education: A Guide to Better Practice*; and *In-Service Education: Materials for Laboratory Sessions*.

Kenneth H. McKinley is Professor and Associate Dean of Education Research and Projects in the College of Education at Oklahoma State University in Stillwater. He is author of *Alternate Instructional Delivery Systems for Rural, Small Schools*, a report for the Joint School Finance Committee of the 40th Oklahoma Legislature; *How Well Do Oklahoma's Rural and Small Schools Prepare Graduates for Higher Education?*, Oklahoma Education Research Symposium IV; and *Teacher Professional Identity and Job-Leaving Inclination in Oklahoma*, Oklahoma State Department of Education. Professor McKinley has published numerous other reports and articles relevant to rural education, Indian education, and international technical assistance.

John Donald McNeil is Professor of Education at the University of California, Los Angeles. He is author of 36 books and more than 200 articles, including *Curriculum: A Comprehensive Introduction* and *Reading Comprehension: New Directions for Classroom Practice*. Professor McNeil is President of the California Educational Research Association.

R. Bruce McPherson is Director of the North Carolina Center for the Advancement of Teaching at Western Carolina University in Cullowhee, North Carolina. He is coauthor of *Managing Uncertainty*, and "State Board Desegregation Policy: An Application of the Problem—Finding Model of Policy Analysis," *Educational Administration Quarterly*.

George E. Melton is Deputy Executive Director of the National Association of Secondary School Principals in Reston, Virginia.

Arlene T. Metha is Associate Professor of Counseling Psychology at Arizona State University in Tempe. She is author of 20 journal articles. Her research has focused on several issues related to sex equity in education, in particular sexual harassment and affirmative action. Her recent research includes two major themes: adolescent suicide and life regrets and priorities of adult men and women. Professor Metha is Associate Editor of the *Journal of Educational Equity and Leadership*.

Mary Louise Mickler is Professor of Administration Educational Leadership at the University of Alabama. She is author of "Accountability: Perceptual Changes over a Decade," *Educational Horizons*; "Viewing Accountability from the Top," *Educational Horizons*; and "Conversations with Ralph W. Tyler" (Parts I & II), *The Forum*. Professor Mickler is author of 12 articles, 8 grant publications, and 4 videotape publications.

Mary Oellerich Dalnoki Miklos is Professor of Mathematics and Science Education at Georgia Southwestern College in Americus. She is author of *Mathematics Competencies for Teachers of Early Childhood*, *Mathematics Competencies for Teachers of Middle Grades*, and *Competencies for Teachers of High School Mathematics*, all published by MM Publications.

Chuck Miles is Manager of Computer Based Training at Johnson Controls in Milwaukee, Wisconsin. He is author of "Energy Management Systems: Why and How They Work," *School Business Affairs*; "Which One's for Me?" *Data Training Magazine*; and "Planning Your Next Off-Site Seminar," *Training & Development Journal*.

Richard Dwight Miller is Executive Director of the American Association of School Administrators in Arlington, Virginia.

Douglas E. Mitchell is Professor of Education at the University of California, Riverside. He is author of 4 books and over 75 articles, including *Work Orientation and Job Performance* and "Authority, Power and The Legitimation of Social Control," *Educational Administration Quarterly*. Professor Mitchell is past President of the Politics of Education Association.

JoAnne Ellen Neil Moore is research assistant for Detroit Public Schools and adjunct faculty member in the College of Education at Wayne State University in Detroit. Dr. Moore is President Elect of the Michigan Educational Research Association and Vice President of the Wayne State University Chapter of Phi Delta Kappa.

Ivan D. Muse is Professor in the Department of Educational Leadership at Brigham Young University in Provo, Utah. He is coauthor of *One-Teacher Schools in America*, published by the Clearinghouse on Rural Education and Small Schools, and of "Teachers in the Nation's Surviving One-Room Schools," *Contemporary Education*. Professor Muse has conducted numerous presentations and workshops and has served as a consultant to various school districts.

Frank E. Nardine is Associate Professor of Educational Psychology at the University of Wisconsin-Milwaukee. He is author of "The Development of Competence" in *Psychology & Educational Practice*, and coauthor of "Social Interaction and Social Literacy" in *Literacy Through Family, Community & School Interaction*. His research includes the study of competence acquisition, parent-child interaction, and family members' perceptions of favoritism.

Neal C. Nickerson, Jr. is Professor of Educational Administration at the University of Minnesota in Minneapolis. He is a frequent contributor to the *NASSP Bulletin* and a member of the NASSP team studying middle-level principals. He has been a principal, assistant principal, and assistant headmaster in public and private schools. Professor Nickerson is a member of the NASSP Assistant Principal Council and Director of the Minnesota Principal Assessment Center.

Betty W. Nyangoni is Chief Attendance Officer in the District of Columbia Public Schools and an adjunct faculty member in the Department of Counseling and Education at Trinity College in Washington, D.C. She has written over 30 articles on wide-ranging topics in education and has conducted over 100 workshops, seminars, symposia, interviews, and oral presentations related to school attendance, truancy, and compulsory school laws.

Allan R. Odden is Associate Professor and Director of the Southern California Policy Analysis for California Education (PACE) Center at the University of Southern California in Los Angeles. He is author of "A School Finance Research Agenda for an Era of Education Reform," *Journal of Education Finance.* Professor Odden is former President of the American Education Finance Association. His areas of specialty are school finance, education policy, and program implementation.

Peter F. Oliva is Professor and Head of the Department of Educational Leadership and Research at Georgia Southern College in Statesboro. He is author of over 40 articles, monographs, and miscellaneous publications, including *Developing the Curriculum* and *Supervision for Today's Schools.* Professor Oliva has been a member of the faculty of the University of Florida, Indiana State University, Southern Illinois University and Florida International University.

Donald C. Orlich is Professor of Education and Science Instruction at Washington State University in Pullman. He is author or coauthor of *Teaching Strategies: A Guide to Better Instruction; Findings from Inservice Education Research to Elementary School Teaching*; and "Federal Educational Policy: The Paradox of Innovation and Centralization," *Educational Researcher.* Professor Orlich is past President of the Washington Science Teachers Association and of the Washington Educational Research Association.

Allan C. Ornstein is Professor of Education at Loyola University in Chicago. Dr. Ornstein is author of more than 300 articles and 20 texts, including *Curriculum: Foundations, Principles, and Issues* and *Introduction to the Foundations of Education.* He has been consultant to more than 40 government and education agencies.

Robert G. Owens is Distinguished Research Professor of Administration and Policy Studies at Hofstra University in Hempstead, New York. He is author of *Organizational Behavior in Education* and coauthor of *Administering Change in Schools.*

Ralph I. Parish is Associate Professor in the Division of Educational Administration at the University of Missouri-Kansas City. He is author of 18 publications relating to change, including *Discontinuation of Innovations*, ASCD; "We Do Not Make Change," *Metropolitan Education*; and "We're Making the Same Mistakes: Myth & Legend in School Improvement," *Planning & Changing.*

Forrest W. Parkay is Associate Professor in the Department of Educational Leadership at the University of Florida. He is coeditor of *Quest for Quality: Improving Basic Skills Instruction in the 1980s* as well as author of *White Teacher, Black School: The Professional Growth of a Ghetto Teacher* and more than 30 articles in professional journals. Dr. Parkay also has an appointment to the Research and Development Center on School Improvement at the University of Florida.

Leonard O. Pellicer is Professor of Educational Administration and Chairman of the Department of Educational Leadership and Policies at the University of South Carolina in Columbia. He is the author of more than 30 articles in professional journals, including "Increasing the Effectiveness of the Personal Interview for Teacher Selection Through the Use of the Structured Approach," *Educational Leadership* and "Job Satisfaction: Its Impact Upon Teacher Atten-

dance," *NASSP Bulletin.* Professor Pellicer is currently chairing the national study of the secondary school principalship under the sponsorship of the National Association of Secondary School Principals.

William Hilmer Peters is Professor of English Education and Head of the Department of Educational Curriculum and Instruction at Texas A&M University in College Station. He is author or coauthor of *Effective English Teaching: Concept, Research, and Practice*; "Future Research in English Education: Some Modest Proposals," *English Education*; and "Teacher Intellectual Disposition and Cognitive Classroom Verbal Reactions," *The Journal of Educational Research.* Professor Peters is Chair of the Conference on English Education, Commission on Research in Teacher Effectiveness of the National Council of Teachers of English.

William H. Pichette is Associate Professor of the School of Library Science at Sam Houston State University in Huntsville, Texas. He is author of "The Evaluation and Professional Growth of School Library Media Specialists," *NASSP Bulletin.* Dr. Pichette formerly served as the Library Supervisor for the Wisconsin Department of Public Instruction.

Lester A. Picker is President of the Pyramid Group in Elkton, Maryland. He is author of "Human Sexuality Education: Implications for Biology Teaching," *The American Biology Teacher.* Mr. Picker is a former faculty member at the University of Maine and the University of Delaware.

William T. Pink is Associate Dean of the Graduate School of Education at the National College of Education in Chicago. He is author of *Schooling in Social Context*, as well as "Academic Failure, Student Social Conflict, and Delinquent Behavior" and "Student Suspension: A Critical Reappraisal," both in *The Urban Review.* Professor Pink is Editor of the *Urban Review* and Research Consultant for the Center for Policy Research in Education (CPRE).

Richard S. Podemski is Associate Dean for Instructional Programs at the University of Alabama. He is senior author of *Comprehensive Administration of Special Education*, published by Aspen Systems Corporation, and author of over 40 articles on a variety of issues in educational administration. Professor Podemski is a former member of the Executive Committee of the University Council for Educational Administration and is currently a member of the Task Force on Administrator Preparation of the Association for the Accreditation of Teacher Education (AACTE).

Linda M. Post is Associate Professor in Curriculum and Instruction at the University of Wisconsin-Milwaukee. She is author of "Individualizing Instruction in the Middle School," *Clearing House* and "Mainstreaming in Secondary Schools: How Successful Are Plans to Implement the Concept?", *National Association of Secondary School Principals Bulletin.*

Diana G. Pounder is Assistant Professor of Educational Administration at Louisiana State University in Baton Rouge. She is author of "The Challenge for School Leaders: Attracting and Retaining Good Teachers" in *Instructional Leadership: Concepts and Controversies*, and "The Male/Female Salary Differential for School Administrators: Implications for Career Patterns and Placement of Women," *Educational Administration Quarterly.* Dr. Pounder's professional background includes 10 years of experience in public schools as a teacher, guidance counselor, and middle school principal.

Robb E. Rankin is Principal of Granby Elementary School in Granby, Colorado. He is coauthor of *The Principalship: Concepts, Competencies, and Cases*, published by Longman. In 1987, he was an International Teaching Fellow in Victoria, Australia in the position of Acting Principal, Lalor East Primary School.

A. Jean Renfro is Education Coordinator of the Alcohol and Drug Council of Middle Tennessee in Nashville. She is author of "Mission Possible: Adolescents Do Not Have To Self-Destruct," *Educational Horizons*. Ms. Renfro provides workshops and in-service programs to school personnel on topics such as chemical dependency and the family, adolescent signs and symptoms, children of alcoholics, effects of drug use/abuse on the classroom environment and the school as a whole, prevention activities for classroom use, and ways in which the teacher and the school can respond effectively to drug use/abuse.

James A. Rentmeester is Employee Assistant Consultant with the Wisconsin Department of Health and Social Services.

Cecil R. Reynolds is Professor of Educational Psychology at Texas A&M University in College Station. He is editor of the *Encyclopedia of Special Education*, and author of "Critical Measurement Issues in Learning Disabilities," *Journal of Special Education*. Professor Reynolds is President of the National Academy of Neuropsychologists and author of more than 200 journal articles.

Alan Riedesel is Professor of Learning and Instruction at the State University of New York at Buffalo. He is author of over 50 articles and 8 books, including *Coping with Computers in the Elementary and Middle Schools*, published by Prentice-Hall, and *Solve It* (problem solving software), published by SUNBURST. He has developed computer-assisted instruction materials for the past 20 years and directed the Software Evaluation Project at SUNY/Buffalo.

Fred Rodriguez is Associate Professor of Education at the University of Kansas in Lawrence. He is author of *Equity Education: An Imperative for Effective Schools*. Professor Rodriguez is Director of the Upward Bound Program at the University of Kansas. He has written numerous articles and books in the area of equity education.

Lowell C. Rose is Executive Secretary of Phi Delta Kappa International in Bloomington, Indiana. He has also served as Executive Secretary of the Indiana School Boards Association and Associate Professor of Education at Indiana University. Dr. Rose was Superintendent of Schools for the Kokomo-Center Township (Indiana) Consolidated School Corporation, and taught social studies in various senior and junior high schools.

Barak Rosenshine is Professor of Educational Psychology at the University of Illinois in Champaign-Urbana. He is coeditor of *Talks to Teachers*, and author or coauthor of "Teaching Functions" in *Handbook of Research on Teaching*; "Explicit Teaching," *Educational Leadership*; and "Unsolved Issues in Teaching Content," *Teaching and Teacher Education*. Professor Rosenshine is the winner of the 1984 award for best article interpreting research into practice awarded by the American Educational Research Association.

Samuel G. Sava is Executive Director of the National Association of Elementary School Principals in Alexandria, Virginia. He is the author of *Learning Through Discovery for Young Children* and of numerous articles in such journals as *Saturday Review* and *Creative Living*. Mr. Sava has been Director of Research for the U.S. Office of Education, Vice President for Education with the Charles F. Kettering Foundation, and Senior Vice President with the Charles Stewart Mott Foundation.

Anthony Saville is Professor of Educational Administration and Higher Education at the University of Nevada, Las Vegas. He is author or coauthor of *Instructional Programming: Issues and Innovations in School Scheduling, The Will of the People: Education in Nevada*, and "Programming Advice for the School Schedule," *Clearing House*. Professor Saville is Chair of the Board of Directors of the Southwest Educational Research Laboratory in Los Alamitos, California.

Richard W. Saxe is Professor of Administration and Supervision at the University of Toledo in Toledo, Ohio. He is author of over 50 articles and books including *School Community Relations in Transition, Educational Administration Today*, and "Interest Groups in Education," *Education and Urban Society*. Professor Saxe is Chairman of the Committee on Higher Relationships of the American Association of School Administrators.

Richard A. Schmuck is Professor of Educational Psychology and Administration at the University of Oregon. He is author of 145 articles and 15 books, including *Group Processes in the Classroom*, now in its 5th edition, published by William C. Brown. He is Associate Dean of the University of Oregon's College of Education.

Gail Thierbach Schneider is Associate Dean of the School of Education and Associate Professor of Educational Administration at the University of Wisconsin-Milwaukee. She is author of "Schools and Merit: An Empirical Study of Attitude of School Board Members, Administrators, and Teachers Toward Merit Systems," *Planning and Changing*; "Teacher Involvement in Program Planning," *Educational Horizons*; and "The Myth of Curvilinearity: An Analysis of Decision-Making Involvement and Job Satisfaction," *Planning and Changing*.

Jack H. Schuster is Professor of Education and Public Policy and Head of the Graduate Program in Higher Education at The Claremont Graduate School in Claremont, California. Dr. Schuster is coauthor of *American Professors: A National Resource Imperiled*, which received the Association of American Colleges' Frederick Ness Book Award in 1986. Dr. Schuster's article, "The Politics of Education in a New Era," received a Distinguished Achievement Award from the Educational Press Association of America. Dr. Schuster has lectured extensively in the U.S. and in addition has presented a series of eight lectures on higher education administration at Nanjing University in the People's Republic of China.

Robert C. Serow is Associate Professor in the Department of Educational Leadership and Program Evaluation at North Carolina State University in Raleigh. He is author of *Schooling for Social Diversity: An Analysis of Policy and Practice*; "Credentialism and Academic Standards: The Evolution of High School Graduation Requirements," *Issues in Education*; and numerous articles on minimum competency testing. Professor Serow is a member of the Editorial Board of *Educational Studies*.

Albert Shanker is President of the American Federation of Teachers in Washington, D.C. He is author of a weekly column in the Sunday *New York Times* entitled "Where We Stand," and of numerous journal, magazine, and newspaper articles. Mr. Shanker is a member of the National Academy of Education and a member of the Carnegie Task Force on Teaching as a Profession.

Thomas A. Shannon, an educator and an attorney, is Executive Director of the National School Boards Association and Executive Publisher of *The American School*

Board Journal, The Executive Educator, and *School Board News.* He also is a Visiting Professor of Educational Administration at the University of Virginia and an Advisory Commissioner of the Education Commission of the States.

Robert C. Shaw is Professor of Educational Administration at the University of Missouri in Columbia and State Director of the Missouri North Central Association of Colleges and Schools. He is author of "Do's and Don't's for Dealing with the Press," "Enrollment Forecasting: What Methods Work Best?", "High School Graduation Requirements—From Whence Did They Come?", all published in the *National Association of Secondary School Principals Bulletin.* Professor Shaw is President of the State Superintendents Association and Treasurer of the Mid-Continent Regional Educational Laboratories.

William R. Shirer is Director of Pupil Services and Instruction for the Mosinee (Wisconsin) School District. He is author or coauthor of "A Practical Approach to School Improvement," *Educational Leadership;* "Why Accreditation is Important," *North Central Association Quarterly;* and School Evaluation Procedures at the University of Wisconsin-Madison. Mr. Shirer is former Deputy Director of School Evaluation Services at the University of Wisconsin-Madison and former Chairperson of the Committee on Theory and Practice of School Evaluation at the North Central Association.

John P. Sikula is Dean of the Graduate School of Education at California State University, Long Beach. He is Associate Editor of the *Handbook of Research on Teacher Education,* and Editor of the Tenth-Year Anniversary issue of *Action in Teacher Education.* He is author of 8 books and monographs and more than 150 miscellaneous educational publications including some 60 journal articles in 35 different journals. Professor Sikula is President-Elect of the National Association of Teacher Educators.

Paula F. Silver (deceased 1987) was Professor in the Department of Administration, Higher and Continuing Education at the University of Illinois in Champaign-Urbana. She was author of *Educational Administration: Theoretical Perspectives of Practice and Research* and more than 50 articles and technical reports. She also served as editor of 3 books and journals. Professor Silver was Associate Director of the University Council for Educational Administration and at the time of her death was President-elect of the Council.

Ronald P. Simpson is Administrator and Secondary Magnet School Program Manager for Kansas City Missouri Public Schools. He served Milwaukee public high schools for 19 years as a teacher, assistant principal, and principal. Dr. Simpson was also an adjunct instructor at the University of Wisconsin—Milwaukee, where he taught the introductory graduate course in administrative leadership.

Paul T. Sindelar is Head of the Department of Special Education at Florida State University in Tallahassee. He is author of "The Effects of Group Size and Instructional Method on the Acquisition of Mathematical Concepts by Fourth Graders," *Journal of Educational Research;* "Teacher Effectiveness in Special Education Programs," *Journal of Special Education;* and "The Effects of Lesson Format on the Acquisition of Mathematical Concepts by Fourth Graders," *Journal of Educational Research.* Professor Sindelar is Chairperson of the Higher Education Consortium for Special Education.

Barbara A. Sizemore is Associate Professor in the Department of Black Community Education Research and Development at the University of Pittsburgh. She is author of "The Limits of the Black Superintendency: A Review of the Literature," *Journal of Educational Equity and Leadership; The Ruptured Diamond: The Politics of the Decentralization of the District of Columbia Public Schools;* and over 50 other articles on Black education. Professor Sizemore is former Superintendent of Schools in Washington, D.C.

Erling Skorpen is Professor and Chair of the Department of Philosophy at the University of Maine in Orono. He is author of "Making Sense of Kant's Third Example," *Kant-Studien;* "Moral Education: Its Historical and Phenomenological Foundations," *The Educational Forum;* and "The Art of Socratic Thinking" in *Thinking Skills: Concepts and Techniques.* Professor Skorpen is Consulting Editor for the *Journal for the Theory of Social Behavior.*

Christine E. Sleeter is Associate Professor at the University of Wisconsin-Parkside. She is coauthor of *After the School Bell Rings;* "An Analysis of Multicultural Education in the U.S.A.," *Harvard Educational Review;* and "Race, Class and Gender in an Urban School: A Case Study," *Urban Education.* Professor Sleeter is past President of the Wisconsin State Human Relations Association and co-chair of the AERA Special Interest Group on Critical Evaluation of Prevailing Theory with Emphasis on Race, Social Class, and Gender.

Larry L. Smiley is Associate Professor of Educational Administration at the University of North Dakota in Grand Forks. He is author of "Student Use of Unscheduled Time," *NASSP Bulletin* and "Why Not An Open Campus?", *American Secondary Education.* Professor Smiley is President-Elect of the National Council of Professors of Educational Administration and Executive Secretary of the Upper Midwest Small Schools Project.

Carol Payne Smith is Professor of Education and Professional Development at Western Michigan University in Kalamazoo. She is author of "A Needs-Based Curriculum for Teenage Mothers," *Education;* "Collective Bargaining as a Springboard to Faculty Development," *Journal of Research in Education;* and "Women's Participation in Michigan's State-Supported Four-Year Colleges and Universities," a research report presented to the Michigan Women's Commission. Professor Smith is former president and current member of the Advisory Committee of the Center for Continuing Education for Young Families at Kalamazoo Public Schools.

Karolyn Johnson Snyder is Associate Professor and Director of the School Management Institute of the College of Education at the University of South Florida in Tampa. She is author of numerous publications, including *Competency Training for Managing Productive Schools, Coaching Teaching: Clinical Supervision in Action,* and coauthor of "Instructional Leadership Training Needs for School Principals," *Journal of Educational Administration.* Professor Snyder is Chief-Editor of the *Journal of the Florida Association of Supervision and Curriculum Development.*

Howard Leonard Sosne is Superintendent of Wayne County, North Carolina Schools. He is author of *Pointers for the New Principal,* a pamphlet published by the National Association for Elementary School Principals; "A Primer for the School Principal," *The Principal;* and "Creative Retrenchment," *The School Administrator.* Mr. Sosne is an Instructor at Duke University and at Appalachian State University and Executive Assistant with the National Academy for School Executives.

Dennis C. Sparks is Executive Director of the National Staff Development Council. He has written extensively in the areas of staff development and instructional improvement.

Bernard Spodek is Professor of Early Childhood Education at the University of Illinois. He has lectured in many countries and has published 20 books, 30 chapters in books, and 40 articles on early childhood education, including *Today's Kindergarten* and *Teaching in the Early Years*.

Walter D. St. John is President of the Management Communications Institute. He has written 3 books and over 50 articles, including "The Best Ideas in Employee Communication," *Communications Briefings*; "Leveling with Employees," *Personnel Journal*; and "Communicating in Time of Crisis," *NASSP Bulletin*. Dr. St. John is a former University Dean and Professor of Educational Administration.

T. Elaine Staaland is State Supervisor of Home Economics Education for the Wisconsin Department of Public Instruction in Madison. She is author of "What is Basic?," *Illinois Teacher* and *Guide to Curriculum Planning in Home Economics*, published by the Wisconsin Department of Public Instruction. Ms. Staaland was speaker on "Home Economics for the 1990s" at the 1987 USOE Home Economics National Conference.

Jane A. Stallings is Director of the Houston Center of Effective Teaching and Chair of Curriculum and Instruction at the University of Houston. She is author of "What Students Should Learn in Schools: An Issue for Staff Development," *NASSP Bulletin*, and is author of over 60 articles and 2 books.

Ronald D. Stephens is Executive Director of the National School Safety Center and Professor of Education at Pepperdine University in Malibu, California. Dr. Stephens is Executive Editor of *School Safety*.

Ruth A. Stephens is Professor of Educational Administration at East Texas State University in Commerce, Texas. She is former elementary school teacher and principal, Codirector of the Meadows Principal Improvement Program, author and director of state-mandated instructional leadership training programs for administrators, and a member of the National Committee on the Preparation of School Administrators of the American Association of Colleges for Teacher Education.

Kenneth Richard Stevenson is Associate Professor and Coordinator of the Educational Administration Program in the College of Education at the University of South Carolina in Columbia. He is coeditor of *The Best of the NASSP Bulletin: Readings in Secondary School Administration*; "Emergency Preparedness Plans—How to Develop, Operate," *NASSP Bulletin*; and "Paying Noninstructional Employees: More May Not Be Better," *School Business Affairs*. Professor Stevenson is Long Range Facilities Planner for Sarasota County School and Facilities Planning Specialist for the Florida Department of Education.

Michael J. Stolee is Professor of Administrative Leadership at the University of Wisconsin-Milwaukee. He is former Dean of the School of Education at the University of Wisconsin-Milwaukee; Special Master for the U.S. District Court, Western District of Michigan; and an expert witness in approximately 40 desegregation cases.

Jim Sweeney is Professor and Section Leader of Educational Administration at Iowa State University in Ames. He is author of "Principals Do Make A Difference—A Report on School Effectiveness," *Educational Leadership*; "Actualizing Administrator Growth—The Assessment Center Concept," *The Developer*; and "Administrator Evaluation—Planning and Process," *Education*.

Marian J. Swoboda is Assistant to the President of the University of Wisconsin System in Madison. Ms. Swoboda is author of "The Society of Outsiders: Women in Administration" in *Strategies and Attitudes, Women in Edu-*

cational Administration; "Equity Policies and Classroom Climate," *Teaching Forum*; and "Moving Forward to Create an Equitable Environment," *Wisconsin Ideas*. She is a Board Member of the Educational Approval Board of the State of Wisconsin, Chair of the College/University Committee of the American Association of University Women, and a Lecturer at the School of Business of the University of Wisconsin-Madison.

Clayton F. Thomas is Assistant Dean of Graduate Studies and Professor of Educational Administration at Illinois State University in Normal. He is author of *Effective Secondary Education*; "Making the Board Meeting Work is Every Member's Job," *Illinois School Board Journal*; and "Affecting Change with Skillful Feedback," *Illinois Principal*. Professor Thomas is past Member of the Executive Committee of the University Council for Educational Administration and past Chair of the NASSP Committee of Professors of Secondary School Administrators and Supervision.

M. Donald Thomas is Senior Partner of Harold Webb Associates in Winnetka, Illinois. He is author of 500 articles and 5 books, including *Your School: How Well Is It Working?* and *Pluralism Gone Mad?*. Mr. Thomas was Superintendent of Schools in Salt Lake City, Utah and a Member of the Task Force on Elementary Education of the U.S. Department of Education.

Robert Thompson is Head of the Department of Professional Development and Graduate Studies at Lamar University in Beaumont, Texas. Professor Thompson is a personnel and labor-relations consultant to public schools and has many years experience as a chief negotiator in public sector bargaining.

Charlene B. Tosi is a Clinical Nurse Specialist in Adolescent Psychology at St. Michael Hospital in Milwaukee, Wisconsin. Ms. Tosi coauthored "Health During the School Age Years" in *Handbook of Community Health Nursing: Essentials of Clinical Practice*. She has written a six-week curriculum for Parents of Early Adolescents and is active in advising and consulting schools on suicide prevention policy, curriculum writing, and program implementation.

Kenneth J. Travers is Professor of Mathematics Education at the University of Illinois in Champaign-Urbana. He is author of more than 20 books and articles, including *The Underachieving Curriculum*. Professor Travers is Chairman of the International Mathematics Committee, Second International Mathematics Study.

Dale W. Trusheim is Assistant Director of Institutional Research and Strategic Planning at the University of Delaware in Newark. He is author of *The Case Against the SAT* and "The SAT and Traditional Predictive Validity: A Critical Assessment," *Journal of College Admissions*.

Ralph W. Tyler is Director Emeritus of the Center for Advanced Study in the Behavioral Sciences. He is author of *Perspectives on American Education, Appraising and Recording Student Progress*, and *Constructing Achievement Tests*. Mr. Tyler was Director of Examinations Staff for the Armed Forces Institutes and Chairman of the Exploratory Committee on Assessing the Practice of Education.

Gerald Unks is Associate Professor of Educational Policy Studies at the University of North Carolina in Chapel Hill. He is author of "The Illusion of Intrusion: A Chronicle of Federal Aid to Public Education," *The Educational Forum*; "The New Demography: Implications for the School Curriculum," *Education and Urban Society*; and "Product-Oriented Teaching: A Reappraisal," *Education and Urban Society*. Professor Unks is editor of *The High School Journal*.

Cynthia O. Vail is a doctoral candidate in Special Education at Florida State University in Tallahassee. She is author of *A Resource Manual to Accompany the Special Educator's Handbook*; "Recording Behavior with Ease," *Teaching Exceptional Children*; and "News for Students with Behavior Disorders," *Journal of Reading*. Ms. Vail has recently received federal funding for a student initiated research grant entitled, "The Effects of Vigorous Exercise on Subsequent Social Interactions of Mildly Handicapped Preschool Students."

John H. Vanderhoof is Technology Education Supervisor for the Wisconsin Department of Public Instruction in Madison. He is a regular contributing author to *Interface*, the Journal of the Technology Education Association. Mr. Vanderhoof is a member of the Board of Directors of the Wisconsin Technology Education Association.

Janet F. Varejcka is Principal of Bennett County High School in Martin, South Dakota. She has contributed articles on effective time management to the educational administration departments of the Universities of Indiana and Oregon. Ms. Varejcka is the first woman president of the South Dakota Secondary School Principals Association and President of School Administrators of South Dakota.

Albert E. Virgin is Educational Planning, Information and Evaluation Services Director for the North York Board of Education in North York, Ontario, Canada.

James Alvin Vornberg is Professor of Educational Administration at East Texas State University in Commerce, Texas. He is author of "A Model for Organizing Your School's Activity Program," *NASSP Bulletin*; "Auditing the Student Activity Program," *NASSP Bulletin*; and "Student Activities—What are the Problems Now?", *Clearing House*. Professor Vornberg is Director of the Meadows Foundation Principal Improvement Program and past President of the Texas Professors of Educational Administration.

John Edward Walker is Associate Professor of Educational Leadership at Arizona State University in Tempe. He is author of "Local Opinion Polling—The Benefits of Polls and How to Conduct Them," *Journal of Educational Public Relations*; "Polls of Public Attitudes Toward Education—How Much Help to Principals?" *NASSP Bulletin*; and "Who Gives Schools A-B Ratings?" *Clearing House*. Professor Walker is former director of the Southwest Center for Community Education Development and past President of the Arizona Community Education Association.

James K. Walter is Assistant Principal of Maple Crest School in Kokomo, Indiana. He is author of "Teacher Evaluation & RIF—Can There Be Peaceful Coexistence?", *NASSP Bulletin*; "Fiscal Management is Everyone's Responsibility," *The School Administrator*; and "The PR Explosion: It is Time to Get Your School Involved," *The Hoosier School Master*. Mr. Walter is codeveloper of the Walter-Carfield Graphic Overlay of Teacher Effectiveness and consultant and frequent speaker to educational forums.

Harold V. Webb (deceased 1987) was President and Senior Partner of Harold Webb Associates, Ltd. in Winnetka, Illinois. He was author of numerous articles in the *American School Board Journal* and former Executive Director of the National School Board Association.

L. Dean Webb is Associate Dean for Administration and Personnel at Arizona State University in Tempe. She is coauthor of *Educational Administration Today*, *Personnel Administration in Education*, and *School Business Administration*. Professor Webb served on the Board of Directors of the American Education Finance Association and edited its Fourth and Fifth Annual Yearbooks.

Gary G. Wehlage is Professor and Associate Director of the National Center on Effective Secondary Schools at the University of Wisconsin-Madison. Professor Wehlage coauthored *Dropping Out: How Much Do Schools Contribute to the Problem?*, and is currently engaged in the study of 15 interventions for at-risk students.

L. David Weller, Jr. is Associate Professor of Educational Administration at the University of Georgia in Athens. He is author of "Attitude Toward Grade Inflation: A Survey of Public and Private Colleges of Education," *Journal of Research and Development in Education*; "A Longitudinal Study of Pass/Fail Grading Practices at Selected Private American Colleges and Universities," *Research in Education*; and "Attitude Toward Grade Inflation: A Random Survey of American Colleges of Arts and Sciences and Colleges of Education," *College and University*. Professor Weller is Associate Editor of the *Journal of Research and Development in Education* and editor of *American Middle School Education*.

Richard Frank Wenzel is Assistant Director of the Division of Transportation Services for the Milwaukee Public Schools. He is author of "Rider Management," *Wisconsin School Board Journal*; "Driver-Rider Rapport," *Chrome Yellow*; and "Transportation is PR," *Chrome Yellow*. Mr. Wenzel is past President of the Wisconsin Association of Pupil Transportation; President of the National Safety Council, School Bus Section; and past President of the Wisconsin School Public Relations Association.

Philip T. West is Professor and Coordinator of the Public Relations Specialization in the Department of Educational Administration at Texas A&M University in College Station. He is author of *Educational Public Relations*, coauthor of *Training the Community Educator: A Case Study Approach*, and author or coauthor of 100 articles. Professor West is editor of *Research and Case Study, Journal of Educational Public Relations* and of *AASA Professor*.

Glenn E. Whitlock is Clinical Director of the Christian Counseling Service in Redlands, California. He is author of *Person Centered Learning*; "A Learning Paradigm at Johnston College," *Journal of Humanistic Psychology*; and *Understanding and Coping with Real Life Crises*. Professor Whitlock was Faculty Fellow at Johnston College and University of Redlands, and Professor of Psychology at the University of Redlands.

James Dale Wiggins is President and Clinical Director of Training Associates Limited. He is author of "The Relationship Between Counselors and Students' Self-Esteem Related to Counseling Outcomes" and "Self-esteem, Earned Grades, and Television Viewing Habits of Students," both in *The School Counselor*; and "Effectiveness Related to Personality and Demographic Characteristics of Secondary School Counselors," *Counselor Education and Supervision*. Mr. Wiggins is editor of *The American Mental Health Counselors Association Journal* and Chairperson of the Alcohol and Drug Abuse Committee of the American Mental Health Counselors Association.

Arthur E. Wise is Director of The RAND Corporation's Center for the Study of the Teaching Profession in Washington, D.C. He is author of *Rich Schools, Poor Schools: The Promise of Equal Educational Opportunity* and *Legislated Learning*. He has also written dozens of articles appearing in the education and popular press. Dr. Wise served as a consultant to President Carter's reorganization project to create the U.S. Department of Education and has served as a consultant to numerous other international, national, state, and local agencies.

R. Craig Wood is Associate Professor of Educational Administration at Purdue University in West Lafayette, Indiana. He is author of over 75 articles and one edited text, *Principles of School Business Management*, published by the Association of School Business Officials, International. Dr. Wood specializes in finance, law, and facilities.

I. Phillip Young is Associate Professor of Educational Policy and Leadership, and Coordinator of Educational Administration at Ohio State University in Columbus. He is author of *Teacher Selection: Legal, Practical, and Theoretical Aspects*, published by the University Council of Educational Administration and of "Predictors of Interviewee Reactions to the Selection Interview," *Journal of Research and Development*. Professor Young is codirector of Midwestern Compensation Associates.

Bettie B. Youngs is Director of Stress and Wellness Research Associates and Executive Director of the Institute for Executive Development. She has published over 100 articles and is author of *Stress in Children: How to Recognize, Avoid, and Overcome It; Helping Your Teenager Deal with Stress*; and *A Stress Management Guide for Young People*; and coauthor of the eight-part video series, *Nutrition and Behavior*. A noted authority on the topic of stress and wellness in the home and workplace, she is an active consultant to school districts, parent groups, educational agencies, and service organizations.

John A. Zahorik is Professor of Curriculum and Instruction at the University of Wisconsin-Milwaukee. Professor Zahorik has over 80 publications in the areas of curriculum planning and instructional analysis, including "Teachers' Collegial Interaction: An Exploratory Study," *Elementary School Journal*; "Teaching: Rules, Research, Beauty, and Creation," *Journal of Curriculum and Supervision*; and "Acquiring Teaching Skills," *Journal of Teacher Education*.

Roger D. Zeeman is Director of Pupil Services for Montgomery Township Schools in Skillman, New Jersey and Child/Adolescent Psychologist in private practice in Bridgewater, New Jersey. He is author of "Collaboration between Private Practitioner, School Psychologist, and Child Study Team," *New Jersey Pscyhologist*; "Occupational Therapy and School Psychology: A Partnership," *New Jersey Journal of School Psychology*; and "Special People-Basic Facts to Help Children Accept Their Handicapped Peers," New Jersey Association for Children with Learning Disabilities. Mr. Zeeman is Trustee of the New Jersey Association of Pupil Personnel Administrators.

Anita L. Zeidler is Editorial Assistant at *Metropolitan Education* magazine and doctoral candidate in Urban Education at the University of Wisconsin-Milwaukee.

Perry A. Zirkel is Professor of Education and Law at Lehigh University in Bethlehem, Pennsylvania. He is author of over 200 publications, including *Digest of Supreme Court Decisions Affecting Education*. Professor Zirkel is former Dean of the College of Education at Lehigh University and an active labor arbitrator.

Guide to Related Topics

ADMINISTRATIVE POSITIONS

Assistant/Associate Superintendent
Assistant/Vice Principal
Central Office Personnel
Department Heads
Principalship
School Business Manager
Superintendent of Schools
Supervisory Personnel

ADMINISTRATIVE PROCESSES

Administrative Authority
Administrative Power
Collective Bargaining
Communication
Conflict Resolution
Decision Making
Delegating Authority
Enrollment Projections
Grantsmanship
Group Processes
Human Relations
Job Descriptions
Management by Objectives
PERT
Planning
Problem Identification
Quality Circles
Time Management

ADMINISTRATIVE TASK AREAS

Administrative Tasks
Budgeting
Curriculum Development
Facilities Planning
Program Evaluation
Public Relations
Pupil Personnel Program
Recruitment of Staff
School-Community Relations
Staff Development
Staff Evaluation
Staff Orientation
Supervision, Clinical
Teacher Selection
Transportation Management

ADMINISTRATIVE THEORY AND RESEARCH

Administrative Authority
Administrative Ethics
Administrative Power

Administrative Roles
Administrative Styles
Administrative Theory
Bureaucracy
Leadership
Organizations: Principles and Theory
Research on Administration
School Climate
Systems Theory
Theory X, Theory Y
Theory Z

ADMINISTRATOR CAREER STAGES AND CHALLENGES

Administrative Accountability
Administrative Preparation
Administrative Salaries
Administrative Status
Administrative Stress
Administrator Effectiveness
Administrator Evaluation
Administrator Inservice
Administrator Turnover
Administrator Unions
Administrators, Beginning
Minority Administrators
Principal Selection
Superintendent Selection
Women in Administration

CHANGE AND PROGRAM IMPROVEMENT APPROACHES

Accreditation of Schools
Change Agent
Change Process
Change Variables
Curriculum Committee
Curriculum Development
Curriculum Evaluation
Curriculum Implementation
Desegregation Plans
Management of Decline
National Reports on Education
Needs Assessment
Program Evaluation
School Improvement and Effectiveness Movements

COMMUNITY-SCHOOL RELATIONS

Advisory Committees
Business/Education Partnership
Censorship
Communicating with the Community

Community School Involvement
Community School Programs
Demographic Trends
Education and Community Views
News Media
Parent Involvement
Parent Teacher Association, National
Parent-Teacher Conferences
Public Opinion Polling
Public Relations
School Boards
School-Community Relations
Single-Parent Families

CURRICULUM AREAS AND ISSUES

Adult Education Programs
Back-to-Basics
Business Education
Career Education
Character Education
Citizenship Education
Computer Literacy
Driver Education
Educational Goals and Objectives
English Education
Foreign Language Education
Gifted and Talented Education
Head Start
Health/Fitness Education
Hidden Curriculum
Home Economics Education
Industrial Arts Education
Instructional Media Center
Mathematics Education
Multicultural Education
Physical Education
Reading Education
Science Education
Sex Education
Social Studies Education
Student-Centered Curriculum
Subject-Centered Curriculum
Textbook Selection
Values Education
Vocational Education

INSTRUCTIONAL METHODS AND ISSUES

Academic Learning Time
Affective Education
Bilingual Education
Class Size
Classroom Management
Cognitive Development
Computer-Assisted Instruction
Cooperative Learning
Direct Instruction
Home Instruction
Independent Study
Individualization of Instruction
Instructional Objectives
Learning Styles
Lesson Plans
Mainstreaming
Mastery Learning
Social Learning in the Schools
Split-Brain Controversy

Teaching Approaches, Future
Team Teaching
Technology Education
Television in Instruction

LEGAL CONCEPTS AND ISSUES

Due Process
Judicial Decisions
Rights: Teachers' and Students'
School Law

PRINCIPLES AND APPROACHES TO ORGANIZING

Administrative Team, District Level
Centralization and Decentralization
Consolidation of Schools
Organizations: Principles and Theory
School-Based Management
School District/University Partnerships
School Districts

PROFESSIONAL ORGANIZATIONS

American Association of School Administrators
American Federation of Teachers
Association for Supervision and Curriculum Development
National Association of Elementary School Principals
National Association of Secondary School Principals
National Education Association
National School Boards Association
Phi Delta Kappa
University Council for Educational Administration

SCHOOL FACILITIES

Emergency Procedures
Energy Management
Facilities Planning
Scheduling, Student

SOCIAL ISSUES

Affirmative Action
Bilingual Education
Compensatory Education
Competency-Based Education
Desegregation Plans
Financing of Schools
Minorities and the School System
Multicultural Education
Sex Discrimination
Sex Education
Sex-Role Stereotyping
Student Pregnancy

STATE AND FEDERAL RELATIONS

Federal Agencies
Federal Role in Education
Funding Methods: State and Federal
State Boards of Education
State Departments of Education

STUDENT PROBLEMS, ISSUES, AND PROGRAMS

Athletics
Corporal Punishment
Counseling and Guidance
Disadvantaged Students

Alphabetical List of Articles

ENCYCLOPEDIA OF

◇

SCHOOL ADMINISTRATION & SUPERVISION

◇

ACADEMIC LEARNING TIME

Academic learning time has three components: (a) the time allocated to instruction of a particular subject, (b) the proportion of that time during which a student is actually engaged in learning activities appropriate to the subject for which time has been allocated, and (c) the level of difficulty of the material being used by the student. In addition, the learning activity in which students are supposed to be engaged must be of value. This should be reflected in the criteria used to determine the extent and quality of that learning. This additional stipulation is what distinguishes academic learning time from time-on-task. When time-on-task is addressed without respect to the value of the activity taking place, students may be considered "on-task" when they are actually engaged in activities which might be classified as "busy work."

Given this definition, attempts to measure academic learning time usually focus on time samples of student behavior coupled with concurrent time samples of teacher behaviors. The measurement also takes into consideration the content of the lesson being taught (so that a judgment can be made as to the appropriateness of the content). The level of difficulty of the material students are working on and the amount of time allocated to instruction of the subject also are considered.

Much of the current interest in academic learning time can be traced to public concern about basic skills and test score outcomes reflected in national reports such as *A Nation at Risk*.

The initial step in increasing academic learning time is to make teachers and school staff aware of its components, as outlined above. One good strategy is to collect data in classrooms before teachers and staff are approached about academic learning time. These data are a powerful motivator for teachers to change their teaching strategies and to gain back time wasted through inefficient classroom management practices. The entire staff must work on the components of allocated time and content so that there is consensus on how class time is to be allocated and what the contents of lessons will be during time allocated to particular subjects. Curriculum alignment will help to bring about a closer match between content and measures of outcome. School staffs may find that they want to measure their students' outcomes in new and/or additional ways in order to determine the quality and extent of learning taking place.

Once these conditions are in place, additional training may be provided to teachers and other staff in classroom management strategies and other pedagogy, such as Madeline Hunter's Workshop, "Essential Elements of Effective Instruction." Peer observations and/or coaching are also effective strategies for increasing academic learning time. They also provide teachers with opportunities to learn strategies and gain ideas from their peers.

Whatever strategies are used, all three of the components of academic learning time, along with the value of the subject matter taught with respect to the outcome measures, must be kept constantly in mind. Increasing one component at the expense of the others will not result in improved achievement which is the goal.

See also Classroom Management; Direct Instruction; Instructional Objectives; Lesson Plans.

—JoAnne E. Moore
Detroit Public Schools

References

Moore, J.E. (1983, October). *Assessing time-on-task: Measurement problems and solutions*. Paper presented at the 1983 Joint Meeting of the Evaluation Network and Evaluation Research Society, Chicago, IL.

Moore, J.E. (1985, April). *Measuring and increasing time-on-task: A cost effective approach*. Paper presented at the 1985 Annual Meeting of the American Educational Research Association, Chicago, IL.

Stallings, J. (1980, December). "Allocated academic learning time revisited, or beyond time-on-task." *Educational Researcher, 8-9*, 11–16.

ACCREDITATION OF SCHOOLS

There has been renewed interest in the mandatory and voluntary accreditation of schools in recent years. Concerns over falling college-board test scores, employer complaints about functional illiteracy of people entering the work force, and criticisms about the qualifications of teachers in the schools have pushed states to develop or revise state accreditation standards. These criticisms have prompted local school authorities to join voluntary regional accrediting agencies. This move to, or return to, accreditation is a response to the demand for accountability from taxpayers and legislators responsible for funding the schools.

State Accreditation

State accreditation usually is a function of a state board of education, the state education agency, or state department of public instruction. Standards for accreditation are drafted and passed by state legislatures, and schools or school districts are required to meet the standards to be or become accreditated. In most cases the entire educational program of a school district is examined, with general regulations for school administration and organization combined with specific regulations for elementary, middle, and secondary curricula.

General administration criteria often pertain to staff qualifications, instructional materials, equipment, physical-plant organization and operation, student attendance and reporting, and programmatic efforts that cross grade levels and buildings. Programs relating to dropout prevention, special education, and courses for the gifted and talented fall into the districtwide category.

Regulations for elementary school accreditation can include requirements for admission, scope and sequence of curricula, teacher licensure, activity schedules for instruction in the basic subjects (reading, mathematics, writing and social studies), class period size, and instructional materials. Building programs for library or media, health promotion and maintenance, physical activity, or counseling are also components of state standards for elementary school accreditation.

Standards for high schools follow similar patterns as those for elementary schools and also include graduation requirements, transfer or correspondence credit, faculty requirements for teaching, vocational and technical education rules, extra- or co-curricular program requirements, along with the admission, instruction, and curriculum regulations identified for elementary schools.

Some states have recognized the middle school as a unique and important component of the educational enterprise. These states have developed separate accreditation standards for middle schools. These requirements include a written statement of the objectives of the school, a description of the curriculum substantiating the fulfillment of the needs of pre- and early adolescents, and a plan for evaluation of school programs.

A state education agency has the responsibility of evaluating schools for state accreditation. The agency's reviews may include on-site program audits and the completion of forms or surveys by school administrators, or often a combination of both. Filling out compliance forms often is an annual activity. On-site visitation is periodic on a less frequent schedule.

Regional Accreditation

Several regional accreditation agencies have established standards for both elementary schools and high schools. A school's membership in a regional agency is voluntary. The North Central Association of Colleges and Schools, headquartered in Boulder, Colorado, is one example. North Central is a partnership of nineteen midwestern and western states dedicated to the development and maintenance of high standards of excellence for schools. In the Association Articles of Incorporation, approved in 1963, the stated goal is one of "improvement of the educational program and the effectiveness of instruction . . .through a scientific and professional approach to the solution of educational problems."

The North Central Association is administered through state offices, either located on a college campus or in the state education agency. State directors are responsible for monitoring the completion of compliance forms and for attesting to the fact that schools meet the standards. The directors represent member schools at an annual meeting of all state representatives. They point to their schools' adherence to accreditation standards.

Periodic, on-site reviews of programs every seven years are another part of the regional accreditation policy. States may couple the regional review with the state review in instances where the schedule and standards are compatible. Schools found in noncompliance with standards are warned. If corrections are not made, the schools are dropped from membership. This authority rests with the state director, who is responsible to the state board for accreditation. The board is elected by the membership and from the membership.

Outcomes Accreditation

The state and regional standards have traditionally focused on the inputs of the educational system. Minimum standards of materials, facilities, and staff were the yardstick for measuring whether a school should be accredited.

The new emphasis is on an accreditation which is based upon the appropriate output, or outcome, of the system. These outcomes can be measured in several different ways. An appropriate testing program is one effective means of measuring outcomes as are follow-up and drop-out studies. In addition, a school or school district sometimes measures outcome by means of a community attitude survey or similar instrument.

The North Central Association has taken a leadership role in the development of outcomes accreditation by a regional agency. Administrators and state directors in the North Central Association saw the need for an alternative approach to elementary and secondary school accreditation, one that would focus on student learning rather than relying primarily on input measures.

This movement was a response to the call of school reformers to make the schools accountable for student performance. It was no longer enough to rely on a standards adherence which allowed little flexibility to the individual schools. The outcomes accreditation approach allows schools more discretion in meeting the intent of the standard which focuses on the quality and equity of student performance.

The basic format of outcomes accreditation begins with the development of a steering committee consisting of staff members along with the selection of an external resource specialist to shepherd the school through the process. The steering committee, with the help of the resource specialist, develops a list of school objectives that are phrased in a manner conducive to the development of instructional objectives. The school staff must reach agreement or consensus on the objectives, and on the specific outcomes desired for the students served. The steering committee will identify major priorities as target areas for study; the priorities will be selected from the objectives developed. The target areas should be consistent with the school's statement of the overall mission.

The next step in the outcomes accreditation process is to collect base-line data to provide an estimate of how successful the school is in meeting its expectations for student performance. This is where norm-referenced tests, criterion-referenced tests, teacher-constructed tests, or other student tests or inventories are used to provide a basis for judgment. The first analysis is to determine which standards are being satisfied, and the second use is to compare those standards found to be below school expectations for their growth.

When discrepancies are found between actual and desired student performance, it is up to the staff and steering committee to review the results. The expectations should be reviewed to determine their reasonableness, and the priorities should be arranged to reflect an accurate picture of what the school can accomplish. The characteristics thwarting the school's attempt to help students achieve should be analyzed, and modifications of programs should be designed to free student achievement from those constraints.

Strategies to reduce discrepancies between actual and desired student performance should be developed to reinforce areas of strength and remedy areas of weakness. A coordinated plan of implementation of the strategies should be determined. Responsibilities for carrying out the activities of the plan should be assigned. The plan should include a timeline of activities for completion of the strategies and evaluation checkpoints for formative evaluation and revision when necessary.

Standards Review

The second major change in the process of school accreditation seen in recent years is a shift in the methods used to review standards. As was noted above, the technique originally designed was to schedule periodic reviews or audits by a team of educators through a one-, two-, or three-day on-site visit. The change to outcomes accreditation has precipitated a change in the review process as well. The new model calls for the assignment or appointment of a review panel composed of three to five educators to monitor standards compliance and to review the outcomes accreditation plan.

The review team would visit the school at least twice during the school's timeline for program implementation. The panel would review the base-line data and the conclusions drawn regarding target areas in need of study and also review the school's plan for improvement strategies. The visits of the review panel would be in lieu of the visit by a larger visiting team, an external team, which is active in the more traditional accreditation audit format.

A school may select one or more programs, such as math and guidance, in the first year. A program subcommittee in each area spends the year determining program expectations. During the second year, one or more additional programs is undertaken, and the second-year committees collect evidence on the expectations written. In the third year, data are analyzed, the second group collects evidence, and a third group becomes active. The fourth year in the cycle is for the audit or review by the external panel, and the fifth year is the time to begin implementation. With different programs beginning and ending in different school years, the evaluation of programs is done in a continual cycle of setting objectives, collecting data, analyzing data, audit, and implementation.

Summary

Accreditation of elementary and secondary schools is on the verge of a new beginning. The call for accountability from the public has encouraged educators to determine just what a school is capable of doing and to measure how well the school is accomplishing its goals. Schools can expect legislatures to continue the efforts to create more regulations that must be met as part of accreditation and, therefore, accountability. Accreditation by outcomes is an appropriate technique to reach compliance and, at the same time, work toward school improvement. If done appropriately, teachers, students, and others associated with the schools can only prosper.

See also Curriculum Development; Curriculum Evaluation; Program Evaluation.

—Peter Burke
Wisconsin Department of Public Instruction

References

State of Oklahoma. (1985, July). *Administrator's handbook for elementary, middle, junior high and high schools.* (Regulations and criteria for accrediting and improving the schools of Oklahoma). Oklahoma City, OK: Department of Education.

Vaughn, J.W. (1986, Winter). "An evolutionary revolution: Some thoughts on outcomes accreditation." *North Central Association Quarterly, 60* (3), 386–97.

Wisconsin School Evaluation Consortium. (1983). *Continuous process program review.* Madison, WI: The University of Wisconsin-Madison.

ADMINISTRATIVE ACCOUNTABILITY

Administrative accountability expresses a relationship between the occupants of roles who control daily work in institutions (administrators) and persons who possess formal power to displace them (reviewers/boards). The scope of this accountability includes *everything* that those who hold powers of dismissal (reviewers/boards) apply to an appraisal of the administrator's work; boards sometimes find it necessary to withdraw their confidence in their administrator. Thus, administrative accountability is the requirement on the occupant of an administrative role, by those who authorize that role, to answer for the results of work expected from him or her in the role.

The enactment of this concept has undergone change in recent years, especially in American public education. In simpler times, local boards relied heavily on the uncorroborated testimony of their administrators, hearing little from external authorities. It was common for administrators to account sufficiently for their stewardship in general terms. Claims that they "did their best" were seldom submitted to rigorous review.

Today, however, many factors have increased state and federal presence at the local level. This presence demands detailed explanations and holds both local boards and administrators to ever-tighter standards and more specific expectations, especially for results achieved. Failure to comply with these expectations carries threats of judicial action, withholding of funds, and/or, in some cases, direct intervention by external authorities in the running of local districts. Accordingly, in order to comply with these external pressures as well as to maintain and build trust with local boards, educational administrators are apt to turn to a number of recently developed management and educational practices intended to meet this demand for greater accountability.

These new practices share certain characteristics—they attempt to increase the clarity of what is expected, what is to be done, how it is to be done, and the results anticipated. This clarity is attained by increasing the degree of rationality employed. That is, the practices are designed to achieve more rational—to tighten the logical systems between administrative means and educational outcomes—school operation in a manner intended to make the institution more efficient, effective, and responsive to the policymaker's expectations.

Measures used to promote this rationality generally come from today's "scientific management" and its educational counterpart. Examples of these management techniques include: planning, programming, budgeting systems (PPBS); management-by-objectives (MBO); operations analysis; systems analysis; program evaluation and review technique (PERT); management information systems (MIS); planning models; cost-benefit analysis; cost effectiveness analysis; systems engineering; zero-based budgeting; and others.

Facilitating the application of these management practices to education are new techniques to assist in sharpening the specificity and reporting of educational outcomes: behavioral objectives; mastery learning; criterion-referenced testing; assessment systems (federal, state, and local); educational indicators; competency-based education (CBE); performance-based education (PBE); performance contracting; educational program auditing; and similar approaches.

With a strong push from federal and state agencies, these new technologies form an accountability system—a system that clarifies expectations into goals and measurable objectives, specifies tasks and delineates conditions, and renders as rational as possible an account of results achieved toward specified objectives. In contrast with earlier convention, the newer approach displays:

Higher visibility of outcome expectations. For example, it is one thing to hold that "each child shall learn to the best of his/her ability"—a lofty hope—and another to state that "every child shall be functionally literate according to the State literacy test"—a narrower, less rhetorical goal, and one that can be measured.

Closer monitoring of educational, managerial and financial processes through greater data gathering capabilities. The advent of modern electronics, the computer, systems-based management and educational technologies combine to create an unprecedented capacity to collect and analyze data. Nearly all elements of the educational, managerial, and financial operations of schools can be traced if desired, often generating more data than can be practically used. Because of this capacity, reviewing bodies exercise tighter controls, holding their administrators more accountable.

Greater efforts to identify and specify educational need. To corroborate subjective opinions of teachers and administrators, greater emphasis is placed on establishing objective criteria of educational need. There are elaborate assessment procedures for analyzing tests and other data. Reviewers search for "hard data" to identify and specify educational need.

More extensive testing and evaluation procedures. Comprehensive efforts are made to establish "proof of results" that students are competent and learning what is expected. Testing has become a national concern, with individual states implementing statewide testing programs and with many districts using these results to judge their own progress.

More involvement of local citizens. As a result of pressures to involve citizens in school governance more directly, citizens other than those serving on the board of education appear on special committees to review programs and advise the board. This involvement broadens decision-making participation. It also serves as a watch-dog function for external agencies, keeping administrators accountable for programs that may be unpopular with local boards.

Greater effort at reporting educational results to the public. Formerly, beyond annual school budgets and infrequent educational statistics, few citizens were informed of their district's educational progress. Reliable comparative data with other districts was even rarer. Now, many state education departments routinely release local educational data for statewide publication. Some districts also prepare elaborate annual educational achievement reports.

Although all these forces act to increase administrative accountability, debate remains whether these new techniques actually produce schools that are administered more efficiently, effectively, and responsibly. Some believe the new procedures trivialize education and give an illusion of rationality to things that are beyond the bounds of knowledge ("hyperrationality"). Others argue that our knowledge of learning and testing is still too tentative for such procedures. Research remains largely inconclusive.

See also Administrative Status; Administrator Effectiveness; Administrator Evaluation.

—Lesley H. Browder
Hofstra University

References

Browder, L.H. (1973). *An administrator's handbook on educational accountability.* Arlington, VA: American Association of Schools Administrators.
DeMont, B.C., & DeMont, R.A. (1975). *Accountability: An action model for the public schools.* Homewood, IL: ETC.
Madaus, G.F., & Stufflebeam, D.L. (1984). "Educational evaluation and accountability." *American Behavioral Scientist,* 27(5), 649–72.

ADMINISTRATIVE AUTHORITY

Authority is a mechanism for encouraging subordinates to behave in accordance with the wishes of organizational leaders. It is only one such mechanism, however, and must be carefully distinguished from three others: power, persuasion, and exchange.

Two Theories of Authority

Two quite different conceptions of the relationship between power and authority are to be found in the literature on these topics. The dominant theory (developed at length in Carl Friedrich's, 1958, work and skillfully applied to educational organizations by Dornbusch and Scott, 1975) sees all social influence as springing from the exercise of power, and defines authority by reference to the social circumstances under which power is exercised.

A second theory of authority holds that authority is fundamentally different from social power. Theorists holding this view generally trace the concept historically. They note, for example, that the English word for authority is derived from the Latin (*auctor*) rather than earlier Hebrew or Greek roots.

The concept of authority also holds that it is a uniquely human form of social control, created whenever some individuals are able to provide security, intimacy, self-worth, or personal potency experiences for others. As Mitchell and Spady put it, "Individuals move toward social relationships which promise to provide these experiences and come to *accept as legitimate* the right of anyone who can create such experiences to guide and direct their behavior." They go on to argue that power resources are actually *derived from* authority through psychological *displacement* from the experiences themselves to various outward symbols that come to represent them.

The differences between the two competing theories of authority are of crucial significance to the development of administrative control systems. If the first theory is right, administrative control is derived through acquisition and judicious use of critical power resources. Developing the legitimacy of popular support for the exercise of power is important only as a means of stabilizing influence and reducing the costs of maintaining organizational control. If the second theory is right, however, administrators who focus their attention on the acquisition and use of power resources are unlikely to generate the types of personal experience that lead subordinates to pursue *voluntarily* organizational goals and comply with the wishes of administrative leaders. From this perspective, administrative authority depends on the development of meaningful relationships between superordinates and subordinates, not from the accumulation of resources or the development of capacities for reward and punishment.

Four Modes of Authority

Whether they embrace the direct experience or the social-approval conceptions of authority, all theorists agree that there are multiple types or *modes* of authority, and that the nature of the influence exercised by a superordinate depends on the particular mode of authority being used. Early in the twentieth century Max Weber explored this issue in depth. He distinguished three modes of authority: traditional, charismatic, and rational-legal. Weber argued that modern social organizations (the bureaucratic forms common to post-revolutionary governments, modern armies, and private corporations) were organized on the basis of rational-legal authority systems. The traditional authority systems of feudal society and the important, but unstable, influence of charismatic individual leaders were, he argued, systematically replaced in the division of labor, formal rules and meritocratic status systems of modernity.

Recent work reveals that Weber's conception of authority was flawed in two important respects. First, his hyphenated "rational-legal" mode of authority fails to distinguish two quite different meanings of the term "rational." In one meaning, rational actions are ones that rely on expert knowledge to link the means and ends of action. The other common meaning of rational does not involve theoretical knowledge, but refers instead to the imposition of order on a situation that is otherwise unorganized. In this second meaning "rationalizing" means routinizing or standardizing actions—creating order through convention or convenience. Authority based on the first notion of rationality is "expert" authority. The second concept of rationality underlies the "legal" part of the rational-legal authority which dominated Weber's original framework. Hence, there are four, not three, basic modes of authority: traditional, charismatic, legal, and expert.

The second problem with Weber's discussion of the various authority modes is his tendency to view both tradition and charisma as awesome, extraordinary qualities that arise only rarely in human experience. Actually, these modes of authority influence behavior in a wide variety of ordinary everyday social settings. All human groups develop traditions soon after they are formed. The "old hands" interpret these traditional norms to newcomers, and their authority is confirmed through acceptance of their right to do so. Cha-

risma is also an everyday experience. Friendship, camaraderie, entertainment, and spontaneous leadership all depend on the easy availability of a certain amount of charismatic authority. Anyone who, by force of personality, sways the behavior of others has charismatic authority.

Distinguishing Authority and Power from Persuasion and Exchange

The social influence processes of persuasion and exchange emerge from the fact that each of the multiple modalities of authority (and power) is linked to a particular domain of behavior. Authority and power can be distinguished from persuasion and exchange. Expert authority, for example, can be used to guide behavior when subordinates sense that they have a problem or need help overcoming technical obstacles. But charismatic authority is needed if social isolation, alienation, or loneliness are the principal impediments to cooperation. Legal authority can be used to routinize and rationalize actions, but it has little effect on the development of self-worth and identity. Traditional authority can convey group identity, but it can also get in the way of a rational attack on social problems.

Persuasion is simply a matter of using one mode of authority to influence behavior directly related to another. Thus, for example, teachers who are seen as subject matter experts may be allowed to establish classroom norms and rules, even if they do not seem capable of enhancing student identity or security. Conversely, teachers who operate as personal mentors may be able to persuade students to follow rules even when they do not seem to be able to create a secure social order. Where persuasion involves authority trade-offs, exchange relationships are created when people are able to trade in power resources. When one person or group has technical superiority and another has economic wealth, they can usually find a basis for accommodation. Where coercive power is not absolute, contracts for exchange of power resources become the norm.

Authority in Administrative Actions

Different administrative patterns or styles are developed through reliance on different combinations of authority and power. The four most common themes of executive action—administration, supervision, leadership, and management—are each supported by one of the four basic authority modalities. Executives who emphasize the administrative dimensions of their work roles will rely most extensively on traditional authority to interpret the goals and work norms of their organizations. Those who emphasize supervisory responsibilities will use legal authority to create standards and set work rules. Leadership oriented executives will use charismatic authority to engage the energies of their subordinates in the mission of the organization, and those for whom management of resources and personnel is the dominant concern will find expert authority an indispensable element in framing key decisions and securing the cooperation of subordinates.

See also Administrative Power; Collective Bargaining; Conflict Resolution; Delegating Authority.

—Douglas E. Mitchell
University of California, Riverside

References

Dornbusch, S.M., & Scott, W.R. (1975). *Evaluation and the exercise of authority.* San Francisco: Jossey-Bass.

Friedrich, C.J. (Ed.). (1958). *Authority.* Cambridge, MA: Harvard University Press.

Mitchell, D.E., & Spady, W.G. (1983, Winter). "Authority, power and the legitimation of social control." *Educational Administration Quarterly, 19*, 5-33.

ADMINISTRATIVE ETHICS

An explicit code of ethics that is binding on its members is one attribute of a profession. A noteworthy example is the Hypocratic Oath in medicine. A code of ethics for educational administrators did not exist before 1966. In 1966, the American Association of School Administrators adopted and published a set of policy statements as a guide to acceptable behavior. This initial statement was followed by the adoption of a ten-standard code of ethics in 1976. This code has been adopted as a standard of ethics by the National Association of Elementary School Principals and the National Association of Secondary School Principals. It is reproduced below.

> The educational administrator:
> 1. Makes the well-being of students the fundamental value of all decision making and actions.
> 2. Fulfills professional responsibilities with honesty and integrity.
> 3. Supports the principle of due process and protects the civil and human rights of all individuals.
> 4. Obeys local, state, and national laws and does not knowingly join or support organizations that advocate, directly or indirectly, the overthrow of the government.
> 5. Implements the governing board of education's policies and administrative rules and regulations.
> 6. Pursues appropriate measures to correct those laws, policies, and regulations that are not consistent with sound educational goals.
> 7. Avoids using positions for personal gain through political, social, religious, economic, or other influence.
> 8. Accepts academic degrees or professional certification only from duly accredited institutions.
> 9. Maintains the standards and seeks to improve the effectiveness of the profession through research and continuing professional development.
> 10. Honors all contracts until fulfillment, release or dissolution mutually agreed upon by all parties to contract.

The adoption of this code of ethics is one of the important steps toward achieving professional status; however, the code is not binding on practitioners. The only action that can be taken by the administrators' associations is to deny membership in the association to anyone found in violation of the code of ethics. Since a person may continue to practice even though denied membership in the professional organization, and many thousands are not members to begin with, the code is not binding on those holding administrative positions in most of the states.

Presently most states do not have a process for enforcing compliance to any code of ethics. Each of the states should establish some process (e.g., ethics commission) to remove the license to practice educational administration from those found in violation of acceptable codes of behavior. A few of the states have established processes to review charges of unethical conduct. This usually consists of legislation which establishes a state ethics commission to hear evidence concerning administrators charged with unethical behavior. In these states, power is given to conduct investigations of alleged unethical conduct and report the results to the hearing body. This type of legislation is needed in each of the states to achieve the principle of a binding code of ethics.

Unethical conduct is perceived by many educational administrators as restricted to criminal acts or to a severely flawed character. Charges of conflict of interest and embezzlement are examples of fraudulent acts. In addition, such charges as malfeasance and bribery may be heard. Administrators who are found to commit immoral acts will usually be removed from office and may in some states lose their license to practice.

Administrative ethics, however, are not limited to these infamous acts. A review of the American Association of School Administrators code of ethics reveals that a violation of some standards of behavior may not be fraudulent before the law. For example, the standards demand that the educational administrator be a caring person in which the welfare of students is central to all decisions. The administrator is obligated to improve the effectiveness of the profession and attempt to correct unwise legislation, and so on. Violations of these standards, however, are not unlawful.

In addition to these officially stated standards of behavior are many informal expectations that legitimize a person in the profession. These might even include manners, dress, and common sense. School administrators who are lazy and fail to perform their tasks well are guilty of unethical conduct. The educational administrator is expected to uphold those unwritten norms of behavior to be promoted to a higher status in the profession and to maintain respectability. For example, a person who frequently is observed to become intoxicated or to engage in improper sexual behavior will not be respected. A certain loyalty to the organization and even to persons is frequently expected. Lack of observance of these normative codes often spells trouble for those administrators who have ambitions to achieve high positions in the field.

School administrators have both externally imposed (e.g., laws) and personal (e.g., matters of personal conscience) obligations for behavior. Laws, board policies, regulations, and the like are obligations imposed externally. However, the administrator is obligated for personal acts of conscience that are well beyond these externally imposed obligations. These obligations of conscience vary in degree of intensity and in importance assigned to them by different school systems. For example, acting in the public interest or maintaining good character has greater intensity than the ethics of form, e.g., mode of dress or conduct of ceremonial functions. On the other hand, the ethics of form (e.g., observing protocol, courtesy, language) may have greater intensity in some school systems than in others.

In summary, educational administrators are obligated to act consistently with the laws, policies, and other externally imposed obligations. They are also expected to uphold certain professional behaviors (e.g., caring, character, loyalty, formalities) accepted by many who practice in the field. Many states have not adopted formal procedures to make an administrative code of ethics binding on those licensed to practice.

See also Administrative Accountability; Administrator Evaluation.

—Ralph Kimbrough
University of Florida

References

Cooper, T.L. (1982). *The responsible administrator.* Port Washington, NY: Kennikat Press.

Kimbrough, R.B. (1985). *Ethics: A course of study for educational leaders.* Arlington, VA: The American Association of School Administrators.

ADMINISTRATIVE POWER

The degree to which administrators in schools are able actually to establish and enforce policies and procedures which reflect their educational philosophy is a strong indicator of the extent to which they hold administrative power.

Power is generally held to be of two classes. Power which comes from the position which one holds in the organization is often referred to as the power of the role or office (sometimes called the authority of office). It is a power which is not person specific; that is, no matter who holds the particular office, this power remains relatively intact. The second type of power is much more reflective of the innate abilities of the individual who holds the particular position and is often referred to as *person-power.* This kind of power is derived from the ability of an individual to convince others that he or she has the "right" answer with regard to a problem or situation. It is not directly related to the position which the person exercising it might hold within the organization.

The strongest kind of administrative power is a combination of these two classes of power. That is, when a single individual is able to utilize his or her personality in the direction of particular goals and, at the same time, has the appropriate level of authority to enforce his or her decisions within the organizational context, then, a very strong level of administrative power exists.

Types of Power

Two major views of administrative power are found in organizational research. One, developed by Etzioni conceptualizes power as the ability to invoke compliance by subordinates to the desires of the leader. The other, developed by French and Raven, views power as an exchange between subordinates and superiors.

Etzioni suggests three sources of power: normative, coercive, and remunerative. Coercive power utilizes force, either physical or threats of physical force, to ensure compliance with the leader's will. Normative power has as its base the utilization of symbolic means of exercising control, such as the priest's ability to withhold sacraments. Remunerative power derives its strength from the ability to give or withhold material goods or resources.

French and Raven suggest five foundations upon which power may be based: legitimate, reward, coercive, referent, and expert. Legitimate power is operant when subordinates perceive that the administrator has the right or authority by virtue of his or her office to make a certain decision. Administrators are almost always given legitimate power to make decisions with regard to routine operational matters such as deciding when schools should close for inclement weather or approving teacher absences. Power based on reward exists when subordinates' willingness to heed the directives of the administrator are tied directly to the administrator's abilities to reward the subordinate through the various instruments at his disposal, such as good evaluations or approval of material requests. Referent power is somewhat a manifestation of reward power but, in this case, the follower sees rewards coming forth because of the association which the administrator has with others within the school organization who are in a position to give rewards or favors. Coercive power is derived from the belief, held by the subordinate, that the administrator has the ability to punish. In schools, that punishment is invariably psychological, i.e., poor classroom or teaching assignments or strict enforcement of regulations with regards to a teacher's tardiness. Expert power has as its foundation the concept that the administrator is able to elicit compliance because of his or her expertise in a particular area. The members of the organization follow this leadership because they trust the ability of the administrator to figure out what is best for their group.

Power Arenas

The ability to exert power can also be viewed as being situational; that is, there may be certain kinds of decisions or certain elements within the organization where an individual can exert power. Pfeffer explains some of these sources of power by concentrating on the abilities of administrators to excel in different arenas. He suggests that there are at least five arenas in which one may gain power for use within an organization such as schools. These arenas are resource provision, uncertain environments, decision process, consensus-seeking, and policies.

Organizations are dependent upon a constant supply of resources in order to remain effective. An administrator who is able to control any of these sources of resources gains power within the organization. Since schools are open systems, adjustments in their operations are often made in order to respond to environmental demands. This constant changing brings with it a rather significant degree of uncertainty. An administrator who is capable of dealing with this uncertainty in an effective manner gains power to affect the outcomes of the system. Another source of power is tied to the organizational decision-making process and the administrator's ability to influence decisions which occur at all of the different levels within the school system. Administrators may also utilize group consensus to strengthen positions with other constituencies or use agreement between a number of constituencies to unite for a common cause. Lastly, the ability to engage effectively the political process is an important source of power.

Power does not, then, come to the administrator simply because of the position held. Effective administrators gain power in a variety of ways with the various constituencies with which they work. For some members of the school organization, compliance may be forthcoming because of their desire to keep their jobs, for others it may be out of respect for the abilities of the administrator, and for others it will be because the person holds a particular position. Since power is necessary to affect change, it is imperative that school administrators understand its various sources and how they can best be integrated to provide for effective administration.

See also Administrative Authority; Conflict Resolution; Decision Making; Delegating Authority.

—W. Hal Knight
East Tennessee State University

References

Etzioni, A. (1964). *Modern organization.* Englewood Cliffs, NJ: Prentice-Hall.

French, J.R.P., & Raven, B. (1959). "The bases of social power." In D. Cartwright (Ed.), *Studies in social power.* Ann Arbor, MI: University of Michigan, Institute for Social Research.

Pfeffer, J. (1978). "The micropolitics of organization." In M.W. Meyer (Ed.), *Environments and organizations.* San Francisco: Jossey-Bass.

ADMINISTRATIVE PREPARATION

The search for the best procedure to prepare educational administrators has heightened in the 1980s. This increase in activity has been led by professional administrator associations and scholars in the discipline of educational administration in response to the national concern for more effective schools. These scholars and practicing school administrators are cooperating to close the gap between the academic content in formal graduate study and the specific professional skills necessary for successful school management. Although much has been written about university-based administrative preparation programs, the literature lacks an extensive research base with clear cause and effect explanations.

Program Ingredients

Surveys providing general descriptions of preparation programs inevitably mask significant variations. Such variations notwithstanding, the surveys suggest common elements found in the programs. They range from offering master's degrees with state certification to offering doctorates in various specializations within administration. These programs contain many similarities in methods of instruction, content of instruction, and field experience. Most programs offer courses which emphasize organizational behavior and theory, theories and methods of educational change and planning, management information systems and human resource management. Also, more specific on-the-job competence and skills are taught (i.e., finance, law, facilities, politics, personnel, curriculum, instruction, evaluation, the principalship and superintendency.) Internships conducted jointly by universities and school districts are vital ingredients of most programs.

Theory and Practice

Recent surveys by the American Association of School Administrators and university researchers found practicing school administrators generally pleased with their graduate programs. However, other surveys reveal numerous complaints from practitioners who find discrepancies between what they do on the job and the training they received in graduate classes.

These mixed opinions about the usefulness and quality of traditional university preparation programs have prompted the growth of nontraditional or external degree programs as well as training programs and academies by national administrator associations, school districts, and state departments of education. The quality of these programs varies, since some place more emphasis than others on the knowledge base, research evidence, and examples of successful practice. Preparation programs which link universities to professional associations and school districts are leading the way in differentiating classroom learning from skills learned on the job. Several encouraging, innovative approaches which will influence administrative preparation for years to come now are under way.

New Directions

Those interested in designing new administrative preparation programs or reconditioning old ones would be well advised to take note of the efforts by the American Association of School Administrators (AASA), the National Association of Secondary School Principals (NASSP), the University Council for Educational Administration (UCEA), and the National Conference of Professors of Educational Administration (NCPEA).

None of these groups is advocating startling change in administrative preparation, but each is widening its examinations of the assumptions upon which current practices and research are based. Cooperation among these groups has produced task forces to test hypotheses and to debate the diverse bodies of literature which give rise to current preparation methodologies. As a result of these inquiries, insight is gained about correspondence between common learnings from the literature of the administrative sciences and the successful application of on-the-job skills. Observers have agreed that the complexities in the study of educational administration can hardly be reduced to a specific list of competencies and skills.

The American Association of School Administrators, in concert with university professors, has produced a set of preparation guidelines which attempt to identify the relationship among the common learnings, conventional wisdom, and practice. *The Guidelines for the Preparation of School Administrators,* 2nd Edition 1983, and the subsequent textbook, *Skills for Successful School Leaders,* are based on seven leadership outcome goals. The Association emphasizes that all school administrators should have a firm grasp of the theoretical foundations and demonstrate the application of the following seven performance goals:

1. Establish and maintain a positive and open learning environment to bring about the motivation and social integration of students and staff.
2. Build strong local, state, and national support for education.
3. Develop and deliver an effective curriculum that expands definitions of literacy, competency, and cultural integration to include advanced technologies, problem solving, critical thinking and communication skills, and cultural enrichment for all students.
4. Develop and implement effective models/modes of instructional delivery that make the best use of time, staff, advanced technologies, community resources, and financial means to maximize student outcome.
5. Create a program of continuous improvement, including evaluation of both staff and program effectiveness as keys to student learning and development.
6. Skillfully manage school system operations and facilities to enhance student learning.
7. Conduct and make use of significant research as a basis for problem solving and program planning of all kinds.

For each leadership outcome goal, these guidelines and the textbook include related competencies and skills. Also, included are appropriate strategies to diagnose student skill levels and program design, delivery and evaluation components.

The National Association of Secondary School Principals' university consortium has produced a special report, *Performance-Based Preparation of Principals*. The project is a product of 15 years of collaborative effort between this association and the university community to improve administrative preparation programs. A set of twelve generic skills have been identified for the principalship. These skills are to be taught and then evaluated through a detailed assessment center approach. Early research findings reveal promise in discovering a clearer understanding of the effects of preparation on job performance. The twelve generic skill descriptors of the assessment center project are problem analysis, judgment, organizational ability, decisiveness, leadership, sensitivity, stress tolerance, oral communication, written communication, range of interests, personal motivation, and educational values.

The University Council for Educational Administration has established a program study center on administrative preparation. It is gathering and processing information and conducting research and seminars to improve its information base and to provide assistance to smaller schools, universities, and state departments. The American Educational Research Association, Division A, and the National Conference of Professors of Educational Administration each conduct critical analyses to expand the understanding and improved practice of preparing educational administrators for the twenty-first century. Some questions go unanswered, but educational leaders are providing many key answers to the effective preparation of administrative leaders.

See also Administrative Styles; Administrative Theory; Administrator Effectiveness; Administrator Evaluation.

—John R. Hoyle
Texas A&M University

References

Hoyle, J.R. (1985). "Programs in educational administration and the AASA preparation guidelines." *Educational Administration Quarterly, 21*, 71–93.

Hoyle, J.R., English, F.W., & Steffy, B. (1985). *Skills for successful school leaders*. Arlington, VA: American Association of School Administrators.

Miklos, E. (1988). "Administrator selection, career patterns, succession, and socialization." In N.J. Boyan (Ed.), *The handbook of research on educational administration*. White Plains, NY: Longman, Inc., 53–76.

ADMINISTRATIVE ROLES

The term role is used in several ways. Sociologically it is defined as a set of expectations which deal with responsibilities and rights. When the role incumbent exercises the responsibilities and rights, that person is performing the role. A second definition comes from drama where a person assumes a "role" to act. The actor becomes another person. Thus, in the role of superintendent one is not one's ordinary self. A third conception is more generalized than either of the above. It is a complex of specific behaviors, or a function, as in leadership role, management role, and decision-making role.

The three concepts are clearly related, differing more in focus and emphasis than in substance. Usually, the terms role and position are synonymous. The "role of principal" means simultaneously the position of principal; the duties, responsibilities and rights attached to the office; and such functions as instructional leadership and administrative coordination.

Role Theory

Roles are defined in terms of expectations. Some expectations are formally spelled out in statutes, rules and regulations, and job descriptions. Others exist as social and professional norms. Expectations may be specific or ambiguous, mandatory or discretionary, uniform or diverse. Groups and individuals may hold highly divergent expectations for a given role, or place expectations in a different order of priority. There is, therefore, always a probability of role conflict.

The behavior of the role incumbent is largely determined by expectations and perceptions of those expectations. Expectations are effective because those holding them also have sanctions at their disposal. Sanctions—rewards and punishments—range from informal to formal, and are effective according to the importance assigned them by the role incumbent. Informal sanctions may consist of no more than expressions of approval or disapproval. Formal sanctions may be as serious as legal action or dismissal from a position.

Roles are interdependent and are usually arranged in some form of network. Some roles are placed in hierarchical order with relevant rights and obligations spelled out. Others may be set in peer relationships. The interaction of mutual role expectations creates much of the organizational structure and operation. Another major determinant of action is the personal orientation of the role incumbent.

Common Administrative Roles

There are many administrative roles in a school system. The following are given as examples: superintendent, assistant superintendent, principal.

The Superintendent. As the chief executive officer of the school board, the superintendent is subject to the expectations of the board, central office personnel, principals and teachers, and related community groups. The superintendent is responsible for working with the board and community groups on matters of goal discernment and resource development and with the staff on the operational policies and educational programs of the schools. In assisting the board by preparing relevant information, the superintendent points out probable consequences of proposed actions, gives professional advice, and devises strategies for implementing policy decisions.

The superintendent's role is that of a generalist concerned with the school system as a whole rather than with specific details of classroom operation. In a large system, primary concern should be with questions of goals, policies, and directions, and with enlisting community understanding of, and support for, schools.

The Assistant Superintendent. In systems too large to be administered by a single superintendent, the work of the central office is allocated to a number of assistant superintendents. Typically, each assistant superintendent is placed in charge of a general area such as elementary education, secondary education, special services, or business administration.

The assistants, together with the superintendent, often form an administrative council, in which competing demands from many parts of the system can be examined in relation to overall needs and resources, and in which policy matters can be operationalized. Assistants are delegated authority and responsibility by the superintendent, and in turn, are accountable to the superintendent. They, too, are concerned with general, systemwide issues rather than with specifics of classroom instruction and learning.

The business aspects of school system operation—finance, accounting, purchasing, plant operation and maintenance—is also placed on this level. Although it is qualitatively different from instructional programs, business operations must be effectively coordinated with them. Hence, the role of business administrator is subordinated to that of the superintendent, an educator.

The Principal. Elementary and secondary schools differ significantly, but the roles of their principals are similar. In both the high school and elementary school, the principal is expected to work with people—teachers, pupils, support staff, and parents. Effective principals in both kinds of schools help other people to work out their best relationships. They help to define and allocate tasks and to coordinate the efforts of many people.

The role of principal as local school leader is widely accepted, but there is often disagreement over how this can be achieved most effectively. On one hand are those who expect the principal to be a line officer, performing mainly line functions such as directing the work of subordinates. Proponents of this position recommend decentralizing much of the administrative management of the system; responsibilities such as budgeting, accounting, and personnel management can then be delegated to the principal. Such delegation, it is held, gives the principal flexibility which allows him or her to establish local priorities and to meet local needs. In this approach, personal concerns and dimensions of administration are minimized.

On the other hand, it is held that, though the principal is formally a line officer, line authority and line functions should be minimized in favor of close working relationships with professional colleagues. Developing education programs and solving related problems are highly complex undertakings and require extensive commitment of all participants. Such commitment is most likely where there are collegial relationships, mutual respect for competence, and free exchange of ideas. Authority differentials are deemphasized in favor of participative decision processes. It is also implied that less of the overall administrative operation will be delegated by the central office.

Generalized Administrative Roles

Certain administrative functions, such as leadership, apply to all administrative roles in the system. Each administrator is expected to perform the functions that are required by his or her position and location. The behavioral implications for the superintendent are distinctly different from those for the principal, for example. Four such roles are discussed to illustrate this point.

Role of the Leader. Much has been written about leaders and leadership. It is agreed that leadership is crucial, but is is not clear exactly what it is and how it operates, nor what behaviors constitute leadership in particular situations. Leadership is concerned first with goal issues: defining, refining, clarifying, and devising strategies for goal attainment. Good leaders have, and are able to communicate, a vision of what is desirable and possible. Second, leadership is concerned with creating good working environments and with stimulating and motivating coworkers. Leaders are able to clarify the roles and role relations required for effective work. They are concerned with excellence, but are also aware that the means employed to achieve excellence may be as important as the ends sought.

Role of the Manager. Efficient management of essential details is of central importance. Although this kind of management is often dismissed as "administrivia," it is necessary. Indeed, the epithet "bureaucracy" is often applied when it fails. Of course, management of detail must contribute to the central tasks of learning and teaching. Thus, supplies must be managed so as to contribute to instructional processes; personnel practices must contribute to motivation and morale. Administrators need not perform all management tasks; they must, however, ensure that tasks are done, and done well.

Role of Facilitator. It is axiomatic that administration exists to make the work of others easier, more effective, and more efficient than would otherwise be possible. For instance, the principal's role is to make it possible for others—professional teachers—to work more effectively than they could do on their own. Hence, one set of tasks for the principal is to reduce or remove impediments to effective teacher-pupil working relationships, to procure resources, to manage, and to coordinate. Administration is a second-order function, coming after learning and teaching, which are the *raison d'detre* of schools. The facilitator gives precedence to instructional values over administrative values and needs.

Role of Decision Maker. Some authorities identify decision making as the central role in the administrative process. Certainly, effective performance of other roles depends on effective decision making. Sensing problems, isolating causes, gathering information, devising possible courses of action, assessing probable consequences, choosing alternatives, implementing them, and monitoring the effects are all crucial to the process.

Many writers emphasize the importance or participation of colleagues in decision making. Not everyone should participate in every decision, however. Such a practice could paralyze a work group. Decisions involving only managerial matters should be made by managers. Involvement should be extended only to those who have a legitimate interest in the decision problem and its outcome. Involvement can serve a useful communication function and can contribute to professional satisfaction. It can also provide information and judgment that would not be available otherwise. To be effective, participation must be genuine, and it must not become so burdensome as to interfere with mainstream work.

See also Assistant/Associate Superintendent; Principalship; Superintendent of Schools; Supervisory Personnel.

—Frederick Enns
University of Alberta

References

Campbell, R.R., Bridges, E.M., & Nystrand, R.O. (1977). *Introduction to educational administration.* Boston: Allyn & Bacon.

Getzels, J.W., Lipham, J.M., & Campbell, R.F. (1968). *Educational administration as a social process.* New York: Harper & Row.

Owens, R.G. (1970). *Organizational behavior in schools* (Chapters 4, 5, 6). Englewood Cliffs, NJ: Prentice-Hall.

ADMINISTRATIVE SALARIES

Salaries are the largest expenditure within a school district's operating budget. In most instances, salaries represent more than 80 percent of the total operating budget. When salary categories are broken down on a per employee basis, the salaries paid administrators represent the single most costly expenditure. Consequently, it is not surprising that those responsible for the overall operation of a school district are concerned about this important source of direct cost.

Other than as a source of direct cost to a school district, salaries paid administrators have several indirect costs associated with them. One indirect cost for salaries paid administrators is the financial support provided to the school district by the taxpaying public. Because salary data are public information and appear often in the printed media, salaries paid administrators can influence the public's willingness to provide financial support for a school district.

Another indirect cost associated with salaries paid administrators is the selection of future administrative personnel. Salaries paid administrators employed currently by a district will influence the number of applications for administrative openings and the number of acceptances for job offers. Astute candidates considering an administrative position will evaluate both their immediate earning potential and their long-range earning potential based on a school district's present rate of compensation for administrators.

Still another indirect cost associated with salaries paid administrators is staff morale. Grievances, turnovers, and dissatisfaction will be prevalent among and between employee groups when administrators are compensated in an inequitable manner. On one hand, if the salaries paid administrators are either low or inconsistent, then administrators will be disgruntled with their rate of compensation. On the other hand, if the salaries paid administrators are too high, then other employee groups will be disenchanted with their rate of compensation.

To ensure the continued financial support for a school district, to increase the effectiveness of selection practices, and to promote harmonious relationships among employees, salaries paid administrators must be perceived to be equitable. These salaries must be perceived to be equitable by the public at large, by the school board members, and by the employees of the district. The likelihood of all three groups perceiving the salaries paid administrators as equitable will depend, to a large extent, on the district using a systematic plan or procedure for compensating administrators; this plan or procedure should be based on up-to-date data.

Equitability

Most administrators of wage and salary agree that a formal plan or procedure is necessary if administrators are to be compensated at an equitable rate. Specific administrative positions and current salary data are variable and subject to changes in educational practices, to market trends, and to economic fluctuations of the economy. Because of the variability of salary data, school districts having a formalized plan for compensating administrators must review the plan at least on a biannual basis, whereas school districts without a formalized plan should take immediate steps to develop and to adapt a plan for compensating administrators.

Regardless of whether a school district is assessing the current method for compensating administrators or is developing a new method for compensating administrators there are two issues that must be resolved apriori. One issue concerns responsibility for the task, and the other issue concerns criteria to be employed for the task. A definitive answer to the first issue does not exist because the responsibility for the task could be delegated potentially to a committee comprised of local school personnel, to a single employee responsible for administering compensation, to an outside agent with special expertise, or to some combination of the preceding options. The final solution will rest with the technical competencies within the district. It also will be determined by the financial resources of the district and by the credibility associated with the source of responsibility.

With respect to the second issue, there exists an almost universal agreement among professionals in the field of wage and salary administration. Criteria to be used either for evaluating the current method of compensating administrators or for developing a new method of compensating administrators are internal consistency and external competitiveness. The internal consistency criterion pertains to the relative worth of a specific position within a school district as compared with other positions within the same district. External competitiveness refers to the actual worth of a specific position within a district as compared with the market value of the same position in other school districts. Because these criteria are fundamental for adequate compensation of administrators both will be discussed briefly.

Internal Consistency. Most administrative positions are essential for the effective operation of a school district, but some of the administrative positions are more important than some of the other administrative positions. To determine the relative importance of each administrative position as compared with other administrative positions, the analyst must use a systematic job evaluation procedure. Results from the job evaluation process should yield a hierarchical ranking reflecting the relative importance of administrative positions for the school district. The internal consistency criterion is satisfied to the degree that the assessed relative importance of the administrative positions corresponds to the actual salaries paid the position holders.

Compensation literature contains several different job evaluation techniques that can be used to assess the internal consistency for salaries paid school administrators. However, most of these techniques represent some variation from one of the basic methods used most frequently within the context of administrative salaries: (a) job ranking; (b) job classification; (c) factor comparison; and (d) point method. These techniques differ with respect to whether the whole job or the different job components are compared either with other jobs or with fixed standards.

External Competitiveness. Actual salaries paid school administrators should be neither too low nor too high but should be competitive with salaries paid school administrators holding similar positions in comparable districts. To assess the external competitiveness of salaries paid school administrators, the analyst must identify comparable districts. Salary data must be collected. Although comparability within the private sector has been defined narrowly, this concept has taken a much broader definition in education. Comparability for school districts has been justified on one or more of the following: (a) tax base; (b) enrollment; (c) geographic region; and/or (d) athletic conference.

Comparable districts should be solicited for data that are used either to assess the external competitiveness of current salaries or to establish competitive rates for future salaries. Because salaries paid administrators are a function of several factors, data will be needed for the number of persons holding each administrative position, the education attainment and administrative experience of these persons, and the dollar value for monthly salaries and fringe benefits earned by position holders. These data are used to develop compensation curves that reflect for each administrative position both the gross income and the relative hierarchical ranking. Competitive school districts will compensate administrators at a rate falling near the average of all compensation curves.

Conclusion

Salaries paid school administrators represent an important source of direct and indirect cost for the school district. Advantages of these costs can be realized and controlled only through a systematic procedure that yields salaries which are internally consistent and externally competitive. If the administrative positions are justifiable and if the performances of position holders are satisfactory, then school districts should be obligated to provide an equitable rate of compensation.

See also Collective Bargaining; Financing of Schools; Funding Methods: State and Federal; Merit Pay.

—I. Phillip Young
Ohio State University

References

Castetter, W. (1986). *The personnel function in educational administration.* New York: Macmillan.

Harris, B., McIntyre, K., Littleton, V., & Long, D. (1986). *Personnel administration in education.* Boston: Allyn & Bacon.

Patten, T. (1977). *Pay: Employee compensation and incentive plans.* New York: Free Press.

ADMINISTRATIVE STATUS

People desire to become educational administrators for several reasons. Among them is the status that accompanies the position. Status includes the many signs and symbols of the position within an organization, such as privileges, size and location of work space, the number of people supervised, and so on. Prestige, rank, and relative standing among others in the organization are also measures of status.

Administrative status has evolved as the society has changed and as the importance of formal education in the society has changed. Over the years the society has moved from a rural to an urban and suburban society. As the density of the population has been reconfigured, the growth and reorganization of schools has led to the need for persons with more specialized skills to deal with the administrative functions needed to educate that population.

The educational attainment of the United States population is relatively high and continues its trend upward. Illiteracy has declined from over eleven percent in 1900 to less than one percent in 1980. Accompanying this phenomenon is the fact that technological growth has contributed to the need for greater specialization; thus, formal education has brought about increases in social, political, and economic status for all of the population.

First there were teachers; then teachers with some administrative responsibilities; still later the principal-teacher; and finally a principal. The principalship is the oldest administrative position in public education, and it rose as a result of the multiroom school operation. A variety of other administrative positions exist at the district level in larger school organizations.

In the mid-1800s, principals' duties were concerned largely with record keeping and reporting. Late in the 19th century the emphasis shifted from records and reports to organization and general management. More recently, the emphasis has identified the principal as supervisor and instructional leader. District-level administrators are responsible more for dealing with the political and financial needs of the schools than for the direct educational activities of teaching and learning.

Formal education institutions have increasingly assumed a function that was primarily the function of the family in previous years. The importance, therefore, of the school has taken on different dimensions recently, and the status of the executive in charge of the educational program has grown accordingly. Educational programs in communities of all sizes have become focal points of the society. Such visibility has brought increased awareness of educational leaders, and has thus increased their status.

There are many factors that influence status. The position of administrator carries with it a certain level of prestige. It denotes the responsibilities of an executive, manager, or leader within an organization. Administrative positions are in the organizational hierarchy such that they must assume greater levels of authority, responsibility, and influence.

The nature of most administrative positions and responsibility requires a broader view of education than is typically required of the teacher. With this greater scope of activity, the administrator is in charge of larger numbers of people, manages larger budgets, and is faced with broader challenges.

All educators must attain prescribed minimum levels of educational preparation in order to be certified. Administrators typically are required to have more training than is required for teachers. They earn higher salaries and frequently have a longer term of contract than do teachers.

Greater status is generally recognized for administrators than teachers; district-level administrators than building level administrators; and administrators in larger schools than those in smaller schools. Administrative status tends to be correlated positively with the notion of "bigger is better."

Administrators can improve their status by assuming more active and visible community responsibilities and by exhibiting the characteristics of leader, executive, and manager. Promoting positive images of schools tends to be impressive to parents and patrons in communities and will surely contribute to the status of administrators. They tend to be public people and are therefore expected by most to be positive models for the general society.

See also Administrative Roles; Administrative Tasks.

—Larry L. Smiley
University of North Dakota

References

Campbell, R.F., Corbally, J.E., & Nystrand, R.O. (1983). *Introduction to educational administration* (6th ed., Chapters 1 & 4). Boston: Allyn & Bacon.

Knezevich, S.J. (1984). *Administration of public education* (4th ed., Chapters 1, 14, 16, & 25). New York: Harper & Row.
Monahan, W.G., & Hengst, H.R. (1982). *Contemporary educational administration* (Chapters 1 & 2). New York: Macmillan.

ADMINISTRATIVE STRESS

Today educational leaders are faced with more pressure, change, and conflict than in any other decade in the twentieth century. The result: a plugged-in, clipped-on, stir-and-serve setting where educational administrators have become less equipped to handle the conflict, change, and stress of their jobs.

Within the administrative ranks superintendents are popularly identified as those individuals most susceptible to stress, primarily due to the nature of their managerial responsibilities. This exclusive assumption has not been supported by the literature and research. Some evidence exists, for example, that coronary heart disease is more common among middle managers than executives. Conflict, anxiety, frustration, and aggression have crept into all administrators' lives with few outlets in work or leisure to relieve their pressures.

In response to this twentieth-century age of anxiety, a proliferation of materials has been produced: an estimated 200,000 books and articles, 1,000 research projects, and 6,000 additional publications catalogued every year. Research in the area of managerial stress in schools has also been voluminous. Thirty-five studies on administrative stress from 1980 to 1985 pertain to the sources of administrative stress and coping techniques used by administrators. Thus, the literature on administrative stress is also significant in volume and diverse in attention.

The word "stress" is one with which both the layperson and professional are familiar. Administrators encounter stress every day. It is as much a part of their lives as joy, happiness, love, pain, and other feelings of euphoria or defeat. However, due to multiple uses, references, and definitions, the exact meaning of stress remains ambiguous.

The Process of Stress

A broad perspective and clear understanding from which to view administrative stress is needed. Such a perspective is provided by a four-stage stress cycle. The cycle begins with a set of demands or stressors (stage 1). For example, a meeting is a demand as is a telephone interruption, but whether it produces stress depends on the individual's perception (stage 2). Does he or she have the time or resources (either mentally or physically) to meet the demand adequately? If not, the manager perceives the demand as a stressor.

It is possible for the same demand to be perceived as a stressor by one administrator and not another. For example, if an administrator perceives a change in board policy as not demanding unavailable resources, a discrepancy will not exist and stress will not occur. However, if another manager perceives this policy change as demanding much time of which he or she has little, a discrepancy exists and stress ensues.

The stress created by this discrepancy results in a stress response (stage 3). It is here that the coping process for administrators begins. They may go through physiological changes (adrenal secretion, increased heart rate, and so on) that prepare them to ignore, flee, combat, or alleviate the stressor. Although the immediate physiological response is the same for everyone, the behavioral and psychological choice is very much a personal matter. It largely depends on the resources administrators have available and what has worked in the past.

The fourth and final stage, consequences, differs from responses because it takes into account the long-range effects of stress due to its duration and intensity. If an administrator does not alleviate some stressors and learn to cope, consequences may arise in the form of serious mental, behavioral, or physical illnesses.

Administrative Stress

A place to begin to understand and cope with the stresses of school administration is with stage 1. What do we know about the nature of administrative stress in schools? Researchers have found that an administrator's typical work is characterized by an unrelenting pace, brevity of tasks, fragmentation in activities, and a constant preference for live action working with people—all contributing to stress.

Numerous research projects involving school managers throughout the United States have disclosed several stressors which are common to all administrators whether they hold the superintendency or building principalship. These include complying with rules and policies, meetings that take up too much time, completing reports and other paperwork on time, gaining financial support for programs, resolving personnel conflicts, evaluating staff members' performance, making decisions affecting the lives of employees, having too heavy a work load, imposing excessively high self-expectations, and frequent interruptions from telephone calls and drop-in visitors.

While these examples represent specific stressors or demands that bother administrators, the general stress categories of school administrators are conflict mediation, task-based stress (accounting the performance of such daily tasks as meetings and paperwork), role-based stress (including administrators' role interactions and beliefs about their place in the organization), and boundary spanning stress (reflecting their dealings with environments outside their administrative control such as community relations). Within school administration, task-based, role-based, and conflict-mediating stresses are common to all administrative occupations; however, boundary-spanning stress is peculiar to public school administrators.

Coping with Stress

An administrator's personality and disposition play an important role in determining how stressful these conditions become. In other words, stressors in stage 1 represent a set of objective demands, which can become subjectively stressful only when administrators perceive them to be. To understand this process of administrative stress, the following definition of stress is posited: "The anticipation of one's lack of ability to respond adequately to a perceived demand, accompanied by his or her anticipation of negative consequences of an inadequate response."

This definition is based on administrators' perceptions of their ability to meet the challenges of their jobs. As defined previously this perception creates a negative stress response when they imagine they do not have the skills necessary to meet a challenge. However, stress can be positive if the skills are present and used to meet the challenge.

With regard to stage 3 of the stress cycle, the literature on coping addresses popular and academic concerns as well as conceptual, theoretical, and empirical investigations. From this body of research several propositions can be offered. First of all, the individual is the most important variable—no one coping technique is effective for all individuals in all situations. Second, coping techniques must be sensitive to cultural, social, psychological, and environmental differences in individuals. In addition, individuals who cope best develop a repertoire of techniques to counteract different stressors in different situations.

The above propositions notwithstanding, identifiable categories of coping have been identified by educational administrators. These include "social support" activities such as having lunch with friends, playing games, and talking with peers; "physical activities," including running, walking, meditating, and playing sports; "intellectual stimulation" such as attending professional conferences and attending cultural events; "entertainment," which encompasses watching television, going to a movie, or taking a vacation; "personal interests" such as hobbies; "self-management" techniques representing such things as practicing time and conflict management principles; and "attitudes" such as positive beliefs and knowing one's limitations.

Thus, if administrators take charge and control the first three stages of the stress cycle, the fourth stage of consequences will not necessarily represent illness but wellness. However, it needs to be emphasized that despite everything that has been researched, written, and spoken about administrative stress, no ready-made stress formula exists that will suit every administrator.

See also Teacher Stress and Burnout.

—Walter Gmelch
Washington State University

References

Gmelch, W.H. (1982). *Beyond stress to effective management.* New York: John Wiley & Sons.

Hansen, P.E. (1986). *The joy of stress.* New York: Andrews, McMeel & Parker.

Hansen, P.E. (1985). *Stress management for the executive* (compiled and edited by Executive Health Examiners). New York: Berkeley Books.

ADMINISTRATIVE STYLES

The topic of administrative styles acknowledges the existence of variations in the performance of administrative responsibilities. Persisting diverse styles confirm that, as work, administration continues to defy standardization. Students of style seek to describe, analyze, and explain practitioners' multifarious approaches to their work. There are two main lines of investigation. Individual executives may be observed for the peculiar ways they perform their tasks over the course of their own career paths. This is style *of* work. Then particular career roles in administration (e.g., principalship, superintendency regional directorship) may be studied to assess causes of influence and the extent to which role incumbents are able to exert influence. This is style *in* work.

An administrative style may be defined as an individual's characteristic way of administering. Styles of work are accounted for psychodynamically. The habits and patterned ways of acting followed by administrators originate in their early career learning. Acceptance by others and the achievement of self-esteem requires the neophyte to evolve an identity or consistency in definition and presentation of self. This, in turn, necessitates resolving inner conflicts stemming from early childhood nurturance. Situational demands impose themselves and, if stressful, reactivate latent anxieties, irremediably coloring the individual's experience of success or failure. It is in early socialization around these emerging patterns of adjustment that styles begin to cohere. With experience and accumulating actions they calcify like the marine secretions on a coral reef. Styles prove remarkably intractable and resistant to change.

Types

Instead of the usual differentiation between individuals who are typecast as autocrat, democrat and, perhaps, the laissez-faire administrator, a more enlightening list is included. Research reveals the following common types of styles: perfectionist, narcissist, paranoid, schizoid, impulsive, combative, and idealist. This is by no means exhaustive, and there are hybrid types combining two or more categories. Any one person rarely fits exactly into one slot.

Perfectionists are obsessed by the need to master detail and to keep on top of things. High standards are set which for their own well-being must be met by themselves and others. This makes the perfectionists prone to rigidity and difficult to live with, especially when they are sticklers for the rules and bureaucratic machinery. *Narcissistic individuals*, by contrast, constantly draw attention to themselves. They feed on hubris, worshipping their own grandiosity. Others are used to mirror back confirmation of their idealized self-images. Those who are *paranoid* are obsessed by threats, searching for signs and enemies. These are then used to justify action. They constantly label, smear and scapegoat various 'out-groups' to secure their own following.

The *schizoid* type comes closest to being organizationally autistic. A very poor grasp of reality and the urge to escape or withdraw from it all has taken root here. This detachment behind closed doors and an inability to communicate creates a power vacuum. Rival factions have free reign. Sometimes individuals are highly unpredictable, and their actions appear to be the expression of mere whim and fancy. These are the *impulsives*. The impulsives are poor planners and subject to violent swings of mood. Subordinates are frequently uncertain where they stand. *Combatives*, by virtue of their toughness, offer others, above all, protection. These people thrive on conflict and adversarial posturing. It is essential to their self-definition. They are both dominant and divisive in their effects. Lastly, there are the *idealists*, who live on hope and assume human nature to be infinitely malleable, perhaps even perfectible. They are romantics and utopians with big visions, but often lack the wheels to make them run.

Utility

No one style type commends itself as intrinsically superior to any other. Case histories and biographies of leaders and administrators in all spheres and at all levels reveal individuals with strengths and weaknesses. Nor is there an ideally best style. Nominating particular approaches as more or less desirable can be done only from a particular ideological standpoint. And since styles are so closely bound up with each individual's basic character structure and identity they are not readily transformable, sloughed off, or exchanged.

There are two courses of action open to administrators. Evidence exists that in early and midcareer individuals are highly susceptible to the influence of mentors. Mentoring is an intensely emotional dyadic learning experience between a venerable elder who dispenses wisdom, and a rookie, who soaks it up. If the encounter is sufficiently congenial to both, some important modeling of relationships normally ensues. Workstyles can be honed through mentoring.

Likewise, systematic reflection on the documented lives of leaders in all cultures and epochs as well as the histories of organizations pays dividends. All sorts of questions can be asked. Traits and attributes admit of comparison, the range of options predating action examined and the subsequent effects on the livelihood of various groups can be traced out. And the important assessment of whether individuals could have acted otherwise is permitted.

Conclusion

Administrative styles have attained importance and recognition only recently, thanks to the emergence of leader and administrator watchers among journalists and academics. Contouring the work of public figures has now become a craft in its own right. Recent analyses have emphasized the significance of collective work styles. However, because the dominant styles of key founding figures in an organization influence hiring and recruitment practices, particular patterns come to perpetuate themselves over time. The result can be regressive, to the disastrous cost of all concerned, when tried and true patterns are no longer suited to changed social conditions. This suggests an inextricable link in practice between work styles, the life cycle of organizations, and social context and the requirement that all three be monitored simultaneously.

See also Administrative Authority; Administrative Power.

—Peter C. Gronn
Monash University
Victoria, Australia

References

Davies, A.F. (1980). *Skills, outlooks and passions* (Chapter 3). Cambridge, MA: Cambridge University Press.

Hodgson, R.C., Levinson, D.J, & Zaleznik, A. (1965). *The executive role constellation*. Boston: Harvard University, Graduate School of Business Administration.

Kets de Vries, M.F.R., & Miller, D. (1984). *The neurotic organization*. London: Jossey-Bass.

ADMINISTRATIVE TASKS

One's concept of administrative tasks depends upon one's perspective. A variety of concepts may exist, depending on whether one is a school board member, a superintendent, a central office person, a principal, a teacher, a member of the support staff, a student, or a parent. The tasks of the administrator have changed over time and will probably continue to change. More specialized roles have developed because of collective bargaining, increased technology, demand for more school services by the public, and an increase in the size of school districts.

Educational Administration and Administrative Tasks

A number of administrative texts do not list administrative tasks in the index. Instead, one will find terms such as "administrative behavior," "administrative functions," "administrative roles," "administrative leaders" and "administrative competencies." The term "management" has been used in some cases to replace the term "administration."

There are at least as many definitions for educational administration as there are for administrative tasks. Basically, educational administration is the use of leadership skills to manage human and material resources in an efficient and effective way in order to meet the needs of students and society. This definition definitely sets the tone that administrative tasks are complex.

The educational administrator must meet the personal goals of those who work within the organization as well as the goals of the organization itself. In order to accomplish this, the administrator has many tasks. These include goal setting, planning, organizing, coordinating, communicating, motivating, facilitating, decision making, and evaluating. Evaluation is necessary to determine the extent to which goals have been met. It is evident that the administrative process is a continuous one. Assistance is necessary if the administrator is going to perform these tasks effectively. This assistance can be provided by administrators at various levels within the organization.

Superintendent. The superintendent would have tasks dealing with the following: (a) school boards, (b) policy development, (c) personnel, (d) school facilities, (e) curriculum and instruction, (f) collective bargaining, (g) transportation, (h) school business management, (i) school community relations, (j) program evaluation, (k) legal matters, (l) periodic reports, (m) in-service education, and (n) evaluation of other administrators.

School board members normally have the most contact with the superintendent since he or she serves as the executive officer for the board. They would expect the superintendent to provide them with information to make informed decisions. Some superintendents also provide administrative recommendations for the board to consider.

Central Office Personnel. Central office administrators would be utilized by the superintendent to perform those tasks which provide support for actions the board directs and also to assist in providing resources and leadership for building-level administrators, teachers, and noncertified staff. Central office administrators' tasks are more specialized than those of the superintendent. The superintendent would be more of a generalist. In large districts all tasks associated with a central office administrator may relate almost entirely to one of the general tasks of the superintendent. One administrator may be totally responsible for transportation, another administrator with curriculum and instruction, another with facilities, and yet another with personnel. In smaller districts, the superintendent and two or three other administrators would perform all of these tasks. Quite often the building-level principal would be enlisted to assist.

Building-Level Principals. Typical administrative tasks performed by the building-level administrator include work related to (a) discipline, (b) student activities, (c) scheduling, (d) curriculum development, (e) teacher evaluation, (f) in-service for teachers, (g) counseling, (h) food service, (i) building maintenance, (j) athletics, (k) hiring new teachers, (l) noncertified staff, (m) student attendance, (n) building-level budgets, (o) school-community relations, (p) student transportation, (q) student records, (r) local and state reports, (s) health and safety of students, (t) student testing, (u) meeting needs of special students, (v) library services, (w) audio-visual services, and (x) textbook adoption.

Building-level administrators look to the central office to perform those tasks which assist them in operating a building. If the building-level principal has some assistants, he or she would normally divide the tasks so that a team approach is utilized to insure that all tasks are performed. Some buildings are operated by associate principals who have the same authority level and can coordinate their activities and manage the building as a team rather than having one person who has ultimate authority.

According to research, principals are key individuals in the development of effective schools. The task of leadership by the principal is an important factor in the success of a school. As a leader, the principal must take responsibility for developing goals for his or her school which will lead to student success. The specific tasks which a principal must perform to meet these goals depend on the situation in which he or she finds himself or herself. Schools may be found in a variety of situations—rural, urban, suburban, low socioeconomic, high socioeconomic, etc. The most important task for a principal is to provide strong leadership which results in a solid team approach to reaching goals at the building level. Teachers are an important part of the team. Building-level administrators must insure that the tasks they perform assist teachers in providing the best instruction possible for students.

The Ultimate Purpose

The result of all administrative tasks should be to provide a better learning environment for students. Parents are interested in seeing their children learn at the highest level possible and thus expect all administrators to perform administrative tasks which fulfill this expectation.

See also Budgeting; Curriculum Development; Facilities Planning; School Community Relations; Staff Development.

—Dale Findley
Indiana State University

References

Knezevich, S.J. (1984). *Administration of public education: A source book for the leadership and management of educational institutions.* New York: Harper & Row.

Wood, C.L., Nicholson, E.W., & Findley, D.G. (1985). *The secondary school principal: Manager and supervisor.* Boston: Allyn & Bacon.

ADMINISTRATIVE TEAM, DISTRICT LEVEL

The concept of team management holds great potential for contributing to school districts becoming environments in which community, board, administration, and staff work together in providing quality education. Interest in team management has been stimulated by the successful experiences of Japanese and American industries and by a growing number of school districts in the United States. Organizational research evidence also has aroused interest. The evidence suggests that educational organizations which implement team leadership tend to enrich the professional educator's sense of self-fulfillment, provide greater job satisfaction, reduce burnout, reduce conflict, increase employee influence upon the work environment, and improve the quality of education. This article offers a definition of team management. It also provides a description of team management function and form and sets forth the characteristics of effective team management on the district level.

Team management is leadership by consensus. With leadership by consensus, the shared leadership empowers individuals in the organization and encourages them to make use of their talents. Leadership which acknowledges the talents of each person and encourages this alternative organization is the type of leadership required for team management. Team management is a consensus decision-making process used within an organization to solve problems collaboratively and creatively. Decision making by consensus is agreeing to implement a decision which is most acceptable to the group as a whole.

Team management has the primary function of collaborative problem solving carried out through the form of multiple interrelated teams within the organization. Individuals who have particular expertise are brought together into teams. They make decisions by consensus; they may not all be in unanimous accord, but they at least agree to implement a decision which is most acceptable to the group as a whole.

The primary function of team management within a school district is to solve problems in a collaborative and creative manner. A productive organization is a cohesive, creative problem-solving organism. Problems and opportunities are stimuli for educational improvement. Teachers, staff, administrators, community members, students, and parents all have some vested interest in the educational enterprise. Each person has a unique view of what the problems and opportunities are for quality education in the district. Each person also has unique talents which may be valuable resources in solving the problems and optimizing the opportunities confronting the system.

Problem solving in a team proceeds through the stages of problem identification, information gathering, alternative solution generation, solution choosing, solution implementation, and solution evaluation. The unique perspectives and talents of various people within the school district should be used appropriately in making decisions at each stage of the process. For example, at the problem identification stage, it may be useful to obtain community members', teachers', and administrators' perceptions of problems in the school district; at the alternative solutions generation stage, it may be helpful to ask individuals inside and outside the system who have expert knowledge to participate. Collaborative problem solving is the merging of individual and/or subgroup energy to solve problems. For people to be willing to give their energy, they need to feel respected, trusted, and rewarded; conversely, they also need to give respect, trust, and rewards to those with whom they work. Creative problem solving is the development of new ways to deal with problems.

The structure or form of the school district which facilitates problem solving is a network of interrelated teams. Horizontal and vertical teams are assembled to make decisions. The team management concept is usually implemented by forming an administrative team which is a group of administrative specialists who meet formally with the chief executive officer and who work together as a team to discharge their decision-making responsibilities with the organization. In large school districts, this team typically includes the superintendent and a cabinet of key central-office administrators; in smaller systems, the team typically includes the superintendent, central-office administrators, and principals. As people in school districts become more experienced and skilled in working in teams, modifications in the team structures may occur. The organizational structure in which team management operates is flexible and characterized by teams with an organic rather than a bureaucratic orientation.

School districts committed to developing administrative teams should be aware of the characteristics of effective team management on the district level and direct their efforts toward creating conditions for successful implementation of the concept. Characteristics of effective team management are team clarity of goals, leadership which empowers, participative decision making, and fluid communication. Effective management teams in school districts have a clear and common understanding of what they are to accomplish and how they will accomplish the task. Members of the team are committed to working together to achieve group goals and give their talents willingly to the work of the team. Members of the team also have a clear understanding of what each team member's contributions are to be and acknowledge the fulfillment of team responsibilities.

Effective management teams also have leaders who have an intention for the team, communicate well with people, organize the team to achieve the intention, give themselves to the work of the team, and motivate others by empowering them. Effective team leaders recognize and respect the talent of team members and give them the power to make decisions. Team members participate in making decisions through consensus. In order to make sound decisions, team members need valid and accurate information; therefore, effective management teams have open and fluid communication to keep all of the members well informed.

Team management on the district level holds great potential for improved educational organizations. Through combining the talents of individuals within the school district on administrative teams, problems confronting education can be solved creatively and effectively. School districts which implement team management can become more productive. They can enrich educational environments.

See also Central Office Personnel; Group Processes; School Business Manager; Superintendent of Schools.

—Nancy A. Evers
University of Cincinnati

References

Bennis, W., & Nanus, B. (1985). *Leaders: The strategies for taking charge.* New York: Harper & Row.

Shaw, M.E. (1981). *Group dynamics: The psychology of small group behavior.* New York: McGraw-Hill.

Wynn, R., & Guditus, C.W. (1984). *Team management: Leadership by consensus.* Columbus, OH: Charles E. Merrill.

ADMINISTRATIVE THEORY

To many administrators, the word "theory" evokes negative feelings and aversive reactions. Theory is too abstract, too academic, too full of jargon, these people believe, to be of any practical use. In fact, all administrative action is grounded in theories of some sort, although these may be only partially formulated and unconsciously applied. The merit of academic or scientific theories, despite their abstruse language and unfamiliar concepts, is that they identify some of the underlying dynamics of organizational events that often elude common-sense understanding.

Theories developed in the behavioral science disciplines (such as social psychology, sociology, and anthropology) can be of immense practical use to administrators who are charged with understanding, predicting, and controlling events in their schools or school systems. The purpose of this article is to illustrate the utility of administrative theory for explanation, prediction, and control in schools. We conclude with a practical strategy for systematically utilizing theories to improve practice and increase professional effectiveness.

The Utility of Administrative Theories

In order to lead effectively and efficiently within an organization, one must first understand how organizations function and how people within organizations tend to behave. This brings us to the first important function of theory, *explanation.* Many organizational theories provide explanations that surpass common-sense interpretations of events and thus expand administrators' understandings. An example of a frequently misunderstood phenomenon is student discipline: despite clear discipline policies and consistent enforcement, many school administrators find that some students repeatedly misbehave, showing up frequently for punitive measures. A sociological theory of compliance developed by Amitai Etzioni demonstrates that coercive uses of power tend to increase participants' feelings of alienation and hostility, thus increasing the likelihood of more disruptive behavior. On the other hand, the use of only normative or symbolic power generally has the more positive effect of raising participants' commitment and appreciation of the organization. This theory is one of many that explain some of the dynamics of organizational life not easily recognized through observation alone.

The most important reason for understanding organizational behavior is to assist administrators to foresee the outcomes of their own and others' actions. This brings us to the second function of theory, *prediction.* Organizational theories are more effective than intuition alone in helping administrators predict the near future. An issue in the popular press serves to illustrate this point. Many legislators and journalists are clamoring for merit pay for teachers, their intuitive prediction being that this will increase teacher motivation. Frederick Herzberg's theory of job attitudes makes it clear, however, that salary does *not* affect motivation in the long run; other factors, such as recognition and opportunities for growth, have a more powerful and lasting effect on motivation. Astute administrators can safely predict that salary increases will not affect teacher motivation, but that other kinds of changes within schools are likely to have more salutary effects on staff (and student) motivation.

The primary reason for wanting to predict the future is in order to exercise some influence over the course of events. This brings us to the third important function of administrative theory, *control.* While there are countless events in the normal course of school life that defy human intervention, there are innumerable other events that spell the difference between excellent and ineffective administrators. Control over the quality of teaching in a school is one of many examples of the utility of administrative theories for control. Victor Vroom's expectancy theory highlights two key aspects of individuals' motivation to perform well.

First, there must be consistent and meaningful rewards (not necessarily monetary) for excellent teaching; second, the teacher must have self-confidence to believe his/her effort will make a significant difference for students. The second of these elements is the more frequently overlooked by administrators in their intuitive attempts to improve teachers' classroom performance. Those administrators who understand the theory thoroughly and act upon it sensitively are those best able to control (and enhance) the quality of teaching in their schools or districts.

These are examples of the utility of theories drawn from the behavioral sciences for purposes of explanation, prediction, and control in schools. In actuality, each substantiated social-science theory contributes to the expansion of the administrator's repertoire of understandings, insights, and strategies. Although the theories cited thus far were developed during the 1950's and 1960's, they remain useful alongside more contemporary views of organizations.

Current Perspectives on Organizations

Two schools of thought that have come to the fore during the past decade yield additional insights into the nature of organizations and the human behavior within them. A brief overview of these viewpoints is provided here.

A number of contemporary theorists maintain that organizations are not at all like natural objects that can be studied dispassionately or scientifically. Nor are they like houses or gigantic shells filled with people. Instead, organizations are the fluid creations or interpretations people place on their experiences in their day-to-day interactions; organizations are no more and no less than the subjective constructions of the people who recreate patterns of interaction day by day.

Administrators who understand that such "psuedophenomena" as authority, leadership, climate, and intelligence are but conventions that are precariously re-enacted each day—and who recognize that others' perspectives are different from their own, though equally valid—are the more likely to appreciate others' views and act accordingly in a sympathetic and constructive manner. This perspective, a phenomenological one, adds an important dimension to the administrator's conception of the school as an organization.

Other contemporary theorists have been developing a critical theory of education which emphasizes how schools perpetuate the inequalities of society at large even while educators believe themselves to be striving toward equity. Critical theorists point to such common practices as within-class "ability" grouping, tracking students, relying on mass-produced text books and instructional programs, and "packaging" school curriculum as if knowledge were a commodity to be distributed; these and other aspects of school life serve to reproduce the existing inequitable power structures of society instead of expanding opportunities for children of the poor and for racial and ethnic minorities. A thorough understanding of this body of thought, the new sociology of education, would help administrators recognize dysfunctional aspects of their organizations and initiate changes to advance the interests of a more truly democratic society.

The Systematic Use of Theory

The ability to use theories from the allied academic disciplines to resolve administrative problems does not come easily, but requires conscious effort and practice. With sufficient mental exercise and repetition, the application of theoretical concepts can eventually feel as natural as driving a car or swimming, and the results of the effort can be at least equally rewarding. Furthermore, the consistent application of theories to practice by administrators would greatly enhance the professionalism of the field of educational administration.

A technique introduced by the Center for Advancing Principalship Excellence to increase the systematic use of discipline-based theory in practice provides concise forms whereby school principals record their analysis of situations that arise in their schools and require their attention. The analysis of each situation includes specifying the likely causes of the current situation and pinpointing all the information needed to formulate a reasonable response.

This is where theory comes into play. The principal can draw upon virtually any theory and consider its relevance to the situation at hand, using it both to gain awareness of non-obvious causal factors and to infer a constructive course of action. It is recommended that the administrator use one theory repeatedly for many case situations until the use of that theory feels natural and yields worthwhile insights into many on-the-job experiences. At that point another theory should be added to the administrator's repertoire and used consciously and repeatedly until it, too, comes to mind naturally.

In this way the administrator's range of understandings and insights grows continuously, and his or her ability to explain, predict, and control becomes even more sophisticated. Given the infinite complexity of schools as organizations, there is no limit to the growth and development an administrator can experience on the job by applying theories to practices.

See also Organizations: Principles and Theory; Research on Administration; Systems Theory; Theory X, Theory Y; Theory Z.

—Paula F. Silver
University of Illinois

References

Bates, R.J. (1983). *Educational administration and the management of knowledge.* Victoria, Australia: Deakin University Press.

Gronn, P. (1983). *Rethinking-educational administration: T.B. Greenfield and his critics.* Victoria, Australia: Deakin University Press.

Silver, P.F. (1983). *Educational administration: Theoretical perspectives on practice and research.* New York: Harper & Row.

ADMINISTRATOR EFFECTIVENESS

Perhaps the single most important benefit of the school-effectiveness research of the past decade is the preponderance of evidence pointing to leadership as one of the forces behind school organizations that scale greater heights. While some have attempted to explain administrator effectiveness by using a simple equation applicable to all schools and situations, an administrator's effectiveness is actually contingent upon the knowledge and skill to assess the situational and organizational characteristics which he or she encounters and the personal characteristics necessary for leadership in a dynamic, challenging environment. This discussion is designed to focus on the characteristics related to administrator effectiveness in the hope that it will serve as a guide or stimulate further discussion.

Personal Characteristics

Virtually hundreds of studies have been conducted to determine the characteristics of successful leaders. Meta-analysis of these studies has led researchers to conclude that the personal characteristics of effective administrators are dependent on the situation. This is hardly surprising. Certain personal characteristics, however, consistently surface as generally more important than others. The personal characteristics discussed below seem especially important for school administrator's effectiveness irrespective of the situation.

Ability to Organize. Leadership follows management. No administrator can succeed unless she/he establishes a routine. The flow of paper, the hectic pace, appointments, telephone messages, memoranda, and hundreds of fragmented activities demand efficiency. A top-flight secretary helps, but an administrator must be organized in order to be effective.

Reasoning. School administrators make a great many decisions in a day. Many seem insignificant unless they are wrong. Effective administrators make good decisions! It is as simple as that. For years, it has been said administrators need common sense. Instead, administrators need uncommon sense: the uncommon sixth sense to know when to make quick decisions and when to identify intended and unintended consequences and systematically analyze them.

Persistence. The framed message which hung on Ray Kroc's wall underlines the importance of persistence.

Nothing in the world can take the place of persistence. Talent will not; nothing is more common than unsuccessful men with great talent. Genius will not; unrewarded genius is almost a proverb. Education will not; the world is full of educated derelicts. Persistence, determination alone are important.

Significant change in schools takes time. Roadblocks and potholes often block the school administrator's path. The effective administrator will possess dogged determination and will to stay the course for the three to five years (or longer) necessary to implement planned change.

Need for Achievement. Drive, determination, energy, and enthusiasm have been championed as desirable personal characteristics for those who lead schools. Who could disagree? Each, however, emanates from the administrator's need to experience success. The effective administrator has an insatiable appetite for results: achievement of students, growth of efficacy of staff, and personal growth.

People Skills. Some call it sensitivity, others interpersonal skills. Typical school administrators spend more than 60 percent of their time in face-to-face communication with individuals or groups. School principals, on the average, spend 80 percent of their time working with people. Administrators at any level need to be good listeners, helpers, encouragers, developers, and persuaders. They must have the ability to resolve conflict. Their behavior in interactions with others should serve as a model for students, staff, and members of the community.

Organizational Characteristics

An administrator should possess, or attempt to develop, certain personal qualities in order to function effectively. However, the organizational characteristics of a school or school district can also influence the extent to which an administrator will be effective in a particular work setting.

An organization is a great deal more than a group of employees producing a product or providing a service, a neat table depicting line and staff relations, or a policy manual with job descriptions. An organization has, in a sense, its own unique persona emanating not only from the people who lead and work in it but from structural and other characteristics. Effective school administrators study the organization, adjust their leadership style, and make decisions which fit the organization's persona. They understand that size, structure, and history of the organization affect every administrative activity.

Size is a prime example. Administrators in large schools realize that they have to work especially hard to keep people informed, to delegate tasks and responsibilities, and to keep the organization as free of bureaucratic impediments as possible.

The structure of the organization also affects how the administrator functions. The organization's philosophy, goals, and past practices influence the extent to which rules, regulations, policy, job descriptions, and lines of communication, and authority are employed for control. Effective administrators understand the organizational structure. They know when to bend the rules or regulations or know when to attempt to widen the boundaries to obtain results.

One other characteristic influences an administrator's effectiveness—the history of the organization. No one factor has more influence on organizational behavior and on beliefs and attitudes than the experience of those in the organization. Past experiences are a subtle but powerful influence on every human activity and decision made in an organization. People often accept or reject an idea, a program, a leadership style, or a decision because of the residue of previous experience. Asking the right questions and acquiring a sense of an organization's history and traditions is an essential prerequisite for effective administration of schools.

Situational Characteristics

An effective administration can be defined as "doing the right things right." "Right," however, is a function of the situation in which administrators find themselves. A great strategy in one situation can cause a disaster in another. There are, however, three situational characteristics which significantly affect all school administrators regardless of title or role: the economic/social climate, the community, and employee characteristics. The first two are, in a sense, external characteristics; the third is an internal phenomenon.

It is unlikely that there is a school organization in this country that is not affected by the economic and social climate. The amount of available resources has a telling effect on organizational decision making. Staff and program development are but a few of the key components of school effectiveness dramatically affected by the health of the budget.

More subtly, and perhaps even more importantly, the status of the economy influences the way patrons view their schools and what they expect from those schools. For example, a field trip viewed as a great experience for students may be seen as a poor use of taxpayers' funds during hard times.

The social climate surrounding schools typically is affected by the economy. For example, as America's corporate sector floundered and unemployment rose, administrators who implemented programs that favored the basics and who ran the proverbial tight ships were more likely to be given high effectiveness grades. Major social or political activity, however, occasionally overpowers the economic climate, which pushed school administrators into managing schools like factories, in order to catch up with the Soviets. Conversely, as a result of social events and the social climate which enveloped schools in the 1960s, schools and their administrators were forced to embrace value clarification and relevance while eschewing the three R's.

The effective administrator is keenly aware of the economic and social environment affecting schools; being out of touch often results in "bad" decisions. "Know the community" could well be the golden rule for school administrators in the latter part of the twentieth century. America's communities have changed dramatically. The school's various publics are no longer passive, agreeable partners on a honeymoon with public education. Patrons and community members ask difficult questions, have great expectations, and are very good at getting what they want. Administrator effectiveness often depends on the extent to which those expectations are met in the eyes of the beholders. The effective administrator analyzes the characteristics of the community and reflects on their implications before making difficult decisions.

Finally, there are the characteristics of the employees. Administrator effectiveness revolves around the leader's ability to achieve results through people. Human resource management may be the most important administrator activity. Yet, each staff seems to have a character or culture of its own. A powerful factor in forming that culture is the background of the staff members, i.e., their experiences within the profession and the organization, and the beliefs and values they bring to the job. To be effective, an administrator needs to understand the pattern of employee characteristics which influence attitudes and behavior. Such knowledge is helpful in making administrative decisions about any effort to shape the culture.

But how does one analyze employee characteristics? Like situational characteristics, some employee characteristics lend themselves to analyses: age, experience, and expertise, for example. Others, such as employee work ethic and self-reliance are more difficult to analyze but still perceptible if an administrator possesses discriminating eyes and ears. Discerning employees' beliefs and values requires care, time and effort, and a well developed sixth sense.

Summary

Few activities are more challenging or important than the administration of American schools. Enhancing the effectiveness of those responsible for leadership should be a national imperative. Those who administer schools must be attuned to the economic and social climates that surround school organizations, as well as to the community the school serves and the characteristics of the organization's human resources. They must understand in an analytical way the organizations they work in, how to work in them, and how to shape and change them. As we continue to train and develop a large number of administrators with these conceptual skills and highly developed people skills that the nature of the enterprise demands, excellence will become a practical reality in schools across the nation.

See also Administrative Accountability; Administrative Roles; Administrative Styles; Administrator Evaluation.

—James Sweeney
Iowa State University

References

Kilmann, R.H. (1985). *Beyond the quick fix*. San Francisco: Jossey-Bass.

Tannenbaum, R., & Schmidt, W.H. (1958, March-April). "How to choose a leadership pattern." *Harvard Business Review, 36*, 95–101.

Yukl, G.A. (1981). *Leadership in organizations*. Englewood Cliffs, NJ: Prentice-Hall.

ADMINISTRATOR EVALUATION

Numerous studies have been conducted on school effectiveness in search of the factors that relate directly or indirectly to student achievement. While a number of factors appear salient, each seems to be contingent upon one powerful factor, strong administrative leadership. The extent to which the administrator is able to establish the mission, plan and organize the work, and release the human potential determines the relative effectiveness of the organization.

Yet, despite virtual unanimity of agreement with the premise, we continue to struggle with efforts to employ performance evaluation as a vehicle for assessing or improving administrator performance. While there may be a number of reasons for this lack of success, it appears that if valid administrator evaluation is to occur, two major questions must be answered: (a) How do we develop evaluative criteria which represent important administrator activities or outcomes related to effective schools; and (b) how do we implement evaluation procedures which promote communication, feedback, commitment, and growth while ensuring fairness and accountability?

Criteria

Historically, criteria have taken varied shapes and forms: personal qualities, goals, functions, and even administrative procedures. Each has limited value; major job responsibilities illuminate best and are the most valid measure of performance.

Most school organizations have job descriptions highlighting major job responsibilities. If they have been updated recently, correlates of school effectiveness are reflected in the job responsibilities. The task is to translate them into evaluative criteria using three key elements: (a) the object of action, (b) the scope of responsibility, and (c) the action verb. For example, curriculum, a major responsibility of principals, becomes the *object* of the criterion. The scope of the principal's responsibility, in most cases, is the attendance center which the principal administers. Other administrators, however, often have broad or overlapping curriculum responsibility. Thus, it is important to clarify that responsibility is limited to elementary, secondary, English, K-12, et cetera.

Next comes the tricky part, choosing the action verb. This is very important since it explicitly clarifies whether the curriculum is to be implemented, articulated, coordinated, or monitored. The action verb leaves little doubt as to what activity is expected. The table, Evaluative Criteria, shows some examples of evaluative criteria with key components for each.

EVALUATIVE CRITERIA

Position	Action Verb	Scope	Object
Principal	Provides	9–12	Functional Curriculum
Assistant Superintendent	Evaluates	Secondary	Principals
Curriculum Director	Articulates	7–12	Curriculum
Superintendent	Implements	District	Goals

Criteria typically are job specific. Some school organizations, however, have chosen to identify responsibilities common to all administrators, such as staff evaluation, budgeting, communication, and team membership. These "team criteria" plus job specific criteria become the evaluative criteria.

A final thought about criteria: While each criterion is important, the situation often dictates the degree of importance. For example, it may be more important for a principal to develop a positive climate this year and work on instructional improvement the next. Climate, for that principal, has more weight this year, whereas next year evaluation for improvement of instruction becomes more important.

Some school organizations have chosen to address this by employing intricate, across-the-district weighting formulas. The formulas look elegant but do not work. Administration, perhaps even more than teaching, is too complex to "formulize." Administrators who are ineffective sometimes receive relatively high overall rating scores. While they may be proficient in carrying out many of their responsibilities, nonperformance or ineffective performance in one or two seemingly less important criteria render them ineffective overall. It makes more sense to identify, through discussion, "key criteria" for each job holder. These, then, provide a focus for evaluation and coaching.

Descriptors

Although evaluation criteria are important, they are frequently insufficient without descriptors. This can be illustrated by using a criterion commonly employed by school systems: "Evaluates the teaching staff." Although this seems straightforward, it is not clear whether the district merely wants valid ratings of teachers or expects more from the principal. The example below is illustrative.

Criterion: Evaluates the teaching staff.
Descriptors: 1. Observes lessons frequently.
2. Confers with teachers and provides positive and evaluative feedback.
3. Provides written lesson observation summaries.
4. Provides valid end-of-year ratings.
5. Develops and monitors growth goals.

Use of the criterion and descriptors makes clear to both the principal and the supervisor what is expected. The school organization expects lesson observation, conferences, lesson observation summaries, end-of-the-year ratings, and growth goals to be of high quality.

One other decision remains. Most summative evaluation instruments utilize a scale to rate performance. The school organization must decide whether to rate each descriptor or merely use each as a guide. Rating descriptors promote more valid assessment because they force the evaluator to assess specific factors before rating the criterion. They have other benefits. Frequently, when a supervisor rates the criterion "satisfactory," he or she may praise the administrator for achievement in one area represented by a descriptor, but is unlikely to point out ineffectiveness or nonperformance in an area represented by another descriptor. Forcing the supervisor to rate each descriptor tends to overcome the leniency tendency and promote more, specific feedback.

Procedures

Developing an evaluation system can be a risky business. Administrators are a bit skeptical; therefore, one needs to be careful. The following are suggestions for school organizations when developing an administrator evaluation system: (a) Go slowly. (b) Communicate, communicate, communicate. (c) Involve everybody as much as needed. (d) Reassure, reassure, reassure. (e) Check on what folks are thinking and feeling. (f) Emphasize benefits.

The best way to assure the administrative team that something is being developed *for them* rather than done to them is to enlist the assistance of a steering committee and charge them with the responsibility for developing a system which helps administrators grow and assures quality performance. It also helps to develop the system on a test and try basis; the committee is kept in place to monitor the system's procedures and instruments, and make revisions where necessary.

A good evaluation system has some basic elements. Every school organization should consider including the following:

1. *Beginning of cycle conference.* Nothing beats a good discussion to kick the process off. This conference clarifies how things will work and begins the coaching process.

2. *Frequent on-site observations.* Great coaches observe performance as frequently as possible. Evaluation procedures should include at least three formal on-site observations, distributed over time, focusing on the key administrative activities identified at the beginning-of-cycle conference.

3. *Follow-up conferences.* Each on-site observation should be followed by a conference designed to discuss achievement and growth. This conference should follow the observation as closely as possible, be of sufficient length, and be followed by a written summary.

4. *Documentation.* There are many ways to document administrative performance. These include plans, testimonials, attendance data, et cetera. The evaluator and evaluatee should examine the evaluative criteria and descriptors and decide how to document performance; each should keep a folder of work samples.

5. *End-of-cycle conference/growth goals.* The evaluator must clearly communicate effectiveness of performance, reinforcing what was done well and pinpointing areas for growth.

Final Thought

Many Americans believe that our schools must provide the thrust to return us to the top of the global, economic, and educational hierarchy. Challenges facing educational administrators are among the most complex and difficult confronting administrators in any profession. If excellence in education is to become a reality rather than a slogan, it will be achieved by energizing the human potential of the dedicated men and women who set the pace in schools across the country. We cannot waste our time and energy merely going through the motions. We need evaluation systems which enhance our most important administrator activity, growth.

See also Administrative Accountability; Administrator Effectiveness; Principalship; Superintendent of Schools.

—James Sweeney
Iowa State University

References

Bolton, D.L. (1980). *Evaluating administrative personnel in school systems.* New York: Teachers College Press.

King, P. (1984). *Performance planning and appraisal.* New York: McGraw-Hill.

Zappulla, E. (1983). *Evaluating administrative performance: Current trends and techniques.* Belmont, CA: Star Publishing.

ADMINISTRATOR INSERVICE

At one time in the not-too-distant past, inservice education for school administrators might have been dismissed as a pure luxury and not a significant issue worthy of much discussion. Recently, however, there has been an increasing awareness that staff development or inservice for educators is not a "frill"; rather, it is something in which professionals need to engage. Ongoing growth and learning are no longer viewed as "add ons." In addition, increasing expectations that school administrators should be viewed as a "key ingredient" in effective schools has led to a situation where there is a real and present need for educational leaders to engage in activities that will help them to understand more fully the complexities and demands of their roles. Inservice education is a vehicle that may assist individuals to learn more about their responsibilities as instructional leaders.

Although the topic of administrator inservice is one that has only recently started to receive systematic attention by researchers and others, there are nonetheless some basic observations that will be made in an attempt to provide some background information and clarity.

General Inservice Characteristics

During the past few years, a number of researchers have been able to make some generalizations about the nature of effective inservice for school administrators that include the following: (a) Effective inservice is directed toward local needs; (b) inservice participants need to be involved in the planning, implementation, and evaluation of programs; (c) active learning processes, rather than passive techniques such as lectures, are viewed as desirable inservice instructional modes: people seek involvement in their learning; (d) inservice that is part of a long-term systematic staff development plan is more effective than a one-shot, short-term program; (e) local school inservice must be backed up by a commitment of resources from the central office; and (f) effective inservice requires ongoing evaluation.

These characteristics derived from research on successful inservice practices suggest that an effective program for school administrators would need to reflect the same features. Over the years, a variety of approaches, or models, have emerged for use in the delivery of administrator inservice. These models can be classified as more or less effective in dealing with these six descriptors of effective practice. A review of the models, then, is another way of increasing basic understanding of the fundamental issues related to administrator inservice.

Administrator Inservice Models

Reviews of existing practice show that there are five major models available for administrators seeking opportunities for inservice education. None of the models is "perfect" in terms of its ability to address all the stated criteria for effective inservice. However, each model enjoys some features that, depending on specific local conditions and other factors, makes it an appealing approach to continuing professional education for a school administrator.

The first model is referred to as the traditional approach to inservice and consists essentially of enrollment by the administrator in graduate-level credit courses at a university. This model, perhaps the most popular, is useful in assisting school leaders to achieve personal goals by earning credits toward an advanced academic degree or additional professional certification. Similar to this approach is the inservice academy, an arrangement where a state education agency or a local school district provides structured classes on topics of concern to administrators. The major distinction of this model, as contrasted with the traditional model, is the fact that the content of learning experiences tends to be tailored more directly to local needs and interests of practitioners rather than the academic expectations of the university.

A third model that is nearly as popular as the university class is the short-term inservice institute or workshop. The distinctive feature here is that the workshop is designed to address topics of immediate concern to participants. Professional associations have long been viewed as the organizations with a primary interest in promoting such opportunities for inservice education. In recent years, however, workshops and institutes have also been offered by universities, state departments of education, and private consulting firms.

The two final models of administrator inservice appear to be promising approaches, but they are not as yet as widely utilized as are the other models. The first of these is the emerging concept of the assessment center. For the most part, this competency-based strategy has been seen as a preservice administrator training device, or at least as a process to be used in selecting candidates for administrative positions. However, the reliance of assessment centers on job-related performance guidelines as targets for professional development makes this approach one that holds considerable promise for use as an inservice training device that is focused on the improvement of job-related skills.

The final model, also an emerging one, is the network, an arrangement wherein individuals with common interests form alliances for mutual support. This type of administrator inservice tends not to be as strong with regard to content as are the other models; however, networking is an approach that helps individual administrators feel a part of a larger group that is willing to assist colleagues with problems that arise as a normal part of the job.

Inservice Issues

Administrator inservice in recent years has been steadily improved because it has become something for which it is increasingly acceptable to expend school district resources of time and money, and also because there are more opportunities for quality learning opportunities than there were in the past. Despite this improvement, however, there are at least two continuing issues that will need to be addressed systematically if professional development opportunities for school administrators are to achieve their fullest potential.

The first issue concerns the ways in which the topics or foci for administrator inservice are selected. Frequently, principals, superintendents, and other school leaders select training according to the extent to which topics are of momentary interest, or because the topics are prescribed as "important" by the local district administration, a state education agency, or some other group external to the individual school administrator. The result is an inservice program that is unsatisfactory because it is not related to the learning needs of individual participants. Work needs to be done in the future in the area of finding more effective needs assessment strategies—either led by professional administrator associations, local school districts, universities, or state education agencies—to increase the likelihood that the content of inservice programs makes sense to participants.

The second issue concerns ways in which inservice programs are evaluated. A consistent criticism of many staff development activities is that they are rarely evaluated to determine strengths and weaknesses and areas for future improvement. This has typically been a problem in administrator inservice as well. Although opportunities for additional programs are increasing, little is done systematically to ensure the programs are of sufficiently high quality to warrant widespread participation by school administrators.

Summary

Inservice education for practicing school administrators is an important tool that may be used in promoting more effective leadership. There are problems that have existed in this area in the past, ranging from limitations on the approaches or models used to deliver inservice to limitations resulting from the lack of effective strategies for conducting needs assessments and carrying out program evaluation. Despite these shortcomings, however, progress is being made to improve the quality of professional development opportunities that are available for school executives.

See also Administrative Accountability; Administrative Preparation; Administrator Effectiveness; Staff Development.

—John C. Daresh
Ohio State University

References

Daresh, J.C. (1984, Autumn). "Status of research on administrator inservice." *National Forum of Educational Administration and Supervision*, 3(1), 23–31.

Hutson, H.M (1981). "Inservice best practices: The learnings of general education." *Journal of Research and Development in Education*, 14(2), 1–10.

Lawrence, G. (1974). *Patterns of effective inservice education.* Tallahassee, FL: Florida State Department of Education.

ADMINISTRATOR TURNOVER

Administrator turnover is a phenomenon that occurs in all organizations. Historically, the causes have been retirements, promotions, transfers, resignations, deaths—to name a few. Beginning in the 1960s, when activists desiring change began exerting pressure on all social institutions, administrator turnover increased substantially. The greatest and most sustained pressure was exerted upon educational institutions generally and upon the administrators who ran them especially. Consequently, public school administration has been more challenging during the last two decades and, as a result, administrator turnover has increased.

Causes and Trends

A major cause of administrator turnover today is mobility. It is often necessary for school administrators to be mobile if they desire to move to progressively higher positions. Many superintendents and a growing number of other administrators, including secondary principals, have held several different positions in different school districts in their careers. Less than ten percent of superintendents have spent their entire career in one school district. Moreover, in school districts enrolling more than 10,000 students, 24 percent of the superintendents have held three or more superintendencies. These mobile administrators are described as being "career bound" rather than "place bound" administrators.

Also, the average tenure in the superintendency is now 7.6 years, with tenure in large, urban districts being even shorter. Consequently, irrespective of reasons, superintendents move on in a relative short time. Reasons cited most frequently by superintendents are promotion and salary increase, change of locations, and conflict with the school board. They also cite inadequate financing, too many demands on the superintendent, lack of time, and collective bargaining as reasons. Other researchers usually note one of the following reasons: failure to work with the school board, failure to understand the dynamics of superintendent-school board relationships (trust, communication, loyalty, integrity), and failure to provide staff leadership.

Administrator turnover in the principalship is attributed primarily to stress, pressure, heavy workload, excessive time demands, and conflicting expectations from constituent groups. As a result of these factors, some principals experience emotional exhaustion, or "burnout." It is noteworthy that all of the reasons cited for leaving the principalship are related to job conditions rather than personal circumstances such as a career change or an opportunity in the private sector. However, it is a sobering phenomenon to note that more than two-thirds of the successful secondary principals are not committed to the principalship as a career. Although approximately one-third of them aspire to the superintendency or a central office position, the others are not firmly committed to careers in school administration. Nevertheless, only a small percent (10 percent) have definitely decided to leave the principalship.

By contrast, almost 60 percent of the elementary principals view the principalship as their final career choice. Most of the others aspire to higher-level positions in school administration. Accordingly, based upon the percentages of elementary principals that desire to remain in the position and pursue a higher position in school administration, it appears that they do not desire to leave school administration to the extent that secondary principals desire to leave it. The environment in which elementary principals function is, however, one that produces considerable stress.

When the larger picture of administrator turnover in public education is examined, it appears that the most serious problems exist at the principalship level, particularly in secondary schools. Because of the heavy workload, excessive time demands, legal-legislative policy constraints, and multiple (and usually conflicting) expectations from constituent groups, principals must spend enormous time and energy bargaining, negotiating, and compromising. It can easily be understood that, after a given period of time, one would wish to move out of this kind of role. Many administrators decide that the rewards are not equal to the daily demands and pressures.

Superintendents, by contrast, do not have the daily demands to contend with that principals face. While they generally deal with major issues and more serious problems, they do not present themselves in daily, rapid-fire order. Also, their policies and decisions are open to more public scrutiny and are more political in nature. Therefore, after a sufficient number of unpopular decisions have been made along with established policies, they may lose the support of the community and subsequently the school board. Astute superintendents usually perceive this problem and move along before they are terminated.

Suggested Solutions

In view of the seriousness of the problem of administrator turnover, it seems that some action is needed in most states to address the situation.

Legislatures, state and local boards of education, and citizens groups might initiate studies of the excessive demands and pressures that are placed on school administrators. Perhaps more administrative or staff support is needed to fulfill the expectations held for administrators. These groups might also determine if school administrators still have sufficient autonomy and authority commensurate with their assigned responsibility. In addition, these groups might conduct in-depth studies of turnover at the state and local levels.

Finally, stronger and more consistent support of school administrators by school board members might enhance the ability of all administrators to perform their responsibilities on a day-to-day basis.

See also Administrative Salaries; Administrative Status; Administrative Stress; Administrator Effectiveness.

—James E. Lyons
University of
North Carolina-Charlotte

References

Byrne, D.R., Hines, S.H., & McCleary, L.E. (1978). *The senior high principalship* (Vol. I). Reston, VA: National Association of Secondary School Principals.

Cunningham, L.L., & Hentges, J.T. (1982). *The American school superintendency 1982: A summary report.* Arlington, VA: American Association of School Administrators.

Pharis, W.L., & Zakariya, S.B. (1978). *The elementary school principalship in 1978: A research study.* Arlington, VA: National Association of Elementary School Principals.

ADMINISTRATOR UNIONS

Since the 1960s, school administrators and supervisors (including principals, assistant principals, directors, and coordinators) have formed local, independent bargaining units, or unions, and have in some cases affiliated with the labor movement. The purposes of these activities include (a) union recognition under state and local policies, (b) collective negotiations of working agreements or contracts, (c) grievance and due process rights, and (d) improved access to power and decision making in the district. In 32 states and the District of Columbia, state public-employment relations laws grant rights to these "middle managers," those who supervise but do not make districtwide policies. The middle managers may petition voluntarily for recognition. The laws have required that local boards of education treat the administrators as the exclusive bargaining agent.

In some cases, furthermore, school administrators have joined with "big labor," affiliating with the AFL-CIO's American Federation of School Administrators, or the Teamsters Union, to gain power and influence with local, state, and federal policy makers. And in a few situations, school principals' unions have actually gone on strike. In a New York City case, the Council of Supervisory Association—the bargaining unit for all mid-rank administrators—joined the United Federation of Teachers, AFL-CIO, on the picket lines in reaction to Black "community control" efforts in the Ocean Hill-Brownsville community to remove 29 White teachers and three principals.

Background

The rise of unionization among administrators is not unique in the labor movement. Industrial foremen created the Foreman's Association of America; its membership reached 70,000 members by 1948, when the Taft-Hartley Law amended the National Labor Relations Act (NLRA) to exclude all supervisors from union recognition. In the absence of a national *public-sector* bargaining law, a number of states have passed their own public-employment relations laws—most of which permit school supervisors to seek union recognition if local members so vote. Eleven states, on the other hand, have followed the NLRA model for the private sector, relieving the local employer (boards of education) from having to recognize its supervisors for collective bargaining. Instead, they seek a "meet and confer" relationship which is advisory but not binding.

A number of reasons have been given for unionization of administrators in education. They include:

1. Mounting teacher power: As teachers' unions gained strength and absorbed increasingly more local resources, principals, assistant principals, and other midlevel administrators found themselves unable to keep up financially (salaries and benefits) and, for the most part, unable to maintain administrative prerogatives in their jobs. Unions of administrators, then, were seen as counterweights to the increased power of teachers' unions.

2. Toughening accountability measures: Central office managers, including superintendents and boards of education, were putting increased demands on principals, often without involving and consulting them in the process. Building administrators found themselves held responsible for policies which they, the principals, had little say in creating; they also found central office management to be increasingly more distant, confusing, yet demanding. By unionizing, prin-

cipals gained (a) a *united voice* in communicating their concerns "downtown" and (b) *bi-lateral* involvement at the negotiating table in establishing management-supervisory relationships.

3. Cut-backs and lay-offs: The 1970s and early 1980s saw the closing of schools and the loss of programs. These constrictions also led to reductions-in-force and lay-offs of administrators and supervisors. To protect jobs and to ensure the use of seniority in determining who is released (last in—first out), school administrators turned to unionization and strong contractual language to see that lay-offs were based on universal criteria (years of experience), not the desire of superintendents to "get rid of" certain unfavored supervisors.

Impact

Collective bargaining for administrators has led to several results. First, clearly, it has raised the salaries and benefits over the last fifteen years as much as 21 percent above those administrators who have not engaged in union activity. In part, this increase has accompanied the improvement in teachers' remuneration; principals now earn upwards of $45,000 to $50,000 in some cities, whereas teachers can earn $38,000 to $40,000.

Second, principals have made their voices heard. Superintendents are careful to consult the president of the administrators' union before making major changes in district policies that affect schools (and which ones do not?). Whereas teachers still wield the greatest political clout, actively helping to elect school-board members who are sympathetic to labor, principals' unions, too, are heard in the halls and meetings where district policies are set. Whether this involvement has led to *better* educational programs is not clearly established. But the involvement of building administrators may mean that sound policies are made, ones that can be effectively implemented in the schools. Principals should, then, have some "input" into setting district policies and procedures, with unions helping to make the administrators' voices audible above the roar of district operations.

The Future

The future role of administrator unions is not clear. Already, some states such as Ohio and Oregon have stipulated that school boards are *not* required to recognize administrators: principals are part of management and cannot and should not divide their loyalties between being unionists and being on-site managers. There is ample precedent in the private sector for treating supervisors that way, although, for many of the reasons referred to earlier, a good case has been made for granting administrators independent bargaining status.

If Congress were to pass a national public-employment bill, like the Wagner Act for industry, principals would be removed from union protection. Should Congress follow the lead of such policies as the Taylor Law in New York, boards would be required to recognize them. Right now, it is a state-by-state issue.

Unionization, also, will depend on the future role and self-perception of administrators. In the press for "effective schools" and improved leadership, principals may be trapped between their loyalty to the profession and their allegiance to fellow unionists; in many districts, principals have shown that collective bargaining and union unity can be forces for real districtwide school improvement and change. Collective power, particularly among the vital middle-rank supervisors, is an important factor in any attempt to make American schools better. Principals' unions appear to be an integral part of this effort.

See also Administrative Salaries; Administrative Status; Administrator Turnover; Bureaucracy.

—Bruce S. Cooper
Fordham University

References

Cooper, B.S. (1979, October). "Collective bargaining for school administrators four years later." *Phi Delta Kappa, 61,* 130–31.

Cooper, B.S. (1977, September). "Federal actions and bargaining for public supervisors: Basis for an argument." *Public Personnel Management, 6*(5), 341–53.

Cooper, B.S. (1978). "The future of school middle management." In D.A. Erickson & T.H. Reller (Eds.), *The principal in metropolitan schools.* Berkeley, CA: McCutchan.

ADMINISTRATORS, BEGINNING

Many events in the employment process and during the first year shape the administrator's work and reputation for the duration of his or her career in a district. First impressions during the interview, promises stated or implied in the early days of the job, and the reactions created by first decisions and appearances markedly affect an administrator's success. The best beginning requires (a) selecting the candidate who best matches the position's requirements and (b) providing the candidate with optimal information as he or she starts work. Underlying both requirements is a commitment to share accurate descriptions of the schools, the responsibilities of the position, the administrator's competencies, and all parties' expectations for high performance.

Selection: Making the Best Match

The goal of the employment process is to match an administrator candidate's qualities to the requirements of the job opening. The process hinges on all parties having adequate, valid information about both the candidate and the position. Essential information about the candidate includes first-hand evidence of previous administrative performance, thorough evaluation of personal qualities through interview and on-site observation, and the review of professional and academic activities and performance. Essential information about the position includes clear statements of the responsibilities of the position, evidence of the character and qualities of faculty and staff, and an accurate picture of both the employer's and the staff's performance expectations of the administrator.

The committee's decision to hire and the candidate's decision to accept must follow a thorough comparison of the job's goals and personal requirements with the candidate's demonstrated competencies. Written descriptions of job responsibilities and of preferred personal qualities provide the employer an objective and legally sound basis for comparing candidates. Similarly, the candidate must carefully rate his or her own personal strengths, weaknesses, and preferences against the demands of the position. Most importantly, neither the employer nor the candidate should agree to a match when significant doubt exists; such uncertainty can seriously handicap the new administrator's crucial first months on the job.

First Months: Base Line for Year One

The thorough interchange of information in the hiring process lays the groundwork for starting the job. Once hired, the new administrator must proceed immediately to clarify employers' expectations for his or her performance, explore areas of high need with the staff, and evaluate operating procedures in the district or school. Over the first months, the review of documents and the interviewing of staff and supervisors will specify for the administrator the various goals others have for him or her. The new administrator will identify the key individuals with whom he or she will be working. Fiscal matters will come to his or her attention. All the while the new administrator will be developing an understanding of the curriculum and school programs.

From the district's perspective, the new administrator should be assisted in the full assessment of the organization and community. Board members, other administrators, faculty leaders, and community members should be available to inform the new administrator about both the current condition of the school or district and the aspirations they and others hold for it. Most importantly, the employing agent or board should not expect the new administrator to make major decisions or changes before obtaining a full understanding of matters relating to personnel, school programs, fiscal responsibilities, and public opinion.

The First Year: Three Priorities

The new administrator will be expected to perform many tasks and to fulfill many expectations; some of these will plainly contradict one another. This fact makes it essential that the administrator (a) have as clear a mandate as possible from his or her employers and (b) have access to his or her employers to clarify and negotiate priorities as the first year unfolds. In reaching an understanding of what is expected, the board or lead administrator must state high priority tasks and functions clearly and provide the new administrator multiple opportunities to check his or her understanding of them as he or she takes action.

The new administrator's early responsibilities are threefold. First, he or she must give ample, timely attention to the operational procedures of the district or building. Procedures and schedules for student and teacher activities, finances, maintenance, and transportation must be clear, well publicized, and educationally sound. The new administrator should deliberately review past and present practices in these areas; informed adjustments can follow when they are obviously merited and clearly explained to those affected by them.

A second major goal must be to cultivate staff leadership. The administrator will be responsible for establishing productive relationships with staff and faculty and for promptly supervising them in a manner which does not compromise those productive relationships. The administrator's initial approaches to the faculty and staff must be open and confident; the goal must be to share expectations, goals, and information with them and to seek comment. A key activity of these first meetings is listening; staff who know the students, know the community, and know the program will teach the new administrator more in the first months than the new administrator can teach them. The administra-

tor, however, should present to the staff and faculty information about him or herself and his or her administrative philosophy: goals for the organization, expectations for a professional working relationship, and supervisory procedures. Similar efforts should be directed at students and the community.

A third focus of activity is long-range curricular and instructional planning. Although this focus is not as immediately pressing as the first two, it is essential that the new administrator establish curriculum and instruction as a primary concern. The administrator should review evaluations of existing personnel, student performance, and programs. The supervision of the staff and faculty, begun within the first month, and the first rounds of interviews and meetings with school and community members will provide important first-hand insight into the needs of the curriculum and teachers.

Based on these interviews, meetings, and performance observations, the new administrator can begin to fashion goals for long-range improvements and further evaluation. Within the first year, the administrator can then offer proposals to advance the curriculum, the quality of instruction, and staff development. These proposals can, in turn, influence the planning of facilities and budget, the personnel decisions, and the public and staff leadership activities of the new administrator. Most importantly, they will stand on a foundation of accurate information about the schools rather than on hearsay or pressure group preferences.

Evaluating Progress: Clear Goals, Good Communication

Under normal circumstances, it is extremely difficult to assess with confidence the impacts of a new administrator in the first year. Surface impressions tend to carry the day while the more lasting effects of the administrator are not evident. To alleviate the ambiguities that inevitably beset both the administrator and the employer in this situation, it is imperative that an evaluation structure be in place at the beginning of employment and that it be used faithfully in the first year.

In brief, the new administrator should (a) know in advance the criteria which will be used to judge his or her performance, (b) have multiple opportunities to meet with his/her supervisor(s) to discuss performance during the year, and (c) receive the final evaluation of his/her performance in writing. The importance of open and frank evaluation of the new administrator cannot be overstressed: it will either strengthen the match of person and job for the benefit of both, or it will precipitate the administrator's timely departure if that match is not beneficial to either party.

See also Administrative Preparation; Administrator Evaluation; Principal Selection; Superintendent Selection.

—Gordon A. Donaldson, Jr.
University of Maine

References

Bolton, D.L. (1980). *Evaluating administrative personnel in school systems.* New York: Teachers College Press.

Gephart, W.K., Ingle, R.B., & Potter, W.J. (Eds.). (1977). *The evaluation of administrative performance: Parameters, problems and practices.* Bloomington, IN: Phi Delta Kappa.

Jentz, B., Cheever, D.S., Fisher, S.B., Jones, M.H., Kelleher, P., & Wofford, J.W. (1982). *Entry: The hiring, start-up, and supervision of administrators.* New York: McGraw-Hill.

ADULT EDUCATION PROGRAMS

Adult education is generally regarded as the practice by which mature persons undertake systematic and sustained learning to bring about changes in their knowledge, attitude, values, or skills for the purpose of addressing needs and facilitating personal and job-related growth. Organized activities designed to teach basic skills, enhance leisure-time activities, and foster professional development are sponsored by different types of institutions for the accomplishment of specific educational objectives. They include courses and other activities which provide no credit as well as those which lead to academic degrees.

Adult education programs are characterized by their response to individual needs and interests, institutional goals, and societal changes, resulting in a continuing increase in the numbers of adult education programs, sponsors, and participants. According to the Center for Statistics, U.S. Department of Education, participants number 23 million adults, more than twice the number of full-time college students and nearly two-fifths of the total number of children and young people enrolled in public schools in the United States. The education of adults contrasts with the education of children in the diversity of sponsors and deliverers of services, in the voluntary nature of participation, in the breadth of subject matter, and in the educational procedures used.

In order to explain adult participation in educational programs, Cyril Houle described those who use education as a means of accomplishing explicit purposes as goal-oriented, those who take part because they derive meaning from the circumstances of learning apart from its content (for example, to meet people) as activity-oriented, and those who seek knowledge for its own sake as learning-oriented. Morstain and Smart have identified six factors which motivate adults to participate in learning activities: (a) valuation of knowledge for its own sake; (b) improvement of occupational performance or status; (c) external compulsion or pressure; (d) preparation for service to others; (e) escape from boredom or frustration through intellectual stimulation; and (f) development of interpersonal relationships.

Leadership in adult education programs includes full-time adult educators who administer and coordinate programs and those who teach or counsel adults, part-time adult educators who perform these functions along with other employment, and volunteer adult educators who serve as program leaders in a variety of settings. Many colleges and universities grant graduate and undergraduate degrees in adult and continuing education. Professional organizations such as the American Association for Adult and Continuing Education provide opportunities for continuing professional development and encourage high standards of professional practice among adult educators.

Sponsors: Agencies and Schools

Some sponsors of adult education programs are agencies for which adult education is the sole function. An example is the community-based literacy training organization. Others, such as schools and colleges, have education in general as their primary service. Organizations such as hospitals offer education as a secondary service. Among other sponsors are businesses and industries that underwrite staff-development and training programs.

Sponsors whose primary service is adult education include the Cooperative Extension Service and community-based adult education agencies. The Cooperative Extension Service, a national informal adult education organization supported jointly by federal, state, and local units of government to prepare instructional material and train local personnel on a continuing basis, is committed to the dissemination of practical knowledge by specialists in agriculture, home economics, youth development, and community development. Community-based adult education agencies include community adult schools; independent residential schools, such as the Highlander Research and Education Center in Tennessee; and private literacy education organizations, such as Laubach and Literacy Volunteers of America.

Sponsors whose primary service to clients is education include four-year colleges and universities; two-year community, junior, and technical colleges; the public schools; and proprietary schools. Recent data indicate that approximately half of all participants in organized adult education were enrolled in four-year colleges and universities, two-year colleges and technical institutes, and in programs sponsored by the public schools. There were more than ten million enrollments in two- or four-year colleges and universities compared with fewer than three million in programs sponsored by the public schools.

The method of delivery, the primary deliverer of adult education programs, and the program emphases vary according to sponsor and locale. In some states, the principal sponsor for general adult education programs is the public school system and in others it is the two-year college. Program emphases tend to reflect the needs and interests of those whom they serve. In some areas, vocational education, basic skills education, citizenship training, and high school completion comprise the principal course offerings; in others, general enrichment, personnel development, and avocational programs are also included.

The practice of using public school buildings for adult education and other community activities dates back to the colonial era. By the end of the 19th century the "Evening School," designed to provide the regular elementary and secondary subjects to working youths and adults, had become a standard component of the program of many public schools. In the early years of the twentieth century, the program of the evening schools began to focus on meeting the academic, vocational, and enrichment needs of adult students; to consider the unique characteristics of adult learners; and to respond to the broader needs of the community of which the school was a part.

In addition to their regular offerings, community colleges provide continuing professional education for a variety of occupational groups. These community colleges also sponsor programs for special groups, such as senior citizens, reentry women, single parents, displaced workers, and others, using a broad range of instructional formats and off-campus locations to bring the instruction to the students. Many two-year community colleges engage in aggressive outreach programs in response to the particular needs of persons in their respective service areas. Four million registrants enroll in noncredit activities in community colleges, compared with roughly two and one-half million in universities and two million in four-year colleges.

The principal function of four-year colleges and universities is to provide educational programs leading to diplomas and/or degrees. Noncredit adult education programs are provided under the heading "continuing education," focusing in particular on continuing professional education.

Proprietary schools provide business, technical, secretarial, and occupational training, using both on-site and correspondence courses as educational procedures.

Sponsors for whom adult education is a secondary activity include cultural organizations, community organizations, occupational associations, government agencies, correctional institutions, health care institutions, and businesses and industries. Cultural organizations include libraries, museums, and public television, where adult education programs become one important aspect of a broader mission and purpose. Similarly, community organizations such as service clubs, political and special interest groups, churches and religious organizations, and health associations are a major source of adult education activities which are secondary to but support the organization's major purpose. Hospitals, in addition to medical treatment and care, provide education to patients in order to assist them to participate in the treatment of their own illness.

Occupational associations and labor unions concerned for the professional development of their members aid them to enhance their proficiencies through professional education. Correctional institutions provide adult education programs to facilitate the rehabilitation of incarcerated prisoners.

As products become increasingly complex and technologically sophisticated, businesses and industries provide educational programs to enable customers and other new product users to use their products successfully.

The armed forces, government agencies, and business and industry turn to education as a means of developing staffs and achieving objectives. The traditional focus has been to provide training as a means of increasing the worker's production. One of the major current developments in adult education has been the rapid change in larger firms from a job-related training focus to a broader concern for human-resource development, with courses ranging from work-related subjects to physical fitness and career planning. Some businesses collaborate with colleges and universities to provide these offerings; others have developed their own educational facilities and programs, in some cases to grant degrees. Government agencies and the armed forces also use adult education programs to increase the skill and facilitate the development of their personnel.

A better educated adult population, work increasing in technological sophistication, and greater amounts of leisure time available to adults, especially older adults, combine to ensure that adult education programs continue their important service of addressing educational needs and facilitating growth among adults in the future.

See also Community School Programs; Independent Study.

—James C. Fisher
University of Wisconsin-Milwaukee

References

Darkenwald, G.C., & Merriam, S.B. (1982). *Adult education: Foundations of practice*. New York: Harper & Row.

Houle, C.O. (1961). *The inquiring mind*. Madison, WI: University of Wisconsin Press.

Knowles, M.S. (1977). *A history of the adult education movement in the United States* (Rev. Ed.). Malabar, FL: Robert E. Krieger Publishing Company.

ADVISORY COMMITTEES

A potentially effective tool in a comprehensive school-community relations program is the advisory committee. Advisory committees, which usually consist of representatives from the community and possibly teachers or students, can help the administrator explore alternatives to problems, plan programs, and evaluate the effectiveness of programs.

There are several advantages of advisory committees. First, research on group decision making indicates that, because a wider range of options are considered, the involvement of individuals representing different points of view can improve the quality of the decision reached. Second, an advisory committee can improve communication and understanding between the administrator and community groups. Third, advisory committees can help generate political support among constituent groups within the community for the committee's decision. Fourth, advisory committees can facilitate the implementation of the committee's solution. Implementation often requires cooperation and support between and among individuals within the school and the community. Those involved in an advisory committee can help the administrator anticipate important implementation problems and recommend solutions.

The administrator should also be aware that there are potential disadvantages with advisory committees. First, advisory committees can consume a great deal of time. In order to facilitate the work of an advisory committee, the administrator may spend time coordinating the work of the committee, providing information to the committee, and helping the committee explore alternatives. Administrators should not establish too many committees; each new one places additional time demands upon the administrator. Second, since advisory committee members may lack perspective regarding school practices or educational issues, the administrator may need to collect and provide background information for the committee. Third, committee members may not understand group dynamics or group decision-making procedures, thus hampering the committee's effectiveness. A successful advisory committee comes into being when the committee can process divergent information and opinions and function well as a group.

Fourth, many times the special interests of individual committee members may conflict with the need for the committee to achieve consensus. Administrators often select members for participation in an advisory committee because they represent a particular point of view. Although different points of view are important on an advisory committee, this may become a problem when a committee member refuses to compromise, believing that he or she must continue to represent a particular point of view regardless of other alternatives being considered. Fifth, permanent committees may search for problems or issues to justify their existence even though the initial issues and problems which led to the formation of the committee have been solved.

Once the decision to use an advisory committee is made, the administrator should consider the following steps in establishing and monitoring the work of the committee. First, the administrator should identify carefully those issues which he or she wishes an advisory committee to address. Advisory committees should address only important issues, and the administrator must be willing to consider seriously and implement, whenever possible, the recommendations of the committee. If the administrator already knows the appropriate response to an issue or if there is little leeway regarding alternatives the advisory committee can explore, then the administrator should implement what he or she believes to be the best practice without involving an advisory committee. The credibility of the administrator is tied directly to his or her willingness to implement the committee's recommendations. Committee members will not serve in the future if they believe their work has been fruitless. Second, committee membership should be selected wisely. Although it is important that members be interested in the issues to be discussed, it is equally important that they have expertise to share, time to participate in the work of the committee, and be willing to participate in the decision-making process.

Third, the administrator must clearly define and communicate to all members of the committee the scope and function of the committee, a time frame for committee deliberations, and constraints regarding the range of alternatives the committee can consider. The more the administrator is able to share information regarding the committee's role and function, the more likely it is that committee members will reach a decision the administrator can endorse. Fourth, the administrator should help identify a committee chairperson who is knowledgeable about group dynamics and provide group decision-making training for the committee, if needed. The work of the committee will be facilitated if an agenda is prepared in advance, supporting information is available when needed, members know the rules which will govern group discussions, voting procedures are agreed upon in advance, and timely, accurate minutes of meetings are prepared.

Fifth, the administrator should monitor regularly the work of the committee and be willing to meet with the committee whenever necessary. Sixth, the administrator should sincerely acknowledge and reward committee members. Since participants contribute a great deal of time and energy, the administrator should recognize their accomplishments. Both official forms of recognition and personal expressions of thanks are appropriate. Seventh, the administrator should attempt to implement as many of the committee's recommendations as possible. If the administrator has done a good job in establishing and monitoring the work of the committee, then the committee's recommendations should be realistic. Further, the administrator will have gained additional benefits associated with increased involvement of community members in the educational decision-making process.

See also Business-School Partnerships; Community School Involvement; Curriculum Development; School District/University Partnerships.

—Richard S. Podemski
University of Alabama

References

Gorton, R.A. (1983). *School administration and supervision* (2nd ed.). Dubuque, IA: Wm. Brown Company.

Kindred, L.W., Begin, D., & Gallagher, D.R. (1984). *The school and community relations* (3rd ed.). Englewood Cliffs, NJ: Prentice-Hall.

New Jersey School Boards Association. (1981). *Working with advisory committees*. New Jersey: Author.

AFFECTIVE EDUCATION

Affective education is concerned with the feelings and emotions related to learning cognitive tasks and social behaviors appropriate to classrooms and schools. It is essential to the *latent* curriculum where students learn who they are in relationship to others and develop ideas of self-worth which may remain with them for a lifetime.

Affective education is also concerned with self-discipline. Punishment is generally ineffective in influencing behavior on a long-term basis; therefore, helping students learn to accept responsibility for their actions and become active participants in the total learning process is a key element of an affective education program. Without it, many children are simply unwilling or unable to deal with the cognitive tasks presented in school.

Researchers have demonstrated that children with adequate self-esteem perform more effectively on school achievement tests than those with low self-esteem. Underachievement is directly correlated with students' negative feelings about themselves. Numerous studies have shown a positive correlation of .5 or higher between the use of affective measures and improved school performance. Feelings of adequacy and acceptance on the part of children are directly linked to successful performance in school.

There are four major ways to implement affective education in classrooms: (a) improving teacher discussion skills, (b) increasing student involvement in cognitive tasks, (c) enhancing students' discussion skills and behaviors, and (d) merging affective and cognitive activities.

Teacher discussion skills that personalize learning are one aspect of affective education. "What are your feelings when you view a polluted river?" is appropriate to a science, ecology, or social studies class. "Why might some people commit crimes against property?" "How might you feel in their situation?" are other questions that personalize learning and are appropriate for consideration by an informed citizen. Personalizing also helps motivate students to explore and to become involved as opposed to being passive participants in the learning process.

Involving pupils in cognitive tasks may be accomplished through relating hobbies or interests to coursework; e.g., the cost of a bicycle or one's batting average may be referred to in mathematics. Improving students' discussion skills may be accomplished by encouraging students to give and receive feedback from peers in such a way that it demonstrates an understanding of another's position.

Finally, the merging of affective and cognitive activities may be taught directly in a unit fashion which might focus on items such as understanding basic emotional needs, examining the impact of our behaviors on the needs of peers, dealing with feelings of anger and frustration related to school performance, and learning to cope with peer conflicts. All of these topics are appropriate and are related to education in significant ways. Such activities may also be integrated or merged with cognitive tasks throughout the day.

Children generally learn well those things in which they have an interest. Affective education is designed to motivate children to become involved and to develop the interest necessary for observable learning to take place.

See also Cooperative Learning; Instructional Objectives; Teaching Approaches, Future.

—James D. Wiggins, President
Training Associates Limited

References

Battle, J. (1983). *Enhancing self-esteem and achievement.* Odessa, FL: Psychological Assessment Resources.

Bloom, B. (1977). "Affective outcomes of school learning." *Phi Delta Kappan, 59,* 193–98.

D'Angelli, A., D'Angelli, J., & Danish, S. (1981). *Helping others.* Monterey, CA: Brooks/Cole.

AFFIRMATIVE ACTION

Affirmative action takes in a wide range of remedies that are primarily designed to overcome the consequences of past and present discrimination. *Affirmative action* is the means for achieving the goals of equal employment and equal educational opportunity. By its very nature, affirmative means to confirm, establish, or assert. Affirmative action goes a step beyond equal opportunity or nondiscrimination by requiring employers to examine and monitor their workforce for underutilization of women and minorities and, where necessary, to set goals for increasing the representation of qualified individuals who are underrepresented and to establish timetables for achieving those goals.

Most of the public controversy over affirmative action stems from a misunderstanding of the concept and its requirements. Although affirmative action may require the establishment of goals and timetables, it does *not* require the adoption of rigid quotas. Nor does it require that the factor of race or sex be the sole or determining factor in making decisions concerning employment or admissions. Rather, affirmative action is a process that is designed to ensure the representation of a number of identified groups.

The legally identified groups (protected classes) which are specifically targeted for affirmative action include minorities (Hispanic, Black, Asian or Pacific Islander, American Indian or Alaskan Native), handicapped, disabled veterans of the Vietnam Era, and women. Goals based on the available pool of qualified individuals are established in each employment category, and, in line with anticipated vacancies, projections of protected-class employees in terms of a percentage or actual numbers are made. District schools are then expected to make "good faith" efforts to recruit and hire qualified protected class members to meet the goals and timetables. The term affirmative action may be relatively new to education; however, the concept of different treatment of different students in order to achieve certain educational outcomes is not new. For example, it has been a widely accepted principle of curriculum to recognize that students differ in abilities, needs, and interests. The recognition of such differences is not only accepted, but is considered as a legitimate basis for the differentiation of instruction.

Legal Basis of Affirmative Action

The term "affirmative action" was first mentioned in federal law in 1935 when the Wagner Act authorized the National Labor Relations Board to order affirmative action as a remedy for unfair labor practices. Affirmative action was given its impetus with the passage of the Civil Rights Act of 1964. Other antidiscrimination legislation and a number of executive orders issued by Presidents Kennedy, Johnson, and Nixon have also strengthened affirmative action by focusing on employment discrimination. The two which have proven to be the most important to the advancement of the concept of affirmative action are the Civil Rights Act of 1964 and Executive Order 11246.

The Civil Rights Act of 1964 prohibits discrimination on the basis of race, color, religion, sex, or national origin, in any term, condition, or privilege of employment. It also established the Equal Employment Opportunity Commission to administer Title VII, that section of the law most important to affirmative action. Title VII of the Civil Rights Act of 1964, considered to be the most encompassing piece of federal equal-employment legislation, does not explicitly require affirmative action. However, if discrimination is found, the Equal Employment Opportunity Commission or the courts may prescribe remedies which may include numerical hiring and promotion goals.

Executive Order 11246 requires all government contractors to have written affirmative action plans which include goals and timetables for increasing the representation of protected classes that have been underutilized in the past.

In addition to these two actions which have specifically addressed affirmative action, there are several other laws that, while *not* specifically addressing affirmative action, do support the "spirit" of affirmative action: These include:

1. *The Equal Pay Act of 1963* which requires all employers subject to the Fair Labor Standards Act to provide equal pay for men and women performing similar work, including executive, administrative, and professional employees;

2. *The Age Discrimination in Employment Act of 1967,* which prohibits employers from discriminating because of age in any area of employment;

3. *The Equal Employment Opportunity Act of 1972,* an amendment to the Civil Rights Act of 1964, which bars discrimination on the basis of sex, strengthens the powers of the EEOC, and expands the EEOC's jurisdiction for the enforcement of Title VII;

4. *Title IV of the Education Amendments of 1972,* which prohibits discrimination on the basis of sex against employees or students of any educational institution receiving federal financial aid; and

5. *The Rehabilitation Act of 1973,* which requires the hiring of qualified handicapped workers, affirmative action for the handicapped and the provision of "reasonable accommodations" for the handicapped.

Affirmative Action in the Schools

The two areas of public education that are most affected by affirmative action are employment and admissions.

Employment. Affirmative action plans may be voluntarily adopted by school districts or they may be required by a court or administrative agency as a result of a discrimination allegation. The courts and administrative agencies have required school districts to apply affirmative action remedies to the employment practices of hiring, retention, promotion, and seniority of school personnel, not only in the instance where there is evidence of current or past discrimination, but even in the absence of evidence of discriminancy intent where data indicate certain protected classes have been underutilized in the past. Although such remedies have been decreed in the past, they have not gone without challenge and have, in fact, increasingly become subjected to challenge. For example, the San Francisco Unified School District implemented a voluntary affirmative action program intended to improve the racial balance among administrative personnel by establishing goals and quotas for the hiring and promotion of minority group members. Shortly thereafter, a class action suit involving 4,000 nonminority certified administrative employees and teachers challenged the defendant school district's affirmative action program, in particular, its goals and quotas for hiring minority group administrative personnel (*Anderson v. San Francisco Unified School District*). The federal district court struck down the district's voluntary quota system on the basis it excluded the plaintiffs from promotion, advancement and compensation since it required virtually all administrative lay-offs to be nonminorities and all appointments to be minorities.

In another case concerning hiring and voluntary quotas, *Szewiola & Joyce v. Los Angeles Unified School District*, the plaintiffs alleged discrimination based on sex on behalf of women who were past, present, or future applicants for a variety of administrative job classifications. Prior to the complaint, the school district had instituted an affirmative action plan to ensure that equal employment opportunity be provided. However, the disproportionately small number of females occupying administrative positions was such that the district, while denying liability, entered into a consent decree instead of litigation. The consent decree established appointment goals for several job classifications. According to the decree, appointments were to be made on the basis of the percent of females qualifying for particular administrative positions (e.g., if the job examination was given and 45 percent of the qualified applicants were female, then 45 percent of the appointments from the eligibility list were to be given to females).

Some of most controversial issues related to affirmative action occur when seniority rights are in question. The courts have been reluctant to approve affirmative action remedies which ensure promotions for underrepresented classes, when they impact upon seniority rights. For example, the courts have not been as inclined to allow quotas for minority group members in promotion cases as they have been in cases involving hiring. Although the United States Supreme Court has not prescribed a complete set of criteria for distinguishing between permissible and impermissible affirmative action plans and their impact on seniority rights, in a significant noneducation decision, *Firefighters Local Union No. 1784 v. Stotts*, the United States Supreme Court did provide some guidance. The Court struck down a decision by a district court that enjoined a fire department from laying off firefighters on the basis of last hired, first fired, as required by its seniority system. The lower court believed that the injunction was necessary to protect gains in minority hiring which had been made under an affirmative action plan previously accepted by the city as part of an out-of-court settlement of a past employment discrimination suit. The Court overturned the injunction and ruled that affirmative action may not be court decreed and may not interfere with seniority systems unless specific past discrimination against those who would benefit from the affirmative action plan has been demonstrated.

The permissability of voluntary affirmative action plans that call for preferential treatment of minorities at the expense of seniority rights was not addressed by the Court in *Stotts*, but will be addressed by a case currently pending before the Supreme Court, *Wygant v. Jackson Board of Education*. This case involves a school district's voluntary affirmative action plan that protected minority teachers from lay-offs by retaining minority teachers in proportion to the percentage of minority students in the district. The lower court has held that the plan was "substantially related to the objectives of remedying past discrimination and correcting 'substantial' and 'chronic' underrepresentation of minority teachers in the district." Given the current public sentiment and makeup of the high court it seems probable that the ruling in this case will focus on issues pertaining to voluntary affirmative action and past discriminatory practices.

Admissions. In addition to employment concerns, affirmative action programs in public education have a bearing on admissions to schools and colleges. The major impact comes from affirmative action's goal of increasing the numbers of women and minorities in programs in which they have traditionally been underrepresented. In some instances these efforts have included preferential admissions and have led to acts or allegations of "reverse discrimination." The majority of these instances of alleged reverse discrimination have taken place in institutions of higher education and have resulted from the selectivity of many colleges and universities, particularly at the graduate or professional levels. (Although there are few selective academic programs at the elementary or secondary level, where they do exist the issues have been similar and the judicial processes or remedies identical to those in higher education.)

The most controversial case involving reverse discrimination in education was *Regents of the University of California v. Bakke*. Bakke, a white candidate who had been rejected by the medical school at its Davis campus, filed a suit alleging that the school's admissions policy which designated that sixteen of the one hundred openings available each year be reserved for minority students was racially discriminatory. The U.S. Supreme Court ruled that Bakke should be admitted to the Davis medical school because its policies had violated both the Fourteenth Amendment and Title VI of the Civil Rights Act by discriminating on the basis of race. However, the Court upheld the use of voluntary special admissions plans that consider race as *one factor* in admissions decisions. Thus, the Court's ruling should not be viewed as a signal to retreat from affirmative action remedies under Title VII.

Conclusion

To date, the impact of affirmative action legislation and judicial support of its intent has been encouraging. In the area of employment where the concept has been widely implemented, affirmative action has brought about a number of changes which have benefited all: employees have gained access to a wider pool of employers, and recruiting, selection, and evaluation procedures have been improved. Similarly, in admissions, institutions have gained access to wider and more representative candidate pools and admissions policies have been improved and made more equitable. Although there have been some proposals to amend or eliminate Executive Order 11246, the concept has gained widespread acceptance in education, and the commitment to its principles is likely to continue even in the absence of legislative or judicial mandates.

See also Judicial Decisions; Minority Administrators; Sex Discrimination; Women in Administration.

—Arlene Metha
Arizona State University

References

Gee, E.G., & Sperry, D.J. (1978). *Education law and the public schools: A compendium*. Boston: Allyn & Bacon.
McCarthy, M. (1984). Recent challenges of affirmative action. *Journal of Educational Equity and Leadership, 4*, 69–75.

ALTERNATIVE SCHOOLS

The phrase "alternative education" is used to refer to learning programs that differ from what is considered to be standard educational practice. Standard practice has the following characteristics: (a) a system of testing and grading that sorts out "good" and "bad" students; (b) a concentration on textbook and workbook learning (c) an emphasis on the unquestioned authority of the teacher and on teacher initiated questioning rather than dialogue; and (d) an adherence to the value of conforming to rules, rituals, and standards set by professional educational authorities who are not themselves classroom teachers.

Educational programs that differ from one or more of these characteristics are frequently called "alternative programs" and schools which do not follow them are called "alternative schools." The word "alternative" is used not to refer to the quality and content of an educational program or institution but to the relationship a program has to the authorities who control public-education funds.

Illustrations of the most frequent uses of "alternative" in the context of education are:

1. Alternative schools as free schools. Free schools are usually private learning situations set up by parents who want their children to have an important voice in determining what they learn. They do not use testing as a mechanism of control, often have no set curriculum, and do not use reward and punishment for disciplinary purposes. Teachers at these schools are chosen for what they know and how they feel about children as opposed to what credentials they have. Free schools are often considered threats to local educational authorities because they withdraw attendance-based funds from school districts and plant the idea that parents and students can control schools.

2. Alternative schools as freedom schools. Freedom schools were established during the Civil Rights movement to protest the segregation of the public schools and the degrading way in which people of color were treated in text books and other curriculum material. They have also been set up more recently in protest of the continuing failure of the public schools to meet the needs of poor people of all colors and cultures.

3. Alternative programs as programs for students who do not respond to what is offered in the standard institution. This can include young people who are physically, emotionally or mentally handicapped, or those who are artistically and intellectually gifted. The use of the word "alternative" in this context is a way of keeping difference out of the mainstream and letting the current educational system maintain the dominance of mediocrity.

4. Alternative public schools. This refers to schools within public school systems (such as magnet schools) which have voluntary admission and which have been allowed to depart from the standard curriculum. These schools are usually tolerated within public school systems because of parental and community pressure. They do not fundamentally change the nature of the systems they are part of, and have a very short life expectancy. . .whence the designation of alternative.

"Alternative" is a word used by people who consider themselves "regular." Many people who are involved in so-called "alternative education" consider themselves to be the legitimate educators and the standard system to be antichild and antilearning. These educators believe that education in a democratic society should embody, on a daily basis, the principles of democracy. In practice this means (a) allowing students the maximum choice consistent with maintaining an orderly and friendly school environment; (b) putting a strong emphasis on collective discussion and decision making; (c) respecting cultural differences and understanding what it means to be a citizen of the world; (d) learning to read as a way of knowing about people and the world and considering the rewards for reading not an A in language but the power of having access to books; (e) writing as a way of communicating with others, not just with the teacher; (f) learning the role numbers play in the world and the way different economic systems measure value in terms of numbers; (g) learning and living in a cooperative rather than a competitive environment; and (h) working to eliminate race, sex and class discrimination in education.

These so-called "alternative schools" should more properly be called "schools for democracy." The tradition of democratic schooling has been developed over the last 250 years by people such as Ben Franklin, Froebel, Rousseau, Pestalozzi, Bronson Alcott, Elizabeth Peabody, Louisa May Alcott, John Dewey, and Angelo Patri. There are many of these schools in the public and private sector, but they are a distinct minority. However, they are not alternative, but different. The question of democratic vs. authoritarian schooling is, in education, similar to political, social, and economic questions about whether this imperfect democracy will move towards greater equality and freedom or towards greater concentration of power and neglect for the less fortunate.

See also Inner City Schools; Magnet Schools; Private Schools; Religious Schools.

—Herbert Kohl
Point Arena, California

References

Kohl, H. (1982). *Basic skills: A plan for your child: A program for all children.* Boston: Little, Brown.

Kohl, H. (1984). *Growing minds: On becoming a teacher.* New York: Harper & Row.

Kohl, H. (1982). *Insight, the substance and rewards of teaching.* Menlo Park, CA: Addison-Wesley.

AMERICAN ASSOCIATION OF SCHOOL ADMINISTRATORS

The American Association of School Administrators (AASA) is the professional organization for nearly 18,000 educational leaders across the United States, Canada, and in many other parts of the world. Founded in 1865, members of the Association include superintendents of schools, other central office administrators, building-level administrators (principals), college and university administrators and professors, and administrators from other local, regional, state, and national educational agencies.

The American Association of School Administrators has demonstrated a firm and continuing commitment to excellence. Its programs and efforts seek to promote excellence in administration, teaching, and learning. It believes the public interest is best served by assuring the availability of high quality education for all; knowledgeable, ethical, and effective administrators, in its view, are essential to achieving educational excellence. The association supports the National Academy for School Executives (NASE) and the National Center for the Improvement of Learning (NCIL). It distributes publications and audiovisual materials designed to increase the knowledge and skills of educational leaders. Moreover, the association engages in governmental relations activities which seek to inform congressional staffs of conventions, minority affairs, and impending legislative issues.

Special groups within the organization work to assist administrators in small, rural, suburban, urban, and regional school districts.

The annual convention and regional conferences are designed to provide educational leaders with knowledge and skills that will ultimately assure better education for students. AASA provides leadership through striving for the development of highly qualified leaders and supporting excellence in educational administration, with emphasis on continuous development of a body of knowledge, a shared vision, a code of ethics, effective communication and appropriate action. The association initiates and supports laws, policies, research, and practices that will improve education. It promotes programs and activities that focus on leadership for learning and educational excellence, and cultivates a climate in which quality education can thrive.

General Goals

Annually the American Association of School Administrators upgrades its long-range plan to establish goals for direction of the organization. The general goals are as follows:

1. *Quality education programs.* To promote and provide leadership for the improvement and advancement of education in order to attain comprehensive, accessible, responsive, relevant and efficient educational programs.

2. *Administrator professionalism.* To increase the awareness, skills, knowledge, commitment, and well-being of educational administrators in order to provide effective organizational management and leadership for learning.

3. *Governmental relations.* To attain laws, regulations, and decisions to improve the quality and effectiveness of education, to interpret these laws, to represent the concerns of the educational administration profession, and to work toward the elimination or modification of those laws, regulations, and decisions that impede educational effectiveness.

4. *Communication.* To engage in an effective program of communication that will foster a climate of understanding in support for quality education and to develop, maintain, interpret, and disseminate information concerning education and the educational administration profession.

5. *Association management.* To manage the organization in an effective and efficient manner.

6. *Research.* To sponsor, conduct, disseminate, and encourage the application of research that contributes to the understanding and effectiveness of education, educational administrators, and education's relevant constituencies.

7. *Technology.* To encourage the development and effective use of advanced educational and administrative approaches and technologies.

8. *Human relations.* To develop further human relations skills among educational administrators and to promote a positive human relations climate.

9. *Relationships with other organizations.* To work with chartered state associations and other organizations to achieve mutual goals.

The national headquarters of the American Association of School Administrators is located at 1801 North Moore Street, Arlington, Virginia.

—Richard D. Miller, Executive Director
American Association of School Administrators

AMERICAN FEDERATION OF TEACHERS

The American Federation of Teachers (AFT), headquartered in Washington, D.C., is an AFL-CIO international union that represents the professional, economic and social concerns of teachers as well as other public-sector employees. With a membership of nearly 620,000 individuals—predominantly K-12 teachers but also higher-education faculty, health-care professionals, and state employees—the AFT is organized into more than 2,000 highly autonomous local chapters. The highest policymaking body is the national convention, where local delegates meet to vote on resolutions and elect national officers. An elected executive council is the body responsible for implementing AFT policies. Among its publications are *The American Educator*, a quarterly journal, and *The American Teacher*, a monthly newspaper. The AFT informs members and others of new ideas and practices in education through its publications.

The Federation was organized in 1916 by eight local teacher unions from across the United States. Starting with a membership of less than 3,000, the union experienced steady growth, despite intensive antiunion campaigns. Throughout the first four decades of its existence, the federation worked hard to improve the economic security and working conditions of teachers and to establish and defend teacher rights. All of these efforts were predicated on the assumption that professionalism in education requires, foremost, a secure and free teaching force, empowered to dedicate its full energy to teaching children.

Also central to the philosophy and history of the American Federation of Teachers has been the promotion of civil rights and equality of opportunity in education. As early as 1918, the American Federation of Teachers demanded equal pay for black teachers and compulsory school attendance for black children. It was among the first organizations to break down racial barriers and insist on full membership for minorities and integrated locals.

By the 1950s, as union locals engaged in repeated struggles to gain professional rights and protections, it became obvious that a binding contract, specifically stating these rights and protections, was necessary. In 1956, delegates to the national convention in Pittsburgh adopted a resolution in support of collective bargaining as a desirable goal. The breakdown occurred in 1962 when New York City teachers, after three months of negotiations, went out on strike to win the first major collective bargaining agreement in the nation. Teacher unionism and collective bargaining for teachers soon became widespread, and the AFT entered a new stage of mature professional unionism.

Professional issues have been central to the Federation throughout its history. State and local affiliates are currently engaged in nationally recognized experiments with internship programs, teacher-research linkages, business-school partnerships, and programs to increase student achievement. Most recently, the American Federation of Teachers, under the leadership of its president, Albert Shanker, has been widely hailed in the media and by civic, education, and business groups as a major constructive force in the education reform movement. To promote the professionalization of teaching, it is also exploring a new, national, profession-based entry exam, formal internships, specialty-board certification, and the restructuring of schools and the teaching career.

—Albert Shanker, President
American Federation of Teachers

Reference

Shanker, A. (1985, Fall). "The making of a profession." *The American Educator, 9*(3), 10–17, 46–48.

ASSISTANT/ASSOCIATE SUPERINTENDENT

Administrative specialists who are a part of the superintendent's staff hold a variety of titles, including deputy, associate, assistant, and area or district superintendent. Of these, the titles of assistant and associate superintendent are most commonly used. Immediately subordinate to the assistant superintendent are usually the directors and coordinators of the major divisions within the school system. Titles of assistant to the superintendent or administrative assistant are usually given to assistants who report directly to the superintendent and who have little or no responsibility for supervising other members of the staff.

Extensive utilization of assistant or associate superintendents in other than large school districts is a practice of relatively recent origin. The rapid increases in school enrollment in the 1950s and 1960s, the number of federal programs which were implemented during the 1970s, and the pressures placed on schools because of changing and expanding expectations of the general public increased the need for central office management at the district-wide level.

The position of assistant superintendent of schools was first created in New York City in 1854. School officials in Chicago in 1870 and in St. Louis in 1868 followed the lead of New York City in utilizing the position of assistant superintendent. Initially, assistant superintendents of schools were assigned responsibilities related to the supervision and coordination of instructional programs at the school-building level, a practice which often resulted in friction and "turf disagreements" between the building principal and the assistant superintendent. The introduction and utilization of line-and-staff and span-of-control administrative concepts from 1890 through 1930 helped to reduce areas of disagreement.

The emphasis on human relations theory characterized by concern for morale, group dynamics, and participative supervision during the period from 1930 to 1950 helped to mature the relationship between assistant or associate superintendents and other members of the administrative staff. Concern during more recent years for such matters as leadership behavior, accountability, and performance evaluation has emphasized the need for a "management team" approach to school administration.

Disagreements between the superintendent and other school district administrators are often the result of the superintendent's failure or inability to define accurately the individual roles and responsibilities of members of the central office staff. Leadership studies indicate that the success or lack of success of school programs is dependent, in part at least, on each administrative staff member's perceptions and expectations of the roles of other administrative-staff members. When members of the administrative staff do not understand what is expected of them or of others on the staff, the result is often confusion, inefficiency, and a lack of continuity and purpose.

The allocation of the work of the superintendent's office among assistants, associates, and other administrators should include delegation of authority to accomplish the tasks which are assigned. Also, the superintendent should work closely with members of the staff and the board of education in developing clear goals and objectives for the school district. Assistants who have a clear understanding of their roles and responsibilities derive a feeling of importance, satisfaction, and pride related to their assigned tasks. The successful superintendent also encourages his or her employees to participate in decisions which directly affect them. Job satisfaction among assistants can be enhanced when the superintendent clearly delegates authority and responsibility, gives clear direction to employees, and consults with employees.

Accreditation and classification regulations of the fifty states vary somewhat in terms of the number of certificated administrators in the central office required for various levels of accreditation and classification. A state or regional accreditation agency usually requires a certain number of certificated central-office administrators in relation to the number of teachers or other professionals employed by the school district. For example, an assistant superintendent might be required when the number of teachers exceeds 100; and an additional central office administrator would then be required for each additional 100 teachers.

In most states the regulations of the state department of education or the policies and standards of regional accreditation agencies specify the professional requirements for those who hold positions such as assistant or associate superintendent. For approximately fifteen years, accreditation agencies and state departments of education have required between 45 and 60 hours of graduate credit, inclusive of the master's degree, for those who hold the position of assistant or associate superintendent. These agencies also usually specify the number of hours required in the areas of administration, supervision, and curriculum and commonly require a minimum of two years of teaching experience as a prerequisite for holding a position of assistant or associate superintendent.

A frustration often voiced by central office assistants is that, although they have the title of the position, they do not have the authority required to meet their responsibilities effectively. These assistants often complain that they believe the superintendent is not sufficiently confident of their abilities to delegate the necessary authority and responsibility for them to make decisions and carry out actions which are in the interest of the school district.

Another frustration voiced by assistant and associate superintendents is that, although the assistant does the work, the superintendent takes credit for the hard work when the board of education or general public judges the performance in a positive light. Conversely, assistant superintendents often complain that superintendents sometimes blame the assistants when negative comments are made regarding the school district's administration and general operation.

Four suggestions for superintendents concerning their relationships with assistants are:

1. Hire the brightest and best-trained assistants the school district can afford.

2. Clearly specify by means of job descriptions and policy statements what each assistant is expected to do.

3. Get out of the assistants' way and do not look over their shoulders or second-guess them. Offer support on a continuing basis and respond to specific requests for advice and counsel.

4. Hold assistants responsible for the success or failure of their portion of the school program, and offer praise when appropriate and constructive criticism when necessary.

See also Central Office Personnel; Superintendent of Schools; Supervisory Personnel.

—Robert Shaw
University of Missouri

References

American Association of School Administrators (1971). *Profiles of the administration team.* Arlington, VA: Author.

Knezevich, S.J. (1984). *Administration of public education* (Chapter 15). New York: Harper & Row.

Owens, R.G. (1970). *Organizational behavior in schools* (pp. 10–28). Englewood Cliffs, NJ: Prentice-Hall.

ASSISTANT/VICE PRINCIPAL

The assistant/vice principalship is an important position in American schools. Although the principal is the instructional leader of a school, most principals, particularly at the secondary school level, have been assistant/vice principals before assuming the principal's chair. In that position, they have been providing valuable help to the principal. In addition, they have been "learning the ropes" about that leadership position. Therefore, it has been said that the assistant/vice principal is a principal in training.

However, in many situations the person who is the assistant/vice principal has decided to make it a career position. For many possible reasons, the assistant/vice principal chooses not to move to the principalship. The reason may be economic, geographic, one of loyalty, or one relating to the person's job description or particular ability.

Regardless of the focus of the assistant/vice principalship—be it a training or career position—the role is a vital one in providing high-quality education. As pressures and demands increase upon schools, the principal should turn to assistant(s) to insure that the goals and objectives of the school are attained.

The teaching-learning process is a sophisticated activity. Those who help teachers teach and students learn must have a high degree of expertise in the area of instruction. The traditional role of an assistant/vice principal as dealing only with student discipline and attendance is passé. Contemporary educational administration calls for much more than that. The assistant/vice principal should be as competent as the principal in instructional areas. The increasing emphasis upon instructional improvement in American schools demands it. A good principal shares responsibility for teacher observation, evaluation, and assistance with assistants. Matters of curriculum and pedagogy are highlighted as the prime focus of a school.

Certainly the management aspects must not be ignored. Assistant/vice principals have often been responsible for such facets of school organization as the master schedule, the school calendar, transportation, and student activities—to name a few. Obviously, those functions are maintained to aid the overall instructional process.

The assistant/vice principal is a member of the school's administrative team. Whether a principal in training or a career assistant, the assistant/vice principal must be judged on the basis of skills and ability. The assistant/vice principal's job preferences must be fully assessed and used. His or her job preferences and abilities may be different from those of the principal. If so, differentiated job assignments and responsibilities will be appropriately forthcoming. Ideally, assistant/vice principals will not be assigned tasks for which they have little interest or skills. All have been successful classroom teachers. Their respective teaching areas may be used when deciding instructional responsibilities. The credibility factor must also be considered when teacher-supervision assignments are designed. Assistant/vice principals may have the responsibility of assisting the classroom teachers in their day-by-day instructional and management functions.

The job responsibilities of principals are many and varied. They have been trained to handle the plethora of duties which must be performed. These duties may be categorized under two main headings: Management and Leadership. Management includes the day-to-day operation and maintenance of the school. It is implementing policies and procedures to ensure a smooth running operation. Leadership, on the other hand, includes working with people to make the organization grow and improve. Both functions are important. Both are foci of the training principals receive.

Because assistant/vice principals perform the same job functions as the principals, they too should be trained in management and leadership. There need be no separate training components exclusively for assistant/vice principals. Naturally, when in-service and other professional growth activities are considered, special program emphases may be made. This is true regardless of job title.

An area for rigorous training is instructional leadership. Whether that is emphasized in preservice or inservice, it is a topic of vital importance to all members of a school's administrative team. Assistance to classroom teachers is one of the most vital activities any administrator performs. Evaluation and supervision for the purpose of helping the teacher perform his or her job as effectively as possible are important facets of leadership.

The typical role of the assistant/vice principal has been primarily one of handling student discipline and attendance. If that is the sole focus of the position, at least two things happen—the talents of the person are not used fully, and job frustration sets in. Remembering that the role of the assistant/vice principal is to be active with the principal in all the school's operations, saddling the individual with *only* student affairs is counterproductive. The strengths of the individual should be reflected in job assignments, not the traditional tasks often found distasteful by the principal. Discipline and attendance are important aspects of a school's operations. However, limiting an assistant/vice principal's duties to them will lead to frustration on the part of the person responsible.

An administrative team functions best when duties are allocated because of ability and interest and not because of some experiential or age "pecking order." The diagnosis of skills each member of the team possesses will lead to appropriate job responsibilities and a lessening of job frustrations. School districts may take advantage of such diagnostic services as the National Association of Secondary School Principals' assessment center activities. Assessment centers are available throughout the country and are appropriate activities for assistant/vice principals at both the elementary and secondary school levels. Through simulation activities, the assistant/vice principals are given a report on how they demonstrate twelve skills which have been validated as necessary for success in administration. Such an analysis is an important help to the process of job assignment which should be built upon an individual's strengths.

As schools increase in size, and as greater demands are made upon administrators, the assistant/vice principalship becomes an increasingly important position. It is a vital component of the administrative team—a fact which must be recognized.

See also Assistant/Associate Superintendent; Administrators, Beginning; Principalship; Student Discipline.

—Neal C. Nickerson, Jr.
University of Minnesota

References

Gorton, R.A. (1983). *School administration and supervision: Leadership challenges and opportunities*, (pp. 105–14). Dubuque, IA: Wm. C. Brown Company.

NASSP Bulletin, May 1980 *64*(436).

Wood, C.L., Nicholson, E.W., & Findley, D.G. (1985). *The secondary school principal, manager and supervisor*, (pp. 263–64). Boston: Allyn & Bacon.

ASSOCIATION FOR SUPERVISION AND CURRICULUM DEVELOPMENT

The Association for Supervision and Curriculum Development (ASCD) is the world's largest professional leadership organization in education. The ASCD has more than 75,000 members. The membership forms a broad cross section of instructional leaders in all 50 states and several other countries. A third of the members are principals, and the rest are about equally divided among other leadership roles, including curriculum directors, superintendents, supervisors, teachers, and professors. The work of the association is conducted by a staff of 65 and countless members who volunteer their time and talents.

Founded in 1943 with the joining of the Society for Curriculum Study and Department of Supervisors and Directors of Instruction, the organization was officially named the Association for Supervision and Curriculum Development in 1946. Its mission is to develop leadership for quality in education for all students. The improvement of education is emphasized by increasing leaders' knowledge and skills in the areas of curriculum development, supervision, and instruction. In addition, the ASCD calls for a balanced curriculum and instruction as a means of enabling all students in a diverse society to learn successfully.

Projects

Each year several projects are designed to contribute to the goals of the association. Some current projects are (a) a network of high schools to examine and plan for the future role of the high school; (b) a network of elementary schools to plan for the teaching of thinking; (c) a policy analysis project that has provided members with information on topics such as increased high school graduation requirements, merit pay, and bilingual education; and (d) a thinking skills project now producing videotapes, resource materials, and other member services advancing the teaching of thinking in the curriculum of the nation's schools.

Major Benefits

Educators join the association for its many benefits. Comprehensive members receive the journal, *Educational Leadership*, newsletters, a yearbook, and three to five books each year on relevant topics. Members also receive special rates on videotapes, other media, and the National Curriculum Study Institutes. They may join the Human Resource Development Program, which offers videotapes and institute packages. Other benefits include an annual conference attracting leading educators from across the country, the Resource Information Service, and reports of special project groups. In addition, membership in state or international affiliates provides collegial relationships with other nearby educational leaders.

Publications

Each member receives eight copies of the award-winning professional journal, *Educational Leadership*, which regularly features theme issues on topics of immediate concern to educators along with articles on various aspects of curriculum, instruction, supervision, and leadership.

Two newsletters, *ASCD Update*, published eight times a year, and *Curriculum Update*, published four times a year, feature background stories on current developments in elementary-secondary education, recent trends in the subject areas, and information about association activities.

All members receive a yearbook, and comprehensive members receive three to five other books on such topics as teacher evaluation, curriculum development, and effective schools. The association also offers a new scholarly journal, *The Journal of Curriculum and Supervision*, by subscription.

The association distributes more than a million printed publications per year. The association also produces videos and other media intended for staff development of teachers and instructional leaders. Examples include the widely-acclaimed "Teachers Teaching Writing" video series and "Effective Teaching for Higher Achievement," a six-part program.

Institutes

During the 1985-86 academic year, 4,000 educators attended the National Curriculum Study Institutes. These two-to-five day meetings are conducted at three levels—awareness, training, and issues analysis—and are designed to provide resources to educators for improving educational practice, research, technology, and instructional materials. Some current topics include thinking skills, curriculum development, supervisory skills, computer education, and effective schools.

Planning for the Future

In the summer of 1985, the Executive Council approved a new five-year plan intended to help educators lead the way into the 1990s. Based on continuous environmental scanning, an internal analysis, and members' ideas, the plan has five areas of focus: (a) education and care of young children, (b) teaching thinking, (c) restructuring the teaching profession, (d) effective leadership and supervision, and (e) technology in the content and process of schooling.

—Diane Berreth, Director of Field Services
Association for Supervision and Curriculum Development

ATHLETICS

Interscholastic athletics are an important part of extra-curricular activities within schools across the United States. These programs provide opportunities for students to develop their athletic potential in a variety of sports. Not only do programs provide for physical skill development, but they also provide experiences in competition and cooperation which emphasizes the utilization of both in an acceptable framework. The goals of group loyalty, responsibility, self-discipline, self-confidence, and fair play are all important components of a quality athletic experience.

Nevertheless, the realization of strong outcomes in athletics has been plagued in many instances by pressure and the desire to win, problems with adequate and fair budgeting, and a lack of trained personnel. The challenge of providing sound educational outcomes in athletics is recognized by all, and the accomplishment of this task should not be compromised in programs that have the welfare of the students as a first priority.

Because athletics have only rarely received full status on any educational level, full support of athletic programs has been an ever-present budgetary problem. For example, new programs in athletics, especially those in girls' sports, have practically doubled the cost in many school districts. Nevertheless, the needs of all programs should receive equal consideration when athletic facilities are scheduled and budgets are allocated. Administrators and athletic directors must communicate and work with the coaching personnel in providing fair and equitable programs for boys and girls.

Outside of the regular and expected costs of the athletic program, an unwarranted strain is placed on cost and resources when there is an unrealistic pressure to win. Community leaders, school boards, administrators and athletic directors must insist on a program of athletics guided by strong educational ideals so that the purpose and cost of interscholastics are kept in a proper perspective.

Another major concern that is directly connected to educational standards has to do with the academic achievement of the student athlete. Americans are virtually unanimous in supporting a requirement for student participants to maintain passing grades and to have acceptable school attendance records. There is a connection between learning and performance in all phases of a student's life. Coaches should encourage excellence in the classroom as well as on the playing field. It is paramount that coaches emphasize the importance of attaining a sound education and demonstrate the importance they attach to academics and the concern they have for students as total individuals—both to the athletes themselves, and to their fellow faculty, parents, and community.

Probably the most crucial issue that administrators and athletic directors face is the shortage of qualified coaches and the use of noncertified coaches. The advent of Title IX, an aging teaching population, and a turnover of coaches because of inherent pressures of the position are reasons for a shortage of qualified coaches. Some school districts have elected to utilize teachers who are not specifically qualified to coach, especially in the junior varsity and freshman programs. Other athletic programs have brought in coaches from outside the school district. These situations cause problems for athletic directors in communication, scheduling of events, liability and general organization, and continuity of the program.

For the most part, there are no immediate solutions to the problems of nonqualified or inexperienced coaches. There are, however, some steps that should be taken when these personnel are hired in the athletic program. First, the athletic director must provide an orientation to the school with an emphasis on the educational ideals of athletics. Second, the personnel should understand the general expectations and responsibilities of coaching students. Third, the athletic director and other experienced coaches should provide clinics and workshops which emphasize techniques of coaching and the prevention and care of injuries.

With respect to *all* coaches in the interscholastic program, the athletic director should follow written policies which provide specific guidelines for the selection, assignment, utilization, training, retention, and minimum qualifications of coaches. An athletic handbook with a statement of school philosophy, policies, and procedures for interscholastic athletics should be given to each coach. Furthermore, an evaluation and/or review process should be established for coaches by the administration and athletic director, and these procedures of evaluation should be made known to all coaches.

For programs to thrive and flourish in interscholastic athletics, school administrators must provide excellent leadership through quality athletic directors and coaches. The quality of the performance of their duties by the coaches working with young athletes will go a long way in determining the quality of the programs and the value of the athletic experience which those on the teams enjoy.

See also Extracurricular Activities; Health/Fitness Education; Physical Education.

—Martha Bagley
University of Wisconsin-Milwaukee

References

Jensen, C. (1983). *Administrative management of physical education and athletic programs.* Philadelphia: Lea and Febiger.

Jones, B., Wells, J., Peters, R., & Johnson, D. (1982). *Guide to effective coaching, principles and practice.* Boston: Allyn & Bacon.

Keller, I. & Forsythe, C. (1984). *Administration of high school athletics.* Englewood Cliffs, NJ: Prentice-Hall.

B

BACK-TO-BASICS

In response to a general lowering of academic standards and declining test scores in reading, writing, and computation, concerned parents, educators, and policy makers began in the mid 1970s to call for a return to the basics. The back-to-basics movement, as it came to be called, has several different components and several different spokespersons.

Advocates of the movement want schools to stress basic subjects—especially reading, writing, and mathematics. They also want schools to reduce the number of electives offered and to increase the rigor of standard courses such as English, science, mathematics, and history. In addition, greater emphasis should be placed on order and discipline. By using more direct, structured methods, teachers should regain the authority and respect they lost during the 1960s and 1970s. Students, therefore, would be given more drill, recitation, and homework. Promotion would be based on demonstrated mastery of skills and knowledge, not on time spent in school. Finally, schools should stress the teaching of morality and patriotism.

During the early 1980s, the back-to-basics movement gained considerable support from an unprecedented number of reports that focused national attention on the need for school reform. Though varied in their assessments of the strengths and weaknesses of schools, these reports all stressed the need to raise academic standards by placing greater emphasis on literacy, mathematics, science, and computer skills. In addition, many reports called for stiffer graduation requirements, more time spent in school, more homework, and more direct instruction.

In response to the demand that schools raise curriculum standards and devote more attention to teaching the basics, every state has implemented statewide testing programs. Several states also require students to pass a basic skills test before graduating from high school.

Effective Basic Skills Instruction

Research on effective teaching has confirmed that there is no single, simple approach to increasing student achievement in the basic skills. The attributes of good teaching vary from situation to situation. Nevertheless, research has demonstrated that *how* teachers interact with students does influence achievement. Generally, effective basic skills instruction is linked to four kinds of teacher behaviors: expectations, direct or active teaching, time on task, and classroom management.

Teacher Expectations. Research shows that teachers behave differently toward students whom they believe to be either high or low achievers, and these differences are related to student learning. Effective teachers believe that they *can* teach and students *can* learn.

Effective teachers convey their positive expectations by avoiding such behaviors as requiring less work and effort from low-achieving students than from high achievers; having low achievers recite less often; giving low achievers less time to answer questions; seating low achievers in a group, usually farther from the teacher; giving low-achieving students fewer prompts when answering questions; criticizing low-achieving students more often for wrong answers; and praising low achievers less often.

Direct or Active Teaching. Effective teachers of basic skills are also more active or direct in presenting content. They spend more time actually teaching and devote less time to seatwork or other activities. In addition, they are more alert for signs of student misunderstanding, and they provide more opportunities for students to practice skills successfully. In general, these teachers actively demonstrate *how* to learn. They do more than simply monitor students' progress on seatwork. They act as models, demonstrating to students how to solve problems and providing regular, consistent, corrective feedback.

Time on Task. Effective basic skills instruction is also characterized by greater amounts of what researchers have termed time on task, academic learning time, or opportunity to learn. Significant differences have been found in regard to the time students actually spend on academic tasks. And, not surprisingly, the more time students spend on reading, writing, and mathematics, the higher their achievement in these areas. Students of effective teachers, for example, may experience nearly 200 more hours of academically engaged time per year than students of ineffective teachers.

Classroom Management. The management techniques of effective teachers are characterized not by what these teachers do *after* students misbehave, but what they do *before.* Efficient use of time, proactive planning, responding to student behavior, and the ability to monitor classroom activities (or "withitness") are among the behaviors effective teachers use.

Current Issues

The back-to-basics movement has sparked considerable debate between proponents and critics, and many questions remain unanswered. What are minimum acceptable standards and who should set them? How should schools deal with students who fail to meet these standards? Can standards be raised without increasing drop-out rates? Are excellence and equal opportunity compatible educational goals? Finally, will the increased use of basic skills competency tests be seen as a form of discrimination against minorities who traditionally score lower on such tests?

Some critics believe that the movement is a simplistic solution to a complex problem and that it sets "minimum" skills as the "maximum." In this regard, some have called for schools to go *beyond* the basics to emphasize the "essentials" of education: for example, the ability to solve problems, think logically, communicate clearly, and distinguish fact from opinion.

The back-to-basics movement has also been opposed because it emphasizes rote, mechanical skills, and it tests students only for their mastery of discrete, easy-to-measure bits of knowledge. Some critics even charge the movement with dehumanizing education and stifling teacher and student creativity and self-direction. The result, they fear, will be students who are overly dependent upon authority.

Finally, some educators have pointed out that it is incorrect to call for a *return* to the basics. Schools have *always* emphasized the basics. In fact, such critics maintain that the tendency of schools to teach only basic reading, writing, and mathematics may have contributed to the problems schools now face.

While the issues surrounding the back-to-basics movement will not be easily resolved, the movement has sparked a healthy dialogue. Various groups are now learning to work together to improve the quality of schools. The movement has reminded administrators, parents, teachers, and concerned citizens of the schools' primary mission—to provide students with the skills and knowledge needed to live satisfying, productive lives.

See also Academic Learning Time; Classroom Management; Direct Instruction; Educational Goals and Objectives.

—Forrest W. Parkay
University of Florida

References

Kohl, H. (1982). *Basic skills: A plan for your child, a program for all children.* Boston: Little, Brown & Company.

Parkay, F.W., O'Bryan, S., & Hennessy, M. (Eds.). (1984). *Quest for quality: Improving basic skills instruction in the 1980s.* Lanham, MD: University Press.

Reed, L., & Ward, S. (Eds.). (1982). *Basic skills issues and choices: Issues in basic skills planning and instruction* (Vols. I & II). St. Louis: CEMREL, Inc.

BILINGUAL EDUCATION

The movement in education toward the development and implementation of bilingual programs has entered its third decade. The term "movement," however, is as accurate today to describe the status of bilingual programs as it was twenty years ago. Bilingual programs are in a state of change, change that is the result of historical and present trends in our world. Only through examining these trends can we begin to speculate on what the future holds for bilingual education.

The First Decade (1965–1975)

Prior to the conceptualization of bilingual education, second language learning was an accepted and preferred institution in our public schools. Children were encouraged to receive instruction in a language other than English. During this first decade a division was created which differentiated between foreign language learning and bilingual education. The origins of the two programs were different, yet their long-term goals very similar.

Both foreign language instruction and bilingual programs addressed the need to prepare children adequately for the pursuit of their life goals. Foreign language instruction, however, had its origins in middle class ideology as an avenue for continued refinement and advancement in society. In contrast, the origins of bilingual education arose through the civil rights movement in this country, addressing the inequalities in education and demanding equal education for all children.

The foundation of bilingual education during this first decade was less than secure. Programs were implemented through a "shotgun" approach, implementing numerous programs prior to the development of materials and curriculum, and before trained teachers were available. These newly established programs also lacked any comprehensive plan for program evaluation, a limitation which to this day has adversely influenced support for continued program development in bilingual education.

The Second Decade (1975–1985)

Early in this second decade teacher training programs were designed to train specifically bilingual teachers. The teacher shortage of earlier programs was diminishing, providing more appropriate instruction for linguistically different children. Legislation addressed concerns with teacher-student ratios in bilingual classrooms, supporting the introduction of language tutors and teachers' aides. Federal and state supported programs gained a reputation for sound program evaluation based on guidelines established to promote bilingual programs.

The movement in bilingual education began to slow noticeably as the decade progressed. Federal and state funding agencies felt the impact of changes in government administrations, with a growing conservative philosophy being characteristic of these administrators. Subsequently, funding sources for bilingual programs were threatened with each new fiscal budget. These cuts in fiscal allocations made way for the disproportionate use of pull-out programs which remove students from classrooms on a part-time basis versus full bilingual programs. The re-emergence of pull-out programs also brought about a re-emergence of views holding bilingual education as a remedial education program.

Changes in administration were not the only factors leading to changes in attitudes toward bilingual education. Available empirical research at that time was minimal, or else too recent to reflect program effects for the first fifteen years. The Office of Planning, Budget and Evaluation of the U.S. Department of Education initiated a review of literature which concluded that the effectiveness of bilingual education was questionable.

In response, several proponents of bilingual education re-examined those studies cited by the Office of Planning, Budget, and Evaluation and others not examined in the report. Indeed there are some bilingual programs which have been unable to demonstrate "appropriate" academic achievement for their students; however, significant data exist to suggest that students in bilingual education programs achieve equally or excel their counterparts in mainstream classrooms.

Future Trends and Considerations

The sociopolitical climate in the United States will play a significant role in the continuation and expansion of existing bilingual-education programs. Opponents of bilingual education are using statistics on drop-out rates and illiteracy as indicators of unsuccessful bilingual programs. Concurrently, proponents of bilingual education are utilizing their educational, research, and political skills in an effort to maintain existing programs.

The future of bilingual education in this country is at present questionable. Current research in education has been focusing on the growing drop-out rates for students, and the widespread illiteracy among adults. The most publicized of these studies are those done with linguistically and culturally different populations, often failing to mention that mainstream individuals are also casualties of the educational system. With such a linguistic and cultural focus in these studies, bilingual/bicultural education becomes a natural target for "failing" to educate.

The growing conservatism and strong nationalism in this country has brought a low tolerance for cultural and linguistic diversity. So, not only are bilingual programs "failing" to educate, they are also being labeled as "anti-American." The national movement towards an "English Only" society is indicative of the mood in this country towards culturally and linguistically different populations. Several states have adopted English as their "official language," and the financial repercussions are evident in the loss and/or cut of funding for bilingual programs.

In light of the growing concern for the future of bilingual education, it seems that, in a discussion of considerations which now are pertinent, we are in fact strategizing for this future. State organizations for bilingual education and the National Association for Bilingual Education are two vehicles for solidifying a common educational, research, and political base for those proponents of bilingual education. The skills and expertise of these individuals are essential to promoting a positive image of bilingual education.

Bilingual educators have developed a strong support network of professionals. The combined skills and expertise of these individuals lends itself to developing an empirically sound foundation for bilingual education which would include components of program evaluation and development and legislative and community support. Through these combined efforts it is feasible that bilingual education may be able to influence the growing conservative and nationalistic trend in this country.

Conclusions

As bilingual education enters its third decade, it finds itself in a precarious position. Social, political, and economic support are questionable. Early research is based on bilingual programs implemented during a period where appropriate resources (e.g., materials, teachers) were almost nonexistent. Later studies are often seen to be based on limited data, coming from programs too new to draw significant conclusions. Thus, conclusions supporting or questioning bilingual education are being examined carefully. These conclusions regarding the effectiveness and need of bilingual education will hopefully be reached in this third decade.

During this new decade bilingual education shares a problem with other school support services, namely, how to justify "need." Ironically, as the number of students dropping out of school, being placed in foster homes, and being sent to juvenile authorities continues to rise, we are told that special programs and support services are not needed in our schools and in fact that these social issues may be a result of existing programs that have "failed."

Culturally diverse school enrollments are rising with each new year. Bilingual education, if it is to continue to exist, must be ready to demonstrate that children in our schools do need the support and benefits provided through bilingual education. Bilingual educators must be ready to provide a strong empirical foundation that will be able to demonstrate need and effectiveness, and also recognize that much of their struggle will occur at a judicial level—emphasizing a need for skills, expertise, and solidarity.

See also Minorities and the School System; Multicultural Education.

—Francine M. Martinez
University of Colorado

References

Baker, K.A., & De Kanter, A.A. (1981). *Effectiveness of bilingual education: A review of the literature.* Washington, DC: Office of Planning, Budget, and Evaluation, U.S. Department of Education.

Fishman, J.A. (1976). "Bilingual education and the future of language teaching and language learning in the United States." In A. Simoes (Ed.), *The bilingual child.* (pp. 229–35). New York: Academic Press.

Willig, A.C. (1985). "A meta-analysis of selected studies on the effectiveness of bilingual education." *Review of Educational Research, 55*, 269–317.

BUDGETING

A *budget* is a financial plan that describes the requested expenditures and anticipated revenues required to operate an educational organization for a specified fiscal year. The essential purposes of a public-school budget are to provide a) legal compliance with fiscal requirements; b) control over public monies; c) accountability to public authority; d) predictability of expenses and revenues; and e) fiscal planning and evaluation. The operating budget provides an annual expression of the values of a school system. When programs and priorities are translated into budgetary dollars, the public can readily observe how the organization is allocating funds among competing programs and services.

Budget Process

As a result of the doctrine of "separation of powers," budgeting is both an executive and legislative activity. The executive (superintendent) proposes, and the legislature (board of education) disposes. Upon formal adoption by a legislative body, a budget becomes a legal document that serves as the basis for actual expenditures, accounting systems, and audit procedures. The five major steps in the process of public budgeting are: preparation, submission, adoption, execution, and evaluation. The third step, adoption, occurs when the legislative branch appropriates specific dollar amounts in various accounts to be spent during the fiscal year. The other four steps are undertaken by the superintendent and staff as part of a process called *executive budgeting*.

Budget Formats and Codes

At the heart of a well-managed fiscal operation is a clearly defined budget coding system. Sometimes called a "chart of accounts" or "expenditure classification," the coding system is keyed to the particular budget format employed by the school system. Typically, a school budget is organized around the following four major expenditure categories and includes specific code numbers for each: (1) *Objects* (salaries, supplies, equipment); (2) *Functions* (instruction, transportation, maintenance); (3) *Programs* (mathematics, science, special education), and (4) *Locations* (Smith Elementary school, Jones High School). Generally, the codes for object and function are mandated by each state, whereas the codes for program and location (usually optional formats) are developed by the school system itself.

The particular budget format and coding system become the engine that drives the entire financial system. The coding system is used by bookkeepers in the business office to record a teacher's salary, by principals to prepare textbook requisitions, and by board members to compare appropriated funds with actual expenditures for specific accounts. Anyone who wishes to understand a public budget document should first learn about the coding system that is used to assign dollars to proper categories. To understand budget codes is to destroy the complex mystique that dominates the layman's view of budgeting.

Site Budgeting

The primary responsibility for submitting a budget request to a board of education rests with the superintendent. Depending upon the superintendent's management style, the role of building principals in the budget process may be limited or substantial. In a highly centralized administrative structure, the role of principals may be confined to filling out requisitions for textbooks after the budget has been adopted. In contrast, an emergent system called "site budgeting" is designed to decentralize the fiscal process by delegating greater management authority and budget responsibility to individual principals. Where is the most expert judgment found for relating financial resources to educational needs? Most likely it is at the building level where more is known about specific pupils, staff, curriculum, and facilities. Site budgeting, which is a major component of decentralized school management, requires that each school be treated as a cost center. This system increases staff involvement in budget planning, moves the locus of budget decisions much closer to the clients (pupils), and can help to reduce arbitrary decisions by a distant central administration.

Role of Principals

As a key member of the administrative team, the principal's role in budgeting includes four major activities. (a) *Budget planning* entails assisting the superintendent in identifying budget priorities and assumptions at the beginning of the annual budget cycle. Principals can suggest ways to improve the process, simplify the forms, and inform the community of school needs. (b) *Program analysis* involves a review of program objectives and evaluation criteria; suggesting curriculum changes; and communicating with staff, students, and parents about programs. (c) *Budget requesting* is the careful review of teachers' requests; setting program priorities for the school; and submitting a total budget request to the superintendent. (d) *Expenditure control* entails a record-keeping system of expenditures and balances at the building level. Also, it includes maintaining an equipment inventory, preparing requisitions, and meeting central office deadlines for various fiscal reports.

Excellence in Budgeting

A number of factors must be present for schools to achieve success in budgeting. The key prerequisite to excellence is a competent superintendent. In addition, it is recommended that school officials consider the following as they assess both their budget process and budget document. The *budget process* is enhanced if there are written board policies on fiscal matters and goals or guidelines that give direction to the annual budget. Compliance with various legal requirements is critical. Attention should be given to ensure adequate staff involvement and citizen participation at budget hearings. Budget priorities should be linked to educational plans in a way that relates program costs with results. The superintendent and board chairperson should review the "bottom line" request in terms of political feasibility in the community. And, of course, the superintendent and business manager should be certain that adequate internal management and accounting controls are in place so that the district can maintain proper accounting of revenues, expenditures, and fund balances.

The *budget document*, if properly prepared, can contribute substantially to administrative excellence. The format should include a table of contents or index, pagination, understandable charts and figures, a letter of transmittal, clarity of style, accuracy of numbers, and a concise "executive summary" that highlights budgetary data. A well-organized budget should include: *assumptions* that underlie the budget, such as projected enrollment, staff, inflation rate, energy needs, and special education needs; an *object budget*; a *function budget*; a *program budget*; a *school site budget*; anticipated *revenues*; comparison with prior years; explanation of tax rates; and a clear explanation of major cost factors such as salary increases and transportation increases.

See also Administrative Tasks; Financing of Schools; Funding Methods: State and Federal; Planning.

—Harry J. Hartley
University of Connecticut

References

American Association of School Administrators (1982). *School budgeting: Problems and solutions.* Arlington, VA: AASA Critical Issues Report.

Greenhalgh, J. (1984). *School site budgeting: Decentralized school management.* New York: University Press of America.

Wildavsky, A. (1983). *The politics of the budgetary process* (4th ed.). Boston: Little-Brown.

BUREAUCRACY

Among classical theories of organizational design, certainly bureaucracy is the one which has the greatest name recognition. Though many theorists have expressed similar principles of classical management of complex organizations, Max

Weber offered a description of an ideal type design based on rational-legal authority, rather than traditional authority or authority that legitimated itself through charismatic leadership. Bureaucracy is defined by a set of related principles which when followed describes an organization which is both rational and efficient, the two underlying primary values of bureaucracy. The principles of organization fall into three broad categories—*structure and function, rewards*, and *rights of individuals*. Among the more commonly listed principles are hierarchy of authority, division of labor, specialization based on expertise, systems of rules, careerism, and impersonal orientation.

Each principle of bureaucracy is intended to enhance rationality and efficiency; however, each may at times become dysfunctional for the organization. For example, highly specialized divisions of labor can lead to boredom; exaggeration of hierarchy of authority can block communications; and systems of rules can become ends in themselves and displace organizational goals. An impersonal orientation, which often ignores personal need dimensions and informal networks, may result in low morale. Careerism with promotion based on seniority and level of expertise can be problematic. Holding a position for some time does not in itself enhance expertise and accrue value to the organization. Yet seniority, in part because it is so much easier to quantify and verify than expertise, is often accorded more weight.

The Bureaucratic School

Schools are said to be more or less bureaucratic, depending on the degree to which they emulate characteristics of Weber's "ideal type." To ask the question, "Are schools bureaucracies?" misses the point. The quick answer to that question is a definitive yes/no. In fact, Gertrude Stein might have responded with—a school, is a school, is a school! The point is that bureaucracy is but one particular set of principles for examining, describing, and understanding school life. A school is no more a bureaucracy than it is a culture, a psychic prison, a political organization, or an organized anarchy. A school is not any *one* of these, yet it may be all of these at one time. Two important questions related to bureaucracy and schools might be raised: In what way(s) does bureaucracy help us to understand better and to work more effectively in places called *schools*? Second, do notions of bureaucracy in any way limit our capacity to understand and deal with the complexity of modern educational enterprises?

Bureaucracy as an ideal-type organizational design is steeped in mechanistic metaphors of the industrial revolution. The change from agrarian-based to industrial-based economies called for new ways of envisioning, planning, accomplishing, and thinking about the work of many people under the umbrella of a single entity. It should not be surprising that the major principles of bureaucratic organizations have been modeled successfully in large industrial settings and in military organizations in which the tasks for subordinates were generally predetermined and straight forward, the environment remained relatively stable, and subordinates behaved and performed compliantly. The degree to which these conditions exist in schools today may call into play various principles of bureaucracy.

Schools are large enterprises which need effective leadership to accomplish a variety of purposes. In support of bureaucracy, it is not too difficult to argue for a system in which people understand their roles, their responsibilities, their rights, and their importance to the organizational outcomes, while individual work efforts are coordinated and planned so that decisions affecting people and outcomes are more rational and efficient, and tend to enhance continuity of purpose and uniformity of activity. Bureaucracy helps us think about, analyze, and attend to particular organizational dimensions which serve the interests of all educational stakeholders. The degree to which bureaucracy helps us to understand, operate, and evaluate school activities is the primary criterion for determining its worth to school leaders. It is not a question of is it?, or isn't it?, but rather . . . Is it helpful?

The limitations of bureaucracy are commonly treated in several ways. The first describes various dysfunctions of the major functions of bureaucratic principles. The second is the inherent conflict between professionalism and bureaucracy. Another limitation of bureaucracy relates to organizational dimensions which are not treated. Failure to treat these areas creates a substantive void for effective principles of management in modern organizations: to name a few—lack of attention to norms of the informal organization, evidenced in cultures and subcultures; human resource issues beyond simple role compliance; political dimensions in and outside schools; and the flexibility to scan the environment and adjust to new demands and new social realities. The obvious danger in looking at schools only through bureaucratic lenses is managerial myopia. Such a condition is often predicated on assumptions that schools are fairly traditional, static institutions. If we could only revisit the conditions which spawned the need for bureaucratic structure and rules, we might once again be able to lead more effective, rational, and efficient school organizations. Perhaps a more appropriate question might be, "To what degree can the administration of schools be nonrational and inefficient yet still meet the multiple missions of today's schools?"

Complexity of Schools

A final consideration is the possibility of some alternative lenses which might help to enlarge our perspectives and help us to clarify the diversity and complexity of schools. The ways we think about and describe the organization, operation, and administration of schools affects the way we define its purposes, its failures, its successes, and its potential. The theoretical and analytical tools we use to describe, examine, and deal with the schools as organizations are mixed blessings.

In one respect bureaucratic lenses may reveal new insights and help account for previously unexplained events. However, at the same time each perspective (bureaucracy being a broad comprehensive one) has its own injunctions or blinders. That is, if one's predominant means of thinking about and dealing with schools reflects the major principles of bureaucracy, it is likely that each problem will be framed in the particular context of a bureaucratic dilemma or problem which then generates a particular set of response possibilities. As in the case with most rational decision-making modes, one framework necessarily eliminates whole categories or possiblities of administrative action. The point is not to eliminate or completely discard bureaucracy as an administrative perspective. One simply needs to ask, which principles of organizational design are appropriate in this case? Do the assumptions and values which undergird traditional notions of bureaucracy match the realities of schools today?

The Modern School

New realities have created a different milieu in which the modern school exists. Changes in family structure and support, the number of families with school age children, major demographic shifts in the general population and in school age children in particular, changes in technology, and the powerful impact of the mass media on social values describe a dramatically different environment in which change and uncertainty appear to be the only constants. There is a need to look beyond traditional descriptions of organizational ideal types. New realities and new conditions demand different configurations, new perspectives and new conceptualizations of what schools as organizations are and what they can be.

The concept of organizational design is based on a system of meaning—forged from experiences with concrete realities and subjective interpretations of those same events. Each person contributes to organizational realities because he or she construes the meaning and attaches importance to particular events and dimensions. Rather than attempting to measure schools against static models or approximations of an ideal type, it seems more useful to tap a variety of perspectives and theoretical explanations. There is place in the study of schools and their administration for complementary and at times contradictory perspectives. If we believe that schools are many different entities at once, then it makes sense to look for multiple ways to describe, understand, and operate in them. Complementary and paradoxical images of schools may emerge from metaphors of politics, culture, entrepreneurial enterprises, networks, transformational entities, nurturing environments, and/or institutions of domination and control. The search for an ideal type might raise the question, which of these is really what schools as institutions are? The answer is: It is all of these. Each, bureaucracy included, represents a part of the constellation of multiple realities we know as school.

See also Administrative Theory; Centralization and Decentralization; Organizations: Principles and Theory.

—Paul V. Bredeson
Pennsylvania State University

References

Blau, P.M., and Scott, W.R. (1962). *Formal organizations: A comparative approach.* San Francisco: Chandler.

Perrow, C. (1979). *Complex organizations: A critical essay.* New York: Random House.

Weber, M. (1947). *The theory of social and economic organization.* (A.M. Henderson & T. Parsons, Eds.) New York: Free Press.

BUSINESS EDUCATION

Historically, business education has provided education regarding aspects of business that concern every member of our society. It provides instruction for those persons who wish to become managers or wage earners in a business occupation. Thus, comprehensive business education programs serve the school population through a relevant curriculum oriented toward providing career direction, a sound foundation for advanced study, and the development of job skills.

Many of the skills taught in vocational business courses are being viewed as essential to the education of all students. The development of skills in business communications, human relations, and good work attitudes have been identified by employers as very important for success in the world of work. In addition, the rapid advent of computer technology has made utilization of the computer in some form an essential part of employment in most occupational areas, and keyboarding skills are needed to input data into computers.

The objectives of a comprehensive business education program are:

1. To educate students for and about business.

2. To provide career information that helps students relate their interests, needs, and abilities to occupational opportunities in business.

3. To educate students about acceptable standards of tasteful grooming, personality, attitude, manners, positive self-image, and appropriate dress in business.

4. To provide instruction in the use of high technology equipment that students will encounter in the work place.

5. To provide educational opportunities for students preparing for careers in fields other than business.

6. To provide a continuous program of planned learning experiences to help individuals (a) produce and distribute goods and services effectively as workers; (b) use the results of production conscientiously as consumers; and (c) make judicious socioeconomic decisions as citizens.

7. To provide instruction that will help students develop a mindset that will enable them to accept lifetime changes that will be demanded of them.

These objectives are attended to in the business education curriculum within the primary occupational foci of accounting, administrative services, and business enterprise.

Some courses, such as keyboarding, may be offered at more than one grade level. Each school district should determine the appropriate level for those courses to be offered within the structure of their individual districts. Keyboarding, for example, should be offered prior to the time that students are expected to do any significant amount of inputting into a computer and should be taught by a business education teacher.

Comprehensive business education programs should include:

Human Relations (including employability skills)
Keyboarding (initially taught at elementary or middle school level)
Business Communications (written, oral, listening)
Technical Skills (as needed for employment or post secondary training)
Dictation/Transcription
Business Occupations
    Methodology of Cooperative Education, Model Office Education
Information Processing (including word processing and data processing)
Business Computer Applications
Career Education and Exploration
Basic Skills (interrelated with vocational education)
Business Procedures
Computerized Accounting
Teaching About Business
    Entrepreneurship/Free Enterprise
    Business Organization/Management
    Basic Business
    Business Law
    Economics

Microcomputers should replace electric typewriters. Although one can point to businesses that use electric or electronic typewriters, the movement toward the automated, computerized office clearly indicates the use of a multi-function machine, a microcomputer.

The future for workers trained in business education is encouraging. Demand for personnel in administrative services is predicted to rise 28 percent in this decade alone; 20 percent of all administrative support positions are unfilled today; and by the year 2000, 80 percent of the total work force will work in information processing fields.

The future for careers in business education is excellent and can lead to an enjoyable and secure future for both men and women.

See also Career Education; Vocational Education.

—Cynthia E. Gallant, Supervisor
Milwaukee Public Schools

Reference

Schrag, A.F., & Poland, R.P. (1986). *A system for teaching business education* (2nd ed.). New York: McGraw-Hill.

BUSINESS/EDUCATION PARTNERSHIP

Industry in the United States has always been closely tied to education. The business and school sectors have defined common goals. For example, business has always provided scholarships and other financial assistance for students, and has given donations to schools for specific buildings or programs.

Recently, the ties between industry and education have been strengthened. Corporations have begun playing an extraordinary role in the education arena all across the country. In fact, American corporations have become the nation's leading education activists.

Corporate Contributions to Education

In the past, humble school officials would go hat in hand to corporations, asking for donations. Benevolent industry leaders would hand over checks patronizingly, treating them as charitable contributions. Today things have changed; corporations are no longer waiting for educators to request money or materials. Corporate America is now taking the initiative, offering deals too good to pass up. Examples abound of companies establishing programs on their own. In Fairfax County, Virginia, twenty-five local businesses pooled their contributions to come up with nearly one million dollars in cash and equipment for a new college prep school of science and technology. National companies such as AT&T, Mobile, Boeing, Honeywell, and Exxon have joined forces with local companies to open state-of-the-art facilities at Thomas Jefferson High school in Annandale, Virginia. These facilities will include a $600,000 telecommunications lab with a television studio and control room, a radio station, a weather station, and a satellite earth station. There will be a biotech lab equipped for genetic engineering experiments in cloning and cell fision, as well as labs for energy, computer, and scientific research.

More Than Altruism

Why the expanded involvement by corporate America? These hard-headed businesspeople are not giving huge sums out of sheer altruism, generosity, and kindness? The leaders of business are painfully aware of the large and ever-increasing gap between what is needed in the contemporary workplace and what is provided by today's educational system. Firms know to their dismay that today's ill-prepared graduates become tomorrow's corporate burden. Statistics bear witness to the fact that what workers don't know can hurt not only them, but their employers as well. The problems may be divided into three areas.

1. *Actual costs.* More than three-fourths of all large U.S. corporations teach remedial reading and writing programs at a cost of over $300 million annually.

2. *Lost opportunity costs.* According to the American Society for Training and Development, corporations lose millions more dollars because of mistakes made by workers who cannot read and write.

3. *Shrinking labor pool.* America's job force is becoming a "seller's market," with a shrinking labor pool of entry-level workers. This means that companies face the prospect of hiring ever-less qualified workers, posing a threat to the promise of prosperity in the new information society.

Nothing Is Perfect

While education and industry may not seem such strange bedfellows once we understand what they have to offer to one another, there are disadvantages to the partnership. Each field has its own priorities. Creating a truly equal partnership is easier said than done. A number of reports have criticized both education and business for pushing their own interests. Some curriculum materials promote specialized products and viewpoints. There are examples of exploitations whereby corporations (because they control the funding) imposed their self-interests on unsuspecting (or helpless) educators and students. Corporations may offer money for research but insist on retaining patent rights and other controls. Some fear that industry will want to divert universities from basic research into commercial product development. Of course, not all the onus is on corporations. There are concerns that schools are just along for the free ride, that once the funds run out the schools will lose interest in further association with corporations.

Advantages of the Partnership

Fundamental in American society is the belief that competition strengthens our country. Training and education systems within American corporations are so vast and extensive that they represent in effect a competitive alternative system to the nation's public and private schools. Because of the profit motive, corporate education is often more efficient than traditional education. It may also be more flexible and open to new approaches. Corporate education comes in a variety of different packages: evening classes, learning on company time, company-sponsored sabbaticals, and the like. Because it is more cost effective to keep an employee than to hire a new one, corporations are chosing to promote training and retraining as a lifelong process.

Schools are recognizing and applauding the fact that corporations are taking their new role as education activists seriously, with determination and imagination. There is a natural relationship between education and industry in that good schools are often the key factor in recruiting the most creative, talented people to a company. Business and education must compliment, not compete.

Guidelines for Establishing a School/Business Partnership

The following aspects of corporate-education partnerships have proved effective across the nation. If you are ready to establish a mutually advantageous partnership, these suggestions can help.

1. *Collaboration.* Establish a steering committee with representatives from the education and business sectors who develop yearly plans and designate standards.

2. *Input.* Sponsor activities at each location in order to brainstorm partnership ideas.

3. *Council.* Review existing, established school/business partnerships to determine areas of mutual concern. Identify what works and what does not.

4. *Agreement.* Establish an administrative agreement that delineates monthly activities and policies governing all phases of planned ventures.

5. *Celebration.* Enjoy the partnership. Plan special events that help all parties learn to respect one another.

6. *Shared Responsibilities.* Ensure equal input and recognize contributions of each side.

7. *Team Concept.* Establish and promote a team concept in which participants assist each other with projects.

8. *Public Relations.* Disseminate information reporting partnership activities to the community.

9. *Network.* Promote a local and statewide network of business/education coalitions.

10. *Critique.* Evaluate activities, provide feedback, and outline recommendations for future projects.

See also School District/University Partnerships; School-Community Relations.

—Bettie B. Youngs, Executive Director
Institute for Executive Development

References

Naisbitt, John & Aburdene, P. (1985). *Re-inventing the Corporation*. Warner Books.

Timpane, M. (1984, February). "Business Has Rediscovered the Public Schools." *Phi Delta Kappan*: pp. 389–92.

Youngs, Bettie. (1981, November). "Business/Education: Synergy at Last." *Thrust for Educational Leadership*. 18–20.

C

CAREER EDUCATION

Career education consists of a comprehensive program that prepares students for careers by relating their education to the world of work. Career education is an instructional strategy that teachers use to increase students' awareness of themselves and occupations as well as to teach students how to make critical life and career decisions. The concept of career education emerged in the early 1970s in response to the perception that traditional education was irrelevant to future life. It was originally designed to be part of a sweeping educational reform emphasizing out-of-school learning, flexibility in school day and school year, lifelong learning, career guidance, community and business participation, and increased use of educational technology. Although some of these changes have been slow to gain widespread acceptance, the concepts of career awareness and linking school and work have become part of many school curricula.

The goal of career education is to prepare students for whatever the next step may be—work, training, or education. In addition to this broad goal, proponents of career education hope to instill in students a commitment to education and an awareness that learning is lifelong. They also hope that students will leave high school with good work and study habits, a positive work ethic, and an awareness of the self as a potential worker in society. The latter implies awareness of one's values, interests, skills, and personality in addition to knowledge about occupations and the skills needed to enter the world of work.

Programmatic Components

Career education has five major programmatic components. First, it is a developmental program, with different vocational tasks (e.g., relating broad interests to occupational areas in grades 6–8) emphasized at each developmental stage. Second, it has an experimental focus, and third, an emphasis on curricular infusion of career-related activities and skills. Fourth, it is systemwide in that all school staff are responsible for career education. Finally, it involves students' families as well as community resources in career education.

One of the tenets of career education is that children develop an awareness of careers and of their own skills and interests as they grow older. These concepts must be learned in some sequential order that matches students' ability to comprehend them. Four stages are typically defined: career awareness, career exploration, career preparation, and the postsecondary stage. Each student progresses at his or her own pace in moving through each stage, but each goes through these stages.

The first stage, career awareness, occurs in the elementary school years. In this stage children are exposed to a wide variety of occupations in order to gain an understanding of work in adult life, and they begin to develop a sense of their own skills and interests. Career exploration takes place in the middle and early high school years (6–10), and emphasizes greater understanding of the world of work and self, along with initial decision-making skills. Career preparation, in the high school years, focuses on greater understanding of interests and abilities and skills, and choosing a field of interest and the level of work desired (e.g., professional or skilled level). This implies self awareness of skills, interests, and values, as well as knowledge of the world of work, and decision-making skills. The final stage, postsecondary, is an occupational-specialization stage, in which students begin to prepare for their chosen occupations, either through schooling, or entry into the work force.

Career education has an experiential focus, emphasizing activities that relate to the world of work. These activities may actually be on the job such as an internship program, or "shadowing" a worker on the job for a day or more. Teachers and counselors may also provide work-related experiences in school, using work sample kits or classroom activities. In addition to the experiential component, career education is designed to be infused into the curriculum at all levels. Thus, classroom teachers must expand their lesson plans to integrate career education activities.

Career education is systemwide. Through curricular infusion, classroom teachers become involved. Counselors are involved often as monitors of career education programs, as liaisons between the school and community, as teachers of career courses, as consultants to teachers, and as referral resources for individual counseling. Administrators are involved in curricular development, as well as implementation and evaluation.

Finally, career education involves families and the community. On one level, career education is easily understood and endorsed by the community in general, and parents in particular. On another level, parents may become closely involved in career education by serving as resources for information about their own careers, or participating in other classroom activities. Most career education programs invite parental involvement through needs assessment and other evaluations as well as providing parents with information on the career-education program so that it may be reinforced at home.

Practical Implications

The programmatic components of career education have several practical implications. First is the issue of evaluation. The developmental focus of career education carries with it an emphasis on evaluating each student individually. Thus, each child is individually assessed for academic or social deficits and strengths with staff designing programs to meet the individual needs of each student. Evaluation also implies accountability. Several career-education programs have specific objectives the school staff must meet and for which they are held accountable.

A second major implication is communication among parents, teachers, counselors, and administrators. The schoolwide emphasis ensures that each student's program will reflect previous experiences. This implies articulation among school staff at each level. Parental involvement is a key component of career education, and also requires a great deal of communication between parents and school personnel.

A third major implication of career training is the need for training. Staff development is critical to integrate career education effectively into the curriculum. Training also is important for teachers, counselors, and administrators for their own growth and development. Career education concepts do not end with high school or college, and school personnel may serve as role models of lifelong learners.

See also Business Education; Vocational Education.

—Nadya A. Fouad
University of Wisconsin-Milwaukee

References

Hoyt, K.B. (1977). *A primer for career education.* Washington, DC: Office of Career Education.

Humes, C.W., & Hohenshil, T.A. (1985). "Career development and career education for handicapped students: A reexamination." *Vocational Guidance Quarterly, 34,* 31–40.

Mailand, S.P., Jr. (1974). *Career education: A proposal for reform.* New York: McGraw-Hill.

CAREER LADDERS

Career ladders are changes in the structure of work. They make it possible for teaching to remain the main focus of effort while opportunities are provided for teachers to advance and progress in their careers in education. Previously the only avenues open to teachers who desired career growth were in supervisory, support, and administrative roles such as curriculum coordinator or principal. Career ladders include established career stages in teaching with mandatory performance standards, defined responsibilities, and a variety of monetary and nonmonetary rewards.

An attempt to focus work incentives to appeal to academically able and talented teachers and potential teachers along with a gradual upward movement through increasingly higher career stages in teaching is the distinguishing feature of career ladders. Research in a variety of work settings indicates that opportunity for growth and advancement is a widely held value. Consequently, career ladders focus on academically able people who are interested in performing and receiving recognition for their performance, have high personal growth needs, can compete successfully in a variety of job settings, seek opportunity, and are interested in influencing the quality of education in the school systems in which they work. The belief is that these people will be attracted to a job structure that recognizes and rewards performance and effort. Career ladders also enable teachers to map their futures by providing career advancements that teachers can plan and prepare for.

Issues Raised by Career Ladders

Career ladder plans that contain substantial changes in the expectations and rewards in teaching bring up several major challenges. First, the single salary schedule, rewarding teachers on the basis of years of experience and accumulated university credits, is a firmly established tradition based on strong norms of egalitarianism among teachers. It was established to prevent abuses of academic freedom, prejudice, and caprice in the treatment of teachers. Many teachers working in the schools have come to terms with this norm and are comfortable with it. Additionally, any redesign of work will cause stress.

Second, career ladders require the investment of additional human and material resources into the schools as part of the commitment to attract and retain the target population in teaching. The motivation behind the movement to establish career ladders and improve the quality of the teaching force is the improvement of schools. Ultimately, evidence that school-improvement efforts are enhanced by career ladders needs to be gathered to sustain the necessary level of support.

Third, career ladders are often funded by state legislatures or school boards, and the political funding process is demanding. Accountability comes at election time. The evidence that a career ladder is succeeding in its goals will not begin to accumulate for some time after implementation; retention of the plan requires resolve, effort, and patience.

Fourth, the establishment of power and opportunity structures for teachers may challenge the leadership abilities of principals. A new leadership team in the school is available to the principal for school-improvement efforts, but it requires the development of team- and group-leadership skills. Power sharing may present a threat to some principals.

Finally, teacher evaluation systems with the ability to distinguish among the good, better, and best teachers need to be carefully developed. Teacher evaluation without a career ladder focuses on decisions to retain, remediate, or fire a teacher and does not distribute rewards. The stakes are greatly increased when career ladder pay and promotion decisions are attached to teacher evaluation. If teachers cannot trust the integrity of the selection of promotion procedures, then the incentives that were the initial impetus behind career ladders are lost.

These are opportunities as well as challenges; each represents a focal point in calls for improvement and excellence in schools. The attractions, retention, and reward of able teachers; increased resources devoted to education; increased societal support and attention for schools; improved evaluation procedures; and the infusion of greater leadership talent on the part of teachers and principals into the systemwide school improvement effort can all emerge from the career ladder development process.

Career Ladder Features

Models of career ladder plans include a mix of features that emphasize either merit recognition or job enlargement. Most plans include elements of both. Merit recognition systems have a long history of spotty success in teaching, but, though job enlargement has been applied in other work settings for many years, it is not common in education.

Merit features of a career ladder plan often include the establishment of multiple steps on a pay system in addition to the single salary schedule. Ranks or titles such as novice teacher, certified teacher, professional teacher, and master teacher are used to describe the steps on the ladder. Teachers who have the requisite years of experience established by the plan (a characteristic that requires vigilance, because the seniority provisions of the current system can wipe out the incentive gains of promotion opportunities) can request promotion to a new rank. The evaluation process takes several forms. The most promising plans rely on multiple lines of evidence of teacher excellence for promotion. Dossiers containing examples of teachers' curriculum development, tests, and lesson plans; student, parent, and peer rating forms; scores on professional or academic ability examinations such as the National Teachers Exam or the Graduate Record Exam; clinical supervision reports; and principal evaluations can be submitted to a panel of teachers, administrators, and parents for evaluation. Evidence of student achievement such as student projects, criterion-referenced test results, compositions, or performances and products in the arts are often included. This process closely resembles the procedures established in universities for retention, promotion, and tenure decisions.

In other systems, merit bonuses are divided among applying teachers on a yearly basis and do not represent a promotion. Rating forms, principal evaluations, or clinical-supervision reports are often used to determine who will receive the merit bonuses. These systems lack the permanence or planning embodied in the notion of career ladders.

Job enlargement features in career ladder plans take two forms—promotions to additional responsibilities in the school carrying with them increased scope of influence, power, and opportunity and payment for specific projects. The first form is more consistent with a career-planning structure, the second distributes opportunity more broadly and encourages enterpreneurship. Both require that judgments of merit are made, but they emphasize increased opportunity as a result of merit.

Under the promotion model, the notion of master teacher is critical. This model requires the articulation of teaching skills and activities far beyond basic competencies in a series of stages delineating professional growth. The stage I, II, or III career ladder teacher is required to demonstrate competence and effort at increasingly more sophisticated levels. For example, at the basic level, state licensure certifies the mastery of a knowledge base and technical proficiency in teaching. Direct observation of teaching under structured clinical settings can be used to diagnose and evaluate the mastery of necessary techniques and the ability to apply them in a classroom. More experienced and proficient teachers demonstrate the mastery of a variety of techniques, plan much of their own work, and evaluate the outcomes of their teaching, applying increasingly stringent standards. Precision judgments about the appropriateness of their professional decisions, the skillful use of a broader range of techniques, knowledge in their subject area, and

application of developmental psychology reflect the quality of their teaching. Their curriculum units, contribution to schoolwide quality, and involvement in the profession can serve as evidence of professional growth.

Master teachers demonstrate all of the foregoing qualities. In addition, they may be involved as mentors for new teachers and in leadership and evaluation decisions in the school. They make difficult decisions, quickly adapt to contextual factors, and apply professional standards and ethics to the school setting.

Implementation Strategies

Whenever an important and far-reaching change in work design is undertaken such as a career ladder, those whose work lives will be affected and whose professional and personal effort is required should be involved in planning, design, and implementation. Career ladder plans that have been carefully articulated philosophically, with the mix of merit reward, job enlargement, and career opportunities explicitly stated have experienced the greatest successes. Teachers form the bulk of the planning committees for these plans, with carefully designed information and feedback systems for the other teachers, so that opportunity for input is legitimate, not a facade. These plans also require real changes, not simply new names for old features in schools, and adequate lead time for development prior to implementation. Administrators and teacher association leaders can provide the necessary leadership with parents, school board members, and other community leaders giving input. It is also critical that information feedback and ongoing revision systems be built into the early stages of a career ladder job redesign effort so that successes can be capitalized on and difficulties quickly diagnosed and addressed.

See also Competency Testing, Teachers; Merit Pay; Teacher Salaries; Teacher Tenure.

—Ann Weaver Hart
University of Utah

References

Hackman, J.R., & Oldham, G.R. (1980). *Work redesign.* Reading, MA: Addison-Wesley.

Hart, A.W., & Murphy, M.J. (in press). "Career ladders and performance appraisal." *The National Forum.*

Malen, B., & Murphy, M.J. (in press). "A statewide decentralized approach to public school reform: The case of career ladders in Utah." *Journal of Education Finance.*

CENSORSHIP

Two definitions of the term "censorship" are current. Both agree that censorship is the prevention or inhibition of a communication. There is disagreement as to whether the term should refer only to governmental agencies, or whether it should be used for any effort, whether by government officials or by private individuals or groups, to limit a student's right to read, to learn, and to be informed, as well as to limit a teacher's right to academic freedom. The broader definition is increasingly used by scholars.

Censorship differs from the selection procedures used in the schools. Selection is professional in nature, relying on the consensus of experts using open procedures, and making learning materials available across a wide range of ideas. Censorship, on the other hand, is negative and exclusive in its effort to prevent exposure to objectionable books, magazines, films, newspapers, dramatic events, or presentations by speakers. Censors tend to act in secretive ways in contrast to the public method used in education for selecting learning materials. Censors use unprofessional methods of book selection, judging books by associations of the author (such as the false charge that Steinbeck was a Communist) or by a single aspect, a method rejected by the Supreme Court in the Miller decision (1973).

Far more students are now exposed to ideas or books that some segments of the public find challenging or objectionable because the school populations grew from approximately 50 percent of the age group in 1900 to about 90 percent by 1980, and school libraries increased in numbers and in diversity of materials.

Major objects of attack have been sex education, evolution and contemporary realistic novels, which became available after World War II in inexpensive paperback editions. *To Kill A Mockingbird, The Grapes of Wrath, The Catcher in the Rye,* and other realistic, well written twentieth century novels were challenged all over the United States. Moreover, publishers have consistently expurgated Shakespeare's plays, novels by Mark Twain, and other literature in school anthologies.

Books are most frequently attacked, largely by persons outside the school. Second in frequency of attack is the school newspaper, often by members of the school staff. Periodicals and films are less frequently attacked. The most frequent charge is obscenity or "bad language," although no court has found any material used in the schools to be obscene. A frequent objection to the school newspaper is that it criticizes the school or related agencies, such as the food service or the bus service. School newspapers are, however, protected by the First Amendment, as several court cases have made clear.

Recent criticisms of the schools have been launched by persons and groups of particular religious, economic, and political persuasion. What began in the early part of this century as a challenge to the teaching of evolution has broadened to include attacks on virtually any instructional material or program with which groups of citizens disagree.

Sixteen surveys of censorship pressures in the schools found more than 800 titles that have been challenged; these are mostly twentieth century books by American authors, including several of the best writers of the twentieth century, such as Hemingway, Steinbeck, Orwell, and Huxley, along with major nineteenth century writers such as Twain and Hawthorne.

Both critics and defenders of currently used school materials have resorted to litigation to support their actions, with mixed results. In the Warsaw, Indiana, controversy, the Third Federal Circuit Court of Appeals upheld the right of the school board to remove what it regarded as improper materials, such as the social studies text *Values Clarification.* In decisions in Ohio and the state of Washington, the appellate courts upheld the use of controversial materials in the schools. The only Supreme Court decision on this matter (as of this writing), *Island Trees versus Pico,* did not resolve the substantive issues involved. It required that a lower court hold a trial on the charge of a student, Steven Pico, that his First Amendment rights were infringed by the removal of eleven books from the Island Trees library. The school did not pursue the case but returned the books to the library.

The school district policy on censorship should be an integral part of the materials selection policy. That policy should make clear the commitment of the school to intellectual freedom. The committee drafting the instructional materials policy should include representatives of the various groups involved in education: students, teachers, media specialists, parents, administrators, and the school board. The instructional materials policy should be officially adopted by the school board. Sample policies for material selection have been published by several state departments of instruction, including Iowa and Wisconsin.

The policy should include the following items:

1. A statement of the philosophy of materials selection such as contained in the American Library Association (ALA) Library Bill of Rights.

2. A statement that the school board is ultimately legally responsible for the selection of the instructional materials.

3. A statement explaining the delegation of this responsibility to professional staff members.

4. A statement of the criteria for instructional materials selection in the school or district.

5. The procedures for implementing selection criteria.

6. Critical terms used in a policy should be defined, e.g. "selection," "instructional materials," "literary merit," etc.

7. Procedures for dealing with challenges to instructional material: (a) A review committee is necessary to deal with complaints, either a standing committee or a special committee for each complaint. The committee should be appointed by the school superintendent and should be broadly representative of all segments of the school and its constituency: parents, students, teachers, media specialists, and administrative staff. Since a report of the review committee would go to the school board, the school board should not be represented on the review committee; (b) the review procedures should be applicable to all individuals, including teachers, librarians, administrators, and board members; (c) the procedures should explain how challenged materials are to be dealt with during the period of reconsideration; (d) only written complaints should be dealt with by the review committee. Informal complaints should be referred to the staff person—teacher or media specialist—who ordered or used the material; (e) the complaint form should ask for identification of the challenged material, an evaluation of the general purpose for the use of the challenged work, and suggestions for an alternative assignment to accomplish the same purpose. A sample complaint form may be found in *The Students' Right to Know;* and (f) the criteria for dealing with challenges should be twofold in nature: Is the challenged item relevant and appropriate to its classroom use? Is the challenged item appropriate for library inclusion by the standards of ALA Library Bill of Rights?

See also Communicating with the Community; Education and Community Views; Instructional Media Center.

—Lee Burress
University of Wisconsin-Stevens Point

References

Bryson, J.E., & Detty, E.W. (1982). *Censorship of public school library and instructional material.* Charlottesville, VA: The Michie Company.

Burress, L., & Jenkinson, E.B. (1982). *The students' right to know.* Urbana, IL: National Council of Teachers of English.

Davis, J.E. (Ed.). (1979). *Dealing with censorship.* Urbana, IL: National Council of Teachers of English.

CENTRAL OFFICE PERSONNEL

Central office personnel are those staff members of a school district who work under the direct supervision of the superintendent. Such personnel are required to assist the superintendent in the implementation of educational policy. The numbers and skills of central office personnel will depend on the size, structure, and particular needs of each school district. The larger and more complex a district is, the greater the number and diversity of personnel required to assist the superintendent in the implementation of policy.

Several types of central office personnel exist in American school districts. Many districts have a deputy superintendent, who reports directly to the superintendent and is responsible for a wide range of activities. In larger school districts, a deputy superintendent may have a number of assistants and be responsible for coordinating their activities. In smaller systems, the deputy may routinely work directly with teachers, counselors, and other members of the staff. Many districts employ a number of assistant superintendents, each responsible for a particular functional area. For example, one assistant superintendent might be assigned to curriculum and instruction, another to personnel, another to business affairs, and another to community relations and special projects. In larger districts, these assistants may report to the deputy superintendent. In other systems, where there is no deputy, the assistants report directly to the superintendent.

Central office personnel also generally include directors who are responsible for specific departments. These departments frequently include general subject areas of curriculum, such as the language arts, mathematics, science, and social studies. They may also include levels of instruction, such as elementary, secondary, and vocational education, as well as guidance services. Directors may also be assigned to departments such as transportation, buildings and grounds, food services, and media/duplication center. Each central office director generally reports to the assistant superintendent responsible for his or her general area or to the deputy superintendent in systems where there are no assistants.

In many school districts, central office personnel may also include a variety of staff members responsible to directors or department heads. These individuals may hold titles such as assistant director, coordinator, supervisor, special assistant, or consultant. They may hold general responsibility for an entire department or responsibility for particular areas within a department. In large school districts, central office personnel may also include professional specialists with general responsibilities who are employed full time. Such professionals may be attorneys, architects, engineers, or medical doctors.

Virtually every school district central office staff includes a number of clerical and other technical personnel such as secretaries, clerk-typists, computer programmers, mechanics, and maintenance persons. A number of these individuals, especially clerical personnel, may report to individual administrators. Others, particularly maintenance people, may be supervised by a single department, such as the physical plant.

Individual school districts generally develop their central office personnel according to the sizes of staffs to be managed, relationships among areas and departments, and the availability of resources. For example, a large school district may require a full-time superintendent of schools, as well as full-time deputy superintendents, directors and department heads, assistant directors, coordinators, professional specialists, and clerical/technical personnel. A small district, with a modest total staff and program, may require only a full-time deputy or assistant superintendent, directors responsible for multiple functional areas, and a clerical staff. Many districts may reconcile the need for central office personnel with limited availability of resources by employing part-time curriculum coordinators, or consultants for areas which require particular expertise or for special projects.

In addition to the challenges of developing a central office staff consistent with both the management requirements and the resources of a school district, this level of personnel is frequently associated with reporting and responsibility problems. Although line and staff relationships within central office personnel are usually clear, their relationships to other members of this district staff can become ambiguous. For example, although assistant superintendents or curriculum directors may exercise considerable influence on the superintendent or deputy superintendent through staff relationships, their formal, line authority over building principals is frequently limited or ill-defined. Under these circumstances, central office personnel may achieve effectiveness only through long periods of experience with line staff members elsewhere in the district, or by working through the superintendent to reach such individuals. The development of these management relationships can tax the time and energy of the superintendent and central office personnel as well as limit the efficiency of the staff as a whole.

See also Assistant/Associate Superintendent; School Business Manager; Superintendent of Schools; Supervisory Personnel.

—Fritz Hess
East Syracuse, New York

References

Campbell, R.F., Cunningham, L.L., Nystrand, R.O., & Usdan, M.D. (1980). *The organization and control of American schools* (4th ed.). Columbus, OH: Charles Merrill.
Kimbrough, R.B., & Nunnery, M.Y. (1976). *Educational administration: An introduction.* New York: Macmillan.

CENTRALIZATION AND DECENTRALIZATION

Centralization and decentralization can be understood as shifts in organizational routines generated by various competing groups and is designed to seek three goals: representativeness (responsiveness), politically neutral competence (accountability, administrative efficiency and managerial effectiveness), and executive leadership (ability to acquire and use knowledge and information). Centralization is the concentration of administration at a single center which is also the locus of power and authority. Decentralization is the delegation of authority to lower levels of a governing hierarchy and/or the devolution of power to lower dimensions of the structure of the organization or the state. Both decentralization and centralization have been chosen at one time or another by groups seeking more power to govern. The decentralization effort known as community control was such an effort. The black and Hispanic communities wanted control over the policy-making mechanisms of public schools which affected the life changes of their children.

A Repeating Cycle

Historically, the governance of schools began as a decentralized decision-making unit. In fact, our earliest political structures may be described as reactions against executive dominance. Our founding fathers struggled over the extent of decentralization in the new government. Federalism is a form of decentralization wherein the main-area governments receive their powers from the constitution, upon which the central or federal government is equally dependent for its sphere of jurisdiction. Constitutionally, it has been made deliberately difficult for the national government to alter the powers of the constituent units, their boundaries, and their forms of government. Control over education was given to the states by the constitution, and that power devolved to local school boards. But, by the middle of the 19th century, the politics of legislatures, elections, and the spoils system led toward an emphasis on neutral competence and executive leadership. A shift of centralization appeared.

As a consequence, in public education the superintendency developed and the efficiency movement prevailed. The professional bureaucracy grew rapidly after this, and its impersonal procedures made some groups feel that neutral competence and executive leadership could not deliver to them their fair share of resources and benefits. A little after the middle of the 20th century, agitation for decentralization once again occurred, this time from black and Hispanic minorities, who felt that city bureaucracies and public schools no longer responded to their needs. Disparities in practice among numerous small units, differences in human and financial resources, economies of scale, conflict with school desegregation objectives, and strong opposing factions cooled the school decentralization trend, and school systems started recentralizing.

Advantages and Disadvantages

Decentralization is widely regarded as a necessary condition for social, economic, and political development and for improving the efficiency with which demands for locally provided goods and services are met. Yet, if efficiency is a condition in which no person can be made better off without some other person being worse off, equality is not assured. Furthermore, if city interests concern policies which maintain or enhance their economic position, social prestige, or political power, their pursuit may not allow for the care of the needy and unfortunate. Whereas some argue that decentralization offers the widest range of choices for development, allocation, and redistribution, others say that redistribution can occur only where the fiscal base is substantial.

Many think that decentralization strengthens accountability because it provides a training ground for citizen participation and political leadership. Still, studies have shown low turnouts, which may be an effect of class and education in local elections. Moreover, some scholars argue that local government, just as central, is equally capable of restraining individual freedom in pursuit of collective action and that it is narrow and sectarian, allowing a local majority to subvert the will of the national majority as in the case of African American apartheid in the South before 1960.

Some scholars see decentralization as a support system for the status quo, where there is a reinforcement of the goals of the dominant groups, an emphasis on material equality as a prerequisite for political equality, and the direction of community activism towards existing patterns of state intervention and subject to the control of the central government through the receipt and use of grants.

Organizationally, decentralization dilutes the power structure by creating more power positions but limiting the organization's dependence on each one. When the major components of an organization are arranged into self-sufficient clusters, each with its own domain, dependence tends to be confined there. The ability of the individual to handle that dependence is of limited usefulness to the organization.

Both centralization and decentralization may be used for a variety of ends, but each should be evaluated on the purpose for which each is employed. Neither should be judged an absolute good in its own right.

See also Consolidation of Schools; Organizations: Principles and Theory; School-Based Management; School Districts.

—Barbara Sizemore
University of Pittsburgh

References

Kaufmann, H. (1969). "Administrative decentralization and political power." *Public Administration Review, 29* (1), 3–15.
Smith, B.C. (1985). *Decentralization: The territorial dimension of the state.* London: George Allen & Unwin.
Thompson, J.D. (1967). *Organizations in action.* New York: McGraw-Hill.

CHANGE AGENT

During the past twenty-five years there has been a considerable amount of research regarding change agents in schools. A *change agent* is an individual who brings about a change in a school system. A major finding in this research is that in loosely coupled systems, for example schools, such a role does not appear to exist naturally nor can an assigned position of "change agent" be effective. In social systems whose survival depends upon pleasing external constituencies (public agencies, schools, etc.), the dynamics of change appear to be so synergistic and political that an identified change-agent role is often a liability. Evidence seems to suggest that many persons in schools can be, and sometimes are, change agents. It is the history of the school and the organizational context of the school that determines who the change agents can be. The magnitude of the change and the organizational context limit what a change agent can accomplish. If making substantive change is the intent, then it is the organizational context that must be affected.

What seems to be known about educational change are the conditions that promote change along with an understanding that anyone who wishes to be a change agent in schools must learn the territory of a particular school culture and develop and create change relationships (conditions).

Role

A careful examination of change roles indicates certain conditions are essential if administrators are to be successful change agents: (a) An administrator, because of an ability to control resources, flow of information and appointments, can use his or her position to facilitate change; and (b) an administrator can make use of the informal networks within a school or district to build support for and implementation of change efforts, recognizing that it is teachers who have the ultimate control and decision-making power regarding what will actually be implemented. If change conditions are to be created and supported, the administrative role must minimally not block and maximally seek ways to solve problems and promote relationships supportive of change within the school. Many administrators do not view themselves as change agents, and it is not critical that they do, only that they support those change agents working in the school.

Trust

If people work in an organizational climate where mistakes are not tolerated, then only the most persistent of innovators and early adopters will be willing to risk change. It is not uncommon for those who may be insecure, threatened, or view themselves as vulnerable, to do all they can to inhibit change. It is therefore crucial that people who are undergoing the risk of change feel that they will be rewarded and supported for their efforts, not only by administrators but by faculty as well.

Participative Decision Making

Change literature suggests that there must be commitment to a change by those who must implement the change. However, commitment and ownership are not conditions that can be "bestowed." They are outcomes that must be earned through the decision-making process. This means that deciding on what the problems are, how problems are defined, and which changes will be implemented to solve them must be shared by those who are responsible politically (administrators) and those who will have to do the day-to-day work of implementing the change (teachers). Participative organizational structures are a must for sharing of power and status. To many administrators, this may seem like losing power or abdicating responsibility. To many teachers, this will seem like a trick or an intrusion into their work lives.

Introducing participative decision making into school settings is difficult. It takes much more time than most people realize. Participative structures represent substantively different organizational structures in schools, and these new arrangements require that teachers and administrators give up the loosely coupled autonomy of existing school structures for more closely coupled and cooperative relationships.

Organizational Understanding

Organizations have cultural scripts and informal networks of people which have the greatest impact upon change efforts and at the same time are the most difficult to discover. Most change efforts are lost within the first months, but those involved do not discover it until much later. A change agent must take the time to learn the territory of a school setting before initiating strategies and attempting to make substantive changes. Without understanding the territory of a school (social context), there is little chance to influence substantive change.

Vision

The change agent must have a clear view of the shared vision for the change effort. If anyone is to keep the change effort on track, it will have to be someone whose major function is to accomplish the change. Schools are busy, interactive places. Needs abound and school must go on every day. Change efforts can easily be derailed by allowing other agendas to push the change effort aside. People can become so busy putting out fires or taking care of nuts and bolts that the change efforts can get lost. The change agent must be tough minded enough not to allow this to happen.

Resources

Although the change agent need not be an administrator in the formal system, the individual must have access to the organization's resources, both human and fiscal. This means that if the change agent is not someone with budget control, someone with fiscal control must be supportive of the effort and willing to direct resources in new and innovative ways.

Internal/External Agents

It is possible to promote insider/outsider roles that facilitate implementation through collaboration with other institutions and organizations. People from outside bring fresh ideas, additional resources, and independence. (When provided an insider role, they are also privy to the very crucial informal information concerning a school culture.) Insider/outsider people can often unblock situations or take risks that insiders are unwilling or unable to take.

Finally, change agents must realize that the stress of change makes the role an ambiguous one, that change-agent roles are temporary, and that there is a "teachable moment" when those in an organization are ready to learn and a time when they need to rest from changing in order to permit the effects of change to produce the desired results.

See also Change Process; Change Variables; School Improvement and Effectiveness Movements.

—Ralph Parish
University of Missouri-Kansas City

References

Argyris, C. (1982). *Reasoning, learning and action.* San Francisco: Jossey-Bass.

Lortie, D. (1975). *School teacher.* Chicago: University of Chicago Press.

Sarason, S.B. (1981). *The culture of the school and the problem of change,* (2nd ed.). Boston: Allyn & Bacon.

CHANGE PROCESS

This article focuses on improving the change process and includes discussions of *mobilization, implementation,* and *institutionalization.* The process works recursively in a field of often competing and conflicting interests where issues of power, authority, resource allocation, and values bump against the dynamics of change.

Mobilization

What gets the change process started is often difficult to ascertain because of the numerous external and internal stimuli impinging on the school, and such factors as when the stimulus emerged, who was present to respond to it, and what the organizational conditions were at that moment.

What is clear is that organizational goal attainment through systematic planning and problem solving ranks low on the scale of stimuli to change. So do the merits of the change itself. Instead, reasons such as improving school capacity to provide better education, improving classroom instruction, reducing student dissatisfaction with the curriculum, or providing opportunities for professional growth, development, and career advancement are all woven into the web of incentives and rewards that affect mobilization. (N.B., These conclusions are not atypical for schools; research is pointing out that similar nonproblem-solving forces are potent change factors in business and industry.)

Given these conditions, regular decision-making opportunities become key levers for prodding change. For school personnel, choice opportunities such as budgeting, scheduling, analyzing test results, evaluation visits, and staff development sessions take no extra energy to create. Then, at other times, additional decision opportunities may have to be created to initiate an innovation (e.g., an analysis of trends affecting the organization and a planned needs assessment).

Often, mobilization hinges on knowing about available curricular and instructional options. Simply being unaware of possibilities can inhibit organizational readiness and inclination to change. Or, knowing about only a few options can skew a response to a legitimate need.

Administrators play a critical role in this regard. They have more opportunities than teachers do to attend meetings and conferences where the focus is often on new practice or process options. They can disseminate the information that may galvanize innovative thinking and turn it into action. If administrators also become advocates of change, they can promote the movement within the system, a subsystem, or individuals. In addition, expert teachers, who are able to make presentations to peers, play an important role in getting other teachers to adopt or develop an innovation.

At the core of mobilization is an organizational climate that values ideas, inquiry, and research, accompanied by incentives for changing. Because rewards from student interaction are significant to teachers, a work environment that promotes positive reinforcement from students, combined with administrative support, recognition, appreciation, and peer interaction, is a powerful force for encouraging initiation of teacher-level involvement in change (e.g., course, units). For a busy staff, however, this energy can be sapped by discipline problems, unresponsive clients, and having to assume responsibility for school management tasks.

Implementation

Innovations are often adopted or developed but never used. Use depends considerably on the size, complexity, and focus (district or organization, subsystem or individual teacher) of the innovation plus local history of change. Innovations may be installed with relative ease or great difficulty.

Adopted innovations that are focused, well defined, carefully developed, and field tested (such as those from the National Diffusion Network) have a greater probability of having a positive impact if implemented as "true" to their original form as possible and given adequate trial time before being adapted. On the other hand, efforts to bring about change that are more general in concept and components, or makeup (e.g., the Hunter Mastery Teaching Model) must go through a process of adaptation to permit tailoring to the local context.

The bigger and more ambitious the level of change, the more interacting variables will be generated (e.g, scheduling, role definitions, materials, time). Although demanding practices or processes have a greater possibility of affecting significant change, they also run the highest risk of failure.

Sometimes implementation is complicated by the attributes of the characteristics of the proposed change itself. Attributes such as complexity, size and scope, and practicality may generate requirements for additional supervision and assistance (e.g., a project director), training, or an extended implementation time line. (N.B., A recent study indicates that it can take up to eighteen months for a user to gain firm mastery over a fairly complex innovation and six months for one that is less demanding.)

For an innovation to be given a fair test, teachers must be committed to gain "practice" mastery over it. There are times when this commitment emerges after rather than before use of the curriculum practice or instructional process. Therefore, assistance to and support for users can be critical to gain this pledge. It can also be critical in dealing with problems that individual teachers might not be able to solve; willingness to try an innovation can erode quickly in the face of a lack of materials, lack of training, schedule conflicts, or other road blocks. And throughout, various staff concerns will arise, ranging from needs for more information about the change to what will be the possible impact of the change on the individuals' organizational role. Hence, administrator interest in and knowledge about what is happening, active support in the form of needed assistance, and possible intervention at a key moment are requisites for successful installation of an innovation.

During implementation, administrators may need to exert pressure to ensure that teachers sustain use. Adding an innovation can be a formidable new task on top of regular work demands; therefore such pressure has to be applied judicioulsy and with sensitivity. A remote, low profile administrative posture in the presence of a demanding innovation adds to the probability of excessive adaptation or eventual discontinuation.

Effective monitoring requires consistent and substantive communication between administrator and teacher. Each lives in a different world. Administrators tend to see implementation as relatively simple and manageable, downplaying logistic demands such as time and training requirements. Being distanced from the classroom, administrators also tend to forget what life is like for teachers working with youngsters all day. They often expect more from the innovation than it can deliver. And teachers, on the other hand, may not appreciate the need for the change within a broader school/community context—a perspective administrators must juggle constantly.

Institutionalization

Despite the pressures on schools to change, opposing pressures to maintain the status quo or to return to old habits are potent, and they endanger implemented innovations. Numerous innovations are put into use, but disappear, wholly or in part, over time. Thus, in most cases, specific attention has to be given to institutionalization—stabilizing the change and making it a routine practice or process.

If the innovation is to be retained and if it is one that can be managed and tracked, even competent users of the practice or process—users who are motivated and committed—do not guarantee institutionalization. For many changes, routinization revolves around firm and helpful administrative commitment and involvement, and with the expectation that progress with the innovation will continue.

On a more specific level, attention to mechanisms of the following kind help make the new practice or process permanent: (a) put it on hard rather than soft money; (b) build it into the schedule; (c) list it as part of the regular curriculum; (d) write a job description for any new staff; (e) join it to others in use; and (f) provide needed training for teachers.

Studies demonstrate that several factors cause changes to be discontinued, either by intent or neglect: (a) personnel turnover—a key person(s) using it, advocating it, and giving supervision to it leaves and there is no plan in place to deal with the impact of the departure; (b) lack of administrator interest in, knowledge of, and support for the practice or process; (c) outright negative opposition, which quickly puts an end to change; and (d) failure of users to gain mastery over the innovation (perhaps because of a lack of trial time or no assistance and training) may result in reduced usage or extreme modification in order to cope with the demands. These causes create an image that the attempted change is of poor quality or of little value in the overall scheme of curricular or instructional priorities. Funding may be cut, which sets in motion a downward spiral of events, usually resulting in student disinterest or dissatisfaction. Teacher motivation to sustain or drop something new is largely in response to student dissatisfaction.

Change processes are rarely discontinued because of results of a formal, organizationally sponsored evaluation. It is unclear whether this is because of the lack of knowledge concerning the evaluation of programs among educators, whether there is too little time available to make institutionalization decisions, or whether the nature of the school as an organization inhibits such a systematic approach.

Conclusion

The change process is a vital factor in a school's continuing effectiveness. Change is everywhere, and the school cannot fulfill its societal mission without confronting it in a considered and responsible way. Much internal change will occur without an innovative response, but, over time, the absence of innovation will erode the health of the institution. Although change is often difficult, it is possible, too. The specific things we now know about change increase the possibility that educators and laypeople concerned about school improvement can make it happen.

See also Change Agent; Change Variables; Needs Assessment.

—Robert L. Larson
University of Vermont

References

Hall, G.E., & Hord, S.M. (1987). *Change in schools: Facilitating the process.* Albany, NY: SUNY Press.

Huberman, A.M., & Miles, M.B. (1984). *Innovation up close: How school improvement works.* New York: Plenum.

Lehming, R., & Kane, M. (Eds.). (1981). *Improving schools: Using what we know.* Beverly Hills, CA: Sage.

CHANGE VARIABLES

Change is a fundamental process in schools, always occurring whether willed or not, whether planned or not. Sometimes the process is evident and of considerable magnitude. Sometimes it works subtly with no visible effect on the setting. As a core societal organization, the school regularly confronts a dilemma: does it maintain passively existing ideas, values, behavior, and institutions, or does it seek actively to change them? The pendulum at the national, state, and local levels swings on this continuum as illustrated by the push for open education with its humanistic elements in the 1970s, and the current decade-old back-to-basics movement with its functional employment goals.

Hence schools are not sovereign systems; they are bound integrally to the wills of their communities and to accompanying cultural, economic, political, and social conditions. It is often difficult for the organization to decide what to accept or reject that is being urged upon it, or to decide to act when it is being urged not to do so.

Caught in this tug between maintenance and change, schools can survive without changing much themselves. As poorly as they might perform in serving children and youth, and as ill as they might become as organizations, rarely does a school go out of business. However, schools can fall out of favor with their national, state, and local supporters, as witnessed by the spate of recent national reports and studies that are in direct contrast to the heyday of the 1960s, when schools were seen as prime agents for social progress and reform, but congruent with the 1950s when similar criticisms were voiced before and after Sputnik was launched.

The School as an Organization

Schools, when striving to improve their effectiveness, do so as organizations possessing (a) goals that are often ill defined, inconsistent, and difficult to measure; (b) a structure that allows its prime delivery system, the classroom, to be linked only loosely to others like it; (c) a technology of teaching that tends to value conventional wisdom, tradition, and experience over research; (d) great variation in commitment to institutional goals on the part of the professional staff and students served; and (e) decision-making processes that commonly do not work according to the rational choice-making model imbedded in literature.

School improvement is also affected by other unique forces. One is that the organization is committed to try to educate all students sent to it, a captive clientele that ranges the spectrum from cooperation to passivity to resistance. Added to this social melting pot are age groups, each with norms and values which change and sometimes clash as the group moves through the system until graduation. A second is that there is little mystique to the profession of education in contrast to those of law, medicine, and theology. Parents and other laypeople have been instructed and socialized by the organization for close to 13,000 hours from the first through twelfth grade; potential experts in teaching and learning abound in every community.

These conditions bear directly on administrators and teachers, the central actors in affecting school improvement. Their roles find them immersed in a hectic, intense, and varied work pace. At the same time, they must control students while simultaneously teaching them new knowledge and skills through channels of values, attitudes, and feelings. For teachers, who can make or break efforts to bring about a change, primary motivation to do their job comes from interactions with students—psychic rewards—not rewards such as money, prestige, and power. Teachers also perform their duties in an environment isolated from meaningful interaction with other adults for most of the day. This solitary pattern of work impedes curricular and instructional planning and problem solving.

Dynamics of Change

In this context of stability, flux, and ambiguity, change appears to be sometimes simple and sometimes complex. One day, in one setting, it seems sensible, straightforward, and relatively easy to effect. Another day, in another setting, that same change seems maddeningly difficult to attain with the most well planned and sophisticated of efforts. And conversely, in the place where the change was not formidable to accomplish at one moment, it can appear impossible to pull off at virtually the next moment.

This conundrum can be attributed to several factors: the nature of the local community and relationships between it and the school; the school's history; its leadership; the professionalism and motivation of the staff; the type of student body; overall organizational health—morale, effective communications; and available and fair allocation of resources. Given this culture it becomes clear why one school might welcome but implement change poorly, and another school might not welcome it at all, and if change has to be implemented, it will be done largely in form but not substance.

Where change efforts are successful, a culture has evolved that nurtures and supports organizational and individual postures towards change, and a capacity for change has developed. Where thwarting improvement is a prevalent norm, the school (and sometimes community) needs to examine itself and how its culture can be modified so desired change will be more possible to accomplish. Institutional norms regarding change can be created quickly at no monetary cost.

Forms and Foci of Change

Three general categories or forms of change exist within schools:

1. Osmotic—those that gradually work their way into the system, usually without the system actively supporting or opposing them (e.g., open education to back-to-basics, student attire or behavior);
2. Mandated—those imposed by laws and regulations (e.g., PL 94-142, state curricula guidelines, budget cuts of declining enrollments leading to course drops because of a loss of funds or staff);
3. Voluntary—those initiated by the organization or a segment of it, or those in which the organization voluntarily participates (e.g., reading laboratory, a new course or unit, technology such as the microcomputer, an environmental studies program, an alternative school).

For a school that wants to improve established curricular practices, instructional processes, or overall effectiveness, there are choices for voluntary change. There may be organizationwide change (sometimes hooked to districtwide efforts); there may be subsystem change through departments, programs, or grade clusters; or there may be change through individual teachers. The focus should be based on an analysis of purpose, need, and capacity to take on, install, and institutionalize something new. Assessing purpose, need, and capacity is important because approaches to change should fit the situation to ensure a greater probability of success. Such an assessment helps the organization determine whether the best route to becoming better is through far-reaching large scale efforts, or through smaller scale, easier to manage efforts that will, over time, have an important impact on improvement efforts. Too often too much stress is placed on overly ambitious projects, rather than on more attainable change targets.

Conclusion

In conclusion, whatever the focus, research and practice reinforce the validity of several assumptions about change. Change is far more a long-term process than an event. It takes time for it to unfold within a setting that possesses numerous distinctive traits. And, change is made by individuals first and then the organization. Its eventual institutionalization depends ultimately on what the teacher thinks and does in the classroom. If enough individuals are involved, then *maybe* the school will change noticeably.

The process of change is a personal one involving feelings, values, attitudes, needs, and perceptions. From these reactions concerns emerge (e.g., needing more information, uncertainty about one's role in relation to the change, wondering about its consequences for students) that can become powerful aids or impediments to the process.

The entire process is rarely a fully predictable one. Countless variables intervene in what might start out to be a fairly neat series of planned steps to achieve goals. Those involved must learn to operate within an often ambiguous, hard to control environment.

See also Change Agent; Change Process; Needs Assessment.

—Robert L. Larson
University of Vermont

References

Association for Supervision and Curriculum Development (1983). *Educational leadership, 41*(3), 4-36.
Daft, R.L., & Becker, S.W. (1978). *Innovation in organizations: Innovation adoption in school organizations.* New York: Elsevier.
Fullan, M. (1982). *The meaning of educational change.* New York: Teacher College Press.

CHARACTER EDUCATION

The basic purposes of education in America have not changed very much. More than two hundred years ago, Thomas Jefferson wrote that education should aim at the "improvement of one's morals and faculties." Similarly, a recent Gallup Poll found that Americans, in overwhelming numbers, said: "Help them (students) develop a reliable standard of right and wrong."

The *Northwest Ordinance* of 1787 states: "Religion, morality, and knowledge, being necessary to good government and the happiness of mankind, schools and the means of education shall forever be encouraged." Ethical principles, in those early days, were extracted from the *Bible, Poor Richard's Almanac, The Declaration of Independence, The Constitution,* and *The Mayflower Compact*. Most people believed that education was of little value unless it was coupled with the moral development of the individual.

Our nation has a core of basic civic values. These values are the ethos of a nation that binds together people from all parts of the world. It is that common ethos that forms the characters of our people. Call it what you will, character education, civic learning, citizenship education, moral training, ethics, or values education; by any other name, it is the same—the ability to participate effectively in the affairs of the nation as a good citizen.

Issues

If schools are to play a more assertive role in character education, several issues must be examined. They are problems which can be overcome if schools are determined to teach Jefferson's "morals" and the standards for establishing right and wrong.

First, one must ask if values can be taught. The answer is obvious; regardless of what we do, values are always being taught. They are taught by what we do, what we say, the literature we read, the activities we conduct, and the behaviors we reward. Character education comes with the territory—it is being taught in schools by choice or by chance.

Second, there is the issue of which values shall be taught. Again, the problem is not a difficult one to overcome. The ethical principles of our society are embedded in the national documents of our nation. They can be extracted from our history, our literature, and our laws. The important consideration is that we select from basic documents and not from works which reflect individual opinions.

Third, there is the problem of pedagogy—how can values best be taught? Here the answer is not as easily established. Methods vary from direct instruction to self-discovery, from values clarification to service experiences. Methods may vary with the teacher and with community expectations. The identification of the most appropriate method, however, is not as important as the content to be taught. If there is a proper curriculum, method will not make a significant difference in what students learn, unless the method contradicts the ethical principles to be learned.

Fourth, the teaching of values requires that schools determine if values are relative or universal. Most philosophers seem to agree that there are values which are constant and that these values should be taught to all. Universal principles of morality form the ethic of a society. They are of inherent worth to individuals and to the entire social order. Character is behaving in accordance with principles that are for the general good—the commonweal of the nation.

Program Development

If we assume that values are taught in our schools by chance or by choice, the first step in establishing a character education program is to determine which values are to be taught. This can be done in one of several ways: (a) establish those values which are found in basic national documents; (b) establish values which are the consensus of the community; and (c) establish values which are supported by philosophy, laws, and ethics.

Once values are identified, curriculum to support the values must be established. Curriculum is the content which makes it possible for values to be taught and learned. Curriculum can be obtained from national documents, biographies, laws, literature, art and music, philosophy, and from many other sources.

Most philosophers of education agree that the next step in character education is to develop thinking skills based on a study of tradition. This can be in the form of history, literature, political science, or the fine arts. Each of the disciplines transmits a unique part of human experience which directly examines moral behavior, rationality, and ethical development. These areas make it possible to study morality as a whole and not as simple moral dilemmas which involve only a few characters in relatively uncomplicated situations.

Having a cognitive understanding of moral principles is a first step. The second step is the opportunity to practice behaviors which express the principles. Schools are the best laboratory for such practice. Under the supervision of moral individuals, students can obtain confirmation of their moral behavior. They can also receive challenges to behaviors that violate moral codes. Thus, character is formed. In this process, it is also important that the school itself—the adults within it—model moral conduct. The character attributes we wish to develop in students must also be exhibited by adults who are attempting to teach character development.

Character education has become a source of conflict in many school districts. The conflict is usually created by concentration on narrow moral issues or on examination of a single piece of literature. Character education is not one moral issue or one textbook—it is a comprehensive program of study. It contains specific ethical principles to be taught, a body of curriculum, and tools to validate that moral behavior has been established. The program is supported by board of education policy, by the behaviors of adults, and by practices of the schools. It is not a program for students; but, rather, a program for the school community.

See also Citizenship Education; Education and Community Views; Values Education.

—M. Donald Thomas, Senior Partner
Harold Webb Associates
Winnetka, Illinois

References

Larkin, B. (1977, September). *Curriculum Report, 7*(1), Reston, VA: National Association of Secondary School Principals.

Pannwitt, B. (1985, May). *Curriculum Report, 14*(5), Reston, VA: National Association of Secondary School Principals.

Ryan, K. (Ed.). (1986, June). *Character development in schools and beyond.* New York: Praeger Press.

CITIZENSHIP EDUCATION

American public education has been built on a tripod of basic purposes:

1. To make people literate.

2. To make people able to obtain work and be economically self-sufficient.

3. To make people good citizens of a democratic country.

Literacy, economic self-sufficiency, and good citizenship have been the core of school curricula and school activities. Despite the many changes in our country, public education has established a common historical theme for the children and young people of the nation—an appreciation for and the practice of good citizenship as one of the three basic purposes of schools.

The founders of our nation knew that democracy required men and women who could govern themselves. As Benjamin Franklin said, "Only a virtuous people are capable of freedom. Nothing is more important for the public weal than to form and train up youth in wisdom and virtue." This basic purpose of educating the young to be good citizens has served us well. It has created a common national character out of great diversity. It has established direction and stability in a world which is often unstable and violent.

Today, as the nation becomes more and more pluralistic, the common traditions of good citizenship are even more necessary. A common core of civic principles is still the basis for stability, progress, order, and public safety. The need to educate our young to be good citizens is as appropriate today as it was in 1776. It is our way of preserving the cultural traditions and principles associated with democracy, with freedom, with rights and responsibilities, and with a government "of the people, for the people, and by the people."

Good citizenship is much more than the study of government. It is an examination of personal responsibilities. It is an appreciation of the need to participate in civic affairs with an understanding of the values which support good citizenship. Good citizens are intellectually honest, abide by the moral codes of society, are active in public affairs, and protect the rights of minorities. Good citizens are thinking individuals who believe in and practice the common "civic virtues" of the nation. An effective citizen is first and foremost a literate person who can read, write, manipulate numbers, and communicate. In addition, effective citizens understand issues, know history, appreciate geography, understand science, and are familiar with the arts. As the school educates children and young people, it also provides them with tools to be good citizens.

The second function of the school in teaching good citizenship is to develop an appreciation for our history, our traditions, our political structures, our laws, and our common basic values. Students must learn to support the following civic principles embedded in our national documents: respect for property, respect for life, appreciation of orderly process to resolve conflicts, equal opportunity for all, protection of individual and group rights, responsibilities exercised for the common good, and an appreciation for diversity. Good citizenship requires men and women who understand democratic societies and who appreciate a democratic society's unique opportunities and its unique requirements on individuals.

The third function of schools in educating for effective citizenship is to nurture thinking skills. Students must be able to examine complex issues, separate fact from fiction, recognize propaganda, and make independent decisions. Effective citizenship requires the ability to think objectively and logically.

The fourth function of schools in educating for good citizenship is to provide students with opportunities to practice good citizenship skills. Students should be given opportunities to examine important issues and to vote for officers. They should participate in establishing rules and regulations and in providing service to others. Students always should have an opportunity to practice good citizenship behaviors in the life of the school.

Effective citizenship can be taught in a variety of ways. Schools have had a vast array of good citizenship programs, such as, (a) citizenship classes—a study of what citizenship is and what is required of good citizens; (b) the study of law—an examination of the legal system and its effect on citizens; (c) classes in social issues—a study of social problems and the responsibilities of individuals to solve them; (d) classes in ethics—the study of ethics and its relationship to good citizenship; (e) the study of biography— an examination of model citizens, with an appreciation of good citizenship traits; (f) the study of history—an appreciation for our form of government and for exercising citizenship behaviors which support the nation; (g) social service programs—engaging students in good citizenship community service activities; (h) awards programs—promoting good citizenship through awards, recognition, and honors; and (i) the study of society in microcosm—establishing simulation societies within which students practice citizenship behaviors.

Good citizenship programs consist of curriculum and school practices. Good citizenship education is embedded in the content of courses and in opportunities to practice good citizenship skills.

Citizenship programs have been criticized by some as indoctrination. That criticism is valid when leveled at programs which promote blind adherence to a school-determined set of good citizenship principles. It is not valid when students are provided opportunities to examine the principles and to make personal decisions about the validity of the principles.

Schools have an obligation to teach good citizenship. It is an obligation which schools have had since the early formation of our nation. Democratic societies require and depend upon men and women who practice effective citizenship behaviors. There are many strategies to teach good citizenship. Programs are available from a variety of sources. The tripod of school purposes still includes the need to teach our young to be good citizens.

See also Character Education; Multicultural Education; Student Culture; Student Responsibility.

—M. Donald Thomas, Senior Partner
Harold Webb Associates
Winnetka, Illinois

References

Butts, R.F. (1980). *The revival of civic learning.* Bloomington, IN: Phi Delta Kappa.
Thomas, M.D. (1981). *Pluralism gone mad.* Bloomington, IN: Phi Delta Kappa.
Westin, A. (1970). *Civic education in a crisis age.* New York: Teachers College, Columbia University.

CLASS SIZE

Few issues rouse stronger feelings among educators than class size, and few have more direct implication for school policy and practice. Teachers believe that the quality of their teaching and their interactions with students decline with an increase in the size of the class. Administrators recognize that per pupil costs increase markedly as class size falls below 25 students. Both points are correct. Thus, proponents of reduced class size and proponents of the economy of larger classes disagree less about the effects of class size on various criteria than the importance of the criteria themselves. Teachers and administrators do agree on the importance of student achievement, a criterion on which the size of the class exerts an inconsistent effect.

Class Size and Teacher Variables

The effects of class size have been assessed on measures of teacher affect and the quality of instruction. Researchers have used measures of teacher morale, attitudes toward students, and job satisfaction among others to tap teacher attitudes. Common measures of the quality of instruction have included time spent in whole class and small group instruction, time spent in independent seatwork, familiarity with students, the amount of individualization, and the degree of teacher control.

According to recent meta-analyses of studies in which these variables were assessed, smaller class sizes yield more positive teacher attitudes toward work and students. Teachers believe that they have greater opportunity to teach effectively in smaller classes. These effects held across levels and instructional content. In general, teachers were more satisfied with smaller classes. Their morale was higher, and they were more likely to be satisfied with their performance.

Effects on teacher affective variables must be interpreted with care: Teacher perceptions do not necessarily correspond to teacher behaviors. For example, in one large-scale, carefully-conducted study, teachers expected smaller class sizes to permit more individualization, more individual interaction, and stronger rapport with students. However, no such differences were observed in their behavior.

Class Size and Student Affect

The effects of class size on student affect have been assessed with measures of self-esteem, attitudes toward school and teachers, motivation, absences, and time-on-task. Such measures have been found to improve as class size falls below 15 students, but only small differences can be expected to occur as class size increases above 20 students.

Class Size and Student Achievement

The same meta-analyses suggest that class size is inversely related to student achievement: Smaller classes yield greater achievement. This relationship is pronounced for class sizes smaller than twenty and attenuated for classes larger than twenty. This generalization has held equally well at elementary and secondary levels and in reading, mathematics, and science classes.

These findings have proven controversial because the effect of class size on achievement gain is small across the range of typical class size. Although achievement in small classes (fewer than 15) will exceed achievement in both average-sized (about 25) and large classes (more than 30), achievement in classes of 25 will exceed only slightly achievement in classes of 30 or more. It is important to note that 20 to 30 is the range across which class size changes are likely to be made.

The Instructional Group

The study of class size as an independent variable is somewhat misleading, at least to the extent that instruction occurs in small groups. Research in which the effects of group size (in classes in which ability grouping is used) are contrasted to the effects of class size (in classes in which whole-class instruction is used) has illuminated this point. Apparently, group size exerts a more powerful effect upon achievement than class size. This generalization fits well both with conclusions drawn from the teacher effectiveness literature, particularly that effective instruction occurs in small groups, and with the shape of the class size-achievement effect curve as described in these meta-analyses.

Consider four classes, two with 24 students and two with 30. One class of 24 students and one of 30 are organized into three groups on the basis of student ability; in the other two classes, whole-class instruction is used. Little difference in achievement can be expected between the 24 student and 30 student classes; these two class sizes lie on the class size-achievement effect curve where increases in achievement with decreases in class size are small. On the other hand, the increment in achievement as group size falls from ten to eight students is larger; these group sizes lie along the curve where its slope is steep.

Although students will learn more in groups of eight (or ten) than groups of 24 (or 30), it does not follow that three groups of eight students will learn more than one group of 24, particularly when the number of teachers and the amount of instructional time are held constant. The class size literature may not be used correctly to justify the substitution of small group instruction for whole-class instruction.

Reducing Class Size

A school district's decision to reduce average class size (from 25 to 20 students, for example) must be weighed on several important criteria. Of course, per pupil costs will increase (by an estimated 25 percent). Teachers are more likely to feel satisfied with their jobs and believe that they are doing better work. In reality, their teaching may not change. Students' attitudes toward school are not likely to change appreciably and neither are other measures of student affect. Student achievement will increase, but not substantially so.

Because reducing class size is costly and because it may not produce any changes in teacher behavior (the changes which are most likely to increase achievement), leaving the development of better teaching to chance is a considerable risk. A district that adopts a policy of reduced class size would be wise to train its teachers to take advantage of this initiative.

Effective teaching, however, is largely unrelated to class size, at least within the range that encompasses typical class sizes and realistic reductions. Good teaching for 20 is good teaching for 25. Although administrators would be wise to prepare their teachers to make full use of reduced class size, its effects will be confounded with the effects of training. Administrators will be left with the question of what might have happened had they provided the training without reducing class size. To the best of our knowledge, no such assessment has been reported in the literature.

Other strategies for reducing pupil-teacher ratios have been suggested and may prove less costly. For example, two or three paraprofessionals can be hired for the cost of a single additional teacher. With staggered scheduling for reading instruction and training of the paraprofessionals, pupil-teacher ratios can be halved for two (or three) classes each period for every period of the day. Flexible scheduling is a second example. If half of the students in every class came to school an hour early and half stayed an hour late, instructional group size would be halved an hour a day for every student. Teachers might also consider recruiting volunteer parents, grandparents, or retired persons to serve in their classrooms as instructional aides. Although paraprofessionals and volunteers cannot be expected to plan an instructional program, with training and periodic supervision, they can be expected to execute one.

In short, the goal of reducing the size of instructional groups is a worthy one. Research has shown that such reductions are likely to lead to increased student achievement. Whether reductions are accomplished through decreasing class size or through other, less costly approaches is not relevant to the issue of achievement. However, the added costs of reducing class size bring added benefits, most notably a stronger sense of satisfaction for teachers and a clearer perception of doing good work.

See also Classroom Management.

—Paul T. Sindelar
Cynthia O. Vail
Florida State University

References

Glass, G.B., Cahen, L.S., Smith, M.L., & Filby, N.N. (1982). *School class size: Research and policy.* Beverly Hills, CA: Sage.

Hallinan, M.T., & Soreson, A.B. (1985). "Class size, ability group size, and student achievement." *American Journal of Education, 94*, 71-89.

Shapson, S.M., Wright, E.N., Eason, G., & Fitzgerald, J. (1980). "An experimental study of the effects of class size." *American Educational Research Journal, 17*, 141-152.

CLASSROOM MANAGEMENT

Classroom management is the teacher's means of establishing and maintaining orderly behavior and preventing disruptions to learning. Teachers apply certain behaviors and activities to classroom management. Good classroom management can be recognized by its effects—students engaged in academic activities most of the time, minimal amounts of disruptive student behavior, and high degrees of student task orientation and commitment to accomplishing the learning goals of the classroom. Although such behaviors are affected by characteristics of the students, their parents, and the school and community, teachers can strongly influence such behaviors through their classroom management skills.

The process of establishing a well-managed classroom has three related phases. Teachers must plan and organize both the physical and the behavioral setting of the classroom prior to the beginning of school; students must be taught appropriate behavior during the first part of the school year; and, finally, the teacher needs to maintain appropriate behavior throughout the year. Within each of these phases are numerous components that contribute to the final product.

Planning

Before the school year begins, important aspects of the management system should be planned. Planning should allow for efficient use of classroom space and time. It should enable the teacher to communicate clear expectations for behavior, and to avoid constant interruptions and slowdowns in activities. Planning before the beginning of school should include the following components:

1. The classroom must be organized and arranged. Placement of desks and other furniture should allow good student visibility, traffic flow, and teacher monitoring, as well as minimize distractions for the students.

2. Expectations for appropriate student behavior should be identified. This is an extremely important component, because the teacher needs to communicate clearly and concretely about desired behavior. Typically, expectations for behavior need to be considered in the areas of student talk, movement about the room, obtaining assistance from the teacher or students, beginning and ending the day (or period), and use of materials and equipment. For example, a common activity such as seatwork requires consideration of whether students may talk, whisper, or maintain silence, how assistance can be obtained from the teacher, and when it is appropriate for students to leave their seats. Similarly, expectations need to be considered for other major types of class activities, such as whole class discussions, presentations by the teacher, small group instruction, and laboratory and outdoor activities.

3. Academic-work procedures are another important area for planning, because student success in learning is a key ingredient in maintaining student motivation. Components for planning include the grading system, monitoring student progress and providing feedback, communicating assignments and work requirements, and setting forth procedures for helping students who have been absent or encounter problems with assignments.

4. Rewards and penalties should also be planned. Although student success and the intrinsic satisfaction of learning are the most desirable forms of reinforcement, it is often necessary to support motivation by using extrinsic reinforcers, such as awards, symbols, privileges, tokens, recognition, and the like. Also, consequences for inappropriate behavior, in the form of penalties, demerits, detentions, a reduction in grade, or withdrawal of a privilege or desired activity will be needed when the natural consequences of misbehavior are not sufficient or immediate enough to act as a deterrent.

Implementation

At the beginning of the school year, the teacher's management task is to teach students appropriate behavior. This is done by discussing general rules for behavior, emphasizing student responsibility, providing reasonable rationales and concrete examples, and inviting student participation. Procedures and expectations for behavior in specific activities (e.g., during discussions students should raise hands and wait to be called on) should be explained as needed over a period of one to several weeks, depending on the age/grade level and complexity of the setting. Careful monitoring by the teacher is especially important during this time so that failure to follow procedures can be handled promptly by reteaching the expected behavior, and so that appropriate behavior can be reinforced. Other important aspects of management at the beginning of the year are to establish appropriate behavior in familiar settings (e.g., whole class activities) before introducing new or more complex activities. It is also important to maximize student success early in the year by choosing academic work that is well within reach of the students' abilities. It is apparent that the teacher's role in establishing a well-managed setting is an active one, and will be enhanced by maintaining a high degree of visibility, being readily available to help students, maintaining frequent eye contact, and staying in charge at all times.

Maintenance

Concepts that are useful in understanding how to maintain a well-managed setting include activity flow, monitoring, positive expectations, and use of reinforcement. Classroom activities define how time is used, and successful managers keep activities moving and they protect students from external and internal interference. Careful monitoring of students is important because it allows the detection of problem behavior before it becomes severe or spreads. In early stages, it is easier to deal with inappropriate behavior by unobtrusive means, such as eye contact, physical proximity, or redirection. Careful monitoring also allows the teacher to identify students with learning problems before a pattern of failure develops. Frequent failure produces a variety of defensive or aggressive responses and needs to be prevented. It is also important to emphasize the expectation that students can behave and succeed. The use of a variety of incentives for appropriate behavior and performance can be especially helpful when students are not highly motivated by grades. The use of reward systems should also be accompanied by an emphasis on the value of learning the content itself in order to foster intrinsic motivation.

See also Direct Instruction; Disruptive Students; Instructional Objectives; Social Learning in the Schools; Teacher Effectiveness.

—Edmund T. Emmer
University of Texas at Austin

References

Doyle, W. (1986). "Classroom organization and management." In M.C. Wittrock (Ed.), *Handbook of research on teaching* (3rd ed.). New York: Macmillan.

Duke, D. (Ed.) (1982). *Helping teachers manage classrooms.* Alexandria, VA: Association for Supervision and Curriculum Development.

Emmer, E., Evertson, C., Sanford, J., Clements, B., & Worsham, M. (1984). *Classroom management for secondary teachers.* Englewood Cliffs, NJ: Prentice-Hall.

COGNITIVE DEVELOPMENT

Cognition is a term used by psychologists to describe the processes of knowing and perceiving. It encompasses the acquisition, retention, and use of information—how people learn; how people know; and how people think about what they know. Examples of cognitive processes are learning, remembering, making judgments, conceptualizing, perceiving, inference making, and using symbols such as words or musical notation. Cognitive development refers to the nature and growth of human intelligence, including the various components of intelligence mentioned above. The developmental psychologist is interested in the nature of these cognitive processes and in the ways they develop or change with maturation and experience.

The Study of Learning and Cognition

One group of psychologists studying learning are the behaviorists. Behaviorists claim that the only way that psychology could be a true science is by limiting itself to the study of observable behavior as opposed to posited and unobservable mental behavior. However, linguists, most notably Noam Chomsky, maintained that the behaviorist explanation of language acquisition was inadequate to account for the many and varied utterances a child makes and for the language complexities of an adult. The linguists believed that the brain is structured to produce language, thereby accounting for human ability to handle language complexities.

Growing out of behaviorism has come a movement referred to as neobehaviorism. B. F. Skinner, a well-known neobehaviorist, contends that behavior, including learning, is a function of external variables. What the individual learns is determined by the availability and administration of reinforcement/rewards from the environment rather than by physiological events or processes such as growth and maturation or deliberative thinking. For Skinner, the effective setting for education focuses on individualized instruction rather than group lectures. With individualized instruction, according to Skinner, each learner can receive direct and immediate reinforcement of mastery of each small segment of the learning task; if there is a lack of mastery, immediate aid and feedback come into play. Programmed learning through texts or machines fulfilled these requisites by providing a systematic presentation of small units of information, each of which was mastered before the learner moved on.

Developmental Psychology

During the height of interest in the behaviorist approach, many scientists, especially in Europe, continued to study and to develop theories of mental activity. Most prominent of these psychologists was Jean Piaget, whose ideas have had a major influence on learning theory. Contrary to behaviorist theory, Piaget proposed that individuals were active participants in learning and active seekers of knowledge, experience, and interaction with their environment. Furthermore, he theorized that differences between children's knowledge and adults' knowledge were not just a matter of quantity. Children, according to Piaget, had a different cognitive structure from adults, and therefore differences in mental skills and abilities between children and adults represented qualitative as well as quantitative differences.

Piaget postulated that there are mental structures that change in form and pattern with maturation and that all individuals progress through the same stages, each of increasing complexity. Piaget's four periods of conceptual development with approximate ages are:

1. Sensorimotor (birth to two years) — All knowing is based on action. A child brings about effects by doing.

2. Preoperational (preschool) — A child shows evidence of being able to think about actions and events not occurring and objects not present. Thinking is centered on the self, and a child is unable to understand other viewpoints.

3. Concrete-operational (K-7 years) — A child has the ability to classify on the basis of more than one characteristic at a time. A child demonstrates conservation, the ability to identify a constant property of a substance such as the amount being unchanged even though the form is different.

4. Formal operations (beginning of adolescence - adult) — Characterizied by ability to do systematic and abstract thinking.

There is evidence that individuals pass through Piaget's stages at different rates, but once a higher stage is reached there is no return to former patterns of thinking.

Piaget's work in defining development in terms of stages has been useful for developmental theorists in other areas. Lawrence Kohlberg, for example, has used the Piaget model to create a stage theory of moral development in which thinking about moral choices progresses from simple to more complex reasoning. Other schools of development theory focus on stages in the use of symbol systems such as language or music.

Developmental psychologist Howard Gardner has proposed a theory of multiple intelligences in which he suggests that genetics, biological maturation, the environment, and an active organism all interact to create the unique combinations of abilities called *intelligence.* Formal education has conventionally concentrated mainly on developing verbal, mathematical, and logic abilities. Gardner identifies other components of intelligence such as social intelligence and musical intelligence. It may be possible for schools to plan activities that encourage the development of these other aspects of intelligence as well as the more conventional verbal/quantitative development.

Information Processing Theory

Recently another approach to studying learning and cognition has been taken. The information processing approach studies the path of information into and through the mind. Using the computer as an analogy, the information processing paradigm sees the human mind as having a fixed, unchanging structure (hardware) with cognition (software) ordered into a flowchart of steps and levels, each of which is essential to the outcome. This approach has combined with advances in computer science to provide psychologists with an effective means of studying human intelligence.

Although there is more than one information processing theory, generally information processing theorists try to study mental operation by breaking knowledge down into its smallest units and tracking them step by step through the mind. In this manner, psychologists have learned about memory strategies and the organization of information in the brain. They have also been able to characterize structural differences between novice and expert performance. The information processing model has contributed greatly to learning theory, and as a result it is now possible to prepare textbook or other instructional materials on the basis of tested learning and instructional strategies which are demonstrably effective in helping students learn.

Psychometrics

Psychometricians maintain that cognitive abilities can be objectively measured by tests, and that people can be effectively categorized by the use of these test scores. Differences among individuals are largely a quantitative matter. That is, differences in knowledge retention or use are mostly differences of degree, and are identified by the amount of the difference in individual test scores.

The most familiar example of a test of cognition is an IQ test. Although the objectivity and bias-free aspects of IQ tests have been questioned, such tests are widely used to provide a measure of innate mental ability. While the IQ test is a modest predictor of success in formal schooling, it does not reveal levels of innate general intelligence. It attempts to measure certain skill attainments, mainly verbal and logical-mathematical, but it is not helpful in clarifying human potential or in explaining learning abilities. Unfortunately, the myth that the IQ test captures and unfailingly measures human intelligence remains a tenet of many educators and even some social scientists. One unfortunate result has been the use of IQ scores in sorting or tracking school children into groups for which expectations of academic achievement are influenced by the test scores.

Some psychologists now believe that intelligence in a malleable trait amenable to development and training. Robert Sternberg, for example, believes that intelligence has been too narrowly defined in the past and includes aspects such as comprehension, problem solving, and understanding of spatial relationships that can be developed. An effort is being made to devise tests that will include a component assessing traits such as social intelligence and creativity, now thought to be aspects of intelligence in a more comprehensive definition of ability.

Implications for Teaching and Education

Since the organization of cognitive science, traditional views of IQ, memory, thinking, and the idea of what constitutes intelligence have been undergoing intense reexamination by researchers. Theoretical and empirical ideas of cognitive skills and abilities are in a state of flux. Yet the research explosion created by the introduction of the developmental and information-processing paradigms already has profound implications for the professional educator. Intellectual skills once thought to be relatively stable over a lifetime now appear to be malleable. Training and practice in reasoning can lead to substantial improvement. The skill and capacity of young children can be greatly increased by teaching them an awareness of their own cognitive processes. Educational materials and courses can be structured to facilitate what psychologists call the *deep processing* of information, incorporating it into a knowledge base so it can be thought about and used, not just stored as temporary memory or recognition learning. It has been shown that the same information may be better absorbed if it is presented in several different forms, since individuals have varying styles of acquiring and remembering information. This finding is consistent with Gardner's theory of multiple intelligences and suggests that educators have been concentrating on fostering only a small portion of actual human potential.

Research findings such as these emphasize the need for both administrators and teachers to familiarize themselves with the principles and operations involved in the learning process and with strategies involved in directing or controlling these operations. Educational materials need to be examined for incorporation or violation of current learning theory. Tools and methods are available to give students insight into how they learn and strategies to enhance their cognitive skills. The rapid growth and increasing sophistication of cognitive science, however, mean that more information can be expected. Those educators best able to help students will be those who monitor theory and research in learning and cognitive development, and update their practices accordingly.

See also Intelligence and Intelligence Testing; Learning Styles; Split-Brain Controversy.

—Frank E. Nardine
Anita Zeidler
University of Wisconsin-Milwaukee

References

Anderson, J.R. (1980). *Cognitive psychology and its implications.* San Francisco: W. H. Freeman.

Gagne, E.D. (1985). *The cognitive psychology of school learning.* Boston: Little, Brown.

Gardner, H. (1986). *The mind's new science: A history of the cognitive revolution.* New York: Basic Books.

COLLECTIVE BARGAINING

All collective bargaining between employer and employees, whether in private- or public-sector employment, is governed by enabling legislation. In the private sector, this legislation is primarily at the federal level (the National Labor Relations Act and its progeny), and, in the public sector, the legislation is primarily state level (variously called labor relations or employment-relations statutes).

Public-employee bargaining first appeared at the state level with the passage of Wisconsin's Municipal Employment Relations Act in 1959 and was established for federal employees by Executive Order in 1961. By 1987, approximately 40 states had enacted enabling legislation or established administrative rulings granting some or all public employees the right to organize. Public-sector bargaining legislation almost always requires that an agreement be reached by providing a mechanism whereby bargaining impasse is to be resolved and establishing an employment relations board or commission to administer the laws. The essential elements of these provisions fall under five headings: (a) unit determination and recognition; (b) the bargaining process; (c) reaching agreement; (d) resolution of impasse; and (e) contract administration.

Unit Determination and Recognition

Statutorily sanctioned collective bargaining cannot occur unless the employee unit is properly organized and certified. The union is certified by means of a voluntary democratic vote of the affected employees. If more than one organization competes to represent the employees, only one will be recognized as the "exclusive bargaining agent." Employers may not intervene either in support of or against any attempt to organize a unit. Bargaining units may enroll as members only those employees with similarity of job interests; thus, teacher units may not enroll custodial or secretarial employees. Disputes over commonality of member interest do not usually arise unless certain employees attempt to form a new unit in response to dissatisfaction with an existing one, or unless an existing union attempts to require that previously nonorganized employees, e.g. interns or substitute teachers, become members.

Employees who do not wish to become members of the exclusive bargaining unit typically are required by collective bargaining agreements to pay to the recognized bargaining unit a "fair share" of regular dues to compensate for the costs of representation incurred in their behalf. Both federal and state courts have uniformly agreed that legislation and contract language requiring such payments does not constitute deprivation of property without due process of law; it is justified in order to prevent nonmembers from taking a "free ride" from the efforts of active, dues-paying members. However, because employee organizations are typically active politically, only a portion of the dues, which must be less than 100 percent and must be determined prior to collection (requiring filing for rebates has been found to be unconstitutional) may be certified as the cost of representation. Litigation over the acceptability of various activities that may be included as costs of representation and how much accounting is required to justify allocations is unsettled at the present time.

The Bargaining Process

The bargaining process is controlled by the local bargaining climate and the formal procedures that are followed. The climate, which can range from adversarial to mutual accommodation, may contribute more to eventual settlement than the substance of the proposals made during bargaining. Climate will vary according to local bargaining traditions, the personalities of the participants, the intensity of particular issues locally, and the bargaining goals (national, regional, local) of the political parties.

In adversarial bargaining, historically the "normal" approach, the climate can range from pure conflict, in which either side, or both, seems intent on reaching its interests by bringing the other side "to its knees," to power bargaining, in which each side recognizes—perhaps grudgingly—the strength of the other and tries to find a basis on which the benefits desired by one can be exchanged for conditions desired by the other. In accommodation bargaining, by contrast, each party recognizes that neither can exist standing alone. Thus, neither opposes, in principle, every request of the other, and exchanges of equal benefit are not strictly required. Instead, proposals are viewed as channels for two-way communication about how to provide maximum benefits to employees while preserving maximum capability of the employer to continue the enterprise.

Congruence of the parties' approaches, whether adversarial or accommodation, facilitates settlement; noncongruence is dysfunctional. When one side views the climate as accommodating, for instance, while the other views it as adversarial exchange, the result is misunderstanding, agreements that are not acceptable, but not wholly unacceptable, or worse, stalemate and impasse.

Before bargaining begins, ground rules to direct the bargaining process should be established. The following topics should be mutually agreed upon: (a) dates and times of meeting; (b) identity of the spokespersons and the role of various members of the bargaining teams; (c) the authority of the representatives to reach tentative agreement; (d) whether proposals may be withdrawn, once made; (e) whether completely new proposals may be introduced as bargaining progresses; (f) whether tentative agreements on single items are conditional upon final ratification of the entire agreement, or whether they remain in effect even if complete agreement is not reached voluntarily; (g) and the confidentiality of the proceedings, including the conditions under which progress may be reported to unit members and the public.

Strategy and tactics are the black box of collective bargaining with there being as many different absolutely confident views of its contents as there are self-appointed experts who have plumbed its mysteries. Decisions that each side should make regarding bargaining strategy include (a) whether to be hostile or friendly, whether to reach for the moon while being willing eventually to settle for much less; (b) whether to introduce a host of unimportant proposals that can easily be "given up" in exchange for the really important ones (withdrawing a proposal from the table should not be confused with an exchange—it is difficult to convince the other side that you have given up something that you never had in the first place); (c) whether to focus on a limited number of particularly important issues; (d) whether to protract bargaining until the other party wears down or to press for a quick settlement (both positions usually favor the employer); (e) whether to insist on child- or teacher-based outcome proof of need for every change proposed; (f) and whether to adopt a willingness to give the other party isolated concessions here and there in order to soften it up for subsequent, more crucial, propositions.

About the only strategy that is wholly dysfunctional in public-sector bargaining is that which states categorically, "Do not agree to anything the other side proposes." The presence of mandatory third-party impasse-resolution procedures results in an abdication of responsibility for participating in the formulation of employer-employee relationships because it constitutes handing the matters over to an arbitrator.

Enabling legislation always mandates bargaining only on a limited range of topics. This arises because of incompatibility between the concepts of locally bargained conditions of employment and the sovereignty of citizens to establish public policy. Thus, whether a proposal is a mandatory or a prohibited topic of bargaining is always an issue in public-sector bargaining. Mandatory topics may be specifically enumerated in the statutes, or generally described as, "wages, hours, and conditions of employment." Prohibited topics may be specifically listed or left to be discovered through litigation. In some states, a third category, permissive topics of bargaining, has been created. These are neither clearly mandatory nor clearly prohibited, yet contain sufficient employer and employee mutual interest that agreement on them may be mutually beneficial.

No clear-cut guidelines exist by which to predict the resolution of a dispute over whether a topic is mandatory, permissive, or prohibited. Many such disputes are rendered academic by transformation of the proposal into so-called impact language. In this approach, the employer's right to make the policy decision unilaterally is not questioned, e.g., to establish class size. But compensation for the resultant changes in working conditions, e.g., increased pay for an increased work load, must be bargained.

Reaching Agreement

Statutory requirements to bargain do not, alone, carry an obligation to reach agreement. All that is required is to bargain in good faith, which is usually defined as being willing to do the following: (a) meet with the other party at times and places of mutual convenience; (b) listen attentively to proposals that are made; (c) respond to proposals (concession is not required—a reasoned "no" is a legitimate response); (d) treat members of the other side with respect; (e) abide by the ground rules established at the outset of bargaining; (f) refrain from appealing past the bargaining team to its constituency; and (g) follow through to abide by proposals accepted by the other party.

Final agreement occurs when the exchange of items of mutual interest, the pressure of state and local issues, and explicit and implicit comparisons between the local agreement and those of reasonably comparable units in the surrounding area converge to convince both sides that the agreement is the best they can obtain under the circumstances. It will not be everything that both sides wanted, but will be the result of compromise, exchange, persuasion, good and bad guesses, and sheer luck. Generally, the closer a proposal and an entire agreement is to those of its comparable units, the more pressure there will be to accept it. This tends to retard the development of creative contract language that will solve local issues on the basis of a unique local bargaining climate. In any event, the bargained agreement does not become the "law" governing employment relations in the local governmental unit until it is ratified by majority vote of both the employer (the school board, for instance) and the bargaining unit members (the teachers, for instance).

Impasse Resolution

Without some sort of external pressure to motivate compromise, the imbalance of power in favor of the employer in adversarial collective bargaining assumes that the process will either result in an agreement that is less than the employees actually deserve or in no agreement at all. In the private sector, this external pressure is the combined law of the marketplace—a law which can be invoked by strikes and boycotts, with the threat of judicial enforcement of labor-relations legislation and the common law of contracts. In the public sector, where strikes are either prohibited or severely restricted by law, compulsory binding arbitration is typically substituted as the primary external pressure to motivate compromise. This is usually referred to as interest arbitration, which is to be distinguished from grievance arbitration, a process designed to resolve impasse over interpretation of a ratified agreement.

Procedures for seeking interest arbitration usually require mediation (third-party attempts to help the parties find a basis for voluntary agreement) and/or fact-finding (third party determination of the actual facts in the dispute, which neither party need heed). Mediation is prior to a formal certification of impasse and arbitral resolution of the dispute. Arbitral resolution is always limited by statute and must always be based on testimony and evidence presented in quasi-judicial proceedings where each side presents facts and arguments supporting its position.

In some states, the arbitrator must select one or the other final offers of the parties in its entirety, whereas in others, the arbitrator is given the latitude to combine elements of each party's positions to create a resolution not entirely contemplated by either. In a few states, the arbitrator is given unrestricted or wide-open authority to reject the positions of both parties and fashion awards according to terms of his or her own sense of what is reasonable. The general rule in all statutes, however, is to place restrictions on arbitrators, whether in limits on the topics which may be arbitrated, the bases upon which awards must be founded, or the magnitude of change which may be imposed.

While the parties are awaiting arbitral resolution of the bargaining impasse, the provisions of the current agreement continue to control employment relations even though it may have expired. The primary exception to this principle is the grievance procedure, the existence of which expires when a collective bargaining agreement expires. Arbitrator rulings are appealable ultimately to courts, but typically must be appealed first through a state employment-relations commission or board.

Contract Administration

Administration of the collective bargaining agreement is the *sine qua non* of collective bargaining. It is goal toward which bargaining is devoted; without it there would be no reason to bargain. Thus, implementing the agreement following the common law of contracts is the final step in collective bargaining. All contract language is to be interpreted according to the plain, ordinary meaning of the words used unless expressly modified. The common law force of this principle is usually sufficient to insure that implementation occurs. From time to time, however, either party may come to the conclusion that part of the agreement is unlawful, hence unenforceable, and proceed to ignore it. More likely, the parties will disagree on what the language actually says, especially when matters arise which were not contemplated by existing contract provisions. Such disputes must have a source of formal resolution, else little motivation exists for either party to comply with the terms of the agreement. This usually begins with a grievance procedure, the exact terms of which are built into the agreement, and may conclude with binding arbitration. Litigation is always available as a last resort, if the issue is a matter of law.

See also Conflict Resolution; Teacher Grievance Procedure; Teacher Strikes.

—Delbert K. Clear
University of Wisconsin-Milwaukee

References

Cresswell, A.M., & Murphy, M.J. (1976). *Education and collective bargaining.* Berkeley, CA: McCutcheon.

Lieberman, M. (1980). *Public sector bargaining: A policy reappraisal.* Lexington, MA: Lexington Books, D.C. Heath and Co.

Richardson, R. (1985). *Collective bargaining by objectives: A positive approach.* Englewood Cliffs, NJ: Prentice-Hall.

COMMUNICATING WITH THE COMMUNITY

There's probably never been a time when it has been more imperative for school administrators to communicate effectively. Voucher proposals, tax-cutting schemes, and other challenges continue to raise questions which administrators are asked to answer. At the same time, schools are losing a resource which used to make communications easier. Two decades ago half of the adult population in any community had students in the schools, providing a ready-made communications link. Today, only about one-fourth of the adults in America have school-aged children. How do they receive their information about schools? Perhaps through the rumor mill, ill-informed outsiders, or superficial television reports.

Communicating both orally and in writing can be rewarding. It provides the chance to meet people, share the successes of the school and the importance of quality education, and to correct misconceptions people might hold. There are some practical tips to remember that will also make oral and written communications more effective.

If there is one way to improve communication, it is through this simple approach—speak and write in English. Most educators have gone through many hours of college classes, sat through numerous meetings on educational issues, or heard other educators converse. In all these situations, there is the risk of being smitten by that common professional language—educationese. The first sign is the use of multisyllable words whenever education is discussed. Teachers talk of learning for "the whole child," and parents wonder if there's any other kind. Board members discuss "vertical articulation," and perplexed reporters question whether a new disease has been discovered in one of the schools.

Too frequently, communication occurs in language noneducators have difficulty understanding. Whether it is using unfamiliar abbreviations or terms such as "cognitive domain," the result is that messages are not received. There are two components for every message: a sender and a receiver. It is imperative to write and speak in terms the receiver will understand.

A special role for the school administrator is to ensure that all staff members use English. Whether it is the teacher writing to a parent, the secretary answering the phone, or a custodian greeting a late afternoon visitor, there are opportunities for all to communicate. And each of those opportunities is a chance to develop greater support. Professional development for the entire staff in this area would be a wise investment.

In addition to speaking and writing English, it is important to communicate the desired message. That sounds simple, but it is not always that easy. The problem is time—or lack of it—and rushing to get tasks accomplished. For example, one September a school principal sent home a note to parents about joining the PTA. He wrote:

Dear Parents:

It's important to join the school PTA this year. If your child returns the PTA form this week, he or she will earn one point in the classroom ice-cream contest.

The principal had urged that it was important to join the PTA, but then cited only one reason to do so. He probably did not mean to indicate that the ice-cream contest was the sole reason, but people could have inferred that. He was probably in a rush and was hoping to save time. He would have been better off, however, writing the note, putting it down for 10 minutes, then reading it with a clear mind to make sure it communicated what he wanted to say.

An even better approach is to find someone on the staff who has a "good feel" for the community—a secretary, fellow administrator, or teacher. Give that person the responsibility of reading communications and critiquing them to ensure that the correct message is going out. It will save time in the long run.

It is especially important for administrators to recognize the advantages and disadvantages of impersonal and personal communication techniques. Both are important. Impersonal vehicles—such as newsletters, news releases, bulletins—will reach a large audience quickly. They are effective in providing general information, but have little value in changing attitudes. The personal touch is necessary if you want to move people to your viewpoint. You need to provide the opportunity for give and take—for people to ask you questions, to raise issues they do not understand. That is when speeches, open houses, and community meetings are important. Many civic organizations have among their members the opinion leaders in your community. Speaking to these and other groups are an important part of your oral communications program.

In summary, the following suggestions are offered for improved communications:

1. Know your audience and gear your presentation to their level of understanding. Not everyone is as knowledgeable as you about education. Ask people who are familiar with the group you are to address about its members.

2. Be concise. Most people are in a hurry and would like to have time to ask you questions. You do not have to describe everything you know in every speech.

3. Be enthusiastic and energetic. If you demonstrate that you are enjoying your subject, the audience is much more likely to do the same.

4. Use audio-visual materials when appropriate. Arrive early at the site of the presentation to ensure that the projector is there and lighting is right.

5. Use handouts. People are more likely to remember your message and might even share the material.

6. Use concrete examples. If they are local examples, that is even better.

7. Use humor, but only if it fits your style.

8. Suggest ways people can act on your suggestions . . . ways they can help teachers and schools.

9. Provide a short, written biographical sketch for the person who will introduce you.

10. Test your presentation with a friendly audience. Communicating is an important part of your job; do it effectively!

See also Communication; Public Relations; School-Community Relations.

—Lew Armistead, Director of Public Information
National Association of
Secondary School Principals

References

Armistead, L. (1982). *Building confidence in education.* Reston, VA: The National Association of Secondary School Principals.

Davis, B.R. (1986). *School public relations: The complete book.* Arlington, VA: The National School Public Relations Association.

Kindred, L.W. Bagin, D., & Gallagher, D. (1984). *The school and community relations.* Englewood Cliffs, NJ: Prentice-Hall.

COMMUNICATION

Communication is the lifeblood of a school district and its schools. Communication is the essence of effective management. It can be emphatically stated that no one can manage any organization well who is not knowledgeable of communication principles and techniques. It can be equally stressed that no school system can achieve its goals without effective internal and external communication.

Responsibilities for Communicating

Everyone in a school district, regardless of title or position, is a vital link in the communications chain. However, it is usually the superintendent and school principal who are ultimately responsible for the overall communications climate. If top-level administrators share information effectively with associates and insist that their associates do likewise, the spirit of information sharing tends to become contagious.

Formal responsibility for school communications can be fixed in either of two ways: (a) decentralized—where several people or departments are made responsible, or (b) centralized—where one person (or department) has overall responsibility. The centralized system is generally recommended since it affords greater control and coordination.

Philosophy and Objectives

Every communication system needs a philosophy. The communications philosophy sets the framework for follow-up policy and procedures. It also sets forth administrators' major beliefs concerning communications.

After the philosophy is established, objectives need to be identified. Primary communication objectives of administrators are (a) to keep staff members fully informed about school objectives, policies, progress, problems, and activities affecting them; (b) to provide staff members with information about personnel practices, including their job responsibilities and standards for measuring their performance; (c) to have key people readily available with whom to communicate; (d) to assure open lines of multidirectional communication; (e) to tell people why things happen and what the event means to them; (f) to have a crisis communications plan prepared; and (g) to provide an effective means of two-way communication with the general public and important special groups.

Communications Needs Assessment

Communications needs assessments should be conducted regularly. A simple yet effective needs assessment answers these questions:

How well does our communications program meet recommended standards?

Is there a written communications plan that includes philosophy, objectives, responsibilities, policies, procedures and identification of target audiences?

What are our biggest communications strengths and weaknesses?

What information should we be communicating to whom? How?

Is information reaching people promptly?

Are we failing to communicate at all on some pertinent matter?

Are we over communicating? To whom?

Are proper channels, preferred information sources, and media being used?

Is feedback provided for and occurring?

Are our communications goals being met?

To identify communication needs, the following should be reviewed: (a) employee opinion polls and community surveys; (b) results of needs assessment; (c) employee grievances and community complaints; (d) annual and long-range district and school goals; and (e) interviews with representative members of staff and community.

Need for and Timing of Communication

In addition to sharing information with the staff and community, administrators need to identify both specific groups and individuals within the school and community with whom to communicate and must determine what information needs to be communicated.

Information that is necessary to share with employees at one level may be unnecessary for people at another level. Actually, there are no hard and fast rules for determining what information should be communicated to whom. Good judgment and knowledge of what people want to know should guide the administrator when deciding with whom he or she should share information.

The goal of managerial communications is to insure optimal sharing of information (neither too little nor too much) with the appropriate people at the right time. It is preferable to communicate with too many people rather than too few and to communicate too much rather than too little.

However, it is not always what, but when, that is important in communicating messages; therefore administrators need to communicate continuously and regularly. Proper timing is imperative! Information should be shared neither too early nor too late. Important and complex information should not be sent late in the day or close to holidays and vacations. Administrators need to be aware of how preceding or following events may affect receptivity to messages.

Media and the Message

Members of the staff and community have definite preferences for the methods used for communicating with them. Using the right medium for the right message improves the chances of gaining a desired response. The over reliance on one medium makes a message less effective.

The best medium depends upon the goals, message content, and intended receivers. Although there is no best medium for all messages, these points are worth noting: (a) sharing messages both verbally and in writing is best for important information; (b) communicating face-to-face is usually desirable; (c) relying too heavily on the written word can be disastrous; and (d) using a variety of media to appeal to the different senses is advantageous.

Four key points to consider when selecting the appropriate communications channels are:

1. The communications channel largely regulates who communicates what to whom.

2. The more channels to which people have easy access the more likely they are to communicate.

3. The more hierarchical levels there are in the network, the more difficult it is to get the message from level to level quickly and accurately.

4. Communication should not be restricted to the formal chain of command. There is a proper time for communicating out of channels and directly with the best informed person.

Organizational Culture

A school's culture directly influences communications effectiveness. For example, some schools communicate formally (e.g., memorandum), whereas others prefer to communicate informally (e.g., chats). Attempting to communicate by formal means in an informal culture is destined to failure and vice versa. The proper climate for effective information sharing is one which encourages criticism, suggestions, recommendations, and the sharing of problems. Recommended administrators' attitudes toward communication are (a) wanting to communicate and to be communicated with; (b) talking on adult-to-adult level on an I'm okay, you're okay basis; (c) seeking to understand as well as to be understood; (d) willing to focus on and listen to the other person; and (e) having the courage to level with others and be leveled with.

Securing Feedback

Feedback is essential but often overlooked. It involves the receiver of a message providing the sender with a response so that the communicator can tell if the receiver understood the intent and content of the communication. In most communication situations, the potential for feedback is available. Effective administrators make a real effort to obtain feedback and to assure the message is understood.

See also Communicating with the Community; Public Relations; School Community Relations.

—Walter St. John, President
Management Communications Institute

References

Begin, D., Grazian, F., & Hanson, C. (1972). *School communications ideas that work.* Woodstown, NJ: Communicaid.
D'Aprix, R. (1983). *Communicating for productivity.* New York: Harper & Row.
St. John, W. (1970). *A guide to effective communication.* Nashville, TN: St. John Enterprises.

COMMUNITY SCHOOL INVOLVEMENT

Changes in the urban population have become apparent since the 1950s, as more low income, minority, and immigrant residents pushed middle-class and white populations to the suburbs. As the white-flight movement increased, urban schools have become more multiethnic while schools in most outlying suburbs have become more homogeneous in terms of income and ethnicity. In the 1960s and 1970s, the frustration of diverse ethnic groups, especially Blacks, found a common "solution" in greater community involvement and even community control of the schools. By the 1980s, the level and tone of conflict over community control, and other forms of community involvement, had subsided as the focus of community concern centered around school closings, budgetary cuts, and general retrenchment policies.

From the perspective of the last 30 years, three forms of community involvement have surfaced. In the first, *community participation,* advisory groups representing the parents and community function at various administrative levels within the school district addressing school and districtwide concerns. The main function of these groups is to make recommendations, not policy, and to serve as a liaison between school and community. School professionals welcome and support this form of community involvement, since their power and authority is retained. This is the most common school-community arrangement operating within school districts today, and it is similar to traditional school-community relations found in administrative textbooks.

With *community control,* the second form, legal provision is made for an elected school board to function at the local school or decentralized level. These school boards are supposed to be representative of the community (which is not always the case); they usually have specific power and authority to operate schools and share policy decisions with the central or districtwide school board. The powers of teachers and administrators are curtailed under this arrangement; therefore, they tend to reject this form of community involvement. A few urban school districts have attempted community control—Oakland, Detroit, and New York City—with resulting controversy and limited success. Major sources of conflict between professional educators and community groups have centered around questions of authority and power to run the schools but has extended to include ethnic interests in hiring personnel and controlling the budget. Only the New York schools retain much of the original concept of community control.

The most recent and future-oriented form of community involvement, the third form, focuses on *community education* which envisions the schools as one, but only one, of the educational agencies within the community—along with other agencies such as libraries, parks, business groups, unions, health and self-help groups. In this case, the school serves as an equal partner—possibly as a coordinating institution in developing educational, recreational, social, cultural, and health activities for the community. The trend of the 1980s and 1990s suggests a move toward conservativism and, along with it, a stabilization of student enrollments, economic growth, and taxes for schools. Only a diversity of community agencies can serve all the needs of the educational consumer, who now includes not only children and youth, but also parents of traditional families, working mothers, childless adults, and aging adults. Indeed, the schools can no longer afford to ignore the fact that we are an aging and small-family society, and that most taxpayers have no children or only one child, or their children have grown up and are no longer in school. Competition for public dollars is expected to increase as the population ages and expresses different needs and interests, and as federal and state governments contract their educational spending in real dollars. If a sense of community is not developed around the concerns of the taxpayers and voting public, then educational spending will suffer. Community education offers the community an opportunity to participate in the schools as a support agent.

Little data suggest that increased community involvement correlates with improved student outcomes or improved school quality. The idea for increasing school-community involvement is based on a combination of tradition, common sense, and intuitive judgment—a general feeling that increased community involvement will benefit the schools. Three approaches to community involvement have been presented—community participation, community control, and community education—with the latter approach providing services and resources to the entire community and thus benefiting the largest number and most varied groups of constituents.

See also Advisory Committees; Centralization and Decentralization; Community School Programs; School Community Relations.

—Allen C. Ornstein
Loyola University of Chicago

References

Ornstein, A.C. (1982). "Community participation in big school systems." *American School Board Journal, 169,* 17-18.
Ornstein, A.C. (1982). "Thinking small for the 1980s." *Clearing House, 55,* 279-80.
Ornstein, A.C. (1983). "Redefining parent and community involvement." *Journal of Research and Development in Education, 16,* 37-45.

COMMUNITY SCHOOL PROGRAMS

Community school programs reflect an expansion of the traditional role of public education. Their basic foundation is the community education philosophy which emphasizes the mutually interdependent relationship of the home, school, and community as they interact in phases of human development and community improvement.

Community education is a way of looking at public education as a total community enterprise; and a *community education program* is a community's comprehensive and coordinated plan for providing educational, recreational, social, and cultural services for all people in the community. A community school is an organizational structure through which the community education philosophy is implemented; and a *community school program* refers to the program operated by an individual school.

Each community-school program is developed and based on the needs and desires of the specific community in which the school operates. Individual community school programs are as varied as the communities in which they are offered. Each is limited only by the ability of people to plan and develop opportunities and their ability to make maximum use of cooperative working relationships among institutions, agencies, businesses, groups, and organizations in the community.

Distinguishing Characteristics

There is almost no public school system or individual school in the country that cannot cite a few program offerings that are comparable to activities and learning opportunities in community school programs. The difference is that the individual offerings are not part of a planned and organized effort to implement a comprehensive program.

Community-school programs are not "added-on" programs or "frills" to win public support. They are the result of a community involvement process designed to develop a plan to provide opportunities for all ages in a variety of areas. Although there is great diversity among community-school programs, they usually include offerings in the areas of academic support and enrichment, recreation and leisure activities, skill development, community improvement projects, volunteer services, social opportunities, and cultural events.

Another distinguishing characteristic is the defined role of a trained community school coordinator/director. The administrative position is designed to assist in planning, implementing, supervising, and evaluating the diverse activities that are part of the community school program, whether they are offered on the school site or at other appropriate community locations.

Impact on Education and Communities

At a time when only one-fourth of American households have children in schools, public schools are often isolated from the larger community. Community school programs provide a way for schools to reach out to the community and work as a cooperative partner to help meet community needs and solve community problems.

The possible benefits to education and communities from well-designed and carefully implemented community school programs are numerous. They have been documented in a variety of studies, including the Congressional committee on the Nature and Prevention of School Violence and Vandalism, the National Conference on Public Confidence and the Schools, and the Council of Educational Facility Planners' Study on the Impact on Energy Consumption. Most recently, studies have documented the influence of parental involvement on academic achievement and the importance of community involvement in improving local educational opportunities.

The key ingredient in whether a community school program is developed and successfully implemented seems to be *attitude*. In the last decade attitudes have been changing in many areas that affect the acceptance of the community education philosophy and the development of community school programs.

See also Adult Education Programs; Community School Involvement; School Community Relations.

—Larry E. Decker
University of Virginia

References

Boo, M.R., & Decker, L.E. (1985). *The learning community.* Alexandria, VA: National Community Education Association.

Minzey, J.D., & LeTarte, C.E. (1979). *Community education: From program to process to practice.* Midland, MI: Pendell Publishing Co.

Mott Foundation Special Report. (1982). *Community education: Partnerships for tomorrow.* Flint, MI: Charles Stewart Mott Foundation.

COMPENSATORY EDUCATION

The term *compensatory education* is a child of the 1960s, and grew from two different seeds of thought. First, several separate lines of research indicated that intelligence and school ability were heavily influenced by experiences during the first few years in a child's life. Second, the country went through a period of intense concern about poverty, coupled with a conviction that a nation such as this should not have such poverty in its midst. When these ideas were combined, the notion of education as a way to *compensate for the effects of poverty* was born.

The original conception of compensatory education carried with it several interrelated ideas. One was that poverty was cyclical. That is, children born into poverty were limited by that poverty and were consequently never able to escape from it. Another important idea was that the key to breaking out of the cycle of poverty was education. A third was that, if education were to compensate for the inhibiting effects of poverty, it would be more likely to have a strong effect if targeted toward the early childhood years. Finally, the notion of altering the life chances of disadvantaged children was important. It was assumed that if children from poor families and poor neighborhoods could receive more or better education, this opportunity would substantially improve their chances for rising out of poverty.

There were two variations on the early childhood theme. One was that poor children entered school behind because they had less exposure to such learning materials as books and fewer opportunities to do things such as going to museums, etc., because of their poverty. Poor children, then, were culturally disadvantaged, or culturally deprived, and their lack of stimulation needed to be compensated for. The second variation on the early childhood theme did not attend so much to the stimulation or lack of stimulation in the poor child's home, but instead attended to the findings that children at young ages were simply more intellectually malleable. Consequently, early childhood was the most propitious time to intervene.

Viewed in this way, compensatory education has a substantially different meaning from *remedial education*. Remedial education is a form of education customarily used by schools to help particular students who happen to have fallen behind. The idea of remedial education is to remedy a specific, identifiable deficiency. A teacher might notice that a child is having difficulty with subtraction, for instance, and send the child to a remedial classroom for special help. The help is considered to be a temporary matter, and the child is not viewed as needing a substantial or fundamental kind of assistance. And remediation is unrelated to family circumstances. But these two ideas—of compensatory education and remedial education—have been persistently confused.

The first significant federal compensatory education program, Head Start, began in 1965 by offering summer-school programs to poor children who would be entering kindergarten the following fall. Early evaluations of Head Start indicated that the summer period was not sufficient to create the sort of dramatic changes in children that had been hoped for, and Head Start eventually evolved into a preschool program which continues today with goals similar to those with which it began.

Other programs continued to emphasize the early childhood years. The second major federal compensatory education program, for instance, Title I of the Elementary and Secondary Education Act of 1965, permitted school districts to use funds for any grade level they wished. The overwhelming majority of districts at that time, and still today, have used federal compensatory funds for early elementary programs. In 1981, Title I was replaced with Chapter 1 of the Education Consolidation and Improvement Act. The purpose of the consolidation bill had more to do with the variety of other federal programs that had proliferated over the years than it did with Title I. Thus, Chapter 1 of the consolidation bill retains Title I in almost unchanged form, while Chapter 2 consolidated some twenty-eight different federal programs into a single block grant. That Title I retained its separate and distinct mission has been interpreted by some observers as an indication of the nation's continued commitment to its goals.

Chapter 1 is now the primary federally-sponsored compensatory education program that targets funds to school districts. It distributes funds on the basis of the number of poor students in the area, but requires that students be selected for service on the basis of their achievement, not their poverty. The intent behind this rule is that children who really do not need services should not receive them. Chapter 1 also requires that funds be spent for services that are demonstrable additions to the education children would normally receive. This latter provision is intended to assure that districts do not misdirect the funds to other purposes, and that they do not use Chapter 1 funds to replace funds they would normally have spent on these children anyway, so that their own funds can be put elsewhere. In order for districts to demonstrate that their Chapter 1 funds have truly supplemented their regular program, they must engage in some complicated fiscal accounting procedures, and many are discouraged from trying innovative programs for fear that they will not be able to convince auditors of the validity of their ideas.

In addition to federally sponsored compensatory education programs several state and local agencies have sponsored their own compensatory education programs, with the designs varying considerably from place to place. Some state compensatory programs are modeled after Chapter 1 and use very similar rules regarding student selection and fiscal accounting. In these states, districts may combine state and federal support into a single program. Or they may divide the terrain between them—serving, for instance, children in kindergarten through third grade with one fund, and children in grades four through six with the other. Other state programs use poverty as a weighting factor in distributing state funds, but make no provisions as to how the extra funds are spent. Still others have redefined the intent of their funds toward remedial education, though they often still label the programs compensatory education. Several, for instance, distribute funds on the basis of competency test scores, not on the basis of poverty, with the express remedial purpose of remedying the students' performance on these tests. And some states distribute funds to schools as a whole, and encourage schoolwide improvements in services rather than restricting services to a subset of children within the schools. Though targeted at whole schools, these programs also usually have a remedial, rather than a compensatory, flavor to them.

Since the 1960s, as both compensatory and remedial education programs have become more routine, a considerable body of evidence has accumulated regarding family poverty and its relationship to student achievement and regarding the effects of the compensatory education programs. This evidence has altered ideas both about what compensatory education is and about what one can reasonably expect from it.

The first, and probably still most important, evidence came in the earliest years of compensatory education. Early evaluations, of both Head Start and Title I/Chapter 1, made it clear that compensatory education, at least as it had been conceived by Congress, would not substantially alter the life chances of its beneficiaries. At best, these programs contributed to modest gains on achievement test scores. The size of the gains has gradually increased over the twenty-year period during which these programs have been studied, presumably as local agencies improve their ability to implement effective programs. These gains have reached a respectable size relative to the gains typically demonstrated in education. But the impact is not going to substantially alter the life chances of disadvantaged children.

The second important body of evidence generated since the 1950s has been with the relationship between poverty and student achievement. We now know that there are families who tend to be continually poor, and whose life histories resemble the originally assumed cycle of poverty. But there are also many other families whose incomes drop below the official "poverty line" for a year or two, and then return to higher levels. And we know that student achievement is affected more by long-term poverty than by short-term poverty, a finding that is consistent with the assumptions of the original compensatory education movement. But there is no known way to allocate funds or to identify students for service on the basis of long-term poverty. Census counts and other indicators identify anyone whose poverty meets its own specified criteria, regardless of how long the family has had that status.

Finally, we have learned that achievement is influenced both by the child's family poverty and by the proportion of other children from poor families attending the child's school. That is, when students attend schools with large proportions of students from poor families, their achievement is very likely to be diminished. Achievement is diminished even among students whose families are not themselves poor, and it is diminished even more when the student's own family is poor.

Yet most compensatory education funds are distributed on the basis of individual poverty, not on the basis of how long a family has been poor or how many other poor children attend the same school. And many schools receiving funds do not have children needing *compensatory* education: They receive funds because some families in their neighborhoods are poor; but the children are not in need of compensation since the families are not

concentrated into a few dense neighborhoods, and/or the families are not suffering from long-term poverty. Consequently, many contemporary programs that are called compensatory education are in fact remedial education. These two terms, which at one time had completely separate meanings, are now often assumed to mean the same thing.

See also Disadvantaged Students; Federal Agencies; Federal Role in Education; Head Start.

—Mary Kennedy
Michigan State University

References

Bloom, B.S. (1964). *Stability and change in human characteristics.* New York: John Wiley.

Kennedy, M.M., Jung, R.K., & Orland, M.E. (1986). *Poverty, achievement and the distribution of compensatory education services.* Washington, DC: Department of Education and U.S. Government Printing Office.

McLaughlin, M.W. (1975). *Evaluation and reform: The Elementary and Secondary Education Act of 1965/Title I.* Cambridge, MA: Ballinger.

COMPETENCY TESTING, STUDENTS

In the widest sense, testing for learner competency is an integral and inescapable aspect of education wherever it is to be found. Implicit in the notion of mastering a body of knowledge or set of skills are the ideas of what it is to get it right and get it wrong. In this sense of testing, it is a major part of the educator's task to identify and correct learner miscomprehension and mistakes and to reinforce correct understanding and performance. Such critique lies at the heart of education.

More recently, however, the notion of competency testing has taken on a far narrower meaning within the context of the educational system. Prompted by state, regional, and national reports that American schools are producing waves of "functionally illiterate" or "incompetent" graduates, a large majority of states numbering over forty have mandated or are considering legislation to mandate statewide competency-testing programs for all students. Though hard evidence that the schools are producing "waves" of poorly educated students is elusive and ambiguous, consisting primarily of variously interpretable declines on standardized achievement and aptitude tests, the policy thrusts of competency-testing programs are clear. First, there is the aim to hold schools more accountable for their "product." Second, there is the aim to shore up the social meaning of the high school diploma by ensuring that high school graduates actually possess specified academic and social life competencies—at least at the minimum.

Testing Technology

Important to this form of competency testing is the relatively new standardized testing technology called "criterion-referenced measurement." Indeed, without the development of this technology, the minimal competency-testing movement would have enjoyed far less policy impact and political support. Until recently, most achievement testing has been "norm-referenced." Here individual student standing in a particular content area is determined by relationship to the scores achieved by one's peers. But once suspicion grows that a fair proportion of one's peer group is incompetent, a high score relative to the peer group indicates little about how one would score relative to the knowledge domain *simpliciter*.

But, since criterion-referenced measures were developed to avoid the problems of inferring from peer comparisons to what a student knows or can do in a content area, measuring instead a student's performance relative only to absolute knowledge-domain standards, the criterion-referenced measurement appears well-suited to the needs of competency-testing programs. Thus, the marriage of criterion-referenced measurement with minimal competency-testing programs appears to be an excellent tool for holding schools accountable for their products and for identifying nonmastery students.

Standard Setting

Criterion-referenced tests need not require the setting of cutoff scores used to separate student mastery from nonmastery in a content domain. These tests can merely be used in a diagnostic setting. Yet the political, social, and educational impact of minimal competency testing derives just from the attempt to establish such cutoff points on criterion-referenced tests. So, too, does the controversy surrounding criterion-referenced, minimal competency testing. For, when cutoff scores are used to determine minimal student competency and, in turn, are used to make decisions about student academic placement, grade promotion, or high school graduation, then the use of criterion-referenced minimal competency tests raises legal, social, and moral issues.

Today, approximately 18 states require a passing mark on a minimal competency test for (normal) high school graduation. Critics, however, argue that all attempts to identify a pass/fail cutoff line are blatantly arbitrary. Moreover, with grade promotion or high school graduation at stake, they note that even if cutoff standards could justifiably be set, students would still be subject to unjust treatment. Because test scores are *fallible* indicators of true achievement, masters can easily be identified as nonmasters and vice-versa. Also, much depends upon whether the school curriculum and in-class instruction cover test content. Lastly, then, are concerns that the majority of those identified as nonmasters will come from the ranks of "disadvantaged" students. As a major Florida court case shows, setting standards on criterion-referenced tests may work against policies designed to increase equality of educational and economic opportunity.

Cautions and Recommendations

The noted psychologist, Seymour Sarason, tells the story of his first day on his first job as a psychologist at a school for the mentally retarded. Upon his arrival, the students executed an ingeniously successful escape from the school's secured grounds. After their eventual capture, Sarason was given his job: Administer a standardized maze test, at which the students all failed miserably!

Linn and Associates drive home the moral of this story for minimal competency testing. They argue that no single competency test, or any individual indicator of achievement, can be relied upon to give an accurate picture of student competency in particular or schoolwide achievement in general. Yet because of the political visibility of statewide minimal competency programs, there is increasing pressure to focus on these test results as the key measure for assessing student progress and school

results. As a result, administrators are discovering that their own performance is increasingly being judged by this criterion. This same lesson is being learned by individual classroom teachers. The unfortunate result is that minimal competency testing, rather than being a small component for the educational purpose of student performance critique, is increasingly *driving* the school curriculum and classroom instruction. This is the classic example of the cart before the horse.

Though educators have been put on the defensive by calls for greater school accountability, it is now an opportune time for administrators and other school officials to embark aggressively on educating politicians, the media, and the public about the limitations, ambiguities, and social consequences of criterion-referenced, minimal competency tests. By themselves, such tests cannot ensure true school accountability; they can only distort it. And, as Ericson elsewhere shows, such tests cannot shore up the meaning of the high school diploma; strong reliance on such tests can only create consequences no one desires. Though criterion-referenced testing technology can help determine what our young know and can do (and even here it is presently useless for testing "higher-order" skills and knowledge), still, like other proposed technological "fixes," it is no cure for the problems of education.

See also Grades and Grading; Graduation Requirements; Test Score Reliability and Validity; Tests, Criterion- and Norm-Referenced.

—David P. Ericson
University of California, Los Angeles

References

Ericson, D.P. (1984). "Of minimal and maximal: The social significance of minimal competency testing and the search for educational excellence." *American Journal of Education, 92*(3), 245-61.

Linn, R.L., Madaus, G.F., and Pedulla, J.J. (1982). "Minimum competency testing: Cautions on the state of the art." *American Journal of Education, 91* (1), 1-35.

COMPETENCY TESTING, TEACHERS

Teacher competency testing means different things to different people. From state school board members to governors, it is a signal to constituents that elected officials care about schools and are actually doing something to improve them. To practicing teachers, it is more often than not viewed as an external threat and insult from individuals who know little and understand less about what schools are for and about the conditions under which teachers must practice their profession. To some school administrators and parents, competency testing is regarded as a way of keeping unqualified individuals out of the profession and for getting the "rascals" out of teaching who should not have been allowed in schools in the first place.

Given these different perspectives, what are the political considerations underlying the rush toward competency testing for teachers? What are some major concerns in the use of competency tests? And what are the chances of improving the testing of teachers?

Political Initiatives

It now appears that legislatively mandated teacher competency testing will spread throughout the fifty states. This activity, however, will continue to focus primarily on testing individuals seeking initial certification and entry into the profession. The opposition to testing practicing teachers for continuing certification or for salary enhancements by professional organizations (e.g., the National Education Association) will significantly delay such uses of testing for the foreseeable future. The specific action taken by the Texas State Teachers' Association in filing a lawsuit in 1985 against a statewide literacy test for practitioners will make other states think twice before moving in this direction in spite of the fact that the court rejected the claims made in the suit now being appealed.

Nonetheless, colleges and state departments of education must continue to develop and implement valid and reliable instruments for testing students applying for certification. Likewise, school districts proposing to use tests for merit pay or movement on a career ladder should make every effort to establish the highest level of validity and reliability possible in such an approach to rewarding outstanding teachers.

Major Concerns

With the scrapping in Arizona of the Arizona Teacher Proficiency Examination (ATPE) in 1985, and the filing that same year of a suit by the Texas State Teachers' Association against the use of the Texas Examination of Current Administrators and Teachers, it became evident to many that teacher competency testing for certification or continuing employment was creating some major problems. Specifically, large numbers of minority students and practitioners were failing the exams, and there were indicators that if testing continued as it was, the profession would become overwhelmingly white in spite of a growing need for minority teachers. In Arizona, for example, approximately 66 percent of the minorities taking the ATPE failed. The toll was especially heavy among American Indian students.

There are many other concerns raised against teacher competency testing that perhaps will never go away. These include questions about cost, content validity, control (who determines what should be tested), limited response format (paper and pencil), and the inability of current tests to measure critical dimensions of teacher behavior (e.g., interpersonal skills).

Nevertheless, in spite of the problems that teacher competency testing has faced, it has contributed to the overall sense of urgency and effort to improve the quality of individuals certified to teach in American schools. Valid tests should force teacher training faculty and school district personnel to reexamine what it is that teachers should know and be able to do, which should lead to reliable standards for success, which is an important step forward.

Standard Setting

Fortunately, the examination of standards is also being conducted in relation to testing and evaluation. Results so far indicate that the seminal work done by the Committee to Develop Standards for Educational Psychological Testing and the current efforts of the Joint Committee on Standards for Educational Evaluation provide hope that the dangerous pitfalls and stumbling blocks for developing truly valid and meaningful teacher competency tests will be overcome.

In its effort to develop a set of "Educational Personnel Evaluation Standards," the Joint Committee has decided that the basic concerns that guided its earlier work in standards development for program evaluation are also relevant to personnel evaluation. These stated concerns (or standards) are intended to do the following: (a) *Utility standards*: To ensure that an evaluation will serve the practical information needs of given audiences; (b) *Feasibility standards*: To ensure that an evaluation will be realistic, prudent, diplomatic, and frugal; (c) *Propriety standards*: To ensure that an evaluation will be conducted legally, ethically, and with due regard for the welfare of those involved in the evaluation, as well as those affected by its results; and (d) *Accuracy standards*: To ensure that an evaluation will reveal and convey technically adequate information to determine worth or merit.

These "Educational Personnel Evaluation Standards" should be available for general use in 1988. It will be especially important for educators and educational groups to keep abreast of the work of the Joint Committee so that they can draw upon its expertise. For it is vital that all of us work together to systematically improve the evaluations of educational personnel whether it be when finishing their education and training in colleges of education or during employment in the schools.

See also Teacher Certification; Teacher Selection.

—Arnold M. Gallegos
Western Michigan University

References

Committee to Develop Standards for Educational and Psychological Testing. (1985). *Standards for educational and psychological testing*. Washington, DC: American Psychological Association, Inc.

Gallegos, A.M. (1984, May). "The negative consequences of teacher competency testing." *Phi Delta Kappan, 65* (9), 631.

Stufflebeam, D.L. (1986). "Professional standards for assuring the quality of educational and personnel evaluations." In R.M. Wolfe (Ed.), *International journal of educational research, 11* (1, chap. 10). Oxford, England: Pergamon.

COMPETENCY-BASED EDUCATION

Of the many innovations in education, the competency-based approach has sparked more debate than most. It generated such attention because of its potential benefits for improving learning and for the major changes it requires in how instruction is planned and delivered.

Much of the early controversy focused on just what competency-based education (CBE) was, how it differed from the traditional approach and what elements make a program or course competency-based. Now that the dust has settled, four major components have emerged that characterize it:

1. The program is based on specific, concisely stated student outcomes (competencies, tasks, skills, etc.). These outcomes are scrutinized for their contribution toward meeting the stated goals of the particular educational program.

Examples of competency statements are "add and subtract whole numbers" and "describe causes and ways to control erosion."

2. Instruction is designed and delivered in a manner that contributes maximally toward each individual student's mastery of the competencies. Approaches being used include modularized materials, computer-aided instruction, group-oriented mastery learning, self-paced learning and others.

3. A high degree of competency mastery is required before moving to the next competency. Usually, this minimum level of unit mastery is the same level normally associated with an "A" in the traditional approach.

4. Students are evaluated primarily on their mastery of competencies—not in comparison with fellow students. Since competency-based education utilizes a high degree of competency mastery, students perform similarly on end of competency tests. Traditional grades can be awarded. The grades are based on the time needed, the number of competencies attained, and the level of attainment above the minimum required.

Although various approaches to competency-based education (such as individualized instruction, personalized learning, mastery learning, and others) differ, these four basic components are usually a part of the program. Different approaches place varying degrees of emphasis on different operational aspects such as degree of self-pacing, focus on individualized vs. group learning, use of correctives, etc. Major questions within the movement include: What competencies are the "right" ones for each course or grade level? Do these competencies include an appropriate mix of skills, attitudes, and knowledge (including higher level knowledge)? How can we deliver instruction in a manner that accommodates the preferred learning styles and individual needs of students? How can we evaluate competency mastery in a fair and consistent manner? How can various CBE approaches such as self-paced learning and flexible learning time be incorporated into the present educational system?

Implementation of competency-based education within elementary, middle and secondary schools (as well as higher education) will, no doubt, continue. The benefits of specifying what students are to learn, giving them the time and help to learn it, and then determining if they learned simply cannot be ignored. As more experience is gained and as more data are collected about what works and what does not, refinements and even wholesale changes will be made in the various programmatic elements of competency-based education. School leaders seeking ways to make dramatic improvements in the teaching-learning process should seriously consider competency-based education.

See also Direct Instruction; Individualization of Instruction; Instructional Objectives; Mastery Learning.

—William E. Blank
University of South Florida

References

Blank, W.E. (1982). *Handbook for developing competency-based training programs.* Englewood Cliffs, NJ: Prentice-Hall.

Bloom, B.J. (1976). *Human characteristics and school learning.* New York: McGraw-Hill.

Instructor (1980, October). Entire issue.

COMPUTER LITERACY

The term *computer literacy* was coined in the 1970s about the time the microcomputer made its debut. Although the concept has not yet achieved teenage status, it has already found its way into many schools and has taken on diverse meanings. Its enthusiastic promoters, while listening to the "microcomputer-in-education-is-a-passing-fad" refrain, have spread the idea far and wide, and educators have implemented varied literacy programs.

The question of whether or not computer-based education is a passing fad is not a trivial one. Vehement critics argue that microcomputers will suffer the same transient fate which radios, language laboratories, programmed learning, and other technologies have suffered. However, their argument, we suggest, is based upon a false premise; namely, that the microcomputer is comparable to previous technologies. In fact microcomputers differ markedly from their predecessors; students, for example, can interact with them, program them, and use them to learn subjects ranging from history to physics and skills ranging from word processing to information search. Because microcomputers have aggressively invaded homes, government agencies, factories and most other institutions, they and the microelectronic allies to which they are connected are creating new educational needs related, for example, to altered job requirements and changed citizenship roles. Given the greater power, versatility, and flexibility of microcomputers, those who compare them with previous technologies and assign them the same fate are walking on thin ice.

Types of Computer Literacy

Assuming that microcomputers are here to stay, what is the status of computer literacy programs today? Four different types prevail: operational literacy, instrumental literacy, literacy as programming, and role-related literacy.

Operational Literacy. In this approach, students are taught simple operations such as using the keyboard, loading software, and storing information; they are also taught the essential functions of the microcomputer through the study of such components as the "microprocessor," "keyboard," and "terminal." Operational literacy is typically taught over a period of four to six weeks in settings other than regular classrooms. Although critics assert that the approach is a trivial one, many schools begin with it. Neither extensive teacher training nor basic curriculum change is required. It tends to promote equitable learning opportunities, and it opens gateways to new learnings for some students.

Instrumental Literacy. In the instrumental approach, students learn to use computers as tools for learning specified subject matters or skills. In the early 1980s, for example, Swedish educators decided to teach students literacy by using computer programs in mathematics and civics courses. Some high schools have sought to incorporate computer programs in all subjects. In clerical courses, for instance, students might learn word-processing skills; in social studies insights into voting behavior through simulations; in physics concepts of gravity via computer demonstrations and so on. Critics of this approach argue that available software is inadequate to afford all students effective literacy opportunities. Advocates stress, however, that the approach provides students an effective and efficient means of acquiring literacy while pursuing already established school objectives.

Literacy as Programming. Advocates of this approach stress the importance of algorithmic thinking. Acquired through computer programming, this type of thinking requires students to learn how to express thoughts in practice language; to divide the overall programming task into small, clearly understood parts; to explain to the computer how the programming problem is to be solved; to break down procedures into simple steps to establish the logical relations among the steps; and, after finding programming malfunctions, to correct them effectively. Those who acquire algorithmic thinking, then, learn procedural problem-solving skills. Advocates contend that students with these skills can use the computer to fulfill their own objectives and not be locked into programs and objectives designed by others. Critics question whether *all* students need or can acquire programming skills and emphasize the high costs of teaching programming skills.

Role-Related Literacy. Educators have conceived at least three types of role-related literacy: worker literacy, citizen literacy, and consumer literacy. Programs to teach these types of literacy are diverse in content and objectives. For instance, some seek to teach consumers the skills they need to locate, acquire and use electronically transmitted information; others hope to teach the literacy future citizens will need in a globally-oriented democracy surfeited with information and pervaded with issues such as equity and privacy; and still others stress the teaching of cognitive skills individuals will require to work in computer-laden environments. Those who support the "passing fad" view argue that too much is being made of role-related literacy. However, advocates stress that if schools do not update programs, their graduates will not have the requisite knowledge and skills to function as workers, consumers and citizens in the future.

Unresolved Issues

Two major issues will continue to confront leaders in the future. One is centered in human equity. Given the greater costs and complexities of the new technologies, computer-literacy endeavors are likely to produce even greater inequities in learning opportunities than have "book-literacy" programs. Discrepancies between urban and suburban programs are already evident as are discrepancies in the literacy programs of given schools and school districts. The second issue is centered in educational quality. Having moved in a short time from simple "operational" concepts of literacy to the more complex "role-related" concepts, the search for effective literacy is not yet ended. The term "computer" in computer literacy highlights only the tip of an iceberg. Future definitions will need to go beyond machines and the means-oriented skills of algorithmic thinking and effectively encompass electronic networks, global data bases, and electronic information processing. Given the vast societal changes wrought by the microelectronic revolution, a more fundamental question arises: What modes of thought must students learn to resolve the major policy problems which now confront human institutions?

See also Computer-Assisted Instruction; Instructional Technology.

—Jack Culbertson
Ohio State University

References

Culbertson, J. (1986). "Whither computer literacy." In J. Culbertson & L. Cunningham (Eds.), *Microcomputers and education. National Society for the Study of Education Yearbook.* Chicago: University of Chicago Press.
Hunter, B. (1984). *My students use computers: Computer literacy in the K-8 curriculum.* Reston, VA: Reston Publishing Company.
Turkle, S. (1984). *The second self: Computers and the human spirit.* New York: Simon & Schuster.

COMPUTER-ASSISTED INSTRUCTION

Computer-assisted instruction (CAI) has been in use since the middle 1970s. Although there are several different definitions, for our purposes, we will define computer-assisted instruction as "a teaching process directly involving the computer in the presentation of instructional material in an interactive mode to provide and control the individualized learning environment for each student. The modes are usually subdivided into drill and practice, tutorial, simulation and gaming, and problem solving."

The effectiveness of computer-assisted instruction, as with all instructional materials, is greatly dependent upon the quality of the instructional program and individual teaching. There are several generalizations concerning its use that can be drawn from the research literature. We can say with reasonable confidence that computer-assisted instruction (a) either improves learning or is equal to traditional instruction; (b) is helpful for all ages—preschool through adult; (c) speeds up learning when compared to conventional methods; (d) fosters positive student attitudes; (e) increases effectiveness when related to positive teacher attitudes; (f) is helpful in review; (g) is particularly well-suited for instruction in science and foreign languages; (h) may lead to shorter retention of presented material than that presented in a traditional manner; (i) is improving in cost effectiveness; and (j) is being enhanced by an ever-increasing number of computer-assisted instruction programs.

Types of Computer-Assisted Instruction

Drill and Practice. Drill-and-practice programs help children remember and use information they have previously been taught. As is true in all types of instruction, drill should occur after a great deal of exploration and concept formation. A drill-and-practice program replaces worksheets, flash cards, and oral drill. A well-designed program can be extremely helpful in mastery of spelling and vocabulary words, improving typing skills, geographic and historical facts, and mathematics combinations.

Many of the better drill-and-practice programs have two or three presentations modes such as "look and remember," "answer the question quickly," and "play the game." For extensive use of drill-and-practice materials a rather large number of computers is required, since this instructional use requires a one computer-one student ratio. When there are a limited number of computers in the building they should probably be used for simulation and/or problem-solving, computer-assisted instructional programs.

Tutorials. Programs that are classified as tutorial are designed to "teach" material. They usually provide a description and explanation of the concept, some illustrations and examples, and questions and remediation. There are so few good tutorial programs available at this time (1987) great care should be taken in their selection. With the present state of tutorial quality, these programs usually make better review or reteaching programs than they do instructional programs.

Simulations. At the present time simulations are one of the best instructional uses of microcomputers. Simulations provide the students with the opportunity to explore "what-if" situations, make decisions, and then react to the results of their decisions. This computer-assisted instruction mode allows the teacher to present artificial versions of real situations that are too costly, time consuming, or dangerous to present, or a situation that occurred in a different time frame.

Simulations can involve historical events with decision making, environmental situations, science experiments, running a business, or career selection. In fact, the extent to which simulations can be used in the classroom is dependent only upon the ingenuity of the developers and teacher creativity in use. The simulation lends itself well to situations where there are few computers in the building. Since the simulation is often a cooperative study between teacher and pupil, the teacher is able to supplement and modify a simulation much better than a tutorial or drill-and-practice program.

Problem Solving. These programs make use of standard and innovative methods of developing pupil thinking and problem-solving skills. The quality of problem-solving programs ranges from poor to excellent. There are, however, enough really good problem-solving programs. A thorough study of this area should be made by the administrator.

Software Selection

Locating good software programs is a major undertaking. Whereas there is some similarity between the search for a good textbook and a good computer disk, there are a number of other factors that must be considered when selecting software. Poor computer-assisted instruction software is often worse than no software at all. A few guiding principles of software selection are

1. Preview the software before you buy it.
2. Find the answers to these critical questions about software:

   (a) Is interest created through the use of an absorbing approach to the material itself?
   (b) Does the teaching method involve the student in thinking? Is it discovery oriented?
   (c) For what audience is the material appropriate?
   (d) What background is required to use the material?
   (e) Is the program effective in the use of students' time?
   (f) Is the program user friendly?
   (g) Is it well documented?
   (h) Is the sequence of topics in keeping with the curriculum?
   (i) Is the material free from subject-matter errors?
   (j) Are the graphics usable?
   (k) Does the program make good use of the computer?
   (l) Is the program cost effective?

3. Involve those who are experts in working with children and instruction in program selection.
4. Consider materials for teacher use.

Computer-assisted instruction can be a very effective part of the school curriculum. However, if computer-assisted instruction is to be educational and cost effective, much more time and study by the administrator, key supervisors, and teachers must be conducted. Studies have shown that use of computer-assisted instruction is directly related to the expertise and concern of the school leadership.

See also Computer Literacy; Instructional Technology; Teaching Approaches, Future.

—Alan Riedesel
State University of New York at Buffalo

References

Bramble, W.J., & Mason, E.J. (1985). *Computers in schools.* New York: McGraw-Hill.
Hall, K. (1982). "Computer based instruction." In H.E. Mitzel (Ed.), *Encyclopedia of educational research.* New York: Free Press.
Riedesel, C.A., & Clements, D.H. (1985). *Coping with computers in the elementary and middle schools.* Englewood Cliffs, NJ: Prentice-Hall.

COMPUTERS, ADMINISTRATIVE USES

Until recently the use of computers for administrative purposes was primarily restricted to large school districts which were able to afford mainframe computers. The advent of the microcomputer has now brought the speed, accuracy, and large-scale data handling capacity of this technology within the grasp of virtually every administrator who wishes to automate a variety of administrative tasks.

Administrative applications of the microcomputer for which specially designed software exists include

1. Attendance accounting. Attendance programs keep track of student absences by periods, classes, and days, produce summary reports regarding types and frequency of absence, and generate form letters to students and parents.
2. Budgeting and financial accounting. These programs automate financial accounts, keeping track of budget categories, expenditures, and income.
3. Grade reporting. This software can compute grade point averages and class rank, produce report cards and transcripts, generate letters to parents regarding student progress, and produce school and district grade reports.
4. Instructional management. This type of software records student progress in achieving course objectives or specific instructional tasks.
5. Inventory. This application is used to keep records of school property and equipment.
6. Library and media center. Library-related software can be used to process acquisitions, maintain circulation records, prepare and update card catalog entries, and develop topical indexes.
7. Scheduling. These programs can produce the master schedule, and conflict matrices, and generate individual student and teacher schedules, class lists, as well as other scheduling reports for block, fixed period, and modular scheduling modes.

8. Staff and student records. Personnel software can store and retrieve quickly a wide variety of information about faculty members, classified employees, substitute teachers, and students.

9. Guidance. Software exists to score standardized achievement and intelligence tests, store student records, and facilitate student decisions about career and college selection.

10. Activities programs. Specialized software exists to manage various aspects of extracurricular programs. One example would be programs which keep track of athletic statistics, facilitate athletic scheduling, and generate individual and team reports.

11. Planning. Software is available to help compute enrollment projections, develop and analyze salary schedules, as well as apply planning techniques, such as network analysis and PERT, to manage time and task functions of projects.

General-use software can also facilitate administrative tasks. Word-processing programs can be used for correspondence, form letters and general mailings, and proposal and report writing. Database packages can be used to manage large amounts of information and can help the administrator conduct research. Accounting and budgeting procedures as well as any data management function involving row and column data tables can be made easier through the use of electronic spreadsheets. Administrators can also tie into national data bases and send electronic mail through the use of a microcomputer and a modem.

Prior to making decisions about hardware and software the administrator must first determine whether transferring administrative tasks to a computer will be advantageous. The chief criterion in making such an assessment is whether the computer application will reduce the amount of time, effort, and paperwork required to accomplish the task. Software programs which are not well designed may in fact increase the amount of time which the administrator must spend in entering, processing, and retrieving data. Tasks for which computer applications are most appropriate are those which are well defined, routine, and/or involve large amounts of data.

Once the decision has been made to computerize a particular task the administrator should review available software to determine which package(s) will best accomplish this task. General-use packages such as word processing, spreadsheets, and databases usually are the most reliable and least costly since they have been on the market the longest, and many of the problems associated with new programs have been corrected. However, adapting these general packages to specific administrative applications may require a great deal of time, expense, and expertise. Specific application software, such as a scheduling package, although tailored to a particular need, will likely be more expensive and may not be fully debugged. The administrator must weigh the advantages and disadvantages associated with these two types of software first before exploring the appropriateness of any specific package.

Guidelines for selecting administrative software are similar to those for identifying good instructional software. The administrator should determine, at a minimum, if the program will produce useful reports, if the amount of time required to enter and process data is justified in terms of the output received from the program, if the documentation is adequate and well written, if the company which sells the software will provide training and/or a toll-free number for user support, if the software is flexible enough to handle future needs, if the software provides adequate security measures to limit access, if backup copies or multiple copies

are available for all computers in the district, and if updates of the program are provided free of charge. Reviews of commonly used programs frequently appear in computer journals. However, the most reliable critics are other administrators who have had experience with a particular program. Many companies will lend programs on a trial basis. The administrator should try out a program prior to purchase and determine first hand if it lives up to its claims.

The selection of appropriate hardware is related to a variety of factors, including the district's prior hardware purchases, compatibility with the types of software selected, cost, capacity to handle future needs, and reliability. The usefulness of any one brand of computer is restricted by the availability of software to handle desired administrative applications. At a minimum, the administrator should determine if the keyboard is easy to use, if the monitor has clear resolution, if the total capacity of the machine is adequate for current and future needs, and if peripherals, such as printers and additional disk drives, are available and appropriate. The district may also consider whether it wishes to network computers among all of the buildings or with the district mainframe so that they may share information.

See also Computer Literacy; Computer-Assisted Instruction.

—Richard S. Podemski
University of Alabama

References

Crawford, C.W. (1985). "Administrative uses of microcomputers, Part I: Needs evaluation." *NASSP Bulletin, 69* (479), 70-72. See also remaining articles in series: *69*(481), 53-60, 95-98; *69*(482), 115-18.

Little, J.R., Mackey, P.E., & Tuscher, L.J. (1984). *Micros for managers.* Trenton, NJ: New Jersey School Boards Association.

Pogrow, S. (1985). *Evaluations of educational administration software.* Tucson, AZ: ED:AD Systems.

CONFLICT RESOLUTION

Conflicts, omnipresent and natural in schools, take at least three forms for administrators: (1) *prescribed* conflict, intentional competition based on standard rules (athletic contests), (2) *emergent* conflict, unplanned battling over incompatible interests (arguments about student discipline), and (3) *destructive* conflict, intentional efforts to dissolve working relationships (teachers' strikes). Prescribed conflict can be ignored, since in the long run it is satisfying even to the losers, but destructive conflict must be avoided. Dealing effectively with emergent conflict will usually ward off destructive conflict. When, however, emergent conflict is seen as just another kind of prescribed conflict, it will frequently escalate into serious cleavage and eventually into destructive conflict.

Emergent conflicts, ranging from mild disagreement to serious cleavage, are of three types: (a) *factual* conflict, perceived differences over the realities of a situation (arguments about what various teachers really believe), (b) *value* conflict, philosophical differences over educational goals (arguments over priorities for outcomes), and (c) *strategy* conflict, intellectual differences over the best way of moving toward a goal (arguments over curriculum choices). Most disagreements about facts, values, or strategies arise over issues that are personally distant, but serious cleavages arise when the parties feel committed to the facts, values, strategies of the argument, and especially when their self-concepts are entailed.

Sources of Conflict

The sources of mild disagreements or serious cleavages in schools can be categorized as (a) *power struggles* between persons and groups, (b) *role conflicts*, and (c) *differentiation of function* among parts of the school.

Power struggles arise when school participants become adversaries competing for commonly desired rewards (merit pay for good teaching), when rewards are scarce (a desirable room for instruction), and when one's professional autonomy is threatened (counselors who want to ignore influence from teachers or parents). Power struggles can result also from teachers' desires to gain personal influence over the school program. Some faculty members might wish to influence the school's philosophy and instructional program; others might wish to gain influence in order to be seen as more effective professionally and to move into administrative jobs.

Most power struggles inevitably involve administrators because the adversaries look to authorities for conflict resolution. In districts lacking widely agreed upon decision-making procedures, disagreements can build into serious cleavages because of conflicting views about appropriate power relationships in the district; i.e., who should be accountable to whom, or who should tell whom what to do and when and how to do it? Power struggles over professional autonomy frequently arise in secondary schools between principals and teachers over supervision (the principal, urged by the superintendent, wishes department heads to supervise teachers, but teachers and department heads agree that supervision by anyone other than the principal threatens both the autonomy and the equality of collegial relationships).

In role conflict, school participants communicate diverse expectations for how particular jobholders should act. Within-role conflicts come from conflicting expectations that an individual roletaker cannot satisfy simultaneously (following the principal's expectations could mean violating the norms of colleagues). Within-role conflicts also arise when the expectations held by others conflict with one's own values, perception of the facts, or professional orientation (a counselor who is expected to support some teachers' punitive discipline methods).

Conflicts among roles occur when the demands of multiple roles are inconsistent (a teacher is simultaneously the head of a curriculum committee and the school's representative to the teachers' union. If that teacher is firm about leaving a curriculum meeting at 4:00 p.m., members of the committee might express disapproval, whereas staying past 4:00 p.m. without a contractual agreement might elicit disapproval of the teachers' union).

Differentiation of function among specialized units responsible for different tasks is a common cause of conflict in schools. Members of various subgroups who have access to different kinds of information from their counterparts in other subgroups are likely to take different views of the facts, to value different objectives, and to entertain divergent strategies for accomplishing tasks.

Often, conflicts arising from functional differentiation are misunderstood as arising from someone's personal incompetence, because most school participants are too close to their own part of the organization to understand the parts

others work in. It is natural, then, to associate the source of conflict with the people toward whom the frustration or irritation is directly felt (after conferring with the principal and the head of research in the district about students' absences, a vice-principal and several counselors spend more time than before contacting parents, working with police, and counseling students with frequent absences. For their part, the teachers view the vice-principal and counselors as incompetent because they are not dealing with the students who are discipline problems in classrooms).

Resolving Conflicts

Successful tactics for resolving emergent conflicts, whatever their type or source, are organized into three steps: (a) distinguish between *miscommunication and conflict*, (b) assess the *seriousness of the conflict* and (c) respond appropriately to the *source of the conflict*.

Miscommunications are not conflicts; they are gaps between intended messages and received messages. They occur when messages sent do not directly reflect intentions, or when messages sent are inaccurately understood. Miscommunications can be reduced by improved articulation and listening. The skills of paraphrasing and summarizing can be used to enhance listening. When miscommunication might escalate into conflict, face-to-face meetings with the parties involved can be helpful. If clarifying the communication accentuates differences between the parties, one can assume there is conflict and proceed to assess it.

One should assess the source of the conflict, and respond accordingly. With power struggles, he or she can talk separately with the conflicting parties about his or her perception of their conflict. Often just bringing an unconscious power struggle into the open with conversation can reduce its intensity and disruption. If, however, the struggle does not subside, it could be recommended that a third party with authority be introduced to help resolve the conflict. That neutral party could be a key administrator or a committee of trusted school participants who represent a legitimate advisory group (the department heads, an administrative cabinet, or a committee of teachers). Once the conflict has surfaced and a tentative assessment of its source has been made, the neutral party should look for ways to engage the conflicting parties in cooperative work toward ends they have in common.

When role conflict is the source, and the above tactics do not work or seem inappropriate, it would be well to ask each party to write three lists addressed to every other party in the conflict as follows: To help me carry out my role, I'd like you to do the following more or better _____ . To help me..., I'd like you to do the following less often _____ ; and..., I'd like you to continue doing the following as you now are _____ . Give the responses to the parties, encouraging each to question others for clarification, but not to argue about the information. After the messages are understood, ask the parties to choose issues to negotiate, with each prepared to offer some temporary behavioral change. The role negotiation takes the form of an exchange: If I do _____ , you will do _____ . After the parties are satisfied that each will receive a return for what they are to give, record the agreement, and move to another issue. Agree on a time and person to check whether the actions occur.

If differentiation of function is the source of conflict, and the above tactics do not work, ask each conflicting party to write descriptions, both favorable and unfavorable, of itself and of the other party. The parties convene next to share their images with one another. Then separate the parties once more, and ask each to recall instances when its behavior supported the impressions of the other party. In other words, each party confesses that it did, at one time or another, behave in ways that might have exacerbated the conflict. Finally, reconvene the parties to share the confessions, and to specify the underlying issues that are pulling them apart. Although this procedure is unlikely to resolve all existing differences, it can set the stage for collaborative problem solving.

Since emergent conflicts are omnipresent and natural in schools, administrators should routinely pinpoint and manage them as part of their job. Success in turning emergent conflict into cooperative problem solving is largely determined by the administrator's skills of diagnosis, confrontation, communication, negotiation, and follow through. When school conflict is openly recognized, dealt with directly, and acted upon fairly, the energy it induces in the participants can be a constructive force for school improvement.

See also Communication; Group Processes; Human Relations; Problem Identification.

—Richard A. Schmuck
University of Oregon

References

Brown, L.D. (1983). *Managing conflict at organizational interfaces.* Reading, MA: Addison-Wesley.

Cole, D.W. (1983). *Conflict resolution technology.* Cleveland: The Organization Development Institute.

Schmuck, R.A., & Runkel, P.J. (1985). *The handbook of organization development in schools,* (Chapter 7). Palo Alto, CA: Mayfield.

CONSOLIDATION OF SCHOOLS

School consolidation has been a major challenge for most school boards in the 1980s. School boards were not psychologically prepared to deal with the drastic decline in enrollment they began to experience after thirty years of unprecedented growth. Occurring during a period of economic decline in which both recession and inflation were prevalent made the task of dealing with the loss in enrollment even more difficult.

The reality is that no process of closing schools is without pain. Students, school staffs, elected officials and local communities all have an emotional interest in maintaining a local building; therefore, the consolidation process must allow an opportunity for participation.

Since declining enrollment is a relatively new phenomenon, new planning models had to be developed for the consolidation and closing of schools. One of the most effective models is that of corporate or long-range planning. This is a method that begins with creative thinking, looks at what is, and tries to predict what will be on the basis of the best, most comprehensive and relevant information available. It helps approach the solution to what is essentially a negative situation in the most optimistic way.

The corporate planning model involves a five-step process:

1. A review of historical, present, and future patterns of enrollment. A review also of the staff, program, finances, facilities available, and the composition of the student body. It also would be helpful to examine the demographic patterns within the community, e.g., mobility, age distribution, and ethnicity and immigration-settlement patterns.

2. Development of various scenarios or plans for dealing with the decline in enrollment—a development which considers and applies rational criteria such as retention of the best facilities in a centralized location; retention of the greatest number of schools in a financially economic organization; a resulting enrollment sufficient to provide enough staff to deliver a quality program; minimum busing; and, wherever possible, keeping the number of moves affecting students during the consolidation process to a minimum.

3. Development of a process for decision making which includes consultation with as many of the groups affected as possible—teachers, principals, senior administrators, finance officials, elected officials, and the community. This is extremely important, as it gives voice to most of the groups affected by school closings. This may be done by having administrators and elected officials meet to share ideas, concerns, and directions, and to establish guidelines for review of schools with serious enrollment declines. Though final decisions ultimately rest with elected officials, meetings should also be held with staff and community consultative groups to obtain their recommendations and suggestions for alternatives or revisions to the plan presented.

4. Implementation of the plan.

5. Establishment of a review and analysis process which includes monitoring the consolidated schools for a specific time period. This allows for a follow-up on how specific plans are working. Surveys or interviews with the staff and parents are helpful in the transitional stage; one can see how smoothly the operation is functioning and can also find out about the staff's and parents' perceptions of the advantages and disadvantages of the process. An important by-product of the whole process is that school-system personnel have an opportunity to engage in dialogue with the community, a healthy process which is often neglected when things are going smoothly.

Although few school closings occur without serious opposition, the long-range planning model provides for consideration of alternatives and a maximum of participation in the decision-making process among those most affected, resulting in a process which explores all feasible options and encourages the broadest ownership of the solution.

See also Centralization and Decentralization; Community-School Involvement; School Districts.

—Albert E. Virgin
North York Board of Education
North York, Ontario

References

Beck, W. (1976, June). "Everybody got into the act when Blackwell closed a school." *American School Board Journal, 163*(6), 35, 46.

Board of Education for the City of North York, Educational Planning, Information and Evaluation Services. (1983). *School Consolidation Policy Review.* North York, Ontario: Author.

Peshkin, A. (1980). "The issue of school consolidation: Perspectives on a fateful conflict." In L. Rubin (Ed.), *Critical issues in educational policy.* Boston: Allyn & Bacon.

COOPERATIVE LEARNING

Today, a major concern in education is how students interact with one another as they learn. The manner in which teachers structure student-to-student interactions will influence how well students achieve academically, how they feel about school, how they feel about teachers and other personnel, how they feel about each other, and how they feel about themselves as learners and as individuals. Administrators and educational leaders need to understand the concept of cooperative learning, as it is one of three learning structures increasingly being used in school settings. Although research clearly indicates that classroom instruction is most effective when it is dominated by student cooperation, competitive and individualistic learning structures presently predominate. It is, however, important that students learn to interact effectively under each goal structure. With such interaction, they will be able to select an appropriate interaction pattern suited to the situation.

In cooperative classrooms, students work together to accomplish shared goals. Students assigned to small groups learn the material and make sure that the other members of the group learn it as well. This positive interdependence, which grows out of a process whereby the students can reach their learning goals only if the other students in the learning group also reach their goals, can be achieved in several ways. Identifying mutual goals, assigning the learning tasks, assigning student roles, giving joint rewards, and dividing materials, resources, and information among members of the group are ways to establish positive interdependence. Individual accountability for mastering the assigned material can be checked randomly by selecting products from each group to grade. Determining the level of each student's mastery is necessary if students are to provide appropriate support and assistance to each other. A criterion-referenced evaluation system is used when the group's performance is compared to a predetermined, specified level of mastery or achievement.

Cooperative learning requires that students use interpersonal and small-group skills appropriately. Consequently, students are taught these skills for collaboration and are encouraged to use them. Finally, students must also be given the time and skills for analyzing and processing how well their learning groups are functioning; they must recognize the extent to which students are employing the necessary social skills to help all members of the group achieve and maintain effective working relationships. It is these verbal exchanges and interaction patterns among students that affect educational outcomes.

The cooperative goal structure differs markedly from the competitive one in which students work against each other to achieve a goal. Under the competitive structure there is negative interdependence among goals achieved, since only one student or a select number of students can attain the goal. Students perceive that they can obtain their goals only if other students in the class fail to obtain their goals. Students work alone to see who is best and, therefore, who will be rewarded. Grades are generally based on the normal curve and evaluation is norm-referenced. Students either work hard to do better than other students or take it easy and even quit because they do not feel they have a chance to win. Rarely is there an opportunity for students to work with others or to practice appropriate social and communication skills except with authority figures.

Cooperative learning can also be contrasted with the individualistic goal structure. In classrooms where these structures predominate, the teacher has students working on their own toward a goal without paying attention to other students. Success depends on the student's own performance in relation to an established criteria. Individual goals are unrelated to those of other students, and rewards are given according to each student's efforts. Students work on their own set of materials at their own pace with little or no interaction among the other students. Goals achieved are independent and unrelated to what other students do.

In many classrooms, students expect to compete with each other and to work alone. It is not uncommon for teachers trained in these models, however, to have students work in groups. However, structuring students to work cooperatively is very different from arranging traditional learning groups. In traditional groups, students may sit in proximity doing their own work and may be free to talk to each other while completing a learning task. In this arrangement, it is not uncommon for one person to do the work while the rest "hitchhike." In a cooperative group all students need to know the material for the group to be successful. This learning environment is carefully structured and managed by the teacher. Cooperative learning leads to effective instruction and should influence the operation of classrooms to a much greater extent.

Implementation

Implementing cooperative learning procedures is not without its difficulties. In order for a teacher to be successful in using cooperative groups, regular use in the classroom over several years must occur so as to allow the teacher to grow in confidence and skill. This is more likely to occur if there is administrative support for implementing the procedures.

Several steps are necessary for successful implementation of cooperative learning procedures and can be facilitated by a supportive administration: (a) Present a general awareness session to all interested teachers; (b) inform parents and school board members that cooperative learning will be implemented by some teachers; (c) identify a few teachers who are interested in further training in all aspects of the concept; (d) develop a support group which provides teachers with time to work together to plan lessons, to observe each other, and to develop curriculum; (e) provide the necessary resources and incentives to keep teachers motivated and unburdened; (f) assist and participate in the group processing in order to facilitate the greatest possible growth and development of teachers and students alike; and (g) plan on a long-term, developmental process for implementation which may require a minimum of two years for individuals to feel comfortable with cooperative learning procedures.

When these steps are attended to, cooperative learning strategies can have a great impact on the operation of an entire school system. Cooperative learning strategies in the classroom will increase important educational outcomes such as achievement, retention, thinking skills, and attitudes toward subject areas while cooperative relationships among school staff members will tend to increase job productivity and morale.

Conclusion

Cooperative learning is a powerful learning strategy. By structuring the classroom to incorporate cooperative learning strategies, along with appropriate competitive and individualistic learning structures, greater achievement and retention by more students can be observed. Superiority of cooperative learning in conceptual learning and problem solving can be shown. Further, greater interpersonal and small-group skills needed to collaborate throughout life are learned and practiced. Higher-level reasoning processes and critical-thinking competencies are developed. More positive attitudes toward school, teachers, peers, and learning are demonstrated. Higher self-esteem based on self-acceptance leads to greater psychological health and better social adjustment. However, effective implementation of cooperative learning takes time, hard work, and continual support at all levels.

See also Instructional Objectives; Learning Styles; Teaching Approaches, Future.

—Richard G. Fox
Susan E. Gruber
University of Wisconsin-Milwaukee

References

Johnson, D.W., & Johnson, R. (1986). *Learning together and alone: Cooperation, competition and individualization.* Englewood Cliffs, NJ: Prentice-Hall.

Johnson, D.W., Johnson, R.T., Holubec, E.D., & Roy, R. (1984). *Circles of learning.* Alexandria, VA: Association for Supervision & Curriculum Development.

Johnson, D.W., Johnson, R., & Maruyama, G. (1983). "Interdependence & interpersonal attraction among heterogeneous & homogeneous individuals: A theoretical formulation & a meta-analysis of the research." *Review of Educational Research, 53,* 5-54.

CORPORAL PUNISHMENT

During the nineteenth and twentieth centuries, the use of corporal punishment in the schools has periodically generated heated public debate. It is one of the most controversial issues in American education, where it is still widely used. With the exception of Ireland, corporal punishment is used in all English speaking countries. It is illegal in Continental Europe, the entire Communist world, Israel, Japan, and other industrialized nations.

Definition

Corporal punishment in the schools is the purposeful infliction of pain or confinement as a penalty for an offense committed by a student. The use of a wooden paddle is the most frequent method of administering it. Corporal punishment also takes the form of confinement in closets, bathrooms, or other closed spaces or forcing students to assume painful bodily postures or engage in excessive exercise. The use of electrical shock and forced eating or exposure to noxious substances falls with the definition as well.

Corporal punishment does not include the use of force, with the incidental infliction of pain, to quell a disturbance or to protect oneself, property, or another person. Nor does it apply to attempts to protect a student from self injury.

Historical Factors

The use of corporal punishment in child rearing and education appears early in the recorded history of western cultures. Its roots in the Old Testament trace to Proverbs (13:24), where Solomon urges that "he that spareth the rod hateth his son, he that loveth him, chasteneth him." In Christian theology, the use of corporal punishment is historically related to concepts of original sin and the need to combat Satan by "beating the devil" out of children. Whippings and floggings were also used to instill character, obedience, and humility.

Corporal punishment had firm roots in colonial America. The birch rod was synonymous with education until secular philosophies and revisions in Calvinistic thinking began to affect education. The first major change occurred in 1867, when the New jersey legislature banned the use of corporal punishment in schools. However, local control prevailed, and it was not until the twentieth century that the ban was taken seriously. For instance, in the school year ending in 1876, Newark, New Jersey, recorded 9,408 beatings in a system of 10,000 students.

In 1972, Massachusetts banned corporal punishment. By 1986, six additional states, most in the Northeast, had banned corporal punishment in the schools. In addition, many of the major cities and many affluent suburbs have eliminated it.

Demography of Corporal Punishment

Studies indicate that the most frequent use of corporal punishment occurs in the South, Southwest, and rural areas of the country. Minority and/or poor children are the most frequent recipients of corporal punishment. Recent research suggests that it is least likely to be administered by educators who experienced it infrequently or not at all in their own childhoods. Teachers who are the most frequent users tend to be more authoritarian, less experienced, and more impulsive than their peers. Cultural differences were suggested in a study in Canada which indicated that people in Ontario were more than twice as likely to favor its use in schools than were people in Quebec.

Data on the incidence of corporal punishment are difficult to interpret. The Office of Civil Rights has conducted a number of surveys which suggest approximately a million cases per year. Because of sampling problems and large numbers of unreported incidents, most experts consider these estimates to be low. Extrapolation from these data and other sources suggest that a closer estimate might be two million.

National surveys of public opinion about the use of corporal punishment reveal support by 60 percent to 80 percent of respondents in random samples. However, the reverse is true in areas where it is not used and where respondents are at least middle class and have college degrees.

Legal Issues

Legal sanctions for the use of corporal punishment in American education derive from the common law doctrine of "in loco parentis," or "in place of the parent." According to *Blackstone's Commentaries of English Law*, a tutor or schoolmaster was allowed the use of "restraint and correction, as may be necessary to answer the purpose for which he is employed." This doctrine implies that schools cannot *completely* replace parental authority, and it is in relation to this issue that much of the litigation regarding corporal punishment has occurred.

The most frequent litigation regarding the use of corporal punishment results from parents' contentions that educators have used unreasonable force. In most states, parents, under torts law, must prove that injury resulted when the physical force was administered with malice and that the resulting damage is long lasting or permanent. A nationwide analysis of cases reported in the press revealed that most were adjudicated in favor of the defendants. However, there are two mediating factors—geographical and economic. Parents in the South and Southwest are much less likely to succeed than those in the Northeast. In addition, economic factors seem to play an important role in determining community standards of punishment. Economically depressed locales, especially those which are largely rural, produce a greater proportion of decisions favoring the schools.

The second class of suits is based on constitutional issues. The most important case, *Ingraham v. Wright*, was decided by the United States Supreme Court in 1977. A 5 to 4 majority denied school children constitutional protection from corporal punishment under the "cruel and unusual punishment" clause of the Eighth Amendment and procedural due process under the Fourteenth Amendment. Legal experts agree that the only constitutionally untested issue is the question of substantive due process, which deals with the limits of allowable force in administering physical punishment. This issue was addressed by the United States Court of Appeals in West Virginia in *Hall v. Tawney*. The Court indicated that there may be constitutional relief in cases of excessive corporal punishment. Since this case was eventually settled out of court, a constitutional test of the limits of corporal punishment has not occurred.

There are no uniform judicial guidelines to resolve the limits of in loco parentis when parents object to the use of corporal punishment. In 1970, the Federal District Court in North Carolina, in *Baker v. Owen*, ruled that parents do not have the right to forbid educators to use physical punishment. Conversely, in 1972, the United States District Court in Pennsylvania in the case of *Glaser v. Marietta* held that parents have the right to prohibit the use of corporal punishment.

Currently, state constitutions have established guidelines concerning severity of injury and reasonableness of force. A review of cases indicates that regional and/or community standards are the best predictors of outcome.

Research Findings

Advocates of corporal punishment generally base their beliefs on personal experience of its effectiveness, religious ideology, and the assumption that it must be available as a last resort to discipline students. Adversaries object on philosophical principle and/or religious conviction. They feel that punishment is generally a poor approach to correction. Their views are generally supported in the research of educational psychologists.

Historical analysis and behavioral research tend to argue against the use of corporal punishment. The major historical argument is that its use always leads to abuse. Nineteenth century writers such as Charles Dickens began a tradition of literature inveighing against the abuses of corporal punishment.

Educational research generally indicates that punishment is an ineffective way to change behavior. While there are no controlled experimental studies of corporal punishment, correlational and survey research indicate it is not needed or is counterproductive. Changes in behavior occur much more readily with the use of reinforcement and modeling of appropriate behavior and by using techniques of positive motivation. There is some evidence that the use of mild criticism may motivate certain types of children, such as those who are very competitive.

A summary of the findings on punishment indicates that it tends to suppress behavior temporarily and does not teach new behaviors. It loses effectiveness if not increased in frequency and intensity. Excessive punitiveness by teachers reduces learning in the classroom. Correlational studies indicate that most violent delinquents were the recipients of excessive corporal punishment. Recent research reveals long-lasting stress disorders result from corporal punishment, especially when administered by punitive educators to young children. Corporal punishment also results in aggressive responses by recipients. In fact, research on aggression indicates that corporal punishment, through modeling, teaches that force is an acceptable way to solve problems.

Despite the arguments of proponents, there is clear evidence that the elimination of corporal punishment in itself does not increase misbehavior of students. Research on discipline reveals that effective approaches do not use it.

Trends and Implications

By 1986, most professional organizations which deal with children's issues had passed resolutions against corporal punishment. These included the National Education Association, The American Psychological Association, The American Medical Association, and The American Bar Association. School administrators and school board organizations have maintained the issue should be decided at the local school level.

Corporal punishment is not recommended in any identified contemporary secular textbook on teaching. The trend among school districts is to eliminate it.

In conclusion, corporal punishment is still used in many school districts where it is strongly supported by community values. However, educators who rationally evaluate the research, literature, trends, and evolving legal issues may find it difficult to defend corporal punishment as a pedagogical tool.

See also Disruptive Students.

—Irwin A. Hyman
Temple University

References

Hyman, I. (1986). "Psychological correlates of corporal punishment." In B. Germain & M. Brassard (Eds.), *Psychological maltreatment of children and youth*. Elmsford, NY: Pergamon Press.

Hyman, I., & Wise, J. (1979). *Corporal punishment in American education*. Philadelphia: Temple University Press.

Publications Catalogue. (1986, Annual publication). Philadelphia: National Center For the Study of Corporal Punishment and Alternatives in the Schools, Temple University.

COUNSELING AND GUIDANCE

Counseling and guidance is a process in which a professionally certified counselor works with students, individually or in groups, to assist them in resolving educational, vocational, personal, and social concerns in order to become mentally healthy, effective individuals, who function at optimal levels in order to achieve full potential. In order to assist students, counselors also work as consultants to teachers, parents, and community agency personnel to help them create home and learning environments that enhance student growth and development.

An effective counseling and guidance program is developmental, preventive, and crisis-oriented. Developmentally, students must resolve concerns that are age-related. For example, developmental tasks of elementary school children include learning basic skills, developing values and appropriate sex roles, adjusting to competitive and cooperative task-related situations, evolving positive attitudes toward work and achievement, functioning effectively with adults and peers, and progressing toward feelings of self-acceptance and self-esteem. The developmental tasks of adolescents include decision making in educational and vocational planning, learning independence and increasingly disengaging from parents, developing opposite sex friends and peer groups, establishing identity, managing emotions, developing integrity and personal values, and dealing effectively with sexuality and issues of intimacy.

Preventive counseling and guidance involves identifying potential problem areas and developing appropriate interventions to resolve these problems. For example, research reveals common correlates among high-risk students and potential school dropouts. As early as fifth grade, students can be identified who are underachieving, unmotivated academically, chronically absent and possibly from single parent homes in which educational achievement of parents and siblings is low. Special programs can be developed for this population. The programs include remediation, individualized instruction, consultation with parents, and referral to community-based resources. Such programs may include individual counseling to improve study skills and increase achievement and feelings of self-worth. Crisis-oriented counseling provides intensive counseling for pregnant teenagers, students abusing alcohol or drugs, neglected or abused children or adolescents, youth from broken homes, and depressed or potentially suicidal youth.

There are more than 200 theoretically different approaches to counseling. However, the trend is toward eclectic counseling, which involves selecting counseling strategies/interventions/techniques that take into account the individual needs of the students. Counseling through learning styles is an eclectic approach that involves (1) assessing individual learning style preferences and (2) prescribing and utilizing counseling techniques that are compatible with these preferences. Students frequently have strong preferences for learning alone versus with peers versus with adults; learning through auditory versus visual versus tactual-kinesthetic modalities; requiring high versus low degrees of structure; or learning through global versus analytic modes. For example, auditory students will respond best to rational-emotive therapy; visual students should be exposed to biblio-counseling, reinforcement techniques which involve charting or graphing behaviors, and to social modeling through the use of videotapes in counseling; tactual-kinesthetic students learn optimally through role-playing situations, mime, psychodrama, or art therapy.

In addition to counseling students individually and in groups, the counselor's role includes orienting students to school; conducting case conferences with other student services personnel; advising students in course selection; assessing students in terms of scholastic aptitude, achievement, vocational interests, and personality, and interpreting results so that students have self-knowledge for educational-vocational decision making; working with administrators and teachers to infuse career education and psychological education into the curriculum; consulting with administrators, teachers, and parents in terms of students' needs; and providing college planning and job placement services. The American School Counselors Association has developed "Standards for School Counseling Programs" as well as role and function statements for both elementary school counselors and secondary school counselors.

The organization and administration of counseling and guidance services vary greatly among school districts. Large, urban school districts frequently establish a central division of student personnel services with a director, supervisors, and inservice personnel which provide educational, consultative, and programmatic resources to school counselors and other pupil personnel services workers. Small rural and suburban school districts may employ a director of student personnel services who is responsible for staffing school student-personnel programs and providing consulting services to school administrators. In any case, the school principal is frequently responsible for the counseling and student personnel services program within the school. The building principal is usually the immediate supervisor of the counselor and charged with evaluating counselor competence. As such, the principal is ultimately responsible for the planning, implementation, and evaluation of the counseling program.

The principal may appoint a coordinator of counseling, who shares some of the responsibility for program development. Appointment of a standing student-personnel services committee can facilitate program development and should be comprised of counselors, social workers, health personnel, school psychologists, teachers, administrators, and representative parents and students where appropriate. The organizational structure of the counseling program may follow a specialist model, with individual counselors responsible for particular grade levels and duties such as orientation, career education, college counseling, or a generalist model, with individual counselors responsible for all grade levels and following the same group of students throughout school. The caseload of counselors varies from 200 to 1,000 students, depending on counselor role and functions and school district resources.

Recent trends in counseling include (a) higher standards for the preparation of counselors, with many states requiring completion of 48-60 hour master's degree programs; (b) increased attention to the needs of special populations, such as the gifted, talented, disabled youth, minorities, and culturally-different youth; (c) the use of computers to facilitate counseling through computerized recordkeeping, course planning and selection, and the use of software packages in college and career planning; (d) inservice education programs for counselors to provide skills training and improved strategies for working with special problems and/or populations; (e) increased professionalism among school counselors, evidenced by participation in the American Association of Counseling and Development and its local, state, and regional affiliates; (f) counselors facilitating parent networking and community agency involvement in mentoring high risk students; and (g) movement away from an emphasis on crisis counseling for a few students toward developmental, programmatic counseling for all students.

See also Drug and Alcohol Use Among Students; Pupil Personnel Program; Student Absenteeism and Truancy; Student Alienation.

—Shirley A. Griggs
St. John's University

References

Griggs, S.A. (1985). *Counseling students through their individual learning styles.* Ann Arbor, MI: University of Michigan, Educational Resource Information Center for Counseling and Personnel Services.

Hansen, J., Stevic, R., & Warner, R. (1986). *Counseling: Theory and process.* Boston: Allyn & Bacon.

CURRICULUM COMMITTEE

One potentially useful approach to improving the school curriculum is the curriculum committee. Such committees can be established for a variety of reasons, including evaluating the curriculum, conducting needs assessments, developing curriculum guides, selecting textbooks, and proposing new curriculum content. The administrator can make an important contribution to the success of curriculum committees by carefully defining their charge; using good judgment in selecting the members; providing appropriate encouragement, recognition, resources, and training; and following through on the committee's recommendations.

Administrative Considerations

An important step at the outset is for the administrator to prepare the charge or mission of the committee carefully, specifying its objectives, function, scope, and authority. A clear, concise, realistic statement of the committee's charge will be effective in avoiding or minimizing subsequent problems.

Once the committee's charge has been defined, the administrator needs to give attention to the composition of the committee and how its members should be selected. Local circumstances will probably dictate whether the committee is selected by soliciting volunteers, by administrative appointment, or by a combination of the two. However, whichever selection method is used, several important factors need to be considered by the administrator. Committee members should possess strong interest in and motivation for pursuing the agenda and objectives of the committee. Casual interest or superficial motivation will not produce a sense of "ownership of the task" on the part of committee members, nor will it overcome problems or obstacles that may be encountered. However, committee members should also be selected for their objectivity. Individuals who are highly motivated but show a strong bias or an "axe to grind" could hinder the committee's effectiveness. Curriculum committee work requires an open mind on the part of committee members and an objective examination of facts and alternatives.

Whereas motivation and objectivity are important characteristics to look for in selecting curriculum committee members, the most significant selection prerequisite should be the prospective committee members' *expertise.* Although several individuals may be interested in serving on a curriculum committee and may possess the desired objectivity, the key question is whether they possess the desirable knowledge and skill. Curriculum committee work is often of a technical nature, requiring specialized knowledge and/or skill, and, unless that kind of expertise is represented on the committee, its efforts may not be productive. This does not mean that parents, students, and other so-called "nonexperts" should not serve on curriculum committees. It is conceivable that such people could make a potentially useful contribution to the committee's deliberations by offering a different perspective or special insight. Nevertheless, it is recommended that curriculum expertise be a prerequisite for the selection of most committee members.

If the committee members have been carefully selected, the functioning of the committee and the likelihood that its objectives will be achieved will be greatly enhanced. The particular *approach* the curriculum committee selects to reach its objectives will depend to some extent on the nature of those objectives. Recommended approaches to curriculum improvement that the administrator and the committee might consider may be found in the references following this article.

Regardless of which specific approach to curriculum improvement is adopted by the committee, most of its members are likely to possess greater specialized knowledge and/or skill in the curriculum than does the administrator. Therefore, the administrator's primary role in working with a curriculum committee should be that of a facilitator and motivator. One important facet of this role is to provide periodic encouragement and rewards to committee members. Committee work is frequently tedious, and periodic recognition of the value of a member's or group's efforts can pay dividends.

The administrator can also make an important contribution to facilitating the work of a curriculum committee by securing necessary resources, removing obstacles, and helping the committee to increase its problem-solving capabilities. In connection with the latter, the administrator may need to provide training—perhaps through the use of a consultant—to the members of a committee on how to function effectively as a group. The members of a curriculum committee may possess specialized knowledge and/or skill in some aspect of the curriculum and yet be relatively naive about the process of working together cooperatively and productively as a committee. Therefore, some type of in-service training may be needed.

Once a curriculum committee has completed its work, the administrator should provide appropriate recognition to the members and should make every effort to implement the committee's recommendations. Studies have shown that one of the major criticisms teachers level at the use of committees is that there is very little administrative follow-through after the committee has completed its task. Whether or not this perception is valid is almost immaterial if committee members believe it to be true. Although the administrator may not always find it possible or even desirable to implement all of the curriculum committee's recommendations, the committee should be provided a rationale regarding the rejection of any recommendations, as well as an opportunity to ask questions of the administrator regarding the outcome of their proposal.

See also Curriculum Development; Curriculum Evaluation; Curriculum Implementation; Program Evaluation.

—Richard A. Gorton
University of Wisconsin-Milwaukee

References

Lowell, J.T., & Wiles, K. (1983). *Supervision for better schools* (Chapter 8). Englewood Cliffs, NJ: Prentice-Hall.

Oliva, P.F. (1984). *Supervision for today's schools* (Chapters 7 and 8). New York: Longman.

Short, E.D. (1982). "Curriculum development and organization." In H.E. Mitzel (Ed.), *Encyclopedia of educational research* (pp. 405-12). New York: The Free Press.

CURRICULUM DEVELOPMENT

Administrators are at center stage in curriculum development. Their role in deciding what should be taught, to which persons, and under what rules of learning is becoming increasingly important. The decline of federal aid, tax limitations on state resources, and disenchantment with categorical programs for given learners has reversed the tendency to develop curriculum by costly additions in courses. Instead, administrators are focusing on maximizing curriculum content and coverage without increasing total resources. Local administrators are considering overall curricular configuration and upgrading teachers through curriculum development.

Although curriculum development is a shared responsibility with curriculum mandates from different authorities—federal, state, and local governments—it is the school administrator who must balance demands, fitting the curriculum parts together, giving over-all emphasis, and helping teachers respond to curricular policies as they create appropriate learning opportunities for the students in their classes. As always, changing social conditions, advances in the subject matter fields, and a new generation of learners hold implications for both what and how to teach.

Issues and Trends

Controversy in curriculum planning occurs because of a difference in curriculum orientation, and because of tensions among curriculum planners at three levels of decision making.

Curriculum Orientations. A big issue in curriculum planning is what orientation—academic, personal or social relevance, or basic skills—should dominate. Recent history has shown swings in direction from academic knowledge (1960s) to humanistic concerns and political action (1970s) to basic skills (early 1980s) to the present focus upon a core of academic content. Each orientation has a corresponding approach to curriculum development. For example, when basic skills are emphasized, curriculum development takes the form of alignment with national and state tests. High performance on the Scholastic Aptitude Test and statewide tests of achievement becomes the goal. "Essential" skills are defined and a list of items is distributed to teachers. Test items and instructional materials are matched to the corresponding skills. Administrators discuss the skill with teachers, making sure that they agree on what each skill objective means in terms of classroom instruction. Student performance is monitored on each skill, and the results from end-of-year testing are used in setting priorities for a subsequent year. Planning ensures that adequate time, materials, and methods will be given to improving performance.

Level of Curriculum. Curriculum is made at three levels. The formal curriculum is produced by state and local boards of education. The institutional curriculum is the curriculum of the total school which reflects the formal curriculum as adapted by the local school. The instructional curriculum represents the teachers' perceptions of what the curriculum means in practice and what teachers actually do. Although administrators are primarily responsible for developing the institutional curriculum, they must attend to the formal curriculum and help teachers develop plans that are consistent with state and district curriculum decisions.

Recommended Approaches

In their curriculum development activity, local administrators attend to important content identified in state frameworks and district curriculum guides. Their unique role, however, is that of creating a school that is characterized in some positive direction and responsive to the community and students at hand. Basic to this task are considerations about curriculum functions, organizing elements, and organizing structures, and, at the classroom level, the selection of learning opportunities.

Curricular Functions. In designing their institutional curriculum, administrators may choose to serve one or more functions—socialization, intellectual development, self actualization of learners. In serving multiple interests, they indicate differentiated functions for programs and courses: (a) *general education*—core courses that all students take; (b) *specialization*—courses for those who intend to pursue an area of study as a vocation; (c) *exploration*—courses that help students learn about themselves in relation to a field of study; and (d) *remediation*—courses for helping students overcome particular deficiencies.

The function of general education is currently at the fore. All students are expected to have common learnings in science, mathematics, language, history/social science, physical education, and visual and performing arts. Administrators are addressing problems of access and coherence. With respect to access they are asking, "What are the trends in enrollment by subgroups? Why has enrollment in some courses increased or decreased? What are the criteria for student access to courses? What do students see as barriers to taking particular courses? If there is tracking, what effect does it have on instruction, content, self image?" In addressing coherence, administrators ask, "Are courses sequential or otherwise articulated? Do teachers and students see connections and continuity? Are courses related to functions of the school?"

Sequence. As a criterion, sequence stresses the importance of having each successive learning experience (lessons and courses) build upon the preceding one but go more broadly and deeply into the matter involved. A second criterion in organizing a coherent curriculum is *integration*—provision for relating key learning in one course to what is taught in other courses. Integration is to help students get a unified view of knowledge and to encourage the application of important concepts, values, and processes.

Organizing Elements. In planning curricula that meet the criteria of sequence and integration, the administrator must identify the elements that will serve as organizing threads. Often these elements are subject-matter theories, concepts, principles, and processes that are to be treated in a number of courses within a program of studies. The subject-matter elements are usually found in frameworks and curriculum guides. In addition to subject-matter elements the administrator must identify the key elements that represent the values of the school—inquiry, social service, creative problem solving. Later, the administrator will want to know how teachers in every course are giving students an opportunity to engage in activities that involve the selected elements.

Organizing Structures. In attending to the organizing structures, the administrator has great influence over the direction of the curriculum. Structure refers to programs, courses, and areas of study that are to be offered. Structure is also related to function and to curriculum orientation. Designating courses by their subject-matter title—mathematics, foreign language—signals an academic orientation. A broad fields designation—women's movement, problems in democracy—indicates emancipation. By offering courses with titles such as stress reduction and expression through the arts, the administrator indicates a concern for individuality and remediation. It is possible to serve both the interests of those concerned with the teaching of powerful intellectual ideas (academic knowledge) and those concerned with critical community needs. Key concepts in mathematics and science, for example, can be taught by selecting an organizing structure that focuses upon a community concern—vocational education, health, or environmental matters.

Although the topic of the organizational structure is important in its own right, the structure offers a good way to acquire and apply the key elements from the subject fields and elements reflecting the institution's values. There are variations in organizing within broad field structures. There may be seminars "in the round" where social problems are addressed by students and teachers who represent several academic subjects, all bringing knowledge of their fields to bear on the problem, or two or more academic courses can be taught parallel to a social-problems course dealing with a theme of importance to the local community. The systematized resources gained in the academic courses are applied in the problems course.

It should be clear that just as administrators should select structure that reflect community interest and give opportunity for acquisition of key elements of subject matter and values, so, too, should teachers be encouraged to select organizing foci—topics, problems, experiments, projects—that will bring coherence to lessons and relate organizing elements to activities that are of concern to students. The administrator's role in instructional decision making includes seeing that the instructional units selected or developed by teachers meet these criteria: (a) Have intrinsic worth; (b) are instrumental in giving students opportunity to acquire the values and subject matter specified as organizational elements; (c) integrate learning from several sources; (d) appeal to the interests and concerns of students; (e) offer the possibility of desirable unanticipated spinoffs; and (f) accommodate a variety of learner abilities, interests, and learning styles.

The learning opportunities that are planned within each instructional unit should take into account the philosophy, rationale, goals, and recommended content for each grade level as given in the state curriculum framework and the suggested instructional strategies and resources found in the local curriculum guide for the course and grade. The school's own organizational threads should be added to the elements given in the framework and guides.

Teachers should have the responsibility to prepare the instructional units or foci and accompanying instructional activities. They should ask, "What questions do my students have that may serve as a vehicle for developing the key elements and their relations? How can I lay foundations and extend the students understanding of the elements? What are the prerequisites for successful participation in the unit and activities I'm proposing? Do my students have these prerequisites, or should the teaching of them be my priority? Why do I think students will find the activities satisfying? Will the unit and activities contribute to a range of outcomes—intellectual, affective, social, cognitive?"

The selection of appropriate teaching methods and strategies—discussion, inquiry, simulation, direct teaching lessons, synectics—should be in accordance with the school's curriculum design—functions, organizational elements, as well as with consideration of learner characteristics and the teachers' preferred methods.

See also Curriculum Committee; Curriculum Evaluation; Curriculum Implementation; Program Evaluation.

—John D. McNeil
University of California, Los Angeles

References

McNeil, J.D. (1985). *Curriculum: A comprehensive introduction* (3rd ed.). Boston: Little Brown.

Short, E.D. (1982). "Curriculum development and organization." In H.E. Mitzel (Ed.), *Encyclopedia of educational research* (pp. 405-12). New York: The Free Press.

Wulf, K.M., & Schave, B. (1984). *Curriculum design: A handbook for educators.* Glenview, IL: Scott, Foresman.

CURRICULUM EVALUATION

Good organizations have clear goals and know how well the goals are being achieved. Evaluation is the process of judging the extent to which goals have been achieved. In good organizations and in good schools, time and money are invested in evaluation. When effectiveness is assessed, all organizational members must pay attention to the organization's goals, which improves the chances that a renewed commitment to those goals will occur. Research studies consistently indicate that successful organizations and successful schools employ people who share a commitment to organizational goals.

It is also clear that external pressure has created compelling reasons to evaluate curricula. More than 40 national reports have been published which identify problems with American education. Whatever the merits of the reports, they have established a widespread belief that something is wrong with education. If what is wrong is particular, not universal, it is necessary to evaluate programs in order to distinguish between what should be changed and what should not.

Another set of reasons to evaluate curricula emerges from recent research on effective schools. These studies have identified factors which correlate with student achievement. Although there are criticisms of many of the studies, they produce an interesting consensus about good school practices which is consistent with common sense. The identification of good school practices can become a basis for evaluating curricular programs.

A final set of reasons to evaluate curricula derives from the needs of teachers. Demographers suggest that the average age of faculties is increasing. Administrators are searching for activities which will motivate teachers, hardened by experience, to renew their enthusiasm for and commitment to teaching. Properly structured evaluation activities can provide such opportunities.

All organizations need clear, systematic procedures for determining how well they are working. These procedures produce decisions about how to allocate resources (time, money, and energy) which are invariably scarce. Curriculum evaluation is in the self-interest of a school system, with or without external motives to conduct it.

Issues and Trends

An administrator facing decisions about how to conduct an evaluation of curricular programs faces a bewildering variety of choices. It is important for administrators to remember that evaluation has become a business in education, with many providers of evaluation service competing for the support of schools. Testing companies, professors, state departments of education, and accrediting agencies claim that their approach to curriculum evaluation will best suit the needs of school districts. It is essential that administrators, prior to examining trends in curriculum evaluation, clarify for themselves general objectives about what an evaluation process should do for their schools.

It is not possible in a short article to review all of the developments in curriculum evaluation. A few trends, however, seem most relevant to school administrators who want to create sound and effective evaluation systems. The most significant of these trends is the growing belief among professional evaluators that curriculum evaluation is more than the aggregation of test scores and less than a full-blown research project.

Evaluation is not research. It is, by definition, judgment about how well something works, designed to produce either a compelling defense of present practices and/or a compelling argument for changing what is done. In that respect, evaluation judgments must be based on credible data, or they will not be compelling. Good evaluation must be *used*. In order for use to result from an evaluation, those responsible for implementing findings must believe them. Many of the giants in the field of evaluation who once believed that hard data about curricular effectiveness spoke for themselves have now come to believe that effective evaluation requires using different sorts of data, believable to those who are involved in the evaluated program, as a basis for evaluation judgments. When evaluation judgments are not believed, evaluation results will be resisted, sabotaged, and largely ignored. (For a detailed discussion of this trend, see the references listed following this article).

There are three areas of curriculum evaluation activities on which school administrators should focus. First, many states have mandated activities which they call evaluation. These mandated evaluations may simply require that achievement tests be given, but may require more extensive reviews of how well a school or school system is doing what a state legislature thinks it ought to be doing. In some states, however, the methods by which a mandated evaluation is conducted at the local level are open to local modification. When this is the case, the ideas included later in this article should be used to increase the chances that the evaluation will produce useful results.

A second area in which great change has occurred involves the evaluations required by accrediting agencies. If a school is accredited, it must complete some sort of evaluation periodically. The form of these evaluations was once standard. Now, however, many of the largest accrediting agencies have promoted variety in the evaluation methods their members use. If this is the case, the school administrator has an excellent opportunity to achieve his or her own objectives for an evaluation at the same time an accreditation requirement is being met.

The third area for consideration involves locally initiated evaluation projects. In this area, consultants abound. The important thing for administrators to remember, however, is that whatever evaluation approach is adopted, it must have acceptable local purposes and employ methods which are consistent with those purposes. Without a consideration of how decisions are actually made in local districts or a concomitant consideration of how large an investment the district can make in getting an evaluation done, no evaluation system will produce usable results.

The most important practice in curriculum evaluation is that the administrator decide, in advance, exactly what purposes the evaluation is to accomplish and what methods will be used to achieve those purposes. To do this, it is recommended that a committee consisting of administrators, a school board member, and teachers be constituted to plan the evaluation. This group can hear options for evaluation presented by representatives from accrediting agencies, universities, the State Department of Education, and private consultants. By clarifying purposes and procedures in advance, however, the school protects itself from aimless and/or extraneous evaluation effort.

Any good curriculum evaluation must involve teachers in assessing the quality of curricular programs. In that respect, it is essential that the administrator guarantee that personal evaluation is a separate and distinct activity from curriculum evaluation. Evaluation is, by its nature, perceived as a threat to teachers. Personnel evaluation is a normal and necessary practice in schools, but should be kept apart from curriculum evaluation. Teachers must participate in curriculum evaluation activities because they, ultimately, will be those who must implement any evaluation findings in their classrooms. Moreover, the discussion among teachers about what works and what does not work in a curricular program is widely believed to be of intrinsic value and widely documented to be all too absent in schools.

Third, realistic expectations for evaluation must be set. Most school evaluations do not produce dramatic results. Programs are neither abolished nor found to be perfect. It is more likely that findings will identify areas of emphasis which could be changed or practices which seem to be effective. The administrator must convince the school board, the other administrators, and the teaching staff that a curriculum evaluation is not going to produce either catastrophic or revolutionary results. It will not, in short, be a panacea. A good evaluation will produce valid and reliable findings about a limited set of important questions. The findings will be supported by credible data. A realistic set of expectations about the process will prevent involved parties from believing that everything they do not like about the program will change as a result of the evaluation and from believing that their worst fears about what might change will actually occur.

Fourth, the administrator must understand that evaluation is a political activity and take measures to ensure that the results are not completely the product of self-interest. Evaluation is political because it results in the allocation of power, status, and money. It is natural that, given the stakes of evaluation, administrators, teachers, school board members, and public interest groups will use the process to further their own ends. It is possible to structure an evaluation process using a system of checks and balances, so that no one group's definition of what a program should be automatically prevails. Such a system is characterized by preplanning, which identifies in advance the rules of analysis that will be used in the evaluation and subjects the tentative findings of the evaluation to the scrutiny of an evaluation policy group, which might include representatives of all the parties who are going to be affected by the evaluation's results.

Finally, the administrator should see to it that the methods to be used in the evaluation are clear, unambiguous, and practical. This can be done by carefully reviewing each task the evaluation project will require before the project begins. The corollary rule is that enough time and/or dollar resources are set aside, in advance, to allow for the tasks to be completed. Well-thought-out evaluation projects can and do fail when those expected to complete a set of tasks do not understand them, find that the tasks do not seem relevant to the project's purposes, or lack the time and money to complete them. Carefully examining the proposed methods for any evaluation project early in the planning process will minimize the chances that the purposes of the project will be thwarted by methods that are too difficult or too impractical to be implemented.

Strategies for Implementation

Successful evaluation projects are planned. Prudent administrators commit their evaluation plans to writing, using a group to do the writing that includes persons from the key groups who will be affected by the evaluation's findings. The final plan is then submitted to the school board for approval. By creating a written plan, two common mistakes in evaluation are avoided. First, no parties can claim that they were not included in the planning of the project and, as a result, refuse to accept the rules of analysis the plan includes. Second, all parties know in advance just what the project entails, what it is for, and what provisions will be made to get the work done.

Successful evaluation projects have a clear focus. Too many curriculum evaluation projects collect too much data to be digested and/or address issues which, while interesting, are not essential. Administrators should insist on a focus in the evaluation project.

Successful evaluation projects do not overload either the school system or those who work in it. Administrators know how much change their schools can absorb at one time, how many dollars are available for evaluation work and follow-up, and how ready school personnel are for dealing with change. An increasing number of administrators have developed, for these reasons, cyclical approaches to curricular evaluation, examining only two or three curricular areas at a time over, for example, a five-year cycle. Such an approach allows for a more gradual phase-in of evaluation findings. At least one accrediting agency, the North Central Association, accepts this model to meet its evaluation requirement. Whatever model of evaluation is used, however, it is the administrator's responsibility to make sure that the project does not overtax the time, dollar, and energy resources of the school system.

Successful evaluation projects anticipate the need for implementation of evaluation findings. A major criticism of curriculum evaluation has been that it does not produce change. Implementation of results is often believed to be the responsibility of someone else. It is the administrator's responsibility to structure a logical, practical implementation process in advance of the evaluation project. An implementation process can be structured by designating a committee or individual to be responsible for implementation, by setting aside budget allocations for implementation, by asking for implementation reports from teachers, or by asking principals to reinforce teachers who use evaluation findings in their classrooms.

In this brief review of curriculum evaluation, it has been suggested that planning evaluations is the key to making them successful. It has also been suggested that the experts in curriculum evaluation support the idea that data collection and analysis should be consistent with the purposes of the evaluation project. Data from many sources should be considered when judging the effectiveness of curriculum. It has been strongly recommended that evaluation projects be realistic and practical, focusing upon important issues and not attempting to assess too many topics at once. Administrators can be confident that when they plan evaluation projects carefully in light of the realistic constraints they face in their school districts, it is possible to establish systematic and effective methods of curriculum evaluation.

See also Curriculum Committee; Curriculum Development; Curriculum Implementation; Program Evaluation.

—William R. Shirer
Mosinee School District
Mosinee, Wisconsin

References

Anderson, S.B., & Vall, S. (1978). *The profession and practice of program evaluation*. San Francisco: Jossey-Bass.

Cooley, W.L. (1983). "Improving the performance of educational systems." *Educational Researcher, 12*, 4-12.

Patton, M.Q. (1978). *Utilization focused evaluation*. Beverly Hills, CA: Sage.

CURRICULUM IMPLEMENTATION

Curriculum implementation historically has been one of the most, if not the most, neglected aspects of efforts to improve the instructional program. Most energy has been devoted to those activities related to curriculum development. The excitement that is found in the creation of new plans can be lost when the time arrives for putting the plans to work in the classroom. The best curriculum plans can be ineffective in influencing classroom instruction if equal attention is not given to curriculum implementation.

Potential Problems

One of the greatest problems with the implementation of curriculum plans occurs when consideration for implementation is disregarded during the curriculum-development stage. Some curriculum plans are developed without proper recognition of limitations regarding such things as financial and physical resources; time; the instructional, administrative, and support staff; and community needs and support. Enthusiasm for implementing a plan will be less than desirable when the people responsible for implementing the curriculum have no input in the development stage, or when a curriculum is adopted that has not been created or adapted locally as a result of an identified need.

Some administrators and supervisors view implementation as something that teachers do automatically, with no assistance other than being handed the curriculum plan. This behavior demonstrates a lack of consideration for the needs of teachers and is not unlike the behavior of a teacher who would hand an assignment to students without providing the necessary instruction.

A serious problem arises when teachers are told to do the best they can with the resources available. This communicates to the teachers a lack of concern about using the curriculum plan, and soon the teachers may disregard it completely. Administrators and supervisors in such school systems should be careful not to identify curriculum documents developed for their schools as being the curriculum that is being taught in the classrooms.

Vivid examples of problems created as a result of inadequate plans for implementation can be provided from past experiences in education. One of the most notable was that of the "new math" of the 1960s. New textbooks were printed, adopted by school systems, and distributed to teachers and students. In far too many instances this was done with little, if any, instruction for the teachers. The result was that teachers resisted, felt inadequate, were inadequate, and generally functioned inadequately in the instruction of students. Another such problem was found with the national science curricula of the 1970s. Those experiences should be sufficient to prevent a repeat of such behavior.

Recommended Approaches

A basic consideration to insure curriculum implementation is to plan the procedures for implementing as part of the curriculum development stage. This begins with a broad base of participation in the development stage by those who will be responsible for implementing the curriculum. Included in this development stage is an accepted recognition of the need for the curriculum being developed, resulting in feelings of ownership by those who will be using the plan.

Once a plan has been developed with proper participation, the plan should be presented for review and acceptance by the administrative, supervisory, and instructional personnel, as well as by the community. Community acceptance regarding controversial areas of the curriculum is especially important if the implementation is to be successful.

A time and sequence of events necessary to implement the plan needs to be established. This is required to determine where and when each part of the plan will be implemented at each level. Those plans and expectations then need to be communicated to all concerned individuals and groups.

An essential activity, many times overlooked, is that of securing input from teachers regarding the help they need to carry out the instructional program required by the plan.

Teachers will need to examine the plan carefully in order to identify those needs. Once they have examined the plan, they will know what will be required to help them implement the plan. Teachers may need help with such things as becoming acquainted with new instructional materials, learning new skills, better understanding the plan, selecting new materials, and generally developing a sense of security in using the plan. Teachers also should be involved in planning for those activities that they need.

Evaluation should be a part of the plan for implementation. The extent to which the curriculum has been implemented needs to be determined. Teachers' responses to the extent to which they are using the curricular plans will provide important information regarding such things as the selection of course content, emphasis on skill development, instructional procedures, selection and use of resources and facilities, and student evaluation. If it is found that teachers are not using the plan for the purposes intended, or are not using the plan as intended, further evaluation is required.

Two approaches can be used for determining reasons for nonuse of a curricular plan. One suggestion is to evaluate the procedures that were used to assist teachers in implementing the plan. Teachers can provide information about those activities to indicate which activities were helpful, which activities were not helpful, and what other activities may be needed if teachers are to use the plan as intended. The other approach is to evaluate the curricular plan to determine its usefulness as a plan for teachers to follow. Information can be gathered about the organization of the plan, the usefulness and clarity of objectives, suggested procedures and resources, and the evaluation strategies. Feedback from teachers regarding those parts of the plan will help to improve the plan as a useful document.

A final consideration for curriculum implementation is to evaluate student learning based on the plan that was implemented. This, then, will provide a basis for evaluating the existing curriculum and the continuance of the cycle of curriculum development.

See also Curriculum Committee; Curriculum Development; Curriculum Evaluation; Program Evaluation.

—Robert Krey
University of Wisconsin-Superior

References

Eye, G.G., Netzer, L.A., & Krey, R.D. (1971). *Supervision of instruction* (2nd ed., Chapter 16). New York: Harper & Row.
Oliva, P.F. (1984). *Supervision for today's schools.* New York: Longman.
Patterson, J.L., & Czajkowski, T.J. (1979, December). "Implementation: Neglected phase in curriculum change." *Educational Leadership, 37*(3), 204-06.

D

DECISION MAKING

Most authorities describe decision making as the process of making a choice from among alternatives. Some make the description broader, including the steps of defining the problem, generating alternatives to solve the problem, evaluating the alternatives, selecting the best alternative, putting the best alternative into effect, and then evaluating the results. In administrative and policy decision making, it probably is best to use the broader description because it helps the decision maker focus on important aspects of the process rather than ignoring them. Although some distinguish between decision making and problem solving, for many practical purposes they are similar. In "real life," as compared to laboratory studies, it is not entirely clear how people make decisions because decision making is influenced by such things as the values of the decision maker, the setting, pressures of the environment, other people and their values, and the like. The influences of these factors are not certain, and they are likely to be complex; they are also likely to interact with each other. Perfect decision making is probably impossible, but focusing on the process and making an effort to improve it are likely to make decision making more effective for both individuals and groups.

Individual Decision Making

The decision maker needs first to determine what the problem or the decision is. The person should try to separate symptoms from problems or problem causes as information and data are collected about the problem. For example, if an administrator observes that a certain school lunchroom is typically too noisy, the noise may be a symptom of other problems, such as inappropriate seating for students, poor acoustics, interpersonal difficulties among certain students, or a number of other things. Next, the decision maker needs to decide what would have to be true—or not true—if the problem were to be considered solved. Doing so will help establish criteria for finding a good problem solution. In the lunchroom example, one might say that noise below a certain level would be acceptable evidence of a good problem solution and the beginnings of a good decision.

Next, the decision maker needs to develop several possible problem solutions. Although brainstorming (rapidly listing alternatives without first evaluating them) is a well-known method for generating alternatives, other methods may be better for a given decision. Also, some

decisions are already dictated by rules, administrative regulations, policies, or law. Hence, the task is simply to choose which rule, regulation, policy, or law applies, and then do what is required, not generate unique problem solutions.

The next step is to select the "best" decision alternative. This is done by assessing such things as how likely the alternative is to work effectively, how much it will cost for a given level of benefit, how well accepted it will be, the extent to which resources are available to implement, what the consequences might be and the like. Frequently, it is helpful to write down the analysis of the alternatives in a systematic way beginning with the statement of what the problem is and the criteria that will be used to determine whether the problem has been solved.

Planning for implementation of the selected alternative is next. Typically an implementation plan will include the following ingredients: what the tasks are; who is to perform each; and the schedule and deadlines for task completion. Essential to an implementation plan is providing for communications to the right people at the right time about the right things. An evaluation of each step along the way and of the final result also is necessary.

Group Decision Making

It is not always best to involve a group in making a decision. If the outcome (decision) is already known and already prescribed, the decision is probably made best by an individual decision maker. The decision also is better left to an individual if the problem is not relevant to members of the proposed group. The decision should not be left to a group if the problem is beyond the group's expertise. On the other hand, there are circumstances which make a group decision almost necessary. A group should be called upon if broad support for the decision is needed, if politics require it, or if different viewpoints and new alternatives and approaches are needed. All such circumstances make a group decision better than an individual decision.

One key to effective group decisions is a leader who knows how to work with groups in decision making. This person is not always the official leader of the group or organization. Besides lacking the needed group skills, this person may cause the group (by virtue of his or her authority, personal power, or other factors) simply to rubber stamp a decision or course of action perceived by the group to be favored by the leader. It is better to have a person skilled at working with groups and a person, perhaps, not involved in the decision itself.

A second key to effective group decisions is documentation of both the group's deliberations and of the outcomes. These written items should be shared with all group members, since they serve as a "history" of the group's work, an important record, and a time-saver to clarify what is being done or has been done by the group in the past. Some groups have a skilled secretary or clerical person, or a noninvolved group member perform this important function. Some groups also keep a running record of group work on tear sheets posted on the wall in front of the group. These notes can be transcribed and copies distributed later to members of the group.

The third key in effective group decision making is awareness and skill of group members in dealing with the interpersonal nature of decision making. Group decision making, for example, typically is slower than individual decision making. Group members unaware of this may become frustrated and alienated from the group and even engage in disruptive horseplay or leave the meeting in angry frustration. "Hidden agendas"—unacknowledged or unspoken values, priorities, methods, or objectives—may complicate group work on a decision. Or, "steam roller" methods by the leader or one or more members of the group may cause some individuals to disengage themselves from the group intellectually and emotionally so that the resulting decision is not supported or is even sabotaged later.

Problems in Decision Making

A number of problems are common in both individual and group decision making: (a) failing to define the problem; (b) failing to secure enough accurate data and information about the problem; (c) using inappropriate methods for making the decision; (d) allowing emotion or nonrational factors to disrupt or hinder the process; (e) not generating enough or the right kind of alternatives if the decision situation permits other than stock or routine approaches; and (f) failing to consider timing an essential element in decision making—deciding too fast or too slowly or implementing the decision with too little speed or too great haste. Although the obvious way to avoid these problems is not to engage in the problem behavior, it is valuable also to reflect from time to time, while making decisions, on the process and components of decision making in order to monitor, evaluate, and improve.

See also Group Processes; Planning; Problem Identification.

—Hugh W. Fraser, Managing Partner
Fraser Associates

References

Gundy, A. (1981). *Techniques of structured problem solving.* New York: Van Nostrand Reinhold.

Janis, I., & Mann, L. (1977). *Decision-making: A psychological analysis of conflict, choice, and commitment.* New York: Free Press.

Sanderson, M. (1979). *Successful problem management.* New York: John Wiley.

DELEGATING AUTHORITY

Delegation of authority is the process which administrators use in allocating authority to the people who report to them. The four steps include assigning duties to subordinates, granting authority to carry out the duties, creating an obligation on the part of the subordinates to assume the responsibility for the tasks, and holding subordinates accountable for results.

Superintendents receive the authority to operate a school district from the local board of education. They must in turn delegate their authority to those who are responsible of carrying out the myriad activities of schools.

Successful administrators are those who can effectively delegate to their subordinates. They train subordinates to use authority wisely, and the administrators are willing to take risks because they cannot be absolutely sure how much authority a subordinate can manage.

Reasons for Delegating

There are many obvious reasons for delegating. Administrators cannot handle every task involved in operating a school district. Therefore, through delegation, administrators can focus their energies on the most crucial, high-priority tasks. Delegation also allows subordinates to grow and develop, which often means learning from their mistakes. In addition, delegation is needed because many administrators lack the knowledge to make all decisions intelligently. Perhaps the most positive reason for delegation is that subordinates will have greater pride in the results which are directly attributable to their own judgments.

Barriers to Delegation

The most common factor that blocks administrators from delegating authority to others is fear. For effective delegation to occur, administrators must be free of the fear of losing control, of losing status, of the tasks being done wrong, and of someone else's ability to do the job as well or better.

Another barrier to delegation occurs when administrators are not clear what their role is and they feel that they must perform all tasks personally. Related to this barrier is the lack of clarity on the part of administrators in stating what should be done.

In order to delegate effectively, administrators must possess a strong belief in themselves. Second, they must be willing to accept the help and support of others. And, finally, they must also operate on the basis of reality and truth.

Guidelines for Effective Delegation

Effective delegation occurs when the following guidelines are met:

1. Subordinates are involved in helping establish their authority and they have a written record which delineates the scope of their authority.

2. Subordinates' authority is tied directly to their responsibilities.

3. Subordinates can normally act without fear of overstepping their authority or having their actions reversed by their supervisors.

4. Subordinates' superiors, subordinates, and peers clearly understand the degree of authority that they have.

5. There is a sufficient control and feedback system regarding the performance of subordinates in carrying out their authority.

See also Administrative Authority.

—Richard Brown, President
Managing, Inc.

References

Bothwell, L. (1983). *The art of leadership* (Chapter 3). Englewood Cliffs, NJ: Prentice-Hall.

Hodgetts, R.M. (1979). *Management: Theory, process, and practice* (Chapter 6). Philadelphia: W.B. Saunders.

Megginson, L.C., Mosley, D.C., & Pietri, P.H. (1983). *Management: Concepts and application* (Chapter 9). New York: Harper & Row.

DEMOGRAPHIC TRENDS

In a recent issue of the periodical *American Demographics*, researchers concluded that the proportion of American children living in families characterized as extremely poor increased from 3.5 percent of the total population in 1968 to 5.1 percent by 1982. In a different report appearing in that same issue, researchers found that children reared in single-parent families had an educational attainment level one full year behind children reared in two-parent families. Although these demographic facts may impress some school district administrators as statistical minutia, a thoughtful application of population demographics can often aid planners in effectively matching district resources with the needs of their school community.

School districts differ in size and resources and in the school communities they serve, yet all school districts are faced with the same challenge: meeting educational needs with available educational resources. Many large, urban school districts in this country are now faced with a school population that is markedly different from previous populations. Large districts, and even many medium sized districts, are now faced with a student body that is increasingly more "needy" than in the past. Not only is this population poorer than in the past, it is also a population lacking those resources typically provided by a traditional, two-parent family. Therefore, many urban districts now provide free lunches and free breakfasts to their students.

Also, some districts provide free textbooks and some waive all student fees for students from poor families. Some districts are faced with a growing population of students that need bilingual instructional services, some districts are experiencing an increase in the number of students requiring exceptional education programs, and many districts provide free health care screening and free immunizations. Juxtaposed against this increasing need is an adult population that is growing both in size and in its reluctance to support these changing needs.

In order to administer effectively, school district administrators must understand not only the demographic characteristics of their student body, but also the demographic nature of the entire school community. In many communities, the school-aged population is only a fraction of the total district population. Additionally, the local adult population may be significantly different in its own needs. Many districts are now facing an increasing population of single-parent (especially female) families. These families may look to the school district to provide services that in the past were provided by two-parent families. Many school districts are noticing an increase in their preschool population and a concomitant increase in pressure for more preschool programs as a substitute for private day-care services. In some urban districts, increases in the minority population translate directly into increasing enrollment pressure on supplemental and remedial programs. Some rural districts have become popular retirement areas, and these districts may be faced with an adult community that has isolated itself from education problems and excused itself from any fiscal responsibility for public education.

Although national and regional demographic trends have an uneven impact on individual school districts, some of these trends are significant and should be monitored by district administrators. Population shifts tied to employment is a demographic trend that should be watched closely. The shift of jobs from the "rust belt" of the Northeast and Middle West to the "sun belt" of the South and Southeast has had an impact upon district enrollments, especially enrollments in large, urban districts. Recent population migrations away from the oil-producing states of the West and Southwest have also had an impact upon school district enrollments. Recent increases in the preschool population, the so-called "echo boom," have occurred in most areas of the country. Another demographic trend that districts should monitor closely is the increase in single-parent (mostly female) families. Data for the federal census indicates that single-parent families have significantly fewer resources than two-parent families. As the number of single-parent families increases in a district, so will the need for special services for this group of children increase. Lastly, census data indicate that the number of children of school age is decreasing while the number of elderly Americans is increasing. As the proportion of nonschool-aged Americans increases, school districts can expect less support for public education and increased pressure to fund public education from less traditional federal, state, and local tax sources.

Locating demographic data and information to use in school district planning often depends on the size of the district. Large, urban districts often have libraries that have been selected as repositories for federal census data. These districts have a convenient source of demographic data reflecting the region, state, and municipality where they are located. Small and medium-sized districts may have to contact the Bureau of the Census directly to solicit the information they need. A good starting point for federal census data is the Data Users Service Division, Customer Service, Bureau of the Census. Another good source of data is the state department of education, or a similar agency, and a department within state government that generates population projections for revenue sharing. The National Center for Educational Statistics, U.S. Department of Education, can also supply useful data and information, and the Educational Resource Information Center (ERIC) of the National Institute of Education is a reliable and comprehensive source. Many municipalities have a planning department that can supply demographic information as well as reports and analysis on local population trends.

See also Enrollment Projections; Financing of Schools.

—William Hinsenkamp
Milwaukee Public Schools

Reference

Hodgkinson, H.L. (1985). *All in one system: Demographics of education—Kindergarten through graduate school.* Washington, DC: Institute for Educational Leadership.

DEPARTMENT HEADS

The role of department head in public schools has been largely neglected in educational research and literature, especially in reform literature which addresses teaching as a career. One thesis in this literature is that the flat career profile of teachers is a restricting factor in attracting and retaining the most dynamic pool of educators. Many reform proposals and policies have addressed this problem by suggesting the development of a career ladder for teachers. Interestingly, the traditional department-head position has not been suggested (or even mentioned) as a rung on the career ladder or as an opportunity for career ascendancy in the teaching profession.

Perhaps the reason for the omission is that the department-head role, as traditionally defined or operationalized, is limited in terms of its perceived organizational importance. Often the position is narrowly conceived, requiring holders of the position to perform tedious tasks which demand little professional expertise—e.g., distribute written information, request and submit budget requisitions, poll the department faculty regarding instructional issues. The job may be designed in such a way that the position is seen by faculty members as little more than a nuisance or busywork, rather than an opportunity for demonstrating professional leadership or for gaining career ascendancy.

Some researchers have suggested that the role of department head be redefined as an instructional leadership position. One alternative is to expand the role of the school department head to include instructional supervision responsibilities. Although this proposal may hold promise for instructional improvement, it may run counter to many of the accepted norms of schools and of the teaching profession, especially norms of professional autonomy and expertise. Teachers may accept supervision from a superordinate (even then, reluctantly), but the practice of supervision by peers has not been widely or readily accepted.

Where peer supervision has been implemented, it has tended to be limited in scope (e.g., teachers receiving peer supervision only on a voluntary basis or from teachers outside the employing school or school district). Similarly, those teachers who serve as peer supervisors may feel uncomfortable with "changing sides of the fence" when having to critique the work of a colleague. Department heads who are expected to supervise faculty may feel that they are taking on administrative functions for which they are unprepared or not well-suited. In other words, "If I had wanted to be an administrator, I would have become one!" For these reasons, defining the department head as a supervisor of department faculty may be a rational or logical approach to expanding the position, but may not be an effective or functional solution given the norms of schools and teachers.

Perhaps a more viable image of the department head would be that of a "team leader" or "resource colleague"— one who provides curriculum leadership and develops and coordinates the instructional program—one who integrates and synthesizes instructional and organizational resources for his/her department or division—one who promotes group cohesiveness in instructional and professional norms and practice—one who acts as a leader or change agent within the department while serving as a representative or spokesperson for the department in the larger organizational context. This expanded role definition, while having more potential for improving instructional and organizational effectiveness than the typical department head role, also promises a more meaningful opportunity or incentive for recognition and fulfillment of leadership potential within the teaching profession.

This alternative definition or image of the department head is little more than words on a page, if the role is not operationalized in a way consistent with the purpose or intent of the position redefinition. In other words, applying a new position description is meaningless without adjusting the corresponding provisions for or structure of the position within the organization. If one of the purposes of the redefined role is to provide an opportunity for career ascendancy and leadership development within the teaching profession, then the position must be seen as one of responsibility and status within the organization, and the position must be filled by teachers who demonstrate leadership potential as well as professional competence and commitment.

There are many ways that an organization can portray the importance of the department head's role in the school. These may include simple "externals" or "perq's" such as private office space (with telephone), shared secretarial help, increased release time and extended contract year to perform duties, or meaningful salary supplements (at least equitable with those of extracurricular positions). Other evidence of the importance of the role is demonstrated by the amount or type of responsibility given to the position. Such responsibilities might include shared decisionmaking with curriculum specialists or building administrators on such issues as instructional revision and coordination, program development and implementation, organizational policies and procedures, and student services. Similarly, the type of teachers chosen as department heads makes a statement about the importance of the role. It may not be sufficient to choose the best teachers, but may be necessary to choose the teachers who have demonstrated their potential for professional leadership and a commitment to increased responsibility and ascendancy within the teaching profession.

The recent difficulty the teaching profession has experienced in attracting and retaining bright, capable, upwardly mobile professionals has been, in part, because of the limited opportunity for advancement, recognition, or status as a teacher. A redefinition and restructuring of the traditional department-head role within schools could offer promise, stimulation, and opportunity to professional teachers that heretofore has not been available in teaching as a career.

See also Administrative Roles; Administrative Tasks; Administrators, Beginning.

—Diana G. Pounder
Louisiana State University

References

Callahan, M.G. (1971). *The effective school department head.* West Nyack, NY: Parker.

Greenfield, W.D. (1985). "Value leadership: The department chair's role in instructional improvement." *Illinois School Research and Development, 21*(2), 22-27.

Sergiovanni, T.J. (1984). *Handbook for effective department leadership* (2nd ed.). Boston: Allyn & Bacon.

DESEGREGATION PLANS

Desegregation has been a major concern of school authorities since the United States Supreme Court ruled in 1954 that school segregation violates the constitutional rights of pupils. Segregation has customarily referred to the separation of black and white pupils in schools; although in its decision concerning Denver, the Supreme Court also stated that Hispanic children have been discriminated against in the Southwest and should be considered as a minority group to be desegregated in that part of the United States.

Although most plans for school desegregation have been mandated by legal authority, there have been school districts which developed and installed desegregation programs on their own initiative. One of the earliest was implemented in Berkeley, California; one of the larger districts to do so was Seattle. The Supreme Court has ruled that school boards have authority to implement plans in the absence of any mandate to do so.

In most cases, however, a court or other governmental agency will require a school system to develop and implement a desegregation plan. Such a required plan may consist of mandatory reassignments of pupils, provide opportunities for pupils to be reassigned voluntarily, or both. Therefore, when the terms "mandatory" and "voluntary" are used in reference to a desegregation plan, they most frequently refer to the methods of pupil reassignment rather than to the motivation underlying the decision to desegregate the school system.

Mandatory Desegregation Plans

It is generally considered that any mandatory plan should require the least effort possible which will result in effective school desegregation. Methods are presented here in order of increasing effort.

Changes in attendance zone lines. If contiguous school attendance zones enroll different racial groups, sometimes merely redrawing attendance boundaries might result in each racial group being represented in each school.

Contiguous pairing. Where predominantly black and predominantly white schools have contiguous attendance zones, pairing may be possible. Instead of having each school enroll all grades for its own attendance area, the two zones may be combined into one, with all children in some grades attending school in one building and all children in the other grades attending in the other building.

Clustering. When more than two racially identifiable schools are in the same area, they could be clustered. If there were two white schools and one black school, each of the white schools might enroll all children in grades 1-4 in its own attendance area plus half of the 1-4 children in the black school. The black school would then enroll all grade 5-6 children in all three attendance areas.

Single grade centers. This is a form of clustering. If the number of schools and children is large enough, one of the schools serves one grade for all of the attendance areas, and the other schools enroll all other grades in their home areas plus a proportion of the children from the zone of the single grade school.

New construction. When it becomes necessary to add or replace school buildings, new schools are located in such a way as to serve a racially representative group of children.

Noncontiguous pairing or clustering. This is the same as the pairing and clustering concepts described above, except that the combined schools are not located in close proximity to one another. This technique usually requires more transportation.

Satellite zones. A given residential area might be assigned to a school at some distance from the neighborhood. Using a six-grade elementary school as an example, children living in the satellite zone attend the distant school for all six grades. While pairing or clustering guarantees that each child experiences at least several grades at a school close to home, the satellite method requires some children to be away from their home area for all six grades while other children never leave their neighborhood school.

Voluntary Desegregation Plans

Voluntary plans are usually not totally optional, since school districts are often required to make voluntary transfers available, and frequently children must be nonvoluntarily transferred in order to make room for incoming pupils who have chosen to be reassigned. However, voluntary plans seem to be accepted by the public as less undesirable than mandatory plans. Voluntary plans usually involve magnet or specialty schools and/or intradistrict or interdistrict transfers.

Magnet or specialty schools. A magnet or specialty school is designed to appeal to parents and pupils through program attractiveness or the service offered. Enrollment by race is usually controlled so that the school will be desegregated.

"Service magnets" are schools that provide a service which is not available at other schools. An example is an "extended day" program, which appeals primarily to single-parent families or families in which both parents are employed outside the home. The program offers child care services both before and after the regular school day. The school day usually consists of a typical educational program.

"Enhanced program magnets" are schools which offer exceptionally strong instructional programs in all subjects or certain specialized areas of study. A college preparatory emphasis is typical of program enhancement across all subjects, whereas a math-science emphasis is an example of specialized programs. Other common specializations include fine and performing arts, career training, and health professions. Educators are constantly developing additional specializations.

"Curricular magnets" provide a special kind of curriculum or special style of instruction. Typical of this type are Montessori, open education, and traditional or fundamental schools.

Majority to Minority Transfers. Often referred to as "M-M transfer," this program makes it possible for individual children to transfer from schools in which their race is a majority to schools in which their race is a minority. In most cases the school district provides transportation. An example of M-M transfer is the "Permit with Transportation" program in Los Angeles.

Interdistrict Transfers. This program involves the voluntary transfer of children from districts in which their race is overrepresented to a district in which their race is underrepresented. In some cases an interdistrict transfer program is developed voluntarily through cooperative efforts of the school districts, parents, and community agencies. The Boston-area Metco plan is an example of this.

In Wisconsin, the state has mandated that school systems in the Milwaukee area consider voluntary interdistrict transfers and has provided financial incentives to both sending and receiving school districts. This is commonly referred to as the "Chapter 220" program.

Federal courts have mandated the institution of voluntary interdistrict transfer programs in several states, including Michigan (Benton Harbor area) and Missouri (St. Louis area). In these cases, where the courts found state culpability for segregation of schools, courts have ordered that the state pay some or all of the cost of the transfer program.

See also Magnet Schools; Minorities and the School System; Multicultural Education; Transportation Management.

—Michael J. Stolee
University of Wisconsin-Milwaukee

References

Foster, G. (1973). "Desegregating urban schools: A review of the techniques." *Harvard Educational Review*, 43(1).

Hawley, W.D. et al. (1981). Volume I: *Strategies for effective desegregation: A synthesis of findings. Assessment of current knowledge about the effectiveness of school desegregation strategies.* Nashville, TN: Center for Education and Human Development Policy, Institute for Public Policy Studies.

Orfield, G. (1978). *Must we bus?* Washington, DC: The Brookings Institution.

DIRECT INSTRUCTION

Direct instruction is a summary term for recent findings on effective teaching. It refers to a systematic method of teaching with emphasis on proceeding in small steps, checking for student understanding, and achieving active and successful participation by all students. The term "direct instruction" is interchangeable with other terms such as "explicit teaching," "active teaching," "systematic instruction," and "interaction teaching."

Although the findings on direct, explicit teaching come primarily from research conducted on effective teaching of reading and mathematics, their procedures are relevant to any instruction where the object is to teach an explicit procedure, an explicit concept, or a body of knowledge. Specifically, these results are most applicable to teaching mathematics concepts and procedures, reading decoding and sight reading, English grammar, historical knowledge, and science knowledge and procedures.

These findings are less relevant for teaching in areas which are implicit, that is, where the skills to be taught do not follow explicit steps. Thus, these procedures are less relevant for teaching mathematics problem solving, analysis of literature, writing term papers, or discussion of social issues. Of course, basic knowledge is an important prerequisite for mastering implicit areas; however, it is not sufficient.

The research has found that effective teachers in explicit teaching use most of the following skills: (a) begin a lesson with a short statement of goals; (b) begin with a short review of previous, prerequisite learning; (c) present new material in small steps, with student practice after each step; (d) give clear and detailed instructions and explanations; (e) provide a high level of active practice for all students; (f) ask a large number of questions, check for student understanding, and obtain responses from all students; (g) guide students during initial practice; (h) provide systematic feedback and corrections, particularly during the initial learning stages; (i) obtain a student success rate of 80 percent or higher during initial practice; and (j) provide explicit instruction for seatwork exercises, and, where necessary, monitor students during seatwork.

The emphasis in direct, explicit instruction is teaching in small steps with student practice after each step, guiding students during initial practice, and providing all students with a high level of successful practice. All teachers utilize some of these behaviors some of the time, but research has shown that the most effective teachers use them, in a systematic manner, almost all of the time.

The Steps in Direct Instruction

Some investigators look upon direct instruction as a set of teaching steps or functions. The following six functions are a useful way to summarize the research on direct instruction or systematic teaching:

1. *Review and check previous work.* When teaching skill subjects such as reading, mathematics, foreign language, and grammar, effective teachers begin with homework correction and a short review of previous work. Students then will be firm in their knowledge and able to apply it to the current lesson. Typical techniques include review of vocabulary or previously learned skills (as in mathematics or foreign language), quizzes on the chalkboard or overhead, or short quiz sheets. These activities usually take from two to eight minutes.

Effective teachers also review materials prerequisite for new learning. They review previous material, for example, before proceeding with science and social studies instruction, and review the steps in effective writing before the class starts an assignment. Less effective teachers review less often.

2. *Presenting new material.* Effective teachers introduce new material or procedures by giving a series of short presentations with detailed instructions and examples and then check for student understanding. When appropriate, the teacher gives both positive and negative examples, and models the steps in procedures. The teacher stays on the topic and avoids digressions because a change of subjects may confuse the learner.

3. *Guided practice.* After each step in the presentation, when teaching concepts and procedures, or after longer presentations when appropriate, the teacher guides the students as they work problems or answer questions. Some teachers use procedures which involve all students, such as having all students work the problems, or, when questions are asked, having each student tell the answer to his/her neighbor, write the answer on a chalkboard, or raise a finger if they agree with someone's answer. The purpose of this guided practice and active participation is to help students become fluent in their responses.

When teaching a procedure with many steps (e.g., computing an average or multiplying by a three digit number), then it may be too difficult for the children and may lead to errors if all the steps are taught at once. In such cases, each step is taught separately and students have guided practice on one step before they are taught the second step. The number of steps which are taught at one time depends upon the difficulty of the material and the ability of the children.

4. *Provide feedback and correctives.* When students make errors or are confused during guided practice, more effective teachers provide hints, break the questions down, and/or reteach the material. Less effective teachers simply give the answer or call on another student.

5. *Supervise independent practice*. After sufficient guided practice, when most of the students can work alone without error, independent practice begins. The purpose of independent practice is to help the students achieve smooth, fluid, automatic performance. Higher level thinking and transfer is facilitated when the basic skills are overlearned and automatic so that learners can then focus themselves fully on the new tasks.

Effective teachers circulate during independent practice, or, if they are working with a second group, show students how to get help if they need it. Frequently, independent practice is continued as homework.

6. *Weekly and monthly review*. Effective teachers have weekly and monthly reviews and testing. These reviews and tests provide the additional (successful) practice that students need to become smooth performers, capable of applying their skills to new areas.

Some Teaching Examples

Direct instruction or explicit teaching is most readily applicable when teaching explicit procedures such as mathematics and science procedures, or in teaching explicit concepts such as parts of a flower, distinguishing fact from fiction. Grammar can be taught explicitly. Whatever the subject, the teacher begins with a review of background material, then presents the new material, then guides students through initial practice, and finally supervises them during independent practice.

Thus, in teaching the concepts of fact and fiction, the teacher would first explain the concepts, and then check for understanding by giving examples and asking the students to explain why each one is fact, fiction, or undetermined. During guided practice, the teacher guides the students as they work many examples—first as a group and then individually—providing corrections and restatements of the rules when students make errors. Finally, students would be asked to list their own examples of fact and fiction, first with feedback from the teacher and then working alone.

The results of research on teaching have shown that, for explicit areas, when teachers modify their instruction and do more direct, explicit teaching, student achievement improves with no detriment to student attitudes toward school or self.

See also Back-to-Basics; Individualization of Instruction; Instructional Objectives; Mastery Learning.

—Barak Rosenshine
University of Illinois

References

Gagne, R.M. (1970). *The conditions of learning* (2nd ed.). New York: Holt, Rinehart, & Winston.

Hunter, M. (1978). *Improved instruction*. El Segundo, CA: TIP Publications.

Rosenshine, B.V. (1983). "Teaching functions in instructional programs." *Elementary School Journal, 83*, 335-51.

DISADVANTAGED STUDENTS

The notion of educational disadvantage became prominent in the mid-1960s when theories regarding the relationships among poverty, race, and educational achievement were developed and debated. Most definitions of "disadvantage" incorporated poverty as a prominent feature, but the mechanism by which poverty was supposed to have an educational impact on children was never resolved. Some theorists argued that poor children suffered from poor nutrition, and that this hindered their ability to learn in school. Others argued that poor children were culturally deprived, or culturally different, or that they simply lacked the material resources, such as books, that were available to other children.

Research indicates that the statistical relationship between family poverty and children's achievement in school is not particularly strong. That is, many poor children do quite well in school, whereas many not-so-poor children do not do well. This fact makes a theory of disadvantage even more difficult to articulate. On the other hand, the relationship between poverty and achievement among *schools* is strong. Schools which serve large numbers of poor students are highly likely to show lower average achievement levels than other schools do, a phenomenon that has yet to be explained adequately.

Problems associated with defining disadvantage and with measuring it statistically have made it difficult for educators to target special services to disadvantaged students. The federal compensatory education program, now Chapter 1 of the Education Consolidation and Improvement Act of 1981 and formerly Title I of the Elementary and Secondary Education Act of 1965, uses a three-stage procedure for allocating funds. First, funds are allocated among counties on the basis of the number of children residing in the county who are counted as poor by the census. Second, states are required to allocate each counties' funds among school districts on the basis of a poverty count measure that the state has available and that the federal educational agency approves of. Third, school districts are required to place their compensatory education programs in those schools with the highest concentrations of children from low-income families. All three of these steps recognize the fact that educational achievement is related to the proportion of poor children in an area; efforts are made to place services in those areas with the greatest numbers of low-income children. However, once the schools are selected, the rules require that individual children be selected on the basis of their achievement scores, rather than on the basis of their family poverty status, so that children who are poor but who have no educational need are not served by the program.

As of 1986, sixteen states also funded compensatory education programs, and four others distributed state funds with a formula that took into account the presence of poor children in the district. Within those sixteen states which provide guidance regarding the use of their compensatory education funds, most require districts to select students on the basis of their achievement scores, and several tie their state compensatory education funding levels to the results of a state assessment.

The nature of services that should be provided to disadvantaged children has also been debated at length. One school of thought, the most prominent one, holds that the most important point of influence is during the preschool years. Services provided at this time can better prepare children to enter school by providing them with basic readiness skills and with the health and nutrition services they need in order to develop properly. Parents are trained to become better educators at home. The federally-funded Head Start program builds on this model, and provides a range of services to three- and four-year-old children from low-income families.

The most extreme alternative view is that services should be provided to adolescents, as a dropout prevention mechanism or as a way of insuring that students have some minimum level of competency before they graduate from high school. Opponents to this view argue that waiting until students are in high school risks losing them altogether, for they become so alienated as to be beyond help by that time. On the other hand, opponents to the early childhood approach argue that children are rarely helped to the point where they no longer need assistance, and it is inefficient to provide extra help year after year for these students as they progress through school. Some research has indicated that early interventions can have long-term effects, but the relative advantages of early versus later assistance have not been studied.

Yet another view argues that disadvantaged children may actually have different learning styles that make it difficult for them to comprehend lessons as they are normally presented; therefore, the important characteristic of compensatory education is not when it is provided but how it is provided. Under this view, the compensatory education program should attempt to teach children by using alternative materials or learning modes. Research has not supported this view, however.

The bulk of services provided by school districts are provided to students who are in the elementary grades. Students are pulled from their regular classes to receive special reading and/or mathematics instruction, provided by specialist teachers or aides. These services may be provided three to five days a week, with sessions lasting anywhere from twenty minutes to forty-five minutes. Available research suggests that the strongest approach is for the compensatory education teacher to use the same curriculum as the regular reading or math teacher, and to work together with the regular teacher to coordinate instruction.

See also Compensatory Education; Dropouts; Head Start.

—Mary Kennedy
Michigan State University

References

Clark, R.M. (1983). *Family life and school achievement: Why black children succeed or fail.* Chicago: University of Chicago Press.

Jencks, C., Acland, H., Bane, M.J., Cohen, D., Gintis, H., Heyns, B., & Michelson, S. (1981). *Inequality: A reassessment of the effects of family and schooling in America.* New York: Harper & Row.

Kennedy, M.M., Jung, R.K., & Orland, M.E. (1986). *Poverty, achievement, and the distribution of compensatory education services.* Washington, DC: United States Government Printing Office.

DISRUPTIVE STUDENTS

Disruptive students are those who are perceived as interfering with the teaching/learning process. It is important that disruptive behavior be understood in the context it occurs since any student may disrupt the orderly flow of activities in a school or classroom; depending on the circumstances, such students may be disturbed or, alternatively, they may simply be disturbing to others. The students of greatest concern to the school disciplinarian should be those who cause physical or mental harm to others. Students who interfere with school activities through vandalism must also be of serious concern to school authorities. When the disturbances are created because students are unusual in their appearance, or because they exhibit unusual behavior or thoughts, disciplinary action may be unwise, or even unlawful.

Identification

Disruptive students are typically identified by the classroom teacher. Teachers handle discipline problems themselves, but they may refer more serious problems to the school principal, vice principal, or other disciplinarian. Alternatively, the teacher may request that a school counselor see the child. If the student is habitually disruptive, or if the disruptive episodes are of a particularly serious nature, the teacher may request that the school psychologist evaluate the student for possible placement in a resource room, or in a class for the socially maladjusted, behaviorally disordered, or emotionally disturbed. Prior to the psychological evaluation, the psychologist will discuss the reasons for referral with the teacher, or with other witnesses to the child's behavior. The psychologist will compile a history of the problem which will include information about the student's family, medical history, and any unusual events in the student's life. This history should also include any special strengths which the family or student may demonstrate; such strengths could provide the building blocks for future remedial programs. The psychological evaluation will include an individually administered test of intelligence, and a battery of achievement tests. Unusually high or low scores on any test should suggest areas for further investigation. Unusually low intelligence test scores might indicate that the student is frustrated in school, or that he or she does not understand the components of appropriate behavior. Very high intelligence test scores may suggest that the student is frustrated in school, or that others do not understand the student's needs or behaviors. Similarly, unusual achievement test scores may indicate that the student's disruptive behavior results from his or her needs not being adequately met.

Evaluation instruments which may supplement identification of disruptive students include several psychological tests which require the child or adolescent to project his or her feelings by telling stories about pictures which are neutral in meaning. If a student repeatedly returns to disturbing themes when taking such tests, the psychologist or psychiatrist will use that information in arriving at a diagnosis for the student. Students with very serious problems may be sent to a special day school, and those with extremely serious problems may be institutionalized. If the psychologist finds no psychosocial basis for the problem, the student may be referred for neurological evaluation. Youngsters with serious conflicts are often referred for further evaluation.

Issues

Since 1978, federal law has required that no student be excluded from school because of a handicapping condition. If certified psychological examiners identify a student as seriously emotionally disturbed, that student may not be expelled from school, but he or she must be provided with appropriate special education in the least restrictive environment possible. An offense which might be punishable by expulsion if committed by a typical student may not be punishable by expulsion if committed by a student who has been found to be handicapped by emotional problems.

In 1954, education was determined to be a constitutional right under the Fourteenth Amendment (*Brown v. Board of Education*). Since 1967, all minors have had constitutionally protected due process rights. Thus, no student may be excluded from school without appropriate hearings which follow due process requirements (*Goss v. Lopez*, 1975). Students' constitutional rights include those provided by the First Amendment. Students may engage in free speech, including free symbolic speech (as in the wearing of armbands), which may not be prohibited unless there is substantial interference with school activities or with the rights of others. The exclusion of students from school or from extracurricular activities will not generally be supported by the courts unless the student presents a substantial or material danger to the school. The courts have generally ruled that any specific disciplinary measures should reflect the educational goals of the school. However, the Supreme Court (*Ingraham v. Wright*, 1977) has ruled that corporal punishment is not cruel and unusual punishment provided that certain specified due process procedures are followed. Futuristic issues may include the right to privacy versus the convenience of psychological testing and obedience to authority versus negotiation between educators and students.

A few research studies indicate that educators may be overly concerned about conflict in the classroom. Classroom disputes, even noisy disputes, often encourage independent thinking and creativity. Since creative behavior necessarily departs from the usual ways of thinking and acting, such behavior may easily be labeled as "disruptive" with unfortunate consequences for students and for educators.

Some disruptive behaviors may be the result of cultural differences; the origins of such differences may be ethnicity, social class, gender, etc. Many cultures are present oriented rather than future oriented; in such cases, students may be more concerned with the joys of the moment than with school work which requires a delay of present gratification for anticipated future rewards. Similarly, some cultural groups emphasize group cooperation rather than individual competition; this may interfere with classwork that requires competitive responses, as in spelling contests. Many misunderstandings can arise when the cultural groups to which school personnel belong differ significantly from those to which the students belong.

Corrective Measures

Disruptive behaviors may be eliminated in several ways: by changing the disruptive student, by changing the setting in which the behavior occurs, and by resolving the problems that are associated with disruptive behavior. Disciplinarians most frequently expect to change the disruptive student. A clear cut example is the use of a variety of drugs, especially with students who are neurologically impaired, very hyperactive, or severely emotionally disturbed.

There is virtually no evidence that either in school, or out of school, suspensions reduce misbehavior. Other forms of punishment, such as corporal punishment, also seem to have little effect unless there is an attempt at changing the environment in which the student works.

Effective environmental change for disruptive students includes "catching the student being good." The student should be helped to discriminate between acceptable and unacceptable behavior, and such discriminations should be reinforced with a variety of rewards (preferably selected by the youngster) and punishments, as well as immediate and specific verbal praise, consistently used. This method includes a phasing out of rewards and punishments as the student's behavior improves. Interested parents can be taught to use this approach. Many parents mistakenly provide rewards before, rather than after, a required behavior.

Other parents provide a plethora of unconditional rewards which may encourage youngsters to focus on the pleasure of the moment rather than on the delayed gratification which is required by school work.

Disruptive students frequently believe that their world is a chaotic one, and the consequences of their acts tend to confirm that belief. With few exceptions, disruptiveness can be greatly reduced by providing a social and physical environment which is predictable; meaningful expectations and orderliness are also helpful. When the boundaries of acceptable behavior are narrow and specific, i.e., "strict", deviant behavior (both disruptive and creative) decreases. Disruptive students are often tense and frustrated; therefore, interventions which lower tension and frustration, e.g., easier work, humor, soft music, dim lights, etc., are likely to result in fewer disruptive episodes.

Resolving the problems associated with disruptive behavior, reaching down into the roots of that behavior, may well be the most effective way to eliminate such behavior or to channel it positively. Most often this approach is also the most complex. Characteristically, disruptive students have needs which are not being met. Very young disruptive children may perceive that they are not sufficiently loved or parented; it is the child's perception rather than what others perceive which must be addressed. In such instances, the use of professional or volunteer surrogate parents, perhaps in the form of long-term "big brothers" or "big sisters", may help the child to pass stages of development satisfactorily. Older children may perceive themselves as incompetent and they may use disruptiveness either as a red herring or as retaliation. Adolescents often mistakenly see disruptiveness as a ticket to peer-group membership: The appropriate use of student patrols for the enforcement of minor regulations (such as "no running in the halls") will often elicit conforming behavior from otherwise disruptive students.

See also Classroom Management; Dropouts; Student Absenteeism and Truancy; Student Culture; Student Discipline.

—Eve E. Gagné
Chicago State University

References

Gagné, E. (1982). *School behavior and school discipline: Coping with deviant behavior in the schools.* Washington, DC: University Press of America.
Kazdin, A. (1984). *Behavior modification in applied settings.* Homewood, IL: The Dorsey Press.

DRIVER EDUCATION

Driver education includes varied efforts, but the term is usually associated with a high school course for beginning drivers.

Issues

Although a number of studies indicate that up to 90 percent of the people believe driver education should be in the school, it has been subject to attack by some educators. Some question its appropriateness on academic grounds. Others say it prevents students from taking "basic" subjects and that parents should teach driving. Supporters counter that the most comprehensive course requires only two percent of a student's high school time and that it meets an immediate need.

Quality is a related issue. Driver educators contend that these classes are usually assigned to teachers who have only a secondary interest in them, that inadequate time is allotted, and that achievement standards are too low.

Driver education is criticized for not preventing more accidents, but many driver educators believe that a short course can be responsible only for knowledge and skills. Other efforts will have to guarantee proper driving.

Controversy surrounds competency-based instruction. Many driver education people believe that students should be required to demonstrate required levels of performance. Others see this as a means to cut costs by allowing students who can meet only very minimum standards to pass the course.

Teacher preservice training is an important concern. The Sixth National Conference on Safety Education recommended at least twenty-four college hours, but the national average is half that.

Trends

In the early 1980s, school boards found themselves with less money. Many decided this called for the elimination of driver education, downgrading it to a summer course, moving it outside the school day, or charging a fee. The number of schools offering driver education as a regular part of the school day declined. Several state departments of education have reduced or eliminated supervisory services.

Parent-involvement programs are supported by many professionals as a way to raise the amount of instruction, hold down costs, build public support, and convey a better understanding of safe driving to parents. Parents participate in orientation meetings and receive an outline of the skills beginning drivers should practice. The parents are encouraged to help their sons or daughters practice those skills.

The Safe Performance Evaluation Project conducted by the National Highway Traffic Safety Administration may influence future trends. This project compared the accident reduction potential of a comprehensive course with a minimum predriver licensing course and with no formal driver education. Following the study, NHTSA released the following recommendations: (a) provisional licensure of novice drivers, (b) modification of the curriculum to yield an objective-based, predriver license program, (c) improved alcohol awareness education, and (d) increasing stress on socioeconomic benefits of driver education.

Modes of Instruction

Instructional plans may include a classroom, simulation, driving range, and on-the-street modes. Schools use one or more of these.

Classroom instruction is part of all approved high school courses. Shorter courses may include as few as 30 hours, whereas others may extend for a semester.

When behind-the-wheel instruction and classroom instruction are the only modes used, each student should receive six hours of actual driving plus twelve hours of observation.

Simulation involves the use of driving simulators before the student begins the behind-the-wheel phase. Simulation may usually be substituted for part of the behind-the-wheel instruction. Students should still receive up to three hours of behind-the-wheel instruction.

Driving ranges require an area where roadways and other driving situations can be laid out. Ranges may require a large capital outlay, but schools have painted markings and placed cones on a parking lot. A range can reduce cost by enabling a teacher to direct several students at once. Some on-the-street practice should follow range practice.

Obtaining vehicles can require a major effort. Free loan vehicles, once plentiful, are almost unavailable now. Schools often must make payments to cover the dealer's costs. Some districts believe it is advantageous to buy or rent vehicles.

Procedures

First, an adminstrator should obtain a good understanding of driver education. The references listed below will be a good start. The American Driver and Traffic Safety Education Association at 123 N. Pitt St., Alexandria, Virginia, is a good source. Several states have safety centers located on a university or college campus. State departments of education should be a primary source.

The amount of money available must be determined and related to the course being planned. A decision must be made as to whether there will be capital outlay for simulators and/or range facilities.

The single most important procedure is the selection of a staff who will make driver education their first priority, have the recommended 24 hours of preparation, have good driving records, and meet other staff requirements.

Other procedures must provide for determining vehicle needs, for obtaining vehicles, and for maintaining them. Insurance must provide for liability protection for everyone concerned and for protection against damage to the vehicles. Furthermore, fitting driver education into the school's schedule and scheduling students within the classes will require planning. A consultant may be helpful.

Finally, if the state provides reimbursement for the program, the administrator must maintain the necessary records and produce required reports.

See also Curriculum Development.

—Robert Freeman
Carthage Senior High School
Carthage, Missouri

References

Freeman, R. (1971). *Checklist for quality programs in driver education*. Washington, DC: Highway Users Federation for Safety and Mobility.

Freeman, R. (1978). "Driver and Traffic Safety Education." *Evaluative criteria for the evaluation of secondary schools* (5th ed.). Falls Church, VA: National Study of School Education.

Freeman, R. (1980). *Proceedings, Sixth National Conference on Safety Education* (Vols. 1-4).

DROPOUTS

Most of the research on high school dropouts has been aimed at identifying those personal and social characteristics of students that make them different from those who complete high school. Researchers have discovered certain common characteristics among those who decide to leave school early. One type of "causal" characteristic is concerned with factors that are beyond the control of the school, whereas a second type of characteristic is more directly related to practices within the school and are therefore open to interventions by educators who wish to prevent students from dropping out.

The best and most recent information we have on dropouts is obtained from the *High School and Beyond* study of some 30,000 students from 1,000 high schools across the country. Questionnaires and tests were given to sophomores in 1980 and to the same students again in 1982. A sample of those who dropped out during this period were identified and queried again. An analysis of the data indicated that two family background characteristics are strongly related to dropping out: socioeconomic status and race/ethnicity. Students from low socioeconomic backgrounds have the highest dropout rates. Using the race/ethnicity factor, Hispanics have the highest dropout rate, followed by blacks and whites. The combination of low socioeconomic background and minority status is a strong predictor of dropping out. Other background factors associated with dropouts are single-parent family, large family, living in a large city, and residing in the South. While these factors are clearly important in understanding the problems students might bring with them to school, there is nothing schools can do to change these background characteristics of their students. These are, however, "givens" which educators must take into account as they seek strategies for providing at-risk youth with a worthwhile education.

The second type of cause of dropping out is associated with the school experiences of students. Analysis of the *High School and Beyond* data revealed that the most powerful determinants of dropping out are low grades combined with disciplinary problems with truancy being the most frequent. Dropouts perceive that teachers do not show much interest in them. Dropouts also believe the disciplinary system in their schools is not very effective, nor fair, in dealing with rule violators.

In summary, if one is a minority and from low socioeconomic background; consistently discouraged by low grades, failure, and signals about one's inadequacies as a student through a perceived lack of caring from teachers; convinced that the school's discipline system is both ineffective and unfair; and has serious encounters with that system, then it is understandable that such individuals become alienated, lose their commitment to the goal of graduation, and seek an escape to a more rewarding environment outside the school.

Most schools have a relatively small percentage of students who are in danger of dropping out. In schools with not more than 100 at-risk students (e.g., 16 years old, six credits or less, frequently truant), there is convincing evidence that this group can be helped through an alternative program. Typically, these programs are designed around a school-within-a-school concept. Evaluations of several of these programs have produced a number of insights about what is effective with the at-risk student. "Effective" means that the drop-out rate is substantially reduced, measured academic achievement is increased, the number of truancy and disciplinary problems is reduced, and several social-psychological characteristics, such as self-esteem and locus of control, show improvement.

The characteristics of these effective programs can be described under four interrelated categories: (a) administration and organization, (b) teacher culture, (c) student culture, and (d) curriculum.

Administration and Organization

The size of the special program may be small—25 to 60 students with two to six faculty. Small size results in effectiveness for several reasons: (a) Face-to-face relationships among faculty and between faculty and students are frequent and natural; (b) teachers can plan together and assist one another; (c) keeping the students on course is easier when there is opportunity for frequent exchanges among those in the program; and (d) the impersonality and "bureaucratic bungling" that both teachers and students often complain about are reduced.

Small size frequently is associated with an important degree of program autonomy. The strongest programs have delegated control over admission and dismissal of students, course content, and scheduling control. Such autonomy communicates a positive commitment by the school to the program and empowers teachers to use their judgment about what is best for their students. This empowerment creates a sense of ownership, accountability, and extra effort that enhances program success.

Teacher Culture

Teacher culture refers to shared beliefs, values, and assumptions that guide teachers' actions and behaviors. All effective programs are characterized by beliefs that at-risk students can learn, become successful adults, and deserve another chance to succeed. A key element in the teacher culture is the concept of "extended role." Teachers see the need to be more than a purveyor of subject matter and disciplinarian and are willing to extend themselves to deal with the "whole child." This means that certain problems in the home, community, or peer group must be dealt with if the student is to succeed. For example, one teacher arranged to help a family join AL-ANON because family problems were clearly preventing a boy from engaging in his school work.

Another important characteristic of the teacher culture is a high degree of collegiality. Programs require teachers to engage in cooperative decision making and sharing in the successes and problems of the program. As a result of the need for frequent interaction among team members, a bond forms. Many teachers value this escape from isolation, report that they enjoy their work, and find collegiality professionally rewarding and stimulating to teach at-risk students. Some of the rewards arise from their success; teachers see formerly failing, hostile, or troublesome youth acquire skills, competence, and a more constructive set of attitudes.

Student Culture

A positive student culture is initiated by staff selection of students who are willing to admit they need help to improve their lives by changing a pattern of unproductive behaviors. Good programs offer students the promise of a fresh start in return for a promise to accept explicit rules and goals. Students unwilling or unable to commit themselves to the structure of the program are eventually terminated. (Yes, there are dropouts from the dropout prevention program.) However, part of the effectiveness of these programs results from their standards of excellence; students acquire an image of pride and success. As one student said, "This (program) is actually tougher than the regular high school, but I need the structure to make it."

Once students accept program requirements and goals, discipline problems are reduced. Students even monitor peer behavior in an effort to promote the program because it is seen as in their self-interest. Students report that their relationship with peers and teachers is more like a "family," which they contrast with the uncaring and unfriendly environment they experienced in the regular high school.

Curriculum

Effective programs must be substantially different from the regular educational program, at least in certain respects regarding the courses and content for students. Individualization, clear objectives, prompt feedback, concrete progress and a high degree of physical activity describe the most common features. In basic skill subjects, variation in performance of students must be expected. Some will read and compute at or above grade level, while others will be far behind. If a sixteen year-old cannot multiply using decimals, that is where the teacher begins. Many students are in need of considerable remedial work, but rather large gains in achievement are often realized. After all, many students who have been truant more than in class can be pushed ahead rapidly once they are on-task and making sustained efforts.

One of the most important findings from research on effective programs is their success in promoting development of social skills and attitudes. At-risk youth need to have social experiences with adults who exemplify characteristics of responsibility, the work ethic, and positive human relationships. These qualities are often germinated in young people through planned "experiential learning." The best programs have implemented a sequence of experiences that begin with all students doing volunteer work at day-care centers, nursing homes, elementary schools or handicapped centers. This is "real work" and it carries with it a high probability of success. A second type of experiential learning has students work under the leadership of a skilled tradesperson in the renovation of an old house or public building, or even the construction of a new house. This is a group experience designed to teach cooperation, responsibility, and only incidentally introduce youth to possible careers in construction.

Subsequently, students are challenged to experience several potential careers by "shadowing" adults as they go about their work in various career clusters. Near the end of the program students are involved in specific job training and a coordinated internship for which they are likely to be paid. Students completing these programs have testified in retrospect that several experiential components were key to their growth and development as young people. Successful completion of alternative programs can be defined as graduation with a diploma, passing GED tests, or successful placement in a private-sector job from which the youth can project a meaningful career ladder.

Keeping students in school should be seen as a necessary but not sufficient goal. In addition to improving students' basic skills, successful alternative programs promote adolescent development both in cognitive and social terms. The goals of promoting social development and responsible citizenship are ones that schools have often been willing to claim, but in truth much of the work is done by the home, church, and community. For at-risk youth, the school must create new opportunities to develop skills, attitudes and behaviors that other youth seem to acquire more easily and naturally.

See also Disadvantaged Students; Disruptive Students; Student Alienation.

—Gary G. Wehlage
University of Wisconsin-Madison

References

Wehlage, G. (1983). *Effective programs for the marginal high school student.* Bloomington, IN: Phi Delta Kappa.
Wehlage, G. (1983). "The marginal high school student: Defining the problem and teaching for policy." *Children and Youth Services Review, 5,* 321-42.
Wehlage, G., & Rutter, R. (1986, Spring). "Dropping out: How much do schools contribute to the problem?" *Teachers College Record, 87,* 374-92.

DRUG ABUSE EDUCATION

Drug education is the first step in the prevention of the problems related to drug use and abuse. Although the terms "drug education" and "drug prevention" have been used interchangeably, they are not the same. *Prevention* is a process, a long-term, on-going commitment to the reduction of drug-use abuse problems in society today. However, people must become aware of the problem before there can be any commitment to solving the problem. This then is the task of drug education. The term "drug" is meant to be all inclusive (alcohol, illicit drugs, prescription drugs).

Schools offer a unique opportunity to take the leadership role in drug education. They are in the business of educating and can most efficiently and effectively provide the foundation of information and skills needed in a drug-education program. Schools can provide an environment for the dissemination of correct information to young people and the community-at-large in a nonthreatening, nonjudgmental manner. Teachers are trained and skilled in communicating ideas and information.

An effective drug education program succeeds in raising the awareness level of all students. To accomplish this, teachers need to be adequately prepared to teach this complex topic by having a solid foundation of accurate and correct information about drugs and how drugs affect the behavior and feelings of the individual, the family, and ultimately the community. It is important not only to know how alcohol works on the body, but it is also important to know that one out of every four children in a teacher's classroom comes from a home in which chemical dependency exists. Many of these children deal with their feelings by becoming the class clown, rebelling against any authority, or withdrawing emotionally and often intellectually from the class.

Many drug agencies provide excellent in-service programs and workshops for teachers. Teachers do not need to become "drug experts," but they do need to begin to feel comfortable with the information they provide in a comprehensive drug education program. They need to know the signs and symptoms of drug use/abuse, the school policy with regard to drug use, and the resources available in the community to help. Therefore, it is imperative that teachers receive appropriate and adequate training with periodic up-dates.

Drug education needs to utilize a basic curriculum framework which can be applied to all grade levels in the school. To that framework can be added grade-appropriate objectives, information, and activities. A general curriculum framework will give some uniformity to the instruction while allowing enough flexibility for teachers to utilize their own background experience, information, and skills. Although a committee might develop the framework, some excellent programs have been produced by companies and agencies, and personnel are usually available to do the training. The programs could be reviewed to see if they are consistent with the school's curriculum objectives.

A drug education program should focus less on drug-specific information. This has been one reason for the ineffectiveness of past drug education programs. In the 1960s, the focus of drug education was on the use of scare tactics. If you drive drunk, you will die! The use of scare tactics as the basis for providing information often caused distortion of the facts. In the 1970s, the information model was developed. Drug education consisted solely of talking about what drugs looked like and what they did, but many of the materials used contained factual errors. However, by the mid-1970s drug education began to focus on correct drug information in tandem with other issues such as poor self-esteem, inadequate decision-making/problem-solving skills, lack of coping skills, inability to handle feelings, poor relationships with others, and lack of assertion skills. The individual who lacked these skills was at very high risk to become involved with drugs, and the risk was increased in the individual who also came from a chemically dependent home.

Today drug education programs need to continue to incorporate skill-building activities. Early studies indicate that teaching assertion skills—saying no—is an effective tool in drug prevention; assertion activities should therefore be included as a part of the drug education curriculum. New health textbooks are also addressing these same topics in conjunction with being responsible for and maintaining good health habits.

Drug education should address both the legal as well as physical/mental consequences of drug use. Information could be provided on how a person's health is affected. The stages of the disease of chemical dependency and the effects seem at each stage could be discussed. The death rate for teenagers is increasing and the leading cause of death among teenagers is drinking and driving. This issue should be addressed in the drug education curriculum in the high school program.

Drug education needs to incorporate activities which address the influence of the media on drug use. By the time today's 18-year-old graduates from high school, he or she will have watched television the equivalent to 24 hours a day for five years. Programs, as well as commercials, tell a person to take something to feel better. Kids tell adults that they use drugs to change the way they feel. The media message is, "You don't have to feel bad or hurt for even one millisecond." A research assignment might focus on the influence of drug advertising. Drug education must address the pressures that exist in society.

Drug education programs need to utilize up-to-date materials and research information. A knowledge explosion resulting from increased and focused research has occurred in the last five years. Materials produced prior to 1979 should be examined for misinformation and inconsistencies. With the advent of new drugs (i.e., designer drugs such as Ecstasy), it is almost impossible for teachers to learn all the current drug information without infringing on time for the more established classroom learnings. Teachers may select responsible and reputable outside sources for information. Certainly, any curriculum materials should include alcohol as well as other drug information. Alcohol is the number one drug of abuse in the United States today.

Finally, drug education must begin early. Kindergarten children can become aware of what they are putting into their bodies. An article in *Early Years* contends that "(t)he war must begin *before* children begin to smoke, drink, or experiment with drugs." Interviews with teenagers who are chemically dependent indicate they began their use at around the age of 11. Because of the increasing emphasis on starting early, programs should include primary-grade level materials.

Schools can not be solely responsible for the process of drug education. Drug education is everybody's business.

See also Drug and Alcohol Use Among Students; Health/Fitness Education.

—Jean Renfro, Education Coordinator
Alcohol and Drug Council of Middle Tennessee
Nashville, Tennessee

References

Campbell, J.R., & Swanchak, J. (1982). "The primary grades: New focus for drug/alcohol education." *Early Years, 13,* 34.
Ombudsman: A classroom community. (1981). Charlotte, NC: Charlotte Drug Education Center, Inc.
Renfro, J. (1984). "Mission possible: Adolescents do not have to self-destruct." *Educational Horizons, 62,* 141-43.

DRUG AND ALCOHOL USE AMONG STUDENTS

Today's society has a drug problem. The school as a microcosm of society also has a drug problem. However, the school should not be blamed for student drug use. Instead, the school should be responsible for addressing any issues that impair learning. Drugs impair learning.

Understanding the Problem

Although drugs may never be seen, subtle changes begin to occur. One of the first signs of drug use is problems in school. As chemical dependency is a progressive illness, it is important that these changes, no matter how small, be recognized and acted upon. The earlier a potential user can be identified, the greater the chance of halting the progression of the illness and of recovery. Teachers are in an excellent position to recognize these signs and symptoms and note changes.

Because of the changing growth patterns of a young person, the progression of the disease from experimental use to dependency can occur in less than one school year. Experimental use usually begins around age 11, unplanned and usually with friends. Early signs include falling grades and changes in behavior and friends. Later stages are characterized by school problems that result in suspension or expulsion, association with drug-using friends, health problems, and memory losses.

Educators need to know how all students, regardless of age, are "set up" for drug use. Chemical dependency tends to run in families. Whether it is genetic, environmental, or a combination of both is still being researched, but information already available indicates that one in four children in a teacher's classroom comes from a home in which chemical dependency exists. Fifty to sixty percent of alcoholics come from a home with at least one alcoholic parent. Children may not be using drugs, but in order to survive in the home they adopt specific behavior patterns. These survival roles will set a child up for later drug use. These roles are also manifested in a teacher's classroom—the class clown, the rebellious or overachieving student, the loner. By recognizing and learning ways to respond appropriately, teachers can diffuse these roles and change behavior patterns, thus lessening the chance for drug involvement.

The risk of harmful involvement due to the family of origin is exacerbated by adolescent growth patterns. Adolescence is a time of conflict and emotional pain coupled with rapid growth physically, mentally, and socially. Adolescents have needs to be met and students see drugs as a viable means of getting those needs met. Programs can be developed that address these needs.

Drugs negatively impact several areas of the adolescent developmental process. As the adolescent seeks to develop his or her own identity—separate from the family—he or she may attempt to show this independence from adult authority by taking on adult behaviors, such as drinking. Peer relationships become primary in the socialization process. Peers provide a support system for the adolescent who may be experiencing feelings of loneliness and alienation. Drug users provide an immediate peer group. An awareness of one's sexuality and the conflicts surrounding sexual behavior often result in feelings of self-consciousness and confusion. Drugs can relieve these feelings of stress and conflict and remove inhibitions surrounding sexual behavior; however, chemical use impairs sexual development. Adolescence is a period of rapid intellectual growth. Drugs are often used in the mistaken belief that they will help achieve a higher level of thought. The result is precisely the opposite; drugs impair, rather than enhance, intellectual growth. Finally, the adolescent begins to develop a sense of self, of abilities possessed, and knowledge of how the self and its abilities fit into the community-at-large. In the drug culture, the individual may measure his or her ability to fit in by the amount of drugs sold and/or used. The conflict of adolescence can be a time for productive health learning and growing, but that same conflict can also make the adolescent vulnerable to drug use.

Addressing the Problem

Schools can provide instructional programs for the faculty and students. These programs could include drug-specific information, but should also enhance skills in problem solving, decision making, and communication, and should assist the student in developing inter- and intrapersonal skills and in building identity and self-esteem. Incorporating these factors into the curriculum will help lessen the young person's vulnerability to drug use, regardless of age. In addition, programs presently being utilized can be coordinated, and materials available for drug programming can be reviewed. School programs can examine alternatives to chemical use and provide outlets for the student's self-development, individuality, and creativity which recognize individual needs, interests, and skill levels.

Schools can establish clear and concise policies and procedures which specifically address chemical use in the school environment. This process should include the development of a philosophy statement with regard to chemical use, abuse, and dependency; a review of the existing policies and procedures for up-date and/or change; development of clearly defined and consistent operational guidelines for responding to drug use in the school; and review and modification, if necessary, of school health and/or liability policies.

In addition, there are other ways in which the school can respond to student drug use. As an alternative to suspension or expulsion, the school could design, develop, and implement skill-building programs for students in trouble, to

be conducted in conjunction with an in-school suspension program. Another alternative might be the establishment of a school support system—by assisting students in forming a variety of groups such as concerned persons, recovering/aftercare, student assistance, peer counseling, insight, staying straight, and children of alcoholics. A core team of teachers could be trained to intervene on problem students and refer them for help. The core team could be responsible for working with the administration to develop school procedures for identification and referral, for implementing and coordinating drug programs, and for serving as liaison to the community to show the community that the schools are addressing chemical use issues. Schools do not need to become involved in therapy or treatment, but schools can develop referral sources for students in trouble.

A program which addresses the factors that make all children vulnerable to drug use and offers them skills and techniques to meet the needs and challenges of growing up will have far-reaching and positive results. They include (a) a greater awareness of the magnitude of the problem; (b) a joint school-community involvement and mutual support in addressing the problem; (c) a catalyst in generating additional community resources and alternatives to drug use for children of all ages; (d) assistance and referral sources; and (e) more focused and coordinated prevention/education programs resulting in greater effectiveness and efficiency.

See also Drug Abuse Education; Health/Fitness Education.

—Jean Renfro, Education Coordinator
Alcohol and Drug Council of Middle Tennessee
Nashville, Tennessee

References

Black, C. (1981). *It will never happen to me.* Denver, CO: Medical Administration Company.
Crowley, J.F. (1984). *Alliance for change: A plan for community action on adolescent drug abuse.* Minneapolis, MN: Community Intervention, Inc.
Rigg, C., & Jaynes, J.H. (1983). "The role of chemical abuse during adolescence." *Focus, 6,* 16-17.

DUE PROCESS

The concept of due process originated in the Magna Carta and was incorporated in the United States Constitution as part of the Bill of Rights. The Fifth Amendment stipulates in part that Congress shall not deprive any person of life, liberty, or property without due process of law. The Fourteenth Amendment, adopted in 1868, imposes these constraints on state governmental action as well. Constitutional due process essentially guarantees *fairness* in the government's treatment of individuals.

To trigger constitutional due process guarantees, the individual first must establish that a personal interest in life, liberty, or property is impaired by the government. In school cases, one's life usually is not threatened, so the application of constitutional due process hinges on whether a liberty or property interest is at stake. Liberty rights have been interpreted as fundamental constitutional rights (e.g., freedom of speech) as well as the right to be free from unwarranted governmental stigmatization. Property rights include real and personal property as well as entitlements created through state laws and regulations (e.g., the right to attend public school).

Interpreting the Fifth and Fourteenth Amendments, the federal judiciary has identified both procedural and substantive components of due process if an individual is threatened with a deprivation of life, liberty, or property interests by the government. Minimum procedures required by the federal Constitution are notice of the charges, an opportunity to refute the charges, and assurance that the hearing is conducted fairly. Originally, procedural due process rights were recognized in connection with judicial proceedings, but such protections have been extended to actions of governmental administrative agencies. Procedural due process assures fundamental fairness in that both sides must be given an adequate opportunity to present their versions of the controversy. State law often goes beyond constitutional minimums in specifying details of procedural requirements such as the length of notice prior to the hearing and the format of the hearing.

In the twentieth century the federal judiciary has also recognized substantive due process protections. Substantive law defines rights in contrast to procedural law that prescribes methods of enforcing the rights. Substantive due process requires the governmental action to be based on a valid objective with means reasonably related to attaining the objective. In essence, substantive due process protects the individual against arbitrary governmental action that touches on fundamental constitutional values.

Procedural and substantive due process guarantees have been at issue in numerous school cases involving various facets of employees' and students' rights. The remainder of this article focuses on principles of law established in cases dealing with student discipline, instructional issues, and teacher termination.

Student Discipline

Substantive due process rights can be impaired if disciplinary action is arbitrary or unnecessary as a means of attaining legitimate school objectives. Courts will assess the validity of the regulation upon which a specific punishment is based and the nature of the penalty in relation to the gravity of the offense. If a given regulation is found to be arbitrary on its face or as applied in a specific situation, substantive due process rights may be implicated.

Most due process claims in student discipline cases have focused on procedural rather than substantive issues. Procedural due process is required when disciplinary action impairs students' liberty or property rights. Students have a state-created property right to attend public school, and school authorities cannot deny this right by suspending or expelling students without affording procedural protections. Procedural safeguards also are required if disciplinary action implicates a liberty right by stigmatizing a student.

The judiciary has recognized that severe impairments of liberty or property interests require more formal procedures, while minor deprivations necessitate only minimal due process. For example, an informal conversation with the accused student (explaining the charges and giving an opportunity for rebuttal) may satisfy procedural requirements in connection with a short-term suspension from school (i.e., one day or less). When students face expulsion (i.e., removal from school for the balance of the term), they must be provided written notice of the charges, the right to counsel, a hearing before an impartial adjudicator, the opportunity to present witnesses and evidence and to cross-examine adverse

witnesses, and a written record of the proceedings. The judiciary has reasoned that school administrators and school boards can serve as the impartial hearing panels in student discipline cases.

State law and school board policies often provide more detailed procedural requirements in connection with suspensions and expulsions than required by the Federal Constitution. Once such procedures are adopted, courts will require them to be followed. In routine circumstances, procedural due process must be provided before the student is removed from the classroom. If the student poses a threat to others or the educational environment, the hearing can be provided after the student's removal.

The Supreme Court has recognized that the procedures required in connection with student suspensions are not constitutionally required when corporal punishment is administered. The court has noted that unlike a suspension, corporal punishment does not impair a student's property right to attend school, and any liberty infringement can be addressed through state remedies (e.g., assault and battery suits). While procedural due process is not constitutionally required when corporal punishment is administered, substantive due process rights may be implicated if the corporal punishment is excessive or inflicted with malice. In addition, state law and school board policies can place restrictions on the use of corporal punishment and can specify procedures that must be followed when this form of punishment is used in public schools.

Although procedural due process may not be legally required when minor punishments are imposed, educators would be well advised to give students a chance to refute the charges before administering *any* punishments. Educators will never be faulted for providing too much due process, but they may be vulnerable to a successful lawsuit if necessary procedural safeguards are not provided.

Instructional Issues

Due process rights have been asserted in connection with a range of instructional issues. Placement decisions, academic standards, and strategies used to assess student performance have been challenged as impairing due process rights.

The judiciary has recognized the authority of state and local education agencies to design the instructional program and to establish academic standards. Courts have been reluctant to intervene in educational policy decisions unless there is clear evidence of arbitrary action or the violation of constitutional or statutory rights. Students in the regular instructional program are not likely to prevail in challenging placement decisions on due process grounds. However, federal and state laws specify procedural requirements that must be followed in placing students in special education classes. Also, changes in handicapped children's instructional assignments necessitate procedural safeguards to ensure that the affected students' parents are involved in the decisions.

While courts have acknowledged that public schools are empowered to establish academic standards, such standards must be applied in a fundamentally fair manner. Students have a procedural due process right to adequate notice of academic requirements. Where receipt of a high school diploma is conditioned on passage of a competency test, courts have reasoned that students must be given notice of the requirement upon entrance into high school to allow sufficient time to prepare for the test. In addition, students have a substantive due process right to fair treatment in that they must have been adequately prepared to satisfy academic standards. In connection with competency tests, courts have required state and local education agencies to substantiate that the instructional program matches the skills and knowledge covered on a test used as a prerequisite to receipt of a high school diploma.

Students also have challenged the evaluation of their academic performance on due process grounds. Courts in general have deferred to the professional judgments of educators and have not required procedural due process in connection with academic (in contrast to disciplinary) decisions. On two occasions the United States Supreme Court has recognized the broad discretion school authorities have in evaluating pupil performance. Only if performance standards are clearly arbitrary or applied in a discriminatory manner will courts conclude that students have due process rights at stake.

Teacher Termination

A nontenured teacher has a property right to employment within the terms of the contract. Thus, discharge during the contract period necessitates procedural due process. Under most circumstances, nonrenewal of a probationary teacher at the end of the contract period does not trigger constitutional due process. Such nonrenewals are not considered dismissals and in general only require notice of nonreappointment unless state law, board policy, or the collective bargaining agreement specifies additional procedural protections. However, if the nonrenewal is predicated on the exercise of constitutional rights or imposes a stigma to the extent that future employment opportunities are foreclosed, procedural due process is required. Also, if the state has created a legitimate expectation of reemployment, the nontenured teacher may have a property interest in procedural due process prior to nonrenewal.

The granting of tenure creates a property interest or legitimate expectation of employment that cannot be impaired without procedural protections. In addition to constitutional minimum requirements, state tenure laws usually contain detailed procedures that must be followed in dismissing teachers who hold continuous contracts. Typically, these procedures specify the date and form of notice of the charges, the format of the hearing, and the grounds for dismissal. Courts will require school boards to adhere to the procedural requirements outlined in state law and to base dismissals on statutory grounds. State tenure laws generally address the following elements of procedural due process:

- Notice of the charges,
- Opportunity for a hearing,
- Adequate time to prepare a defense,
- Access to evidence,
- Representation by counsel,
- Hearing before an impartial tribunal,
- Opportunity to cross-examine adverse witnesses,
- Decision based on evidence and findings of the hearing,
- Written record of the hearing, and
- Opportunity to appeal an adverse decision.

Some states by law specify requirements for evaluating performance prior to termination and for providing teachers an opportunity to remedy deficiencies. Such statutory requirements must be followed for a termination to be upheld. In usual cases, procedural due process must precede dismissal, but under emergency conditions, teachers can be suspended with pay pending the hearing.

While a termination hearing must be fundamentally fair, it does not have to follow the judicial rules of evidence or mirror the formality of judicial proceedings. The school board is considered sufficiently impartial to serve as the tribunal in termination cases, even in situations where teachers have been in an adversarial relationship with the board (e.g., engaged in a strike). Courts are hesitant to substitute their judgment for that of school board members in connection with teacher dismissals. However, courts will intervene if the school board has not followed the prescribed procedures or if the dismissal is clearly arbitrary or predicated on impermissible reasons. If a due process violation is established and results in actual injury, courts may assess damages to compensate the individual for the injury suffered.

Conclusion

Governmental action impairing an individual's life, liberty, or property rights triggers constitutional due process protections. In the school context, substantive due process requires governmental regulations to be fair and reasonably calculated to achieve legitimate governmental objectives. Procedural due process ensures that decisions are made in a fundamentally fair manner. There is no fixed set of procedures that is applicable under all circumstances. The judiciary has recognized that due process entails a balancing of the individual and governmental interests affected in a given situation. If the liberty or property deprivation is minor, only minimum procedures are required; more formal and elaborate procedural safeguards must be employed when the impairment of liberty or property rights is substantial. State laws and school board policies often specify more detailed procedural protections than constitutionally required, and school authorities must adhere to these legal mandates.

See also Judicial Decisions; Rights: Teachers' and Students'; School Law.

—Martha M. McCarthy
Indiana University

References

McCarthy, M., & Cambron, N. (1981). *Public school law: Teachers' and students' rights* (Chapters 5 and 11). Boston: Allyn & Bacon.

Nowak, J., Rotunda, R., & Young, J.N. (1983). *Constitutional law* (pp. 443-96, 526-81). St. Paul, MN: West.

Rapp, J.A. (Ed.). (1984). *Education law* (sections 6.09[4][c], 9.05). New York: Matthew Bender.

E

EDUCATION AND COMMUNITY VIEWS

It has been said with more than a kernel of truth that, if you walk down the main street of any community, you can learn what education is like in that community. Communities and schools find themselves in a symbiotic relationship in which each influences the other. The school experiences joy, for example, when the community contributes lights for the football field. It experiences pain when the community curtails its financial support. The community is ecstatic when the school's football team wins a state championship. It is aroused when it is suggested that its school be closed and consolidated with a neighboring community's school.

American schools are closer to the public than are those of any nation in the world. The school board, which is elected by the people in most communities of the nation, is one of the governmental agencies close to the public, one against which the people can take direct action if they are displeased.

The school administrator must be an expert in many fields: curriculum, instruction, supervision, and all the ramifications of administration, not the least of which is school-community relations. It is important for the administrator not only to *respond* to community views but to *solicit* them.

An administrator can gain some conception of the views which communities throughout the nation hold toward education by consulting the annual Gallup Polls of the Public's Attitudes toward the schools. Every year the Gallup pollsters ask the public to rate its schools and to point out the biggest problems.

When asked what the biggest problems are with the public schools, the public has rather consistently placed lack of discipline at the top of its list. Other problems perceived by the public as serious are use of drugs, poor curriculum/poor standards, difficulty in getting good teachers, and lack of proper financial support.

Interestingly, the public rates the schools in its own communities higher than it rates the schools nationally. This observation should make the school administrator realize that the better the relationship between the school and the community, the more likelihood there will be of the public's satisfaction with its local schools.

School administrators cannot wait until citizens of the community approach the school to express their views. They must reach out to the community and involve it continually in the affairs of the school. Among the means of engaging the community in school affairs, including the making of curriculum decisions, administrators have found the following effective:

1. A curriculum needs assessment can be conducted periodically to find out the curriculum goals and objectives advocated by the community. Repeatedly surveying the views of the community by means of questionnaires, the administrator asks the public to indicate the goals and objectives it feels to be important for the schools. A curriculum needs assessment reveals gaps in the school's curriculum as perceived by the public, faculty, and students. The data from the needs assessment instruments are used to establish priorities for the school's curriculum.

2. Provision can be made for a standing Advisory Committee composed of members of the community. This committee serves in an advisory capacity to the school administrator. It helps set priorities; it serves as a sounding board; it provides channels for input from the community; and it often helps prevent or deflate controversies. Some school districts appoint community advisory committees for each school; other school systems limit advisory committees to the school system as a whole. With increasing emphasis on the individual school as the locus of improvement, school administrators should give greater consideration to establishing advisory committees for every school.

3. Efforts can be made to involve the community in the day-to-day affairs of the school. Several programs that have proved successful for doing this are

Parent Volunteers. Parents offer their time and skills to help faculty in their classrooms as resource persons and unpaid aides. They tutor; they demonstrate skills; and they help the teachers with clerical duties. The parent volunteers serve as the school's links to the community and can be a force for shaping community views toward the school.

School-Community Partnerships. More and more schools are entering into partnership arrangements with businesses and industrial organizations of the community. School administrators today recognize that education extends beyond the walls of the school. Enterprising administrators make use of the educational forces existent in the community through encouraging organizations in the community to supplement the school's curriculum by providing work and training experiences for youth of the community.

Reports of School Progress. Many school systems periodically send out newsletters, bulletins, and reports to the public. Some schools publish comprehensive annual reports of school progress. These various publications should provide accurate up-to-date information about the school, its goals, and its problems.

The history of American education demonstrates that the community has had and continues to have a significant impact on the curriculum of the schools. Whether we are talking about community views toward religion, censorship, sex education, education for the handicapped, or other controversial issues, community attitudes and mores do have a bearing on what is taught in the schools. The wise administrator keeps abreast of community thinking and tries to gain support for changes which he or she wishes to make in the curriculum.

See also Business/Education Partnership; Public Relations; School Community Relations.

—Peter Oliva
Georgia Southern College

References

"The annual gallup poll of the public's attitudes toward the public schools," *Phi Delta Kappan*, annually, Fall.

English, F.W., & Kaufman, R. (1975). *Needs assessment: A focus for curriculum development*. Alexandria, VA: Association for Supervision and Curriculum Development.

Orlosky, D.E., McCleary, L.E., Shapiro, A., & Webb, L.D. (1984). *Educational administration today* (Chapter 13). Columbus, OH: Charles E. Merrill.

EDUCATIONAL GOALS AND OBJECTIVES

A central task of school and district leadership is the clarification of goals or basic purposes. While the general purpose of schooling—the education of children—is clear, many questions remain about who is being educated, how education should take place, and what the characteristics of an educated student are. When the members of a school agree on the answers to these questions, they can work together more effectively. Without such understandings, conflict, drift, and wasted resources result. Goals provide a succinct, general statement of basic purposes, while objectives provide more specific guidance on how to operationalize those purposes.

Functions

Goals and objectives serve three distinct functions. First, they provide the school with legitimation or assurance to the outside world that the "right" things are being done here. Goals signify that legislative mandates and the interests of community members, parents, and professional associations are taken into account. Second, goals, and more specifically objectives, provide targets for formal accountability systems. These include teacher and administrator supervision, evaluation procedures, and program evaluations. Third, goals and objectives coordinate the actions of all members of the organization and orient them to take the initiative to achieve common ends. To serve this function, goals must become part of the culture—that is, the generally accepted understandings about how things ought to be.

These functions suggest different criteria for goal statements. The first function is best served by goal statements which show that the school or district is working toward a legal mandate or the interest of some valued constituency. Where many constituencies make competing demands, goals must often be stated vaguely to avoid giving offense. The second function is best served by statements that are clear, reality oriented, and verifiable. Often it is useful to quantify objectives. In any case, they should be stated so that observation can determine how well they have been achieved. The third function can be partly served only by statements of goals and objectives. Such statements must be reinforced through frequent repetition by administrators and teachers and by the development of symbols, myths, and rituals that remind and reinforce the staff of the sacredness of goals.

Building goals into the school culture is especially difficult, but also especially worthwhile. When goals become part of the culture, motivation to achieve them and punishment for deviating from them comes from within the group. Administrative efforts to motivate staff to achieve goals are supported by the group itself. Group commitment can even be maintained after changes in administrations.

Tensions frequently arise among these three functions. For instance, it can be difficult to state objectives specifically enough to be easily measured without giving offense to an outside group that opposes that purpose. Similarly, the need to adjust goals to new social pressures can lead to strong resistance when the local culture is firmly committed to initial purposes. Finally, too much attention to writing goal statements for an accountability system can create a culture hostile to those goals. On the other hand, the three functions can be mutually reinforcing. The happiest situation for a school is the one where formal accountability systems reinforce goals that are central to its culture and supported by key outside constituencies. The art of goal setting is reducing the tensions among these three functions.

Development and Maintenance

While one can develop goals that meet the first two functions as isolated events, building goals into an educational organization's culture is a neverending process. There are some times when pressures to change goals are especially intense. These include the arrival of a new formal leader (especially a superintendent or principal), legal pressures for change such as a state-mandated planning process, major changes in funding or the student population, or the realignment of a school board. Even between these relatively dramatic events, pressures to change goals occur frequently. Yet, if goals change with every new development, there will be no continuity in the life of the school, no concentration of efforts to achieve goals. Thus, while the administrator must occasionally guide the reformulation of goals, the more common task is maintaining existing ones.

When a conscious realignment of goals is necessary, three interrelated steps must be taken: diagnosis, stating the goals, and adjusting the system to them. Diagnosis is needed because goals are never developed in a vacuum. They must reflect organizational and legal constraints, objective conditions, and constituency interests. The organizational constraints for a school include district goals. These cannot be contradicted, but they are usually broad enough to allow a range of school goals. The district's goals are developed within the constraints of state and federal mandates.

Objective conditions include increases and decreases in the student population, changes in aggregated student characteristics (demonstrated achievement, values, interest in school) and funding shifts. A school that makes higher-order cognitive development a central goal may have to change priorities if there is an influx of students who consistently have problems in developing competence in basic literacy skills.

A variety of constituencies make demands upon a school. Taxpayers stress cost cutting, and parents want a good education for their children. Parents may be divided into groups with different interests—gifted education, a strong sports program, and more attention to bilingual education—depending on the needs of their children. There are also constituencies within the school that represent occupational (librarians, curriculum specialists, counselors) and discipline (history, science, English) specialization. The administrator's (the school principal's or district superintendent's) own interests are especially important. That person will be most responsible for gaining acceptance of those goals; therefore, the final statement must be something he or she can support wholeheartedly. People will sense the authenticity of his or her commitment to it. If that commitment is not firm, others will be less likely to adopt the goals.

The second step is the statement of goals and objectives. The two key tasks here are to find the right levels of specificity and difficulty. It is easier to tell if specific objectives are reached, but they can be too rigid in rapidly changing situations. Broad goals provide general guidance that is useful in situations not anticipated when they were written, but they can also degenerate into platitudes. Easily quantified goals increase precision, but they create other problems because they are often given more attention than they warrant intrinsically. For instance, when high achievement becomes a goal, parts of the curriculum that are not easily tested are put at risk.

Generally, objectives should be set at levels that are difficult but attainable. People tend to work to the objectives set for them. When those objectives are low, relatively little will be accomplished. More challenging objectives will elicit greater effort and greater results. However, goals that are too difficult discourage people from trying to achieve them.

The third step is adjusting systems to match the goals. Some of the important systems that need scrutiny include budgets, schedules, the curriculum, discipline codes and supervision, and evaluation procedures. These can actually work against new goals. For instance, a schedule with frequent class changes undercuts the goal of increasing instructional time; and requiring district office approval of small expenditures works against increasing building-level innovation. Supervisory procedures must also be adjusted to ensure that information is collected on relevant goals.

One recurring question is whether goals should be developed through a participatory process using some form of committees. It has generally been argued that participation increases the "ownership" of new goals among the staff, but the evidence for this proposition is mixed. Teachers are often willing to let others set goals and objectives and are more interested in having input to the procedures and systems for achieving those goals. They may resent the time spent on committee work. Even if participation does increase ownership, it will only do so for those who are on the committees. There is often too little interaction between the people on the committee and others for the sense of ownership to spread.

Nevertheless, there is a good reason for staff participation in the development of goals: it increases communication. The inclusion of teachers helps administrators gauge staff interests and provides information on such conditions as student learning and disciplinary problems. Such information helps in diagnosing the situation. Formulating goals with the staff helps to determine if the intended purposes are being adequately communicated, if objectives are too easy or hard, and if they have the right level of specificity. Staff input will also help identify the systems that need to be adjusted to the new goals. Finally, the process is educational for those who go through it. The committee members will form a small nucleus who are well informed about and likely to be committed to the goals.

The tasks required to maintain goals are similar in kind to those needed to "sell" the staff on reformulated goals. Three kinds are required. The first is the articulation and communication of goals. The formulation of a written statement is only the start of this process, which takes place both formally and informally. When announcing new actions, the administrator can indicate how they are intended to meet goals. Proposed changes can be reviewed for their fit with goals. The administrator can communicate goals by example either by acting to help achieve the goals or by telling stories about individuals who do. An important principle here is consistency. Administrators make many decisions and hold countless conversations each day. Goals are communicated most effectively if the same message comes through in all these acts.

The second task is reinforcement. Sometimes this can be done simply by noticing an action and encouraging it. Because educators have difficulty in telling how well they are succeeding, any notice by knowledgeable adults can be reinforcing. The principal is especially well placed to provide frequent verbal encouragement. In other cases special awards or rewards will be necessary.

The third task is protecting goal-achieving activity from interference. Such interference can come from without or within. Administrators must sometimes decide what not to tell teachers because it will be distracting and unsettling. They may also have to appeal decisions from superiors in the district office or from state or federal agencies that impede goal achievement. Sometimes selectively ignoring information or creative disobedience is necessary. When interference comes from within, it may be necessary to remove or isolate the source. Depending on the situation, this may be done by teacher transfers or changing student assignments.

The biggest difficulty with written goal statements is building them into the culture: getting them off the paper and into the minds and hearts of the people who must accomplish them. Otherwise goals will serve an external legitimation function but have little impact on the day-to-day life of the school or district. This task is easier if the written statements reflect, reformulate, or reconcile goals that are already held by the staff. Even then a conscious, continuing effort is required to educate and sell staff on a set of goals. It will only succeed when the administrator has a clear vision of and deep commitment to those goals.

See also Curriculum Development; Demographic Trends; Education and Community Views; Planning.

—William A. Firestone
Rutgers University

References

Hampton, D.R., Summer, C.E., & Webber, R.A. (1978). *Organizational behavior and the practice of management* (3rd ed., Chapter 8). Glenview, IL: Scott, Foresman.

Kottkamp, R.B. (1984). "The principal as cultural leader." *Planning and Changing, 15*(3), 152–61.

ELEMENTARY SCHOOLS

The elementary school encompasses prekindergarten through grade 6, with programs for students between the ages of 4 and 12. Just as elementary schools vary in size, organizational and community expectations also vary. Even so, the primary purpose of the elementary school is to provide an environment in which each student can develop as an individual and as a functioning member of society. This rather lofty goal has received even more emphasis in recent years as school improvement has become a critical issue across the nation.

In considering student development, perhaps the most important goal of the elementary school is to make every student an accomplished reader who is skilled in both oral and written communication. This goal gained national prominence during the "Right-to-Read" movement of the 1970s. It is considered even more essential today.

The Elementary School Principal

The head of an elementary school is charged with a myriad of responsibilities that significantly affect the learning of elementary school students. In addition to the tasks of building management and school-community relations, the principal is responsible for student, staff, and program development. Until recent years, it was rare to find other administrative positions in the elementary school; the principal, usually with secretarial help, carried the entire burden. With additional emphasis on the instructional leadership of the principal, including teacher appraisal, assistant principals are becoming commonplace.

Elementary School Curriculum

The curriculum within an elementary school, based on the school's goals and objectives, provides for a various array of learning experiences, reflecting recognition of the individual differences found in learners from this age group. Basic skills in communication, computation, and health care are introduced during the early years. As the student matures and masters these basic skills, content or knowledge areas are added. A traditional curriculum includes language arts, arithmetic, social studies, science, art, music, and physical education. A disturbing trend at this time is the increase in state-mandated curriculum, a movement which would eliminate community input in curricular matters.

In order for the curriculum to serve students appropriately, an effort is made to keep the student-teacher ratio low. Elementary school students differ in their mode of learning, and elementary-school teachers must vary their teaching styles and their use of teaching materials and resources. Other differences, such as achievement, ability, interests, and maturity, must also be considered in the delivery of instruction.

Educational Program

Each school district should have carefully delineated goals and objectives upon which the educational program is based. This is to ensure that the program offered reflects the nature of the students and also that of the community which supports it. The school population must be considered as student competencies and performance standards are set. The scope and sequence of the curriculum provide the bases for selecting, planning, and evaluating instructional units.

Thorough instructional planning is a key ingredient in an effective school program. The principal takes an active part in this planning and encourages teacher collaboration. This promotes the understanding of the relationship of learning goals from one grade to the next and ensures that no gaps exist within the educational program.

In implementing the school program, perhaps the most important decision an administrator makes is in selecting well-qualified, competent, and committed teachers who have high expectations for student achievement. In order for these good teachers to teach at an optimum level, the principal must provide a positive school learning climate. This climate extends far beyond a comfortable physical environment to include teacher and student morale, cooperation, trust, attitude, and productivity.

Evaluation of the educational program is an on-going, complex responsibility. It may be more feasible to separate the program into components and evaluate one component at a time, such as the reading program for all grade levels. Evaluation should assess how well the goals and objectives of the school have been accomplished. Careful evaluation may lead to a change in specific goals or objectives, continuation or modification of the existing program, or addition or deletion of program components.

Evaluation of the instructional process is an administrative and supervisory responsibility. Proper appraisal of teacher effectiveness leads to improved student learning through staff development, in-service training, effective use of materials, and other resources made available by the principal.

Grading Arrangements

Prior to 1960, most elementary schools contained grades 1 through 6, typically located in the same building. Kindergarten and, in some districts, prekindergarten have since been added. Today it is common to find the primary school, with prekindergarten through grade 2 or 3, and the intermediate school, with grades 3 through 5 or 6, as well as other grades combinations. All seem acceptable, with existing facilities often the deciding factor on which grades may be assigned to a particular building.

From an administrator's point of view, these graded arrangements are efficient, practical, and noncontroversial. However, they do not allow for the diversity found in individual students, such as in learning style, ability, interest, and maturity. In an effort to meet these diverse needs, individual teachers often incorporate some form of grouping within the classroom, instructing differently for each group.

Another option for individualizing instruction is nongraded grouping within the same grade level where students from two or more classrooms are appropriately grouped and instructed according to need. Multigrade level or cross-grade level grouping is a third option. Students are grouped for appropriate instruction, disregarding existing grade levels. These options can be integrated into a graded system to whatever extent the administrators and teachers desire.

A schoolwide nongraded approach, effectively implemented only after careful, deliberate, and sound planning, does take into consideration the diversity of students of the same age. Technological advances make this approach more practical than it has been in the past, but its management is difficult and its staff must be prepared and highly committed.

See also Back-to-Basics; Individualization of Instruction; Middle/Junior High Schools; Preschool Education.

—Ruth Ann Stephens
East Texas State University

References

Glickman, C.D. (1985). *Supervision of instruction* (Chapters 2, 11, & 15). Boston: Allyn & Bacon.

Hughes, L.W., & Ubben, G.C. (1984). *The elementary principal's handbook* (Chapters 5, 6, and 11). Boston: Allyn & Bacon.

Lipham, J.M., Rankin, R.E., & Hoeh, J.A. (1985). *The principalship* (Chapters 5 & 6). New York: Longman.

EMERGENCY PROCEDURES

Providing a healthful and safe environment for students and staff is one of the most important responsibilities that educational institutions assume. Though incidences of serious injury and death in educational settings are relatively few, the potential for a major catastrophe does exist. The probability of injury or death can be greatly reduced by instituting and maintaining a comprehensive emergency-preparedness program. Such a program should address the ten considerations described below.

First, emergency plans should be developed through a participatory approach. Staff members who will implement safety and emergency procedures working with experts such as fire marshals, who have specific technical knowledge, produce the most workable plans. Second, such plans must be committed to writing and made available to those who will implement the procedures. Written plans assure accurate communication. Third, effective plans address the wide range of emergencies that might occur in educational settings. Emergencies result from fire, tornado, chemical spills, intruders on campus, bomb threats, mechanical malfunctions, and other situations unique to specific geographic settings.

The fourth component of a successful safety preparedness program is assignment of specific responsibilities to each staff member. At the beginning of the year each person should be given specific emergency procedure tasks related to the plan, and alternate persons should be designated for every assignment. Fifth, good fire safety and general emergency programs specify alternate procedures to be used if the primary emergency plan cannot be implemented. Backup warning systems and secondary escape routes are two examples of needed alternative procedures. A sixth step is the identification of a unique warning system for each type of emergency. The alarm for fires needs to be different from that for tornadoes if students and staff are to react correctly.

The seventh consideration in developing an effective emergency-preparedness plan focuses on the unique requirements of all populations served by the educational institution. For example, orthopedic, trainably, emotionally, and profoundly handicapped students will require special procedures and attention during a crisis. Eighth, emergency-preparedness plans work only if they are practiced. Each type of emergency should be simulated sufficient times for students and staff to become proficient in implementing specified procedures. Because emergencies occur at any time and at any place, practicing the use of alternative routes from primary spaces and practicing of emergency procedures from spaces other than "home base" are important.

The ninth factor in the development of an effective emergency preparedness plan is standardization. Many educational institutions have developed a specially designed document in which each section is color-coded for each type of emergency. Each page of the document is dated so that, if procedures change, each volume can be checked to verify that it is current. Tenth, fire and other emergency programs are effective only to the extent to which they are emphasized. Administrators, staff, and community must make safety a high priority if any emergency preparedness plan is to be successful. Regular discussions of safety procedures should be held at staff meetings, in classrooms, and at parent/citizen meetings.

See also Assistant/Vice Principal; Delegating Authority; Planning; Principalship.

—Kenneth R. Stevenson
University of South Carolina

References

"Fire. These procedures protect handicapped kids." (1986, May). *Executive Educator, 8,* 24.

Johnson, G.K., & Beck, R.R. (1986, January). "The Arrowhead Elementary School tornado safety program." *Journal of School Health, 56,* 33.

"Quick! Tell me how to buy security and fire safety equipment." (1984, August). *American School Board Journal, 171,* 12.

EMPLOYEE DRUG AND ALCOHOL PROGRAMS

School systems develop Employee Assistance Programs when significant persons within the system recognize that alcohol and drug problems are affecting roughly the same percentage of the staff as are affected in other organizations. The primary motivation to implement an Employee Assistance Program is to intervene with alcohol/drug affected members of the staff and assist them to obtain treatment. Members of the staff who are in trouble with alcohol or other drugs negatively affect not only students but also other staff members and, at times, the school system's reputation as an institution of learning.

Most school systems functioning without an Employee Assistance Program tend to deal with drug/alcohol affected employees by transferring them, counseling them to find another school system, terminating them, or by simply living with the employees who have a problem. With such a program, troubled employees usually find their way to treatment and recovery, which leads to considerable improvement in functioning and, of course, a better institution of learning.

Implementing a Program

1. Form an advising committee. It is important that the advisory committee be comprised of a cross-section of the staff at all levels within the school system. Membership should include a mix of people ranging from school board members to members of the teacher's union. When all levels of the staff are involved in the complete process of im-

plementation, there is considerably more support for the program. Employee Assistance Programs can often be a common ground for union and management as they both have a mutual concern—seeking help for a human being in need.

2. Appoint an employee assistant program lead person or director. The advisory committee needs to identify a person who has serious interest and enthusiasm about the prospects of this program. The lead person should be someone who is a good listener, very caring about people with problems, and trusted by almost everyone. This person should be someone who has adequate time to oversee the program.

3. Develop policy, procedures, and program detail. Some of the issues needing attention by the advisory committee and lead person would include confidentiality, job security, insurance coverage, eligibility to use the program, and types of problems to be addressed.

Alcohol-and drug-dependent people have a major impact on all family members; therefore, the advisory committee needs to decide whether or not family members are eligible for program use. Alcohol and drug dependencies often surface to the untrained person as legal problems, divorces, financial problems, troubled children, domestic violence, health problems, and performance problems on the job.

Staff rarely seek treatment for their alcohol and drug related problems; instead they will seek help for symptoms relating to a marital problem, financial difficulties, trouble with a child, or conflict with a parent. Drug/alcohol dependencies lead to on-the-job performance problems. Therefore, school boards need to establish a clear disciplinary and referral process which can be used by management to confront and refer the troubled employee to assessment and treatment. Performance slippage will be demonstrated by absenteeism, tardiness, missed committee meetings, late lesson plans, being late with grading tests and papers, mood changes, and complaints from the staff, students, or parents. Persons who are in supervisory positions need to be trained in methods of recognizing performance slippage, and how to use the disciplinary process to offer help to the troubled employee. It is important that discipline be used only for performance problems, not for personal problems causing performance slippage.

Discipline. While there are multiple ways to approach procedures for discipline, a common method is the four-step progressive process as follows: *Step one*, oral warning; *step two*, written warning; *step three*, suspension; and *step four*, termination. Without an employee drug-and-alcohol program, troubled individuals are taken through the disciplinary process often to termination. What differs with an Employee Assistance Program is that the troubled employee is offered help at each step of the disciplinary procedure. Administrators are taught to confront the employee with specific data regarding performance slippage. If something personal is causing the decline in performance, professional help is suggested. Each confrontation should be done out of care and concern for the employee and his or her job, never out of anger or hostility! The documentation should begin when there has been a *pattern of performance slippage*, but not for an isolated incident. When sufficient performance data have been documented, a caring confrontation is done with the offer of assistance. The troubled employee can accept or reject the offer of help at each step in the disciplinary process. The offer of help is never in lieu of discipline; it is in addition to discipline. Should the employee agree to seek help, the supervisor contacts a resource person for a referral.

Resource Person(s). Some school systems use one person only for supervisory referrals, and others use a model involving multiple resource persons. In any event, a resource person is one who can maintain confidentiality, understands chemical dependency, is caring, and has a thorough understanding of community resources. The resource person receives the documented data, has a meeting with the troubled employee, and sets an appointment for the troubled employee with an appropriate assessment agency. The resource person(s) should receive extensive experiential and didactic training on responsibility, referral procedures, community resources, etc.

Assessment Procedures. Assessing a troubled employee should be done by a certified alcohol and drug counselor so that an accurate picture of the whole person can be completed. The assessment agency assesses whether the problem is alcohol/drug related and, if so, develops a treatment plan based on the severity of the problem. The assessment will include a close look at (a) physical health, i.e., liver damage, kidney damage, blood pressure, vitamin deficiencies, etc.; (b) social life, i.e., family (is the family still together?), friends (does the person still have friends?), activities and recreation (is drinking the only means of recreation?); (c) emotional, chemical dependency involving denial, delusional thinking, guilt, shame, fear, and often times suicidal thinking, etc.; (d) spiritual life; complete spiritual bankruptcy occurs in late stages of chemical dependency.

Treatment. The assessment agency will determine the most effective treatment program for the troubled employee and the members of his or her family. Treatment can vary from detoxification in a hospital setting, followed by inpatient treatment, to outpatient therapy or Alcoholics Anonymous. One aspect of treatment will necessitate the troubled employee admitting his or her own powerlessness over the drug of choice, and seeking the help of a superior being.

Reintegration. Most treatment agencies communicate with the troubled employee regarding what he or she might face upon returning to work. If relationships were seriously harmed, the alcohol/drug counselor will want to work with key school personnel in providing assistance for the troubled person's return. Because recovery is a life-long process involving a total life-style change, the recovering person must feel support for recovery in the work setting.

Conclusion

Although no solution to the problem of employee drug-and-alcohol abuse carries with it a guarantee of success, school systems which have involved the faculty and the staff in planning an Employee Assistance Program and have developed and implemented clearly-stated policies and procedures have been able to provide effective assistance to abusers. These systems have coordinated the efforts of the entire school community in addressing this difficult issue.

See also Drug Abuse Education; Drug and Alcohol Use Among Students; Personnel Policies.

—James Rentmeester
Wisconsin Department of Health and Social Services

References

Presnall, L.F. (1981). *Occupational counseling and referral systems*. Salt Lake City, UT: Utah Alcoholism Foundation.

Redeker, J.R. (1983). *Discipline: Policies and procedures*. Washington, DC: The Bureau of National Affairs, Inc.

Wrich, J.T. (1980). *The employee assistance program*. Center City, MN: Haselden.

ENERGY MANAGEMENT

Today's school administrators and supervisors are faced with escalating operating costs and closer scrutiny of their budgets. One of the contributing factors to these rising costs is the energy needed to operate the heating, ventilating, and air conditioning equipment in their buildings.

An inefficient use of energy compounds the problem. Maintenance and custodial personnel are often not properly trained to maintain and operate heating and air conditioning equipment efficiently. In spite of their best efforts, they frequently support old control systems designed before energy efficiency was important. Their duties and responsibilities do not always allow them to perform adequate maintenance.

All of these situations result in an inefficient operation of the energy equipment. Inefficiency puts an increased demand on the energy budget.

The Solution

Many steps can be taken to reduce energy costs and still meet the diverse and specialized needs of a school building. One such step is installation of an energy-management system (EMS). An energy-management system monitors and controls heating and cooling systems. The monitoring reduces the consumption of energy in the school.

Additional benefits may be enjoyed from an energy-management system besides energy savings. Existing controls are brought up to date, ensuring their proper operation and aiding the conservation effort. The automatic control saves time for the custodial staff. This allows the maintenance and custodial workers to do things they normally have little time for, including adequate preventive maintenance of the heating, ventilating and air conditioning systems.

What's Available?

Today's rapid change in technology applies to energy-management systems. These changes allow the unique environment of a school district to capitalize on the benefits of an energy-management system.

Digital system controllers combine the efficient operation of direct digital control with energy-management features of a larger system. These controllers use expanded control algorithms and provide more accurate, faster control with system feedback. This simplifies complex pneumatic control systems by performing many of the functions normally requiring additional pneumatic hardware. The reduced complexity can lower maintenance costs and reduce the possibility of energy-losing breakdowns.

Digital system controllers in multiple buildings can be tied together to provide centralized monitoring and control of each building. They can be connected by using proprietary lines, fiber optic cable, leased or dial-up phone lines, radio frequency communications, or point-to-point microwave transmission. Such a network allows closer monitoring of the use of energy and helps spot problems early. Personnel can then correct the problems before large amounts of energy are wasted. Energy-management systems save energy by providing control for electrical loads, heating and cooling systems, and chillers and boilers. Load control includes lighting control, a limit on demand to reduce the rate of using electricity, and duty cycling to reduce total consumption. Heating, ventilating, and cooling control incorporates supply air reset and enthalpy switchover to control the mechanical energy expended to condition the school air. It also includes an optimal run-time program to ensure the equipment runs only when needed. Chiller control uses condenser water reset and chilled water reset to lower the input power required at the chiller plant. Chiller sequencing selects the optimum combination of chillers for most efficient operation. Hot water reset controls the energy consumed by the school's boilers.

There are several alternatives to funding an energy-management system. The system can be purchased outright, requiring a capital investment. Some programs provide guaranteed savings with either the vendor or the school district owning the system. It may be more feasible to lease a system rather than buy one. Remote monitoring services may be available from a vendor who uses a single system to provide energy savings for several locations, none of which could justify an EMS on their own. Some vendors also provide assured performance agreements, and, if energy savings do not exceed their estimates, they pay the difference between the actual savings and the estimated savings. Still another alternative is the fixed budgetable service agreement, which includes building equipment operation and monitoring, scheduled maintenance and repair, and performance reporting and review of energy savings. This agreement includes periodic service charges and assures positive cash flow.

Summary

An energy-management system monitors and controls energy consumption by reducing equipment operating time, optimizing equipment performance, and monitoring equipment operation. It can be an effective part of an overall energy-management program for a school district, but it will not solve all energy problems alone. Administrators and supervisors must determine where energy is being consumed in their school buildings and then develop some realistic guidelines and expectations from an energy-management program. Maintenance must also be included as a vital part of that program. Finally, both management and the maintenance staff must commit themselves to make the program and system work effectively.

See also Facilities Planning.

—Chuck Miles
Johnson Controls
Milwaukee, Wisconsin

References

Michigan School Business Officials. (1984). *Total school energy program, energy, conservation techniques for schools*. Lansing, MI: Author.

Payne, F.W. (1984). *Energy management and control systems handbook*. Atlanta: Fairmont Press.

Thuman, A. (1985). *Energy management systems sourcebook*. Atlanta: Fairmont Press.

ENGLISH EDUCATION

In its history as a formal school subject, English has been defined both as a skills subject—traditionally, the skills of reading, writing, speaking, and listening—and a content subject—traditionally, the study of language, literature, and composition. When referring to the skills of reading, writing, speaking, and listening, elementary educators frequently use the term "language arts;" when referencing the content of language, literature, and composition, secondary educators frequently use the term "English."

The skills model is historically antecedent to the content model, for initial literacy was the prime demand early in the history of English as a school subject; the content, or cultural heritage, model came later and reflected a need for a unifying method of instruction. Elementary schools have tended to maintain a language arts approach, that is, a language skills approach, while secondary schools have tended to maintain a content approach focusing on the literary genre, the grammar of American English, or the principles of rhetoric and composition. In an attempt to combine the two emphases, the term "English language arts" has been employed to designate a developmental approach to the discipline, grades K-12.

The Need for a Unifying Theory

Unifying theories not only of English language arts but of other disciplines have been sought for a number of years. Greatest emphasis in this direction for English language arts emanated from the Anglo-American Conference on the Teaching of English in 1966. A structure of English was constructed by James Moffett. Moffett argued that English has been misconstrued and mistaught because we confuse content with skills and have made English an *about* subject rather than a *how to* subject.

There have been many attempts to define the discipline, but it is not enough merely to define the content and/or skills of the discipline. English educators must also describe its *teaching*. Teachers and administrators need to consider a model of the teaching of English language arts that attempts to define the broader dimensions and provide a framework through which one may view factors limiting the English language arts teacher's choices.

An Organic Field Model of the Teaching of English was proposed by Peters, Grindstaff, Hanzelka, and Olson. According to this view, the teaching of English language arts is constrained by at least two major sets of variables: content and context. The *content* variables are substance (literature, language, rhetoric), skills (reading, writing, listening, speaking), and process (affective, cognitive, creative); the context variables involve community (social/psychological, economic, linguistic), policy (human, legal, fiscal, physical), and profession (teacher, department, the larger profession).

Content and context, of course, do not exist in isolation from each other. While they are often analyzed separately by the researcher and scholar, in practice they interact extensively in the English language arts classroom. Both provide the framework within which the teacher must work. Together, they constrain what the teacher can do. This model suggests that it is only when the substance, skills, and processes of English language arts intersect that we have an accurate representation of the *content* of the disciplines. It also suggests that, when the community, policy, and professional variables intersect, we have a true reflection of the *context* in which English language arts is taught. Finally, the model suggests that, when these two intersecting sets of variables come together, the teaching in the English language arts classroom is most effective. Thus, the model provides a framework for a multidimensional conception of the English language arts teacher's craft. The model is suggested as a guide for the teacher, the administrator, and the curriculum supervisor; it can also provide a reference point for both research and criticism.

A Professional Summons

Many English language arts educators believe that research findings must complement theories of English language arts teaching. The challenge for professionals—theorist, researcher, administrator, and classroom teacher alike—is to participate fully not only in dialogues but in the testing, improvement, and dissemination of ever-increasingly sophisticated models for the teaching of English language arts.

See also Bilingual Education.

—William H. Peters
Texas A&M University

References

Dixon, J. (1975). *Growth through English set in the perspective of the seventies*. London: Cox & Wyman.

Moffett, J., & Wagner, B.J. (1976). *Student-centered language arts and reading, K-13*. Boston: Houghton Mifflin.

Peters, W.H., Grindstaff, F.L., Hanzelka, R.L., & Olson, M.C. (1987). *Effective English teaching: Conception, research and practice*. Urbana, IL: National Council of Teachers of English.

ENROLLMENT PROJECTIONS

Although long-range and short-range planning in a school district cannot proceed until a reasonable projection of district enrollment in the future is available, districts often fail in their attempt to secure this critical planning information. Enrollment projections affect not only planning for school facilities, but also critical-operations areas such as teacher staffing, pupil transportation, school lunches, exceptional-education programming, federal and state mandated program enrollments, and so forth. In states that allocate state support to public education on the basis of district enrollment, a significant portion of the district's operational budget is tied directly to accurate enrollment projections.

The need for accurate enrollment projections is clear, yet most districts estimate future enrollments by utilizing methods that are not tied to established statistical methodology. Most school districts instead employ a methodology that can most accurately be described as the "best guess" approach to enrollment forecasting.

In the early and middle 1960s, public higher education faced a critical need to align bulging student enrollments with available facilities. Because the field of long-range planning was not well established in American higher education, colleges and universities were faced with an unexpected, substantial increase in freshmen enrollments. When the baby boom generation reached college age, American colleges and universities were not ready to provide them with the facilities they required. The baby boom of the 1960s resulted in a concomitant building boom which ended in a building "bust" in the early 70s as the baby boom generation graduated. Along with the empty student dormitories, one of the earliest casualties of this experience was the "best guess" method of forecasting student enrollments.

Generically, enrollment forecasting methods currently utilized in public school districts can be roughly divided into two approaches. In the first approach, enrollment trends are statistically "uncovered" in a database of historical enrollment data. These trends are then extrapolated into the future. In the second approach, a historical database of enrollment data is analyzed to discover enrollment trends, and then these trends are tied to district policy decisions. Policy decisions combined with historical trends are then utilized to produce enrollment projections. In the first approach, enrollment projections are dependent primarily upon the behavior of numbers; in the second approach, however, historical trends are tied to the impact of school-district policy and to the combined behavior of individual members of the school community.

Although enrollment projections tied to the behavior of numbers is an approach that has been widely used and often used successfully, it is not sensitive enough to provide reliable enrollment estimates in a management atmosphere that is becoming increasingly complex. Additionally, it only works well where enrollments are either increasing or decreasing in an orderly fashion; that is, it does not model curvilinear trends. Whereas in the past small districts could estimate future enrollments by simply extrapolating enrollment patterns of the past, managers today must anticipate a future complicated by federal and state mandates and increasing public pressure for fiscal accountability. Future enrollments can be projected as similar to past enrollments only when future district policy will be similar to past policy.

Another reason for abandoning the former method of enrollment projecting is related to the changing demographic characteristics of most school districts and to the insensitivity of this method in reflecting these changes. Most large, urban districts have experienced increases in their minority enrollments in recent years. Additionally, large, medium, and small districts have experienced changes in their local birth-rate as well as changes in the proportion or "mix" of the school-aged population. Many districts are now experiencing an increase in students at the preschool and elementary-grade level and a decrease of students at the middle- and high-school level. Many school districts are also now confronted with a school-aged population that is proportionally smaller than it was in the past. A smaller school-aged population not only means fewer school-age children to serve, it also means less support for school programs, school facilities, and less sensitivity to school problems in the adult population.

The second method or approach to projecting student enrollments, the policy driven model, has a better record in generating consistently accurate estimates of future student enrollments. This approach has produced consistent results because it not only utilizes statistical trends and patterns from a historical database of enrollment history, but also because it identifies and incorporates those district policy decisions that are likely to have immediate and long-range impact upon district enrollment.

The following scenario describes the use of the policy driven enrollment projection model applied to a mythical district called "Sample." Historical enrollment data for the Sample district indicates that preschool enrollments account for about thirty percent of the available preschool population; however, last summer the school board decided to expand the preschool program from three elementary schools to five schools. Additionally, local private schools have recently established or expanded preschool program offerings in the district.

In developing an enrollment projection for next fall and for the next five years, the district administrators must incorporate the following data into their short and long range enrollment estimate: the district's current and historical live-birth rate, the traditional enrollment "draw" of parochial schools in the district (i.e., the percent of the available school-aged population that enrolls in private school), the estimated impact of expanding preschool offerings within the district, the historical and projected enrollment rate of district preschool children into district first-grade classes, and the estimated number of years the new policy will remain in effect. Any enrollment estimate based solely upon the historical live-birth-to-preschool enrollment pattern would clearly be inaccurate, given the likely impact of the school board's policy change and the expansion of preschool offerings by private institutions within the district.

See also Administrative Tasks; Demographic Trends; Planning.

—William Hinsenkamp
Milwaukee Public Schools

Reference

American Demographics.
U.S. Bureau of Census. (Annual). *Special studies, current population reports.* Washington, DC: U.S. Government Printing Office.

EXTRACURRICULAR ACTIVITIES

Extracurricular activities is the term used to denote activities in which students participate that are not part of the main course of study at a school or which are scheduled at other than required school attendance hours. Another term, "student activities," is often used interchangeably; however, this second term is also used when referring to activities in which students may earn credit or which are scheduled during normal school hours. The passage of time has tended to blur the distinction between the terms and where "curricular" and "extra curricular" lines are drawn. Generally these activities center around several areas, including student government, publications, athletics—both in inter-scholastic and intramurals—fine arts as music, drama, and forensics, special interest clubs, school spirit, student-recognition groups, social events, and assemblies.

Extracurricular activities add to the school's program certain dimensions which are often otherwise unattainable. These activities motivate students, develop their leadership skills, promote good self concepts, and help students put to practical use skills learned in the classroom. The activities promote school spirit and attendance and provide alternative ways for students to develop their talents within the educational setting. Extracurricular activities are today considered an important part of the schools' programs. Also research indicates that the most common characteristic among successful people is that they were involved in student activities at school.

Students participate in activities for a number of reasons. Chief among these is the opportunity to socialize with peers for personal enjoyment as well as to achieve success and be recognized by others. As important as participation is, there is evidence that the percentage of students involved varies with the setting and the sociological variables of given time periods. There are many students who do not participate in student activities. A primary reason for noninvolvement is the after-school employment in which students engage. Other reasons for noninvolvement include the lack of relevancy of activities to students' needs or interests, scheduling of activities, and control of activities by social cliques/groups. Today, the alternative activities competing for students' time are many. For an extracurricular activity to be successful, it must provide for some student control, encourage voluntary participation, contain real experiences, offer socializing within the context of the activity, and provide experiences and rewards not otherwise available.

Students should have a major role in organizing and leading extracurricular programs. Student councils often provide leadership for the entire program. Frequently, student councils charter new organizations or clubs (a new science club may be established, for example). The student councils initiate efforts and provide seed monies for the new organizations. Student councils sponsor leadership workshops to train students as leaders of programs and clubs. Student surveys can be initiated to identify needs which are not being met and to focus efforts on meeting the needs.

The administrator's role in operating a successful program is to provide the necessary leadership to organize and stimulate activities, either from direct action or by appointing an activities director who will be responsible for the daily operation. Successful activities programs differ in design; however, there are some identifiable dimensions which contribute to the success of the programs.

The total program, as well as individual activities, should have written and well defined objectives or purposes. A set of guidelines or policies should be developed to provide parameters in which to operate the program. A policy committee made up of teachers, administrators, parents, and students may be organized to help provide input to these guidelines and general aspects of the program. Certain policies should be adopted as official statements by the board of education.

The principal should recruit and appoint faculty sponsors from well qualified, interested teachers. These sponsors should be compensated in their job assignments and salaries. The selection and supervision of sponsors is critical in order to offer quality programs and to properly supervise participating students. In-service programs should be arranged to help sponsors properly administer their assigned activities.

Job descriptions should be developed for the director of activities and for the individual activity sponsors. When sponsors are compensated for their work, they should also be evaluated with mutually agreed criteria.

Financial support of activities is a major problem in most schools as many activities are not supported by state or local funds. Money raising projects such as sales, admissions charges to events, in-school sales (as vending machines), organization dues, and booster club efforts are all sources of support utilized in addition to appropriated funds. Annual budgets should be developed for each activity, and all fund raising efforts should be approved under predetermined guidelines by the principal. All funds should be under control of the school and accounted for by using standard accounting procedures. Personnel who handle funds including students, teachers, and office employees should be trained in procedures utilized to protect these monies.

Evaluating extracurricular activities has recently become the focus of outside groups such as parents and politicians because schools have not put adequate effort into evaluating activity programs. A regular formal evaluation of the total program should occur. Criteria used in evaluating programs should include examining the range and balance of activities offered, student participation, attainment of goals, and opinions of students, parents, and faculty. Also individual activities should be evaluated to determine their effectiveness in meeting student needs and educational purposes. As a result of this process, recommendations for changes should be developed and implemented by the principal and sponsors.

Like most nonrequired programs, student activities are plagued with a number of problem areas which continually reappear. Broad-based participation of all students has been identified as a concern as many students do not participate; likewise, over emphasis on participation for some students may be a detriment (at least in the eyes of politicians) to grades. Recruiting, selection, and compensation of sponsors are problems in many schools. Perpetually, financing of extracurricular activities is a concern because a large portion of the expenses must be raised by the students or the activity itself.

See also Athletics; Student Newspapers.

—James A. Vornberg
East Texas State University

References

"Student activities." (1985, October). *NASSP Bulletin* (Eight Articles, 1-39). Reston, VA: National Association of Secondary School Principals.

Sybouts, W., & Krepel, W.J. (1984). *Student activities in the secondary schools.* Westport, CT: Greenwood Press.

FACILITIES PLANNING

Planning can be defined as purposeful preparation culminating in decisions which provide a basis for subsequent action. It is, in effect, deciding in advance what is to be done. Specific techniques and methodologies for planning facilities vary with both the particular personalities and backgrounds of the school officials and the nature of the particular situation which surrounds the need to engage in a planning activity.

The school facility is a means to an end. Its major contribution is to help create an environment which is most advantageous to the success of each student in accomplishing the desired learning outcome in the instructional program. The facility, therefore, is important in the overall educational process. It serves to reflect the educational hopes and desires of the community.

Gathering essential information from the school's community is the beginning of the total school facilities planning process. Several steps are involved in moving the development of a comprehensive plan for a school system to the actual occupancy of satisfactory physical facilities.

The first of those necessary steps is some form of needs assessment. In the determination of needs, there are both quantitative and qualitative aspects that must be considered. Among them is an analysis of the educational program. At this point the general educational plan merges and becomes a part of school facilities planning.

The educational plan implies the type or quality of education desired, but not necessarily the quantity of spaces and equipment to be provided. The number of pupils to be housed determines in large part the quantity of each kind of facility that will be required in order to carry out the desired educational program. There is a multiplicity of factors that affects future enrollments and makes forecasting a difficult, and often precarious, undertaking.

Assessing needs begins, therefore, with knowledge regarding both present and future enrollments. Enrollments are affected by changes in birth rates, overall population growth and decline, varying economic conditions, changing land-use patterns, and factors such as the holding power of public schools and nonpublic schools. The school census is one of the more important pieces of information that can be used for adequate assessment of the quantitative aspects of school facilities needs.

Projecting enrollments over both the short term and the long term is necessary if appropriate facilities planning is to occur. Enrollment projections can be done in several ways, such as analyzing census data in an historical context and making projections based on that history; using analogy with a neighboring school district of similar demographics; relating school enrollment to total population; using a saturation analysis of available land in the district; and using the average survival ratio technique to estimate future student enrollments.

Appraising the adequacy of existing facilities is a second and important part of assessing needs. Two questions must be answered here: (1) To what extent do existing facilities meet program needs? (2) What resources are available to bridge the gap between existing and needed facilities?

Facilities appraisal is based on the collection of detailed information from records and from on-site inspection. One of the major purposes of a building survey is to determine the extent to which the existing plant can be used in the long-range program. This determination depends to a great extent on the quality of the facilities, their suitability as it relates to safety and health, and the extent to which they allow the desired educational program to be realized.

The location of the facilities in relation to the population to be served is a consideration in assessing facilities. Safety and convenience are factors that must be taken into account, assuring that hazards which might threaten safety and welfare are generally eliminated.

There are several instruments available that have been developed to assist school officials in evaluating facilities that already exist and helping to determine the kinds of facilities that are needed. Most of them are similar in content, and vary primarily in focus or approach. Such instruments are valuable aids for systematic data collection and analysis.

An important part of the assessment of needs is the ability to finance facilities that might be required. School districts have varying abilities to pay for their undertakings. Specific solutions to identified problems or needs are often dependent upon the financial resources that are available. Decisions ultimately made about adding or altering facilities are tempered by the amount of financial resources that can be raised.

Facts do not automatically lead to the formulation of recommendations. They provide the baseline data that need to be synthesized in order to develop a plan of action. Plans of action can be either short term (those solutions needed immediately) or long term (those solutions which have some luxury of time before having to be invoked).

The guidelines that might be used in facilities planning should include the following: (a) review the educational plan, (b) calculate the teaching stations needed and other space requirements, (c) determine both the qualitative and quantitative aspects of each space, and (d) prepare written specifications for the facilities. Each component should be characterized by sufficient specificity to leave no doubt regarding the direction or intent of the plan.

Determining who should be involved in facilities planning is neither an easy nor an unimportant task. A large number of educators, consultants, and community members constitute the team that researches, studies, and discusses the application of the community's resources and desires; it is only with adequate resources that appropriate facilities can be obtained. Generally, the direction of such a team falls under the guidance and responsibility of the superintendent of schools.

The involvement of educators is not necessarily limited to administrators. Considerable information and opinion of value can be gained from classroom teachers and support personnel in the school district. Board of education members should be represented to the extent that their interest and time available for such participation is present.

Consultants to be used fall into two categories. First is the consultant who is trained in specific areas that become necessary for carrying out facilities planning. Such persons are educators with particular expertise in curriculum, evaluation, management, and facilities planning. Educational consultants who specialize in planning activities also are within this group. The second type of consultant is the engineer and architect who lend expertise of a specialized nature. City and regional planners may be involved where and when appropriate. They possess knowledge about the community that may prove invaluable in overall planning of educational facilities. With their knowledge and expertise in regard to education in the context of the state, state education agency personnel are often able to supplement the local educators, planners, and contracted consultants.

Facilities planning, at some stage, requires the services of legal counsel. Although a lawyer may not be required at all steps in the process, he or she cannot be ignored at appointed times. When construction occurs, contractors can and should become a part of the planning team.

Finally, an important constituency that should be included in facilities planning is that of lay citizens. Members of the community have an interest in schools and how they carry out their mission. Groups of citizens can be called upon to assist in a variety of ways, from determining the nature of the educational program to identifying potential problems, to helping sensitize the general public to issues about schools, and to lending invaluable assistance in passing bond issues. Participation by students can result in similar outcomes.

As with all types of planning, facilities planning is not free from potential problems and obstacles. Facilities are generally expensive; the cost concerns many people in school communities. Tax monies are required to provide school facilities, and few community patrons are willing to allow taxes to run rampant.

Enrollment declines that occur in school districts often create problems of a different and difficult nature. School facilities are not the most easily adapted to alternate uses, and school districts frequently find themselves operating and maintaining buildings that are not optimally used. The extreme case is when a building must be closed entirely, and an alternate use found for it.

The needs of education are evolutionary and result in the need to provide differing facilities. The continual upgrading of facilities to accommodate changes in educational programs creates problems and obstacles of varying magnitude. Legislative mandates are of consequence in this regard and must be answered if the overall educational program is to be responsive to the demands of the society.

Facilities planning is no small task of the educational administrator. It requires vision, frequent attention, and expertise of varying degrees. The absence of facilities planning is manifest often in educational programs and organizational structures that are dependent more upon the available facilities than on sound educational principles. Providing facilities, therefore, should not be done in a haphazard fashion or without forethought of purpose.

See also Energy Management; Emergency Procedures; Planning.

—Larry L. Smiley
University of North Dakota

References

Castaldi, B. (1987). *Educational facilities: Planning, modernization, and management.* Boston: Allyn & Bacon.

Hawkins, H.L. & Lilley, H.E. (1986). *Guide for school facility appraisal.* Columbus, OH: Council of Educational Facilities Planners, International.

FACULTY MEETINGS

Faculty meetings have long been a part of organized education. In some schools, they occur only once or twice a year, but in most schools they are scheduled on a regular basis. Irrespective of their frequency, faculty meetings represent an opportunity, in a fragmented school day, for all the faculty members and the administrators to come together to address a topic or problem of general interest or concern.

Planning

Like any other meeting, a faculty meeting must be carefully planned in order to be successful. An administrator sometimes may feel that some topic or problem has been identified as important as long as no further planning is necessary. Such a superficial approach to planning a faculty meeting is not likely to produce satisfactory results.

The first step in planning a faculty meeting is to determine whether, in fact, there is a need for a meeting. Teachers frequently report that faculty meetings are primarily held because the administration wants them, and that what occurs during a meeting could be handled in a different way. It makes little sense, for example, to schedule a faculty meeting in order to make several announcements that could just as easily have been disseminated in written form in the teachers' mailboxes.

If, on the other hand, an administrator is persuaded, after examining the situation and talking with several key members of the staff, that a problem or topic has surfaced that can *best* be addressed through a faculty meeting, then an advance agenda will need to be prepared. In preparing the agenda, the administrator should solicit the ideas and concerns of the faculty. According to teachers, too many faculty meetings are held that are not relevant to the interests and concerns of the faculty. While an administrator need not limit the agenda of a faculty meeting to teacher concerns, the faculty should receive consideration in developing the agenda for a meeting. If faculty members do not believe that issues and problems important to them are being discussed at the faculty meetings, eventually they are likely to feel that the meetings are not relevant, and their participation may become marginal.

In preparing the advance agenda, the administrator should also give consideration to establishing time limits for the discussion of each topic. Such time limits will represent only estimates of how much time will be needed to dispose of a particular matter, and they can be varied during the meeting. Their value is in helping to avoid the problem of spending excessive time during a meeting on a single topic or two, and not enough time on the rest of the agenda.

Attached to the advance agenda should be background material that will be helpful to faculty members in understanding a certain topic or problem that is to be discussed at the faculty meeting. For example, if a faculty meeting is going to focus on suicide prevention, then relevant articles and/or reports should be attached to the agenda, and faculty members should be instructed to read these materials before the meeting.

Once the agenda and related background materials have been prepared, they need to be distributed to the faculty members at least a week prior to the meeting. While there may be certain occasions when this will not be feasible, in general the administrator needs to give the faculty plenty of advance notice of the topics to be discussed at a meeting so that the members will have an opportunity to be thinking about those topics and will have enough time to read the background materials.

It is acknowledged that some faculty members may not use the advance agenda and related materials for the purposes intended, but this possibility should not be used as an excuse for not providing the rest of the faculty with the necessary information before the meeting. If the administration has solicited input from the faculty in deciding on the need for a meeting and in the development of the agenda, then its members are likely to treat the advance agenda and related materials seriously.

Conducting the Meeting

Assuming the guidelines for planning a faculty meeting have been followed, the groundwork for holding a productive and satisfying meeting has already been laid.

Before the formal part of a faculty meeting begins, it may be desirable, depending on local circumstances, for the administrator to schedule a short social period with refreshments in order to provide faculty members with an opportunity to visit with each other. This kind of social activity can build good will and put people in a positive frame of mind before they begin to address problems and topics. However, it should be noted that this type of social activity can also make it more difficult to begin the meeting on time.

At the beginning of the formal part of the faculty meeting, the administrator (or whoever is chairing the meeting) should review the agenda and explain why the meeting is necessary and why the topics are important. In addition, especially during the first part of the meeting, but also periodically during the meeting, the administrator needs to encourage the active participation of those in attendance. Obviously, participation will be more difficult in a large faculty, but by dividing the faculty into smaller subgroups for purposes of discussion and brainstorming, this problem can be minimized.

During the meeting the administrator may need, depending on the situation, to play a variety of leadership roles. These leadership roles have been characterized in various ways by different authorities on group dynamics, but basically they fall into two broad categories: (a) task-accomplishment behaviors and (b) human-relations behaviors. The task-accomplishment behaviors include, for example, the provision of orientation to a group regarding important goals, tasks, and roles; asking for suggestions and ideas; identifying and clarifying issues and alternatives; recommending a procedure for solving a problem; summarizing the main idea of the discussion; providing feedback on the group's performance; and following through on decisions made during the meeting.

Although the task-accomplishment behaviors are important contributions to achieving the goals of a productive and satisfying meeting, it is likely that certain human-relations behaviors will also be needed in order to achieve those goals. The human-relations behaviors include behaviors such as encouraging everyone to participate and demonstrating openness to the ideas of others; relieving tension when it occurs by humor or a change of pace; acknowledging feelings and attitudes which, if not recognized and dealt with effectively, could impair a group's success; and attempting to resolve disagreements constructively.

It should be emphasized that it is not necessary or even desirable in all situations for the administrator to assume the total responsiblity during a faculty meeting for *initiating* all of the task and human relations behaviors. Both categories of behaviors are important to the success of a meeting. However, the administrator should also attempt to encourage and facilitate others to initiate these group-leadership functions and thereby broaden the leadership capacity and contributions of the faculty.

Follow-Up Activities

One of the common complaints of teachers about faculty meetings is that there is very little follow-through on what occurs during the meetings.

Part of the problem may be that, all too frequently, there is no written record of what transpired during the meeting. This is unfortunate. If an administrator feels it is important to gather the entire faculty together for a meeting, then it would seem at least desirable—if not essential—to provide a written record of what took place during the meeting. Therefore, it is recommended that the administrator appoint someone to take minutes during the faculty meeting, and that these minutes be distributed within a few days after the meeting. If faculty meetings are held frequently, the minutes can be attached to the advance agenda for the next meeting. The minutes should include the names of those who attended the meeting (or, in the case of a very large faculty, those who did not attend) and should provide a brief summary of what was discussed, which decisions were made, and what follow-up steps and deadlines are needed.

Follow-up steps after a faculty meeting might include, for instance, investigating questions that were raised during the meeting but could not be immediately answered, appointment of a committee to make recommendations on a problem that was discussed, or implementing a change in procedures that was agreed upon at the meeting. Unless there is appropriate follow-up action after meetings (usually by, but not limited to, the administration), then faculty members will soon begin to doubt the value of such meetings, an attitude which is likely to affect their participation during and after future meetings.

A Concluding Note

Faculty meetings should be scheduled only when they represent the best means for accomplishing a particular goal or objective, and when adequate preparation has been given a priority. Given adequate preparation, effective use of task-accomplishment and human-relation behaviors, and appropriate follow-up steps after the meeting, faculty meetings can lead to productive and satisfying results.

See also Communication; Group Processes; Human Relations; Planning.

—Richard A. Gorton
University of Wisconsin-Milwaukee

References

Gorton, R. (1983). *School administration and supervision: Leadership challenges and opportunities.* Dubuque, IA: Wm. C. Brown.

Gorton, R., & Burns, J. (1985, September). "Faculty meetings: What do teachers think of them?" *The Clearing House, 59*(1), 30-33.

Schmuck, R.A., & Runkel, P.J. (1985). *The handbook of organizational development in schools.* Palo Alto, CA: Mayfield Publishing.

FACULTY WORKSHOPS

The profession is deeply committed to the concepts of staff development and in-service education. States and local school systems have been pouring generous sums of money into projects and programs for continuous upgrading of school personnel.

Although the members of a faculty, as a rule, subscribe to the need for staff development, they often question the value of specific in-service activities. One of the key methods of delivering staff-development activities is the workshop in which a group of teachers is brought together for a limited period of time for instruction by a consultant/lecturer.

The term "workshop" conveys the notion of hands-on experiences through which teachers may gain or improve specific knowledge and skills. Leadership in providing staff development is one of the many tasks of the administrator or supervisor. Those charged with this responsibility can avoid some of the pitfalls in organizing and conducting workshops if they would follow a few rather simple guidelines. We discuss these guidelines in reference to a functional model which can apply to most managerial activities, including workshops. This model consists of three components.

Planning

Input should be obtained from the faculty. Most frequently input is gathered through a survey of in-service needs of teachers in the individual school and/or school district. After the faculty has had an opportunity to express its needs for staff development, a representative group of teachers in cooperation with administrators and supervisors should establish priorities. Then the local school's staff development plan should be coordinated with the district's.

Workshops should be tailored to the needs of teachers in an individual school. The more remote the activities, the less effective they generally are. More and more responsibilities, including staff development, are being placed on the local school, as the individual school becomes recognized as the most viable locus of change.

Objectives of each of the staff development activities should be clearly stated. Those charged with planning a workshop should define objectives in terms of the accomplishments which teachers are expected to achieve as a result of the workshop. Faculty development activities tend to be of two types. First, some workshops are designed to enable teachers to do their present jobs better. Second, workshops are sometimes planned to help teachers develop new skills. Some educators refer to the first type of workshop as in-service education and the second type as staff development.

Some incentive in addition to personal growth should be incorporated into the planning. One such incentive is released time. Workshops ideally should be scheduled on school time. Some school systems provide for staff-development days, pre-school-year and post-school-year planning. Other incentives are college or in-service credits and tuition paid by the school district. School systems cannot expect teachers always to pay for their own staff development and always to undergo training on their own time. It needs to be recognized that the state and local school systems must support staff-development programs.

Implementing

The program must be tailored to the objectives. Workshops can fail when the activities are not aligned with the objectives. Teachers come to the workshop expecting certain learning activities. They are rightfully dissatisfied when the workshop trainers have departed from the planned objectives.

Consultants/instructors should be chosen carefully. Planners have several decisions to make in staffing workshops. They need to select the most qualified instructor they can obtain within the limits of their budget. They should be absolutely certain that the consultants they choose have the qualifications to deliver the programs. They often must choose between someone from within the system and someone from outside the system. There are pros and cons to the use of each. Sometimes an in-district consultant can deliver a program as well as or better than an outside consultant. Sometimes the expertise does not exist within the system and outside consultants must be called in. Those from within know the system better and are available for follow-up. On the other hand, teachers often want to hear from outsiders, particularly well-known consultants, to gain new points of view.

Activities should meet both the perceived needs and actual needs of faculty. Needs as perceived by teachers and actual needs are not always the same. Consequently, both kinds of needs must be dealt with. Teachers tend to favor two types of programs. They like motivational speakers—those who can make them feel good about themselves and the profession. They also like and want hands-on experiences. They want training which will help them with tomorrow's class. When workshops extend over several days, it is often desirable to schedule an entertaining speaker who can amuse the audience and put the participants in a receptive frame of mind. There are a number of skilled motivational speakers on the lecture circuit who have the capacity to delight their audiences while delivering a relevant message and useful information. These speakers are in constant demand to appear before teacher groups. Some of these speakers deliver their message in the best tradition of "show-biz."

For one- or two-day workshops, planners will be well advised to concentrate on practical application. It is perhaps an unfortunate situation but teachers reject what they term "theory." They are impatient with abstractions and want the "nitty-gritty." Instructors, therefore, should bootleg theory under the guise of practice. In this respect, workshop consultants commonly teach inductively, beginning with practice and then inferring theoretical principles as opposed to starting with theory and then providing for practice.

Evaluating

Evaluation of the workshop should be conducted at the end of the workshop by a person(s) designated by the planners, not by the consultant/instructor. An impartial evaluation is sought, and a person who is neither instructor nor participant is in the best position to do this. An evaluation form should be designed, and all evaluations should be anonymous.

Follow-up evaluation is essential. Workshop evaluations often begin and end with participants filling out the evaluation form at the conclusion of the program. These forms generally reveal participants' reactions to the program— whether they liked it or not, whether facilities were adequate. What they cannot tell is whether the workshops actually made any difference in the participants' teaching. Few workshops actually provide for follow-up by the consultant/instructor or other person. It would be particularly beneficial if the consultant/instructor, though he or she may come from outside the system, could be brought back one or more times to visit classrooms and meet with teachers to see if they were translating what they learned in the workshop to the classroom. In some respects, it would be more beneficial if fewer workshops with follow-up evaluation were conducted than more workshops without follow-up evaluation.

The workshop is a time-honored vehicle for delivering in-service education. By following a few simple guidelines, administrators and supervisors can make workshops more effective and more appealing to teachers.

See also Communication; Group Processes; Human Relations; Staff Development.

—Peter Oliva
Georgia Southern College

References

Harris, B.M. (1980). *Improving staff performance through in-service education.* Boston: Allyn & Bacon.

Marks, J. R., Stoops, E., & King-Stoops, J. (1985). *Handbook of educational supervision: A guide for the practitioner* (3rd ed., pp. 205-207). Boston: Allyn & Bacon.

Oliva, P.F. (1984). *Supervision for today's schools* (2nd ed., Chapter 9). White Plains, NY: Longman.

FEDERAL AGENCIES

An estimated two hundred federal aid-to-education laws have been enacted since 1787. The implementation of each becomes the responsibility of either an existing or a newly created federal agency. Thirty or more agencies administer hundreds of federally financed educational programs. Virtually every facet of schooling, from day care through postgraduate, is affected by the actions of federal agencies. Their power and scope is enormous; however, they are a relatively new phenomenon: between 1787 and 1941 only about 15 federal laws directly affecting education were enacted; since World War II, Congress has passed at least 185 education bills.

An important characteristic of federal agencies is that their jurisdiction and action are primarily *categorical*; they are earmarked for specific issues, such as vocational education or special compensatory programs. Federal agencies have traditionally used six methods to affect educational policy. They *stimulate* program development, providing differential funding for needs in specific areas (the Elementary and Secondary Education Act [1965] is an example of this method); *regulate* the activities of state and local education authorities (programs for the handicapped and bilingual education illustrate this method); *generate and disseminate new knowledge* (e.g., the activities of the National Institute of Education and the National Center for Educational Statistics); *provide* services (consultants and technical assistance in specialized areas exemplify this method); *focus attention* on perceived national needs (reports on teacher shortages or special needs of students, for example). And they *grant general aid* to state and local educational authorities. Block grants illustrate this method. It is important to recognize, however, that these methods are not aimed at developing a *rational* plan of federal intervention in educational policy. Rather, they reflect the outcome of political bargaining and coalition formation. They are a patchwork quilt, not a blanket.

Federal agencies are most effective in making a lasting impact on schools when the policy they advocate is structural or organizational, creates a specialized constituency, and is easily monitored. Thus, programs for school breakfasts and mainstreaming are likely to stay in place. Federal efforts requiring changes in classroom teacher effort or methods are the least likely to leave a permanent impression. Further, where the federal agency has created *new* educational *institutions*—for example, day care centers—the impact has been more apparent and long-lasting than in working through the existing K-12 system.

Many federal agencies having no apparent responsibility for education are heavily involved in training and research. The Defense Department has programs to upgrade the skills of recruits. The Labor Department operates manpower training programs. Through the Job Corps, the Office of Economic Opportunity improves the skills of dropouts. The National Science Foundation trains teachers and finances research. School districts have received grants from federal agencies attached to the following departments: Health and Human Services, Defense, Agriculture, Interior, State, Transportation, Housing and Urban Development, Justice, and Labor. The Department of Agriculture is second only to the Department of Education in expenditures for education, and the Department of Defense is a leader in developing curriculum materials for its dependent schools.

Most education-related federal agencies are housed in one of the six Offices of the Department of Education, created in 1979 and controversial since its formation. A brief discussion of the Department of Education is necessary, for its future is inextricably tied to the issues and trends of all educationally related federal agencies. The Department consolidated and centralized the activities (depending upon who is counting) of between 28 and 42 federal agencies. Its formation did not result, however, in fewer federal agencies funding education. Proponents of the Department cite the efficacy of bringing most federal educational agencies under one roof and argue that education is an important *national* endeavor that warrants cabinet-level status. Opponents see it as an extension of federal intrusion into an area that is constitutionally mandated to the states. It is also the beneficiary of the frustration and controversy that accompanied school desegregation, bilingual education, and mainstreaming. Neutrals acknowledge the importance of education but question whether far-removed federal bureaucracies can appreciate, let alone solve, local problems. Virtually all recognize the difficulty of finding "the right answer" from "the right agency" within the Department, and the Department's paperwork approaches the notorious.

The federal educational climate changed decidedly in 1981. It became apparent to most that "the federal era" in education (1965-81) was over, and federal agencies would not have the power nor the personnel they once possessed. However, there is an axiom in social science that, once federal agencies are set in motion, they tend to continue on course unless a *very strong* external force is applied. From this flows the "law of incrementalism": *mostly what will be is mostly what has been.* This suggests that, unless the executive and legislative branches become aggressive, federal agencies will continue in much the same form, fulfilling most of the same functions. But irrespective of their resolute ability to survive, they cannot escape trends that become part of the federal agenda.

For example, the Education Consolidation and Improvement Act, enacted in 1981, introduced two fundamental changes in the pattern of federal funding and agency administration. First, Chapter One of the act replaced Title One of ESEA giving *states and local education agencies primary* responsibility for carrying out the federal education program designed to meet the educational needs of disadvantaged children (the old ESEA Title I). Chapter Two united forty-two programs into "block grants" for improving basic skills and support services as well as special projects. The administration of all Chapter Two programs was vested with state—not federal—agencies.

Under Chapter Two, federal money becomes available through direct grants or through block (entitlement) grants. Direct grants are for programs having "national priority," and recipients must meet federal agency criteria published in the *Federal Register*. Block grants are awarded to states after they have determined how the funds are to be distributed in accordance with intended federal priorities. Block-grant funds have been reduced yearly since 1981. With the passage of legislation mandating reductions in the federal debt, this pattern will likely continue, and federal agencies may exert less influence on educational policy.

Historically, federal agencies have not played a major role in the financial support or control of schooling. The period 1965-81 witnessed unprecedented federal agency growth, and proponents of federal involvement presumed a long-term trend. A more accurate analysis may be that it was an aberration in the history of federal-agency participation which is unlikely to be repeated unless there is a national crisis in education so enormous that state and local units are truly overwhelmed. Then they will turn to Washington, for that is the historical context of federal agencies and education.

See also Federal Role in Education; Funding Methods: State and Federal; State Departments of Education.

—Gerald Unks
University of North Carolina-Chapel Hill

References

Advisory Commission on Intergovernmental Relations. (1980). *The intergovernmental grant system: An assessment and proposed policies.* Washington, DC: ACIR.

Jones, C.O., & Thomas, R.D. (Eds.). (1976). *Public policy making in a federal system.* Beverly Hills, CA: Sage.

Seidman, H. (1970). *Politics, position power: The dynamics of federal organization.* New York: Oxford University Press.

FEDERAL ROLE IN EDUCATION

The national government's involvement with schools and colleges has evolved very slowly—and with considerable ferment—over a century and a half. Although the national government has been reluctant to intrude on the traditional autonomy of the education process, the federal role began to expand in scope and dollar amounts beginning with World War II, and then escalated sharply in the 1960s. Five periods of federal involvement in the educational process are discernible.

Establishing the Framework

Neither the U.S. Constitution nor the accompanying Bill of Rights refers to education. Indeed, during the Constitutional Convention of 1787, education was mentioned only once (in connection with a proposal to establish a national university). Nonetheless, as early as 1785 the Continental Congress had enacted the Survey Land Ordinance to dispose of a portion of federal lands in the sparsely settled Western territories for the purpose of endowing public schools. And in 1787, that policy was affirmed with the passage of the Northwest Ordinance which (in perhaps the first unequivocal expression of support for education by the embryonic national government) proclaimed that: "Religion, morality, and knowledge being necessary to good government and the happiness of mankind, schools and the means of education shall forever be encouraged."

Invigorating the Practical Arts

The Land-Grant College Act of 1862, better known as the "Morrill Act" (named for the Vermont Congressman who was its principal sponsor), cast the federal government in a new role, that of pressing colleges to engage in more practical pursuits, specifically, instruction relevant to "agriculture and the mechanic arts." Over the next three-quarters of a century, federal involvement in education was manifested primarily in the modest level of support for those land-grant colleges. That support was bolstered somewhat by the Hatch Act of 1887 (which added agricultural experimental stations) and the second Morrill Act of 1890 (which provided for annual grants to the land-grant colleges). The Vocational Education Act of 1917 (the Smith-Hughes Act) extended the federal role a step further via grants-in-aid to public schools to promote vocational education. In all, though, until the outbreak of the World War II, the federal government's involvement in education had been decidedly sporadic and marginal.

War and Science

The nation's immersion in World War II prompted unprecedented interaction between research universities and the government. This partnership was most dramatically evident in the historic "Manhattan Project," which gave birth to the atomic bomb. Meanwhile, the Servicemen's Readjustment Act of 1944 (the famous "G.I. Bill") provided returning veterans with billions of dollars for education and training. Three further developments, among many, served as milestones during the post-war era:

1. Federally sponsored research expanded after the War with the creation in 1950 of the National Science Foundation.

2. The National Defense Education Act of 1958 (prompted by the Soviet Union's successful launch of the Sputnik satellite the year before) reflected Congress' acceptance of increased responsibility for education. This multi-faceted legislation stimulated colleges to engage in teaching and training activities deemed important to the national defense, in particular, science, mathematics, and foreign languages.

3. With higher education rapidly expanding, the Higher Education Facilities Act of 1963 propelled the government into a new arena—subsidizing construction on college campuses.

Expansion and Regulation

A new era in the federal government's support of education began in 1965 as the heavily Democratic 89th Congress (1965-67), spurred on by President Lyndon B. Johnson (who had been elected by a landslide in 1964), enacted two sweeping education measures. Both were "omnibus" bills; that is, they encompassed a number of loosely related Titles (now called Chapters). And both laws were "categorical;" that is, they were restricted in their coverage to specific, defined purposes, rather than providing "general" aid to education. First, the Elementary and Secondary Education Act of 1965 substantially broadened the federal commitment in education; it is justly regarded as the nation's "first great breakthrough in Federal school aid." Title I of this Act authorized an unprecedented billion dollars annually to be allocated among school districts with large numbers of children from low-income families. Within months of the passage of the Elementary and Secondary Education Act, the Higher Education Act of 1965 became law. At its core, Title IV created several student financial-assistance programs; these have since evolved—especially via the Education Amendments of 1972 and 1980 and the Middle Income Student Assistance Act of 1978—into multibillion dollar grant and loan programs which benefit several million college students each year. The Higher Education Act of 1965 has been reauthorized periodically by Congress, most recently in 1986 for a five-year extension through 1991. Two additional developments highlight this era:

Government Regulation. In the 1970s, Congress and the Executive Branch began to require more fiscal accountability by colleges for their use of federal monies. The federal government also insisted upon compliance with national social-policy objectives, most notably legislation and regulations designed to protect employees (for example, occupational safety and health, labor-management relations, and the provision of employee benefit-plan information) and to prevent discrimination on account of race, gender, or age.

U.S. Department of Education. By a razor-thin margin, Congress established in 1979 (effective 1980) a cabinet-level Department of Education. An education office had first been created in 1867, but throughout its numerous transformations that office had been relegated to subcabinet status within larger administrative units (from 1953 to 1979 as part of the U.S. Department of Health, Education, and Welfare). Despite the longstanding concerns of some critics about the threat of "federal control," education—after nearly two centuries—had been "promoted" to cabinet status within the federal government.

The Federal Role at a Plateau

Since the 1980 national election, the Reagan Administration has attempted to limit the federal role in many areas of national life, including education. But, while the Administration persistently has sought sharp cutbacks in federal support of education, the Congress, being more favorably disposed to a significant federal role in education, consistently has resisted the President's initiatives. To date, Congress has prevented serious rollbacks in either the size or scope of federal support. Thus the federal influence in education, having steadily expanded in recent decades, is at a plateau; as of 1987, an uneasy tension prevails between the executive and legislative branches over the desirable extent of federal support of education.

The Federal Policymaking Process

A review of federal policymaking in education suggests several important characteristics:

1. Federal support for education is *sizable*. Appropriations for fiscal year 1987 (ending September 30) amounted to $19.5 billion, not counting federal education and training programs funded apart from the U.S. Department of Education. Of that total, the biggest segment—$8.2 billion or about 42 percent—goes for student financial aid programs.

2. Despite its magnitude, the federal role in education has always been *subordinant* to that of state and local education agencies. Federal support has never amounted to more than a small fraction of the $240 billion funding from all sources for elementary, secondary, and higher education.

3. Federal policy in education, as in numerous other policy areas, is *fragmentary* and *diffuse*, a product of innumerable actions—major education bills and obscure specialized programs alike. The consequence is "a bewildering hodgepodge of enactments strewn across dozens of federal agencies and congressional subcommittees." In fact, there are hundreds of federal education and training programs, and less than a fifth of them are overseen by the U.S. Department of Education. Education-related programs are to be found in almost every major agency, with large-scale activities being carried out, to illustrate, by the Departments of Defense, Health and Human Services, Energy, Agriculture, Interior, and the Veterans' Administration—and on it goes.

4. Federal education policies have always been targeted to achieve specific purposes. Instead of providing broadly-cast general support for education, policies have been more narrowly *instrumental*, that is, designed to promote other societal objectives. For example, in the nation's earliest years, public land development was an objective achieved in part through "education" policy. In more recent years, two broad objectives, among a multitude of others,

have been salient: promoting equality of educational opportunity and stimulating nationally-needed research and development.

5. Although the federal role in education is usually discussed in terms of policymaking by the executive and legislative branches, the federal *courts* have often played a highly influential role in shaping education policy. Among numerous examples of pivotal U.S. Supreme Court decisions are *Brown v. Board of Education* (1954; school desegregation); *Engel v. Vitale* (1962, church-state separation); and *National Labor Relations Board v. Yeshiva* (1980; collective bargaining).

Viewed across the span of two centuries, the federal government balked initially at becoming involved with education issues and, accordingly, participated in relatively minor fashion until recent years. That support has now reached massive proportions. Despite that growth, however, the current level of federal support still constitutes only a small proportion of total revenues derived from all sources—including state, local, and private sources—that serve to finance education.

Compelling national priorities that vie with education for perennially scarce resources, coupled with swelling federal budget deficits, contribute to the uncertainty of the federal education role in future years. Ultimately, the dimensions of that role are not circumscribed by any "higher law"; the scope and size of the federal government's involvement in education is, and will continue to be, shaped by the will of the American polity.

See also Federal Agencies; Funding Methods: State and Federal.

—Jack H. Schuster
Claremont Graduate School

References

Clark, D.L., & Amiot, M.A. (1983). "The disassembly of the federal educational role." *Education and Urban Society, 15,* 367-87.

Miller, R.A. (Ed.). (1981). *The federal role in education: New directions for the eighties.* Washington, DC: Institute for Educational Leadership.

Schuster, J.H. (1982). "Out of the frying pan: The politics of education in a new era." *Phi Delta Kappan, 63,* 583-91.

FINANCING OF SCHOOLS

Public elementary and secondary schools in the United States are financed with a combination of local, state, and federal revenue. Local revenues, primarily from property tax, historically have been the major source of school revenues. Indeed, early in the twentieth century, property taxes provided nearly all school revenues, with the states providing only small amounts, and the federal government barely any revenues.

Heavy reliance on local property taxes, however, produces the fiscal inequity that for years has been characteristic of public school financing because property wealth per pupil, the local property tax base, is distributed unequally across school districts in most states. At a given tax rate, districts highest in property wealth per pupil are able to raise more money per pupil than districts with an average level of property wealth per pupil, and several times more than districts poorest in property. In many states, the ability to raise local property tax revenues might vary by a factor of seven to one across districts. As a result, revenues per pupil range considerably, with the differences related directly to local property wealth per pupil. High revenue per pupil districts usually are high in property wealth per pupil and able to produce handsome revenues with below average tax rates, while low revenue per pupil districts usually are poor in property, having modest revenues per pupil even though usually levying above average tax rates.

These fiscal inequities were the subject of several court suits in the 1970s, beginning with the 1971 *Serrano v. Priest* case in California. These cases argued that the linkage between spending and property wealth violated state equal protection and education clauses. In 1973, a U.S. Supreme Court decision in *San Antonio Independent School District v. Rodriguez* held that these inequities did violate the federal constitution; and, as a result, cases were brought in nearly half the states. In half the cases, state courts overturned the school finance structure, but upheld them in the other half.

An actual court mandate or threat of one, in part, led 30 of the 50 state legislatures to enact school finance reforms during the past fifteen years. All reforms were designed to distribute more aid to districts poor in property wealth per pupil. These reforms were primarily responsible for increasing the state role in financing schools during the past decade.

As school finance reform proposals were debated in legislatures, the full complexity of school finance problems emerged. Spending differences in some states were related to average district household income as well as property wealth per pupil. In some districts, moreover, concentrations of low income students lived in districts high in property wealth. Further, legitimate reasons were articulated for spending more on some students, such as low achieving, limited-English-proficient, and physically and mentally handicapped. Some districts with higher costs caused by sparsity, rural isolation and higher prices for educational goods also required more funds per student. Interrelationships between taxpayer equity and student equity in school-financing schemes also became clearer.

In the late 1970s, an equity framework for sorting out these school-finance objectives was developed; it provided not only a conceptual framework for organizing school-finance equity issues but also a methodology for assessing equity under different equity goals. The framework includes four key components.

The first is specification of the group for whom equity is desired. The primary groups of concern are (a) students who receive educational services; (b) taxpayers who provide the resources to finance schools; and (c) teachers and administrators who provide educational services. The second is specification of the object that is to be distributed equitably within the group. Different objects are appropriate for different groups. Possible objects for students include current operating expenditures per pupil, state and local revenues per pupil, instructional revenues per pupil, class size, and allocated instructional time. Possible objects for taxpayers include total taxes paid, taxes paid as a percent of household income, and whether an equal tax rate produces an equal level of revenues per pupil from state and local sources. Possible objects for teachers include salaries, promotional opportunities within teaching, and working conditions such as class size. Clearly, there are several potential objects for each group of concern.

The third factor includes the equity principles used to judge the distribution of objects for the group of concern. There are three main principles. The first is horizontal equity. This would require equality of distribution of the objects of concern, and is a standard school-finance equity principle for students. The second is vertical equity which allows different amounts for differences considered legitimate. For students, the vertical equity principle allows extra revenues for special student needs such as handicapping condition and for special district needs such as sparsity and price. For taxpayers, vertical equity allows higher income taxpayers to pay a higher percent of their income in taxes, the progressive burden of tax incidence. For teachers, vertical equity allows teachers with greater responsibilities and longer work years to earn a higher salary. The third equity principle is nondiscrimination; it identifies variables that should not be associated with differences in the distribution of objects such as property wealth per pupil and household income, the traditional school finance problem.

Finally, the fourth factor includes the statistical measures used to assess the equity of the system once a group, object, and equity principle have been selected. Since different statistics have different characteristics, the selection of a specific statistic also entails value judgments. Usually, the coefficient of variation is used to assess the equity of a distribution, and the correlation and wealth elasticity are used to assess the relationship between revenues per pupil and property wealth per pupil.

Conclusions about the equity of a state school-finance system vary with the group, object, equity principle and statistic chosen, and the time period over which the tests are made.

School finance formulas historically have not been related explicitly to such an equity framework but easily can be. For flat grant programs, the state pays each district an equal amount per pupil. For low or minimum foundation programs, the state identifies an expenditure per pupil level the state will guarantee by providing state aid to make up the difference between what a required local tax rate will raise and that minimum level. Both reflect a variation of the student equality principle for state and local revenues per pupil. The variation is that the state is responsible only for a minimum level of spending, or for revenues that would provide all students with at least a basic education program. However, this value perspective, which prevailed in the pre-1970s era, produced the fiscal inequities described in the first few paragraphs and was challenged in the courts.

Today, states are moving to much higher level foundation programs, where the minimum expenditure per pupil level is set at the previous year's average or even at a level far above the average, such as the 60th or 75th percentile. This reflects a closer approximation to the student equality principle. Full adherence to equality of expenditures per pupil would require a full state funding program, such as programs in California and Hawaii, in which the state sets essentially the same expenditure per pupil level for all schools and districts.

The vertical equity principle for students is reflected in extra revenues provided, either through categorically funded programs or pupil weighted programs, for students from low income backgrounds, with limited-English-proficiency, handicapping conditions, special gifts and talents or in vocational programs. Price adjustments to recognize the varying purchasing power of the educational dollar across regions in a state, and higher costs due to density, sparsity, or rural isolation reflect vertical equity for districts.

The nondiscrimination principle is embodied in district power equalizing, guaranteed tax base, or resource equalizer formulas in which the state, for a given tax rate, guarantees equal revenues per pupil—for all districts—from a combination of state and local sources. Districts are allowed to set different tax rates, and thus spending levels. Spending differences result, but from tax effort differences, not wealth differences. When such formulas include both property wealth and income measures of fiscal capacity, they help keep spending related to neither property wealth nor average district household income.

These mechanisms to create equitable state school-finance structures are still funded by a combination of state, local, and federal sources. The federal role peaked in 1979 at 9.3 percent; it has fallen to about 6 percent and is unlikely to rise in the near future. The state role has risen to nearly 50 percent, and several states, although they increased taxes to finance new and expensive education reforms, have not been able to break the 50 percent level. Local sources have fallen from above 50 percent in the 1960s to about 44 percent.

Finally, both traditional and new sources of school revenues produce modest, annual increases in education funding. The best state lotteries produce $100 per student, not insignificant, but not large compared with a national average expenditure per pupil of $3400. Even increasing the state sales tax a penny (a method for financing popular education reforms) produced a twenty percent increase in revenues in only one state—South Carolina. While property taxes produce the bulk of local revenues, the tax and spending limitation fever is still high, keeping property tax increases low. Local education foundations can provide some additional revenues, but the largest to date have produced less than a one percent increase in the budget.

See also Funding Methods: State and Federal.

—Allan Odden
University of Southern California

References

Berne, R., & Stiefel, L. (1984). *The measurement of equity in school finance.* Baltimore, MD: Johns Hopkins University Press.

Garms, W.I., Guthrie, J.W., & Pierce, L. (1978). *The economics and politics of public education.* Englewood Cliffs, NJ: Prentice-Hall.

Odden, A., McGuire, C.K., & Belches-Simmons, B. (1983). *School finance reform in the states, 1983,* Denver, CO: Education Commission of the States.

FOREIGN LANGUAGE EDUCATION

Foreign language education has undergone rapid changes in the last few years. In the 1960s and 1970s, the predominant methodology for teaching a second language was the "audio-lingual approach," which viewed language learning as habit formation. Basic patterns of the language were taught through dialogue memorization and then extended in pattern practice drills. Although proponents of an audio-lingual approach claimed that it would teach students to communicate in a second language, very few students ever reached that goal, since they rarely had the opportunity to go beyond rote-level practice in their daily learning activities.

In the early 1980s, leaders in foreign language education and the American Council on the Teaching of Foreign Language, the national organization of foreign language teachers, began to call for the development of communicative skills and proficiency in a language as legitimate, valued goals of second language instruction. Critics of foreign language instruction in the 1970s pointed out that students might have developed *linguistic competence* in a language (the ability to produce discreet sounds, vocabulary, grammatical forms, even whole sentences) but that they had not developed *communicative competence*—the ability to interact appropriately in a spontaneous interchange involving the exchange of new, unknown, realistic information and ideas. They pointed out an obvious, but previously unobserved, point that students learn to communicate only if they engage in communicative and information-sharing activities, every day in every class session.

In 1981, in a move to work toward the establishment of nationally agreed upon goals and outcomes of the study of a second language, the American Council on the Teaching of Foreign Language, published its *Provisional Proficiency Guidelines*. Looking at communicative skills as the major goal of second-language instruction, these guidelines give both generic and language-specific descriptions of language learners' abilities at succeeding levels of proficiency development. These descriptions, based on the Foreign Service Institute's oral interview test, indicate communicative skills that learners display and types of communicative interactions that learners carry out as they progress from the novice state to the superior level in proficiency. While they are heavily influenced by the oral interview, the guidelines nevertheless provide descriptions of proficiency in all skills areas (including listening, speaking, reading, writing, and culture).

These proficiency guidelines have already made a strong impact on the profession. Some states are requiring prospective foreign language teachers to be tested on their language proficiency as part of the certification process. At several United States universities, students will have to pass an oral proficiency exam to meet a language requirement at a certain level, regardless of how many credits they have accumulated. State task forces on curriculum development have used the proficiency guidelines for developing suggested learning outcomes for foreign language programs and for determining curriculum development.

The impact of the proficiency movement is also being felt in the foreign language classroom where teachers are now re-evaluating their instructional strategies in light of how well they develop students' proficiency. In particular, the following principles are useful for fostering proficiency:

1. *Maximum and consistent use of the second language in all classroom activities.* The one variable that is known to affect language acquisition is the amount of time students are exposed to and use the second language. Since the classroom is probably the only location where students are likely to use the second language, teachers are encouraged to conduct all classroom activities in that language and to teach students vocabulary and structures for interacting in those activities.

2. *Opportunities and training in asking questions and in initiating communication.* Like classroom interactions in other disciplines, teachers in the foreign language classroom usually ask the questions, and students answer them. However, in the proficiency guidelines, one skill that raises a student's rating in proficiency is the ability to ask questions and to initiate a communicative exchange. Therefore, teachers today are planning activities in which students both ask and answer questions, including pair-work interactions, classroom interviews, and role-playing.

3. *Opportunities for extended discourse.* Another characteristic that typifies more advanced proficiency in the guidelines is the ability to engage in extended discourse—that is, the ability to say several utterances in response to a question or a topic, rather than the typical one-sentence answer to a question that we find in most classrooms. Given the generally large number of students in foreign language classes, it is difficult to provide for the type of uninterrupted, continuous individual speech needed to attain that goal. Thus, more and more, teachers are using pair-work activities (such as describing a picture to a partner or talking about one's weekend) as a means of promoting extended discourse.

This is a time of excitement in foreign language education, as teachers rededicate themselves to the goal of teaching their students to communicate and re-educate themselves in instructional strategies and classroom activities for reaching that goal.

See also Bilingual Education; English Education.

—Constance K. Knop
University of Wisconsin-Madison

References

Brumfit, C. (1984). *Communicative methodology in language teaching: The roles of fluency and accuracy.* Cambridge, England: Cambridge University Press.

Grittner, F.M. (Ed.). (1985). *A guide to curriculum planning in foreign language.* Madison, WI: Wisconsin Department of Public Instruction.

Higgs, T.V. (1984). *Teaching for proficiency, the organizing principle.* Lincolnwood, IL: National Textbook Company.

FUNDING METHODS: STATE AND FEDERAL

As alternative funding methods, discretionary and formula funding are based on different assumptions and have different impacts. Under discretionary funding, the basic assumption is that all eligible recipients will not receive equal unit shares and that the administering agency will determine which eligible recipient will receive the funds and how much will be awarded to each recipient. An additional assumption is that the funding decisions will be made by the executives in the granting agency and that the criteria used in determining the eligible recipients and award amounts will be considered to be subjective. The typical assumptions under discretionary funding are that all recipients may not recognize the merits of the activity, that all may not have the expertise to carry out the program, or that demonstration or experimental programs may be a more appropriate use of funds than broad implementation of the activity.

Under formula funding, the basic assumption is that all eligible recipients in equal circumstances will receive equal unit shares. The role of the executives in the granting agency will be ministerial rather than discretionary and the appropriateness of the amount of the award to each recipient can be verified and agreed to by an independent third party. The typical assumption is that each eligible recipient recognizes the merits of the activity being funded and has the capability to implement the program.

Funding at the State Level

The formula funding mechanisms most common in use among the states are flat grants, foundation plans, percentage equalizing, guaranteed tax base, district power equalizing, and full state funding. Categorical funding (i.e., money that can only be used for a specific defined purpose) is most commonly distributed by the flat-grant mechanism where aid is allocated on a per unit basis (e.g., per pupil, per instructional unit, per mile) without regard to district wealth or tax effort, or a variant of it called the *excess cost formula*. According to this variant the state (or federal government) pays a specified percentage of local expenditures above some minimum amount. Currently no state uses the flat grant to allocate general aid (money that can be expended for any education related purpose). Rather, one of the other mechanisms are used. Of these, full state funding, where the state pays for the entire cost of education in the state, is used by only two states. States may, and very commonly do, use one formula for the allocation of general aid and other formulas for the allocation for different categorical aids.

Under the foundation plan the state establishes a minimum support level per pupil (F) that the state guarantees will be provided each district in the state that makes a specified local tax effort (r). State aid is determined by the following formula:

$$SA_i = SC_i (F - r AV_i)$$

According to the above formula, state aid (SA_i) is the difference between the foundation support level (F) and the local share (r AV_i), multiplied by the student count (ADA, ADM, weighted pupils, etc.). The local share is determined by multiplying the required local effort (r) by the districts assessed valuation (AV_i).

Under the percentage equalizing formula there is no state-guaranteed expenditure level or required minimum tax effort. Instead, the focus is on equalizing a district's capacity in reaching its self-determined expenditure level. The state provides a specified percentage of that expenditure, the percentage being a function of the district's relative wealth. State aid is determined by the following formula:

$$SA_i = SC_c \left(1 - f \frac{AV_i}{AV_s}\right) E_i$$

In this formula the function f is the local share of expenditures whose value is determined by public policy. Once f has been determined, the relationship of the assessed valuation per pupil in the local school district (AV_i) to the average assessed valuation per pupil in the state becomes the determinant of what percentage of a locally determined expenditure level (E_i) will be provided by the state.

The guaranteed tax base (GTB) plan has the same philosophical basis as the percentage equalizing plan: equalization of fiscal capacity and local determinatioon of expenditure. This is accomplished by the state determining an assessed valuation per pupil (AV_o) that it is willing to guarantee to each district. State aid under the GTB is calculated by the formula:

$$SA_i = SC_i (r AV_g - r AV_i)$$

According to this formula, state aid is the difference between what the district actually raises at a given tax rate and what the same tax rate would yield if levied against the guaranteed tax base.

The final formula used in the allocation of state aid is the district power equalizing (DPE) formula which is expressed as:

$$SA_i = SC_i (E_i - r AV_i)$$

Under DPE the state establishes a schedule of effort, usually expressed in mills, and the expenditure (revenue) guaranteed at each level df effort. The district then chooses the expenditure level it desires (E_i) and the state pays the difference between the chosen expenditure level and what would be generated if the scheduled tax rate associated with that expenditure level (r) were levied against the district tax base (AV_i).

Funding at the Federal Level

Formula funding at the federal level is used to distribute the largest share of educational dollars. Funds through the largest program, Chapter 1, are allocated to each state by a flat grant based on the number of children of poverty in the state weighted by a factor to recognize cost differentials among states. The specific formula funding for other programs varies (e.g., funding for vocational education is based on a formula which takes into consideration two factors: the state's median personal income and population to be served). Under the Education for All Handicapped Children Act, the principal portion of the federal funds is allocated to each state on a formula basis under which each state receives a uniform amount per handicapped child being served in the state.

Discretionary funding is also used at the federal level in the allocation of education aid. Notable among these programs funded with discretionary funds are bilingual programs. Funds are for demonstration programs, and local school districts make application directly to the Secretary of Education. In determining which local school districts will receive the grants, the secretary considers a variety of factors, including the distribution of linguistic minorities and their relative needs.

The block-grant approach, the approach used by the federal government to allocate aid under Chapter II of the ECIA and the term used by a few states to describe their systems of funding special programs, combines some of the elements of both discretionary and formula funding. In the case of Chapter II funds as distributed to states on an objective basis (the state's share of the country's school age population) and 80 percent of this is redistributed by the state to local districts using a distribution formula which combines enrollment with adjustments for "high cost" children. The remaining 20% may, however, be distributed as discretionary grants.

Current Issues

Discretionary funding has been the subject of some controversy and criticism. On the one hand, discretionary funding increases the leadership opportunities of the granting agencies. Demonstration, model, pilot and "lighthouse" programs can be funded. In the current school reform era, the popularity of discretionary funding appears to be increasing as a way to promote high visibility/low cost activities and also to encourage local school districts to undertake specific activities. The assumption is that the promotion of designated programs and services will have a "spin-off" benefit to other local school districts. On the other hand, history has shown that too often when the funding for the activity is terminated, the activity is terminated with little residual impact. Thus, one may question the ultimate worthwhileness of the expenditure. Of equal concern is the disequalization that occurs when some districts are the recipients of discretionary funds and others are not. For those and other reasons, discretionary funding and categorical funding have lost favor over the years, while formula funding, especially equalization formula have gained favor. This trend is expected to continue.

See also Financing of Schools.

—L. Dean Webb
Arizona State University

References

Augenblick, A. (1984). "School finance in the 1980s, part I: Alternative approaches to providing state aid for schools." *ERS Spectrum, II*(2): 38-46.

Johns, R.L., Morphet, E.L., & Alexander, K. (1983). *The economics and financing of education* (4th ed.). Englewood Cliffs, NJ: Prentice-Hall.

Jones, T.H. (1985). *Introduction to school finance technique and social policy.* New York: Macmillan.

G

GIFTED AND TALENTED EDUCATION

Gifted and talented children have special needs that must be met if they are to fulfill their potential. In addressing those needs, education programs should provide gifted and talented children with equal educational opportunity. These programs will help develop individual minds and, in the process, refine a precious national resource.

Gifted and talented children are traditionally the top 3 percent to 5 percent of the population. Specific gifted categories include general intellectual ability, specific academic aptitude, visual and performing arts, creativity, and leadership. The first three attributes are most commonly served in gifted and talented programs.

Problems

The field of gifted and talented education has been plagued since its inception with charges of elitism and special privilege. Many educators and parents remain insensitive to the special needs of gifted and talented children. In addition, gifted and talented professionals have paid insufficient attention to the problems of culturally different, economically disadvantaged, and underachieving gifted children. However, with a higher priority and more adequate identification and programming, these problems can be ameliorated.

Identification

Identification criteria are as varied as gifted and talented categories. Ideally, a program's criteria should match its curriculum. General intellectual ability and specific academic aptitude programs use IQ and achievement test criteria. These tests, however, would be an inaccurate and inefficient way to identify children for a visual and performing arts program. Such programs usually have professional artists evaluate the talents of potential children.

Districtwide intelligence tests are often a first-level screen for students with general intellectual ability. The cut-off score establishing eligibility for intellectual ability gifted programs is usually 130. Similarly, academic aptitude tests identify students with specific academic aptitudes. Students must score in the ninety-ninth percentile on one or two academic aptitude tests to be eligible for a specific aptitude gifted program. Some programs combine high intellectual ability and high achievement programs. Few pro-

grams select only for creativity and leadership. Instead, these traits are incorporated in intellectual ability and specific academic aptitude programs. Creativity tests and actual performance typically identify children with these abilities.

Relying only on tests to determine eligibility, however, causes many gifted children to be overlooked. In addition to districtwide and individual tests, most programs use teacher nominations and behavioral characteristic rating scales, such as the Renzulli and Hartman *Scale for Rating Behavioral Characteristics of Superior Students*. Parent, peer, and self-nominations also help to identify gifted and talented students.

Curriculum Models

The Guilford/Meeker *Structure of the Intellect* model, Renzulli's *Triad Enrichment Model*, and Bloom's *Taxonomy of Educational Objectives* are the most influential curricular models in gifted and talented education. However, many other useful models exist in the field.

Programs

A variety of programs or student groupings is available. Full-time homogeneous classes, full-time heterogeneous classes, and several part-time grouping programs meet the needs of gifted and talented children. Special day classes are generally the most effective approach to educating the gifted child. These classes consist entirely of gifted and talented students who are brought together for at least one complete school day. Special day classes may be conducted one day a week, a few days a week, or throughout the entire week. The length of a program is a measure of the community's commitment to gifted education as well as the amount of funds and experience available in the district.

Part-time and cluster groups are the most common approaches to gifted and talented education. Part-time groupings or "pull-out" programs remove identified gifted and talented students from the regular school program and group them together for part of the school day to attend qualitatively different classes or seminars. This approach offers the student a brief opportunity to explore problems in more depth or to become involved in a more engrossing advanced activity. However, it is plagued by scheduling difficulties and a lack of curriculum coherence.

In cluster groupings, gifted and talented students remain in the regular classroom and receive instruction from the regular classroom teacher. Typically, teachers must complete gifted teaching certification, and instruction is expected to be qualitatively different from regular classroom teaching. This approach requires no extra expenditure of funds. The most significant problem with cluster groupings is that many communities that claim to offer a gifted cluster program in fact provide only a regular honors or advanced-placement class, leaving gifted and talented students underserved.

Enrichment activities are usually combined with other approaches. Students remain in their regular classrooms and receive advanced materials and/or special opportunities in addition to their regular educational program. This approach gives the student exposure to a wide variety of activities and materials that are qualitatively different from regular instruction—for example, oceanographic projects, theatrical performances, museum tours, and literary studies.

Independent study may mean receiving instruction from a mentor or enrolling in a correspondence course. Typically, however, independent study involves working with a teacher on a student-designed course. This approach, like enrichment, is most useful when combined with other more substantive approaches.

Acceleration, placing students in more advanced grades or classes, is another popular approach to gifted education. Grade-skipping is the classic method of acceleration. Subject-skipping accelerates the student in a specific subject or class. Telescoping condenses or collapses the high-school program into two or three years. A student's level of maturity is the independent variable most frequently used to determine whether acceleration or enrichment is the better course.

Post-secondary educational opportunities are usually available for some portion of the school day. This approach allows gifted high-school students to grow at their own pace and, in some cases, to advance through the educational system more rapidly. These opportunities expose gifted students to a plethora of course offerings not available in high school.

See also Learning Styles.

—David M. Fetterman
Stanford University

References

Clark, B. (1983). *Growing up gifted: Developing the potential of children at home and at school.* Columbus, OH: Charles E. Merrill.

Davis, G.A., & Rimm, S.B. (1985). *Education of the gifted and talented.* Englewood Cliffs, NJ: Prentice-Hall.

Fetterman, D.M. (in press). *Excellence and equality: A qualitatively different perspective on gifted and talented education.* New York: SUNY Press.

GRADES AND GRADING

Evaluation of student performance has long been recognized as an integral and indispensable part of the learning process. While grading is at best inaccurate and unreliable, the fact remains that grading is not only inevitable, it has been so ingrained in the educational process that to negate its use would thwart its primary function—the assessment of learner outcomes. Traditionally, grades have served as marks of quality control for the school, the public in general, and prospective employers. For schools in particular, grades have been used to determine how well students have met academic standards, performed in relation to certain teacher expectations, and as an expression of the results of student performance on examinations.

Historically, discontent and experimentation have characterized the grading process. Prior to the turn of the twentieth century, experimentation with a variety of grading practices existed, with three marking systems playing a predominant role—descriptive terms, numerical scales, and alphabetical letters. By the turn of the century, however, acceptance of alphabetical symbols had become widespread and strongly supported by teachers, students, and parents. The popular appeal of what has been aptly characterized as the "four little gods (A,B,C,D) and the little devil (F)" has resulted in unwavering faith and obeisance. Despite this general acceptance, dissatisfaction has remained regarding the inaccuracy and inadequacy of both measuring and evaluating student performance. Foremost among these concerns were the grade's inability to have consistent and universal meaning to those interpreting the grade and the grade's inability, if solely reflective of performance, to describe intellect or application. Grade interpretation is often complicated by not knowing which of three philosophies may be held by the grader: (1) the degree of gain in achievement from the beginning of the marking period or course to its conclusion; (2) the overall level of the student's performance in relation to group norms; and (3) the amount of achievement a student demonstrates in relation to his or her own potential.

During the decade of the 1960s, concern about grading equity became widespread, and serious exploration and study of promising innovative practices were initiated. The academic mood called for a break with traditions in grading and the advent of alternative strategies to student assessment practices most commonly used—numerical (0-100) and letter grading (A,B,C,D,F) scales. Unfortunately, these efforts to improve marking and reporting were directed more toward manipulation of alphabetical symbols (e.g., substituting S, U for A,B,C,D,F) than resolving issues of grade reliability and validity and addressing the question, "What do grades mean to those who read them?" In addition, parents and prospective employers called for reporting systems which would differentiate among factors such as achievement, effort, and personal behavior, and would adequately assess students' learning strengths and weaknesses. At the same time, concern was expressed for simplifying grading practices, deemphasizing grades as the focal point of instruction and redirecting students and teachers toward the essence of learning. As a result, a variety of grading alternatives were proposed. Pass/Fail sought to encourage students to explore courses which they might not normally take for fear of a poor grade. Multiple Marks were designed to assess both cognitive and affective development. Contract Learning offered students the opportunity to be responsible for a self-paced predetermined achievement level. Checklist system personalized skill development and utilization. Anecdotal records provided greater in-depth analysis of the learner's potential and progress. Pupil Profiles emphasized line graphs which charted student's accomplished objectives. Mastery learning sought to document the learning process through criterion-referenced materials.

Implications for Administrators

Clearly, utilization of any one grading system is inadequate for summarizing student performance; evaluating performance requires careful reflection and reporting on many aspects of student cognitive abilities and affective behaviors. This is evident when considering the major purpose for grading: facilitating the educational development of each student in relation to his or her ability. The effectiveness of any system should be judged by this criterion. Prior to the development of any adequate reporting system, four salient functions of grading should be considered: (a) instructional, (b) informative, (c) guidance and counseling, and (d) administrative.

The instructional function for teachers and students requires a reporting system which accurately assesses student performance in relation to learning potential, achievement of course objectives, and the assessment of academic strengths and weaknesses. The informative function addresses the question of valid and reliable reporting of student achievement to parents and prospective employers in relation to the objectives of the curriculum. Guidance and counseling needs focus on both cognitive and affective development for viable educational and vocational planning as well as on information relative to social and personal adjustment problems. Administrative functions center around promotion/graduation decisions, placement of transfer students, and for college admission/prospective employers decisions.

In essence, a multiple marking system must be devised if student achievement in both the cognitive and affective domains is to be meaningfully reported and if confidence is to return to student evaluation. A viable grading system must assess achievement, personal and social characteristics, effort, and work habits. The leadership of administrative and supervisory personnel is necessary if educators are to answer the challenge of developing creative solutions to the grading dilemma.

See also Graduation Requirements.

—L. David Weller
University of Georgia

References

Geisinger, K.F. (1980). "Who is giving all those A's?" *Journal of Teacher Education, 31*(2), 11-15.

O'Conner, D. (1979). "A solution to grade inflation." *Educational Record, 60*, 295-300.

Weller, L.D. (1984). "A longitudinal study of pass/fail grading practices at selected private American colleges and universities, 1969-81." *Research in Education,* (31), 41-61.

GRADUATION REQUIREMENTS

One hallmark of educational systems is the authority to establish minimum standards for awarding school diplomas. In the United States, this power is vested in state and local governments which typically prescribe the number of course credits or units that students must complete in order to graduate from high school. Underlying these requirements is the assumption that state and local governments will provide a framework for disseminating socially useful knowledge and skill to all segments of the school-age population. Accordingly, courts have upheld academic standards for graduation on the grounds that universal exposure to the core culture is a compelling state interest. Nevertheless, state policy-making in this area has been circumscribed by a strong tradition of local educational autonomy. For that reason, the requirements issued by state school boards and legislatures have often been minimal and loosely formulated.

Much of this has changed in recent years. Since the mid-1970s, nearly every state has increased the amount of coursework needed to earn the diploma, especially in the core subjects of English, mathematics, science, and social studies. Whereas fifteen or sixteen credits was once the minimum courseload, the total today is closer to twenty. In addition, many states now require that students pass a minimum competency test of basic skills at some point during their high school careers.

By most accounts, these changes have come about in response to growing public concerns about the quality of secondary education and about the "meaning" or value of the high school diploma. Specifically, it is believed that educational attainments among American youth have been artificially inflated by the adoption of less demanding academic standards which have allowed a sizeable number of students to coast through twelve years of formal education without acquiring the knowledge and skills that are expected of high school graduates. According to the report of the National Commission on Excellence in Education, the schools' efforts to address a broad range of social demands have diverted them from their traditional academic mission and have produced a permissive, "cafeteria-style" curriculum in which academic subjects may be subordinated to the personal interests of the student. The expectation, therefore, is that increased credit requirements in the core subjects will direct enrollments back toward the traditional or basic courses, and that the adoption of minimum competency testing will provide a means for identifying and remediating students who are deficient in reading, arithmetic and other fundamental skills.

Carnegie Units

The unit system of high school graduation requirements has long been a source of controversy among educators. According to James Conant and others of its defenders, the combination of core and elective requirements symbolized "the twin ideals" of the comprehensive high school: common learning outcomes and opportunity for individual development. Critics, however, have described the unit system as a mechanical contrivance that insures the orderly progression of students through the grades but contributes little to the quality of curriculum and instruction.

The standard unit was devised by the Carnegie Foundation for the Advancement of Teaching as a solution to several problems associated with local diploma examination. By defining graduation requirements in precise measures of class time, the Carnegie unit represented a decisive step toward a nationally standardized high school diploma. Furthermore, the new system helped to reduce failure and dropout rates by basing grade promotion and graduation on coursework rather than on separate yearly or semester examinations.

For most of this century, high schools followed a conservative interpretation of these requirements in which students were obliged to pursue a uniform sequence of grade-level courses in the core subjects. Beginning in the 1960s, however, the core requirements were interpreted much more loosely, in order to address contemporary demands for relevance and equity in school programming. As students' interests became an increasingly important factor in curriculum decisions, enrollments shifted from the traditional courses to a burgeoning group of innovative or experimental electives. Although there has been little hard evidence to link these changes to the concurrent decline in student achievement, it appears that the rise of the elective curriculum permitted more students to complete high school with only a fleeting exposure to conventional academic content.

Competency Requirements

Minimum-competency testing is based on theories of mastery learning and criterion-referenced testing. It assumes that certain basic skills, notably reading and computation, are needed to succeed in adult life, and that such skills should and can be mastered by all students before high-school graduation. Testing typically begins in tenth or eleventh grade, in expectation that pupils who initially fail the exam can reach the desired level of proficiency through exposure to intensive remediation. While some states use minimum competency testing solely for diagnostic and remedial purposes, most require or permit school districts to withhold diplomas from anyone who has not passed the exam by graduation day.

Competency requirements have been the target of several lawsuits which have charged that the denial of the high school diploma solely on the grounds of failure to pass a minimum-competency test is a violation of students' constitutional rights to due process and equal protection of law. The most important rulings in this area have come in the case of *Debra P. v. Turlington*, in which federal courts first suspended and then reinstated the statewide diploma penalty in Florida. The *Debra P.* decisions are noteworthy for introducing the concepts of curricular and instructional validity as criteria for judging the legality of the minimum competency testing requirements. By these standards, state and local systems may be required to show that all of the material used in the diploma test has been included in school curricula and actually taught to all students.

Policy Implications

As the *Debra P.* case suggests, the graduation reform movement raises a number of issues about the social, academic, and administrative consequences of the new requirements, including the following:

Quality Control. Despite the widespread interest in restoring the traditional curriculum, most state-level requirements continue to be subject specific rather than course specific. That is, they indicate that students must take an extra year of English or social studies without specifying the courses that must be taken. In many cases, the possibility is left open that the additional requirement can be met by enrolling in an elective, such as film studies or science fiction, rather than grammar or literature. A similar situation occurs with respect to competency testing in that relatively few states have adopted a single, uniform standard. Instead, districts are allowed to develop or purchase their own instrument and set their own cut-off scores.

Costs. Estimates of the start-up and annual costs of competency testing have exceeded $50 million in the larger states, depending on the scope and frequency of testing and on the amount and quality of remediation offered to students. By contrast, the costs involved in requiring additional coursework can often be met by shifting resources from marginal or undersubscribed programs to the core subjects. One criticism of this approach, however, is that it simply requires pupils to take "more of the same" and diverts attention from underlying curricular weaknesses.

Student Achievement. Most minimum-competency testing programs have reported substantial reduction in the number and proportion of students unable to pass a competency test. However, the absence of solid research and evaluative data makes it difficult to tell whether these apparent improvements reflect a genuine trend toward permanent mastery of basic skills or are merely short-term fluctuations. For similar reasons, it is not possible to determine whether the upsurge reported during the mid-1980s by the Scholastic Aptitude Test and other measures had anything to do with the imposition of additional course requirements for graduation. Over the years, few studies on the effects of Carnegie units have been reported, and such evidence as does exist indicates little if any relationship between the number of credits required and the amount of subject material learned.

Educational Opportunity. Some educators believe that unless accompanied by close attention to the problems of academically marginal students, the new graduation requirements will lead to increased dropout rates. The evidence on this point is not conclusive. Although the proportion of students completing high school has dropped from 78 percent to about 72 percent since 1972, there is nothing to indicate that many students have been pushed out of school either by the course or competency requirements. In most states, minimum-competency testing failure leads to diploma denial for only about one percent of the graduating class. As is often the case with such statistics, however, these general findings mask specific instances of deprivation or disadvantages. For instance, the diploma denial rate is especially high among groups that have only recently been allowed to enter the educational mainstream, such as low-income blacks and pupils classified as educably handicapped.

To summarize, the best-case scenario for the graduation reform movement would be for there to exist (a) close articulation between state and local policies, (b) a willingness to support the new requirements with appropriate and necessary resources, (c) demonstrations of a positive impact on student achievement, and (d) sensitivity to the possible adverse impact of these policies on groups that have historically not been well served by the educational system.

See also Competency Testing, Students; Grades and Grading.

—Robert C. Serow
North Carolina State University-Raleigh

References

Conant, J. (1959). *The American high school today*. New York: McGraw-Hill.

Jaeger, R., & Tittle, C.K. (1979). *Minimum competency achievement testing*. Berkeley, CA: McCutchan.

National Commission on Excellence in Education. (1983). *A nation at risk*. Washington, DC: U.S. Government Printing Office.

GRANTSMANSHIP

The process by which funds are secured for a particular program from a source outside the applicant's organization usually involves the identification of potential funders, the development of the proposed program consistent with a potential funder's purpose and policy, and the creation and submission of a document called a *grant application* which describes the proposed program in detail.

The initial phase of the process is the identification of potential funders. Federal, state and local governments; national, local, charitable, and corporate foundations; churches and united community charities provide financial support for particular programs which achieve their objectives. Important sources of information about funders include the

Catalog of Federal Domestic Assistance, which details all federal grant-in-aid programs; *The Foundation Directory*, which describes the giving levels and patterns of major foundations in the United States; *Corporate 500: Directory of Corporate Philanthropy*, which describes the giving of large corporate donors; and annual reports and other publications of national, state, and local funders. Many of these may be found in local community or college libraries. Often personal contact is helpful to obtain information as well as establish a liaison between the applicant and a potential funder.

Important questions to consider when selecting a potential funder include the following: (a) Are the objectives of the proposed program compatible with the aims of the funder? (b) Does the applicant's organization qualify for aid from this particular source? (c) Is the size, cost, and scope of the proposed program consistent with those usually supported by this funder? It is also important to learn the rules or policies governing the submission of grant applications, funding cycles, and deadlines. This information will determine the final form in which the grant application is presented. For example, a local foundation may require a letter describing the program and costs, whereas a federal agency may require a lengthy narrative constructed according to a given outline together with several forms and supplementary documents in order to consider a request for funding.

Despite differences in final form, the following sequence provides the outline for most grant applications and a useful format for planning: (a) abstract; (b) introduction; (c) problem statement; (d) program purpose; (e) program method or activities; (f) program evaluation; (g) institutional commitment and future funding; (h) budget and budget narrative.

The Abstract is a summary of the entire document; its length depends on the rules of the funder. Usually, it is written last and includes a brief statement from each of the sections of the document.

The Introduction introduces the applicant organization and establishes the organization's capability to complete the proposed program successfully. The size, program, objectives, and expertise of the organization; its experience with similar programs; and the relationship of the proposed program to the ongoing program of the organization are all important considerations.

The Problem Statement describes the specific need or problem which the proposed program will address. Sources of documentation may include a review of pertinent literature, the findings of an advisory committee, records of the applicant's organization, or a survey conducted among potential participants or beneficiaries of the proposed program. The survey explains the problem and affirms its significance. These data should assist the reader in understanding the dimensions of the problem. The problem should be capable of being addressed by the program described in the grant application.

The Program Purpose consists of a general statement of intent which links the applicant's capability and the problem to be addressed with the general aim of the program for which funding is being sought. The major focus of this section is a series of objectives which identify the specific, measurable outcomes of the program and which describe the consequences of the program rather than the process. The outcomes and consequences should address the problem described in the preceding section.

Program Methods or Activities addresses such questions as how the program objectives will be accomplished and why the applicant has chosen this particular methodology. The document may list the activities necessary to accomplish each objective. It specifies a time frame in which each activity is to be performed. The document also stipulates the budgetary and personnel resources required for each activity.

Program Evaluation describes the process and criteria for determining the effectiveness of the objectives, once they are achieved. Objective data should be used to document the results of a program. The evaluation section also delineates how the program will be monitored in order to assure that the activities are completed in a timely manner and that appropriate changes are made in order to enhance program effectiveness and solve unforeseen problems.

The section on Institutional Commitment and Future Funding reaffirms the link between institutional and program objectives, describes how the institution will manage the program, and explains how the institution will continue the program in the future after the grant has ended. A letter from an administrator of the institution is an important way to document this support.

Budget and Budget Narrative address the overall cost of the program, the portion to be underwritten by the institution (called matching funds), and the amount being requested in the grant. Matching funds may comprise goods and services purchased by the applicant. Direct costs include personnel, fringe benefits, consultants and contracted services, facility costs, equipment costs, travel, consumable supplies, printing, and other costs. Indirect costs are a percentage of the direct costs assessed by the institution for administering the grant. The total cost of the program to the funder is the sum of the direct and indirect costs, less matching funds contributed by the applicant. The Budget Narrative provides a rationale for each item in the budget and justifies each expenditure on the basis of the program objectives.

A final review of the grant application should ascertain that the document is carefully and precisely written. The application must conform to the policies and objectives of the funder. It should describe a reasonable and attainable solution to the problem. The various sections of the document should fit together as a cohesive whole.

See also Funding Methods: State and Federal.

—James C. Fisher
University of Wisconsin-Milwaukee

References

Catalog of Federal Domestic Assistance. (1986). Washington DC: U.S. Government Printing Office.

Corporate 500: Directory of Corporate Philanthropy (4th ed.). (1985). San Francisco: Public Management Institute.

The Foundation Directory. (1985). New York: The Foundation Center.

GROUP PROCESSES

Committees, boards, and informal workgroups are the vehicles by which educational decisionmaking takes place. Unfortunately, they can also be mechanisms for wasting time and making poor decisions. Administrators need a high level of knowledge and skill in working with groups to be effective. While the knowledge level can be increased through reading and study, group process skills are learned through practice and experience. For this reason, school officials should encourage employees to attend workshops and classes which provide practice in the development of skills in group processes.

Group process is a broad term encompassing many kinds of activities that are used by groups to carry out their stated function. These processes are most helpful in areas such as evaluating, decision making, agenda setting, problem solving, and goal setting. The selection of the most appropriate process to facilitate a group's objective most often rests with the group's leader.

Leadership in educational groups is not the same as leadership on the battlefield. Group leaders are actually facilitators who help the members accomplish the task to which they have been assigned or for which they have volunteered. Effective group leaders begin each meeting by clearly stating the purpose of the meeting and clarifying the procedures that will be used to accomplish the group's purpose. It is also helpful to state the amount of time the group has available at this meeting and when the meeting will adjourn. If a prepared agenda is available, it should be reviewed with the group. If an agenda is not available, one should be prepared quickly, using a chalk board or a large sheet of newsprint so everyone can see and participate. The agenda will help keep the group on the topic of the meeting.

The leader should encourage everyone in the group to participate in the discussion. This means drawing out the shy member and occasionally discouraging the constant talkers. Statements such as, "John, what do you think?" or "Mary, could we come back to that point later? I would like to hear what some of the others feel." are appropriate statements by a group leader. Effective leaders also summarize frequently, pointing out what the group has agreed upon thus far and what business remains unfinished.

An example of a process that is sometimes used in helping groups reach decisions is consensus decision making. This process is effective when small groups, usually less than ten, need to reach decisions that need the support of everyone in the group. This process replaces voting as a decision-making activity. A group consensus is achieved when each member either verbally agrees with the decision or will go along with it without attempting to sabotage it later.

The process of achieving a consensus involves each person stating a position, concerns, ideas, and feelings on a particular topic. Members then discuss their thoughts and feelings until they appear to have achieved a common position. At that point the leader states what the common position appears to be, and each member then, in turn, either agrees or disagrees with the decision. An individual who disagrees with the conclusion explains why he or she

disagrees. When all members of the group have spoken, the discussion turns to those who disagreed. The ensuing discussion most frequently results in a modification of the original position. Another survey is then taken. If there are still disagreements, the process is repeated until a decision that all can accept is reached. At no time is voting appropriate when a consensus model is being used. A consensus decision-making model takes time, but results in a decision that the group will support. Groups that use a voting process will often reach decisions that are supported by a majority, but the minority is still large enough to prevent the decision from being carried out.

Problem solving is another group process and one that can be an enjoyable task if some creativity is used. In its simplest form, problem solving involves the collection and examination of alternatives and the selection of one or more alternatives as a preferred course of action. Creative brainstorming, in which the participants contribute ideas as rapidly as possible without evaluation, is one effective and enjoyable process for identifying courses of action. These ideas, once recorded on paper, can then be evaluated and the best ideas placed in priority order for further action.

Regardless of the process selected for carrying out the group's purpose, it will need careful monitoring and nurturing. The leader must observe which members of the group are contributing to the task at hand and which are not. Behaviors that are helpful should be encouraged and complimented. Those that are not should be ignored unless the unwanted behaviors are interfering in the group's success.

In the consideration of group processes, care should be given to the physical setting to encourage interaction. Tables and chairs arranged so that the participants can face each other is essential. To the extent possible, participants should be treated as equals regardless of title or rank; otherwise, productive interpersonal communication is unlikely to occur. Following the above procedures will greatly enhance group meetings.

See also Advisory Committees; Curriculum Committee; Decision Making; Planning.

—Clayton F. Thomas
Illinois State University

References

Holding effective board meetings. (1984). Arlington, VA: American Association of School Administrators.

Schein, E.H. (1969). *Process consultation: Its role in organization development.* Reading, MA: Addison-Wesley.

Zander, A. (1982). *Making groups effective.* San Francisco: Jossey-Bass.

HANDICAPPED STUDENTS

The term "handicapped children" is defined in the Education of the Handicapped Act (Public Law 94-142 Sec. 3(a) in 1975 and reclassified as Sec. 1400 in 1981) to mean "mentally retarded, hard of hearing, deaf, speech and language impaired, visually handicapped, seriously emotionally disturbed, orthopedically impaired, or other health impaired children with specific learning disabilities, who by reason thereof require special education and related services." Further, "special education" means "specifically designed instruction, at no cost to parents or guardians, to meet the unique needs of a handicapped child, including classroom instruction, instruction in physical education, home instruction, and instruction in hospitals and institutions." The term "related services" means "transportation, and such developmental, corrective and other supportive services (including special pathology and audiology, psychological services, physical and occupational therapy, recreation, and medical and counseling services, except that such medical services shall be for diagnostic and evaluative purposes only) as may be required to assist a handicapped child to benefit from special education, and includes early identification and assessment of handicapping conditions in children."

M-Team Process

Students having a handicapping condition are identified through a referral and screening process which has been approved for each local education agency by its state education agency. Once a student has been referred for having a suspected exceptional education need (EEN), a multidisciplinary team (M-Team) process is set into motion. As the team functions, several decisions must be made. The team must first determine if the child has a mental, learning, emotional, or physical disability, next determine the handicapping condition as enumerated in the law, and finally determine whether or not exceptional education services are needed to supplement or replace regular education.

The multidisciplinary team has the expertise which is needed to assess the learning needs of children with suspected exceptional education needs. The findings and recommendations of the team are made to assist the school board through the director or program designee in making placement decisions appropriate to each child's needs. Each member of the team must use a variety of assessment tools and procedures in order to document the nature and extent of the child's need. In addition, the team must make recommendations for any program and/or service based on the specific needs of the student.

This all must be completed in a timely fashion as specified in the law. Parental consent must be given in writing prior to evaluation and again prior to placement in a program. Furthermore, it is advocated that parents be involved in every step of the process so as to avoid any misunderstandings and to ensure that they are informed of the findings. Their input will usually be beneficial in developing a program which can be reinforced in the home setting. Fairness guaranteed by law is ensured to parents and the child through due process procedures, including the right to a hearing and appeal.

Finally, once an exceptional educational need is established, the child is placed in an appropriate program. Program options which might be recommended range along a continuum from supporting teachers in regular classrooms to highly restrictive educational arrangements. However, most students with such needs are served in resource or self-contained programs within a school. The placement must occur within the least restrictive environment which is consistent with the student's educational needs and, insofar as possible, with nonhandicapped children. In addition, a written individualized educational program (IEP) must be prepared for each handicapped child and must state present levels of functioning, long- and short-term goals, services to be provided, and plans for initiating and evaluating the services.

Strategies for Serving

When handicapped students are served in the least restrictive environment, curricular and instructional adaptations and modifications will have to be made to meet the child's individual needs and will vary based on the teacher's training and philosophy. These strategies will affect the curriculum, environment, and the methods used within the educational setting. Technological and mechanical adaptations may be necessary for some types of handicapping conditions, particularly for those students with physical, hearing and visual impairments. Curricular and instructional modification may occur in both social and academic areas.

Procedures such as direct instruction, consideration of learning style, multisensory approaches, structural management, stimulus reduction, cognitive behavior modification, and other techniques should be considered. The student's work should be on a level commensurate with his or her abilities. Clear instructions should be given. Occasionally, there will be a need for adjustments in the way tests and assignments are given and completed. The room arrangements might also need adjustment and could include working with students in cubicles or quiet areas, in small groups, and in the large group setting.

Approaches to working with the emotional, social, and behavioral functioning of a student with handicaps may vary as well and, again, may include a range of instructional and interventional responses. Various types of counseling may be provided for both the child and his or her parents. Increasingly, direct instruction in social skills has been shown to be effective in improving the academic and social functioning of the child.

The programs of many handicapped students call for some level of mainstreaming to facilitate both social integration and academic achievement. In addition to mainstreaming, some students may need alternative programs in order to function. Some will need programs which will focus on basic academics, while others will need preparation in vocational training or college preparation. Some students will require a combination of the above. The curriculum, environmental structure, and instructional methodologies should be established for each student and should be based on the data collected during the assessment process. Currently, curriculum-based assessment is a technique used by classroom teachers to ensure that progress is being made toward meeting the student's individualized educational need.

Issues and Trends

Many of the factors discussed above have influenced the future directions of the education of students with handicaps. More students are being educated in the least restrictive environment. These students are being taught in the regular education setting, are remaining in school for a longer period of time, and are being exposed to transition programs to facilitate their movement into the world of work. Schools are also working more closely with community agencies to meet the needs of the older students.

The issue of identification and labeling has led to schools developing "noncategorical" special education programs where students with similar characteristics are placed in the same program. This model is based on students' education need rather than diagnostic label. Teaching methods used with many of the students tend to be similar for all students, especially across students in the mildly handicapped areas.

The issue of effective instruction also is being addressed. More data collection is occurring to demonstrate the effectiveness of intervention. There is a trend to implement strategies that have been researched rather than those which have been used in the past in spite of their ineffectiveness.

The field of education for the handicapped is moving toward a more data-based approach. The legal issues have forced professionals in the field to take a close look at what they are doing. What we have learned at this point in time is that there is not much "special" for special education students with mild handicaps, since the methodologies employed represent the best of educational practices appropriate for all students. A corollary lesson is that special education is probably better used for students with severe handicaps, given the need for radical revisions of the curriculum, the environment and instructional methods.

See also Cognitive Development; Individualization of Instruction; Learning Styles; Mainstreaming.

—Richard G. Fox
Susan E. Gruber
University of Wisconsin-Milwaukee

References

Buchwach, L.T., Silverman, R., & Zigmond, N. (1978). "Teaching secondary learning disabled adolescents in the mainstream." *Learning Disabilities Quarterly, 1,* 62-72.
Hallahan, D.P., & Kauffman, J.M. (1982). *Exceptional children* (3rd ed.). Englewood Cliffs, NJ: Prentice-Hall.
Ysseldyke, J.E., & Algozzine, B. (1982). *Critical issues in special and remedial education.* Boston: Houghton Mifflin.

HEAD START

Project Head Start is a Federal program that provides comprehensive developmental services for low-income preschool children. It grew from a program spending $95 million in 1965 to $1,131 million in 1987 and serving 452,000 children of ages three to five. The children are cared for by 80,000 employees and 670,000 volunteers. The average cost per child in 1987 was $2,445 per year.

Head Start's children come from a wide range of backgrounds and from every part of the nation. They are black (40 percent), white (32 percent), Hispanic (21 percent), Asian (3 percent), and America Indian (4 percent). Many come from migrant families and from mountainous areas. A fourth of their parents are unemployed. Many are single.

Although directed by the federal government, Head Start is a decentralized program administered through state offices and 11 regional offices. Further, 1305 grantees receive federal funds for administration. The children are cared for in 24,120 classrooms. The members of the Head Start staff are both professional and paraprofessional.

A Comprehensive Services Approach

Head Start was preceded by a considerable body of psychological research stressing the importance of early experience. In 1965, a panel of experts chaired by Dr. Robert Cooke prepared a memorandum of *Recommendations for a Head Start Program* that included all of the basic elements of today's Head Start program and clearly articulated its philosophy of comprehensive services: (a) improving the child's physical health and physical abilities; (b) helping the emotional and social development of the child by encouraging self-confidence, spontaneity, curiosity and self-discipline; (c) improving the child's mental processes and skills with particular attention to conceptual and verbal skills; (d) establishing patterns and expectations of success for the child which will create a climate of confidence for his or her future learning habits; (e) increasing the child's capacity to relate positively to family members and others while at the same time strengthening the family's ability to relate positively to the child and his or her problems; (f) developing in the child and his or her family a responsible attitude to society, and fostering constructive opportunities for society to work together with the poor in solving their problems; and (g) increasing the sense of dignity and self-worth within the child and his or her family.

Head Start's services are intended to be tailored to the needs and resources of local communities. Parents are encouraged to participate in decision making, as volunteers and as staff members (32 percent of the staff are parents of current or former Head Start children), and to participate in classes and other activities to enhance their own growth and development. Each program has a social services component that links its families with community services.

The Head Start Performance Standards require that every child be given a comprehensive health screening. A child suspected of having a health problem is provided medical or dental diagnosis or a nutritional assessment as indicated. The child is then treated and given needed follow-up treatment. Head Start provides meals and snacks that make up at least 50 percent of the child's required daily nutritional intake.

About 13 percent of the children have some specific handicapping condition such as a speech defect. Special education and support services are provided to meet the individual needs of handicapped children and their families. The children are mainstreamed with nonhandicapped children.

Evaluation

Head Start has been extensively evaluated. Immediate gains of 5 to 10 IQ points are relatively easy to observe. However, an early study using an *ex post facto* experimental design found no long-term gains in achievement. Later longitudinal studies found lasting effects.

In order to study this complex program, large samples, longitudinal experimental designs with random assignment of children, sensitive instruments, sophisticated field work, and advanced statistical techniques are required. When these requirements have been ignored, evaluations of Head Start have tended to find no difference between treatment and control groups, but have not had the statistical power to demonstrate that the difference was present but not observed. In contrast, studies which have met these requirements have generally found large and lasting effects.

The outstanding early intervention evaluation was that of the Consortium for Longitudinal Studies, a group of 12 investigators of early intervention programs, some of which served as models for Head Start. Many years after the initial well-designed studies, they gave a common set of posttests. The Consortium found the following:

1. Early intervention programs significantly reduced the number of disadvantaged children assigned to special education classes and significantly reduced the number of disadvantaged children retained in grade. These effects lasted through high school and became stronger over time.

2. Preschool programs produced a significant increase in the IQ and school achievement of low-income children through at least the critical early primary years.

3. Children who attended preschool are more likely to give achievement-related reasons for being proud of themselves.

A recent study by one of the Consortium's programs, the High/Scope Perry Preschool Project, found that this early intervention program has benefits that last into early adulthood. In addition to improving school success and achievement, the program helped prevent delinquency and teenage pregnancy and improved the likelihood of employment. A cost-benefit analysis determined the net benefit to society to be $28,933 for a year of preschool.

Head Start's influence on education can be seen in the increase in preschool programs in the United States, from 11 percent of all children in 1965 to 39 percent in 1985. The public schools are increasingly adding preschool components.

Issues

Some future issues for Head Start include the use of computers in preschool, optimizing individual child planning, and implementing better mental-health services. Head Start is seeking to facilitate the transition of Head Start children into the public schools so that (a) records are transferred and used, (b) children develop school coping skills, (c) parents learn to communicate with public school teachers, and (d) Head Start and public school staffs are sensitized to students' needs.

While the weight of scientific evidence now finds preschool an effective intervention for disadvantaged children, the question that remains is: Why does it work? A current study aimed at examining changes in family dynamics in the families of Head Start children may throw some light on this question.

It is possible that as knowledge about children advances we may find improved approaches to serving disadvantaged children. With new approaches, Head Start could be modified or replaced. Nevertheless, Head Start continues as a growing, evolving program with a billion dollar budget serving more than 450,000 children.

See also Compensatory Education; Federal Agencies; Federal Role in Education; Preschool Education.

—Bernard Brown
Administration for Children, Youth and Families
U.S. Department of Health and Human Services

References

Berrueta-Clement, J.R., Schweinhart, L.J., Barnett, W.S., Epstein, A.S. & Weikart, D.P. (1984). "Changed lives: The effects of the Perry Preschool Program on youths through age 19." *Monographs of the High/Scope Educational Research Foundation.* Ypsilanti, MI: High School Foundation.

Brown, B. (Ed.). (1978). *Found: Long-term gains from early intervention.* Boulder, CO: Westview Press.

Consortium for Longitudinal Studies. (1983). *As the twig is bent—lasting effects of preschool programs.* Hillsdale, NJ: Erlbaum.

HEALTH PROBLEMS AND HEALTH SERVICES

Administrators can affect the health of the school by choosing a school health program that can benefit the students, the school personnel, and the community. Before selecting a program which will benefit the total school population, a principal or superintendent should have an understanding of the health problems common to elementary, middle school, and high school students. He or she should be aware of any special problems.

Problems in the Elementary School

Health problems among elementary school children are related to the discovery of physical, emotional, or mental discrepencies that interfere with learning. These can sometimes be linked with visual or hearing deficiences which can be detected through screening programs.

The most widespread health problem is dental cavities, with 90 percent of the children experiencing a cavity by the age of twelve. Another problem is communicable disease. Some communicable diseases are controlled with immunizations, but there is always the possibility of an epidemic. Chicken pox, streptococcal throat, lice, and impetigo are infectious diseases transferred quickly in the school environment. Policy on how to handle communicable diseases is a necessary part of a school-health program.

Chronic health problems common to this age group are diabetes, asthma, allergies, and cancer. Acute health problems which cause missed days are usually related to upper respiratory problems and the common flu. Child abuse and neglect are health problems that need to be handled discreetly and effectively when a suspicion arises. Most states require reporting suspicions of child abuse.

Problems in the Middle School

Because of the rapid physical, emotional, and mental development of middle school students, developmental stresses can interfere with learning. Common health problems are scoliosis, due to rapid growth; eating disorders and depression, due to changes in relationships and the emerging feelings toward self; and school phobia due to the pressure of achieving.

Areas of health promotion to be targeted include drug abuse and smoking, positive self-esteem building, sex education, responsible decision making, and coping strategies for handling stress.

If administrators want to focus on one population which will benefit the most from intensive health services, the middle school is the most vulnerable and open to health-promotion services.

High School Students

High school students are constantly being troubled with minor health problems. Acne, influenza, mononucleosis, sports injuries (the knee, particularly), and menstrual problems afflict students from one day to the next. High school students also have major health problems. Teenage pregnancy and sexually transmitted diseases must be dealt with. The abuse of alcohol, drugs, and cigarettes cannot be ignored. Depression is a mental-health problem. Many high school students lose their lives or are injured in automobile accidents.

Emphasis should be put on peer counseling and peers teaching peers. The areas that are the most important to address in delivering health services are sexuality, positive mental health, the use and abuse of substances, and accident prevention.

Delivery of Health Services

Health services can be delivered with minimal amount of coverage based on state law requirements, or with a thorough coverage of all levels of prevention. Elementary students need to be screened for vision and hearing deficiencies and taught proper hygiene and safety rules. Middle school students need more sophisticated health-promotion strategies, and high school students need interventions from a team of professionals.

To deliver health services in all areas requires the administrator to look at the total school-health program based on the health problems and needs of each school population. Health services can be delivered in cooperation with a health department, by hiring a nurse to coordinate the school health program, and/or by hiring school health aides to cover the first aid and sudden illness portion of the school-health program.

If the school administration decides to employ a nurse, the nurse should have a Bachelor of Science degree in nursing with additional credits in education and counseling. Some states require that school nurses be certified to work in the school. The nurse is prepared to assess health needs in individuals, families, groups, organizations, and communities, and to provide comprehensive health care in a school setting. The responsibilities of the nurse include managing the total school health program; delivering health services, i.e. screening and conducting health exams; acting as an advocate for the school in the community; providing health counseling to students, parents, and school personnel; planning and implementing the health education program in line with the state laws; and evaluating the effectiveness of these services. Further delineation of these roles can be found in the *Guidelines for the School Nurse in the School Health Program*, published by the American School Health Association.

The purpose of the school-health program is to enhance the health of the students, school personnel, and the community. Administrators need to decide the level of delivery of services needed to achieve the highest level of health possible.

See also Drug Abuse Education; Drug and Alcohol Use Among Students; Health/Fitness Education; Sex Education.

—Charlene Tosi
St. Michael Hospital
Milwaukee, Wisconsin

References

American School Health Association (1974). *Guidelines for the school nurse in the school health program*. Kent, OH: Author.

Anderson, C.L., & Creswell, H. (1980). *School health practice*. St. Louis, MO: C.V. Mosby.

Petrowski, D. (1984). *Handbook of community health nursing* (Chapter 6). New York: Springer.

HEALTH/FITNESS EDUCATION

Health/fitness education is receiving attention from school administrators across the United States. This curiosity is the result of societal concerns about healthy and active lifestyles. This view is exemplified by public interest and participation in exercise, stress management, weight control, and proper nutrition. However, recent educational reform studies depict school health and physical education as "curricular frills" not deserving of allocated time during the school day. An important question surfaces for administrators: Is health/fitness education basic to elementary and secondary children and youth? This article replies to this central question, while providing a brief overview of relevant research, key curricular issues, program content, and administrative roles.

Research

In 1980, a significant government report, *Promoting Health/Preventing Disease: Objectives for the Nation* specified 226 health objectives to be reached by 1990. Three of the objectives are targeted for youngsters: 60 percent will attend daily physical education classes, 70 percent will have fitness levels tested, and 90 percent will be engaged in activities that enhance the cardiorespiratory system.

National fitness studies by the President's Council on Physical Fitness and Sports and the Department of Health and Human Services tested almost 30,000 youngsters ages 6-18 and have concluded the following: cardiovascular strength and endurance is lacking; flexibility is poor; muscular strength needs improvement; and obesity is a problem for many youngsters. Most children do not participate in daily physical-education classes. Elementary and secondary children generally attend physical-education classes once or twice a week. The studies show that students get most of their activity out of school and are not participating in the type of experiences that contribute to health-related physical fitness.

Many experts feel the causes of unfit students can be attributed to ineffective physical education curricula, lack of parental encouragement to exercise, poor nutrition, inadequate sleep, substance abuse, and sedentary habits. In addition, some researchers are discovering evidence of high cholesterol levels, high blood pressure, obesity, and other conditions that predispose one to heart disease. Research in several states and in one national sample in the 1980s found student-health knowledge to be below acceptable levels. Comprehensive school health instruction, taught by a qualified staff, is an afterthought in most school districts nationwide.

What are the implications of these investigations for administrators? First, health/fitness education should be an *integral part* of the school curriculum at the elementary and secondary levels. Second, intervention using a structured health/fitness curriculum is necessary to influence one's knowledge base and activity levels. Third, influencing and even changing the health/fitness behaviors of youngsters is imperative prior to adulthood.

Curricular Issues

Many misconceptions persist about definitions of health education, physical education, and health/fitness. School health instruction should include the following areas: personal health, nutrition, safety and first aid, family life and sex education, substance abuse, community health, consumer health, environmental health, and prevention and control of disease and disorders. The major goal of physical education is lifetime participation and play requiring a dominant motor emphasis. Motoric skill and physical fitness are enhanced by engagement in exercise, sports, games, dance, gymnastics, aquatics, and outdoor adventure activities.

Important questions emerge: How does health/fitness differ from, and should it replace, traditional health and physical education? What is the purpose of health/fitness education? What content is to be learned in health/fitness education? What should students be able to do and know? Should the curriculum be primarily cognitive or psychomotor in nature? Who should teach this subject matter?

Program Content

The purpose of health/fitness education is to provide learning experiences that contribute to a healthy lifestyle and knowledge about the connection between motoric activities and wellness. Ultimately, the goal is to help students accept the responsibility for positive lifestyle changes. The scope of the program includes activities with clear health-related benefits. Health/fitness education would focus on aerobic activities (those raising the pulse rate) that promote lifelong physical fitness such as jogging, cycling, walking, swimming,

dance, and rope jumping. Themes would include cardiovascular endurance, muscular strength and endurance, stress management, flexibility, and body-weight fitness (including nutrition).

Health/fitness education can be implemented in one of two ways. It can be the *curriculum model* for physical education. Second, health/fitness education can be a component part or unit within a movement education or sport education model. Health/fitness education uses a prescriptive approach based upon entry level assessments (AAHPERD Health Related Physical Fitness Test; Lifestyle Physical Fitness Test; lifestyle inventories; wellness profiles; cognitive tests) for each individual. A secondary physical education textbook for students entitled *Fitness for Life* provides a conceptual approach to health/fitness using the lecture-laboratory method. The text helps students construct programs accentuating lifetime fitness. Topics such as threshold of training, exercise and fat control, skill related fitness, exercise cautions, and attitudes about fitness demonstrate contrast with the traditional physical education programs that emphasize games, relays, and team sports.

At the elementary level, an appetite for health/fitness can be built by integrating positive attitudes, skillful movement, and knowledge that promote a lifetime of physical activity. Since exercise is part of the solution to a healthy lifestyle, administrators should analyze the content of current health and physical education programs to locate a place for health/fitness education.

Administrative Roles

Administrators can be a catalyst for changing deficient physical education programs. The initial step, when promoting programmatic change, is to spark faculty interest in current program evaluation with the explicit purpose to facilitate revision. Quality physical education, with a health/fitness component, requires resources and support. Administrators should garner local commitment to include students, parents, and community agencies. Administrators must expect student gains in physical fitness and health knowledge. This will necessitate a planned curriculum and instruction a minimum of three times a week.

As with other curricular areas, it is essential to hire and motivate competent teachers. Principals should advocate the use of specialists in physical education who have extensive knowledge in the subject matter. At the elementary level, classroom teachers cannot and will not be effective changing student behaviors in health/fitness education. Most classroom teachers lack the knowledge, time, and interest to teach health/fitness. The specialist should serve as a positive role model for children and youth. This person should be prepared in anatomy, physiology, kinesiology, fitness, motor learning, evaluation, and pedagogy. Inservice training should be provided to update the obsolete teacher's knowledge and skills.

Youngsters are not as active as they appear. The evidence is clear. Administrators must begin to value and implement better physical education programs, of which health/fitness education is an integral part. Schools can be *effective* if societal values about healthy lifestyles are mirrored in the classroom and gymnasium.

See also Drug Abuse Education; Health Problems and Health Services; Physical Education; Sex Education.

—Craig A. Buschner
University of Southern Mississippi

References

American Alliance for Health, Physical Education, Recreation and Dance. (1980). *Health related physical fitness test manual.* Reston, VA: The Alliance.

Corbin, C., & Lindsey, R. (1983). *Fitness for life.* Glenview, IL: Scott Foresman.

U.S. Department of Health and Human Services (1985). "Summary of findings from national children and youth fitness study." *Journal of Physical Education, Recreation and Dance, 56*(1), 43-90.

HIDDEN CURRICULUM

Underneath what we are overtly teaching in mathematics, social studies, language arts, science, and the other subjects in the curriculum is a hidden curriculum. There are always tacit social and institutional values that are taught to students simply as a result of students being in school for many hours, days, and years. While the teaching of these values may occur in an almost unconscious fashion, they are among the most powerful messages communicated by the school. A good deal of research has shown that the hidden curriculum present in schools may sometimes reproduce the class, race, and gender divisions in the larger society. Unless educators understand the social values that educational institutions may tacitly teach, they may unfortunately be contributing to such inequality in the larger society.

The hidden curriculum includes three areas: (a) the norms and values taught by the school structure and by the classroom interaction between the teacher and the students; (b) the hidden social messages that are present in the curriculum materials themselves; and (c) the knowledge that is *missing* in the overt or planned curriculum.

Two questions need to be asked about these three areas. First, what is tacitly taught to all students? Second, what is differentially taught—that is, what is taught to some identifiable groups of students and not others?

Norms of conformity and competitiveness seem to be taught to all students. Competitiveness is reflected in the extensive amount of individual and group testing and evaluation that is carried out in American classrooms. Since educational and social mobility are seen to be dependent on grades, it is claimed that students learn that grades, not necessarily appropriate learning or the wish to learn more, become the most important goal.

The depth of these messages is often specific to group membership, however. In classroom interaction patterns, students may be treated differently, depending on their social class, sex, or race. Girls may unconsciously be given less encouragement in science and mathematics, for example. Boys may be subtly encouraged to play in ways that are considerably more aggressive and physical than girls. Teachers may deal with behavior problems in a stronger manner with poor or black children than with white or more affluent ones, or a self-fulfilling prophecy may operate concerning teachers' expectations and pupil achievement.

These differences demonstrate the importance of recognizing how education may be linked to the social division of labor outside of the school. Thus, some investigators have found that the classrooms attended by affluent students are more often organized around norms of flexibility, self directiveness, discovery learning, and individualization. The classrooms that working class and poorer children attend may stress punctuality, neatness, and habit formation. In this way, students are prepared for an unequal occupational ladder. A number of commentators have argued that because of this differentiated teaching, schools are not fulfilling their function of enhancing equality of opportunity, but instead may be ratifying already existing inequalities.

In the overt curriculum, there is a *selective tradition* that operates. Some groups' knowledge is taught while other groups' knowledge is omitted. Issues raised here focus for instance on the history that is found in textbooks. Many of the books stress military history, presidential administrations, or the perspectives of industry. The contributions of populist groups, labor, minorities and women are still underrepresented, although gains have been made over the years. In curricular materials in other subject areas, similar problems have been found to exist. Both the presence of the knowledge of a limited portion of our population and the relative absence of the perspectives of working people, minorities, and women create an imbalance that also contributes to the hidden curriculum.

It is worth noting, however, that some aspects of the hidden curriculum are *positive*. In most classrooms, the mere fact that there are often large numbers of students and limited time and resources means that students need to learn cooperative behavior. Many schools do exhibit democratic norms and processes that may counterbalance some of the negative effects of the hidden curriculum.

The presence of this tacit set of messages has implications for how we evaluate classrooms and curricula. Usually, educators' evaluation is based on gains in achievement scores. However, this may not be sufficient. Sometimes classroom material and techniques may increase achievement, but may also communicate subtle norms and values that we do not wish to be taught. Because of this, any thorough evaluation should integrate an assessment of the planned curriculum with the hidden curriculum to make certain that gains in the former are not contradicted by losses in the latter.

Dealing with the hidden curriculum requires that administrators and teachers become knowledgeable not only about educational matters but about the structures of inequality in this society. To combat the negative effects of this valuable substratum of schooling, administrators need to ensure that teachers have sufficient time and resources to examine closely the social and political assumptions within the practices and materials they will be employing in their classrooms and that conditions supporting reflective and self-critical teaching are established.

See also Curriculum Development; Social Learning in the Schools; Student Culture; Values Education.

—Michael W. Apple
University of Wisconsin-Madison

References

Apple, M.W. (1982). *Education and Power* (Chapters 1, 3, 4 and 5). Boston: Routledge and Kegan Paul.

Apple, M.W. (1979). *Ideology and curriculum,* (Chapters 3, 4 and 5). Boston: Routledge and Kegan Paul.

Giroux, H. & Purpel, D. (Eds.). (1983). *The hidden curriculum and moral education.* Berkeley, CA: McCutchan.

HIGH SCHOOLS

Whereas the boundaries between secondary schooling and college-level education have been relatively clear and stable throughout the history of the high school in America, the boundaries between elementary schooling and secondary schooling have been a perennial source of ambiguity. Well into the 1930s, the dominant organizational pattern was the eight-year elementary school and the four-year high school: the so-called 8-4 plan. This entrenched the concept of twelve years of schooling (plus kindergarten) prior to college which continues to persist as the basic pattern in America.

However, rising concerns about the educational propriety of such a structure for young adolescents and the difficulties of articulating between the elementary school and the high school gave rise to the junior high school movement in the 1930s that continued to influence the structure of secondary schooling into the 1950s. This yielded the six-year elementary school, three-year junior high school, and the three-year senior high school (the K-6-3-3 plan). The theory of the junior high school (normally embracing grades 7, 8, and 9) was that it would serve as a transition from the self-contained classroom of the elementary school to the departmentalized structure of the senior high school. In practice, many junior high schools offered a curriculum intended to permit students to explore subjects that had been unified into broad areas, such as social studies, manual arts, and general science as preparation for selecting the specialized courses of study to be pursued in the senior high school.

Sweeping demographic shifts, beginning in the 1960s, triggered important structural changes in high school organization: (a) the percentage of youth in the population declined, with the result that many school districts found that they had excess buildings; (b) population declines were unequal across the age-cohorts that schools served; and (c) mobility of families exacerbated the decline in some communities, while other communities experienced increases in the school-age population. Seeking to minimize cost by getting maximum use from existing buildings, many school districts modified or abandoned the K-6-3-3 plan in favor of a "middle school" plan which facilitated much greater flexibility in shifting groups of students from overcrowded buildings to those which were underutilized.

By the late 1980s, much shuffling of students within school districts to deal with declining enrollments had made it difficult to generalize as to the organizational structure of the high school and its articulation with the lower schools.

However, by the mid-1980s, about 8,200 of the 16,000 American high schools were four-year senior high schools. Another 4,400 were combined junior-senior high schools, and some 3,200 were three-year schools comprised of grades 10 through 12. The remaining schools had different organizational patterns, with about 600 being "specialized" or "magnet" schools (that emphasize curricula in such areas as the sciences or the arts) and a few (though growing in number) "schools of choice," or alternative schools. The schools in this latter group attempt to provide programs to meet the special needs of either unusually able and/or talented students or, more likely, students at risk of failing in the "standard" schools.

Since the 1930s, a public policy of consolidating small school districts into larger ones (in an effort to reduce costs and improve educational opportunity in rural areas) has created a consistent trend toward larger high schools. Whereas there were 127,531 districts in 1932, by 1982 there were 16,000. Larger, consolidated districts tended to merge their small scattered high schools into larger, centralized units. By the 1980s, about half of the high schools in America enrolled fewer than 600 students, but these students were a minority of the student population in the nation. The majority of students attended much larger suburban and urban high schools, many of which enrolled 1,500 students and upward.

Issues

Two key policy issues have formed the core of public debate over secondary schooling:

1. *Purpose of secondary schooling.* Major competing orientations have been that (a) schools should prepare students for admission to college, (b) they should prepare students for the world of work, and (c) they should seek to fuse academic studies with practical, work-oriented studies. However, high schools have also increasingly been expected to expand their mission to implement other, broader social policies through educational offerings. These range from teaching the effects of alcohol and drugs to driver education, from sex education to the nutritional benefits of dairy food products, from patriotism to the benefits of the free-enterprise system. By the late 1980s, the purposes and priorities of the American high school were still a major subject of public policy debate.

2. *Open and equal access to the high school.* Whereas until late into the 1800s public policy generally accepted that access to a high school education was a privilege limited to students who were found acceptable by those in control of schooling and could afford it, after 1874 a major long-term trend in public policy was to make high schools freely accessible to all youth regardless of where they lived, their social status, their abilities, their sex, race, economic condition, ethnicity, or religion. Further, in order to meet the educational needs of this increasingly diverse population, the scope of the curriculum of the public high school has been steadily broadened and extended.

Widespread and intensive desegregation efforts, begun in the 1950s and still in progress in the 1980s, have been a highly visible contemporary example of the persistent issue of open and equal access to high school as public policy. The rise in bilingual education, moves to address equity issues in high-school education for women, and the rapid development of programs for students with handicapping conditions are further visible evidence of the vitality of this issue.

These two public policy issues—purposes of secondary schooling and universally equal access—have remained central over the course of time as emerging social, cultural, political, and technological developments have required iterative adjustments in secondary education. The trend in these public policy issues over the course of more than a century had, by the 1980s, resulted in a profusion of goals and purposes in high schools whose priorities were unclear and whose curricula were laden with a wide range of offerings.

Trends

The report, *A Nation at Risk*, ushered in the reform movement of the 1980s with a scathing indictment of the high school based upon declining scores of students taking the then-widely-used Scholastic Aptitude Test. In reaction, regulatory actions by the states generally increased the numbers of courses required of students, stiffened requirements for graduation, increased required testing of students, and sought to assure minimum competency of teachers.

By the mid-1980s, it was clear that continuing profound demographic changes had presented the high school, as an institution, with a historically novel conundrum that may overwhelm it and which—at the very least—signals the need for more major changes in the future. For example, fewer children were being born, and the school-age population shrunk overall 14 percent in the late 1980s as compared with 1970; at the same time the over-50 age-group was steadily increasing its percentage of the composition of the population. Thus, the population as a whole was aging in proportion to the population of high school students.

Perhaps of greater significance, however, are demographic shifts occurring in the age group that the high schools serve. In 1980, about 33 percent of all white Americans were 19 years of age or younger while 43 percent of Hispanics and 40 percent of black Americans were in that category. Clearly, as the high-school-age population of white students declines irreversibly, the percentage of Hispanic and black students will comprise an increasing percentage of the population served by high schools. In view of evidence that Hispanic and black students have tended to be served less successfully by the high school, this looms as a historically significant trend. Further, minority youth have in the past gone on to higher education in fewer numbers and suffered higher rates of unemployment. In short, the demographic trends strongly suggest that high schools in America face a period requiring considerable change if they are to be successful in meeting the educational needs of the new population that is emerging.

Analysis of the composition of the population of preschool-age children who were living in 1986—and who would predictably be of high school age in the near future—revealed that perhaps even more significant changes are to come. For example, whereas in 1955 60 percent of American households were composed of a working father, a mother-housewife, and two or more school-age children, by 1985 only 7 percent could be so described. Thus it has been estimated that 59 percent of the children born in 1983 will live with only one parent before reaching the age of 18—that is, before completing high school. Of this cohort of children, about 40 percent will be born to parents who will separate and/or divorce before the child leaves high school, and 12 percent will be born out of wedlock. In short, the demographic trends indicated by the mid-1980s (when approximately 30 percent of the school population comprised minority students) that the ratio of minority students to white students in the population of high schools will increase markedly by the 1990s, and, further, that the family background of the students will shift remarkably from the traditional family to newer patterns that are emerging.

See also Alternative Schools; Elementary Schools; Magnet Schools; Middle/Junior High Schools.

—Robert G. Owens
Hofstra University

References

Boyer, E.L. (1983). *High school: A report on secondary education in America.* New York: Harper & Row.

National Center for Education Statistics (1980). *1980 survey of high school and beyond.* Washington, DC: U.S. Government Printing Office.

HOME ECONOMICS EDUCATION

Home economics, a school discipline within vocational education, is based on the study of home and family as other vocational disciplines are based on business, industry, and agriculture. Home economics is concerned with the provision of educational opportunities that enable young people to prepare for work in the home and family and to explore and prepare for jobs that originated from home and family functions. Through class participation students gain career development skills, job and employability skills, skills related to home and family living, and the basic skills of reading, writing, oral communication, and computation. There is also emphasis on helping students develop thinking skills, such as the ability to identify problems and propose and evaluate ways to solve them; to secure, organize, and use information; and to develop individual and group participation skills.

The general goals for a middle/junior high and senior high-school home economics program include

1. Developing knowledge and skills for assuming the responsibilities of home and family living.

2. Exploring opportunities and developing abilities to work in a chosen home economics related occupation.

3. Developing greater understanding of basic educational and general employability skills through class participation.

The formal home economics program commonly begins at the middle/junior high school level. A quality exploratory program should be required of all students and should include at least 180 hours of instruction in course offerings that meet every day for at least twelve weeks. The national vocational student organization, Future Homemakers of America, can be an important component of the program at this level.

In order to meet the diverse needs of high school students, the high school vocational home economics program usually offers courses that relate to the home and family emphasis and to the job emphasis. In most cases, the courses are elective, semester offerings with limited prerequisites. The following subject-area courses are included in the home and family emphasis: family relations, food and nutrition, child development/parenting, consumer education, textiles/clothing, and housing/interiors. In some schools these subject areas are combined to create year-long offerings.

The job exploration and preparation course offerings help students to prepare for home economics related occupations, including food services, child services, human services, clothing services, and, housing services. Service occupations are among those in which the market for qualified workers is growing most rapidly. To prepare for entry-level jobs and/or advanced training, students should have opportunities to participate in a developmental sequence. This sequence should include at least a one-semester introductory course related to the specific career cluster, followed by a two-semester course offering which combines related classroom instruction and a supervised on-the-job work experience related to the student's career objective.

In addition to providing the regular program, home economics teachers, because of their professional preparation, can also offer leadership and instructional expertise in various "special" programs related to teen parenting, school dropout prevention, and other student and societal concerns. An FHA/HERO chapter which provides leadership, service, and educational opportunities should be an integral part of the high-school program. FHA (Future Homemakers of America) chapters emphasize preparation for community and family life while recognizing that family members fill dual roles as wage earners. HERO (Home Economics Related Occupations) chapters emphasize preparation for jobs and careers in home economics related occupations, recognizing that wage earners fill multiple roles as family members. FHA or HERO chapters may be incorporated into the program through in-class and/or out-of-class chapters with one or more advisers per school.

Curriculum trends include (1) the examination and development of strategies for incorporating thinking skills and problem solving approaches as a part of home economics content, (2) the increased consideration of family from both an individual and a societal point of view, including the reciprocal relationships of family and work, and (3) the deliberate identification of and the provision of instruction to enhance basic skills and general employability skills. Program trends include (1) increasing male enrollment and participation, (2) varied, school-community specific, specialized programs to meet needs of special populations, (3) student-centered instruction and leadership, and (4) utilization of new technologies to enhance instructional methods.

See also Sex Education; Single-Parent Families; Vocational Education.

—Elaine Staaland
Wisconsin Department of Public Instruction

References

Brown, M. (1987). *A conceptual scheme and decision rules for the selection and organization of home economic curriculum content*. Madison, WI: Wisconsin Department of Public Instruction.

Handbook for youth centered leadership. (1982). Reston, VA: Future Homemakers of America, Inc.

Laster, J. (1986). *Vocational home economics curriculum: State of the field*. Peoria, IL: Glencoe Publishing Co., Bennett & McKnight Division.

HOME INSTRUCTION

Teaching one's children at home and in as much of the world around the home as possible was the predominant method of schooling for most children until the 20th century. Since then, our society has developed in ways that can foster the educational institutionalization of our young while parents work or otherwise engage their lives during the school year. Yet many parents, because of geographical isolation or personal conviction, when presented with the choice of sending their children to school or not, still choose to teach their own. Accurate figures for the number of parents teaching at home are not available, but it appears these numbers are small but growing. As more two-income families emerge who are willing to pay for others to oversee their children, schools will continue to have plenty of enrollment. Home schoolers pose no immediate or future threat to the supply and demand for schools.

Some of the most common reasons parents teach their children at home are because they feel their child's learning is not being adequately developed by school methods or is otherwise unsuited for conventional school; they believe raising their children is their business and not the government's; they enjoy being with their children as they learn and do not

want to give that up to others; they want to provide their children with more time and freedom to explore their own interests in a variety of environments; they want to prevent their children from being hurt, mentally, physically and spiritually.

Parents' rights to choose the education they want for their children are well-established and upheld in many court decisions. There are no federal guidelines regarding home instruction, and decisions about home schools are left up to individual states and school districts.

Many states have passed home-schooling legislation to be used by parents and schools; other states provide for the decision to be made locally. The courts have ruled that the state has but a minimal interest in supervising home schools. Their only legal concerns are to be certain that home schooled children are ready to assume citizenship in our democracy once they leave school. Given this minimal criterion, schools should refrain from prosecution of parents and instead cooperate with them to arrive at a mutually satisfying arrangement. Besides, the benefits of encouraging, alternative-learning opportunities cost the school nothing; it costs a great deal of time and energy to prosecute home schooling cases through the courts.

There have been instances when schools have brought parents into court. Schools tend to get bad publicity from these cases, especially when such families clearly teach their children because they enjoy a close and loving relationship with their children and the family is threatened with being separated. Even when schools win these cases, they do not gain much because the family can move to a friendlier school district or out of the state.

Rules and laws regarding home schooling vary from state to state. In those states that have home-schooling legislation the potential home educator usually deals directly with a state authority that provides approval and regulation of the home-school plan in accordance with the appropriate statutes. In those states without home-school legislation, most typically states in the Northeast, decisions regarding home schooling are left to the local school district. The part of this article which follows applies mainly to states that leave these decisions to each school district.

Guidelines for School Officials

After parents notify a school of their intent to teach their children at home, it is common for them to provide a teaching proposal, curriculum, and method of evaluation to be considered. The proposal is usually a detailed statement about why the parents want to teach their own and how they are going to do it. The parents sometimes refer to local and legal precedents that indicate their right to teach their children at home.

Giving the school's curriculum outline for each grade to the parents will be a great help to them since the home educators then will know what standards a school expects from its own students as well as theirs. Being open to new curriculums and approaches by home schools can provide schools with many new ideas and suggestions about how children learn.

Unburdened by time constraints and large classes, home educators can allow their children's abilities to develop naturally in an unforced manner. Home educators have time to foster independent thinking, helping their children learn how to learn and giving much of the responsibility for learning to the child. At home, the three "r"s are no longer facts one memorizes and uses just for tests and are disconnected from real life. Learning becomes a process that is part of daily life, not something that can take place only in schools in the presence of teachers.

In states that allow local governance of home schools, school boards can require some type of evaluation of the home school, usually on a yearly basis. The portfolio method of evaluation works well for home educators, but if the parent or school wants tests, standard basic skills tests can be administered at home or at school. Parents are usually required to keep records of their children's activities and time spent learning. These matters and the frequency of testing are best arranged when the parents and the school discuss the home-schooling program.

Officials often question parents' abilities and qualifications as teachers. Most private schools do not require state certification of their teachers; a B.A. in any major field of study is sufficient. Even without a degree many parents successfully teach at home by using an accredited correspondence course, or by hiring a professional tutor. They validate their teaching skills with the preparation and presentation of their home-school proposal and on-going progress reports of their work. Some home educators enroll their children in programs that make their home a "satellite school" of the school in which the children would otherwise be enrolled, thus sharing teaching responsibilities with a recognized school. In some states a home school can simply register itself as a private school.

Another objection is the lack of socialization that home schools provide. However, one spends little time in school socializing compared with the time spent in silence receiving instruction from the teacher. When socialization does occur in school, it is usually dominated by peer pressure to conform to what "all the other kids" do. Many parents teach at home solely because of a school's social life. They see to it that their children participate in church and community events, group lessons, and with the neighborhood children after school for socialization.

Lack of resource facilities can be a problem for home educators. Here a cooperative school can excel in community relations and innovation by opening its doors to home educators during school hours. Home educators, coming to school by choice and for their own purposes, can show full-time students by their part-time presence that there are some things taking place in school that are so interesting or so useful that people actually choose to do them. This will also provide feedback to the schools and teachers about the attractiveness and effectiveness of teaching and the classroom environment. They rarely get such feedback from students who attend "because I have to."

The school's responsibilities depend upon a state's position regarding home schooling, but it is typical to ensure that learning is taking place and to fulfill any obligations agreed to in a family's home school plan. In evaluating home school students, officials judge progress by using the same standards they apply to their own students. With these standards, it can be determined whether a home student should pass to a grade level equivalent to a grade in school. If necessary, remedial work can be assigned to home students.

Offering help and materials to home students will further insure financial aid to the school since no state requires that "attendance" in school must mean only the physical presence of the student in the school building; "attendance"

is usually interpreted as taking part in an educational activity that is approved by the school. School districts can register home students in their schools as participants in a special program to collect state aid.

Parents' responsibilities also vary from state to state, but in states without any home school laws they usually notify their local school in advance of their desire to teach their children at home; their school-age children should be in a state-approved school until they have been granted permission to attend a home school. By submitting agreed-upon methods of evaluation and meeting their proposal's goals as supported by the journals and records (some parents provide monthly progress reports) they maintained about their child's time spent learning, families fulfill their duties.

In many ways the educational problem of children in modern society is the gradual extinction of the community of networks by which children used to be prepared for society. School officials can address this problem positively by helping, not hindering, home schoolers, thereby making their school less of an institution and more like an extension of the community and home.

See also Curriculum Development; Independent Study; School Boards; State Departments of Education.

—Patrick Farenga, President
Holt Associates, Inc.
Boston, Massachusetts

References

Holt, J. (1983, October). "Schools and home schoolers: A fruitful partnership." *Phi Delta Kappan, 49,* 2-5.
Holt, J. (1981). *Teach your own.* New York: Delacorte Press.
Pagnoni, M. (1984). *The complete home educator.* Burdett, NY: Larson Publications, Inc.

HUMAN RELATIONS

People are gregarious, feeling, striving human beings who most often work and play in groups. The field of human relations is concerned with the behavior of individuals in groups as well as the relationships between groups of individuals. This human interaction is the key to achieving both personal and group objectives and is a vital skill for all who work in the field of education.

It is not uncommon for individuals to fail because of their lack of human relations or "people" skills rather than because of their lack of knowledge or expertise. The development of people skills begins early in life; children observe others and become socialized. Unfortunately, the role models for children are not always the best, and there has been almost no formal education to develop human relations skills.

Human-relations skills are critical for all who work in the field of education because a great deal is at stake. The future of children's education depends heavily upon a board of education that can make decisions in a controlled, creative, and knowledgeable environment. Likewise, administrators must provide leadership in helping groups interact and be productive with a minimum amount of destructive conflict. Teachers must also have these skills to be able to plan the curriculum with colleagues, teach students with widely varying backgrounds, and, at the same time serve as the students' role model. Thus, people with different socio-economic, ethnic, and racial backgrounds must learn to interact effectively in the education process.

The ultimate objective is to have people achieve a high level of mutual acceptance of each other, a level where people share ideas and feelings in an open and trusting way without the threat of criticism or reprisals. This objective is sometimes difficult to achieve because of a lack of under-standing stemming from widely different backgrounds of students, teachers, administrators, and members of the school board. Achieving this objective requires skill in inter-personal communications, conflict management, and group processes.

Some important interpersonal communications skills are those of listening, understanding, and responding with one's own ideas and feelings. Listening is distinguished from merely hearing and includes understanding what is heard to the extent that the listener can paraphrase it accurately to the satisfaction of the speaker. Part of understanding some-one also includes the ability to interpret accurately their hidden messages as well as their nonverbal behavior.

Administrators in particular need a high degree of skill in dealing with conflict. Some conflict needs to be pre-vented, some to be managed, and some to be resolved. Conflict can be destructive on the one hand and, on the other, provide the stimulus for action; it can result in better decisions and create cohesive groups. Administrators need first of all to have a good conceptual understanding of conflict, including the forms it takes, possible causes, and available strategies for dealing with it. They also need to know the probable consequences of each strategy. For exam-ple, a negotiation strategy can have an outcome which is entirely different from the outcome of an avoidance strategy. Each may be appropriate in a given conflict situation.

A knowledge of various group processes and the skill to facilitate them are also important human-relations abilities. Processes that lead to better understanding between individuals and groups and that help them set goals, make decisions, and resolve conflict need to be a part of every administrator's repertoire. Administrators and supervisors need to avoid behaviors that manipulate, create facades, and deal superficially with feelings of others.

See also Change Process; Conflict Resolution; Group Processes; Teacher Satisfaction.

—Clayton F. Thomas
Illinois State University

References

Gordon, T. (1977). *Leader effectiveness training.* New York: Wyden Books.

Griffith, D. (1956). *Human relations in school administration.* New York: Appleton-Century-Croft.

Schmuck, R. & Runkel, P. (1985). *Handbook of organization development in schools.* Palo Alto, CA: Mayfield.

I

INDEPENDENT STUDY

Independent study is the student's opportunity to choose "what" is to be learned, "how" it is to be learned, and "when" it is to be learned. It is the student's self-directed pursuit of academic learning. In its broadest meaning, independent study embraces a process in which students take the initiative to determine their learning needs, formulate learning objectives, identify the resources for learning, and decide upon the appropriate learning activities.

Independent study is based upon five assumptions. First, independent study assumes that students grow in their needs and abilities to be independent as an essential element of maturing. Second, independent study assumes that the student's experiences are a rich resource for learning and should be used in one's learning. Third, independent study assumes that each student has a different degree of readiness for learning. Fourth, independent study assumes that learning experiences should be organized as task-accomplishing or problem-solving learning projects. Fifth, independent study assumes that students are motivated by internal rewards.

The content of independent study can be as diverse as its forms. Projects may include a study of a topic not covered in the course; a deeper probing into a topic introduced in a course; reading more books; writing more papers; doing more experiments; or doing more difficult work. A common kind of independent study in English consists of picking an author, a period, or a literary movement and doing extensive reading. In science, a student can do research in botony, microbiology, or zoology. In mathematics, students can work at their own pace in algebra and geometry. Students are free to do independent study in any course offered in the curriculum, preferably in a subject they are studying.

There are a variety of ways a student can go about designing a plan for independent study. Perhaps the easiest is to have the student begin by answering the following questions: (1) What is the topic I am interested in? (2) What questions do I have about the topic? (3) What do I need to know to answer the questions? (4) What sources can I use to obtain the information? (5) What activities should I engage in to gather the information? (6) How should I organize the information to answer my questions? (7) How will I report my answers? After the students answer these questions, they are ready to design an independent study contract which is a binding agreement between the student and the teacher specifying the learning objectives, the resources and strategies, the form of the completed work, and the criteria for evaluation.

Independent study has many benefits. It focuses the attention of the teachers and students on the elements of effective teaching, expecially the relationship of objectives, procedures, materials, and evaluation. Independent study enables students to develop their interests and abilities; it also teaches them to become responsible for their own learning, which is the most important reason for including independent study in our classrooms today.

See also Gifted and Talented Education; Home Instruction; Instructional Objectives; Learning Styles.

—Mark A. Krabbe
Miami, Ohio University

References

Brookfield, S. (1985). *Self-directed learning: From theory to practice.* San Francisco: Jossey-Bass.

Dressel, P.L., & Thompson, M.M. (1973). *Independent study.* San Francisco: Jossey-Bass.

Knowles, M.S. (1975). *Self-directed learning.* Chicago: Follett.

INDIVIDUALIZATION OF INSTRUCTION

The need for individualizing instruction has become increasingly apparent in the last twenty years. Historically, educators were content to teach to the mythical average student. The teacher designed a good lesson on a particular subject, taught that lesson to the whole class, assigned follow-up activities, answered questions, and proceeded to the next subject, which was taught to the whole class in the same manner. Some students learned exceptionally well, others were average, and still others fell farther and farther behind.

Several national issues have caused this scenario to change. In fact, this type of teaching, although still prevalent in our schools, is not considered creative or effective instruction.

The issues of multicultural education and mainstreaming of handicapped students into regular classrooms have forced a rethinking of traditional methods of instruction and have had a profound and lasting influence on the definition of effective classroom instruction. In addition, the current trends toward competency-testing of students, academic excellence, and the need for technological skills and computer literacy have served to establish more firmly the necessity for individualizing instruction in today's classrooms. In some cases, it has become law. For example, Public Law 94-142 mandates that an individualized educational program be designed to meet specifically the learning needs of any child who has been diagnosed as having exceptional education needs.

Defining the term "individualizing instruction" requires viewing the concept as both an educational philosophy and as a method of organizing classroom instruction. As a philosophy, it means assessing the instructional needs of each student (diagnosis), and providing learning opportunities which are designed to meet the identified needs (perception). As a method of organizing classroom instruction, it demands a much more comprehensive definition. Individualizing instruction requires a determination of what areas are included in the term "individual student needs," and what resources and/or options are available to structure the learning environment to meet prioritized needs.

Individual Student Needs

Determining individual needs requires assessment in the areas of intellectual development, physical development, learning style, personality, special aptitudes, cultural experiences, and background experiences.

Intellectual development requires looking at both a student's I.Q. (intelligence quotient) and stage of intellectual development. The range of intellectual abilities in any classroom will vary. Physical development when combined with corresponding emotional changes can influence student motivation, behavior, and classroom performance.

Learning styles focus the preferences of a student when he or she is involved in learning tasks. For example, a need for a quiet area free from distractions may be necessary for some students. In addition, different senses are used by students in the learning process. To meet these needs, a variety of materials and activities must be used in a classroom.

Personality is another factor that must be considered. If a student is outgoing, withdrawn, or anxious, then some learning experiences will be more appropriate than others. Different aptitudes, talents and areas of interest must be determined and cultivated in students. The identification of these can allow a teacher to build on the strengths of each student.

Cultural and background experiences can have a significant influence on how an individual student approaches the learning process. Also, this can affect how a student generalizes concepts and information.

In any classroom, the possible combinations of these learner needs will cause a wide range in the levels of achievement for any given subject area. This is true even when efforts are made to group students who are on the same level of achievement (homogeneous grouping).

Two facts become readily apparent when one considers learner needs. First, assessment is a complicated and difficult task, and, second, total individualization of instruction to meet the possible combinations of student needs, in any classroom, is difficult to justify because of cost. Given this conclusion, how do educators provide learning experiences that can be effective for individual students?

Available Options

There are variables in any instructional program that can be manipulated to provide options for individual student learning. Once skill level in a particular subject area is determined, modifications can be made in the following ways:

1. *Learning objectives for students.* These can be different for some students, even though the content and skills to be learned are the same for all students. Breaking down tasks into smaller steps, decreasing the amount of work required for some students, extending time periods, and allowing students to self-pace are some of the ways that can be utilized by teachers.

2. *Tasks and materials.* Many teacher-made and commercially produced series, programs, systems, kits, and packages are available. Cost factors and expertise in selecting appropriate tasks and materials are important considerations in this area.

3. *Methods of presentation.* How content is presented can be varied through the use of lecture, discussion, small group work, and independent study. In combination, these methods can and do provide different ways for students to learn required skills.

4. *Evaluation of learning outcomes.* The ways that are used to determine whether a student has learned required material can be varied to include formal tests, assignments in class, and use of individual student folders; another way is by means of student demonstrations and products, e.g., reports, exhibits, models, and displays.

This overview of individualizing instruction describes what has become a key focus in our schools and a critical challenge for our educators.

Current Practices and Future Trends

Current classroom practices range from instruction that is designed to teach the mythical average student to the use of a variety of approaches to individualized instruction. These approaches include use of learning centers, media labs, modularized packages on specific skills, open experiences, and computerized instruction.

One approach that holds a great deal of promise in helping to individualize instruction effectively is that of computerized instruction. Currently, over 50 percent of our schools are using computers for some level of instructional purposes.

There are three functional areas of computer use:

1. *Computer-assisted instruction (CAI).* This has been the area of primary use of computers in schools. The computer assists teachers in instruction. Programs to provide drill and practice, tutorial assistance, and demonstrations are available and in use. These programs allow self-pacing of students, immediate feedback, and independent use. They can provide one-on-one review and practice which teachers are unable to provide due to time limitations and class size. Also, simulations and instructional games can be motivational and fun for students.

2. *Computer learning environments.* Some of the functional areas of computer use in this approach are data processing, numerical analysis, and artificial intelligence.

3. *Computer-managed instruction.* This use of computers provides a possible avenue to assist teachers in the diagnostic, prescriptive and management activities that are an integral part of individualizing instruction. It allows for testing students, immediately directing them into appropriate skill activities, and keeping a detailed record of student achievement. Both students and teacher have ready access to skill attainment information.

Given the impressive options which exist to help individualize instruction, why are many classrooms unable to make the transition into new and more effective individualized teaching strategies? There are many reasons. Much of the available material is expensive, and evaluating these materials to determine which to use can be time consuming. But one of the main reasons centers around the question of how to individualize instruction.

Strategies for Implementation

Successful implementation must occur at three levels: the district level, the school-building level, and the individual classroom level.

1. *District level.* A commitment on the part of school boards, staff and parents is critical to the success of an implementation strategy. This means that there must be agreement that individualizing instruction as a philosophy and as a method can and should occur. This agreement should then be reflected in the stated goals and policies of the district. The next critical step is the allocation of resources for achieving the goals. These resources include, but are not limited to the following: (a) financial allocations for materials and in-service training of the staff; (b) central office staff (supervisors and curriculum specialists) who are trained in individualizing instruction and available to assist schools in implementation; (c) curriculum committees which provide for teacher input and/or specialists with expertise in evaluating and selecting materials, programs, and texts; and (d) if computers and computer programs will be utilized, there is a need for expertise in evaluating and selecting equipment and programs (software). In addition, computer literacy will be required for the staff at all levels.

2. *School building level.* The administrator and specialists at the building level must have an understanding of methods and materials to be used in implementation. They need to serve as a resource and support system for classroom teachers. In addition, the following activities should be addressed at the building level: (a) Define specific areas in which inservice training of teachers must be provided in teams or individually; (b) structure time for teachers, to develop specific plans for implementation in the classroom; (c) review plans with teachers and organize necessary resources and timelines for implementation; and (d) communicate with parents what their role will be, and how implementation will occur.

3. *The classroom teacher.* In their detailed planning, teachers should (a) identify subject area in classroom instruction to be the initial focus of individualized instruction; (b) determine which students will be involved at the beginning of implementation; (c) develop specific timelines and detailed plans for expanding the program; and (d) define the resources/materials that will be necessary to support the implementation and to carry out the expansion phases.

If teams of teachers undertake the planning, this can be very beneficial for implementation. It allows for a peer support group which can be nonthreatening and provide assistance for individuals on the team.

In summary, successful individualizing of instruction requires involvement at all levels of a school district. It demands a commitment to allocate resources, plan in detail, carefully evaluate available approaches and materials. Everyone should plan on moving slowly and deliberately toward implementation and expansion.

See also Computer-Assisted Instruction; Direct Instruction; Independent Study; Learning Styles.

—Linda Post
University of Wisconsin-Milwaukee

References

Charles, C.M. (1980). *Individualizing instruction* (2nd ed.). St. Louis: C. V. Mosby.

Coburn, P., Kelman, P., Roberts, N., Snyder, T., Watt, D., & Weiner, C. (1985). *Practical guide to computers in education* (2nd ed.). Reading, MA: Addison-Wesley.

Glass, R., Christianson, J., & Christianson, J. (1982). *Teaching exceptional students in the regular classroom.* Boston: Little, Brown.

INDUSTRIAL ARTS EDUCATION

America's schools are answering a new call for the technological literacy of students leaving our secondary schools. This challenge is being met primarily by those teachers trained in the Industrial Arts, but who are now designing and teaching "Technology Education," a new term, which describes programs rapidly replacing traditional industrial arts. The change reflects an understanding of a new mission, content base, and teaching methodology.

Industrial arts education, until the technology education movement, remained rooted in the subjects of Woodward's Manual Training High School—those of woodworking, metalworking, and drawing. Plastics, graphic arts, and electricity-electronics were added only after they were fully established in our culture. These craft- and trade-oriented programs are wholly inadequate in answering the call to technological literacy. What is needed are courses and programs which provide the student with broad understandings of the systems of technology early in the educational process, while providing specific job-skill experiences in the upper levels for those who will earn their livelihood as they create, use, service, and teach technology. The purposes of technology education are to:

1. Provide all students with experiences designed to introduce them to the concepts and systems of technology, not only industrial systems, but those principles of technology applied in medicine, business, agriculture, and all areas of our society.

2. Provide all students with a sense of well-being relative to their ability to use technology to enhance their lives, to make good decisions about the use of technology, and to solve technology-related problems.

3. Provide experiences which will prepare students to find employment as those who are skilled in creating, using, servicing, and teaching technology.

Technology, by definition, is the application of scientific principles, resources, and tools, to extend human potential and/or to modify our environment. Four categories of human productive behaviors form the basis for the structure of the Technology Education Program. People are productive as they engage in *manufacturing, construction, communication,* and *transportation.* The study of these systems will provide a student with a fundamental knowledge of technology.

Course work in technology is generally formalized for the first time in grades six, seven, or eight, although many opportunities for integrated "technology units" exist at the elementary school level. A minimum of eight semester courses should be offered at the high-school level, with larger school districts able to offer many more. A balanced representation of each of the systems should be the goal of curriculum planners, whatever the size of the school.

Technology educators have not only adopted technology as their content base, but differ from industrial arts practitioners in other ways. Rather than focus on individual take-home projects, technology teachers use many short-term activities and experiments to teach the concepts of technology. Activities are often of a problem-solving nature and encourage

Socratic questioning and divergent thinking. The project-plan sheet is replaced with a statement of a technological problem for which students, frequently working in groups, will research and test potential solutions. Technology teachers emphasize the process and not the product both in their teaching approach and in their evaluation design.

Teaching at the occupational-preparation level requires that teachers coordinate the use of community resources, organize cooperative education programs, and work closely with both universities and junior/technical colleges and institutions. Partnerships with business and industry are crucial.

The new technology teacher is also considering ways to improve the physical plant (shop) by replacing the industrial look with a laboratory or classroom look. New equipment frequently requires a clean environment. The "new look" also attracts more female students and more academically able students than traditional industrial arts programs.

The Industrial Arts Student Association and the Vocational Industrial Clubs of America provide students with programs for the development of leadership skills needed for occupational success. These clubs are an integral part of the technology education program and are not to be viewed as an optional or extracurricular activity.

As our society knocks on the door of the 21st century, we must ask ourselves about the type of education which will enable our citizenry to deal with the technological aspects of our society. Traditional industrial arts education clearly falls far short of what is needed, but great promise exists in the emerging field of Technology Education.

See also Educational Goals and Objectives; Career Education; Curriculum Development; Technology Education.

—John H. Vanderhoof
Wisconsin Department of Public Instruction

References

Illinois State Board of Education. *The Illinois plan for industrial education: A planning guide.* Macomb, IL: Curriculum Publications Clearing House.

Snyder, J.F., & Hales, J.A. (1981). *Jackson's Mill Industrial Arts Curriculum Theory.* Charleston, W VA: West Virginia Department of Education.

Technology Education: *A Perspective on Implementation.* Reston, VA: International Technology Education Association.

INNER CITY SCHOOLS

Inner city schools are found in the ghettos of most large cities. As such, they have a tremendous importance on the kind of education received by ghetto youngsters because of the overall characteristics of most ghetto communities.

Such disadvantaged areas, or ghettos, have the following commonalities that directly influence the schools found in the ghetto, and inner city schools are the schools of the urban ghetto: (a) high-population densities, mostly minority, with a large male mobility rate; (b) high birth rates for minorities as opposed to Whites (2.4 per female for Blacks, 2.9 for Hispanics, and 1.7 for Whites); (c) high death rates due to violence in the ghetto and especially high infant mortality rates; (d) high rates of unemployment (especially among minority youth); (e) high welfare dependency based upon unemployment, higher illegitimate birth rates, and the feminization of poverty (50 percent of children in female headed households were in poverty in 1984 as opposed to 40 percent

in general for the ghetto); (f) high incidences of substandard housing and overcrowding, which are reflected in overcrowded inner city schools; (g) high crime rates which decrease availability of social services at the expense and need for more police services; (h) large minority populations that are highly concentrated and that dominate the area, neighborhoods, and schools; and (i) inner city schools that reflect the failures and traumas of the community, and ultimately define, organize, limit, and cripple the aspirations and achievements of minorities attending these schools. Inner city schools are constant reminders of our failure to provide equal opportunities for all citizens, especially minorities.

Like the ghettos that these schools are found in, inner city schools have definite characteristics, and these characteristics define the challenges ahead for educational reform. Inner city schools are therefore an integral part of an urban ghetto and all it characterizes. Aside from this, there are two other characteristics that are most noticeable: (a) inner city school facilities are the most overburdened, unequal, and insecure of all urban schools; and, (b) inner city schools have more problems than other urban schools and produce the greatest challenge for educators. The problems are enormous in terms of reform and change in public urban education.

Inner city facilities tend to be the oldest; have the largest numbers of students per school; have the highest numbers of newly credentialed teachers (also nontenured and emergency credentialed teachers); have the largest teacher and administrator turnover rates of any of the urban schools; have the greatest demand upon teachers' time and energies in terms of discipline, instruction, lesson planning, and class sizes; and have the highest absentee rates among school personnel of any urban schools. Inner city schools utilize more substitute teachers per school than any of the other types of urban schools.

Inner city schools have more problems than other urban schools because they have more students who have reading and achievement problems and whose scores are the lowest in most school systems, have the highest student truancy and drop out rates (e.g., 50 percent to 63 percent of inner city students in the Los Angeles schools drop out before graduation, with the overall average for Los Angeles being 42 percent, keeping in mind that the L.A. schools have 80 percent minority enrollment), have the greatest number of discipline and vandalism problems of any schools (e.g., it is estimated that the average teacher spends 80 percent of his or her time in disciplining and 20 percent in instruction), have the greatest transient rates of any schools (especially in the urban centers experiencing traumatic immigration growth), and have a greater amount of "teacher burnout" than any other type of school. Inner city schools have the lowest overall tenure averages for teachers in their schools.

Teachers in inner city schools face enormous problems, and they are ill-trained for handling these problems. With inner city youngsters who are almost 100 percent minority in racial and ethnic background, teachers face greater challenges in three task areas with students: (1) gaining their attention, (2) maintaining their attention, and (3) increasing their attention and directing it towards goals, short or long range. Teachers of inner city youngsters must be prepared to deal with kids that bring to school some well-defined "deficits": attentional deficits, behavioral deficits, learning deficits, nutritional deficits, and affectional deficits as a result of family instability and improper role models. Students with such deficits score low on IQ and other standardized tests, read and speak poorly, and often perform below grade level on other tasks; they are not motivated towards the traditional academic goals that most teachers hold, and are more prone towards toughness, hostility, violence, sexual license, and differentness in behavior as a result of the social and environmental influences in their daily lives. School is secondary in their priorities.

Teachers in inner city schools, regardless of background, including race, know very little about their students. Few know that black children are twice as likely as white children to die in the first year of life, three times as likely to be poor, four times more likely not to live with either parent, five times more likely to be on welfare, six times more likely to be unemployed and unable to find work, and seven times more likely to be more sexually active than other teens of that age. As a result, what is rapidly developing in many ghettos and inner city schools is a permanent underclass which makes the tasks of the school impossible in light of the social and economic realities influencing the lives of inner city youngsters.

That is not to say that all inner city schools are failing. There are some successful inner city schools, but they are exceptions. Successful inner city schools demand an almost perfect balance of available resources, strong assertive leadership from a determined principal, a supportive community with parents directly involved in the process, *and* a cadre of well-prepared, trained teachers for the inner city experience. It is being done in some schools.

The prescription for a successful inner city school is twofold: strong, experienced, assertive principals and skilled, dedicated, creative teachers. The emphasis for both is upon experience—neither should be new to the profession. Teachers must have acquired the essential survival skills such as the (a) ability to understand and use developmental and remedial reading procedures; (b) ability to organize and structure specific classroom procedures; (c) ability to reconstruct syllabi, texts, and materials in terms of the background of students; (d) ability to adjust to truancy, absenteeism, and new entrants to the classroom; (e) ability to discipline and handle group behavior; (f) ability to translate street language and knowledge into specific classroom use; (g) ability to counsel and work with community and parents; and (h) ability to use creative flexibility and innovation in lessons with a greater emphasis on individualized instruction.

Principals must be able to (a) set rules and codes of school conduct and vigorously enforce them; (b) select the best available teachers and demand accountability in terms of achieving common selected goals; (c) get constant feedback from parents, teachers, students, and community; act on that feedback, and be a change agent; (d) be an instructional expert in allowing for teacher creativity, selecting specialists in such areas as reading and counseling, providing for lower class sizes, and demanding such things as lesson plans from teachers; (e) provide for critical in-service education for all front-line and in-school contact staff and to provide for paraprofessional and parental aides; (f) provide strategies for accountability and competency-based training; and (g) provide for strategies for total community, wider family, university, and general public involvement in the urban core experience. The success or failure of the inner city school depends upon the principal-teacher relationship; both must be in close harmony with the above stated objectives. The key to holding both together is experience. Inexperienced principals and/or teachers unravel success: on the job training is costly and unproductive. Teacher- training institutions must assist principals and teachers in the above goals and assist in specialized training for inner city schools.

The Supreme Court in *Plessy vs. Ferguson*, 1896, enunciated the principle of "separate but equal," but it took until the Brown Decision of 1954 to convince the public that segregation was wrong and unconstitutional. Voluminous evidence from social research proves the contradictions in separate but equal. Yet our inner city schools remain largely segregated, socioeconomically separate from the other schools, and inherently unequal in what they have to offer, how they offer it, and what they do. Few understand that these "minority" students are fast becoming the "majority" in our schools (inner city schools, 1986, represented 50 percent of all urban-school enrollments). The social consequences of an inferior education for these youngsters is tantamount to national suicide. Inner city schools are the critical link for any reform in public education. And this is the challenge!

By the year 2000, one out of every three Americans will be non-White. The minority numbers are now so large that if they are not educated, all of us will have diminished futures. This is the new reality in schools and society. We can no longer afford to allow our inner city schools to be the worst examples of public education in America.

See also Demographic Trends; Minorities and the School System; Multicultural Education; Student Culture.

—Alfred Lightfoot
Loyola Marymount University

References

Borman, J., & Spring, J. (1984). *Schools in central cities*. New York: Longman.

Hodgkinson, H. (1985). *All one system*. Washington, DC: Institute for Educational Leadership.

Lightfoot, A. (1985). *Urban education in social perspective*. Washington, DC: University Press of America. Reissued from the 1978 Rand McNally publication.

INSTRUCTIONAL MEDIA CENTER

As the curriculum patterns for individual schools have emerged, developed, and changed over the years, so have the services and operations of the school library. Influenced by national trends, state standards, regional accrediting agencies, financial resources of the school districts, and an increased number of trained and certified library media personnel, the small book room containing a few old textbooks and the classroom collections in the elementary grades have become central collections containing many types and formats of print and nonprint instructional materials with their accompanying hardware. These collections and facilities are called by many terms such as instructional resources centers, instructional media centers, and learning resources centers. The term instructional media center will be used in this article.

The instructional media center program is a vital and basic part of the school, providing quality education by enriching the total educational process. Through a program of unified media services, it serves as the instructional materials center, providing the learning resources necessary to meet the needs of the school's curriculum and acting as an integral support for the school's goals and objectives. As members of the instructional team, the staff helps define and plan learning activities and a program structured to meet the needs of the students and curriculum served.

Program Design and Implementation

The school administrator can make an important contribution to the success of the total educational program by carefully guiding the development of the instructional media center program through the planning stages with the help of appropriately trained instructional media personnel and staff. While developing the plan for the implementation of an instructional media center program, an administrator should give the following processes careful attention:

1. Defining the purposes of the instructional media center program. It is critical that the identified purposes be determined before other decisions relating to staffing services, equipment, or facilities are made,

2. Integrating the instructional media center program with other programs of the school. An effective program is dependent upon the support of the school board, the superintendent, the school principal, and upon a mutually supportive partnership between teachers and instructional media personnel. Attention should be focused on the center as a multifaceted learning laboratory which supports, complements, and expands the work of the classroom.

3. Participating in instructional design, course development, and the creation of alternative modes of learning. The program must be an integral part of all curricular activities. Instructional media personnel should be represented on all school curriculum committees and should be involved with all additions, deletions, and revisions of the school's instructional program so that the instructional media service can accommodate these changes. The program should also provide regular in-service education to each school's staff in the following areas: (a) awareness and use of available resources and technology; (b) application of instructional technology; and (c) techniques of local production of instructional materials and software.

4. Developing budget criteria and budgets. The budget and accounting system for the instructional media center programs should follow the accounting system of the state. Each school should have a budget allocated to the operation of its program. This portion of the school budget should be managed by the instructional media specialist.

5. Developing policies controlling the operation of the instructional media center program. Each school should have a written policy manual governing the program. The policies should be in strict accordance with the policies of the school district. They should include but not be limited to (a) materials and equipment selection, (b) use of the collection and of the media-center materials and equipment acquisition, (c) reconsideration procedures, (d) lines of authority, (e) public relations, (f) weeding and maintenance of the collection, and (g) program evaluation.

6. Providing program activities that respond to curriculum goals on a day-to-day basis. The instructional media center program should provide resources and technology to assist all teachers and students in their educational programs. Developing flexible operations that encourage users in problem solving, interest fulfillment, and creative expression is necessary. The program should also provide opportunities for exploration independent of the stated curriculum. In order to meet curriculum goals, the program must maintain professional resources for teachers, inform them about new materials and equipment, and involve them in purchasing decisions.

7. Providing orientation and instruction in media skills to students and staff. The program should provide detailed instruction in instructional media including the use of audio visual materials and equipment for all students K-12. It is recommended that instructional media specialists and teachers cooperatively determine what will be taught in this skills program. The program should also provide instruction as needed to all members of the staff in the proper use of materials and equipment.

8. Providing local production capabilities. The instructional media center program provides the materials, equipment, and technical assistance necessary to allow teachers to produce certain instructional materials neither readily available nor commercially accessible, but which would be beneficial in the teaching-learning process. A wide range of resources such as cameras, lettering sets, mounting and preserving equipment, recording equipment—both audio and video—and related software should be available for this purpose. Involvement of students in this activity can be extremely beneficial.

9. Developing and maintaining the collection. The media staff is responsible for the development of a balanced, relevant collection. This determination should be made based on the curriculum and student population being served. The staff is responsible for the care of the collection. The program should also be able to provide information concerning resources available in other locations such as other school districts, public libraries, and state libraries. If district instructional media programs are developed, computer online bibliographic searching services should be made available.

10. Building a public relations program that communicates the role of the instructional media center and its contributions to the goals of the school. The instructional media specialist should collect, analyze, and disseminate information on the program, its services, and its needs, in order to extend public awareness and generate support.

11. Performing on-going evaluations in light of stated objectives and making program modifications. The instructional media specialist should provide for a continuous process of evaluation involving instructional media staff, administrators, teachers, and students in the assessment of program components. The results of these evaluations should then be applied to planning for program modification, budgeting, in-service training, collections development, and public relations.

12. Reporting to administrators, teachers, and students relative to the program. Communication with the community being served is vital to maintaining an instructional media center program. Reporting may be accomplished in a variety of ways, including formal reports, oral reports, displays, and newsletters. The use of various instructional media should be considered.

13. Examining newer technology such as microcomputer/CD-ROM storage, interactive video systems and networking systems. The instructional media specialist should provide leadership in assessing the potential of new media and technology in instructional and managerial processes.

Conclusion

The instructional media center program represents a combination of resources which includes people, services, materials, equipment, and facilities. Its prime responsibility is to facilitate the teaching-learning process by providing resources and services which satisfy both individual and instructional needs of students in an atmosphere which promotes inquiry, creativity, self-direction, communication of ideas, and the ability to use rational processes. In this manner, the program provides a learning environment in which individual differences and enrichment needs can be met as students attain basic skills and achieve identified goals.

An effective instructional media center program is dependent upon the support of the school board, the superintendent, the school principal, and a mutually supportive partnership between teachers and instructional media center personnel. Teachers, as members of this instructional team, keep instructional media center staff informed about curricula and assignments. Teachers also participate in the planning of instructional media skills instruction, evaluating learning resources, motivating students to use media, and implementing the instructional media center program within the context of curricular areas. Attention is focused on the instructional media center program as a multifaceted learning laboratory which supports, complements, and expands the work of the classroom.

See also Independent Study.

—William Pichette
Sam Houston State University

References

Gillespie, J.T., & Spirt, D.L. (1983). *Administering the school library media center.* New York: R. R. Bowker.

Turner, P. (1985). *Helping teachers teach: A school library/media specialist's role.* Littleton, CO: Libraries Unlimited.

Wehmeyer, L.B. (1984). *The school librarian as educator.* Littleton, CO: Libraries Unlimited.

INSTRUCTIONAL OBJECTIVES

Two essential decisions in planning education at any level and in any area are means and ends. *Means* are the learning activities, teaching methods, and educational materials used to bring about accomplishment of the ends. The ends are the outcomes sought. Most typically they are statements about knowledge, skills, and attitudes students are to possess as a consequence of the means.

Ends are usually referred to as aims, purposes, goals, or objectives. Although some writers use several of these terms interchangeably, it is possible and helpful to distinguish among them. Using the basis of the educational level for which they are intended, three types of ends can be differentiated. Aims or purposes refer to the highest level of ends. They are broad policy statements that the district sees as outcomes for the students' total education. Goals are broad ends associated with a subject-area program, course or unit. They are the outcomes sought, for example, in the school's English program, an English course, or a particular English unit. Objectives or instructional objectives are the ends for use by teachers, usually on a daily basis. They are outcomes for one or more class periods, lessons, or learning activities. The district-level aims and the district- and school-level goals both give direction to the classroom-level instructional objectives.

Functions of Instructional Objectives

Instructional objectives are indispensable to teaching. They aid in making decisions in four areas: (a) They define the direction of educational development. Instructional objectives unify and give meaning to classroom events; (b) They facilitate the selection of learning activities. Without instructional objectives, the choice of activities as well as materials would be difficult if not impossible; (c) They define the scope of what is to be taught. They identify the nature and limits of the content that is to be taught and learned; and (d) They serve as a basis for evaluation. Instructional objectives are essential for appraising the adequacy of the session or lesson.

Because of the power of instructional objectives in shaping every aspect of a classroom lesson or session, they must be formulated with great care. Most writers say that instructional objectives are the single most important decision to be made in preparation for teaching.

Dimensions of Instructional Objectives

Instructional objectives are by no means simple, standardized formulations concerning what students are to acquire. They can vary in relation to a number of dimensions: substance, level, focus, form, target, and time. Those who formulate instructional objectives need to be aware of these dimensions.

Substance. *Substance* refers to the specific types of learning that students are to acquire. The substance can be knowledge, skills, or attitudes. *Knowledge* refers to facts, concepts, and generalizations that the teacher wishes the student to learn. The focus is on knowing. *Skills* refer to abilities or operations that the student is to acquire. Skills include basic skills such as word-attack techniques in reading, thinking skills such as weighing evidence, and social-personal skills such as group leadership. The focus is on doing. *Attitudes* refer to appreciations, feelings, and values. Attitudes are judgments that the teacher wishes students to accept or to develop for themselves. The focus for attitudes is feeling.

Level. *Level* refers to the degree of complexity of the substance. Some instructional objectives such as recalling facts from a story are relatively simple, while others such as explaining the causes of the 1929 economic depression are more complex. Bloom and his colleagues have developed a taxonomy of six progressive levels of development: knowledge (remembering or recalling information), comprehension (understanding and relating information), application (using information in new situations), analysis (reducing information to its constituent parts), synthesis (combining information to create new patterns or structures), and evaluation (judging the value of information). In the area of skills, a helpful set of categories for manipulative skills consisting of observing (watching an experienced performer), imitating (acquiring basic rudiments), practicing (repeating the sequence of actions), and adapting (perfecting the skill) was developed by Harrow. Within the attitudes area, levels of complexity are provided by Krathwohl, Bloom, and Masia. Their categories are receiving (willing to attend to the phenomena), responding (actively attending to the phenomena), valuing (behaving in a consistent, stable way), organization (creating a system of values), and value complex (internalizing values to the point that they automatically govern behavior).

Although all of the categories in each of the areas are useful, formulating instructional objectives can be simplified by compressing the levels into just two: lower level and higher level. *Lower-level* objectives are those that call for knowledge and comprehension, observing and imitating, and receiving and responding. All of the other categories can be labeled *higher-level objectives.*

Focus. Instructional objectives are narrower than aims or goals, but they exist in varying degrees of breadth. Some instructional objectives deal with a very specific skill or segment of knowledge such as identifying grammatical errors in prose paragraphs. These are *narrow* objectives. Others deal with more general learnings such as gaining understanding of the countries of the Middle East. These objectives have a *broad* focus.

Form. The dimension of form has to do with how the objective is stated. Three commonly used forms are behavioral, conceptual, and topical. An objective stated in *behavioral* form is one in which the behavior that the student is to display as evidence of acquiring a specified learning is identified. An example of a behavioral objective is the following: "Given a list of fifteen contemporary authors, the student must be able to name one work of at least ten authors." This objective states who is to perform the behavior, identifies the behavior, states the product of the behavior, describes the conditions under which the behavior is to occur, and provides a standard for judging success.

An objective stated in *conceptual* form is one that expresses a content concept or generalization such as the following: "The lower the price of a product, the more people will buy it." Conceptual objectives are widely applicable truths that scholars have derived from study in their disciplines.

An objective in *topical* form is one in which the knowledge, skill, or attitude to be learned is announced. Neither student behaviors nor generalizations are included in this form. "To study Arctic climate" and "To understand decimal fractions" are examples of topical objectives.

Target. Target refers to the person or persons for whom the objective was formulated. Objectives can be formulated for the *student*. That is, they deal with what the student is to come to know, do, or feel. Or, they can be formulated for the *teacher*. When the teacher is the target, the objective states what the teacher is going to do to bring about learning on the part of students.

Time. Time, the last dimension, refers to the point when the objective is to be achieved. All instructional objectives are relatively immediate, but they can vary concerning when their achievement is to occur. An objective can be the *present* time. These objectives identify ends that are to be achieved in one time. These objectives identify ends that are to be achieved in one or two class periods or sessions. An objective can also be for a *future time*. These objectives state ends that need a week or more to achieve.

The various combinations of these six dimensions of instructional objectives can lead to many different kinds of instructional objectives. No one kind of instructional objective is absolutely better than or preferable to another kind. Instructional objectives are good or appropriate to the extent that they are consistent with and lead to the accomplishment of district aims. If district aims, for example, emphasize the development of basic skills and knowledge, one would expect to find many instructional objectives that stress knowledge and skill substance at the lower levels, have a narrow focus and behavioral form, are directed to the student, and are to be accomplished during the present. If district aims have a self-actualization focal point, one would expect to find many instructional objectives that highlight attitude substance along with knowledge and skills at both levels of complexity, have a broad focus and topical form, are directed to the student, and are to be accomplished in both the present and future. If district aims stress thinking and problem solving ability, one would expect to find many instructional objectives that deal with knowledge and skills at the higher levels, have a broad focus and conceptual or topical form, are directed to the student, and are accomplishable in both the present and future.

Trends and Issues

Two significant trends in instructional objectives are the use of the behavioral form and the stress on skills substance. Advocates of the behavioral form can be traced back to at least the 1920s, but the behavioral form, or behavioral objectives, as they are usually called, began to be a major movement in the 1960s as a result of the writing of Mager and others. At present, behavioral objectives have become so commonplace that many think of them as synonymous with instructional objectives. This confusion can result in failure to accomplish district aims or the alteration of district aims if the behavioral form of the instructional objective is incompatible with district aims.

Behavioral objectives have many strengths, but they also have weaknesses. The strengths typically associated with them are that since they require the teacher to identify the behavior that the student will display to indicate mastery, they have more precision and clarity than other forms of objectives. Also, because they specify student behavior, they establish the instructional activity and thereby facilitate instruction. Further, because they carry standards for achievement as well as describe outcome behavior, they make evaluation a simple process.

The criticisms of behavioral objectives usually center on their conception, their use, and their effects. Critics of behavioral objectives say that student behavior cannot be taken as evidence of student learning because a one-to-one correspondence between the two does not exist. Much learning occurs that does not result in overt, classroom behavior. Even if behavior could be taken as evidence, behavioral objectives are difficult to formulate, the critics contend. It is especially difficult to write behavioral objectives in the attitude substance area, for example. And, when instructional objectives are framed in behavioral terms, dangerous side effects develop, the critics say. Since it is easier to use the behavioral form for simple learnings, complex learnings are often ignored. Also, because of the effort involved in specifying objectives in behavioral form, teachers, once they have written them, may tend to use them repeatedly. That is, they may result in rigidity when spontaneity is needed.

The second trend, stressing the skills substance, is of more recent origin than the behavioral objectives movement. It is a result of the decline in basic skills achievement as revealed in national examinations in the 1970s. In response to the decline, schools have increased their attention to reading, mathematics, writing, and other basic skills. They have emphasized skills substance and de-emphasized attitude substance, and to a lesser extent, knowledge substance areas. At present, especially in the elementary grades, skill substance instructional objectives are used to the near exclusion of other substance areas. This trend, like the behavioral form trend, is appropriate if it is directly related to the district as well as school goals.

Conclusion

Few, if any, decisions made by the classroom teacher are more significant than those regarding instructional objectives. In describing the outcome of a single learning activity, these objectives have the capability to shape every aspect of a lesson or session and therefore must be formulated with great care.

See also Cognitive Development; Competency-Based Education; Curriculum Development; Educational Goals and Objectives.

—John A. Zahorik
University of Wisconsin-Milwaukee

References

Bloom, B. (Ed.). (1956). *Taxonomy of educational objectives: The classification of educational goals, Handbook I: Cognitive domain.* New York: David McKay.

Harrow, A. (1972). *A taxonomy of the psychomotor domain: A guide for developing behavioral objectives.* New York: David McKay.

Krathwohl, D., Bloom, B., & Masia, B. (1964). *Taxonomy of educational objectives: The classification of educational goals, Handbook II: Affective domain.* New York: David McKay.

INTELLIGENCE AND INTELLIGENCE TESTING

Schools are the largest users of individual intelligence tests. They also use group intelligence tests. Individual intelligence tests are necessary for accurate diagnosis of children's learning and emotional problems and require extensive training and supervised experience in their use. A graduate degree in school or clinical psychology is regarded by most professional organizations as the minimally acceptable credential for use of these tests. Group intelligence tests are used in screening for overall intellectual level when great accuracy or detailed information is unnecessary.

The widespread use of group intelligence tests coincides for the most part with the growth of the individual intelligence test. During World War I, a committee of the American Psychological Association developed the Army Alpha and the Army Beta, the first widely applied group intelligence tests. Current group intelligence tests are all similar in format, presenting multiple choice items with four or five distractors in reusable test booklets with separate answer sheets. Since group intelligence tests lack the flexibility of individual tests, most group intelligence tests consist of a series of multilevel tests, each designated for a particular age, grade, or ability level.

The two most widely used group tests of intelligence are the Otis-Lennon School Abilities Test and the Cognitive Abilities Test. The Otis-Lennon is almost entirely a test of verbal intelligence with five separate levels from grade one to 12. The Cognitive Abilities Test has 10 levels, spanning Kindergarten through grade 12. Although the Otis-Lennon yields a summary of IQ, the Cognitive Abilities Test does not, deferring to three separate scales, verbal, nonverbal, and quantitative.

Intelligence tests are useful in the diagnosis of all disorders of learning and nearly every mental disorder of children and adolescents. Intelligence testing is a controversial activity, however. Alan Kaufman has, over the past decade, attempted to bring together the positive aspects of intelligence testing and describe a method by which intelligence test results can be used to improve educational decision making and specific aspects of programming. Kaufman refers to this model as the *intelligent testing philosophy*. The intent of the intelligent testing model is to bring together empirical data, psychometrics, clinical acumen, psychological theory, and careful reasoning to build an assessment of an individual. An intervention to improve the life circumstances of the individual then can be worked out. The promulgation of this philosophy was influenced by many factors, but particularly by extremist approaches to the use of intelligence tests.

Conventional intelligence tests and even the entire concept of intelligence testing have been the focus of considerable controversy for several decades. The past two decades have witnessed intelligence tests placed on trial in the federal courts in the famous Larry P., PASE, and Marshall decisions. State legislatures (e.g., New York's "trust-in-testing" legislation) have enacted laws relating to intelligence tests. Tests have come to the attention of the layperson. They have been discussed in open scholarly forums such as the recent debate by Reynolds and Brown. At one extreme of the issue are those who contend that IQ tests are inherently unacceptable measurement devices with no real utility, while at the other extreme are such well-known figures as Richard Hernstein and Arthur Jensen, who believe the immense value of intelligence tests is by now clearly self-evident. While critics of testing demand a moratorium on their use, psychologists are often forced to adhere to unreasonable and rigid administrative rules that require the use of precisely obtained IQ scores when making placement or diagnostic decisions, with no consideration for measurement errors, the influence of behavioral variables on performance, or appropriate sensitivity to the child's cultural or linguistic heritage.

A middle ground is sorely needed. Intelligence tests need to be preserved, along with their rich clinical heritage and their prominent place in the neurological, psychological, and educational literature. At the same time, the proponents of tests need to be less defensive and more open to rational criticism of the current popular instruments. Knowledge of the weaknesses as well as the strengths of individually administered intelligence tests can serve the dual functions of improving examiners' ability to interpret profiles of any given instrument and enabling them to select pertinent supplementary tests and subtests to secure a thorough assessment of the intellectual abilities of any child, adolescent, or adult referred for evaluation. High reliability and validity coefficiency, a meaningful factor structure, and normative data obtained by stratified random-sampling techniques, though clearly necessary, do not ensure that an intelligence test is valuable for all or even most assessment purposes. The skills and training of the psychologists engaged in using intelligence tests will certainly interact with the utility of intelligence testing beyond the level of simple actuarial prediction of academic performance.

With low IQ children, the primary role of the intelligence tester is to use the test results to develop a means of intervention that will "beat" the prediction made by global IQs. A plethora of research during this century has amply demonstrated that very low IQ children show concomitantly low levels of academic attainment. Despite cries of bias, without appropriate intervention, low IQ blacks and other minority children have the same high probability of school failure as do white middle class low IQ children. The purpose of administering an intelligence test to a low IQ child then is at least twofold: first, to determine circumstances and, second, to articulate circumstances that defeat the prediction.

For individuals with average or high IQs, the specific task of the intelligence tester may change, but the philosophy remains the same. When evaluating a learning-disabled child, for example, the task is primarily one of fulfilling the prediction made by the global IQs. Most learning disabled children exhibit average or better general intelligence but have a history of academic performance significantly below what would be predicted from their intelligence-test performance. The "intelligent tester" then takes on the responsibility of designing a set of environmental conditions that will cause the child to achieve and learn at the level predicted by the intelligence test.

When psychologists engage in intelligence testing, the child or adult becomes the primary focus of the evaluation and the tests fade into the background as only vehicles to understanding. The test setting becomes completely examinee oriented. Interpretation and communication of test results in the context of the individual's particular background, referral behaviors, and approach to the performance of diverse tasks constitute the crux of competent evaluation. Global test scores are deemphasized; flexibility, a broad base of knowledge in psychology, and insight on the part of the psychologist are demanded; and, the intelligence test becomes a dynamic helping agent, not an instrument for labeling, placement in dead-end programs, or disillusionment of eager, caring teachers and parents.

Intelligent testing individualization becomes the key to accomplishment and is antithetical to the development of computerized or depersonalized form reporting for individually administered cognitive tests, and should lead to differentiated instruction. The intelligent-testing model is inconsistent with "checklist" approaches to the development of individual education plans as well. It is a mode of true individualization and does not lend itself to mimeographed individual education plans that are checked off nor with special education programs where all children are taught with the same methodology of instruction. Intelligent testing seeks differentiated instruction driven by student characteristics. Intelligent testing urges the use of contemporary measures of intelligence as necessary to achieve a true understanding of the individual's intellectual functioning. The approach to test interpretation under this philosophy has been likened by Kaufman to that of a psychological "detective" and requires a melding of clinical skill, mastery of psychometrics and measurement, and extensive knowledge of cognitive development and intelligence.

Clinical skills with children are obviously important to the intelligent tester in building rapport and maintaining the proper ambiance during the actual testing setting. Although adhering to standardized procedure and obtaining valid scores are important, the child must remain the lodestar of the evaluation. Fully half the important information gathered during the administration of an intelligence test comes from observing behavior under a set of standard condition. Behavior at various points in the course of the assessment will often dictate the proper interpretation of test scores. Many individuals earn IQ scores of 100, but each in a different manner, with infinite nuances of behavior interacting directly with a person's test performance.

Knowledge and skill in psychometrics and measurement are requisite to intelligent testing. The clinical evaluation of test performance must be directed by careful analyses of statistical properties of the test scores, internal psychometric characteristics of the test, and data regarding its relationship to external factors. Difference scores have long been of inherent interest for psychologists and educators, especially between subparts of an intelligence scale. Difference scores are unreliable, and small discrepancies between levels of performance may be best attributed to measurement error. If large enough, however, difference scores can provide valuable information regarding the choice of an appropriate remedial or therapeutic program. The psycho-metric characteristics of the tests in questions dictate the size of the differences needed for statistical confidence in their reflecting real rather than chance fluctuations. Interpretation often requires integrating clinical observations of the child's behavior with data on the relationship of the test scores to other factors, and with theories of intelligence.

One major limitation of most contemporary intelligence tests is their lack of foundation in theories of intelligence, whether these theories are based on research in neuropsychology, cognitive information processing, factor analysis, learning theory, or other domains. Nevertheless, many profiles obtained by children and adults on intelligence tests are interpretable from diverse theoretical perspectives. Theories then become useful in developing a full understanding of the individual. Well-grounded, empirically evaluated models of intellectual functioning enable one to reach broader understanding of the examinee and to make specific predictions regarding behavior outside of the testing situation itself. One will not always be correct; however, the intelligent tester has an excellent chance of making sense out of the predictable individual variations in behavior, cognitive skills, and academic performance by involving the nomothetic framework provided by theory. The alternative often is to be stymied or to rely on trial-and-error or anecdotal, illusionary relationships when each new set of profile fluctuations is encountered. Theories, even speculative ones, are more efficient guides to developing hypotheses for understanding and treating problems than are purely clinical impressions or armchair speculation.

Through the elements of clinical skill, psychometric sophistication, and a broad base of knowledge of theories of individual differences emerges intelligent testing. None is sufficient; yet when properly implemented, these elements engage in a synergistic interaction to produce the greatest possible understandings. The intelligent-testing model places a series of requirements on the test but also on the tester; not every test can be used intelligently nor can everyone be an intelligent tester. The examiner's breadth of knowledge of psychometrics, differential psychology, child development, and other areas is crucial. Equally, the test must have multiple scales that are reliable, with good validity evidence, and be standardized on a sufficiently large, nationally stratified random sample. The test must offer the opportunity for good clinical observations. Without all of these characteristics, intelligent testing is unlikely to take place; when it does, however, the child is certain to benefit.

See also Cognitive Development; Handicapped Students; Individualization of Instruction; Tests, Criterion- and Norm-Referenced.

—Cecil R. Reynolds
Texas A&M University

References

Kaufman, A.S. (1979). *Intelligent testing with the WISC-R.* New York: Wiley-Interscience.

Reynolds, C.R. (in press). "Intelligent testing." In C.R. Reynolds and L. Mann (Eds.). *Encyclopedia of Special Education.* New York: Wiley-Interscience.

Reynolds, C.R. & Brown, R.T. (Eds.) (1984). *Perspectives on bias in mental testing.* New York: Plenum.

J

JOB DESCRIPTIONS

One of the most effective ways of managing a school district is to employ the use of job descriptions. A set of clearly written job descriptions is exceedingly useful in defining areas of responsibility and authority, clarifying relationships, establishing accountability, and determining standards for evaluation and performance appraisal.

There is no one best method of writing job descriptions. However, certain elements tend to appear in most job descriptions. These elements include the title of the job, the duties to be performed, the authority and responsibilities of the job, reporting responsibilities, and the specific qualifications necessary for successful performance.

Job descriptions which center around major areas of responsibilities are more useful than those that list specific duties. This allows employees more flexibility in performing their duties and encourages individuality and creativity. In addition, when the limits of authority which go with each responsibility are contained in job descriptions, employee accountability is greatly enhanced.

Job descriptions which indicate the reporting relationships can assist in clarifying lines of authority and minimizing misunderstandings. By specifying the reporting relationships, employees will clearly know who their supervisors and subordinates are.

Writing Job Descriptions

The first step in preparing job descriptions for a school system is to conduct a job analysis. This involves finding out what employees do; why they perform certain tasks; how they do the job; what skills, education, or training are required for the job; and the relationship the job has to other jobs.

There are three commonly used approaches to conducting a job analysis: (a) the detached approach, (b) the analytical approach, and (c) the cooperative approach. The detached approach is used when an objective statement of duties is desired. When utilizing this method, those occupying the position are not consulted because the focus is on the job performance, and the relationship of the underlying skills, knowledge, and behaviors comprising that job performance.

The analytical approach is the process of recording information about the work performed by an employee. By using a personnel specialist within the district or an outside consultant, information is obtained through direct observation, individual and group interviews, questionnaries, and/or the diary method. Job descriptions based on the results of the job analysis are then written.

The cooperative approach includes all levels of employees in the process of writing job descriptions. The primary advantage of this process is that it promotes the involvement of all people concerned.

Many authorities recommend the following step-by-step cooperative approach because it provides both an analysis of the school system's objectives as well as an examination of its structure:

1. Inform the faculty and staff of the benefits of a job description program.

2. Identify the procedures to be used in developing specific task descriptions.

3. List the functions to accomplish the school system's goals and objectives.

4. Analyze the organizational structure in order to determine who is doing what and what is not being done.

5. Insure that all employees in a specific category help determine the job description for that category.

6. Review and make adjustments to the job descriptions.

See also Administrative Roles; Career Ladders; Delegating Authority.

—Richard Brown, President
Managing, Inc.

References

Debore, R.W. (1982). *Personnel administration in education* (Chapter 4). Englewood Cliffs, NJ: Prentice-Hall.

Job descriptions in public schools. (1984). Arlington, VA: Educational Research Service.

Redfern, G.B. (Winter, 1984). *ERS spectrum*, (21-26). Arlington, VA: Educational Research Service.

JUDICIAL DECISIONS

A court's decision has force within the boundaries of its jurisdiction. Usually, the decision applies both to the immediate parties and to future cases that have the same circumstances. This effect on the future is called *stare decisis* (let the decision stand), or more familiarly, *precedent*. Under this principle, previous decisions at the same or higher level of the judiciary within that jurisdiction are predominant, and those from other jurisdictions may be persuasive. This tradition provides stability and predictability to the law.

Nevertheless, the law is and must be flexible enough to adapt to changing social conditions and to respond satisfactorily to exceptional individual circumstances. Principal sources of this needed flexibility and equity are powers given to the courts to distinguish factual circumstances from what otherwise would be controlling precedent and to reverse their own previous decisions, particularly at the Supreme Court level. Reversals and modifications of the law through constitutional amendments and statutory changes provide other means of flexibility.

The United States has a dual system of law under which state and federal courts have overlapping authority. Within each of these two tracks the judiciary ordinarily is organized into three levels: numerous trial courts, a limited number of intermediate appeals courts, and one high (usually, but not always, called *supreme*) court. The state's highest court is the supreme authority as to the interpretation of that state's law. In a parallel way, the United States Supreme Court is the highest authority as to the meaning of federal law. Since the U.S. Supreme Court has a nationwide jurisdiction, its decisions apply to the entire country.

The rate of education-related litigation has exploded since 1954. This striking increase continues to accelerate. A recent study revealed that the number of suits involving students increased 243 percent from 1977 to 1980. An overview of the Supreme Court's leading decisions affecting education illustrates the extent and nature of this trend.

Supreme Court decisions were sporadic in the first half of the century. Notable were *Pierce v. Society of Sisters* (1925), holding unconstitutional a state statute requiring attendance at only public, not private, schools, and *West Virginia State Board of Education v. Barnette* (1943), holding unconstitutional a school board decision to condition attendance upon saluting of the flag.

The first major modern decision was *Brown v. Board of Education* (1954) in which the Supreme Court reversed the constitutionality of separate but equal governmental treatment of blacks. In *Brown I* the Court ruled that official segregation of children in public schools solely on the basis of race, even though the physical facilities and other tangible factors may be substantially equal, violates the equal protection clause of the Fourteenth Amendment. In *Brown II,* the following year, the Court returned the case to the federal trial courts for the implementation of desegregation "with all deliberate speed."

The next decade gave rise to a handful of landmark decisions, starting with *Abington School District v. Schempp* (1963), in which the Supreme Court held that Bible reading and organized prayer in the public schools violate the establishment clause of the First Amendment. In *Epperson v. Arkansas* (1968), the Court similarly held that a state law forbidding the teaching of the Darwinian theory of evolution also violates the establishment clause. During the same year the Court held that the dismissal of a public school teacher for criticizing the local board's allocation of school funds without proof of knowingly or recklessly false statements violates the free expression clause of Amendment I. The First Amendment's free speech rights were extended to students in the final school decision of the decade, *Tinker v. Des Moines Independent Community School District* (1969). In *Tinker* the Court held it unconstitutional to suspend public school students for the peaceful wearing of armbands or other symbolic expressions of opinion unless the administration proves that material interference or substantial disruption of the school's operation did or would occur.

In the 1970s, the number of significant Supreme Court decisions concerning education more than doubled. In 1972, the Court denied the constitutionality of applying a state compulsory education law to children beyond the eighth grade (*Wisconsin v. Yoder*), and it defined the "liberty" and "property" interests of publicly employed teachers under the due process clause (*Board of Regents v. Roth; Perry v. Sinderman*). During the following year, the Supreme Court ruled in *San Antonio Independent School District v. Rodriguez* that education is not a fundamental federal right, and, thus, that a state's school funding system based on local property taxes does not violate the U.S. Constitution. Students' rights under the Constitution were more clearly defined in a cluster of decisions in the mid-70s. In *Goss v. Lopez* (1975), the Court held that under the due process clause students are entitled to informal notice of charges and, if the student protests, an explanation of the charges and the opportunity to tell his side of the story for suspensions of up to ten days. In *Wood v. Strickland* (1975), the Court held that school officials are liable when they know or should have known that they were violating the constitutional rights of students.

Revealing limitations to the expansion of students' rights in *Ingraham v. Wright* (1977), the Court refused to hold corporal punishment as violating the "cruel and unusual punishment" language of the Eighth Amendment and the procedural due process guarantees of the Fourteenth Amendment. In the same year, the Court similarly spelled out limits in the constitutional rights of teachers, holding in *Mount Healthy School District v. Doyle* (1977) that a teacher could be terminated for constitutionally protected conduct if the board proves that it would have independently reached the same decision for legitimate reasons. The qualified First Amendment in *Mount Healthy* was extended to private teacher expression in *Givhan v. Western Line Consolidated School District* (1979).

The explosion of education litigation continued in the early 1980s. Significant U.S. Supreme Court decisions included *Stone v. Graham* (1980), which held unconstitutional a state statute requiring the posting of the Ten Commandments in every public school classroom; *Board of Education v. Rowley* (1982), in which the Court interpreted the Education for All Handicapped Children's Act as providing largely procedural rather than substantive standards for special education students; and *Island Trees School District v. Pico* (1982), in which a variously divided Court spelled out limitations on the right of school boards to remove school library books.

See also Rights: Teachers' and Students'; School Law.

—Perry A. Zirkel
Lehigh University

References

Marvell, T., Galfo, A., & Rockwell, J. (1981). *Student litigation: A compilation and analysis of civil cases involving students, 1977-81.* Williamsburg, VA: National Center for State Courts.

Reutter, E.E., Jr. (1982). *The Supreme Court's impact on public education.* Bloomington, IN: Phi Delta Kappa.

Zirkel, P. (Ed.). (1978, 1982). *Digest of Supreme Court decisions affecting education.* Bloomington, IN: Phi Delta Kappa.

L

LEADERSHIP

Leadership is demonstrated in almost every walk of life—in the home, in the school, in the community, in the nation, in the world. There are examples of leadership in the fields of religion, politics, military, business, academics, athletics, and combinations of these. Some of the leaders have been in their positions for a long time; some have been like meteors in their rise and fall, but all of them have been acknowledged for their leadership. Each of us can name several people who are outstanding leaders, and yet we may not have analyzed why those named succeed as leaders.

Among the factors which influence leaders' success are luck, election, determination, manipulation, and inherited position. The idea of manipulation may appear to be negative, but it can be positive. Manipulation is merely a leader's employment of strategies to get others to do what the leader wants them to do. Manipulation can be ethical, and it must be part of the leader's role.

Rather than list the qualities which are ascribed to leaders—qualities which are obvious to most people—an analysis of those qualities usually cited reveals that there are several basic overriding descriptors which emerge: (a) problem-solving ability, (b) decisiveness, and (c) judgment. All three of these descriptors are based upon analytical skills tempered with intelligence and wisdom. Many leaders have demonstrated their ability to be decisive, but their judgment became their downfall. In a few words, the essence of leadership is wise decision making.

No matter how leadership is defined, the only essential ingredient is followership. Without followers, there is no leader. The second major factor is how one keeps the followers. The leaders whose followers are fickle and temporary cannot survive. There are theories which seek to explain the best ways to lead; such theories set forth reasons for a leader's survival. Other theories are based on the factors which are inherent in successful leadership and on the resolution of institutional needs compared with individual needs, and related concerns. No matter which theory is followed and no matter what the qualities of the leader, it is essential that the leader have loyal followers. Without the loyalty of the followers, the decision-making skills of the leader will go for naught; information received by the leader may be distorted, decisions made may be undermined, and implementation of activities may be stymied. Decision making and loyalty are integrally related if leadership is to be successful.

With these essentials as givens, the leader must have a clear sense of mission and the ability to communicate that mission to all concerned in and out of the institution served. A clearly articulated statement concerning the mission will eliminate excuses from followers concerning direction. The leader must face pressures, must analyze trade-offs, must be aware of political implications of his actions, must face consequences, and must present the type of image deemed appropriate by the followers and by the employers. All of these concerns may evoke criticisms among the constituents, but as long as the mission is served, they are the prerogatives of the leader. Thus, a clear sense of mission must be grasped and promulgated by those who are responsible for leading an enterprise.

In order to clarify this sense of mission in school districts, there are school-board policies. These policies cannot be taken lightly. In fact, they have the authority of law for those employed by the school district. A policy can be a haven for the leaders when discretion is not the issue. All policies have the backing of the school board, and so the leader cannot be blamed for implementing policy. Following policy is a security for the leader, but this approach may be an excuse for not exercising judgment. Leadership skill is not put to the test when routine, mandated decisions are made. It is in the area of discretion where a leader exercises judgment. In the absence of a mandate, a law, a court decision, a policy, a rule, a regulation, the leader must make decisions. If these decisions result in unpopular and/or unfavorable consequences, the price the leader may pay is dismissal.

Partly for self protection and partly for goal achievement, the superintendent of a school district must make certain that the board's policies are clear to the board, to the staff, and to himself or herself. The principals of a school must also make certain that the policies are clear to all, and they must make rules which are in harmony with these policies which provide direction and clarity of mission within their buildings. Teachers must establish classroom rules and procedures in harmony with district policies and building regulations so that they can implement the same mission. Flexibility and individual talents must not be stifled in this consideration. There is room for divergence and creativity if an organization is to be dynamic, but without the clarity of mission from the top leader to the least among the followers, there can be confusion and organizational chaos. Because the leader is the most visible target of critics, it behooves the leader to clarify that mission.

Having a clear sense of mission does not preclude the change-agent role of the leader. In fact, change may be the mission. It is important, however, for the leader to know what is expected in a particular position—whether the leader is expected to maintain the status quo, to initiate minor change, to initiate major change in the school, among the staff, in the community. In a sense, there will always be a change in the status quo due to the individual styles that each one brings to the leadership position. A change of leadership will inevitably bring about some change in the institution. But the leader must be careful to weigh any planned change in terms of goals, purposes, traditions, and related issues affecting the schools. Support bases tend to disappear when change threatens the "wrong" people. What is successful in one situation may be a dismal failure in another situation. Hence, it is necessary to assess the ever-changing nature of the leadership role, the need for appropriate decisions, and the need to have a sense of mission which must be communicated to all concerned persons.

The aspects of leadership discussed in this article, although not all-inclusive, are critical. The ingredients of successful leadership are vast and varied. Research studies have resulted in many conclusions, some of which can be stated succinctly as follows:

1. Most theories of leadership focus on either the task aspect or the human-relations aspect of the role. A few theories focus on both aspects. Emphasis in current theories seems to be more related to the human relations aspect than to any other single factor.

2. Studies of leadership traits and qualities are repetitive and do not account for the intangibles which affect success or failure. Yet skills in problem solving, decision making, and judgment are crucial for success.

3. A leader must be flexible enough to use a variety of leadership skills and behaviors, but consistency seems to be desired most by followers.

4. Leadership requires the blending of skills and the artful application of them so that goals will be achieved.

5. Designated leaders have authority and some power, but they must be aware of the informal leaders who have power also.

See also Administrative Roles; Administrative Styles; Administrative Theory; School Improvement and Effectiveness Movements.

—Mel P. Heller
Loyola University

References

Boles, H.W. (1984). *Introduction to educational leadership.* University Press of America.

Knezevich, S.J. (1984). *Administration of public education: A source book for the leadership and management of educational institutions.* New York: Harper & Row.

Wright, P.L. (1984). *Improving leadership performance.* Englewood Cliffs, NJ: Prentice-Hall.

LEARNING STYLES

Every person has a learning style regardless of IQ, achievement level, or socioeconomic status. Certain elements of style are biologically imposed; others develop as an outgrowth of individual life experiences. However, longitudinal studies demonstrate that, during selected periods of maturation, individual styles change, and that change is predictable. Although style can change over time as a result of maturation, strong preferences change only over years. Furthermore, preferences tend to be overcome only with high internal motivation; teachers cannot identify students' styles easily without appropriate learning-styles instrumentation. Significantly, increased academic achievement and statistically improved attitudes toward school—in addition to better behavior—result when students are taught in ways that complement their styles.

Each person's style comprises a combination of environmental, emotional, sociological, physiological, and psychological elements that permit individuals to receive, store, and then use the knowledge or skills to which they are exposed. Most people have between six and fourteen elements that influence their styles strongly; some have more or fewer. Of the two million or so human beings tested, few have evidenced fewer than three. Husbands and wives tend to have many elements of style that are different from each other. Children often do not reflect their parents' styles. And, in the same family, siblings appear to be more different from each other than similar. Of interest is that in a survey of 2,000 teachers and administrators in a metropolitan area, fewer than 25 percent were aware of the relationships between learning style and brain behavior. The two, however, tend to go hand in hand.

The Environmental Elements

Individuals tend to be influenced by the environment in which new and difficult learning is being attempted. Some require bright light, a quiet room, and a hard wooden, plastic, or steel seat and desk; others prefer music or the sound of waves, winds, or singing; the latter often prefer soft illumination and an informal design—pillows, a lounge, carpeting, or even a bed *when concentrating on difficult material.* Temperature also affects certain people—some prefer a warm room, whereas others prefer a cool setting consistently.

Although some people are unaffected by certain elements, the need for a quiet room, bright light, and a formal design appears to be characteristic of strongly sequential, analytic learners, whereas the reverse is often representative of simultaneous, global processors. As a result, the extremes of both types learn in exactly opposite conditions from each other and thus require different study environments and classrooms. Experimental research conducted by St. John's University's Center for the Study of Learning and Teaching Styles, New York, has demonstrated that consistently higher achievement occurs when students are permitted to learn in environments responsive to their strong preferences, in contrast with those same persons' grades in incongruent conditions.

The Emotional Elements

The emotional elements that affect learning include motivation, persistence, responsibility, and the need for structure as opposed to options and choices. Motivation changes easily; within weeks of working in responsive instructional situations, students express significantly better attitudes. Persistence appears to be a sequential, analytic trait; global people often prefer to begin several tasks simultaneously and work at a few at a time—as opposed to focusing on one until it has been completed. As a result, globals can remain on-task, but require many different, less lengthy tasks to continue on focus than analytics do. Responsibility tends to be a characteristic of conforming students—they do what they have been told to do. Less responsible youngsters often are nonconforming and can be worked with satisfactorily when (a) the importance of what is required is explained; (b) they are spoken to like a colleague; and (c) they are provided choices of how what is required may be demonstrated. Some people require a great deal of external structure; others like to do things their way; the latter often are internally structured. Interestingly, high schools tend to reward conformity, and nonconformists seem to respond better to alternative schools rather than comprehensive high schools.

The Sociological Elements

Some people do their best thinking alone; the presence of others distracts them. Others work better in pairs or in teams. Some like to work with authoritative teachers, whereas others prefer collegial teachers. A small percentage cannot concentrate with anyone nearby and, simultaneously, may not have the independence skills to learn alone; many of these achieve well with the use of media—computers, language masters, videotapes, filmstrips, and so on. Others achieve best with multimedia packages. Such aids enter into specific instructional method for underachievers who learn well with such help. Many students can learn with combinations of the above—alone, with others, with media. The latter group often comprises people who enjoy variety rather than routines and patterns when studying. When students are assigned to groups based on their sociological preferences, they achieve significantly better than when they are assigned to incongruent groups.

The Physiological Elements

Perceptual strengths—the senses through which individuals tend to remember best—develop gradually with maturation. Most young children begin to remember by experiencing new situations; their ability to recall tactually (by holding and manipulating materials) develops next. Then they become able to remember what they see and, eventually, read; last to develop is their memory through auditory exposure. The most difficult way to learn new, demanding material is by hearing it.

Most instruction occurs by teachers talking or questioning; only 30 percent of people remember best that way. Research has demonstrated that, when students are *introduced* to new material through their *strongest perceptual strength* and then have it *reinforced* through their secondary and tertiary strength, they learn three times the amount they do when they are introduced to new and difficult information through their secondary or tertiary modalities.

Some people need to eat, smoke, drink, or chew when learning; others do not. Some are early morning, or late morning, high-energy preferents; others cannot concentrate on difficult material until afternoon—or even evening. It is not that people cannot *function* at the wrong time of day (for them); they just cannot absorb new and difficult material as easily then as they can during their high-energy periods. Again, prize-winning research has evidenced the significantly higher achievement scores that occur when students are taught during their best—rather than their worst—chronological periods.

Mobility is a necessary activity for many; too often, however, youngsters who require it are labeled hyperactive. Healthy, energetic children—particularly boys, need to move a great deal; such children *learn through activity rather than passivity*. Schools ignore this physical need and demand passivity of many who cannot sit still for more than 12 to 15 minutes at a time.

The Psychological Elements

During the past decade, we have learned that people who tend to begin processing in a "left style" learn in very different conditions from those who process in a "right style." For example, right-preferred students (a) are less bothered by sound/noise when studying; (b) prefer dim, rather than bright, illumination when studying; (c) tend to require an informal, rather than a formal, design; (d) are less motivated in school than lefts; (e) are less persistent; (f) prefer learning with peers more often than lefts; and (g) prefer tactual to auditory or visual stimulation as a learning mode—even at the high-school level and among the gifted. Apparently, students who are right- and left-preferred have different environmental and physiological needs within the classroom, as well as different motivational and personality characteristics. In addition, lefts learn most easily in a sequential, analytic style, whereas rights prefer a simultaneous, holistic global style.

Identifying Learning Styles

The Center for the Study of Learning and Teaching Styles, St. John's University, New York, has experimented with different learning styles tests for various purposes. The tests that consistently have discriminated significantly among extreme populations are the (a) *Learning Style Inventory: Primary Version* for children in grades K-2; (b) the *Learning Style Inventory (LSI)* for students in grades 3-12; and (c) the *Productivity Environmental Preference Survey* (PEPS). These are the three instruments that have been used most widely throughout the United States and the ones employed in experimental studies at The Center for the Study of Learning and Teaching Styles.

Learning Style Variations

Gifted and talented students have learning styles that are different from each other's and also styles that differ from those of underachievers. Differences exist between the styles of Caucasians and southeastern Orientals; between the learning disabled and average achievers; and between secondary students in vocational education and those in comprehensive high schools. Indeed, whether or not teachers respond to the different styles among their charges appears to determine the amount of academic success each student experiences.

See also Classroom Management; Direct Instruction; Individualization of Instruction; Split-Brain Controversy.

—Rita Dunn
St. John's University

References

Dunn, R., & Dunn, K. (1978). *Teaching students through their individual learning styles: A practical approach.* Englewood Cliffs, NJ: Prentice-Hall.

Learning Style Inventory (LSI) (Dunn, Dunn, & Price, 1984). Obtainable from: Price Systems, Box 1818, Lawrence, KS: 66044.

Learning Styles Network Newsletter. (1979, 1980, 1981, 1982, 1983, 1984, 1985, 1986). Jamaica, NY: St. John's University's Center for the Study of Learning and Teaching Styles.

LESSON PLANS

One of the controversial topics in the realm of teacher expectations is that of preparing lesson plans. The controversy generally focuses on the reasons for, the format of, and the use of lesson plans. Debates on the merits of lesson plans generally indicate some lack of understanding between administrators, supervisors, and teachers in reference to the three topics (reasons, format, use). Administrators and supervisors must assume the responsibility for helping teachers to understand the function of lesson planning within the instructional program.

Establishing Purpose

An initial consideration for administrators and supervisors is to determine what purpose lesson plans are to serve in the school system. Purposes can be separated into administrative and supervisory expectations. An administrator's perspectives about teaching and teachers as professionals will strongly influence his or her reasons for requiring teachers to prepare and/or submit lesson plans.

Administratively, lesson plans can serve the purpose of verifying that teachers are involved in planning their work, and this can serve as an item on the administrative evaluation. This type of purpose generally elicits negative reactions from teachers, who wish to be treated as professionals and dislike the use of lesson plans for purposes of evaluation and inspection.

Another administrative purpose for requiring lesson plans is to give direction to substitute teachers. Teachers generally understand and accept this purpose as being reasonable, but only if there is considerable potential for obtaining substitute teachers who are able to carry out the plans. If the school system does not have a pool of qualified substitute teachers, this purpose also is likely to be rejected by teachers. Selecting this purpose for requiring lesson plans needs to be a part of the larger view of the use of substitute teachers. If substitute teachers are only expected to monitor a group of students for a specified time period, with little or no expectation for continuing the instructional process, this purpose will not be accepted by reasonable professionals.

Supervisory purposes focus more strongly on the "fit" or appropriateness of daily/weekly lesson plans with the short- and long-range goals and objectives of the instructional program. An implication here is that such short- and long-range plans exist for the school system. The respect for planning must be demonstrated by the instructional leaders if they expect teachers to demonstrate respect for planning. With a focus on this purpose, teachers will not feel "singled out" as the only individuals in the organization being expected to plan. Teachers and supervisors will be better able to work together in achieving the goals and objectives of the instructional program when they can focus on the relationship between those goals and objectives and the teachers' lesson plans.

Planning has been identified as one of the factors influencing teacher effectiveness. Lesson plans can be a useful tool in working with a teacher who may be having difficulty.

Selecting a Format

Professional education programs for preparing teachers include work that requires the preparation of lesson plans. The format of the plans used varies with the expectations of the instructors. Teachers who have been prepared at different times and different places may be accustomed to using different formats for their lesson plans. Administrators and supervisors, consequently, cannot expect that all teachers will respond in the same way when asked to submit lesson plans. Teachers will need to be informed about the format expected.

Lesson plans commonly used in preparatory programs usually include basic elements such as objectives of the lesson, procedures or activities, and evaluation. These may be expanded to include items such as motivation, introduction, presentation, developmental practice, and/or assignment. These depend on personal preference. Those espousing the Hunter model for effective teaching may select the elements of that model, although it should be recognized that not all of the elements of the Hunter model will necessarily be included in every lesson.

The format selected is secondary to the purpose for the lesson plan. The purpose should dictate the format. This needs to be discussed with teachers so that there is a clear understanding and acceptance of that relationship. Input from teachers can be useful in blending the format with the purpose. This is especially true if more than one purpose is to be fulfilled.

Using Lesson Plans

Lesson plans should be used for the purposes which have been specified. First, a lesson plan serves as an outline for a lesson which a teacher intends to teach. Lesson plans also can be used by substitute teachers so that the plans of the regular classroom teacher can be carried out. If the substitute teacher is a marginal teacher, the lesson plans may need to be different from those used for supervisory purposes.

A lesson plan can be an effective supervisory aid when working with any teacher. The plan provides information necessary for a supervisor to understand and evaluate what is happening in a given classroom. This is especially true if the supervisor is observing the teaching-learning experience.

Most teachers accept the requirement of lesson planning as a professional responsibility. Some may express resistance if the purpose is not clear, if the format is not related to purpose, or if experience indicates that the lesson plans are not used for their intended purpose. For instance, if plans are required for the purpose of assisting substitute teachers and subsequently are used for the purpose of administrative evaluation, teachers can be expected to object. On the other hand, if there is clarity of purpose, consistency in application, reasonableness in format, and equity in expectation, most teachers will support the concept of lesson planning.

See also Instructional Objectives; Planning.

—Robert Krey
University of Wisconsin-Superior

References

Dave, R. (1971, September). "Plan books are a waste of time!" *Today's Education, 55*(6), 49.

Gage, N.L., & Berliner, D.C. (1984). *Educational psychology* (3rd ed., pp. 594-99, 611-13). Boston: Houghton Mifflin.

Hunter, M., (1985, February). "What's wrong with Madeline Hunter?" *Educational Leadership, 42*, 57-60.

M

MAGNET SCHOOLS

The magnet school has become a popular method of innovation in the organization of elementary and secondary education. From a few schools in large urban districts a little more than a decade ago, the magnet-school movement has grown to more than 1100 schools in more than 130 urban school districts. The magnet school has become well known as a strategy for school desegregation, primarily because it offers an alternative to mandatory assignment, or "busing." However, there are four innovative elements which characterize magnet schools and differentiate the magnet-school model for the organization of public education: (a) a role in voluntary desegregation within a district, (b) a special curricular theme or method of instruction, (c) choice of school by the student and parent, and (d) open access to students beyond a regular school-attendance zone.

The initial models for magnet school curricula were the specialty schools in public education, such as Bronx School of Science, Boston Latin School, and Chicago's Lane Technical High School, which have served selected students for many years. However, the specialty schools admit students by examination or other measures of performance or ability, and they serve mainly highly gifted students. The basic idea of a magnet school is to attract and enroll students based on their interest, either in a particular subject, such as science, art, or business, or in learning through a different instructional approach, such as an open school. By attracting students with common educational interests, but diverse socioeconomic backgrounds, the goals of a magnet school are to attain a racially heterogeneous student enrollment and provide a unique educational experience.

In practice, school districts have incorporated many curricular themes, methods of instruction, and unique educational services in designing magnet schools. Currently, magnet schools are equally prevalent at the elementary and secondary level. The curriculum of a magnet school might involve a whole school, a school-within-a-school, or a part-day program within a school. An important element in the development of magnet schools has been the local flexibility in program design to meet local needs. Federal support has stimulated the creation of magnet schools in many urban districts, but program innovation and development has mainly been the result of local initiatives. For school districts, magnet schools provide a way to offer specialized curricula and instruction, and thereby increase the diversity of educational programming without the necessity of increasing diversity in each building in the district.

Although communities generally become interested in magnet schools as an alternative method of desegregation, a magnet school usually succeeds or fails according to the quality of education it offers. The magnet-school model has several advantages in providing a positive academic environment that are related to the self-selection of students—first, students are generally surrounded by students with similar interests and motivation, and, second, the decision to enroll may increase the student's own motivation toward education. Self-selection of teachers and administrators can also increase the quality of the educational environment.

However, there are two major potential problems that can arise with efforts to create a unique educational opportunity in a magnet school. First, some districts establish magnet schools that are highly selective in admitting students according to achievement or ability, which sometimes leads to charges of elitism. But, even in the large majority of magnet schools that only require passing grades for admittance, districts may have to address the issue of whether magnet schools create programs within a school or differences in the quality of education between schools. Second, a magnet school has to deliver what it has advertised and promised in order to maintain a voluntary enrollment. An innovative program in quality education must be developed and implemented, but the curriculum also must be within district guidelines in order to allow students to transfer in and out of the magnet school.

With respect to the goal of desegregation, the magnet-school concept has proven to be effective in desegregating targeted individual school sites. On a districtwide basis, magnet schools have been most successful in helping to reduce racial isolation when used in combination with other methods of desegregation, such as pairing, rezoning, and two-way busing. Key factors in magnet schools having positive effects on desegregation are a strong policy commitment by district leaders, an effective plan for district-wide recruitment of students, and an equitable method of admitting students.

A distinguishing characteristic of a magnet school with high quality education is coherence of the theme, curriculum, staff, and teaching methods. This means that the elements for producing education are consistent with the magnet school's special purpose and goals, i.e., it is not a magnet school in name only. Some districts have found that the "whole-school" model is the most effective way to develop a unique educational environment, and a positive identity for the magnet school. With this model, an existing school can be significantly changed through building rennovations, staff selection and assignment, and redesign of the curriculum. However, many successful part-school magnet programs have been designed and implemented within existing schools. Principal leadership and district support and flexibility are important ingredients for success of a magnet school using either model.

There are several critical issues that must be resolved for magnet schools to be effectively initiated, and continued, in a district. The overall district plan for magnet schools should be based on a broad consenus of community needs and interests in education innovation; the plan should not reflect only narrow interest groups or the interests of district leaders. The planning and development of each magnet school should involve teachers, parents, and community resources. To anticipate public charges that only a small proportion of students benefit from magnet schools, the program should be conceived as part of a larger district plan for improving the quality of education and open, equitable access should be central to the design of magnet schools.

Extra funds are likely to be needed for program planning and start-up of magnet schools, and annual per-pupil costs are usually slightly higher than the costs for other schools (generally due to transportation and teacher salary differences). Some districts try to seek funds from sources other than tax revenues, particularly if the total number of students that can enroll in magnet schools is small. Magnet schools can create competition between schools for students, teachers, and financial resources. To ensure that competition remains healthy, the development of a magnet school should be carefully monitored to avoid detrimental effects on the selection of the faculty, the makeup of the student body, and the programs of any existing school. The district should keep open the option of adding new magnet schools if there is sufficient interest.

See also Desegregation Plans; Educational Goals and Objectives; High Schools; Planning.

—Rolf K. Blank
Council of Chief State School Officers

References

Blank, R.K., Dentler, R.A., Baltzell, D.C., & Chabotar, K. (1983). *Survey of magnet schools: Analyzing a model for quality integrated education.* Final Report of a National Study for the U.S. Department of Education. Washington, DC: James Lowry and Associates.

McMillan, C.B. (1980). *Magnet schools: An approach to voluntary desegregation.* Bloomington, IN: Phi Delta Kappa.

Raywid, M.A. (1986). "Family choice arrangements in public schools: A review of the literature." *Review of Educational Research, 55*(4), 435–69.

MAINSTREAMING

Public school administrators are charged with the responsibility of educating students with and without handicapping conditions. With increasing frequency these students are being educated with each other through a process called *mainstreaming*. While not a new concept, mainstreaming recently has been surrounded by a great deal of misunderstanding and controversy. To understand mainstreaming, it is necessary to review its definition, history, implementation practices, and continuing questions surrounding it.

Definition

Mainstreaming has come to mean two things, one of which encompasses the other. In its broadest sense, mainstreaming refers to making educational placement decisions for handicapped children that provide maximal opportunities for interaction with their nonhandicapped peers. This broad definition of mainstreaming refers to educating students in the least restrictive appropriate placement with a variety of program options. One of these is that of placement in a regular class. It is this option that has given the term "mainstreaming" its second, more limited, meaning: education of students with handicaps in classes with nonhandicapped students. This is only one option and is not appropriate for all students with handicaps.

Consequently, when the term "mainstreaming" is considered to be synonomous with education in regular classes, concern is generated regarding the appropriateness of educational programs for the student with a handicapping condition as well as for the nonhandicapped students who must now share the teacher's instructional time with an individual who may have more intense educational needs. There is also an incorrect belief that mainstreaming will result in the wholesale return of handicapped students to regular classes and that handicapped students no longer will be taught by specially trained teachers.

It has been pointed out by many, however, that mainstreaming is not (a) the elimination of special education programs; (b) the indiscriminate placement of students in regular classes; or (c) the overextension of regular class teachers to teach students for whom they were not specifically trained. Mainstreaming *is* intended to be a carefully considered decision to provide educational experiences for students in a manner that minimizes the differences between students with and without handicaps. This is accomplished by providing education in the least restrictive placement option appropriate for meeting all the student's educational needs.

Events Preceding Mainstreaming

In the early years, students with handicaps were separated from other students. One of the earliest practices was that of total isolation in institutions. Individuals identified as having handicaps were removed from their communities and placed in geographically-isolated residential settings. Few, if any, individuals with handicaps were found in public schools.

In the 1950's, when public school districts began to assume responsibility for students with handicaps, a great deal of emphasis was placed on identification of these students and the subsequent removal of them from regular classes. Often, these students were taught by less capable teachers; the instructional materials were inferior, and the budgets for the programs were small. Additionally, the students' classes were frequently physically separated from those of their nonhandicapped peers. Often, they were either educated in segregated schools or in classes in school basements. There were few opportunities for the students with handicaps to interact with their nonhandicapped peers. While some may have thought that specialized programs would improve conditions for handicapped students, separate programs did not lead to the existence of quality of educational programs.

An analysis of early programs revealed the following: (a) comparisons of test scores of mildly retarded students in regular classes with the test scores of mildly retarded students in special education classes revealed no significant differences; (b) there were large numbers of minority students in classes for the handicapped; (c) handicapped students taught in self-contained programs were denied the opportunity to interact with nonhandicapped students; and (d) students assigned to classes for the handicapped perceived themselves as less able, and their perceptions served as self-fulfilling prophecies. The intention was to provide different and improved services to students with handicaps, but it became apparent that this was not happening.

Both the courts and the U.S. Congress responded to this situation. In the early 1970s, several court cases indicated a judicial preference for the education of students in regular classes and schools with other students without handicaps. Section 504 of the Rehabilitation Act of 1973 and the Education for All Handicapped Children Act of 1975 (PL 94-142) demonstrated support for mainstreaming. Section 504 states that a recipient of federal funds cannot discriminate against a person solely on the basis of a handicap and that the recipient must provide education to students in the least restrictive environment. Public Law 94-142 guarantees a free appropriate education for all handicapped children and, just as in Section 504, requires that education for students with handicaps be provided in regular classes and such students removed only when appropriate education can not be provided with supplementary aides and services.

Implementation of Mainstreaming

Successful mainstreaming is dependent upon a number of factors. Among these are the availability of a full continuum of educational placement options, appropriately prepared teachers and administrators, and careful determinations of the educational needs of students with handicaps.

Educational Placement Options. As previously discussed, many consider the term "mainstreaming" to be synonomous with placement in a regular class. In fact, placement in a regular class is only one option from a wide range of possibilities which must be available to meet mainstreaming's goal of minimizing differences and separation of students with and without handicaps. For some, placement in a regular class would work contrary to the goal. That is, the consequence of placing a student who can not benefit from instruction in the regular class, even with supplementary aides and supports, would probably add to the differences between that student and his or her peers. For such a student, placement could actually serve to restrict further his or her learning and development rather than facilitate learning and development.

Districts in which mainstreaming is being successfully implemented have available a full continuum of educational options. Or, if the district lacks its own mainstreaming options, it can get help from neighboring districts through cooperative arrangements. The options may vary from district to district but basically include the following: (a) placement in the regular class with or without support; (b) placement in regular class with or without class supplementary instruction; (c) placement part-time in special education class with the rest of the time in a regular class; (d) placement full-time in a special education class in a school with nonhandicapped students; (e) placement in a segregated school with other handicapped students; (f) home instruction; and (g) placement in a residential school.

Personnel Preparation. Prior to the mandate for mainstreaming, students with special education needs were taught only by teachers trained in special education; often the students were educated in segregated schools. Consequently, there was little opportunity for teachers of nonhandicapped students to learn how to interact with and teach students with handicaps. For many teachers, the initial reaction to the prospect of having students with handicaps in their school and classes is one of great concern and fear. Often, the source of this concern is lack of knowledge and experience about students with handicaps.

Many states now require that education students preparing to teach nonhandicapped children take at least one course designed to increase their understanding of handicapped children. While this is minimal, it is a positive attempt toward assuring that teachers in the future will have some information regarding methods for accommodating students with handicaps in integrated schools and regular classes. To deal with the current situation, school districts with successful mainstreaming programs have instituted extensive inservice training programs for their staffs. The content of such training programs has included an introduction to the characteristics of students in need of special-education services. The in-service programs have dealt with the needs of handicapped students and have outlined methods for teaching mainstreamed students.

Determining Least Restrictive Alternatives. A third important component of successful mainstreaming is the process employed in determining the appropriate least restrictive placement for students. Several provisions in PL 94-142 are designed to assure that appropriate decisions are made.

Public Law 94-142 requires that each student with a handicapping condition have an individualized educational program. This program is developed with information obtained as a result of multidisciplinary assessments and joint planning by professionals, parents, and, whenever appropriate, the student himself or herself. Included in the individualized educational program is a statement of the student's current level of functioning and a description of the annual goals and short-term objectives. Also included is a description of the type of special educational services and program-placement options that are necessary to accomplish the goals and objectives delineated. To assure that consideration is given to providing education in the least restrictive alternative, PL 94-142 specifically requires that a description of the proportion of time the student will spend in the regular class be included in the individualized educational program. This may be seen as giving the developers of the student's program the responsibility of making plans that do not always include the placement of students with handicaps in regular class programs for at least some time of the day.

It is important to emphasize that placement decisions are based on all the goals and objectives specified in the student's program, not just those related to social-skill development. Decisions are not to be made to place students in regular classes just so that they can interact with their nonhandicapped peers; the placement must also provide for in optimal learning opportunities in other areas of development.

To assure that students continue to be provided with learning opportunities in the most appropriate placement, PL 94-142 requires that a review of the individualized educational program be made annually and that appropriate modifications be made at that time.

Ongoing Questions

Much more must be tried and learned before all the questions about mainstreaming are answered. Some researchers continue to seek answers regarding the best strategies to assure the maximal academic and social integration of students. Some are concerned about the effect of mainstreaming efforts on nonhandicapped students in the regular school and classes into which the handicapped students are integrated. Effective integration into regular classes is dependent upon adjustments being made in the regular class to accommodate handicapped students. A question raised by many is, how will students with special educational needs be accommodated in the future along with decreasing budgets and increased class sizes due to increasing enrollments?

The benefits of mainstreaming can be many for students with and without handicaps. However, these benefits are realized only with a philosophical commitment to it and careful implementation of procedures. Appropriate decisions must be made and educators must be prepared to deal with consequences of the decisions.

See also Handicapped Students; Individualization of Instruction; Judicial Decisions.

—Donna H. Lehr
University of Wisconsin-Milwaukee

References

Paul, J.L., Turnbull, A.P., & Cruickshank, W.M. (1977). *Mainstreaming: A practical guide.* New York: Shocken Books.

Schultz, J.B., & Turnbull, A. (1985). *Mainstreaming handicapped students: A guide for classroom teachers.* Boston: Allyn & Bacon.

Stainback, W., & Stainback, S. (1984). "A rationale for the merger of special and regular education." *Exceptional Children, 51,* 102–11.

MANAGEMENT BY OBJECTIVES

Management by objectives may be defined as the process wherein management provides a structure for individuals and subsystems of the organization to relate their objectives to those of the larger system. The objectives should be determined cooperatively and administrators should be evaluated on the achievement of the results. The crucial element in the concept is the linkage of management and objectives, and its import goes beyond merely linking two well-established notions. The critical decision centers on which factor is primary. Every formal organization incorporates both objectives (ends) and a management function (means). However, one perspective might relate, systematically, organizational objectives to worker performance in order to improve the management function. On the other hand, an organization might view management as an important tool to assure that a large and complex organization can maximize the achievement of its many and diverse goals. Granted, all organizations are interested in both, and the differences of emphasis may be subtle. The differentiation does, however, demonstrate the ways schools have adapted these management concepts.

Originally developed in the business and industry sectors in the 1950s, management by objectives came to the attention of public schools in the 1970's and 1980's. During these years, there was strident public demand for increased accountability, productivity, and efficiency. Both programmatic and management aspects of the schools were under sharp criticism. This approach to management seemed to be an answer to such criticism.

Basic Functions and Concepts

The essential function of management by objectives is that of increasing the effectiveness of schools by determining the objectives; relating the objectives to the management or administrative system of the school (who does what and how roles interrelate); and using appraisal data to make decisions on personnel, financial resources, and time resources. In this sense, management by objectives reflects a general systems orientation: a set of discrete elements in mutual interaction and interdependence which in turn produces a total characteristic effect.

School systems incorporate a wide variety of organizational goals. The nature of these educational goals is usually unique to each hierarchical level. Thus, school district-wide goals are incorporated in the district's philosophy or policy. These are most frequently general and ". . . this we believe . . ." statements. District administrative goals are designed to implement school-board policy goals and tend to be operational and indicate how professionals intend to achieve the broader goals.

The situs of operational goals is primarily the school building, for it is here that teachers interact with pupils. Building goals reflect how groups of teachers design and implement specific programs for specific groups of pupils under the overall school district policy and administrative parameters. Individual teachers establish objectives for individual pupils via the individualized instructional program.

The central concepts applicable to all the hierarchical levels include the following processes:

1. Define the organization's goal(s). These must be clear and easy to comprehend.

2. Identify performance indicators. Criteria must be set to determine if, and to what extent, the goal has been reached.

3. Assess the feasibility of performance. If not feasible, objectives become "pie in the sky" or mere aspirations, and progress toward them is not really measurable.

4. Determine alternative strategies. These are multiple paths to goal achievement; therefore, all reasonable alternatives should be identified and tested. The best alternative should be selected.

5. Implement the selected alternative, monitor its performance, and evaluate the performance. The inputs allocated to goal achievement should be related to the measured level of goal achievement. On the basis of these data, decisions may be made regarding the propriety of goal definition, performance indicators, etc. Changes in some or all previous steps may be justified, and thus incorporated for the next cycle.

Schools as organizations are not monolithic, with one set of goals applicable at all hierarchical levels. As was pointed out earlier, there are general systemwide goals, administrative (or management) goals, school building goals, and teacher (individual or group) goals. If one views management by objectives as a general system in its application to schools, the goals at the several hierarchical levels must be reconciled and interrelated. Thus school-system goals—often what the schools should accomplish—are spelled out by school boards. The superintendent as chief administrator designs a management system using the previously described concepts. As the system moves from general to specific, from policy formulation by the school board to policy implementation by the teacher in the classroom, it reflects the hierarchy of goals. Administrative units, the Division of Curriculum and Instruction, for example, set division objectives in its area of specialization which are consistent with districtwide goals. This division may have responsibilities for (a) developing curriculum and instruction policy proposals, (b) consultation and advisement with principals and teachers, and (c) initiation and coordination of teacher and administrator efforts to improve curricular and instructional activities. If the division chose to implement management by objectives, it would follow the basic steps previously cited as central concepts.

Application

Individual school buildings are the organizational units where management by objectives in education has enjoyed its greatest visibility. In those systems where MBO has been most fully implemented, building principals and their teachers determine the responsibility and authority accruing to the building unit. This provides a picture of the scope of management decisions the group may make. Typically, the areas of curriculum and instruction discretion are well defined. For example, the school district policies in these areas and the responsibilities of the Division of Curriculum and Instruction suggest that individual building professionals may tailor programs to fit the needs of the pupils enrolled in a given school as long as district-wide policies are followed. Thus, in high schools, certain physical science courses must be provided, but the specific courses, and their unique instructional strategies, materials, and equipment may be determined by the teachers and/or principals with the approval of the Division of Curriculum and Instruction.

In a high school with several gifted students, the teachers and principal may design an Honors Biology course. Course objectives would be developed to fit the unique need but still would be compatible with the overall objectives of the Division of Curriculum and Instruction as well as districtwide policies.

For each course objective, measurable performance indicators are developed to determine the extent to which the objective is met. In Honors Biology, one objective is the development of an understanding of molecular biology—an understanding of DNA (deoxyribonucleic acid) and its replication, for example. The companion performance indicator might be that 90 percent of the students can explain DNA with 90 percent accuracy.

The next step in the process is to develop an appropriate and feasible strategy to achieve the objectives in the course. Alternative strategies are described and analyzed. In most cases, there are considerable variations in both costs and benefits for the several strategies. In Honors Biology, the teachers and principal with consultation from specialists in curriculum and instruction, might suggest three alternative instructional strategies: (a) conventional lecture-discussion-demonstration, (b) laboratory and problem solving, and (c) computer assisted instruction with laboratory.

A form of cost-utility analysis could be employed. On the basis of past experience, research and the experience of school systems with similar strategies, the teachers and principal select the strategy that appears to provide the most cost-effective approach given the funding and other constraints in this school. Therefore, in our example, computer-assisted instruction with the laboratory might yield the highest level of expected achievement of performance, but it is not feasible to equip the school with both computers and laboratories. Possibly the laboratory and problem solving strategy is relatively costly, but its probability of achievement of objectives is considerably higher than the conventional strategy. In any event, the feasible strategy with maximum cost-effectiveness is selected.

Once selected, the strategy must be operationalized into a work plan and tasks. A team of teachers is assigned to develop and implement an integrated set of course activities. This becomes a set of job descriptions and job expectations tied directly to the measurable course objectives. At this point the administration (management) dimension becomes highly visible. The teachers and principal as participants have determined: "If we do this, then we should expect these results." A basis for accountability has been built.

A monitoring capability should be built into the operationalized plan. This is necessary to get an accurate picture of what is actually happening and thus avoid major problems. It is also important to document unanticipated conditions which influence the achievement of objectives.

At the end of the Honors Biology course an assessment should be made. Each measurable objective should be related to its performance indicator. Data gathered from the monitoring process should be related to performance. These, along with expenditure and other related data, should be reviewed to provide answers to questions such as (a) to what extent are objectives appropriate? (b) to what extent are performance indicators appropriate? (c) to what extent is the strategy cost-effective? and (d) to what extent is the management system effective? Answers to these questions are useful in making decisions as to whether one should repeat, modify, or abandon the project.

The Honors Biology scenario is useful in demonstrating several concepts of management by objectives. The objectives of several levels of the organization are interrelated. The Division of Curriculum and Instruction has an objective of providing advice and consultation to principals and teachers as well as the initiation and coordination of teacher and administrator efforts to improve instruction. This objective was met as the division's input was incorporated and as the teachers and principal developed their objectives, performance indicators, and strategies for Honors Biology.

The effectiveness of the management system likewise reflects the performance of division personnel, the principal, and the teachers. Each is accountable for a performance which is related to objectives of the given unit within the organization. District-wide goals are tested for feasibility in that Honors Biology may or may not manifest goal achievement.

See also Administrator Evaluation; Competency Testing, Students; Instructional Objectives.

—Walter G. Hack
Ohio State University

References

Knezevich, S.J. (1973). *Management by objectives and results.* Arlington, VA: American Association of School Administrators.

McDonald, C.R. (1982). *MBO can work!* New York: McGraw-Hill.

Odiorne, G.S. (1965). *Management by objectives.* New York: Pitman.

MANAGEMENT OF DECLINE

The *management of decline* is a task most educational administrators were not trained to undertake. It has never been part of university curricula. Nor has it been an aspect of the practical experience an administrator acquires once assuming an administrative role.

For the entire post-World War II period until approximately 1970, American public schools were on a projectory of expansion created by population growth and suburbanization. Then, for the first time in nearly forty years, birth rates and enrollments fell, creating an initial wave of decline demanding the attention of administrators. For some years it was possible for them to ignore these trends, largely because the public continued to demand improvements such as new services and reduced class sizes. However, in the mid-1970s the national economy suffered from the twin problems of recession and inflation (dubbed "stagflation"). This economic climate helped create taxpayer revolts throughout the country and in some cases forced school systems to close or brought them to the verge of collapse, such as New York City experienced in 1975. During this second wave of decline, school administrators first began to talk seriously about school closings, early retirement, and other cost-saving strategies. The American public pressed school officials not only to reduce expenditures but also to improve the quality of programs.

With the inception of the national reform movement in 1983, however, this second wave of decline seemed to dissipate. Once again, the public mood shifted; additional expenditures were justified by governors, legislators, and school boards in the interest of improving the quality of public education. Enrollments began to increase in elementary grades. Many administrators took these as signs that decline was a thing of the past.

Despite the shift of public attention in the mid-1980s, there are several indications that the management of decline will continue to command the attention of administrators. First, decline in American secondary schools will remain until 1990 or later, presenting even more difficult political problems than those which school systems faced when coping with the loss in elementary-school enrollment. It has proven difficult to close elementary schools because of community opposition; the problem is greatly magnified at the secondary level. Second, decline is likely to be a recurring phenomenon in many school systems because, with an increase in state and federal assistance, they have become less dependent on the local property tax in recent years. These intergovernmental aids are more volatile, depending on the political party which controls Washington and statehouses and fluctuating with the changing fortunes of broader economies. As the society grows older demographically, pressure to reduce educational budgets in favor of other public services will intensify, regardless of the level of government.

Third, the public's raised expectations for its schools may lead to ever sharper scrutiny of school budgets, particularly in the nation's large cities, where high minority dropout rates have become a national issue.

At first blush, there is no reason to believe that the management of decline should require strategies and techniques any different from those confronting an administrator in periods of growth or stability. In a very general way, this assumption is true. Yet as any administrator will readily confirm, context is a vital consideration to be taken into account before any "textbook" principles are applied. In fact, the research literature on decline, both in education and in other domains such as business, indicates that the context of decline presents special problems. These require administrative responses frequently different from conventional practice. The literature suggests some things which improve the administrator's chances of a successful outcome as well as actions which generally are to be avoided.

Conflict

The first notable difference characterizing organizations undergoing decline is the presence of conflict. Organizations can grow gradually over time with little opposition. In periods of growth, resistance to change can be defused because some individuals stand to gain from any improvement. Decline, however, generates losers who can effectively mobilize to protect the status quo. The management of decline requires a strategy for minimizing this conflict while achieving necessary reductions.

Uniform or Selective Cuts

Frequently, an administrator has the discretion to choose a cutback strategy. Should all programs be cut by a uniform amount, or should cuts be made selectively? It may be better to eliminate certain programs or services altogether rather than to whittle away continuously at all programs. Again, however, these substantive considerations must be balanced with political realism. The administrator faces a choice between across-the-board freezes or cutbacks, in which everyone is asked to make a similar sacrifice, and selective cutbacks, where some may be minimally affected by cuts or remain untouched, while others bear the burden of decline. The first course may be politically more appealing in the short run, since opposition will usually remain unfocused.

By contrast, whenever *particular* programs or units such as schools are cut or eliminated, the administrator confronts focused opposition from employees and consumers who will be affected. It may be possible to isolate these opponents. However, the more such cuts are contemplated at one time, the greater is the possibility that a coalition of opponents will mobilize, capturing media attention and pressuring board members (who may be sympathetic to them) to oppose the administrator's efforts.

An important initial consideration is whether the decline is likely to be temporary or of long duration. Enrollment declines generally represent long-term trends. By contrast, a revenue shortfall in state monies may occur once or episodically. Temporary revenue shortfalls can be met with short-term expedients such as deferred maintenance of facilities, a budget freeze, or some other device which is easily reversed when the fiscal climate improves. However, enrollment declines require a long-term response strategy. Administrators initially are inclined to treat all decline as a temporary problem. But delay or temporizing measures can turn out to have higher costs than directly confronting the problem through coherent planning. End-of-the-year spending freezes, for instance, implicitly assume that in the next year operations can return to "normal." They are politically acceptable because everyone sacrifices a little. However, this is a risky strategy, as some school systems have learned, if the budget overruns are allowed to accumulate and, worse still, are disguised through dubious accounting devices.

What to Cut

The decision as to what should be cut has both substantive and political dimensions. From a strictly political point of view, if the administrator has a mandate from the board of education to make cuts but would prefer that they not occur, popular programs such as athletics can be targeted. This strategy sometimes is counterproductive because the conflict cannot always be guided once it erupts. From a substantive point of view, there are no clear rules on what programs to sacrifice. If cost-savings can be found in noninstructional areas, these frequently are taken first, with the hope that programs will be minimally affected. Improved accounting, for instance, can reduce cost overruns. Efficiencies in management of investments and reserves, in delivery of food service, transportation, plant maintenance, and other aspects of business operations can have beneficial results. Postponement of improvements in the physical plant can be an expedient answer, although many school systems have learned that they must pay back dearly in the long run for such decisions. Another cut which is popular with school boards and with the general public is reduction of administrative staff. In general, none of these areas will be helpful if a substantial budget reduction is contemplated. Well over half of the budget in public school systems is consumed by instructional salaries.

If instructional programs must be cut, the typical decision employed by administrators has been to minimize damage to the overall integrity of programs. This principle has been operationalized in myriad ways. Should split-grade classes be created to reduce excessively small, costly classes? How important are auxiliary personnel compared with the classroom teacher? At the high school level, should advanced courses with small enrollments be dropped, or should remedial classes be sacrificed? Each of these choices must be made with an eye to less costly, equally effective alternatives. Our current knowledge about effective instructional programs and services should be considered. University specialists frequently will offer their help if asked. In making program cuts, administrators must be aware of statutory and accrediting requirements, as well as constitutional protections available to children, which cannot be abrogated due to financial exigencies.

The literature on decline indicates that program cuts do not always harm the instructional program. While clear examples exist where Draconian cuts have harmed children, reductions sometimes have led to improvements in the quality of programs. Adversity and opportunity are closely linked and can force rethinking of traditional approaches. The idea that instructional cuts can be beneficial only makes sense, however, if the cuts are made in a timely way and not deferred until a crisis occurs. In a crisis, orderly planning is no longer feasible. Instead, the focus is on damage control. While this crisis approach gives administrators a mandate to cut, they cannot really do so effectively because too many options have been foreclosed by their inaction.

Perhaps the most controversial area of cuts in the instructional program has been school closings. The traditional delivery of educational services through neighborhood schools has favored the development of strong individual school identities and public loyalties. Opponents of school closings have raised several challenges to the justifications usually offered by administrators. First, critics assert that expected cost-savings are overstated, particularly when existing personnel are merely absorbed elsewhere in the system without corresponding staff layoffs or attrition.

This argument's credibility frequently hinges on how well the administration has documented the case for a closing. A second challenge is that some children who must move to a new school will be treated unfairly because of the distance or danger of the new routes they must travel. Usually this issue has arisen where attempts are made to close schools located in predominantly black, Hispanic, or other minority-group neighborhoods. Such considerations should be weighed carefully before a proposed policy is developed. Critics are concerned also with the impact of the closing on the long-term health of particular neighborhoods. As an alternative to abandonment, alternative uses of facilities have been developed successfully in many communities. A critical decision must be made whether to sell or lease the property. The latter may be desirable, assuming the condition of the facility and its location would make it attractive for reopening when enrollments rise again. Some decisions to sell closed schools have proven unduly hasty because facilities shortages began to recur in the mid-1980s.

Decision Processes

Still another issue in the management of decline is not when or where to cut, but from a procedural viewpoint, precisely how. Here the conventional wisdom of school administrators to involve everyone in decision making at least nominally sometimes has proven disasterous. The idea that cutback management is rational-technical in nature leads to the erroneous assumption that the ingredients of consensus are to be found in open discussion by all affected parties. Often, this approach merely gives opponents time to organize and forestall any meaningful change. Administrators have learned that cutback management requires political bargaining in which they may play the pivotal brokerage role. This approach to leadership may be the only realistic one in highly emotional situations where there are many potential losers, and it may require coalition building. In other words, administrators must assume a more explicitly political dimension to their role.

Alternatives to Cutbacks

Political leadership also is necessary to generate improved revenue through lobbying and grantsmanship. Administrators have been somewhat slower than teachers unions to shed the myth that education and politics do not mix. As state leadership in funding and regulating public education increases, an important strategy for preventing or ameliorating decline is to be found in revenue-generating strategies with state education departments, legislatures, and foundations. Increased revenues and favorable regulatory treatment can go a long way toward offsetting the need for expenditure reductions.

See also Consolidation of Schools; Enrollment Projections; Funding Methods: State and Federal; Planning

—James G. Cibulka
University of Wisconsin-Milwaukee

References

Dean, J. (Ed.). (1983, February). "The politics of school closings." [Special issue]. *Education and Urban Society, 15* (2), 147–261.

Levine, C.H. (Ed.). (1980). *Managing fiscal stress: The crisis in the public sector.* Chatham, NJ: Chatham House.

Zerchykov, R. (1983). *Managing decline in school systems: A handbook.* Boston: Institute for Responsive Education.

MASTERY LEARNING

Emphasizing the principle that learning is a function of time and other aspects of opportunity to learn, mastery learning aims to improve the achievement of all students through organization and delivery of instruction according to the following four-phase cycle: (a) teach according to stated objectives; (b) test to determine mastery and identify learning errors; (c) reteach nonmasters while extending or enriching the learning of masters; and (d) retest. Mastery learning also emphasizes alignment of curriculum, instruction, and testing through use of criteria-referenced (i.e., mastery) pretests, formative tests, and summative tests to record and guide student progress. The emphasis on explicit corrective instruction for students below mastery level distinguishes full-fledged mastery learning from many mastery-type approaches that (only) emphasize selection and mastery of specific learning objectives.

Mastery learning can be delivered through direct instruction for the whole class, through individual and small-group learning, or some combination of these organizational patterns. Whatever the pattern, mastery learning can and should accommodate established pedagogical principles such as positive reinforcement for success, emphasis on higher-order learning, provision of appropriate cues and feedback, motivation through high-interest material and active learning, and recognition of diverse student learning styles, particularly in corrective instruction. Thus, while mastery learning is an instructional process which does not directly provide teachers with skills in classroom management or presentation of material, it incorporates and helps to organize many of the elements frequently associated with effective instruction and effective teaching.

Whole-group mastery learning in elementary and secondary schools has been particularly developed by and associated with Benjamin Bloom and colleagues such as Lorin Anderson, James Block, Thomas Guskey, and developers of the Chicago Mastery Learning Reading Program. Approaches emphasizing individual and small-group learning and continuous progress have been developed by Alan Cohen and others such as John Champlin and Albert Mamary of the Johnson City, New York, public schools. Mastery learning at the post-secondary level is particularly associated with the Personalized System of Instruction developed by Fred Keller to provide individualized, continuous-progress learning.

Mastery learning programs also differ in how materials are selected and developed. One approach emphasizes teacher development of materials and methods as part of classroom planning for instructional improvement. Other approaches emphasize centralized development or purchase of curriculum materials in a mastery-learning sequence. One advantage of the latter approaches is that they greatly reduce the burden placed on individual teachers.

Research demonstrates that, when properly implemented, mastery learning can bring about impressive gains in student achievement. Experimental studies conducted by Benjamin Bloom and his colleagues show that, when mastery learning is combined with other improvements (e.g., in instructional materials and technology, motivation and guidance of students, teaching practices, emphasis on higher mental processes), achievement can approach or equal the two standard deviation levels (above "regular" instruction) attainable through one-to-one tutoring. Instructional programs in Johnson City, New York, Canaan, Connecticut, Red Bank, New Jersey, and other school districts demonstrate that achievement increases of nearly this magnitude can be attained through outstanding implementation of mastery learning throughout a school or district. In addition, mastery learning has been identified as a component associated with the success of some unusually successful schools in several effective schools studies.

Although successful programs thus demonstrate that mastery learning can provide a scaffolding for effective instruction and assessment, many implementation problems are present and frequently result in ineffective arrangements that merely process students through a discrete continuum of low-level skills and subskills. In addition to neglect of higher-order skills, problems most frequently encountered involve inadequate delivery of enrichment extension for masters, overemphasis on auditory learning, insufficient planning time and technical assistance for teachers, overemphasis on testing, and fragmentation of instruction due to stress on isolated skills.

Prerequisites for successful implementation of mastery learning include provision of (a) staff and program development time as part of the regular school day; (b) staff developers and other instructional support at the school building level; and (c) arrangement to minimize record-keeping burdens. Technical prerequisites include avoidance of the tendency to overtest and the need for planning to (a) establish appropriate priorities among instructional objectives; (b) organize and sequence objectives into appropriate units; (c) effectively orient students; and (d) set rational performance standards.

Other issues which must be resolved for successful implementation of mastery learning involve problems inherent in allocating sufficient time for students to attain mastery, in delivering and supervising instruction in an organic rather than a bureaucratic manner stressing paper-and-pencil monitoring, in coordinating instruction across and within grade levels, and in ensuring that arrangements for homogeneous or heterogeneous grouping (or some combination) are productive. (Heterogeneous grouping typically requires much more planning and resources to be implemented effectively than does homogeneous grouping, but homogeneous grouping is particularly susceptible to problems associated with low expectations and slow pacing for low achievers, especially at poverty schools in the inner city).

In general, successful mastery learning requires that instructional arrangements be made manageable and feasible for the average teacher, and thus requires substantial resources to ensure that teachers have sufficient planning time, instructional materials, and technical assistance, and are not responsible for an unmanageable number of low achievers. In practice, unfortunately, mastery learning frequently is viewed (incorrectly) as a cheap and easy way to improve achievement by merely specifying required objectives and collection of data on student mastery. Mastery learning also is highly susceptible to misinterpretation and misimplementation by administrators and teachers who find it convenient to overemphasize low-order skills which are easiest to teach and test. For these reasons, many mastery and mastery-type programs have been unsuccessful, thus tending to discredit the potential of an approach that can produce enormous achievement gains. From this point of view, the future of mastery learning probably will depend substantially on explicit recognition of the administrative and organizational prerequisites for successful implementation.

See also Academic Learning Time; Direct Instruction; Instructional Objectives; Tests, Norm- and Criterion-Referenced.

—Daniel U. Levine
University of Missouri-Kansas City
—Beau Fly Jones
North Central Regional Education Laboratory

References

Block, J.H., & Anderson, L.W. (1975). *Mastery learning in classroom instruction.* New York: Macmillan.

Guskey, T.R. (1985). *Implementing mastery learning.* Belmont, CA: Wadsworth.

Levine, D.U. (1985). *Improving student achievement through mastery learning programs.* San Francisco: Jossey-Bass.

MATHEMATICS EDUCATION

A knowledge of the elements of mathematics is essential for effective citizenship in modern society. In recognition of the importance of mathematics, all countries, from those in early stages of development to those that are highly industrialized, such as Japan and the United States, give the study of the subject a prominent place in the school curriculum. Mathematics education is the study of the teaching and learning of mathematics, particularly in the school setting. In this study, the domains of mathematics and of education are joined and interact. For example, when dealing with the concept of number, there is concern with the mathematics of number and of number systems. There is at the same time a concern with cognition, as found, say, in the work of Piaget.

Elementary School Mathematics

In the elementary school, a beginning is made in building basic mathematical competencies. Often, "arithmetic" is used to refer to the content of elementary school mathematics. But this term is only a short-hand reference for the array of competencies that constitute an adequate preparation for more advanced study. These competencies include the ability to count, to perform simple computations (involving whole numbers of one or two digits), to estimate quantities (such as areas of rectangles), to organize data, and to read and interpret simple tables and charts.

Secondary School Mathematics

As the study of mathematics proceeds through the grades, its content becomes successively more abstract and powerful. A knowledge of algebra, the mainstay of secondary school mathematics, permits a more general grasp of relationships between quantities (introductory algebra) and an introduction to mathematical structures (such as number systems), as encountered in more advanced algebra.

Traditionally, college-preparatory mathematics in the secondary school has culminated in the calculus—a powerful method of mathematical analysis that enables one to deal with rates of change, heat flow, and a myriad of other problems in science and engineering.

Recently, a report of the National Science Board recommended that secondary school mathematics be broadened in scope, in terms of numbers of students who engage in its study as well as the kind of mathematics that is offered. Such mathematical topics would include probability, statistics, graph theory, and algebraic structures.

Calculators and Computers

The invention and rapid development of computing devices (due primarily to the silicon chip, a device that enables the storage and retrieval of enormous amounts of information in a very small space) has profound implications for mathematics education. Calculators, with their ability to perform a variety of arithmetical operations, have a natural place in the school program—not only in mathematics, but in other subjects, too. However, there has been resistance to the use of calculators, especially in mathematics classes. A common reason given is the fear that, in using these devices, students will become overly dependent on them, use them as crutches, and as a result mathematical competencies will diminish, not grow.

Research in the field of calculators and mathematics education does not support such fears. To the contrary, many experiments point to the benefits of calculators in promoting an investigative approach to mathematics, and to developing estimation skills. It is likely that barriers to the use of calculators and computers are due to natural hesitancy in accepting change and in the lack of appropriate curricular materials that take advantage of calculators and computers.

Drill vs. Understanding

A major issue facing mathematics educators is that of the relative emphasis that should be given to drill and practice as opposed to meaning and understanding. For example, when teaching the basic facts of arithmetic, such as $2 \times 3 = 6$, should the teacher stress simply remembering the "two times table," or should a great amount of attention be paid to understanding that 2×3 can be thought of as "two groups of three," as in "two groups of three marbles?" A rationale for memorizing basic facts is that as students advance in their study of mathematics they need a storehouse of skills upon which they can quickly and accurately draw (for example, as they do long division). But justification for emphasizing understanding can be found when a student forgets a basic fact and must reconstruct it. At that time, the meaning of 2×3 as "two groups of three" is useful in finding the answer: 6.

Attitudes Towards Mathematics

Various measures of attitudes towards mathematics have been developed, such as Mathematics and Society (the role of mathematics in today's world), Mathematics and Myself (how mathematics relates to one's self-concept) and Mathematics in School (how mathematics is regarded in the classroom setting). The general decline of students' attitudes towards mathematics as they move through the grades is of great concern to mathematics educators. The National Assessment of Educational Progress found that among nine-year-olds, mathematics is their favorite subject. With thirteen-year-olds, mathematics was the second most liked subject. But seventeen-year-olds listed mathematics as their least-liked subject.

A Challenge

As we move from the twentieth to the twenty-first century, a serious challenge faces mathematics educators. The central role of mathematics in a high-technology society will continue—and likely increase. However, since mathematics is a living, growing subject, the kind of mathematics that is learned in school must change. Just as the 1960s saw a "revolution" in school mathematics in order to update the subject, there must continue to be developments in the curriculum, and in how the subject is taught, in order that we might offer the kind of education required by today's, and by tomorrow's, society.

See also Computer-Assisted Instruction; Computer Literacy; Technology Education.

—Kenneth J. Travers
University of Illinois

References

National Council of Teachers of Mathematics. (1982). *Mathematics for the middle grades*. Reston, VA: Author.
National Council of Teachers of Mathematics. (1985). *The secondary school mathematics curriculum*. Reston, VA: Author.
Papert, S. (1980). *Mindstorms*. New York: Basic Books.

MERIT PAY

The primary goal of evaluating teachers on the basis of merit is to reward outstanding teachers for their efforts and success. Designing a system to achieve this goal is a complex task which must take into account various organizational and behavioral considerations. The purpose of a merit system is to establish a salary scale on the basis of merit. Teachers with merit are given salary increases.

Defining Merit

The most difficult task facing teachers, administrators, and school board members as they attempt to deal with recent pressure for merit evaluation systems is to reach agreement on the meaning of "merit." Problems arise when the assumption is made that everyone has a common understanding of merit. In reality, definitions vary from stringent (excellence, superior performance) to vague (effective performance). To some individuals, merit implies a monetary reward, or an increase in salary, while to others it means nonmonetary recognition, or little more than a pat on the back.

Merit plans based on the premise that superior performance will be rewarded should differ significantly from plans which focus on effective performance. The first design assumes that only a small percentage of teachers is meritorious or superior and that those teachers are identifiable; these plans typically specify a quota or percentage of teachers who will be recognized for excelling in their roles. Thus, merit plans which focus on superior performance are perceived as a means of identifying teachers at the extremes and recognizing the added effort which is expended by those excelling.

In contrast, the approach which defines merit as a reward for effective performance differs conceptually from a plan rewarding superior performance. In a plan rewarding effective performance, all teachers should theoretically be eligible to receive merit recognition if they perform their jobs as expected. Problems arise when the language of merit plans focuses on effective behavior, but rewards based on superior performance are distributed. When this occurs, teachers who do not receive a merit reward infer that they are ineffective. Worse yet, the public assumes the same.

Rewards

Rewards associated with merit plans may be either extrinsic or intrinsic in nature and may relate to various levels of need experienced by individual teachers. Extrinsic rewards are typically monetary in nature, or relate to benefits not associated with the job. Examples are money, medical/dental coverage, life insurance, and retirement benefits. These rewards relate to lower-order, physiological and security needs and often prevent dissatisfaction but do not necessarily lead to satisfaction. In addition, extrinsic rewards tend to be short-term, rather than long-term, and are soon forgotten.

Intrinsic rewards, on the other hand, relate to the higher-order needs of self esteem, recognition, work itself, and self-actualization. They may or may not have monetary implications; however, in contrast to extrinsic rewards, intrinsic rewards relate to the job. Examples of intrinsic rewards are promotions, praise, public recognition, additional instructional materials, additional work responsibilities, and the approval of out-of-state travel for the purpose of attending professional meetings. Unlike extrinsic rewards, these have been found to lead to long-term job satisfaction.

Research studies which investigated the rewards desired by teachers found that when given a variety of extrinsic and intrinsic rewards from which to choose, teachers were more likely to choose conference attendance and selection of instructional materials. In addition, teachers desired increased autonomy (being allowed to do what they think is best), expanded responsibilities, and opportunities to develop professionally. Teachers also placed considerable value on the administrator's ability to remove impediments to competent teaching—discipline problems, frequent interruptions, excessive paperwork. In essence, teachers expressed a belief that special recognition in the form of money was often contrary to their concept of professionalism.

These results indicate that merit systems based exclusively on extrinsic rewards will not serve as motivators for many teachers. In fact, for some teachers a monetary merit plan may be offensive to the point that it serves as a disincentive to improve performance. Furthermore, as a result of the reward system, teachers' short-term personal goals are frequently accomplished at the expense of long-term personal, professional and organizational goals.

Methods of Evaluation

Regardless of the rewards, merit systems must have specified evaluative criteria on which decisions will be based. For the sake of simplicity, many plans focus on quantitative criteria which are easy to document. For instance, one might assume that students will achieve at a higher level if their teacher is not absent frequently; therefore, teachers may receive a bonus if their number of sick days does not exceed a specified amount. Another assertion may be that continuing professional development will improve teacher effectiveness; thus, rewards may be given for successful completion of approved coursework. These measures indicate verifiable, indisputable criteria; however, they cannot truthfully be called "merit systems." They may be the bases of an incentive program, but a system that does not reward differentially according to evaluation of the quality of work is not merit pay.

Therefore, in order to differentiate among teachers' performances, goals and objectives frequently focus on less concrete evidence of accomplishment. A typical example is the use of student achievement data as evidence of effective teacher performance. Objections to the use of achievement data are that such measures ignore student variability, socioeconomic backgrounds of students, and peer group pressure, all of which have been found to affect test score results. Furthermore, these tests often determine curriculum content and ignore the broader, global goals of education such as reasoning, logic, appreciation, and critical-thinking skills. Teachers, therefore, feel that the use of such evidence as the sole measure of their effectiveness provides a distorted and often inaccurate assessment.

Criteria of Effective Teaching. In order to include within their merit plans evaluations of teaching (instructional) performance, criteria of effective teaching which are research-based and measurable must be specified and communicated to all teachers. These criteria should be listed in behavioral terms and written in such a fashion that they may be shared with and understood by teachers. For each behavior, a definition should be provided and measurement criteria stipulated. These behaviors should be derived from a collaborative review by administrators and teachers of existing research regarding effectiveness.

In order for the evaluation system to be viewed as reliable, one with which administrators are comfortable as they make merit decisions, the observation tools should be explicit enough to assure that multiple observers would draw similar conclusions if assessing the same teacher's performance. To accomplish this difficult task, administrators and teachers should be trained and familiar with a variety of observation techniques. Observation strategies should be shared with teachers and assurance provided that data collected will be as objective as possible.

Assessment of Special Assignments. Merit plans must account for the variability among teaching assignments. As a result of declining enrollments, many teachers are now shared between buildings, have split assignments, or occupy combination administrative-teaching positions. Thus, special accommodations must be made within evaluation plans for teachers with unique assignments. For example, special-education teachers and allied-arts teachers are frequently assigned to multiple buildings and often are unsure to whom they report and by whom they will be evaluated. Unfortunately, they are frequently lost in the shuffle. Therefore, plans must specify how and by whom these teachers will be evaluated.

Furthermore, many staff members hold positions which require duties other than direct instruction. The success of special-education teachers, social workers, psychologists, and counselors often depends on their ability to write well and complete reports in a timely fashion, to understand federal and state guidelines, and to interact effectively with parents. Thus, comprehensive merit plans must recognize these special job responsibilities.

Documentation Procedures. In order for an evaluation system to be used for merit decisions, administrators must adequately document each supervisory encounter. Legally, teachers are entitled to be informed of all formal statements which exist regarding their performance. Furthermore, they have the right to challenge, in writing, any written statements with which they disagree. Thus, submitted plans should specify the documentation procedures which will be used. Proper documentation procedures will assist administrators in supporting their merit decisions. If teachers should challenge decisions based on the evaluation system, administrators will need to provide evidence which supports the conclusions they have drawn.

In some merit plans, the burden of documentation has been placed on the teachers. Teachers, once informed of the performance standards, compile a portfolio which supports their contention of superior performance. The portfolio is then reviewed by a team of administrators, supervisors, and teachers who forward recommendations regarding merit to the superintendent. This process often protects administrators against allegations of bias and poor reliability of evaluation techniques.

Success Factors

In the few instances where merit systems have experienced success, a number of supporting factors have been identified. In cases of success:

1. Merit reward systems were based on effective, objective, and consistent evaluation procedures, and decisions were based on valid and verifiable measures of superior performance. Teachers understood criteria by which they were evaluated, and they received feedback from the evaluation process.

2. The superintendent was an effective leader who sold the plan to the staff and worked to win board approval. School board members and administrators were committed to making the merit plan work.

3. Merit plans were developed with input from individuals from all levels of the hierarchy and were not perceived as being pushed from the top down. Teachers were involved in the development of the merit system, and adequate time was allowed for development and implementation of merit plans.

4. Teachers were allowed to create individual performance objectives. Rewards which were personally and professionally satisfying to teachers were determined. Merit systems allowed for differential acquisition of rewards based on individual needs.

5. Merit plans defined a teacher's role in the broad sense and allowed for recognition in areas outside of instructional performance.

6. Adequate financing existed. Rewards were available to all who qualified. The amount of money offered provided a real incentive to improve immediate performance.

In instances of failure, which constitute the vast majority of attempted merit plans, the above principles were generally violated.

Conclusion

In order to respond to the public's demand for increased accountability of teacher performance, school board members, administrators, and teachers must begin with an investigation of current evaluation practices within their district. Only by doing so will they be able to determine whether or not a merit system is necessary and, if so, whether the present evaluation system provides adequate, differentiating evidence on which to base merit decisions.

See also Career Ladders; Staff Evaluation; Supervision, Clinical.

—Gail Thierbach Schneider
University of Wisconsin-Milwaukee

References

American Association of School Administrators. (1983). *Some points to consider when you discuss merit pay*. Arlington, VA: Author.

Astuto, T.A., & Clark, D.L. (1985, January). *Merit pay for teachers: An analysis of state policy options*. Bloomington, IN: Indiana University, School of Education Educational Policy Studies Series.

Murnane, R.J., & Cohen, D.K. (1986, February). "Merit pay and the evaluation problem: Why most merit pay plans fail and a few survive." *Harvard Educational Review, 56*(1), 1–17.

MIDDLE/JUNIOR HIGH SCHOOLS

The middle grades, 5 through 9 inclusive, are found in more than thirty different organizational structures in the United States. These range from schools with one grade through many different combinations of grades, including K-12. The two predominant patterns, however, are the junior high school, typically grades 7 through 9, and the middle school, grades 5 or 6 through 8. Schools having just grades 7 through 8 are called middle schools or junior high schools.

The Junior High School Movement

The junior high school movement began in the early years of this century, with 1909-1910 generally agreed upon as the year the first junior high opened. The basic concepts underlying the junior high school movement were formed first by the Committee of Ten in 1892 and then by the Committee on Economy of Time in Education (1913) and the Committee on the Reorganization of Secondary Education (1918). These concepts included (a) better provision in the school progam for the needs of adolescents; (b) provision for the exploration of pupils' interests and abilities; (c) individualization of the instructional program; and (d) better articulation between elementary and secondary education.

Administrative and structural practices proposed by some of the committees and introduced into the early junior high schools included flexibility, departmentalized studies, and the earlier introduction of secondary studies.

The movement gained momentum so rapidly that, by 1918, there were 557 junior high schools in the United States. The growth continued until, in 1965, there were approximately 8,000, including both 7-9 and 7-8 schools. The movement was not without its problems. As early as 1920, some observers noted that, while the form of reorganization was to be found in hundreds of school systems, real reorganization was being attempted in only a few.

Program Characteristics. Widely different ideas about the purposes of the junior high school ranged from a simple belief in the downward extension of senior high school programs and activities to the call for an entirely new program addressing the uniqueness of early adolescence. Proposals advocated by those who favored a new program included full departmentalization, interscholastic athletics, sophisticated social activities, and an emphasis on academic requirements.

The concept of exploration, the provision of guidance services as an integral part of the school program, co-curricular activities within the school day, and flexibility in staff and student scheduling were among the positions advocated by those who saw the new school as one that should provide a new program, designed to meet the unique needs, interests, and abilities of early adolescents.

The latter group accepted six general functions as descriptive of the mission of the junior high:

1. *Integration.* The group called for the systematic integration of previously acquired educational outcomes and the continuation of a well-integrated general education for all students.

2. *Exploration.* The provision of opportunities to develop a widening range of cultural, civic, social, and recreational interests.

3. *Guidance.* Help for students in making intelligent decisions about their future educational and prevocational opportunities, in making decisions about their immediate and future vocational opportunities, and in their growth toward the maximum development of their personal powers and qualities.

4. *Differentiation.* The provision of different educational facilities suited to the varying needs, interests, backgrounds, capacities, and personalities of early adolescents, appropriate to their future educational and vocational needs.

5. *Socialization.* The provision of opportunities for social growth and participation to enable pupils to adjust to their present and future complex social structures.

6. *Articulation.* The provision of a gradual transition from elementary to secondary education to ensure the continuous adjustment of the educational program to the maturity and previous educational experiences of the pupils and to prepare them to participate as effectively as possible in all of their present and future learning experiences.

The apparent prevalence of the belief in the downward extension of senior high school programs, particularly the movement of secondary education into grades 7 and 8, did meet one of its proponents' goals, reducing dropouts, but with it came the charge that junior high schools were only "little high schools" and not a new or unique program for early adolescents. There were many exceptions, but the presence and promotion of interscholastic athletics, complete departmentalization, marching bands, evening social activities, yearbooks, and the like fueled the opponents' arguments. Critics were echoing the earlier charge that reorganization was everywhere, but real change was hard to find. From this concern, widespread reorganization of middle-grades education began in the early 1960s.

Along with the disappointment that accompanied the failure of many junior high schools to fulfill their mission of providing a unique program for a unique population, other reasons also gave impetus to the call for change. Chief among these were the earlier maturation of girls and boys and the problems local districts faced with building usage, enrollment patterns, desegregation, and other such matters.

The Middle School Movement

The rationale advanced for the new *school in the middle* called for many of the same functions and attributes that had been proposed for the junior high school over the previous half-century. Among these were articulation, exploration, transition, earlier maturation, better building usage, enrollment problems in the local districts, and similar themes that had been a part of the creation of junior highs. Similar to the earlier movement, the reorganization of the middle grades to the new middle school, grades 5-8 or 6-8 primarily, gained impetus rapidly.

Today, more schools in the United States have the 6-7-8 grade organization than the 7-8-9 grade organization. The former represent approximately one-third of the total number of middle grades schools; the latter represent approximately 25 percent. Combining the 5-8s with the 6-8s raises the number of middle schools to approximately 40 percent of the total. Schools with only grades 7 and 8 are about one-fourth of the total. It is impossible to determine how these would split as junior high schools or middle schools as that varies from district to district. The trend to 6-7-8, away from 7-8-9, is clearly established.

In the early years of the middle-school movement, many proponents of the junior high and of the middle school proclaimed the virtues of their particular preference and the evils of the other. Today, there is a growing trend to the use of the term "middle level" to describe middle grades, whatever the building may be named, or whatever configuration of middle grades it may contain. This movement is symbolic of the coming together of the best of both institutions, both in personnel and programs.

Program Characteristics

1. *Adviser-advisee programs* are regularly scheduled times when students have the opportunity to interact with peers and/or staff members about school-oriented concerns.

2. *Block schedules* provide large blocks of time (multiple periods) in which teachers or teams of teachers can organize and arrange flexible groupings of students for varied periods of time.

3. *Common learnings* are that portion of the curriculum considered essential for every student.

4. *Continuous progress* is a system that enables students to move through a learning program on the basis of the successful completion of learning objectives at their individual rate of speed without skipping or repeating.

5. *Correlated or integrated curriculum* is an arrangement that features a conscious effort to relate various subjects to one another.

6. *Exploration* provides curriculum experiences designed to help students explore their changing needs, aptitudes and interests.

7. *Individualized instruction* is instruction that provides alternate routes and rates for student achievement of common or unique objectives, based on diagnosed student needs.

8. *Interdisciplinary team* is a team of two to five teachers who teach a common group of students. Utilizing block scheduling techniques, the team plans programs, groups students, schedules classes, and evaluates students and programs cooperatively.

9. *Multiage grouping* is the grouping of students from more than one grade or age level in the same class to facilitate continuous progress.

10. *Peer counseling* is the process by which counselors help middle-level students share viewpoints and experiences that may benefit other students facing similar problems.

11. *Peer teaching* is the planned use of students in a tutorial role.

12. *Team planning* is the process followed by a group of teachers who plan interdependent instructional objectives, evaluation procedures, and management techniques appropriate for a common group of students. This may or may not result in team teaching.

13. *Unified arts/allied arts* is a coordinated program that provides exploratory opportunities within the humanities, the practical arts, and the fine arts.

This list is not all-inclusive, but it does represent several of the characteristics commonly found in true middle-level schools, regardless of the middle grades they serve. The future of middle-level education may well depend on the ability of middle-level educators to convince boards of education and the general public of the need for a school between elementary school and high school. Available research provides no evidence that middle-level students achieve better in one kind of middle-level school than in any other, or in middle-level schools as compared to the inclusion of the middle grades in an elementary or secondary configuration.

Student Characteristics

If achievement were the only goal of education, there would be no need for middle-level schools or programs; but since there is more to a comprehensive education than achievement alone, middle-level education is supported by the following perceptions about the student population:

1. Early adolescence is a time of phenomenal growth, a time that produces dramatic differences among youngsters of the same age and exhibits rapidly changing growth and behavior patterns in individual children. Between the ages of approximately 10 and 15, young people go through the most radical and dramatic changes that human beings experience.

2. Early adolescence is the time when the adult personality is largely developed. The value formation that takes place in early adolescence, to a greater degree than at any other time in life, determines the kind of adult the individual is going to be. The adolescent forms self-concepts and arrives at many of his or her answers to fundamental questions and ultimate determinants of behavior.

3. Early adolescents face seemingly impossible choices that place them under heavy emotional pressures. They face critical decisions that test their values and ethics at a time when these are being formed.

4. Early adolescents are the least understood and the most misunderstood of any age group. Their normal behavior is unacceptable to many adults.

5. Early adolescents need a supportive, protective, controlled environment in which to experiment with the ideas and relationships that are a normal part of maturation.

Issues

School closings, consolidations, and enrollment shifts were the primary causes for the decline of middle-level schools in the early 1980s. However, beginning with 1984, the trend reversed, and the number increased by more than two hundred over the previous year. Emphasis on middle-level research, the movement of slightly more than half of the states to some kind of middle-level certification, new graduate and undergraduate programs of middle-level teacher and administrator preparation, and an increased awareness of the critical nature of the developmental stage that is early adolescence have focused attention on middle-level education.

A key to understanding the important role the middle-level school plays in the critical developmental period known as *adolescence* is to be found in the fact that it represents the first opportunity these students have to study with teachers who are subject specialists and, at the same time, the last opportunity they will have to do so without the pressure of Carnegie units, grade-point averages, or credits toward graduation.

See also Curriculum Development; Elementary Schools; High Schools; Student Culture.

—George E. Melton, Deputy Executive Director
National Association of
Secondary School Principals

References

Arth, A.A., Johnston, J.H., Lounsbury, J.L., & Toepfer, C.F. (1985). *A consumer's guide to middle-level education.* Reston, VA: The National Association of Secondary School Principals.

Gruhn, W.T., & Douglass, H.R. (1947). *The modern junior high school.* New York: Ronald Press.

Lounsbury, J.H., (Ed.). (1984). *Perspectives: Middle school education, 1964-1984.* Columbus, OH: The National Middle School Association.

MINORITIES AND THE SCHOOL SYSTEM

The United States is experiencing profound demographic changes. One such change is the significant increase in the growth of its minority populations. By 1990, according to the demographic projections, minorities will constitute 20 to 25 percent of our total population, while the percentage of minority school-age youth will be more than 30 percent. The majority of school enrollments in 23 of 25 of the nation's largest cities comprise minority students. By the year 2000, in 53 cities the minority population will be in the majority. The conclusion for schools (at all levels) is inescapable: Minority students are now heavily enrolled in American public schools and will continue to be; an increasing number of them will be eligible for post-secondary education.

Although there is growing recognition of these changes, there is also apprehension that this society's educational institutions are not responding quickly or adequately enough in developing policies that will maximize the contributions to be made by the escalating numbers of minorities in the population. Planning on the basis of this demographic information is essential if educators are to make sure that the largest number of minority students do well in our schools and thus become eligible for post-secondary education.

Diversity and the Role of the School

These changes have brought about a new recognition of America's diversity and an awakened interest in the ethnic roots of its peoples in recent years. Conceivably, this awareness and interest spring from the urgent demands of ethnic groups for acceptance and recognition; conceivably, they also arise from a new focus on cultural backgrounds and social history. In any case, attention to the fundamental diversity that marks the American population is a welcome reversal of the time-honored view of the United States as a "melting pot" which was expected to mold all of our country's ethnic varieties into a single common "American." The time has come to celebrate the diversity that characterizes a country in which some three hundred different native American Indian tribes were joined by numerous peoples from every continent and every country on this planet. The time of arrival was equally varied, stretching over a period of three hundred years. The overwhelming features were diversity and variety. It seems time for our schools to recognize this pluralism as a source of past, present, and future richness and creativity rather than of possible division and conflict.

Celebration of America's diversity has not always been the approach in our nation. Pressures toward conformity and fears of whatever was strange and different underlie a long and dreadful record of suppression of native and immigrant cultures by the dominant society. In this unfortunate process, much that could have been learned from a whole universe of diverse cultures has been lost.

At the present stage in America's growth, there is a new effort to "validate"—that is, recognize and to prize—the full range of ethnic groups and cultures which have contributed and continue to contribute to our country's life and development. Yet, even in the present day, in some communities this effort runs counter to persisting discrimination, racism, prejudice, and suppression of ethnic groups and cultures.

American schools are the primary agency for the transmission of our nation's culture. Increasingly, they are being urged to develop a more pluralistic attitude with respect to the diversity that students bring into all of our classrooms. Historically, the role of the school was one of stressing conformity, rather than diversity. Today, in greater numbers, schools are now beginning to question this philosphical orientation. Should the role of the school be one of stressing conformity and of neglecting an ever-growing population of diverse cultural groups found in our society? Many educators believe the role of the school should be one of endorsing diversity which enhances the recognition, acceptance and appreciation of our diverse population.

One of the major stumbling blocks to this educational concept of pluralism is that many teachers are the products of an education and a society that refused to accept any variation from the predominant Anglo-American norms. Teachers, as well as those who are preparing to teach, are now being asked to shift gears, to adjust to a new kind of world view. Many are reluctant to change.

It is not difficult to convince America's teachers that pluralism rather than uniformity represents social reality in this country, although some teachers meet homogeneous classes, sometimes in rural areas, sometimes in suburbs, and sometimes in ethnic or racial enclaves in our cities. Yet teachers, who are aware of the diversity of our population now must seek elements which were omitted from their own education at all levels. Specific information about America's pluralism is needed. Professional skills and materials to move toward education which is truly equitable now are necessary. Today, there exist wide variations in the extent and the degree to which equal and adequate educational opportunities are available to children and youth in American society. Greater disparities and inadequacies attend educational provisions for the culturally diverse in spite of implied constitutional guarantees for equal educational opportunity. There is agreement among many analysts that one cause of these conditions is inadequate national commitment to education and the educational enterprise. Nor is there a tangible enduring sensitivity to the vicissitudes of a "multicultural" education and its necessity for relevant learning.

The elimination of this inadequate commitment requires an educational system prioritized and geared to accommodate cultural diversity. It will also require educators adequately prepared and favorably inclined to work effectively with children of different ethnic groups and/or other cultural identities to achieve equity education.

Equity education is based on the premise that all students—regardless of race, color, national origin, sex, native language, age, social or economic status, family structure and lifestyle, religious preference, or exceptionality have the right to an education of equal quality.

Summary

During this century, perhaps no concept has given educators more difficulty than that of equality. As administrators and teachers, we have gradually come to realize the inequities that have existed in our educational systems. When all present and future factors and conditions are considered, the need for more competent teachers becomes apparent. Equity education calls for teachers who have powerful teaching skills, who are committed to education for all children, and who are resourceful enough to accommodate children with special needs. Education programs (at all levels) must begin to assume responsibility for seeing that their programs and training reflect the diversity of this nation through their staffing, materials, methods, strategies, resources, and participatory models and practices.

See also Demographic Trends; Desegregation Plans; Minority Administrators; Multicultural Education.

—Fred Rodriguez
University of Kansas

References

Appelton, N. (1983). *Cultural pluralism in education.* New York: Longman.

Banks, J.A. (1984). *Teaching strategies for ethnic studies (3rd ed.).* Boston, MA: Allyn & Bacon.

Barnett, M., & Harrington, C.C. (Eds.). (1984). *Readings on equal education.* New York: AMS Press.

MINORITY ADMINISTRATORS

Typically, increases in minority populations have spurred interest in hiring minorities for administrative posts in education. Protests and public demands for minority representation, especially in the 1960s and early 70s have hastened the effort at all levels. Without these developments, districts have been less responsive to minority representation in the administrative ranks. Furthermore, minority candidates most often consider pursuing such posts fruitless. Where applications are pursued, minority applicants see their being hired as a matter of race or sex rather than one of professional competence.

Hiring practices in educational administration have become much more formalized over the past twenty years. Approaches used do not guarantee fairness, but they help to reduce the margin of error in efforts that seek out competent employees from among those who apply. Since schools at the elementary and secondary levels represent arms of local institutions, public and professional perceptions and sentiments in local circles remain dominant in determining whether a member of majority or minority would be suitable for an available administrative post.

Where the competencies of minorities are desired and sought, the recruiting task may require an extension of routine practices to assure maximum exposure to the total population of minorities who might be qualified to apply. In some instances, for example, public notices of vacancies are not sufficiently "public." Many are published irregularly, and then posted on bulletin boards or walls seen only by the most ambitious. Following up on public vacancy notices by sending timely personal invitations to individuals directly or through consulting firms and other professional groups might assist.

Another recruiting strategy which would offer broad returns would be to strengthen procedures already in place at the various applicable entry levels. Districts, for example, can exploit the supervision function at the building level where the greatest day-to-day contact is made with minority classroom teachers. Local administrators can assist routinely in the identification of prospective administrators as a function of their evaluation responsibilities.

Districts can also increase and strengthen the pool of available candidates for administration by helping to stimulate interest in such a career at a much younger age. The effort would foster more advanced preparation among the minority population for those planning to select administration as a career. The Future Teachers of America at the high school level is in the most advantageous position for this.

The ultimate responsibility for the quality of selection rests with the the superintendent, the director of personnel services, and the board of education for local schools. The director of personnel services must be sensitive to the subtleties of judgement that are inherent in the act of selecting minority candidates. At the same time, the superintendent and the board of education have to be capable of working with public and professional sentiment to allow the minority person selected an effective fit in the organization—one where professional competency has an opportunity to override issues of race or sex.

The selection process should show that a competent minority person for administration will be just as distinguishable from the incompetent as is the competent majority member under the same conditions.

Career Considerations

Administrative systems have usually had an "expected route" that persons followed to obtain positions. Minorities may or may not have been privy to the process as groups or as individuals. Increases in federal programs and grants with "minority representation-in-supervision" riders attached called for unprecedented, and sometimes unorthodox, ways of gaining minority representation on administrative staffs. In part, the outcome was not always positive. At times such actions earmarked positions and function for blacks, Hispanics, and/or women. At other times, they created new, "dead end" jobs and brought on over- and underfilling of positions as nonminority professionals attempted to adjust their credentials to address their own expectations and protect their own interests. It called for "crash" courses and programs to qualify minorities for available positions and, among other things, appeared to alter organizational decision paths and create other administrative strategies to deal with the changing composition of the management staff. Questions arose soon thereafter about the extent to which minorities gained access to decision-making positions and responsibilities.

A district's "promotional attitude" (i.e., how the organization's members feel and what they believe about the competencies and fitness of minority groups for positions of responsibility) tends to control much of what underlies these kinds of promotional efforts. Its character is reflected in remarks and behavior of individuals concerning minority applicants—even apart from general community sentiment. It is an important ingredient for successful promotional results with minority candidates.

The character of the district's attitude is set at the uppermost levels of the organization, i.e., by the superintendent and the board of education. Other formal and informal leaders in the bureaucracy contribute—some extensively. The outcome of their activity affects fair and equitable treatment as to qualifications, standards, and conditions by which promotions are gained.

Standards for promotion in administration are oftentimes less at issue than conditions of promotion. Residency requirements are an example. As long as housing patterns are not open to minority applicants to the extent that employment opportunities may be, such requirements tend to have a negative impact on the minority applicant in spite of the perceived value of the requirement per se.

The success of district promotional efforts grows from established trust, loyalty, and organizational identification as shared by employees at all levels. Technically, these efforts appear as upgrading strategies which districts can design to enrich the way in which personnel function in regard to movement to higher level positions. The efforts include offering wide professional experiences which allow the minority administrator to see value in the work that has to be done. Specifically, minorities are exposed to a variety of functions at one level which would be required to manage well at a higher level. Beyond broadly constituted day-to-day functions, these efforts mean assuring professional opportunities to intermingle and articulate minorities' work with other professionals. Finally, it includes someone properly monitoring tasks so that the administrator's work is consistent with the task description and with due rewards and compensation administered upon completion of the task.

These strategies tend to stress the importance of teaching individuals ways to support each other by helping parties to network and communicate effectively.

See also Inner City Schools; Minorities and the School System; Multicultural Education; Urban School Districts.

—Ronald Simpson
Kansas City, Missouri Public Schools

References

Abney, E.E. (1980). "A comparison of the status of Florida's black public school principals, 1964-65/1975-76." *The Journal of Negro Education, XLIX*(4), 398–406.

McLane, H.J. (1980). *Selecting, developing and retaining women executives* (chapters 7, 8 and 9). New York: Van Nostrand Reinhold.

U.S. Equal Employment Opportunity Commission. (1980). "Table 1. Occupational employment in public elementary and secondary schools by race/ethnic/sex group, 1980." *Elementary-Secondary Staff Information (EEO-5), 1980,* 22–211. Washington, DC: Author.

MULTICULTURAL EDUCATION

Multicultural education may be viewed by some educators and administrators as an ill-defined concept which lacks substance. It may be seen as merely another educational fad of short life expectancy that does not merit serious attention. But, for proponents of multicultural education, it remains a viable vehicle for affecting education changes within American public schools. In this article, the concept of multicultural education will be examined by considering what it is, why it is, and how it relates to school administration.

Much has been written concerning the goals and purposes of multicultural education. An analysis of the literature shows these premises: (a) The American society is characterized as a mosaic of different cultural groups; therefore, cultural diversity is a fact of American society. (b) Cultural diversity is a resource that should be preserved and extended in American society. (c) Since the school is society's major socialization agency, it should assume the responsibility of preserving and extending this resource. (d) The school should promote educational equity by treating diverse cultural groups as equally legitimate and by teaching positively about them. Individuals should not be penalized because of their group membership, but judged on their abilities and talents.

Various programs that are called multicultural education were developed on the basis of these premises. The most prevalent conception of multicultural education is the one that acknowledges, accepts, and respects all diversity within the human experience. *Diversity* includes not only those of cultural or ethnic nature, but also an unlimited number of other possible types of diversity (e.g., gender, age, handicapping conditions, social class, economic status). Educational institutions should adopt the premises of multicultural education by integrating information about contributions and perspectives of different cultural groups into the entire curriculum and by using teaching strategies that build on different students' learning styles.

In practice, the pluralistic idea of multicultural education as proposed by its advocates has not been fully realized by educational institutions. One of the major reasons for its slow acceptance and inclusion in the existing school curriculum can be attributed to the lack of administrative commitment at all levels.

According to Sander and Wiggins, educational institutions have been influenced by four major paradigms of administration, each with its own emphasis on efficiency, effectiveness, responsiveness, or relevance. Efficiency refers to the capacity to produce the maximum of outcomes with limited resources, energy, and time. The concept of efficiency is associated with that of economic rationality. It is concerned with seeking the means and procedures that are most suitable for attaining specific results and goals, independent of their human and political content or of their ethical nature. As a criterion of administration, effectiveness is essentially concerned with the attainment of educational objectives and closely related to the pedagogical aspects of the educational system. The concept of responsiveness is associated with the political demands of the external community. It is a criterion of performance that measures the capacity to produce the solution or response desired by the participants of the larger community. Relevance is a criterion of performance measured in terms of significance, value, and importance. It is oriented toward the improved quality of human life. Historically, school administration has been operating with an emphasis on efficiency and effectiveness and not on administrative relevance and responsiveness.

An emphasis on the technical criteria of efficiency and effectiveness tends to be nonsupportive of multicultural education, at best, and usually militates against its implementation. For example, the state of the economy has required schools to prioritize programs; the schools must deal with large cutbacks in local, state, and federal financial supports. As far as administrative efficiency is concerned, only minimal attention and support have been given to multicultural education, since it is viewed as an add-on. To school administrators, the major concern in multicultural programs appears to be essentially affective rather than cognitive.

Thus, programs have tended to emphasize self-esteem, ethnic identity, cultural awareness, and ethnic holidays while ignoring hard-core areas such as institutional racism, sexism, discrimination, equality, and equity issues. Multicultural education, conceptually, has evolved through three stages. Since its inception, multicultural education has advanced to an integrated process from the simplistic acknowledgement and celebration of group diversity by highlighting ethnic foods, holidays, and heroes. Finally, a comprehensive philosophy has been adopted that embellishes the total educational process enabling all students to achieve educational equity.

Multicultural education must permeate the total educational environment in public school programs and not just be an addition to the regular school curriculum. As student populations have become increasingly diverse in terms of culture and ethnicity, it has become necessary for administrators to possess a knowledge base, a set of attitudes and values, and a philosophy of education that is multicultural. The strength of multicultural education lies in its pedagogical soundness, for it emphasizes social skills and behavioral competencies necessary to function in a pluralistic society.

Multicultural education is also strongly related to the political and cultural dimensions of school administration. According to Sander and Wiggins, the political dimension is important for the educational system. In a pluralistic society, different cultural and subcultural groups present different interests and sometimes conflicting values with regard to what kind of education should be prescribed for their children. The greater the strategic capacity to meet the social necessities and political demands of the community, the more effective will be the administration of education. Responsiveness, in this sense, is the criterion in the political dimension. Educational administrators must be capable of identifying the needs of the community and must act upon them accordingly.

The cultural dimension of administration has to do with the values and beliefs of the people who participate in the educational and social system. The role of educational administrators is to coordinate the activities of the persons and groups who participate in the educational process in the community with the objective of improving the quality of human life in society. Relevance should be the basic criterion that guides this activity.

The major stumbling block for educational institutions in promoting administrative responsiveness and relevance is the lack of competency among administrators in administering the multicultural population. Smith and Boyer point out that administrators have not been prepared to understand the motives, profiles, and perceptions of today's multicultural, multilingual, and multiethnic school populations. The administrators are effective when they develop a knowledge base regarding the mores and folkways of the persons and groups being served within the educational system. Preparation for administrators should include internships in settings that reflects ethnic and cultural diversity.

School administration serves individuals and society. The recognized human diversity reflected in school populations and the needs of the community must be taken into consideration when making curricular, structural, or policy decisions. Multicultural education is a useful frame of reference which school administrators can adapt to meet the needs of their diverse school populations.

See also Educational Goals and Objectives; Minorities and the School System; Minority Administrators; Student Culture.

—H. Prentice Baptiste, Jr.
University of Houston

References

Baptiste, H.P. (1980). *Multicultural teacher education: Preparing educators to provide educational equity.* Washington, DC: AACTE.

Sander, B., & Wiggins, T. (1985). "Cultural context of administrative theory: In consideration of a multidimensional paradigm." *Educational Administration Quarterly, 21*(1), 95-117.

Smith, J., & Boyer, J. (1984). "Educational administrative competency for multicultural populations." *Educational Considerations, 11*(2), 7-9.

NATIONAL ASSESSMENT OF EDUCATIONAL PROGRESS

The National Assessment of Educational Progress is designed to inform the American public about the proportion of American children and youth who are learning what the schools are expected to teach and about the changes in these proportions which have occurred over the years.

Origin

In 1963, Frances Keppel, then U.S. Commissioner of Education, found that there was no dependable information available to report to the people and the Congress about the progress being made by students in the nation's schools. Yet the primary duty of the commissioner as specified by the law is to report on the progress of education throughout the nation.

To remedy this deficiency, he asked Ralph Tyler, a veteran educator, to assemble a group of researchers in education to draft a plan by which this needed information could be periodically obtained. The resulting draft was reviewed and criticized by members of the commissioner's staff, by leading technicians in the field of educational evaluation and by leaders of educational organizations and associations. The revised draft became the basis for the work of the Exploratory Committee on Assessing the Progress of Education. This committee was asked to work out the details of the plan and develop the necessary instruments for assessment. Its work was supported by the Carnegie Corporation of New York.

What Learnings to Assess

Several problems were encountered in developing such an assessment. The first was to identify what the American people expect the schools to teach and what they expect the children to learn. The following procedure was developed to solve this problem.

Leading scholars in school subjects were asked to specify what in their subjects the schools should teach. These lists were then presented to school administrators and teachers at their professional meetings with the request that they identify from the lists those things that their schools were teaching. Finally, panels of parents and other citizens were brought together in four different regions of the country for a weekend to discuss this list of what school personnel reported they were teaching. Each panel was asked: Do you think this is important for students to learn? Is it something you want your child to learn?

The product of this procedure was a list of learnings considered important by scholars in the school subjects that were being taught in the schools and were considered important by parents and other citizens. These became the content of the assessment.

Assessment at What Age?

There is no common curriculum throughout the nation. In teaching reading in the primary grades, for example, some schools begin with phonics to help students attack new words. Others begin with oral words most children know and help the students to recognize these words in print. Still others follow different paths such as the structure of language.

Although there is no common approach used by all schools, by the end of the third grade, or age 9, all schools expect their students to have learned to read and comprehend simple readings such as fairytales, newspaper articles, and the directions for assembling toys. Hence, an assessment of nine-year olds should provide an indication of the number of children who have learned to read such simple prose. Similar situations exist in arithmetic, spelling, and writing.

There is no common curriculum throughout the country in the middle grades. However, most schools have similar expectations regarding the important things that students will have learned by the end of the seventh grade, or age 13. Therefore, age 13 was chosen as an age group to be assessed.

At age 17, most young people are completing high school, and an assessment at that age should furnish indications of the proportion of youth who have learned what the high schools are expected to teach. Finally, to obtain some information about the permanence of school learning, the assessment was planned to include young adults between 26 and 35 years of age.

Designing a Sampling Procedure

The plan called for the assessment of a probability sample of young people in each of the four major geographic regions of the United States, regions that are thought to differ in the educational attainments of their young people. To facilitate the work of the assessors, a geographic unit was chosen as the primary sampling unit. This unit was the attendance area of the public secondary school. All young people in that area were identified, those in public elementary and secondary schools and those in private schools. From this list the desired number of students was selected randomly. Dropouts were identified in residential samples.

Assessing Important Learnings

The best estimate of the time required if each individual student were to demonstrate validly and reliably what he or she had learned in a particular subject is fifteen hours. This included the time involved in performance testing as well as the time utilized in paper-and-pencil tests. Since it was not possible to obtain from most schools fifteen hours of testing time, the plan called for matrix sampling. Fifteen students were selected from each classroom. Each of them took a different one-hour test. In this way, in one hour the class could be tested by fifteen subtests which together would comprise the valid and reliable sample.

To reduce the influence on test results of reading skill in subjects other than reading, the National Assessment presents the directions and essential information on tape recordings which can be understood by poor readers as well as good ones.

The Initial Assessment

During the school year, 1969-70, the initial assessment was made. It included three subjects, but this number proved to be more burdensome than the assessment staff could shoulder. Since that time, only two of the ten subjects have been assessed each year. The reports of the assessments have been in terms of the percent of the particular group of students who answer the questions or perform the exercises correctly. These groups are (a) students from each of the four regions; (b) those from inner city, rest of the city, suburban fringe, small towns, and rural areas; (c) those whose parents have completed no more than the elementary school, the high school, some college; and (d) black students, nonblack.

On each subsequent assessment of the same subject, the results of previous assessments are included in order to show progress or lack of it.

Illustrative Assessment Results

The early assessments found that the groups of students in which relatively few were learning what the schools were teaching were those from families in which the parents had little or no education. Most lived in inner cities or in rural areas. Later assessments found that these groups made more progress from 1970 to 1980 than other students, a fact usually explained by the greater attention then given to so-called disadvantaged children together with increased resources allocated for their instruction.

The interest of the public and of policymakers in national assessment has been increasing, and the results reported are viewed by many as the educational scorecard of the nation.

See also Curriculum Development; Educational Goals and Objectives; National Reports on Education.

—Ralph W. Tyler
Center for Advanced Study in the Behavioral Sciences

References

Department of Elementary School Principals in Cooperation with NEA Center for the Study of Instruction. (1968). *National Assessment of Educational Progress: Some questions and comments.* Washington, DC: National Education Association.

Tyler, R.W. (1971). "National assessment: A history and sociology." In J. W. Guthrie and E. Wynne (Eds.), *New models for American education* (pp. 20-34). Englewood Cliffs, NJ: Prentice-Hall.

Tyler, R.W. (1986). "Assessing the educational achievements of large populations." In *Changing concepts of educational evaluation.* [Monograph]. *International Journal of Educational Research, 10,* (1, 91-97). [New series; formerly *Evaluation in Education: An International Review Series*]. Oxford, Eng. and Elmsford, NY: Pergamon Press.

NATIONAL ASSOCIATION OF ELEMENTARY SCHOOL PRINCIPALS

Founded in 1921 by fifty principals attending an education convention in Atlantic City, New Jersey, the National Association of Elementary School Principals (NAESP) was accepted as a department of the National Education Association a few months later. In 1970, members voted to return the association to its original status as an independent, autonomous organization.

The association serves more than 22,000 elementary and middle school principals throughout the United States, in ten Canadian provinces, and in 40 countries overseas. The schools administered by its members enroll approximately 30 million children in grades kindergarten through eight. The association's activities at the national level are buttressed by a network of state affiliates, all of which are represented through an elected board of directors.

Its major goals are to serve as an advocate for children and youth, especially by ensuring them access to an excellent education; promoting and maintaining high professional standards and creative leadership among principals; heightening public awareness of the early years as the foundation for all subsequent academic achievement; and representing the professional concerns of principals before national decision-making bodies such as Congress, the Executive Branch and its constituent agencies, and other education groups.

The association's activities have been stimulated in recent years by the "effective schools research" of the late 1970s and early 1980s which indicated that one of the critical components of excellent schools is strong leadership by the principal in setting high standards of performance for the staff and students. Accordingly, the association emphasizes professional development through vehicles such as its National Fellows program and seminars at its annual convention; the recognition of a National Distinguished Principal from each state, in conjunction with the U.S. Department of Education; advocacy through its federal relations program for the inclusion in mathematics and science legislation of funds for the training of principals; and an array of publications that stress the application of research to practical, daily problems encountered by principals.

Among the association's most important services to members is a Legal Assistance Program that has two broad purposes: to help members pay for legal aid in contesting job-related actions such as denial of due process and impending demotion or dismissal, and to insure members against financial liability in legal suits brought against them.

National Association of Elementary School Principals publications include *Principal*, an award-winning journal published five times a year; *Communicator*, a monthly newsletter designed to keep members informed of pending legislation and association activities; the biannual *Education Almanac;* and occasional studies such as *Standards for Quality Elementary Schools* (1984) and *Proficiences for Principals* (1986). These major publications are supplemented by frequent, year-round mailings that focus on single issues such as the content of successful early childhood education programs and teacher evaluation.

The association is headquartered at 1615 Duke St., Alexandria, Virginia, just across the Potomac River from Washington, D.C.

—Samuel G. Sava, Executive Director
National Association of Elementary School Principals

NATIONAL ASSOCIATION OF SECONDARY SCHOOL PRINCIPALS

The National Association of Secondary School Principals has grown from its original membership of 78 principals from seven mid-Western states in 1916 to its present 38,000+ membership from every state and 40 foreign countries. Originally located in a small office on the campus of the University of Chicago, the association is presently headquartered in its own building in Reston, Virginia.

Membership in the association includes a wide variety of people interested in secondary education. Although most members are principals and assistant principals in public, private, and parochial middle-level schools and high schools, a large number of members are teachers, department heads, central office administrators, professors of secondary education, and retired educators.

The association works cooperatively with and encourages membership in principals' organizations in the fifty states and the District of Columbia as well as overseas. In an additional effort to bring services to the members, a network of field consultants is sponsored to provide a direct link between the national office and the individual members.

Setting the association's goals, priorities, and policies is an 18-member board of directors. The board consists of two members from each of seven geographical regions of the country, plus two members elected at large—one a middle-level principal and the other an assistant principal. The president and president-elect of the association also serve on the board of directors. A steering committee composed of the president, the president-elect, and a board member chosen by the board acts as an administrative body to facilitate operations of the association between meetings of the board. Under the leadership of its executive director, a headquarter's staff of eighty persons works to serve the needs of the association members. The staff includes experts representing virtually every aspect of educational administration. The association sponsors opportunities for professional growth through conferences, institutes, and an annual convention.

Direct field service is available through the offices of urban services, professional assistance, professional development, research, and legal and legislative services. Members are represented in federal government matters through testimony, letters, and direct contact with congressional and administration officials. Publications help keep members abreast of the latest trends and current thinking in the field. These include the *NASSP Bulletin*, *NewsLeader*, *Curriculum Report*, *Legal Memorandum*, *Practitioner*, *Schools in the Middle*, *Tips for Principals*, *AP Special*, *School Tech News*, and numerous special monographs and research reports.

Major activities in the field of student activities include administration of the National Honor Society, the National Junior Honor Society, the National Association of Student Councils, and the National Association of Student Activities Advisors. Through its office of professional assistance, the association has developed fifty assessment centers in thirty-seven states and three foreign countries in cooperation with districts and universities in an effort to identify and select school administrators with the best potential for success.

Behind the National Association of Secondary School Principals' design for service are several goals: to provide a national voice for middle-level and high school education; to support promising and successful educational practices; to protect the security of middle-level and high school administrators; to provide for conventions and meetings of middle-level and high school educators; to conduct research of use to practitioners; to provide opportunities for the examination of important issues facing middle-level and secondary education; to influence federal legislation and maintain contact with federal agencies; to encourage student achievement and performance; and to cooperate with other administrator and educational organizations.

—George E. Melton, Deputy Executive Director
National Association of Secondary School Principals

NATIONAL EDUCATION ASSOCIATION

The National Education Association is the nation's largest professional organization, with 1.8 million members. Its mission is "to elevate the character and advance the interests of the profession of teaching and to promote the cause of education in the United States." Its objectives have remained constant since the association was founded in 1857.

Members of the association include men and women who work at every level of education. Almost three-quarters of the nation's elementary and secondary teachers are members, and the association also represents more higher-education faculty than any other organization. Administrators are members of many of the association's 12,000 affiliates, and three administrators currently serve on the board of directors.

Policies are determined by the delegates to the association's annual representative assembly. With 8,000 elected delegates, the representative assembly is the world's largest democratic deliberative body. The policies adopted by each year's representative assembly direct its work in local school districts, at the state level, and federally at the nation's capital.

Locally, members of the association work with school officials and community leaders to attract talented young people into careers in education. The members also work locally to achieve other goals and objectives. They engage in collective bargaining to improve salaries and working conditions for teachers. Among the association's community outreach projects is an effort to help the general public understand the educational resources which students need to succeed in their learning and development.

A variety of other projects that aim to explore new approaches to learning at the school building level are under way. Through the Mastery in Learning Project, for instance, school faculties in communities across the United States are piloting innovative learning strategies designed to redefine successful learning as more than just a passing grade.

Similarly, through Operation Rescue, local members are developing projects to rescue at-risk students from illiteracy and dropping out. The association regularly publicizes the strategies perfected at the local level by projects such as Operation Rescue as models for other communities to consider.

State governments are now the nation's primary source of educational funding, and, at the state level, members work to impress on state political officials the importance of full funding for education. National Education Association political activities seek to elect and return to office those candidates committed to providing local school districts the fiscal support essential to excellence in education.

At the national level, the National Education Association is the nation's premiere advocate for education in Washington, D.C.; its lobbying efforts on Capitol Hill have helped enact landmark legislation to ensure access to quality education for the disadvantaged (1965) and the handicapped (1975). In 1979, the association was the nationally acknowledged leader of the successful drive to create a United States Department of Education and assure education the cabinet-level voice and visibility it so long deserved.

It has also helped lead efforts to secure full civil rights for all Americans and has played a key role in fighting sex and racial discrimination in the nation's schools.

At the national level, the association sponsors programs designed to focus public attention on the needs of America's schools and colleges. By sponsoring annual observances such as American Education Week and network television advertising, it has raised the level of public support for education.

The association also serves as a leading national repository of statistical research about education. This research has provided timely information on topics as varied as class size and tax support for education for more than one hundred years.

In addition, it is also the nation's largest publisher of professional materials for educators. Its Professional Library includes over 300 titles for professional development. The Educational Computer Service, established in 1983, publishes the only teacher-tested systematic guidelines for evaluating educational software products.

The National Education Association is headquartered in Washington, D.C. For more information, write: The National Education Association, 1201 16th Street, NW, Washington, D.C. 20036.

—Mary Hatwood Futrell, President
National Education Association

NATIONAL REPORTS ON EDUCATION

International competition for economic and political advantage has brought a proliferation of educational recommendations that are broad in scope and intended for all public schools across the United States.

Specific technology required in domestic and foreign markets has raised political and corporate interest in the preparation of natural talent at the precollegiate level. Optimism among noneducators is very high with regard to the recommendations provided by national task forces and commissions.

This new enthusiasm has provided the synergism for an increasing number of governors to work closely with legislators to formulate state law for education. In turn, an attempt has been made by legislators to include educators from universities, the state department, local school districts, and state teacher and administrator associations. These well-intentioned cooperative ventures are not always harmonious during the formulation of new legislation. Each of the constituents has pride of turf and authorship. The resulting legislation in many states has not pleased all parties invited to participate in initial drafts for legislative review.

State school board members are the first link with national reports. Their responsibility includes an analysis of content and recommendations from national reports and their applicability to overall state educational goals. State school board members have the responsibility to act as a clearinghouse and connector between ideas initiated by national reports, legislation to follow up on the recommendations, and the local school board's policies for implementation.

Once approval has been given and the bills become law, considerable time must be given for public review and explanation. Follow-up by members of legislative committees and state department of education employees must take appropriate time to allow questions to be asked by rural, suburban, and urban board members, superintendents, principals, teachers, and volunteer groups interested in education. Sufficient lead time before legislation is implemented will assist in ownership and provide for budget appropriations at the state and local level.

National reports over the past decade have provided something for everyone and have not left many areas of public education untouched. However, demographics of education, kindergarten through graduate school, reveal two major problems which the national reports and recommendations do not adequately address.

First, an already large number of school-age minority students comprise the high-risk population who do not finish school and are among the increasing number of unemployed. In one example, recommendations resulting from existing national studies have focused attention on legislation for higher standards for high school graduation. For a majority of minority students, this action will bring added frustration for those not having success with present requirements and expectations. Only a few suggestions or recommendations have been made for assisting the high-risk student who is continuing to contribute to the increasing number of dropouts. Legislation being drafted at the state level in response to national reports also lacks measures to prevent or curtail the problem of students who do not graduate from high school.

Second, demographics indicate a short supply of youth available for jobs, precipitating a national interest in what schools should be doing for our country. An increasing number of the youths available for jobs in the future will be of minority origin. It is important that each state analyze existing, pending, and future legislation to see if provisions are included for assisting minority youth to be academically prepared for higher education and job-skill training. Strategies to carry out well-intentioned legislation fall far short at this time of influencing or making a difference to the individual student who has the potential for making a difference in the community, state, and country. Several disjointed efforts to ameliorate problems at the national, state, and local levels have not been addressed with regard to national reports or recommendations.

The effects of national reports on teachers under contract have been minimal at this time. The empowerment of teachers to have a larger role in decision making, as recommended by one report, has created a discussion of the relationship of empowered teachers and building principals. This discussion may change the present role of a principal as an instructional leader. This role has recently been in vogue as a style for practicing principals; it has been a role for those in preparation for principalships to emulate.

Minimally, other changes for teachers triggered by national reports are changes in certification practice, increased emphasis on periodic staff development, and regular utilization of testing to measure growth in academic achievement on objectives initiated at the state level.

Greater interest has evolved in testing and academic progress on the state level as a direct response to concerns aimed at public education by national task force reports. Classroom teachers are reporting a sense of anxiety caused by pressures from local and state boards of education adopting recommendations to study the individual classroom, school, and district academic-achievement results. The fact that comparisons are being made beyond the local level to composite comparative results for the nation is reinforcing anxieties. Initial reactions by teachers are generally negative in regard to limiting the curriculum focus to a state or national set of objectives to allow comparability of results.

Job satisfaction surveys conducted recently with classroom teachers indicated a majority of teachers are dissatisfied with their job. One of the more prevalent complaints was a lack of opportunity to present what teachers felt was an appropriate curriculum for local student needs, rather than one based on a national curriculum or conforming to the demands of a profit-making testing company.

A number of national reports have cited the need for changes and improvements in teacher preparation that should be considered by teacher preparation institutions. Classroom instruction, which includes the use of objectives and testing for results, can and will be included in the development program for new teachers. The inclusion of new methods of instruction and technique brought by new teachers will eventually infiltrate and reduce teacher anxiety caused by new requests and mandates emerging from national reports.

The national reports have promoted teacher and principal training institutions to initiate their own forums to discuss and report the needs and shortcomings in their existing programs for the training of treachers and principals. The inclusion of university and college personnel interested in educational issues provides an opportunity for an alliance between national agencies, state departments, and local school districts. Universities, through their research efforts, are suggesting productive alternatives and solutions to many problems plaguing public schools. The prospects are exciting for a unified effort in behalf of students who represent the future of the country.

National task forces and commissions are proving to be of invaluable service to everyone interested in education. Their reports and recommendations are making positive differences in our political and economic relations with other countries.

See also School Improvement and Effectiveness Movements.

—Donn W. Gresso, Vice President
The Danforth Foundation

References

Deal, T.E. (1985). "National commissions: Blueprints for remodeling or ceremonies for revitalizing public schools?" *Education and Urban Society, 17,* 145-46.

Goodlad, J.I. (1984). *A place called school.* New York: McGraw-Hill.

National Commission on Excellence in Education. (1983). *A nation at risk: The imperative for educational reform.* Washington, DC: U.S. Department of Education.

NATIONAL SCHOOL BOARDS ASSOCIATION

The National School Boards Association, headquartered in Alexandria, Virginia, is a not-for-profit organization whose primary mission is the general advancement of education through the unique North American tradition of local citizen control. In this way, public elementary and secondary school policy is decided by members of the local school board, the vast majority of whom are elected and are directly accountable to the community. The association promotes the betterment of education through services to state school boards associations and local school boards, by maintaining liaison with other education organizations and governmental authorities, by providing a national and federal forum for the local school board perspective on educational issues, by increasing school board impact on federal education laws and regulations, and in court cases relating to education.

Federation members are the 49 state school boards associations, the Hawaii State Board of Education, the District of Columbia Board of Education, and the Virgin Islands Board of Education. Nearly 1,900 local school districts are direct affiliates.

The association represents the interests of school boards before Congress; provides development programs for school board members; provides school district management services; and offers to the school board movement a variety of other services, including the annual convention.

The Federal Relations Network, comprising up to three school board members in each congressional district, plays a major role in the association's education-advocacy program in Washington, D.C.

Three major publications are produced by the National School Boards Association: the award-winning monthly magazine, *The American School Board Journal;* the monthly magazine, *The Executive Educator;* and the biweekly newspaper, *School Board News.*

Seven special groups play a significant role in the National School Boards Association's effort to serve school board needs:

—The Council of Urban Boards of Education focuses on serving the needs of urban school boards.

—The Council of School Attorneys focuses on issues of school law.

—The Large District Forum focuses on the needs of large nonurban school districts.

—The Rural District Forum serves the special needs of rural school board leaders.

—The Federation Member Executive Directors' Liaison Committee serves as the forum for maintaining relationships between the top administrative levels and the federation members.

—The Forum of Federal Policy Coordinators focuses on the administration of federally funded programs.

—The Conference of School Boards Association Communicators serves the needs of the Association and its federation members' professional communicators.

The National School Boards Association also maintains liaison with other groups, including the National Caucus of Black School Board Members, the National Caucus of Hispanic School Board Members, and the National Caucus of Young School Board Members.

The National School Boards Association represents about 97,000 school board members who serve the nation's 15,350 public school systems. Its policy is determined by a 150-member Delegate Assembly composed of active school board members from across the country. Translating this policy into action programs is a Board of Directors consisting of twenty members and four *ex officio* members. The executive director, assisted by a professional staff, administers programs.

—Thomas A. Shannon, Executive Director
National School Boards Association

NEEDS ASSESSMENT

Educational needs assessments provide information to be used to identify, set, refine, and select appropriate educational purposes and priorities. Needs assessments are accomplished through a process of involving educational partners—learners, educators, members of the community—to obtain data on gaps between expectations and performance. A "need" is a gap between *what is* and *what should be* in educational results. A needs assessment is a process for identifying, documenting, justifying, prioritizing, and selecting needs to be reduced or eliminated. From the resulting information, decisions are made concerning what to change, continue, and/or modify in the educational process.

An important distinction between means (how we do something and what we use to do it) and ends (accomplishments) must be maintained. A needs assessment addresses only gaps in ends, not gaps in means. Given the identified needs, appropriate means may be selected.

The following are ten general needs assessment steps:

1. *Decide to develop a plan using data generated from a needs assessment.* A plan is a blueprint for action which includes functions to be completed to meet selected needs. Planning, using needs assessment information, includes commitment by all planning partners to act, not just react to current demands and crises.

2. *Select the needs assessment and planning level.* There are three possible levels of needs assessment and planning. One is the course level which is concerned with the results of day-to-day teaching and learning. Another is the school level which has a focus upon completion of programs and the impact of the total curriculum. The third is the societal and community level, which is concerned with what learners are able to do, accomplish, and contribute to their society after completion of all the educational experiences and accomplishments.

3. *Identify the needs assessment and planning partners.* The planning partners will both guide the process and "own" it when it is completed. Appropriate partners include those (a) who will be affected by the results (students or inservice trainees), (b) who will implement the plan (educators), and (c) clients (or society), who receive the results. They should be nontoken representatives of actual constituencies.

The partners may supply judgments concerning perceived or sensed needs. However, when gathering needs information, an additional reality is critical: hard data-based needs derived from performance observations of the actual human and organizational gaps in performance.

4. *Obtain the needs assessment and planning partners' participation and active commitment.* Partners should be told what will be expected of them, when to act, what expenses will be paid, and the extent to which their contributions will be used. Affirm that, if any partners are not active participants, they will be replaced, and, if necessary, replace them. Commitment is demonstrated first by verbal acceptance and then by continuing actual contribution.

5. *Obtain acceptance of the needs assessment and planning level.* Have the partners understand and select one of the three levels of needs assessment and planning (step 2); each one should identify, define, and justify gaps in results between *what is* and *what should be*. By considering the array and advantages and disadvantages of the alternative frameworks, the partners will make a choice based upon what will be accomplished and missing.

6. *Collect needs data (both internal and external).* Internal needs data concern performance discrepancies *within* the education system (at the course and school levels); external (societal and community level) needs data concern performance discrepancies of completers (e.g., graduates) in their (and your) world. Both external and internal needs data should target gaps in results and should include the perceptions of the planning partners *and* the actual performance discrepancies collected from controlled, objective observations.

7. *List identified and documented needs.* Devise a set of agreed upon needs. Make certain that they relate only to gaps in results (at one or more of the "levels" of concern) and not with gaps in resources or methods. Substantial agreement should be obtained before moving ahead.

8. *Place needs in priority order.* The three partner (learners, educators, community) groups will prioritize the needs by (a) reconciling the sensed needs with those based upon the hard data; (b) deriving a common set of needs which are supported by both the hard and soft data (and request additional data if there are differences); and (c) setting priorities among the needs by asking, "What will it cost to reduce or eliminate the need?" and "What will it cost to ignore the need?" "Cost" may be seen in both financial and quality-of-life terms.

9. *Reconcile disagreements.* Differences among partners usually are based upon one or more individuals clinging to a pet solution, process, or course title and not being willing

first to examine gaps in results to which such "solutions" may be responsive. Such process-orientation may be reduced by asking, "What result will come about *if* your suggested method or solution is implemented?" Such a request to move from means to ends, repeated as often as required, will frequently focus the individual's attention on needs and not wants. Blockage to the resolution of disagreements usually flows from a desire of some to select a means before identifying and justifying a gap in ends (a "need").

10. *List problems (selected needs) to be resolved and obtain agreement of partners.* A problem is a need selected for resolution. No gap in results, no need. No need, no problem. Before completing this ten-step process, make certain that the needs assessment and planning partners agree to the final results and the selected problems. If they do not, revise as required by cycling back through the previous ten steps until substantial agreement is obtained. When there is agreement, publish the list and provide for the selected need and problems being used for further action and evaluation.

These ten steps provide a partnership-derived set of identified, defined, justified, and selected needs. From these, problems may be stated and defined as gaps in results to be closed. These will provide the criteria for measurable objectives which will serve as the basis for further planning and the identification and selection of justifiable methods and means to meet the needs and resolve the problems.

Many tools, techniques, and methods for needs assessment exist and may be used or modified (the references provide a useful starting place). When there are no sensible resources, designing one's own makes sense. Be certain, however, to identify and assess needs as gaps in results, not as discrepancies in money, people, methods, or other resources.

See also Curriculum Development; PERT; Planning.

—Roger Kaufman
Florida State University

References

Kaufman, R. (1982) *Identifying and solving problems: A system approach* (3rd ed.). San Diego, CA: University Associates.

Kaufman, R., & Stone, B. (1983). *Planning for organizational success: A practical guide.* New York: John Wiley.

Witkin, B.R. (1984). *Assessing needs in educational and social programs.* San Francisco: Jossey-Bass.

NEWS MEDIA

School officials and representatives of the local news media depend on each other to inform the community about what is happening in the schools. But this mutual dependence is not always beneficial, according to many educators, who complain that news coverage about schools often is negative. Indeed, stories about high dropout rates, low standardized-test scores, financial crises, and violence in the schools are common in newspapers and on radio and television news programs. Most school public relations experts agree that the kind of news coverage—positive or negative—that schools receive depends at least in part on how effectively school officials work with local reporters and editors.

The plain fact is that schools depend on the news media more than the media depend on schools. To work effectively with reporters and editors, several basic tenets about the news media need to be understood. First, the press is a basic institution in American society (or any democratic society). News people feel strongly about keeping the press free from government control, and they take quite seriously their role as watchdog over other public institutions, including schools. In this country, most news organizations are commercial operations, and, therefore, they generally publish or broadcast news that will increase their readership and thus improve business; what constitutes "news" is any new or unusual information the editor deems newsworthy, regardless of the impact the information might have on the schools and school officials.

Reporters are paid to bring in solid, accurate, balanced stories with colorful quotes from experts and parties involved in the stories. The point for educators: Recognize that reporters simply are doing their job when they pursue you for information and quotes. The perception among school leaders about the negative effects of press coverage persists despite evidence to the contrary: For example, a recent study of newspaper coverage about education showed that nine out of ten articles about local schools were either positive or neutral; half the school superintendents in the study, meanwhile, said news coverage about the schools was mostly negative.

News coverage of schools often comes down to a matter of perception; it therefore is to the school official's advantage to encourage good relations with local reporters and editors. The best way to accomplish this is to be honest and candid, and to speak in plain language, not the jargon of the education profession. Accessibility is essential: Reporters work on tight deadlines, and they usually need facts and comments quickly—sometimes at odd hours. It is wise as well as courteous to return reporters' telephone calls as soon as possible; school officials also improve the likelihood of getting accurate, complete, and balanced news stories if they respond promptly.

School administrators should attempt to know reporters by name and to try to accommodate their deadline schedules. Whenever possible, school administrators should provide reporters with advance notice of important school events. Some school systems, for example, send out press releases about upcoming school board meetings, specifying which agenda items are most important. Many school systems regularly send out press releases, make telephone calls, or produce video footage highlighting special achievements by students and the staff to spark ideas for news features; this works best if you schedule your contact with the press for a slow news day, when editors are more likely to be searching for stories. The key to getting news coverage, according to many school leaders, is making sure the news media are aware of the accomplishments and successes of students and the staff in the schools.

School officials who are experienced in dealing with the news media say it is wise to designate a school spokesperson to serve as press liaison. For example, many school systems make it a matter of school policy for the president of the school board to handle all press inquiries about key board decisions. In many school systems, all requests for information from the media must go through the superintendent or the schools' public-information officer.

An important part of building a good professional relationship with the news media is establishing trust. This means respecting the local reporter's sense of professional ethics and fair play. Rules of thumb include (a) never say "No comment"; (b) make available promptly on request any information that legally should be made available to local citizens; and (c) tell the whole truth, unless state sunshine laws prohibit discussion of a sensitive topic with the press. School leaders adept at working with the local press generally agree that it is not wise to request that information given to a reporter be kept "off the record." For one thing, reporters are not bound ethically to keep information out of the news. Some school officials effectively use the "backgrounder"—an information session, usually held to explain a sensitive issue, wherein reporters agree ahead of time not to identify their sources of information. It is best, also, not to ask to review a story before it is published or broadcasted; a better idea is to offer to clarify information or answer additional questions reporters might have. Additional advice from school officials and news media representatives: do not try to bribe reporters with gifts, exclusive stories, or invitations to social events; do not attempt to go over a reporter's head by complaining to the editor about a story; and do not blame reporters for headlines (they don't write them) or for

editorial positions taken by the news organization's management.

See also Public Relations; School-Community Relations; Student Newspapers.

—Kathleen McCormick
Washington, D.C.

References

National School Boards Association. (1982). *Becoming a better board member: A guide to effective school board service.* Alexandria, VA: Author.

National School Public Relations Association. (1985). *PR survival packet.* Arlington, VA: Author.

Saxe, R.W. (1984). *School-community relations in transition.* Berkeley, CA: McCutchan.

ORGANIZATIONS: PRINCIPLES AND THEORY

To many faculty members and administrators an organization probably represents little more than a place of work. However, organizations possess additional characteristics and functions that need to be understood if the theory and practice of education and administration are to be improved. In the following sections several major organizational concepts will be presented, followed by a discussion of how these concepts impact on the management of human resources.

Typologies for Classification of Organizations

Peter Blau and W. Richard Scott have classified organizations into four types on the basis of the primary recipients of benefits from the operations of the organization. These organization types include (a) mutual benefits associations, in which the membership is the primary beneficiary; (b) business concerns, in which the owners are the primary recipients of benefits; (c) service organizations, in which clients are the primary beneficiaries; and (d) commonwealth organizations, in which the primary beneficiary is the public.

Schools fit best into the category of service organizations and therefore face several problems typical of organizations within this category. First, the clients of a service organization, such as parents, may not know what will best serve their interests and so may be vulnerable to exploitation by and dependency on the professional. The professional must walk a fine line, on one hand being careful not to lose sight of the welfare of the client, through concern with status, career, or administrative problems, while at the same time being careful not to become a "captive" of the clientele, relinquishing power to decide what service will be provided. For example, the interest of students may not be served best by treating students like customers of a business concern and giving them whatever they want. Another problem often faced by service organizations concerns the sensitive nature of the professional-client relationship in which conflicts or problems of professionals may affect the well-being of clients.

Presenting a somewhat different view, Amitai Etzioni has classified organizations in terms of their predominant compliance pattern. In coercive organizations, lower status participants are controlled by the exercise of coercion, resulting in the alienation of these participants. Utilitarian organizations on the other hand depend more on remunerative controls over lower status participants; in turn, these participants are involved in a calculative manner. In normative organizations, legitimate control and a high degree of commitment by the lower status participants are evident. Colleges and universities fall into this normative category.

A third typology for classifying organizations has been proposed by Talcott Parsons. In Parsons' typology, organizations are classified in terms of their primary orientation, i.e., the primary goal and function of an organization within the more inclusive system, society. These organizational categories include (a) economic organizations, those oriented primarily toward economic production; (b) political organizations, those oriented toward attaining and allocating power; (c) integrative organizations, those contributing primarily to the efficiency of individual members of society, rather than the effectiveness of society as a whole; and (d) pattern-maintenance organizations, those designed to serve cultural, educational, or expressive functions. Parsons noted that all organizations that are integrated well into society serve all four functions to some degree; thus, these categories are based on primary function, not exclusive function. Schools fit best into the category of pattern-maintenance organizations since they serve primarily educational functions.

Daniel Katz and Robert Kahn have proposed a typology similar in some respects to that of Parsons. Classification is based on the major or geneotypic function—the nature of the work of an organization, or its activity as a subsystem of society. Productive or economic organizations are directed toward creation of wealth, manufacture of goods, and provision of services. Maintenance organizations are concerned with socializing people for roles in other organizations and in society. Adaptive structures are those designed to create knowledge, develop and test theories, and apply information to problems. Finally, managerial or political organizations are those directed toward controlling, coordinating, and making decisions about persons, other resources, and subsystems. In this typology, schools are classified as maintenance organizations; they socialize students for various roles in other organizations and society. However, research activities of universities also serve an adaptive function, creating knowledge and applying it to problems of society.

The four organization types described by Katz and Kahn are representative of four more general themes which underlie many different typologies for classifying organizations. If models are constructed to illustrate these general classifications (i.e., economic, political, adaptive, and maintenance), each model must include the influence of the other three themes. That is, the functioning of an organization which is primarily economic is influenced by political, adaptive, and maintenance interests. Similarly, functioning of a political organization is also influenced by economic, maintenance, and adaptive interests. Input and output differ among these four models according to relevant resources, needs, and goals. However, input for all four models must include human resources and their management.

When this general classification scheme is used, schools fit all four categories to some degree. Although not primarily economic, schools are concerned with preparing persons to be productive economically, and there is concern with producing a quality product—the student. Although not primarily political, schools are concerned with training citizens for future participation. Schools are easily classified as maintenance structures since another function is preparing replacements for members of existing structures. Finally, schools are also adaptive organizations, addressing the needs for efficiency and creating an evolving order.

Management of Human Resources

As noted above, human resources and their management serve as input in all four general models of organizations. Thus, many important functions of administrators concern personnel. For example, among major administrative functions described by Stephen Knezevich, several relate clearly to the management of personnel. The ability of an organization to pursue an objective requires the identification, employment, and assignment of human resources. In addition, personnel must be stimulated or motivated to move toward the objective. An administrator may also be called upon to diagnose and analyze conflict among personnel, to coordinate efforts of personnel, and to facilitate communication.

Many of the personnel problems faced by educational administrators arise from conflict between the bureaucratic structure and orientation of school and the professional orientation of teachers. The classic model of a bureaucratic organization is characterized by a hierarchical authority structure, division of labor with a high degree of specialization, a formal system of rules and regulations, impersonality, and emphasis on competency. Conflict arises because teachers with a professional orientation expect to be allowed greater autonomy and flexibility and place greater emphasis on individual client needs and interpersonal relationships.

The history of administrative theory shows a move away from classical organizational thought, characterized by the bureaucratic model, toward a human relations approach, focused on building and maintaining harmonious human relationships within the organization. In administrative theory, the human relations approach was followed by the behavioral approach, an adaptation and fusion of the classical and human relations approaches which also included findings from research in the behavioral sciences. In practice, however, most schools still fit, to some degree, the classic model of bureaucratic organization. Therefore, educational administrators must have special skills to develop strategies for meeting the basic needs of the organization in ways that minimize conflict with the professional orientation of the staff.

See also Administrative Theory; Bureaucracy.

—Gladys Johnston
Arizona State University

References

Mentzberg, H. (1979). *The structuring of organizations.* Englewood Cliffs, NJ: Prentice-Hall.

Parson, T. (1981). "Social Systems." In O. Grusky and G.A. Miller (Eds.), *The sociology of organizations* (pp. 98-109). New York: The Free Press.

P

PERT

Program Evaluation and Review Technique, usually identified by its acronym PERT, is a management tool developed in the late 1950s in the military and private sector and adapted to education in the 1960s. It is built around the central concepts of networking and systems analysis. A complex project may be broken down into its component parts, and then reorganized into a network of tasks which highlights the complex interrelationships among the separate tasks. In the reorganization, or system synthesis, interrelationships and interdependencies influence the sequences and time allocations made for each component task or activity. As these determinations are made, the notions of evaluation and review are introduced—and hence: Program Evaluation and Review Technique.

In 1957, the Lockheed Missiles and Space Company along with the consulting firm of Booz, Allen and Hamilton developed the Navy Fleet Ballistic Missile System by employing a prototype PERT. The concept was subsequently applied to government research and development projects which were first-time or one-time only efforts where no established routines or experience could be used as a basis for system synthesis.

The primary impetus for the application of PERT in an education setting came about with the work of Desmond Cook in 1964 under a grant from the U.S. Office of Education, "The Application of PERT to Educational Research and Development Activities." Early applications of PERT to educational projects included the planning and construction of a school building, developing a K-12 curriculum in mathematics, planning a school census, developing a summer maintenance program for school buildings, and designing a school tax levy campaign.

Steps in Constructing a PERT Network

Individual projects that might employ PERT are usually unique and therefore there is considerable variation in the nature of the steps used. However, general practice suggests the following:

1. The nature of the project and its objectives are clearly defined. The PERT chart has a discrete beginning and an end (achievement of the objective). Between the beginning and end are several intermediate objectives. Thus, in the initial plan explicit objectives are set forth and all the tasks and jobs necessary to accomplish the intermediate and final objective are identified.

2. A network is constructed using the tasks, jobs, intermediate objectives, and final objectives. This network shows the planned sequence of tasks leading to accomplishment of objectives, along with the interdependencies and interrelationships between and among tasks and objectives.

Networks are composed of activities and events. Activities are individual tasks or jobs which must be done to reach an objective. On a PERT chart they are illustrated by a line which depicts the time and work necessary to accomplish the objective. An event illustrated by a circle represents a start or end of an activity. Some events are milestone events (intermediate objectives or accomplished workpackages), while others are interface events. The latter are instances where two separate networks or subnetworks within a larger network incorporate an event common to both. For example, in constructing a school building the construction of footings must be completed before structural steel is erected, and both tasks must be accomplished before walls are laid up.

3. Time estimates are made for each activity leading to the completion of the task or event. Few if any projects do not have time constraints—earliest time for beginning and the latest time for completion. Major considerations in time estimates are (a) the relative firmness of these two constraints, (b) the relative activity of time estimates for the complex of activities leading to the completion of tasks and events between the beginning and the end, and (c) the recognition of constraints and dependency in the sequence of events. If all activities could occur simultaneously, then the time estimate for the entire project would be equal to the time estimate of the one activity of the longest duration. Thus, network construction must precede the time-estimate step.

In order to calculate a time estimate for the whole PERT system, one must recognize that considerable uncertainty exists in all nonroutine projects. Estimates reduce uncertainties in terms of the time required for accomplishing each event, and for accomplishing a series of events which have constraints or dependencies. Because of the latter situation, estimates must also be made in terms of the earliest time an event can be accomplished. In the same situation, it is also necessary to estimate the latest time an event can be accomplished without delaying the completion of the entire project. To illustrate these estimates, the critical path (or least time-consuming path) through the PERT network is determined. In nearly all projects one finds slack or free time in the critical path. The presence of constraints and slack time provides a cue for the evaluation and review—the E and R in PERT—of network adjustment in order to meet the overall completion deadline of the project.

Time estimates are made on two bases: deterministic, when one has previous experience with the task; and probabalistic, when uncertainty exists. Since PERT is usually applied to new or unique projects, some probabalistic estimates are usually required. These are derived from three estimates—optimistic, most likely, and pessimistic. A statistical procedure, the Beta distribution, is used to establish the expected elapsed time for each activity. It is

$$t_e = \frac{a + 4m + b}{6}$$

where m is most likely time, a is the optimistic time, b is the pessimistic time and t_e is the expected elapsed time.

4. After time estimates are made for each activity in the network, it is necessary to establish the activity starting time and completion time. A time estimate is computed. This establishes the earliest time an event can take place as well as the latest time which will still not delay the completion of the total project. Scheduling adjustments may involve adding resources, redefining activities, paralleling or eliminating activities, or modifying objectives of the project.

In recent years, the basic concepts of PERT have been operationalized with the incorporation of contemporary management concepts. This has increased its capability in dealing with complex planning projects. Management information systems are used to access a rich data base. Sophisticated computer programs can expedite the incorporation of projections and analyses of multiple alternatives as part of the evaluation and review phases of PERT. Multiple constituencies may now be involved in educational policy and decision making in an interactive mode. In short, the rationality of PERT can now accommodate many more alternative strategies to reach a given objective. In turn, these alternative strategies can be used to relate the programmatic feasibility to multiple alternative objectives.

See also Planning.

—Walter G. Hack
Ohio State University

References

Candoli, I.C. (1984). *School business administration: A planning approach* (chapter 3). Boston: Allyn & Bacon.

Cook, D.L. (1966). *PERT applications in education.* Washington, DC: Cooperative Research Monograph, U.S. Office of Education, Department of Health, Education, and Welfare.

Van Dusseldorp, R.A., Richardson, D.E., & Foley, W.J. (1971). *Educational decision-making through operations research.* Boston: Allyn & Bacon.

PARENT INVOLVEMENT

Researchers, practitioners, and policymakers have included parent involvement in their lists of components of effective schools. Acknowledgements of the importance of parent involvement are based on the following: Two decades of research on family environments reveal that children whose parents continually support and encourage their school activities have an advantage in school, and more recent research on the practice of teachers describes the positive effects which result when teachers involve parents. *Not all families*, however, know how to become involved in school-related activities and *not all schools* actively encourage and direct parent involvement. Indeed, there is little agreement on the most useful types of parent involve-

ment, or on how to solve the problems of designing, implementing, and evaluating successful parent involvement programs. From surveys of teachers, principals, parents, and students, from workshops with teachers, and from research, five main types of parent involvement have been identified in comprehensive programs for home-school relations.

Obligations of Parents

The basic obligations of parents involve the development of home conditions that change over the school years to support their children's growth and learning. Parents serve as managers, monitors, and socializers at home, usually without consultation with the school. Most parents meet their children's basic needs, although some may need assistance from administrators, teachers, or community social service agencies. Because parents vary in their experiences and skills, some schools take active roles in helping parents understand and build positive home conditions for their children's school learning and behavior. Schools keep in touch with parents by means of publications and workshops. They sponsor programs on parenting, child development, and home conditions. School personnel discuss with parents the practices that contribute to student success in school.

Obligations of Schools

A second type of parent involvement common to all schools is communication from the school to the home. The school has an obligation to inform parents about school programs and their children's progress, and parents are expected to act on the information they receive. All schools send memoranda, report cards, and notices of special events to the students' homes. Some districts offer computerized messages that parents can access by telephone to learn more about school programs and policies.

Surprisingly, large numbers of parents are excluded from some of the most common communications with schools. In our survey, more than one-third of the parents had no conference with a teacher during the year. About 60 percent never talked with a teacher by telephone. Although most teachers (more than 95 percent) reported that they communicated with some parents, most parents were not involved in deep or frequent discussions with teachers about their children's program or programs.

Parents of students at all grade levels need clear information on the objectives and specific skills for each subject each year; on grading practices and test results; on course requirements and consequences of course selections; on standards for promotion and graduation; and on other important district, school, and classroom matters.

School administrators and teachers can vary the form, frequency, timing, content, contacts, and likely results of information sent from the school to the home. They can influence whether the information can be understood by all parents and whether parents can work with school administrators and teachers if their children's attendance, grades, conduct, and coursework are not satisfactory. Communications can be designed to encourage and improve two-way communications from school-to-home *and* from home-to-school.

Parent Involvement at School

A third familiar type of parent involvement brings parents to the school building. This includes (a) parent volunteers at school and in classrooms; (b) parent attendance at school events to support their children's efforts; and (c) parent participation at meetings and workshops to build personal skills.

There are benefits from parent volunteers and participants at the school building. Teachers and the staff are assisted in classroom management, instruction, or nonteaching duties, and they see that parents are interested in school improvement. Our research suggested that having some parents active at school influenced teachers to request other parents to conduct learning activities with their children at home.

Parent Involvement at Home

The fourth major type of parent involvement is assistance with learning activities at home. This type of parent involvement may occur with or without specific advice and direction from teachers.

General Skills. Parents may be asked to assist the child to build skills that are useful in school, but that do not duplicate the teacher's efforts. The teacher may request parents' assistance to help students learn to manage study habits, follow school routines, develop problem-solving skills, good sportsmanship, shopping and budgeting abilities, to critique television shows and other media productions, and to build or improve other social and personal skills. Or, the parent may be asked to reinforce certain school-related behaviors using a schedule of rewards set up in cooperation with the teacher.

Specific Skills. Parents may be asked to assist their children in reviewing, completing, or extending specific skills that students are working on in class. Students could receive help in reading, science, art, music, mathematics, language arts, social studies, and other subjects. Our researcher asked: What happens when teachers engage all parents—not just those who know how to help on their own—in learning activities at home with their children? We studied fourteen techniques that teachers use to involve parents with their children in reading, discussing, tutoring, signing contracts, and playing learning games. Parents learned how to teach the child at home by observing teachers in the classroom.

Effects on Teachers' Practices. Teachers reported widespread use of techniques that involve parents with their children in reading-related activities. Principals tended to encourage teachers to involve parents in reading activities more than other subjects. Teachers who frequently used home learning activities were able to involve parents of all educational backgrounds—college education, high school, or less than a high school diploma. Other teachers claimed that parents who had less education lacked the ability or willingness to help their children with learning activities at home.

Effects on Parents. Parents who were frequently involved by teachers in learning activities at home (a) recognized that the teacher *worked hard* to involve parents; (b) received *most of their ideas* from the teacher on how to help their children; (c) felt that they *should help* their children at home; and (d) *understood more* this year than last about their child's education. Parents rated these teachers higher in

teaching ability and interpersonal skills. Principals, too, recognized teachers who were leaders in the use of parent involvement by rating them higher, overall, in teaching ability.

Effects on Students. We studied the effects of teachers' use of parent involvement on a small sample of students for whom fall and spring achievement test scores were available. With important characteristics statistically controlled, students made greater gains in reading achievement if their teachers frequently used parent involvement. We did not find this pattern for gains in mathematics scores which tended to be influenced by other school and family factors. Also, fifth-grade students whose teachers and parents used frequent parent involvement practices reported more positive attitudes toward school, more similarity and familiarity between the school and their family, and they did more homework on weekends.

Grade level was the most important influence on teachers' uses of parent involvement at school or at home and on parents' feelings of confidence about helping their children. Teachers of first-grade students made more frequent uses of parent involvement than did teachers of third- or fifth-grade students—a trend that worsens in the middle and high school grades. However, many parents help their children through high school with or without instructions from teachers, and many more—across the grades—would benefit from directions from their children's teachers on how to help with specific skills needed for progress and success in school.

Governance and Advocacy

A fifth type of parent involvement includes parents in decision-making and activist roles in governance and advocacy groups.

Governance. Parents participate in the PTA/PTO or other organizations, formal and informal school committees, Parent Advisory Councils (PACs) or other councils at the school, district, or state levels. These groups may work as advocates for children by supporting school improvement plans, helping to formulate school policies, reviewing school budgets, conducting fund raising, observing community relations, and participating in political awareness activities. The decision-making bodies are part of the official structure, under the leadership of school, district, or state administrators.

Advocacy. Independent advocacy groups, unions, or clearinghouses are typically initiated and supported by parents and other citizens who are interested in maintaining and improving the quality of the public schools. These groups serve as self-directed reviewers, reporters, and, some say, "loving critics" to provide parents and others in the community with information about schools and other educational issues. They may analyze budgets, conduct workshops, work to increase funding, review legislation, or serve as "watch dogs" for school fairness and against discrimination in desegregation, special education, bilingual, and other policies and practices. Although advocacy groups are independent of the schools, they are often involved in cooperative efforts with schools in the interest of school improvement.

Conclusion

The five types of involvement are not mutually exclusive. In a comprehensive program, all types of parent involvement will be effectively practiced, and all parents at all grade levels at least will be involved in purposeful communication with the school and in the education of their own children. We are only beginning to understand which types of parent involvement lead to specific student, parent, and teacher outcomes. Administrators can help teachers successfully involve parents by coordinating, supporting, funding, and rewarding cooperative, on-going programs of parent involvement.

See also Community-School Involvement; Parent Teacher Association, National; Parent-Teacher Conferences.

—Joyce L. Epstein
The Johns Hopkins University

References

Epstein, J.L. (1986, January). "Parents' reactions to teacher practices of parent involvement." *The Elementary School Journal, 86,* 277-94.
Gordon, I. (1979). "The effects of parent involvement in schooling." In R.S. Brandt (Ed.), *Partners: Parents and schools.* Alexandria, VA: Association for Supervision and Curriculum Development.
Rich, D. (1985). *The forgotten factor in school success: The family—A policymaker's guide.* Washington DC: The Home and School Institute.

PARENT TEACHER ASSOCIATION, NATIONAL (NATIONAL CONGRESS OF PARENTS AND TEACHERS)

The National PTA—the National Congress of Parents and Teachers—is the nation's oldest and largest child-advocacy association. The PTA was founded in 1897 to help parents learn to be better parents, to protect children, to strengthen the home-school relationship, and to support our nation's schools.

In local communities and across the nation, the National PTA advocacy has been instrumental in supporting compulsory public education, including kindergarten; establishing the juvenile-justice system; starting hot lunch programs in schools in order that all children would have at least one nutritious meal a day; field testing the Salk polio vaccine; leading the fight against drug and alcohol abuse by young people; speaking out for adequate funding for public education; and challenging the use of public funds for nonpublic schools.

Today the 6.1 million PTA members, organized into more than 26,000 local units in the 50 states, the District of Columbia and U. S. Department of Defense schools abroad, sponsor programs and activities that address many of the same issues that concerned the PTA's founders. Through PTA, parents and teachers are carrying out programs to improve the lives, health, and safety of our nation's children and to help them become responsible citizens. In addition, the PTA continues its tradition of striving for excellence in education and assuring that access to an excellent education is open to *all* children.

Among current activities of the National PTA are programs to support our public schools, educate parents about AIDS, prevent drug and alcohol abuse, and assure that each child has the opportunity to participate in cultural activities. There is so much that parents need to know today—so much that PTA can help them learn. Therefore, PTA has programs and publications to help parents start their chil-

dren on the right road to learning, raise self-disciplined children, safeguard their latchkey children, and talk to their children about the important decisions that they must make as they grow up and learn to deal with their sexuality.

Also, because every recent study on excellence in education has found that one of the major factors that makes a school effective is the degree of parent and community involvement, PTA has developed programs to help parents play a constructive role in the schools and take an active part in their children's education.

PTA membership is open to everyone, with or without children. When members join a PTA, they become an important part of a national network of parents, teachers, school administrators, and people who care about children. Working together through the PTA these millions of members can accomplish much more than they could alone or in groups that are not a part of a nationwide effort. In today's shrinking world, our children's lives are shaped by what happens to *all* children. The PTA's commitment, therefore, is to work for all of America's children, those in our members' homes and local communities and those living thousands of miles away.

The PTA sponsors three national observances—National PTA Child Safety and Protection Month in November, National PTA Drug and Alcohol Awareness Week the first full week of March, and Teacher Appreciation Week the first full week of May. It cosponsors American Education Week in November. There are two National PTA offices—the national headquarters in Chicago and an Office of Governmental Relations in Washington, DC.

For more information, write to the National PTA, 700 North Rush Street, Chicago, IL 60611.

—Ann P. Kahn, Past President
National Congress of Parents and Teachers

PARENT-TEACHER CONFERENCES

Parent-teacher conferences are as familiar as school itself. For many teachers and parents, the conference is the only time they share for discussing their mutual interest—the child. Almost all teachers meet with some parents each year, but they do not confer with the parents of all the children in their classroom. More than one-third of the parents surveyed in Maryland did not confer with their child's teacher during a school year.

Types and Purposes

There are two main types of parent-teacher conferences—group and individual. *Group conferences* include "back to school night" meetings, workshops or discussions on special topics, or grade level meetings. These are used to discuss programs, policies, and issues of importance to all parents and children. *Individual conferences* focus attention on one child's work and progress to increase the parent's knowledge about the child as a student, to increase the teacher's knowledge about the student as a child, and to identify academic or other problems that need improvement to increase the student's success in school. Individual conferences may be *informal* (parents may come unannounced to teachers' regular "office hours" or before or after school) or *formal* (scheduled on a day or evening when the students are excused from school, or at any time at the request of the teacher or the parent).

Both types of conferences are important at all grade levels, but in many districts there are no formal structures for meetings between secondary school teachers and parents. Some districts have taken aggressive and important leadership to include elementary, middle or junior high, and high schools in their conference days. They have tested and improved procedures to schedule and coordinate parents' visits with teachers of several academic subjects in secondary schools (see references from Indianapolis and Houston Public Schools).

Improving Individual Conferences

Conferences can be beneficial meetings or perfunctory rituals. Some schools and districts have made advances in the organization of parent-teacher conferences in elementary and secondary schools to involve more parents and to make the conferences more productive. There are structures to guide teachers and parents in useful activities *before* the conference, *in conference*, and *after* the conference.

Before the Conference. Parents must know about the conference schedule well in advance. They may select the time for their conference, or choose among alternatives provided by the teacher or coordinator of parent-teacher conferences.

Because time is usually limited, it is important for teachers and parents to plan the agenda. Teachers may use a standard form to list questions and concerns and to summarize specific information about each student to discuss with each parent (e.g., achievement test scores, report card grades, attendance record, homework completion, classroom behavior, etc.). Parents could be provided with a similar form to prepare a list of their own and their children's questions and concerns prior to the conference. Administrators and teachers may prepare a list of questions that parents are likely to ask and may distribute these to parents to assist their planning.

To meet the needs of parents and to increase attendance at conferences, some districts provide special services, including transportation, baby sitting at the school, translators for non-English-speaking parents, evening hours, and conferences for noncustodial parents of children from single-parent homes. Some districts conduct media campaigns, using public service radio, television, billboards, newpapers, advertisements, and public relations programs to publicize the importance of attending the conference and to ask businesses to permit parents to take a few hours off to attend conferences at school.

In Conference. There are many topics for parents and teachers to discuss that are important for student success in school in addition to the traditional overviews of achievement test scores and report card grades. These include the student's rates of progress from the beginning of the year in different subjects, parent and teacher expectations for the student, student's social skills, interactions with peers, personal development, special interests and talents, work habits, attitudes, attendance, behavior, participation in class, homework and home responsibilities, and specific academic and behavior problems that need improvement, including parent involvement in learning activities at home coordinated by the teacher to improve students' skills.

Teachers have the major responsibility to establish good rapport with each parent. Teachers should assume the parent is caring and helpful, and that the parent will follow through on plans that they develop together and that are clearly presented. Parents can often provide new and useful information to teachers on the child's special talents, interests, and strengths; the parent may suggest ways for the teacher to deal with weaknesses. It is a general rule of good conferencing for the teacher to stress the child's positive qualities and then constructively discuss any important areas that need improvement. If problems are identified, specific action plans must be made to correct them.

Conferences should be carefully timed to give each parent equal time. If more time is needed, the conference may be continued on another day or, evening, or by phone. Each conference should conclude on a positive and friendly note.

After the Conference. The teacher and parent should talk with the student about the conference, each stressing the importance of meeting the other, emphasizing the positive assessments that were exchanged, and discussing areas that need improvement.

The real work begins *after* a parent-teacher conference. The teacher, parent, and student must be ready to work toward the successful completion of agreed-upon plans for improvement. This requires continued parent-teacher communication about the student's instructional program, additional work to be completed at home with assistance or supervision from parents, and periodical evaluations of the student's progress and success.

Teachers and parents should evaluate the conference, including their satisfaction with their use of time, the quality of the information obtained and given, new knowledge gained about the family or about the school, the specific plans to help each child, arrangements for follow-through on the plans for improvement, parent's willingness to attend the next conference, and other suggestions for improving conferences in the future.

Teachers should also evaluate the conference procedures. Have all the parents of all the children in the class attended a conference? Was the scheduled time adequate? The teacher should assess the additional needs of parents that were revealed at the conferences. Thought should be given to any changes which seem to be needed in the forms used to prepare for the conferences and to evaluate the conferences.

Principals or coordinators should synthesize the evaluations from teachers and parents and discuss suggested changes with the staff. School administrators and teachers can work together to locate, adopt, or redesign conference procedures that work in other schools or districts; and to establish useful schedules and evaluations in their own schools.

The Need for Research

What types of conferences or what combinations of meetings are most successful for increasing parent-teacher communication and for improving students' skills and behavior? How can each school get the greatest number of parents to confer with teachers in ways that help the students? Research that addresses these questions is not available. Anecdotal evidence suggests that conferences are useful for improving parent, student, and teacher attitudes, and for boosting student effort and achievement. With an impressive media campaign and support from businesses to permit working parents to visit the schools, the Houston School District reported 63 percent of all secondary students' parents and 77 percent of all elementary students parents attended formal individual conferences on a designated Conference Day. Research and evaluation (including annual small scale, in-house studies by school staffs, and large-scale comparative studies by research scientists) are needed on conference structures, processes, and their effects on teachers, parents, and students.

See also Parent Involvement.

—Joyce L. Epstein
The Johns Hopkins University

References

Epstein, J.L. (1986). *Effective parent-teacher conferences: A summary of school practices.* Baltimore: The Johns Hopkins University Center for Social Organization of Schools. Parent Involvement Series, PI #12.
Houston Independent School District. (1985). "Operation failsafe: Involving parents in career decision-making." In J. Frymier (Ed.) *Methods for achieving parent partnerships, Project MAPP.* Indianapolis, IN: Indianapolis Public Schools.
Indianapolis Public Schools. (1985). "Parents in touch conferences." In J. Frymier (Ed.) *Methods for achieving parent partnerships, Project MAPP.* Indianapolis, IN: Author.

PERSONNEL POLICIES

Public education within the United States is a state responsibility rather than a federal obligation. States have delegated a substantial amount of this responsibility for education to local boards of education. These local boards act as agents of the state and assume much of the responsibility for actually operating a local school system.

As agents for the state, school boards must employ a large number of personnel to carry out their mission. In fact, the single largest employer in most towns, cities, and counties is the local school board. Given the large number of employees required to operate a school district, it is not surprising that school boards spend a considerable amount of time on personnel issues.

The actual time spent on matters relating to personnel by local boards of education has been estimated by some authorities to be greater than the actual amount of time spent on any other single aspect of the educational process. Local school boards acting as agents of the state are responsible for the procurement of new employees for the district, the management of existing employees within the district, and the termination of employees leaving the district. To execute these personnel responsibilities in an equitable and an efficient manner, school boards should rely on formal personnel policies.

The content of formal personnel policies should reflect the philosophy of the board and should be broad enough to cover most issues occurring with respect to a particular personnel practice. Each policy should be codified and placed in a binder which is made available to all those of concern. The advantages of having acceptable and accessible personnel policies will outweigh by far the disadvantages of not having formal personnel policies.

Advantages of Personnel Policies

Formal personnel policies can serve as an avenue of legal defense for local boards of education. When a legal issue occurs due to a personnel action taken by a local board of education, the first source of data sought both by attorneys and by courts is the local board of education's policy pertaining to the issue under contest. If the local board of education has adopted and has followed the policy and if the current policy does not violate existing federal and state legislation, then the policy can be used to defend the personnel actions taken by a local board of education.

School districts are dynamic rather than static entities, and over a period of time both new school board members and new employees must be inducted to fill the roles vacated by others. The transition and the orientation of these new persons can be facilitated by formal personnel policies. Personnel policies serve as a source of historical information, provide direction for current actions, and communicate future expectations.

For many personnel issues a single correct answer does not exist and local boards of education have at their disposal a considerable amount of discretion. The actual choice of one alternative over another alternative should be based on the policies of local school boards. Personnel policies of local school boards provide direction for choosing an alternative that is either consistent with previous actions taken by local school boards or congruent with goals newly established by local boards of education.

Finally, formal personnel policies facilitate administrators in carrying out their responsibilities. To operate a school system in a manner consistent with the philosophy and the expectations of a local board of education, school administrators must develop personnel procedures and must expend funds to implement these procedures. Personnel policies provide administrators direction for developing personnel procedures and authority for spending monies.

Policy Development and Evaluation

Formal personnel policies of the school board are different from personnel procedures developed by school administrators. The former should be abstract and should reflect the philosophy of the local school board while the latter should be operational and should provide the method and the means for executing the philosophy of the school board. When the line between policies and procedures becomes blurred, neither instrument will function appropriately. Policies become too restrictive and procedures become too inflexible.

To establish effective personnel policies, the school board must make sure that the development and the evaluation processes operate concurrently. Either school board members or school district personnel must identify a specific need, and this need must be evaluated by both groups. The groups must determine if the identified need is addressed by existing policies, is reoccurring, or can be fulfilled by a simple administrative procedure.

Once a genuine need for a formal personnel policy has been established, the local school board should direct school administrators to prepare an initial draft of a proposed personnel policy. In preparing the draft of the proposed personnel policy, school administrators might confer with outside consultants having special expertise in the area, with state school board associations having archetypical policies on the topic, and/or with other school districts having developed similar policies. After the proposed policy has been drafted, the draft is submitted to the local school board for modification or for tentative approval.

When the local school board has given tentative approval to the proposed personnel policy, the proposed policy should be circulated throughout the school district, and reactions should be solicited from all employees. Feedback obtained from employees should be considered and evaluated by the local school board, and directions for preparing a second draft of the proposed personnel policy should be given to school administrators. This draft must be reviewed again by the local board of education and should be submitted to the local school board attorney for legal verification.

After the local school board attorney and the local school board members have concurred with respect to the draft, formal action in an official school board meeting is required to adopt the personnel policy. To insure that the personnel policy has been implemented correctly and that the personnel policy continues to serve the need for which it was established, the policy should be reviewed on a periodic basis. By incorporating within each personnel policy a sunset procedure, the local school board can provide a schedule for revising the policy.

See also Principal Selection; Rights, Teachers' and Students'; Staff Evaluation; Teacher Selection.

—Marvin J. Fruth
University of Wisconsin-Madison
—I. Phillip Young
Ohio State University

References

Castetter, W. (1986). *The personnel function in educational administration.* New York: Macmillan.
Harris, B., McIntyre, K., Littleton, V., & Long, D. (1979). *Personnel administration in education.* Boston: Allyn & Bacon.
Patten, T. (1977). *Pay: Employee compensation and incentive plans.* New York: Free Press.

PHI DELTA KAPPA

Phi Delta Kappa is an international professional fraternity for men and women in education. The membership is composed of recognized leaders in the profession and graduate students in education whose leadership potential has been identified. Members include classroom teachers, school administrators, college and university professors, and educational specialists of many types. In Phi Delta Kappa, however, they find a fellowship based on common interests and ideas devoted to the promotion of free public education.

The purpose of Phi Delta Kappa as stated in the fraternity's constitution is as follows: "The purpose of Phi Delta Kappa shall be to promote quality education, with particular emphasis on publicly supported education, as essential to the development and maintenance of a democratic way of life. This purpose shall be accomplished through the genuine acceptance, continuing interpretation, and appropriate implementation of the ideal of high-quality leadership through research, teaching, and other professional services concerned with and directed to the improvement of education, especially of publicly supported and universally available education."

There are currently 625 Phi Delta Kappa chapters throughout the United States and Canada, including Puerto Rico, the Isthmus of Panama, and Guam, as well as international chapters in the United Kingdom, West Germany, Korea, Belgium, Thailand, Italy, Okinawa, and the Philippines. Approximately half the chapters are based on college or university campuses within graduate departments of education. The other half are community based. Membership in good standing is approximately 130,000.

Phi Delta Kappa has an educational foundation which was created in 1966, when George H. Reavis, an outstanding Kappan and Ohio educator, made a large gift to Phi Delta Kappa. Reavis envisioned that the foundation would provide resources to expand greatly the fraternity's programs. The foundation is incorporated as a nonprofit charitable organization and is directed by a five-member board of governors. Three are appointed by Phi Delta Kappa's Board of Directors and two are appointed by the dean of the Ohio State University College of Education.

Some of the programs funded by the Phi Delta Kappa Educational Foundation are sixteen Fastbacks annually, two Monographs annually, Reavis Reading Areas, Gerald Howard Read International Seminar Scholarships, Scholarship Grants for Prospective Educators, Cooperative Workshop Series, Distinguished Lecturer Series, Fastback Author Lecture Seminars, Staff Associate Program, District Conference and Biennial Council Foundation Lecturers, Gabbard Institute on Issues in Education, and Annual Summer Writing Workshops.

As of 1986, the endowment of the foundation was $1,750,000. A fund drive is conducted annually among the membership to increase the endowment. Annual contributions exceed $300,000.

—Lowell C. Rose, Executive Secretary
Phi Delta Kappa International

PHYSICAL EDUCATION

An important part of the elementary and secondary school curriculum is the program in physical education. This program should offer developmental physical activity in sport, dance, play, and exercise. The program should provide an understanding and appreciation of a variety of sports and physical activities, and the relationship that these movement experiences have with healthful living. School board members and administrators can make an important contribution to the success of the physical education program by scheduling daily physical education, providing adequate facilities, and supporting excellent instructional practices.

The Need for Physical Education

A vital need for physical education, K-12, is apparent when a connection is drawn between the ability to move and the ability to learn. Students who participate in a regular and vigorous physical education program are more alert and ready to assume an attitude of learning. It is important for students to experience a balance between work and revitalizing activities such as those found in physical education. An awareness of this kind of balance provides an excellent example of how stress-relieving activities can enhance the quality of day-to-day living.

Moreover, there is a need for programs which encourage students to work well together and promote positive experiences in physical activity. Such programs offer a variety of physical skills that challenge and encourage students to progress physically and emphasize leadership, fair play, teamwork and a genuine concern for other students.

An Exemplary Program

School districts are challenged to offer quality programs that provide equal opportunity for all students in physical education. School officials must allow these programs sufficient time during the school day. The scheduling of physical-education classes in accord with organizational convenience may not provide enough time for students to experience a continuous, full program of physical education. If physical education is to become an integrated and meaningful part of the total curriculum, students must participate on a regular basis and receive credit for the successful completion of this class experience. An excellent program should provide daily physical education, K-12, taught by a certified teacher in physical education. Units must be of sufficient length to allow real, not superficial, skill development. Without confidence through competence, it is unlikely that students will enjoy participation.

In addition, school districts should recognize the need for adequate and safe teaching facilities that allow for a variety of activities to be offered to meet the needs and interests of all students. These facilities should include the following teaching stations: gymnasium, outdoor playing fields, swimming pool, dance area, and weight room.

Trends in physical education underscore the importance of individualizing levels of activities for students. Students who are more familiar with certain skills may pursue higher level activities, and those who need more help with the beginning skills should participate in appropriate and progressive learning activities. Physically handicapped or special education students may be scheduled into many of the regular physical education activities; students with more limiting disabilities should have a special class in physical education. When students experience individualized programs that challenge their bodies and minds, they feel better about themselves as individuals, and this benefits other areas of school instruction.

The traditional emphasis of physical education programs has been on competitive team sports. The new emphasis is on a balanced curriculum which stresses individualized instruction, student involvement, innovative programs, equalization of opportunity, and utilization of community resources. The inclusion of lifetime sports and fitness activities complements the individualized emphasis in the curriculum. Lifetime sports such as swimming, tennis, golf, cycling, racketball, cross-country skiing, badminton, dance, archery, camping, canoeing, orienteering, and sailing are examples of activities for the curriculum. Orientation and participation in fitness programs should take place throughout the K-12 curriculum. An understanding of the human body and how it responds to and benefits from exercise and activity are important competencies for students to achieve.

Suggested Delivery Systems

The most important aspect for the realization of quality programs is the physical education teacher. An excellent teacher should be a role model epitomizing personal health and fitness, enjoyment of sport and physical activity, fair play, and sensitivity to student needs. It is the teacher's task to develop and provide activities that are relevant to the knowledge, attitudes, and values of the students.

The physical education teachers within a school district should coordinate a sequential arrangement of activities, K-12. Students should participate in activities which help them develop basic forms of locomotion and participate in low-organized games and rhythms in the early years, dis-cover and develop their physiological and psychological potentials, develop skills in lifetime sports, enjoy physical activities and desire to participate throughout a lifetime in healthful movement activities, and demonstrate positive ideas about social behavior and interactions while participating in sports.

In planning lessons, teachers should organize activities so that all students are actively participating during the major portion of the class period. Specific plans for further lessons should be guided by an awareness of current progress and interaction and involvement of the students. All students may not be of the same skill level or progress in the same manner. The utilization of handicap systems, differentiated goal setting, and organizing teams based on skill and experience are ways to work with different ability levels. Since it is impossible for the teacher to be attentive to all individual differences at one time, it is beneficial to utilize team teaching, teacher assistants, or student leaders in working with small groups.

A continuing responsibility of the school administrator and the physical education administrator is evaluating the physical education program to determine to what extent objectives are being met and to identify areas of the learning situation that need improving. In developing the criteria for check lists or other appraisal instruments, the following aspects of the program need to be considered: program activities, time allotment, class size, facilities and equipment, budget and quality of instruction. Self-evaluation, evaluation by peers, evaluation by supervisory personnel, and evaluation by students should be encouraged to provide information for refining and improving the existing curriculum and instructional program.

See also Curriculum Development; Curriculum Evaluation; Health/Fitness Education.

—Martha Bagley
University of Wisconsin-Milwaukee

References

Getchell, B. (1986). *Physical fitness: A way of life.* New York: Macmillan.

Nichols, B. (1986). *Moving and learning: The elementary school physical education experience.* St. Louis: Times Mirror/Mosby College Publishing Co.

Wessel, J.A. & Kelly, L. (1986). *Achievement-based curriculum development in physical education.* Philadelphia: Lea & Febiger.

PLANNING

The chief purpose of administrative planning is to provide direction for an organization. Planning always occurs within a context that provides limits for the planning process. These limits must be understood so that planning neither (a) exceeds the limits and thereby produces irrelevant and impossible goals, nor (b) is needlessly restricted by erroneous assumptions of narrow limits. Planning gives the administrator a valuable tool to keep the organization from merely drifting along, its course determined primarily by external factors.

A related corollary purpose of planning is to allow the administrator to achieve goals in an effective and efficient manner. Planning enables the administrator optimally to select, combine, and direct resources to goal achievement. It enables the avoidance of excessive false starts, duplication of effort, and other causes of resource attrition.

The Planning Team

There are some types of planning that the administrator can do effectively without involving anyone else. Individual planning is often the most suitable tool for short-range planning, planning that involves only the administrator's personal resources, and planning in pursuit of clearly articulated and validated goals. Personal plans and techniques of time management are examples of this type.

However, most significant organizational planning generally requires a planning team. There are two reasons for this. The first reason stems from the fact that effective planning is generally dependent upon access to the best, most relevant information. Different people are generally the best sources of relevant information, either because of their personal knowledge and expertise or because of their access to sources of relevant knowledge. For example, in the case of planning a new pupil personnel policy, the school counselor very likely would furnish both. A second reason for using a team for planning is that the plan will eventually be implemented. (At least this is the intention of planning.) The conformity of plan implementation to the original intentions of planning will to a large extent be a function of the faithfulness with which the plan is monitored. People who have been involved in the development of a plan will have a vested interest in its implementation and are likely to be highly effective monitors of that implementation.

The composition of the team should reflect both these concerns. Ideally, the team should include everyone who has a stake in the process that is being planned or in the outcomes of the process. Obviously, to include everyone will not always be possible; but the administrator should select a team that includes representatives from the various points of view and sources of knowledge that have relevance for the plan and from the various groups that will be affected by the implementation of the plan.

Since different planning areas require different expertise and have different impact targets, it is reasonable to expect that planning for different organizational concerns will require different planning teams. This concern for obtaining the best expertise for each planning area, however, must be balanced against the administrator's need for consistent, comprehensive overall planning. The administrator needs to ensure that different plans are neither redundant nor conflicting.

A possible solution to balance these two concerns is the formation of a central planning team made up of the chief sources of general expertise that have a vested interest in the ongoing welfare of the entire organization. For example, a principal of a large high school may form a central planning team consisting of him/herself, the assistant principals, the department chairs, the student affairs coordinator, the programming director, and the president and another representative from the parents' association. To strengthen the planning efforts of this team in particular areas, additional members, with more limited planning responsibilities, may be recruited from representatives of feeder schools, community agencies, or whatever other groups and organizations can contribute to or will be impacted by the planning process.

The Planning Process

The first step of the planning process is to clarify the purposes of the process. This basically requires seeking some significant answers to what is, on the surface, a simple question: "What is it we are trying to accomplish?" Or, as it's more commonly phrased: "What are our goals?"

This question is deceptively simple. The search for goals is too easily constrained by what the organization has done in the past. Many of the current troubles of high schools can be traced to the operating assumption that they are in the business of keeping students in school until they graduate rather than the business of preparing them for a changing society that recognizes multiple literacies and a personal adaptability as the prerequisites for success at any level. Effective planning builds upon the foundation of a successful identification and clarification of the relevant goals of the organization.

One useful procedure that has been developed to help a planning team systematically generate and compare goals combines elements of the Delphi Technique and the Q-Sort. In applying these combined procedures, each member of the planning team, using both personal expertise and that of sources to which he or she has access, generates a list of goals for the total organization or for the specific area under consideration for planning. Separate lists are then aggregated into a single list which is submitted to individual team members to distinguish (using Q-Sort methodology) between more important and less important goals until the single most important goal is distinguished from a cluster of second priority goals which in turn are separated from goals of lesser importance. Prioritized clustering of goals takes place until all goals on the list have been accounted for. These individual rankings are then recorded, aggregated, and returned to team members, showing them their own rankings and the group's rankings of each goal. Team members are then asked to consider their individual rankings in light of this group information and once again proceed through the Q-Sort to rerank the goals. The summary information on the reranked goals serves as the basis for the team's final analysis, discussion, and decision regarding the specification and prioritization of the goals to be pursued in planning.

Hoyle describes two other techniques for planning: the Nominal Group Technique and the KIVA Method. The Nominal Group Technique, in certain situations, will enable the planning team to reduce effectively the amount of time required for planning. This technique proceeds in five steps: (a) the silent generation of goals by individual team members, (b) the oral sharing of individual goals with the entire team, (c) the group clarification of goals, (d) an initial vote and discussion of voting results, and (e) the final vote to give direction to the group. The KIVA Method fosters integrated longitudinal planning by having different groups of team members serve as past, present, or future "experts" to present independently relevant historical background, current events, and future scenarios to the other members of the team. These separate presentations are then considered as a whole by the entire team as the basis for planning.

Any of these techniques or their combinations and variations may be valuable to the planning team, but none of them is magic. They will be productive only to the extent that planners are committed to a search that will generate and honestly examine the merits of the full range of organizational goals. Two somewhat opposite considerations are pursued by all these techniques. On the one hand, the fertile generation of goals is promoted by protecting the independent and often creative thought of individuals. On the other hand, a consistent and coherent direction for the organization must be achieved. The successful planning process is one that uses specific techniques to serve both these values.

Implementing the Plan

A final step in planning is the determination of who is responsible for monitoring the implementation of goals and how information on implementation will be reported back in order that plans can be modified. It should be noted that persons with particular responsibilities will do subsequent detailed planning, as individuals or in small groups. Economic allocation of resources can be achieved if this subsequent detailed planning is guided by appropriate techniques such as the Gannt Chart or Program Evaluation and Review Technique (PERT).

It is also important for the planning team to consider how pursuit and achievement of the separate goals will affect each other. For this purpose, the team is well advised to construct a cross-impact matrix with all the team's designated goals listed in prioritized order along both the horizontal and vertical axes of the matrix. Each cell in the matrix should contain the team's prediction of how each goal listed on the horizontal axis will affect each goal listed on the vertical axis. We can then examine each row of the matrix (designated for a particular goal) to see how the columns (i.e., the other goals) are likely to affect it. These anticipated impacts, and others which emerge, should be monitored as the plan is implemented. Such a strategy paves the way for effective evaluation of the organization's operation.

See also Needs Assessment; PERT; Problem Identification.

—David A. Erlandson
Texas A&M University

References

Erlandson, D.A. (1976). *Strengthening school leadership.* Danville, IL: Interstate Printers and Publishers.
Hoyle, J.R., English, F.W., & Steffy, B.E. (1985). *Skills for successful school leaders.* Arlington, VA: American Association of School Administrators.
Naisbitt, J. (1982) *Megatrends.* New York: Warner Books.

PRESCHOOL EDUCATION

Preschool education is the education of children before first grade. This includes kindergartens, nursery schools, child-care programs, and programs for children with special-educational needs.

Preschool programs are designed to increase children's intellectual, social, and language competence and to provide them with skills in self-expression. Preschools also prepare children for the elementary school as well as for participation in society at large. In many ways the preschool acts as a bridge between a child's family and the larger community. Child care centers provide extended day preschool programs to serve children of parents who work. Head Start and similar programs provide education, health, and social services for children from low-income families. There are also preschool programs available for bilingual children and children with various handicaps.

Although various forms of preschool programs have much in common, they have developed independently. Friedrich Froebel originated kindergarten in Germany in about 1835. The original program was aimed at helping children understand the unity of man, God, and nature through a set of symbolic activities. Manipulative materials (*gifts*) were used in prescribed ways along with arts and crafts activities (*occupational*) and songs and games.

Froebel's ideas were brought to America by German immigrants in the 1850s. English-speaking kindergartens developed shortly thereafter. By the beginning of the 20th century, kindergarten education was offered to poor children by philanthropic agencies. Public schools and other agencies were also providing kindergartens. With the development of the child study movement and progressive education, kindergarten programs were reformed to conform to American concerns and to new views of children's needs.

The nursery school, developed in 1911 by Rachel and Margaret McMillan in England, was designed to serve the needs of poor children. Health, nutrition, and social services were provided along with education. As nursery schools developed in America, they tended to serve more affluent children and became primarily education oriented. The Montessori method developed in Italy at about the same time, also originally to serve poor children. Its focus was on education of the senses, along with teaching reading and writing and providing exercises in practical life.

Child-care centers were first established in the 1850s as places to care for children, with little concern for their education. Since then, all such centers provide an educational component, although much of the long day is given over to the feeding, resting, and recreation of the children.

Preschool programs are sponsored by a variety of public and private agencies. Kindergartens are most often found in public elementary schools, as are preschool programs for handicapped children and programs for special populations of young children. Nursery schools, Montessori schools, and child-care centers are usually sponsored by private agencies as nonprofit or profit-making enterprises. While most kindergartens—like nursery schools—operate as half-day programs, schools are increasingly offering full-day kindergarten programs. Prekindergarten programs are also increasingly being offered by public schools.

The proportion of children enrolled in preschool education has been steadily increasing over the past decades. In 1960, for example, fewer than 30 percent of all 3- to 5-year-olds were enrolled in preprimary programs. In 1984, over 36 percent of all 3- and 4-year-olds and more than 92 percent of all 5-year-olds were enrolled.

Learning in Preschools

Many preschool programs use play as a learning medium to enable children to learn about their inner and outer worlds. Children use play to organize what they learn, creating conceptual schemes and developing new modes of self-expression. Activity periods support play; children play in different classroom centers. A block-building area allows children to create wooden block constructions, using various toy accessories. Children act out various adult roles in a dramatic play area, reflecting roles at home and in various community activities. An arts and crafts center allows children to draw, paint, build, and shape two- and three-dimensional constructions. An area is set aside to allow children to use manipulative materials such as puzzles, pegsets and mathematics materials. A music area offers musical instruments, records, and a place to listen or move to music. A library area provides a quiet space to acquaint children with printed language materials. Preschools also provide outdoor space for active play, such as running, climbing, or digging in a sandbox.

Play activities alternate with quieter activities in the daily schedule. As children grow older, there is less emphasis on play and more on required activities in the preschool. Children take the responsibility for caring for themselves and the environment. The children's world is extended as excursions are taken beyond the confines of the school. Opportunities for learning in the areas of literacy and numeracy are also provided. A good preschool program is rich in resources and learning opportunities.

In recent years, a range of preschool program alternatives have developed, including those with an emphasis on academic learning. Program models differ in goals as well as in curriculum experiences offered and teaching methods used. Some programs are built upon specific developmental theories; others have a more eclectic base. There is no clear evidence that one program approach is better than others. In addition, the different goals and values underlying alternative programs make comparisons a problem.

Preschool Teachers

Preschool teachers are predominantly women. Public school teachers are generally prepared in four-year college or university programs; they receive state teaching certificates. Nursery school teachers and child care practitioners may be prepared in four-year college programs, in one-to-two-year community college or vocational programs, or in high-school vocational programs. Requirements for these practitioners are embedded in the state licensing regulations for centers.

Recent Developments

Research over the past few years has demonstrated that preschool education can have pervasive and long lasting effects, especially for educationally at-risk children. This knowledge has led to the increased availability of preschool programs. States are stepping up support for full-day kindergartens and prekindergarten programs. In addition, the continued increase in the number of mothers of young children who are working has intensified the need for child-care services. As the number of young children continues to expand in the years ahead and as their educational and other needs receive added attention, one can expect to see continued growth in the field of preschool education.

See also Compensatory Education; Elementary Schools; Head Start.

—Bernard Spodek
University of Illinois

References

Consortium for Longitudinal Studies. (1978). *Lasting effects after preschool.* Washington, DC: U.S. Government Printing Office.

Evans, E.D. (1975). *Contemporary influences in early childhood education.* New York: Holt, Rinehart and Winston.

Spodek, B. (Ed.). (1982). *Handbook of research in early childhood education.* New York: Free Press.

PRINCIPAL SELECTION

One of the most important personnel decisions made in any school district is the selection of a building principal. There is a high level of agreement among practitioners, researchers, and policy makers that the leadership of the building principal is an essential ingredient for successful or excellent schools.

Practices followed in the recruitment, interviewing, and selection of a building principal must be in accordance with appropriate federal and state statutes, and with locally adopted policy statements and the provisions of negotiated contracts. Discrimination with regard to members of a *protected class group* must be avoided (i.e., discrimination on the basis of race, color, religion, sex, national origin, age, or handicapping condition is not permitted). Affirmative action practices to recruit applicants from protected class groups are recommended and, in some instances, may be required. Unqualified persons, however, do not need to be employed simply because they are members of protected class groups.

Qualifications and Predictors

One of the first steps in the selection process is determination of the qualifications which will be required of applicants for the position. Some requirements may be "necessary, but not sufficient," i.e., applicants may be excluded from consideration for the vacancy if they do not possess required levels of training or do not meet requirements for professional licensing or certification. Other qualifications listed should be selected on the basis of known levels of validity about the degree to which these qualifications serve as *predictors* of principal performance in the school or school district. Each school district must refine and validate its own system for selection of principals, and the predictors used must be ones which have been shown to permit selection of principals who meet district expectations. A highly successful principal in one school or school district may be only mediocre, or even unsuccessful, in another school district. Thus, predictors which have proven to be successful in one district may or may not be appropriate for use in another district.

Predictors used for principal selection should have *content validity*, i.e., the predictors should relate in a direct manner to the knowledge, skills, and behaviors necessary for job performance. Predictor validation for a specific school or school district requires the assessment of the relationship between potential predictors of principal performance and criterion measures of actual performance of principals employed in the job.

Since few school districts have established the predictor validity of qualifications used in principal selection, most districts would be best advised to use a *compensatory model*, rather than a *multiple-cutoff* model, in evaluating qualifications of applicants. In a multiple-cutoff model, a low rating on any single qualification may lead to exclusion of the applicant from further consideration. In a compensatory model, a rating is given to each applicant for each of the qualifications listed, and a single score is computed for each individual; thus, a high rating for one of the qualifications may compensate for a low rating on another qualification.

The predictors most used by school districts in principal selection are application data or data from the resume or vita, letters of recommendation or reference forms, transcripts of academic and professional training, and structured or unstructured interviews. Other predictors might include achievement tests, documentation of past performance, or data from an applicant's participation in an assessment center. On-site visits or observations are also used by a number of school districts.

Recommended Practices

Several predictors should be used. These predictors should be identified by the school district before applications are solicited. Requirements which will exclude an applicant from further consideration should be noted in the job announcement; these requirements should be limited to levels of required academic preparation and eligibility for required licensing or certification if local validation of other predictors has not occurred. A standard process for evaluation of academic credentials, with a definition of ratings to be given to either or both academic grade point average and the content of the preparation program, should be established and used if academic credentials are to be included in the qualifications. A standard rating scale should also be used for evaluating related professional work experiences, if prior experience is to be used as one of the qualifications. (Caution should be exercised in using prior work experience as a basis for excluding an applicant from consideration since this might, in some instances, be *prima facie* evidence of discrimination if experience has not been validated by the district as a predictor.) A standard application form, with the same types of information requested of all applicants, is preferable to the use of individually submitted resumes or vita.

Structured interviews should be used rather than unstructured interviews. If a commercially available structured interview is used, available data about the interview's content validity, predictive validity, and lack of disparate impact among protected class groups should be known before the instrument is used in the selection process. Use of multiple interviews, and multiple interviewers, is recommended. Directions or training in the rating of an applicant's responses in an interview should be provided, if possible, to persons who will conduct interviews.

The finalists for a job might be selected on the basis of standard ratings given to evaluation of academic preparation, evaluation of academic performance, evaluation of an application form, ratings of related work experiences, and ratings given for structured interviews. For those selected as finalists, participation in an assessment center would be recommended. The National Association of Secondary School Principals Assessment Center, available in most states, is designed to assess skills required for building administrators. This Assessment Center has carefully documented ratings with high levels of content validity and predictive validity for persons placed in roles as principals. Information from an assessment center, in combination with ratings from the screening process and ratings of other predictors (e. g., on-site visits, achievement tests, and documentation of past performance) can provide comprehensive information for use in the selection of the successful applicant.

See also Administrator Effectiveness; Administrators, Beginning; Principalship.

—Edgar A. Kelley
Western Michigan University

References

Heneman, H.G., Schwab, D.P., Fossum, J.A., & Dyer, L.D. (1983). *Personnel/human resource management*. Homewood, IL: Richard D. Irwin.

Schmitt, N., Noe, R., Meritt, R., Fitzgerald, M., & Jorgenson, C. (1985). *Criterion-related and content validity of the NASSP Assessment Center*. Reston, VA: The National Association of Secondary School Principals.

PRINCIPALSHIP

If one person is to embody the purpose, programs, and atmosphere of a particular school, that person is the principal. The principal is not only the controlling authority by virtue of the position but must also be the instructional leader. The demands made of principals and schools in general have escalated with society's widespread demand for quality, both in schools and school systems; quality is society's criterion of school effectiveness. The principal is the one person who is directly involved in every aspect of the school's operation and is responsibile for that "quality." The efficiency and effectiveness of a school rely directly on the principal's performance. Outstanding schools have outstanding principals.

What is it that makes a principal "outstanding," "effective," or "efficient?" Countless books, articles, research projects, and personal opinions are permeated with specific practices and traits that are shown to be characteristic of "good" schools and "good" principals. These elements can be broadly categorized into professional and personal skills. The principalship can be examined by these dimensions to ascertain the critical elements in the principal's role.

Professional Skills

The principal may be viewed as an administrator, supervisor, or manager of the school. The specific practices that are observed, categorized, and learned in preparation programs or in continuing professional development can be subdivided into the areas of curriculum, instruction, supervision, evaluation, organization, finances, and political processes. These areas—the traditional "functions"—for which a principal is responsible comprise the elements which are found in job descriptions; they encompass the knowledge and skills which are covered in employment interviews and performance assessments. Collectively, however, they constitute a myriad of proficiencies the principal needs to possess to perform the job in a capable manner.

Curriculum. A school's curriculum runs much deeper than the stated goals and objectives for the subject areas or particular courses. First, a principal must have extensive knowledge regarding students' growth and development. At what point are children ready to begin to read? What expectations should be held for adolescent boys and girls? How important is the desire to complete high school for all students? These questions illustrate that, if principals are to work with students, they must know students' needs and development patterns in order to shape a "relevant" curriculum.

A concomitant area that must be addressed prior to the development of a curriculum is the consideration of the particular community's values and goals. For a school to be responsive to a locale, the values and goals of that community must be manifest in the school's curriculum.

After the students' needs and community's values have been assessed, a curriculum of concepts and skills can be established for subject areas or particular courses utilizing a staff with interest and expertise in the curriculum areas. The principal needs to coordinate these initial elements; monitor the content and sequencing; keep abreast of major curricular shifts in emphases; be familiar with the curricular materials, particularly regarding possible controversy or challenge; and provide the necessary resources for support of the curriculum.

Instruction. Even the most well-planned curriculum will be ineffective without proper instructional techniques and strategies. The historical roots of the principalship come from that of the head of the school being the "principal" or master teacher. The principal must be an expert in the teaching-learning process. The validated principles of teaching and learning must be delineated, understood, and applied to ensure that all students' achievements match their potential. Teaching methods and strategies must be regularly observed and assessed, with feedback given to teachers to identify strengths and weaknesses in their teaching skills. An understanding of teaching styles and students' learning styles must be developed with appropriate matches being made. The principal needs to apply scheduling and grouping practices which effectively meet the needs of the students and the staff.

Throughout the instructional process, the principal should set and model expectations that all students can learn and that all teachers can provide the necessary instruction for optimal learning to occur. A safe and productive climate for instruction to occur needs to be established and maintained as a cooperative school project, with the principal being the key figure.

Evaluation. Once goals and objectives have been established for the curriculum and for the instructional process, including students' and teachers' performances, a determination must be made whether or not those goals are being met. Assessments are conducted through a variety of means, both formal and informal; the assessments cover students' achievement, staff performance, and curricular goal attainment. With that objective data, decisions are made regarding assistance and remediation plans, staff development, employment retention or dismissal, and alterations or modifications of the curriculum. The evaluation process should always be viewed as a helpful one, aimed at personal or organizational improvement, not negative or destructive. Care should always be taken to follow properly established evaluation policies and procedures and adhere to due process for all evaluations of students, staff, or program. Also included in the principal's evaluation process should be self-examination of the principal's performance.

Organization. Within the area of administration, organizational tasks can be viewed as the major ones carried out by a principal. With organizational tasks kept in the proper perspective, a principal can organize the school's day-to-day functions and pay the necessary attention to the other domains.

The principal is the key determinant in the conceptualization and enactment of the school's mission. The allocation and arrangement of a staff in such a way as to accomplish that mission is a vital function of the principalship. Acquiring a competent staff is an essential factor in that mission. If a principal is skilled in the recruitment, interviewing, selection, assignment, and orientation of a staff, his or her job is made considerably easier and more enjoyable by being surrounded by capable and skilled teachers. Once the staff is acquired, the organizational structure and administrative arrangement of the school must be set to work toward the mission and meet the needs of the students, the staff, and instructional program.

Additional considerations in the organizational domain include the collection and use of school and student data, the development of effective and equitable schedules, and the oversight of the operation and maintenance of the physical plant.

While the principal has primary responsibility to the school, he or she must be constantly aware that the school is a part of a larger organization—the district, state, and national educational systems. Procedures and policies which are consistent with existing policies, contractual agreements, and legal parameters should be developed and implemented.

Finances. The fiscal responsibility of the principal varies widely from district to district, but a few elements are universal. The principal must understand the district's budget. The principal's responsibilities include planning, preparing, and defending the school's budget. A budget is merely a dollar representation of the school's program; budget allocations for particular areas should represent corresponding instructional program emphases. The resultant school budget is then managed within the allocated resources, utilizing cost-effective practices at all times. The final fiscal duty of a principal is to interpret the budget priorities and constraints to the staff and community.

Political Process. The principal generates public support for the school's program and represents that program in an effective manner. Principals analyze and communicate with the local community, work with parents and citizens in resolving community issues, and establish positive relationships with the home, school, and the district. An understanding of the local, state, and national political scene is crucial in this endeavor. Principals must be able to work with local boards of education, legislators, and government officials at all levels to represent the school's and education's agenda. Knowing how the system works and being able to use that information for the benefit of the school is a vital ingredient in an effective principal's performance.

Representing the school to the community and the larger educational society is paramount. Clear, concise, correct communication, both written and verbal must occur. Necessary pertinent information should be shared with all interested or affected parties to keep them informed regarding school happenings.

These professional skills cover a wide array of competencies which a principal must possess to be an effective administrator. But a capable, proficient principal has an additional dimension.

Personal Skills

The style or charisma of a principal can set the climate or "culture" of the school. The principal who is eager to improve, not satisfied with the status quo, open to new ideas, and avid to learn regulates the tone of the building. This individual is more than the administrator, supervisor, or manager; he or she is the commanding authority and influence of the school. Particular traits and skills which are considered personal skills fall under the areas of leadership, communication, and group processes.

Leadership. The nature-nurture issue of leadership is not to be resolved here—whether leaders are "born" or "made"—but it is a fact that the principal's leadership is essential for schools to be productive. For leadership to be effective, there needs to be "followership." An effective principal inspires all concerned to join in accomplishing the school's mission, applies effective human-relations skills, and establishes cohesiveness among the staff members to work toward a common goal. In addition, he or she encourages the leadership of others and involves staff, students, and community members in the decision-making process as appropriate. Responsibilities are delegated. Human, material, and financial resources are identified and creatively utilized to achieve the school's goals.

A pervasive element in all of this is the principal's vision as to where the school should be in the scheme of the community. A principal who has that vision, is able to articulate it, and, most importantly, can enlist others to pursue it is a leader.

While working toward that end, a principal must continually assess the situational context and adjust his leadership style accordingly. Different situations require different behaviors, either directive, facilitative, supportive, or participative. As effective leaders, principals vary their styles from a demand for immediate action, to helping someone get the job done by providing the resources, to expressing encouragement and appreciation for other's efforts, or to working actively with individuals and groups.

Communication. The image principals project tends to form the perception of the school itself. Principals must understand how to make that image an effective and useful one. Clear and concise verbal and nonverbal messages need to be given so that the message is understood by the intended audience. Facts and data should be applied to clarify or defend positions in an objective manner. The philosophy, functioning, and practices of the mass media should be understood. Principals persuasively articulate their beliefs and effectively defend their decisions. Besides being adept at expressive communication skills, principals need to practice astute receptive communication. A principal must be a careful listener if he or she is to hear others clearly and interpret thoughts perceptively. High-level thinking skills are demanded. Foremost in the entire realm of communication is a consideration of others. A principal models the behavior which he or she expects of others.

Group Processes. Although the principal is an essential figure in the school's operation, he or she is not the only one in the school! Many other people are involved. The proficient principal is one who capitalizes on the commitment and energies of his or her assistants to assure schoolwide accomplishments. Others need to be involved in setting short- and long-term goals. Principals have to resolve difficult situations by the use of conflict-resolution methods. Various decision-making techniques need to be utilized. The staff, students, and community should be involved in decision making; they should be involved according to their interest, expertise, and constituency in particular situations. They should have something to say about a consensus or a conclusion. The principal also serves to motivate the school to achieve intended outcomes.

The principalship involves a complex interaction of professional and personal skills. A principal with vision and with the ability to carry out the school's goals can make an enormous difference in a school. He or she has much to say about the achievements of both the faculty and the students.

See also Principal Selection.

—Robb E. Rankin
Granby Elementary School
Granby, Colorado

References

Lipham, J.M., Rankin, R.E., & Hoeh, J.A. (1985). *The Principalship: Concepts, competencies and cases.* New York: Longman.

National Association of Elementary School Principals (1986). *Proficiencies for principals.* Alexandria, VA: National Association of Elementary School Principals.

PRIVATE SCHOOLS

Private schools are so diverse in purpose and governance that they defy neat definitions. These differences often lead to misconceptions. For some people, private school means a segregated school; for others, private means parochial or church-sponsored; still others think private education is by definition antidemocratic or socially exclusive. Even private school people themselves confuse the terms "private," "nonpublic," "independent," "parochial," and "denominational."

The common characteristic of private schools is governance under private rather than public auspices. A definition based on the absence of public funding is inadequate, because varying, although small, degrees of tax aid may go to private schools. With that aid go small and subtle degrees of public control; governance, on the other hand, remains private regardless of sources of funding or control.

Various names have been used to describe these schools. At one time the preferred term was "nonpublic," because "private" seemed too exclusive. The term "nonpublic" implied "*anti*public" to some, and most private schools do not want to be labeled as opposing public education. The term currently being used is "private education," referring only to K-12 education; as a reflection of that preference, the Office of Nonpublic Education in the U.S. Department of Education is now called the Office of Private Education.

The Council for American Private Education, a coalition of fifteen private elementary and secondary school associations is the central agency to speak for private education. Representing schools which enroll more than 85 percent of all private school students, the council includes the National Catholic Educational Association and the U.S. Catholic Conference (3.2 million students); the National Association of Independent Schools (316,000 students); the Lutheran Church-Missouri Synod (183,000 students); the National Society of Hebrew Day Schools (85,000 students); the Seventh-Day Adventists (75,000 students); and other small groups such as the American Montessori Society and the Friends Council on Education. The remaining 15 percent of private-school enrollment is largely found in the fundamentalist Protestant schools, smaller denominational schools, and the alternative school network.

Elements of Private Schools

The executive director of the Council for American Private Education defined the common elements of private schools as follows:

1. Each private school is different and, in diverse ways, autonomous. The differences, for example, between two Quaker schools anywhere are as great as between a

public and private city high school. No two of the ten thousand Catholic schools are alike; independent schools are appropriately named.

2. Private schools, regardless of the absence of denominational affiliation, emphasize the character and moral development of the student at least as much as academic training. This is not surprising, given the religious underpinnings of the vast majority of the schools and the strong tradition of character building that has been central to private schools since their colonial-period beginnings. Two factors which aid private schools to pursue this objective are (a) the strong commitment within the school community to both human and academic excellence as goals of the school and (b) the freedom to pursue these goals in ways which work best in each school.

3. Private-school teachers demonstrate levels of commitment beyond their relatively low levels of compensation. Although many have never had formal teacher training, the qualities most frequently exemplified are those of commitment to growing children and knowledge of the subject he or she teaches. The teacher's life-style and personality are viewed as integral components of good teaching.

4. Private schools view size as a critical factor in their effectiveness. The small size of many private schools contributes to an atmosphere or climate which facilitates the development of interpersonal relationships (students learn at least as much from each other as they do from teachers), the ability to introduce innovation and change, and the establishment of conditions in which performance and accountability are closely tied to each person's feeling of concern for the success of the school.

5. Private schools tend, both because of the denominational ties and traditional academic orientation, to be vitally concerned with imparting to students a common body of knowledge and ideals.

6. Private schools are able to select their own students. On the one hand, private schools exist primarily, but not exclusively, to serve the children of particular segments of the population. On the other hand, there is a conscious decision made by parents about their children's schooling—a situation that usually results in a general agreement with and enthusiastic support for the school's goals and style by school families.

7. Most private schools have a strong commitment to the enrollment of minority students. Millions of dollars are being devoted annually to scholarship aid for minority children by private schools. Because of their commitment to strong academic and moral education, private schools are increasingly sought after by minority families, particularly blacks.

8. With only 11 percent of America's school children enrolled in them, private schools are themselves clearly a minority. On occasion, they present points of view which are distinct from those held by a majority of citizens. In fact, many of the constitutional cases involving private schools have to do with matters of conscience and often unpopular belief.

Private education is characterized by private governance, wide diversity among schools, the autonomy of individual schools, a concern for character and a moral context for learning, teacher commitment, size which facilitates personal relationships, tradition as a source of common values and learning, selective admission, and commitment to minorities and minority opinion.

See also Religious Schools.

—John C. Esty, Jr., President
National Association of Independent Schools

Reference

Esty, J.C. (1982, March). "American private schools: A definition." *National Association of Secondary School Principals Bulletin, 66,* 4-9.

PROBLEM IDENTIFICATION

The key activity of school administrators is decision making. The decisions that must be made tend to arrive on the administrator's desk as problems seeking solutions. There is seemingly no end to them. Often administrators feel like Alpine hikers, hip-deep in snow, with the rumble of the avalanche suggesting even more imposing problems shortly to arrive. Given the prevalence of problems, administrators accept the designation of problem solver virtually without question, and usually with enthusiasm.

Yet, the identification or finding of problems is just as critical as their solution. Is every problem that an administrator encounters ready for solution? How can one choose among a number of problems with apparently equal claim for attention? Is the administrator more than simply a problem recipient? These questions imply that in problem processing, skills of identification must be wedded with capacities for solution. For some, problems must be redefined; some problems must be addressed before others; and, at times, the administrator must initiate problems.

The steps of problem processing in the school organization are clear. First, problems well up in both the internal and external environments; the wise administrator keeps a weather eye open for both types. Problem sensing (or environment scanning) is a particular responsibility of the administrator. Second, problems are screened for feasibility. Potentially unproductive or tangential problems are buffered through the use of strategies (e.g., stalling or ignoring) that are only intermittently effective. Those advance problems have their own devices (e.g., generating a crisis; finding a vulnerable, sympathetic person or office elsewhere in the organization) for pushing through administrative defenses.

Third, problems that are accepted by administrators (happily or grudgingly) must be distributed in the organization. The administrator cannot solve every problem. Many are delegated to fellow administrators, to teachers, to parent groups, to student groups, or, increasingly, to coalitions drawn from these different constituencies. It is here that various demands can be negotiated. Fourth, decisions are made, and a problem solution is advanced into a fifth implementation period. As implementation proceeds, the administrator gets feedback from the organization. A sense of how an approach to a problem may or may not lead to a solution begins to emerge. In the final step, if the feedback is positive, the problem can be given a polite burial. If the feedback is negative, the problem must be resurrected and returned to the problem-distribution point, with hopes for greater success the second time around.

The problem is under indentification until it is distributed, and even an individual or group assigned to handle a problem will continue to redefine it close to the point of decision. The solution that begins to emerge will interact with the problem, not simply complement it. And the point at which a solution is applied (e.g., a classroom) may yield a somewhat different definition of the problem. Problem identification begins early and ends late.

Administrators might best consider themselves problem managers, rather than mere problem solvers. They orchestrate problem processing (or management) within the educational organization, for they encounter the people of the organization with an intensity unlike that of any of their colleagues. Problem management provides a means for analyzing and discussing the course of organizational problem finding and solving.

For instance, the problem given to an administrator exists in a context where value (or urgency) must be compared with priority (or importance). There will be differences of opinion as this dialogue is joined, and the administrator acts as the moderator. The administrator guides the problem to the next point of analysis, where the problem is defined through the counterpoint of available information and hypotheses about the nature of the problem. These two stages comprise problem identification, or problem finding. Subsequently, in problem solving, there are two more such dialectic exchanges. The solution is analyzed through the contrast of possible solutions and feasibility factors. Finally, implementation is considered as planning, and its tasks are placed in juxtaposition with participation needs. What does the plan look like? Who is going to do what?

Negotiator, facilitator, intellectual guide, detective—the role of problem manager is more complex, safer, more time-consuming, and more effective than that of the solitary, all-responsible problem solver.

The administrator as problem finder must distinguish between given problems and discovered problems. Some problems are well-defined and routine, and the administrator can turn quickly and confidently to problem solving. But, in other instances, problems are obscure and idiosyncratic, and the administrator must look behind the given problem solving. The administrator who needs time to probe and think must delay the given problem. Some administrators literally use a bottom desk drawer or a third tray of their in-out basket to store such problems. Stored problems sometimes solve themselves. Others change their shape and intensity without any help from the administrator. Still others must be rescued from the drawer or tray because delay will not be acceptable within the organization.

Administrators accept and reject and discover problems. They also initiate problems, when they want to influence the organizational agenda in a direct manner. Further, they use a predictive mode when they look to the future and raise problems which do not require immediate solution, but which have a shaping effect on the institutional future.

Administrators who engage in problem identification (or finding) need to be aware of the types of variables which influence their behavior during such activity, including those that are personal (e.g., job security, location within the bureaucracy) and those that are organizational (e.g., time available; the duration of the problem).

The ability to coalesce support around critical problems is an essential task of leadership. A problem which rallies collective commitment will move through the entire problem cycle, and its solution will have significant impact. Problem solving can be repetitive and mundane, but problem finding and problem management draw upon the creative skills and imagination of the school administrator in determining not only the shape of a particular problem but the range of problem possibilities.

See also Administrative Tasks; Decision Making; Delegating Authority; Leadership.

—R. Bruce McPherson
Western Carolina University

References

Hanson, E.M. (1979). *Educational administration and organizational behavior* (pp. 361-81). Boston: Allyn & Bacon.

Kolb, D.A. (1973). "Problem management: Learning from experience." In S. Srivastva (Ed.), *The executive mind* (pp. 109-43). San Francisco: Jossey-Bass.

McPherson, R.B., Crowson, R.L., & Pitner, N.J. (1986). *Managing uncertainty: Administrative theory and practice in education* (pp. 271-86). Columbus, OH: Charles E. Merrill.

PROGRAM EVALUATION

A school's program is evaluated by many different persons: students, teachers, parents, district officials, the school board, and the community. Some of this evaluation will be formal, explicit, and overt; much of it will be informal, implicit, and covert. The administrator, who wishes to maintain a central voice in determining the direction of the educational program, must have a working knowledge of the purposes and procedures of evaluation and of the various types of evaluation that are applied. His or her own timely, systematic evaluation not only enables the administrator to provide direction for the educational program but provides a structure that helps shape the evaluations of other groups and individuals.

Alternative Evaluation Models

Ernest House has identified eight major approaches to evaluation. These may be summarized as follows.

1. *The Systems Analysis Model.* The systems analysis approach includes such techniques as program-planning budgeting systems, linear programming, and cost-benefit analysis. It includes economists and managers, concerned with achieving efficiency, in its intended audiences.

2. *The Behavioral Objectives Model.* The behavioral objectives approach makes use of prespecified behavioral objectives and quantifiable measures of goal attainment (such as achievement tests). It is the approach typically favored by psychometricians.

3. *The Decision-Making Model.* The decision-making approach seeks to determine whether the educational program is effective and what action needs to be taken to make it more effective in terms of the overall educational goals. Because it focuses on decisions, it is of great use to principals and other administrators.

4. *The Goal-Free Model.* Goal-free evaluation is concerned not only with educational outcomes but with *all* the effects of a treatment or program. Goal-free evaluation takes its direction from an analysis of consumer needs, e.g., student and parent needs, rather than from producer goals, e.g., board policy.

5. *The Art Criticism Model.* Critical review, parallel to art or literary criticism, provides an approach to evaluation that seeks to improve standards for the educational program and heighten the awareness of its consumers.

6. *The Accreditation Model.* The accreditation (professional review) approach uses self study and a panel of professionals to determine how the educational program measures against criteria established by the accrediting agency or professional association.

7. *The Quasi-Legal Model.* The quasi-legal approach, as the name implies, uses procedures parallel to those used in courts of law. Arguments, for and against a program, are presented to a jury (or "blue ribbon" panel or commission) which then examines the evidence to seek resolution of the issues.

8. *The Case Study (Transaction) Model.* This approach uses case studies, interviews, and observations to focus on the program processes and how the program looks to different individuals and groups involved in or affected by the educational program. It seeks to present the essential elements of the program as they are seen by clients and practitioners.

House describes and analyzes these different models. The reader would be wise to gain a working acquaintance of them in order to understand the evaluation options that are available and to understand the evaluation assumptions and priorities of other groups.

Evaluation for Decision Making

All of the major approaches to evaluation have value for an administrator, particularly since individuals and groups from the school district, the community, the state department of education, and various other agencies will be making evaluations of the school for their particular purposes. For purposes of managing the school, however, the principal is probably best served by using a model that facilitates the decisions that must be made to guide and operate the school.

Perhaps the best known and most readily usable of the decision-making approaches to program evaluation is the CIPP model proposed by Daniel Stufflebeam. CIPP stands for the four types of evaluation that take place in the evaluation process: context, input, process, and product. *Context evaluation* flows out of planning to serve decisions about program goals and objectives. *Input evaluation* serves decisions about the selection and allocation of program resources. *Process evaluation* supports decisions required to control the operation of the program, while it is in action, by providing feedback to decision-makers that will enable necessary modifications and other supplementary decisions to be made. *Product evaluation* looks at the attainment of program goals and objectives, both during and at the end of a course of action. These four types of evaluation operate together to provide a systematic approach to evaluation for the practicing administrator.

Responsive Evaluation

An application of the content, input, process, and product model may be productively coupled with *responsive evaluation*, as proposed by Egon Guba and Yvonne Lincoln. Guba and Lincoln believe that an effective evaluation and the decisions that flow from it are dependent upon the claims, concerns, and issues put forth by a variety of stake-holding audiences. These audiences include faculty, other administrators, students, parents, board members, and others. Each audience views the educational program in a different way, each view colored by self interest and a unique perspective.

Why should the administrator be concerned with these different views? Several reasons may be given. First of all, the evaluation and the decisions that flow from it can be enriched tremendously through the contribution of the unique insights and information provided by the members of each audience. Second, it seems clear that each audience

interprets and judges the educational program according to its unique views. Utilizing the unique views of the separate audiences in framing the evaluation and explicating the decisions that flow from it not only enriches the evaluation but increases the likelihood that each audience's point of view will be incorporated into the evaluation or at least be complementary to it. Finally, an implementation of any decision must involve members of all stake-holding audiences if the decision is to work. Individuals who have had substantial roles in structuring a decision will be invaluable allies in monitoring its faithful implementation.

Two-way communication with the various audiences of an educational program is essential throughout the evaluation process, but perhaps it is most critical in the stage of context evaluation. Many educational programs regularly function with inadequate, outdated, or noncomprehensive goals. The apparent belief seems to be that it does not matter much what your educational goals are so long as you are effective in accomplishing them. Put in these terms, the position is ludicrous. There is no point in doing something well that is not worth doing. An organization that does not regularly re-examine its goals in a comprehensive manner that incorporates the views of its stake-holding audiences is an organization that will become increasingly irrelevant to the environment it is trying to serve and will become increasingly ineffective.

The administrator should organize a planning team that meets on a regular basis to consider the goals of the educational program. Planning team membership should consist of representatives of the educational program's various stake-holding audiences. The team should probably meet near the end of each school year to consider the events of the past year and to establish goals for the next. It should also set a regular schedule for meetings to consider specific strategies in pursuit of goals, to review data that have been collected on goals, and to consider possible refinement and modification of goals.

The planning team can assist the administrator in input evaluation by reviewing strategies that the administrator has designed for the selection and allocation of personnel and for setting aside time and obtaining material resources to implement the educational program. The team's involvement at this point provides its members with the opportunity to visualize how decisions about goals can be translated into action, to express their points of view about these strategies, and to communicate these strategies back to the audiences they represent.

The planning team serves a similar function in process evaluation. The administrator should make available to the team materials that provide an ongoing description of the process as it is implemented. This description of the process should identify barriers to program implementation and defects in the strategies that have been devised. The administrator continues to work with the team to maximize the value of their unique insights in shaping strategies and refining goals.

Finally, the administrator needs to see that data are collected on outcome measures (product evaluation) that relate to goals and objectives. These data need to be relayed to the planning team so that effective decisions can be made regarding the continuation, termination, modification, or refocusing of the goals and strategies of the educational program.

At this point, if the input, process and product evaluations have been faithfully carried out and reviewed during the year, the stage is nicely set for the team's annual consideration of its goals. Thus, the process of program evaluation never really ends. It tells the administrator where the educational program is going and where it needs to go. It is an early warning system about defects in program goals and strategies. It is the principal means by which the administrator can make the educational program relevant and responsive to the many valid claims and requirements that are placed upon it.

See also Change Process; Curriculum Evaluation; Needs Assessment.

—David A. Erlandson
Texas A&M University

References

Guba, E.G. & Lincoln, Y.S. (1981). *Effective evaluation.* San Francisco: Jossey-Bass.

House, E.R. (1980). *Evaluating with validity* (chapters 2 and 3). Beverly Hills, CA: Sage.

Stufflebeam, D.L., Foley, W.J., Gephart, W.J., Guba, E.G., Hammond, R.L., Merriman, H.O., & Provus, M.M. (1971). *Educational evaluation and decision making.* Itasca, IL: E. Peacock Publishers.

PUBLIC OPINION POLLING

National polls of public attitudes towards education began in 1969. George Gallup, with the financial support of the Kettering Foundation, conducted the first national poll. These polls over the past decade and a half have provided a barometer of the public's attitudes toward education.

There are a number of reasons why public support for education has increased during the past few years. Through increased opinion polling, school administrators have asked the general public to respond to critical local educational questions. Not only did they ask individuals to rate the schools by using Gallup's questions, but they also asked them to respond to current problems and innovative programs being explored by the local school board. This public interaction with the school district has provided a vehicle whereby local citizens feel that their ideas and opinions are both respected and used by the school-administration team in decision making. It is this process that builds bridges between the community and the school; the public's ownership in the schools is enhanced; and it is an excellent public relations technique.

Opinion polling can also determine those school practices and policies that need changing. Nationally, student discipline continues to be a major problem in public schools. If this is true when polling locally, renewed efforts need to be made to correct the problem. Many school districts have involved community members as part of a district-wide task force to help remedy the discipline problems found in many public schools.

Recommended Approaches

When polling, it is crucial to have a clear purpose in mind. Simply using the questions in the latest Gallup poll might not be germane to local needs. On the other hand, Gallup polls are an excellent source for determining selected scientifically developed and tested questions that could be adapted to the local setting. Local opinion polls provide an opportunity to compare local attitudes towards education with national attitudes. The more recent Gallup polls will usually provide questions that are of current interest and should be perused as one begins to develop a local instrument. Polls can also be adapted demographically by including categories not found in Gallup polls. For instance, you might have a high number of retired citizens living in your school district and wish to poll their attitudes towards education. Where Gallup has three age categories (18-29 years; 30-49 years; 50 and over), you can include a fourth category, 65 years and older.

Each local district is unique. Questions can be tailored to gain feedback on special concerns or programs. For example, a local district might have a serious chemical abuse problem. Community feedback as to what the school should do regarding approaches to the problem could be solicited. According to the responses, a plan of action supported by the community would be implemented. It is this kind of sensitivity and follow up of community concerns that builds public trust and confidence in education.

Other Considerations

What polling method should the school administrator use when seeking feedback? Should it be a survey sent home with the students, a mailed questionnaire, a personal interview, or a telephone interview? Sometimes feedback is targeted to parents. If this is the case, one needs to decide on the method. In elementary schools a survey sent home with the child might provide an adequate response to insure the validity of the study. An 80 percent return is necessary in order to assure the responses are representative of the parents polled. Mailing the questionnaire with an enclosed self-addressed envelope is a better approach at the high school level. Advance publicity of the upcoming survey and purpose as well as follow-up letters and phone calls will help increase the return.

Three out of four citizens in many local neighborhoods do not have children attending public schools; therefore, it is imperative that these residents be included in most opinion polls. These people pay taxes, too, and as the retirement portion of our society lives longer, and on fixed incomes, it is critical that public schools keep them not only abreast of school needs and programs but also solicit their feedback. Since it is difficult to receive a high return with the mailed questionnaire and the personal interview is costly in terms of time and money, the telephone interview is recommended as a more viable approach locally.

Ninety-five percent of the residents of the United States have telephones. By securing a random sample of telephone numbers for a given area (or random digit dialing) a relatively small number of calls can be made to determine the public's attitude towards education. The responses can be generalized to a given community based on the sample and sampling error. Members of a school parent association or booster club are often recruited and then trained in the do's and don'ts of phone interviewing. Interviews must be confidential. All interviews should be done during the same week, eliminating a faulty result caused by events that tend to happen when polling extends over a long period of time. Every effort should be made to contact those residents listed in the random sample. During the evening from 6:00 p.m. to 9:00 p.m. is the best time to call. If people are busy or eating, be courteous and call back later. If a person does not speak English, give his or her number to an interviewer who is bilingual. The results of the poll should be shared with members of the community.

Whether to poll or not to poll is no longer something an effective administrator should think about; it is absolutely essential. Education is too important not to include the community as a powerful resource in providing answers to questions of educational excellence.

See also Education and Community Views; Public Relations; School-Community Relations.

—John E. Walker
Arizona State University

References

Babbie, E.R. (1973). *Methods survey research*. Belmont, CA: Wadsworth.

Bailey, K.D. (1982). *Methods of social research*. New York: Free Press.

Dillman, D.A. (1978). *Mail and telephone surveys: The total decision method*. New York: Wiley.

PUBLIC RELATIONS

An overriding purpose of school public relations is to bring the schools closer to the people they serve. Such an intimacy is predicated on the mutual recognition and acceptance of diverse though relevant needs, interests, and aspirations and is best accomplished though a structured and continuous flow of information from school to community and back again. A corollary purpose is to unite and engage the wholesale efforts of school personnel in achieving this vital intimacy while maintaining a strong sense of esprit de corps. The thrust of school public relations is therefore dual in nature, comprised of external and internal functions.

Obtaining and sustaining public support has always been a major concern of boards, administrators, and friends of education who have long realized that the success of any school enterprise is rooted in public support. Public support represents badly needed human and financial resources without which an educational program is in jeopardy.

When organized and implemented effectively, a school public relations program generates information and activities that help to assure for a district the public support it needs. Unfortunately, some of the same school officials who perceive a need for public support do not see this need filled by a school public relations program which they generally equate with a high-powered Madison Avenue approach. This is the reason why school public relations programs are often called school-community relations and public information programs. These name changes are not-so-subtle attempts to avoid the stigma educational critics frequently assign to orchestrated public relations efforts, which they view as a composite of an inordinate amount of publicity coupled with exaggerated praise. The same is true of school personnel who don the garb of a public relations specialist, but go by the appellations of community relations, public information, and media specialists, or directors thereof. Still, there are appreciable numbers of school public relations specialists who carry the title of "director of public relations." Again, while many educators have felt that school public relations should be viewed as a vehicle for disseminating information, contemporary postures have increasingly stressed not only patron and staff involvement in public-relations processes but also marketing strategies that depict the value of an education.

Although many school districts have public relations programs and specialists, a substantial number have either poorly formulated public-relations policies or none at all. An outgrowth of district values and goals, a well-developed policy designates who should be doing what when channeling information, organizing activities, and assessing the program itself. In providing a plan of action, a policy helps to make the untypical commonplace. This policy is never so extensive as to eliminate discretion nor so terse as to obscure direction.

Without a written policy, a school public relations program may be short-lived. This kind of program usually emerges as an attempt to accomplish a single goal, such as the passage of a bond issue. Having accomplished its goal, the program and the person in charge of it quickly fall by the wayside. The result is a muddling through until the next crisis arises. An unwritten policy evinces lack of commitment, and a single-purpose orientation is the antithesis of true school public relations.

But policies do not develop themselves. They are developed by sincere and dedicated people, boards and administrators who recognize their importance and community members whose values and goals they will ultimately reflect. Ideally, policy-development activities should include a broad sampling of the total community, representative of parents, nonparents, senior citizens, business leaders, staff, and students.

School personnel hired as public relations specialists must perform a variety of tasks, most of which require good writing skills, a knowledge of layout and design, and some experience with photography. The more common of these tasks embrace the preparation of school-community newspapers, board meeting reports, staff newsletters, brochures, and press releases. Infrequently, specialists are involved in the preparation of literature directed toward the passage of bond and building campaigns and in the conducting of surveys that typically precede them.

Lately, the job of this specialist has come to include working with people as well as with paper and typewriter. These people-oriented tasks have specialists organizing and offering varying degrees of leadership to citizen advisory committees of all kinds and developing programs that address the needs of single parents with children, senior citizens, and the general community, as in community education. More recently, they have established school-business partnerships. Also, a small but growing cadre of specialists are exchanging paper and typewriter for a computer keyboard and a television screen. With increased use of computer and video technology in school and home, this task will gain prominence.

Despite task complexity, some role incumbents are initially without sufficient expertise to assure a first-class performance. They learn on the job. Chosen from the rank and file of classroom teachers, their credentials generally consist of a major or minor in English or journalism. Others possess expertise more directly related to the school public-relations function. They hail from one or more of the following fields: journalism, radio, television, advertising, and public relations. Still others have expertise precisely suited for the job at hand, having obtained a graduate degree from a higher educational institution with a training program in school public relations.

In the small school district, the superintendent performs public relations tasks. The school public-relations specialist is most commonly found in the suburban district, where public relations tasks may be shared with building principals but coordinated by a centrally located specialist. In the large district, public relations tasks may be carried out by many administrators or centralized and supervised by a high-ranking administrator to whom several specialists report.

The best approach to school public relations is the one that gives everyone in the district a special part to play. Of all the groups to be alerted to the importance of school public relations, the classroom teacher rates top priority. Teachers have considerable access to the home through their students, from whom parents get most of their information about schools. Therefore public relations in-service for teachers is vital. But no school group, boards and administrators included, should be excluded from in-service activities.

The value of a school public relations program is frequently questioned because it is difficult to put a price tag on its outcomes. Parental involvement, a goal of most boards and administrators, signals democracy at work. The assumption is that involvement stimulates ownership and support. Similarly, involvement tends to resolve conflict at the lower levels of its inception. Another assumption is that students are likely to become more interested in school if their parents share this interest. When involvement is extended to include the entire school staff, the notion of a school family takes on importance.

Equally elusive is the value of paper products, such as newsletters, newspapers, and brochures, flooding the school and community. Yet without the information they contain, patrons grow suspicious, and rumors are abundant. Likewise, school personnel not privy to information have poor morale. A well-informed staff and community feel a part of the school and are more likely to identify with and support its goals.

The value of the academic image a given school district projects is elusive; much of it may be attributed to the quality of a school public-relations program. If the image is substantial, people, wanting their children to have a fine education, tend to move into the district. This desire raises property values. A district with a good image also attracts good teachers.

To put a price tag on the happiness of a child is difficult. Yet if a public relations program is truly at work, school should be a second home. Unhappy students quickly become discipline problems, poor learners, hookey players, and dropouts.

Even when complaints are few, adult attendance at school functions and in community-education programs is high, curricular support is always forthcoming, financial referendums constantly pass, and school-business partnerships flourish, a dollar value cannot be conveniently placed on a school public relations program. Yet such outcomes are invaluable to school districts dependent upon public support to make the difference between mediocre learning and a good education. Perhaps the real value of a public relations program is in results consonant with a district's goals.

An effective public relations program does not occur overnight. It takes work and the contributions of many people. Stemming from a well-formulated public relations policy, it has continuity and financial support and usually a specialist to carry it out. While evaluation is elusive and largely devoid of a specific dollar value, it is essential. Only when evaluation occurs can a school district have confidence in the direction of its public relations program. If it helps to accomplish goals, it is above value.

See also Public Opinion Polling; School-Community Relations.

—Phil West
Texas A&M University

References

Bagin, D., Ferguson, D., & Marx, G. (1985). *Public relations for administrators.* Arlington, VA: American Association of School Administrators.

Holiday, A.E. (Ed.). (1980 & 1982). *The public relations almanac for educators* (Vols. 1 & 2). Camp Hill, PA: Educational Communication Center.

West, P.T. (1985). *Educational public relations.* Beverly Hills, CA: Sage.

PUPIL PERSONNEL PROGRAM

Our society is based upon many philosophical values. Among these are an appreciation for the worth and dignity of every individual, the realization of individual differences, and the recognition of the inherent right to self-direction and choice. The purpose of a pupil personnel program is to actualize these values by integrating individually oriented professional services within the learning environment in order to facilitate the optimal development of each pupil. Consequently, this program of services, known as the pupil personnel program, is guided by each school's and community's goals for the education of its pupils.

The main components of a pupil personnel program are traditionally identified by the disciplines, roles, or job descriptions of the professionals who comprise the team. In an integrated pupil personnel program, the following services need to be coordinated in order to provide maximum assistance to the pupil: guidance, social work, school psychology, health education and nursing, attendance and welfare, testing, individual assessment, evaluation and research, and special education (including speech and language). While each specialist may be identified as having a specific role and may operate relatively independently of others, this traditional professional territoriality should give way to a collaborative effort with the one essential purpose of effectively identifying and meeting the needs of the pupils. It is through this integration of individual knowledge and skills within the team that a comprehensive service delivery system is best developed. The success of a pupil personnel program is dependent upon the extent to which this coordinated team of teachers, administrators, and pupil personnel staff work together to facilitate the maximum development of all students. Therefore, the importance of individual roles is superseded by the various functions of the team, and duplication or overlap in services is minimized.

The major functions of a pupil personnel team are assessment, consultation, and intervention integrated within a service continuum aimed at the needs of individual pupils. The foci of these functions are the individual pupil and significant others, such as family, peers, and teachers, within the school system and community.

Priorities in pupil service programs should be developed from identified needs. Needs assessment is the foundation of a comprehensive and effective program, and decisions regarding both the goals of the program and service delivery should be based on these objective data.

The role of the administrator in the management and coordination of a pupil personnel program generally entails leadership and supervision skills in the areas of planning and program development; staff selection, allocation and development; budgeting and fiscal management; and program evaluation and reporting. It is generally accepted that, regardless of the size or administrative structure of the organization, it is important to have one designated central administrator assume the responsibility for the pupil personnel program. This individual should be part of the major administrative decision-making body. Having this administrative direction will provide a focal point for program planning and evaluating purposes. It will also provide a centralized source of information and input to appropriate policy decisions and enhance annual and long-range districtwide budget development.

There is no single best way to organize a pupil personnel service program. Each school develops an organizational framework to ensure that pupil personnel services function effectively, members of the staff are assigned properly, and services are coordinated smoothly with one another, with other aspects of the school program, and with other services available in the community. Regardless of the organizational arrangement, it is essential that the professional responsibility be directed toward the student rather than the service. A large school district might have an assistant superintendent responsible for pupil personnel services. This administrator would supervise and coordinate directors of each of the services such as guidance, psychology, special education, etc. In a medium-sized district an assistant superintendent for pupil personnel might directly supervise all itinerant pupil personnel staff, including social workers and psychologists. A staff assigned to one particular building would be supervised by that building principal. In a small district, a director of pupil personnel services, reporting to the superintendent, may coordinate the pupil service program for the entire district and have other responsibilities as well. Whatever the organizational arrangement, input to the top decision-making group and complementary accountability are necessary.

The administrator's role in program evaluation is critical. Several principles must be incorporated in any successful evaluation. Evaluation must relate directly to the stated program objectives, be part of the initial program design, and be an ongoing, cooperative effort. The results of the effort should be communicated to all concerned. In many ways, program evaluation is the most important of all of the administrative activities, for without it there can be no justification for the continuation or expansion of a set of services.

See also Counseling and Guidance; Support Staff, Professional.

—Marvin J. Fruth
University of Wisconsin-Madison
—Eileen McCarthy
Director of Special Education,
Rockland County, New York

References

Hummel, D.L., & Humes, C.W. (1984). *Pupil services: Development, coordination, administration.* New York: MacMillan.

National Association of Pupil Personnel Administrators. (1973). *Pupil personnel services.* Washington, DC: Author.

Stoughton, R.R., McKenna, J.W., & Cook, R.P. (1969). *Pupil personnel services: A position statement.* Washington, DC: National Association of Pupil Personnel Administrators.

Q

QUALITY CIRCLES

Quality circles are being found in an increasing number of industrial organizations worldwide. Private-sector interest in their use may be traced to concerns about industrial quality and productivity which have declined over the past decade. Many firms have also come to view quality circles as vehicles to enhance the quality of working life, to utilize employee creativity, to improve communication between workers and management at all levels, and to build morale.

A quality circle in industry is a small group, usually of eight to twelve persons, which meets regularly to solve problems of concern to employees. Individuals in the same work area volunteer to join the group, and they usually receive specialized training in problem identification and analysis. They are also trained in data collection and analysis techniques. Meetings are held weekly for one hour on company premises. Most firms schedule meetings during working hours to avoid overtime costs. The members are encouraged to identify problems needing attention and to focus on those which are of highest priority to the group.

Once a problem is selected, members state it clearly and begin to collect information on the causes of the problem, often using graphs and other basic statistical techniques. The members then generate as many solutions to the problem as possible, evaluate these, and develop recommendations for management action, usually based upon information relating to costs and benefits. When the members of the quality circle are ready, they share their recommendations with management in a formal, structured presentation.

At the presentation, the members define the problem, present data that support the problem statement, summarize the solutions considered, identify and justify the solution chosen, and offer suggestions for implementing the solution. Presentations are attended by top management and others interested in the problem. Managers often ask questions, and they customarily inform the quality circle members of when to expect a decision regarding the recommended solution.

Several features of quality circles make them potentially more effective than many of the task and advisory groups commonly found in schools and school districts. The agenda items and priorities of the quality circle are set exclusively by the members, thus increasing the likelihood that real needs of members and their constituents are addressed. Membership in the quality circle is voluntary, reducing the risk of administrative stacking. The members receive training that is not restricted to immediate organizational needs but, rather, applies to a broad range of problems that may be chosen for study.

The processes within quality circles are designed to optimize effectiveness. Members must conduct thorough analyses of the problems that they seek to solve, and quantitative methods are used to provide insight into important dimensions of the problems. Quality circles inhibit the rush to solution which can dominate traditional work groups. Members are not asked to select from a list of decision options developed by someone else but, rather, to develop their own solutions to problems that they identify. Cost-benefit techniques permit measured consideration of the advantages and disadvantages of each option. The key benefit of quality circles in school districts may lie in face-to-face presentation of the group's work and final recommendations to the responsible administrators. The administrator's response may not be favorable, but a negative response calls for thoughtful consideration.

The decision to use quality circles in a school district, perhaps initially on a pilot basis, should be made deliberately. The superintendent should answer several important questions: (a) What, specifically, can quality circles be expected to accomplish? (b) Will the school board support the program? (c) What will the program and materials cost? (d) How will unions react? (e) Does the school district have a person available to coordinate the program?

The professional literature of elementary and secondary education that discusses quality circles consists largely of descriptive overviews, opinion articles, anecdotal reports of implementation, and recommended training materials. To date, systematic research on the effectiveness of quality circles, while generally supportive, is scant and available only in unpublished sources. Further research, wide publication of results, and more public debate are needed. In spite of their apparent strengths, quality circles have yet to prove themselves in school districts.

See also Decision Making; Delegating Authority; Group Processes; Problem Identification.

—Robert J. Beebe
University of Mississippi

References

Bonner, J.S. (1982). "Japanese quality circles: Can they work in education." *Phi Delta Kappan, 63,* 681.

Chase, L. (1983). "Quality circles in education." *Educational Leadership, 40,* 18-26.

Zahra, S.A., Beebe, R.J., & Wiebe, F.A. (1985). "Quality circles for school districts." *Educational Forum, 49,* 323-30.

R

READING EDUCATION

The primary purposes of reading, and therefore reading instruction, are for use as a means of information gathering and as a means of recreation. At a fundamental level, reading has long been viewed as a significant contributor to our republican form of government; a literate and well-informed populace is considered instrumental in preserving and extending our form of self-governance. As our society continues its apparent transition from an industrial base to one of technologically oriented information processing and service, the ability to read will continue to hold a position of importance. Notwithstanding the foregoing, there are some current estimates that by the year 2000 two of every three adults in the United States will be functionally illiterate. If such predictions hold true, our populace could be schismatized beyond reconciliation. The mingling of a continuing, if not increasing, need for reading ability and the dire prediction of the lack of success of reading instruction prompts consideration of the trends and issues of, and the approaches toward, reading education.

The trends and issues of the art and science of reading education include a plethora of topics which span the theoretical and applicative considerations of research and instruction. These efforts may be broadly divided between considerations of reading as a process and considerations of reading as a product. This division derives its logic from the fact that reading is a cognitive activity and, as such, the process of reading can not be readily observed. As a result, the observation of reading is dependent upon those products or behaviors which are accepted as being representative of reading.

Much of the recent research, whether process or product oriented, has focused on a reconsideration of the existing information base with the result of reaffirming and extending the knowledge base. As cases in point, the corpus of present day research has modestly extended the findings and implications of original efforts. Recent writings regarding schema theory, which deals with the way our minds organize information, has reiterated the writings of Immanuel Kant (1724-1804). Studies of the automaticity of function, the process through which well-practiced events are executed with less and less conscious control, has reaffirmed the writings of Edmund Burke Huey in 1908. Laser assisted eye movement cameras have shown the validity and reliability of the 1890s and 1900s writings of Catell, Dodge, Dearborn, and Woodworth regarding how the eyes function while reading. Computer assisted electrothermography has reaffirmed the works of Broca (1824-1880) and Wernicke (1848-1905),

who concluded that language functions were localized and specialized within particular areas of the brain. Present efforts combining computer technology and cognitive psychology appear to be leading toward a more sophisticated understanding of learning, thinking, and reasoning and are likely to offer reconceptualizations of the teaching and measurement of reading.

In addition to considerations specifically oriented toward reading, trends and issues within related topics are affecting reading instruction. Notable among these are accountability, minimum competency testing, criterion- versus norm-referenced testing, qualifications of the personnel employed, censorship, and the confusion generated by the inconsistent defining and use of terms such as "dyslexia" and "learning disabled."

Consistent with the diversity of the perspectives of reading and the concomitant trends and issues, approaches to the teaching of reading have taken many avenues. These approaches are generally based in one of three orientations with the generic classifications of (a) skills/subskills, (b) holistic, and (c) interactive. The skills/subskills designation, also referred to as a bottom-up model, considers reading to be basically a process of translating, decoding, encoding, and recoding. The skills of reading are then themselves divided into subskills. Those following this orientation believe that the sophisticated reader has so well integrated the skills of reading that he does not have to attend to them. From this approach, the teaching of reading emphasizes the subskills through practice with easy materials until integration occurs. Critics have maintained that the learner's ability to comprehend can suffer because the learner must pay undue attention to the separate parts of reading.

The holistic designation, also referred to as a top-down model, considers reading to be a high-speed process which does not require the recognition of every letter or word. The reader's language and mental abilities are regarded as integral in the construction of meaning from printed materials. Based on these abilities, the reader predicts the author's message and samples only as much of the print as is necessary to confirm or reject the prediction and make new ones. The approach to teaching reading assumes that beginning readers have only begun to develop an awareness of oral and written language patterns and as a result need to be in an environment which is replete in language and language-based activities. Critics of this approach have maintained that readers' performance may be limited due to a lack of the skills necessary to deal with unknown words.

The interactive designation, also referred to as the combination or simultaneous model, combines the opinions of the first two. Comprehension is believed to be dependent on both the printed information and the information in the reader's mind. As comprehension may be prevented when an integral skill or bit of prior knowledge is missing, the skilled reader is thought to compensate by using one or more word-identification techniques. Beginning reading instruction emphasizes component skills which, when mastered, become the foundation for emphasis on a meaning-oriented process. Critics have raised the concern that such an approach may lead to a lack of emphasis of either orientation and result in confused, unskilled readers.

The predominant reading-education delivery system utilized is a basal reading series. Basal reading series overwhelmingly employ a skills/subskills orientation with the holistic or interactive orientations serving subsidiary roles. The materials incorporated within a basal series typically include readers, workbooks, and teacher's editions as well as supplemental materials such as computer programs, records and tapes, duplicating masters, classroom libraries, and overhead transparencies. Scope-and-sequence charts are generally provided to indicate the topics covered and points within the reading series where the topics are introduced, extended, and reinforced. The traditional pacing has been learning to read during the first three years of school and reading to learn in the years subsequent to third grade. Assuming a normal progression on the part of the learner, the middle, junior, and high school years emphasize the development of study skills and literature appreciation.

See also Competency Testing, Students; Curriculum Development; Tests, Criterion, and Norm-Referenced.

—Roger J. De Santi
University of New Orleans

References

Harris, T.L., & Hodges, R.E. (Eds.). (1981). *A dictionary of reading and related terms.* Newark, DE: International Reading Association.

Huey, E.B. (1968). *The psychology and pedagogy of reading.* Cambridge, MA: MIT Press.

Singer, H., & Ruddell, R.B. (Eds.). (1985). *Theoretical models and processes of reading* (3rd ed.). Newark, DE: International Reading Association.

RECRUITMENT OF STAFF

The quest for excellence in schools is a quest for excellence in teaching. Aside from the principal, the factor which makes a difference in teaching and learning is the quality of the faculty. With the private sector offering more to able people than public schools typically provide, there may be fewer teachers for more positions. Therefore, it behooves school districts to establish appropriate mechanisms for the recruitment of teachers.

Attracting Good Teachers

It has been said that quality athletic programs at the college level do not recruit athletes; they select them. Their programs are so successful that good athletes naturally want to gravitate to them. So it can be with school districts. Over time, the reputation of a school system as a good one can prompt prospective teachers to seek out the system rather than vice versa. The key to positive image building is a commitment on everyone's part to settle for nothing but the best. Everything, including the simplest communication,

even the answering of a telephone, should be guided by high standards. When people inquire about positions in the system, they should be treated as if they are the best applicant for the job.

Some school districts find it helpful to develop a recruitment brochure to send to applicants. A well-written brochure which accentuates the district's positive attributes can be an excellent tool for attracting good applicants. Research findings show that prospective teachers are influenced by factors such as students' academic achievement, good discipline, class size, a variable fringe-benefit plan tailored to individual needs, and, to some extent, geographic and community factors.

Establishing an annual budget for recruitment is one way to demonstrate that recruitment activities are valued. The recruitment budget is a capital investment in the future and should not be the first dollars removed when shortfalls require a "tightening of the belt." A good recruitment budget should include monies for travel, for advertisements in professional journals, for printing brochures and other documents, and for bringing quality recruits to the district for interviews.

The development of a recruitment plan for the district provides a framework to guide recruitment activities. The plan should be written with input from the school board, professional staff, teachers, and the community. It seems best not to adopt a recruitment plan as board policy but rather as a dynamic tool which can be changed as needed. The plan should include any affirmative-action procedures required by governmental agencies along with local requirements judged appropriate. However, insofar as possible, the emotional issues of race and sex should not cloud the central function of good recruitment activities; namely, the central function is the employment of quality teachers.

Any workable recruitment plan should be based on the fact that recruiting is a continuous process. Although a well-developed plan may establish key dates and persons responsible for activities, in actuality recruiting never stops. Everyone should be sensitized to the search for quality teachers. They should constantly look for the kinds of teachers who show promise for continuing the district's program of excellence. Additionally, someone in the organization should be responsible for maintaining an active pool of viable candidates. Adding the personal touch of follow-up and contact from time to time sends a signal of friendliness that may be the deciding factor in an applicant's choosing one position over another.

New Developments

The advent of shortages in certain teaching areas requires finding ways to attract qualified applicants, albeit for a short period of time. Short-term teachers whose ultimate occupational goals are outside the teaching profession can provide a tenable solution to teacher shortages in critical areas. Teaching can provide able college graduates with a place to start while waiting to move on to another profession.

Many of the studies, especially of high-school education, have recommended the practice of having private enterprise work cooperatively with the public schools by encouraging some of their employees to teach on an adjunct basis similar to what frequently takes place in community colleges and universities. Additionally, the opportunity to work in the private sector during summer months can provide an incentive for some persons to choose teaching.

The endowed chair has long been a practice of the university community. Offering an endowed chair at the high-school level is one way of attracting able teachers and of adding to the academic climate of public institutions. The "artists-in-residence" program where talented artists practice their craft in the school setting is a variation on a similar theme. Surrounding young people with quality teachers and quality performers not only makes knowledge and skills more accessible, it offers an opportunity to see models of competence at work.

See also Affirmative Action; Competency Testing, Teachers; Staff Orientation; Teacher Selection.

—John M. Jenkins
University of Florida

References

Engel, R.E., & Nall, R.L. (1984, February). "Recruiting shortage area teachers: Is there a more effective way?" *National Association of Secondary School Schools Bulletin, 68*(468-471), 105-09.

Goldstein, W. (1986). *Recruiting superior teachers: The interview process* (Fastback #239). Bloomington, IN: Phi Delta Kappa Educational Foundation.

Jenkins, J.M. (1984). "Selecting staff." In *Instructional Leadership Handbook*. Reston, VA: National Association of Secondary School Principals.

RELIGIOUS SCHOOLS

Just as the decade of the 1970s was a period of crisis for many religious schools in the United States, the 1980s have witnessed their return to public favor as examples of successful education. Scarcely ten years ago, enrollment, staffing, and financial problems led many prognosticators to foretell a dismal future for religious schools.

The truth about the fortunes and misfortunes of religious schools is somewhere between these two simplistic portrayals of gloom and euphoria. Five major developments which indicate both the strengths and problems of religious schools will be discussed in this article.

Enrollments

Catholic school enrollments began to fall well before public school enrollment declined. From their high point of 5.6 million in 1965, they have continued downward. In the decade of the 1970s alone, Catholic schools witnessed better than twice the enrollment losses of the public school system. This led to the public perception that private religious schools were having problems.

Trends in the Catholic schools disguised the growth of religious school enrollments in other denominations. In recent years, all non-Catholic religious schools experienced significant increases. Lutheran enrollments overall were up 35 percent. Most dramatic was the better than six-fold increase in Evangelical ("born-again" Christian) school enrollments. By one estimate they constituted over a fifth of all private school enrollments.

Private School Quality

During the early years of the decline in Catholic school enrollment, officials worried about Catholic school quality and attempted to make improvements. By the 1980s, public perceptions of private school quality had changed dramatically, fueled by concern over public school quality. A spirited academic debate has occurred since 1984 as to whether private schools do a better job of educating youth than do public schools. According to James Coleman and his colleagues, as well as Andrew Greeley, private secondary schools are more academically challenging and have closer working relationships with and support from parents. If continued research documents the relative success of private schools, despite what academic critics of the research say, this may encourage more "comparative shopping" by parents and lead to a possible rise in religious school enrollments. Of course, not all religious school patrons select a private alternative out of disapproval of public schools. Among those for whom this is an issue, however, the recent trend toward the development of public specialty and magnet schools may make public schools look attractive once again.

Staffing

One of the most significant developments in parochial schools in recent years has been the decline in the number of "religious" personnel who teach and administer in them. Beginning in the 1950s, members of religious orders staffed Catholic schools in declining numbers. Schools either had to be staffed with more costly lay teachers or be closed. As a matter of philosophy, many schools were closed by the religious orders which founded them. Today this is no longer a burning issue. It has proven possible to retain the religious emphasis and special character of most schools despite their being staffed by lay persons.

In the 1980s, an issue of concern among parochial school educators is state regulation of staffing requirements. States vary widely in this regard, but some evidence indicates that the public school reform movement is spilling over into the private sector; efforts to improve the quality of public school teaching increases pressure to extend the reach of the state to all schools. Concern over home schools has focused this debate, even though many religious schools predate the home school movement.

Financing

Religious schools in the United States receive few public funds apart from indirect services. Consequently, they must rely on tuition and subsidies. This fact has encouraged economical, efficient management. It also has forced many schools to close because sufficient tuition and/or subsidies could not be raised, particularly where enrollments are declining. In many of these same schools, the decline in religious personnel to staff the schools required sizable budget increases to hire lay persons. While this trend peaked some years ago, a further labor-cost squeeze has occurred in Catholic schools as church policy changed to require that the remaining teachers who are members of religious orders be paid at parity with lay staff.

In order to improve their financial stability, most Catholic dioceses require their schools to engage in "development." This involves self-assessment, mission and goal setting, marketing, and fundraising. The sophistication required to accomplish effective development is considerable. Many high schools have development directors, and, in addition, the school's principal usually has to give much attention to financial management.

Public aid to private schools or their patrons remains controversial. According to survey research, low-income and minority parents especially would be likely to switch from public to private schools if they were given an appropriate voucher or tax credit. Nonetheless, these groups and the general public remain divided on the issue of public support for private schools.

The main arguments in favor of aid are that the present situation imposes unfair financial hardship on private school patrons by forcing them to support both public schools and their private school, while the general public enjoys a reduced tax burden by being relieved of the responsibility for the private school segment of the population. This ostensibly restricts parental choice according to income and opens private schools to charges of elitism. Proponents also point to the possibility that a more vigorous competitive climate for public schools would improve their performance. In addition, they point to the inequality of resources within the public school sector and the racial and income stratification this represents, arguing that aid to private schools could hardly make matters worse.

Critics of private school aid respond that the growth of private schools would drain off the most talented and highly motivated pupils from public education and would increase separatism. They question whether aid would increase the supply of private schools available or reduce tuition. They doubt whether most parents would be sufficiently informed or would care enough to demand good schools. Many religious school groups oppose direct aids or vouchers, arguing that tax credits are more appealing because they might involve less direct public regulation.

Notwithstanding this divided public opinion, judicial decisions continue to be hostile to the concept. However, the U.S. Supreme Court did uphold a Minnesota tax deduction statute in *Mueller v. Allen* on grounds that it applied both to public and private school costs.

Another important financial issue is how to support impoverished inner-city Catholic schools which serve poor and minority pupils. Many are attached to parishes which lack the money to continue supporting them. Most bishops are committed to keeping such schools open but find the costs increasingly prohibitive. Since these schools are an important avenue of social mobility for many blacks and Hispanics who attend them, and who lack the resources to move to more advantaged suburban school systems, their demise would be a national misfortune.

Relations with Public Schools

The U.S. Supreme Court raised a storm of controversy in its *Felton* decision. By prohibiting the delivery of compensatory education services at private school sites under terms of the Elementary and Secondary Education Act of 1965, the Court jeopardized an important political compromise reached between public and private school supporters twenty years earlier, which had made possible the passage of the Elementary and Secondary Education Act of 1965. The Court did not set forth a clear standard which might guide public and private school educators in selecting a "neutral site" for delivering educational services to private school pupils.

Initially *Felton* reopened old tensions between the two groups, but in many places they have worked together to develop a new, legally acceptable delivery system. At the same time, a less highly publicized development has been occurring in various states. Cooperative linkages are being built with the encouragement of the federal government and some state departments of education.

Conclusion

In some respects, religious schools are enjoying in the 1980s a popularity and well-being which reverses their dismal prospects only a decade earlier. Yet enrollment, staffing, and financial problems persist. It is worthwhile recalling that, throughout their history, these schools have been in jeopardy either from external or internal pressures. Today their strength, as in the past, lies in their ability to be different from public schools and to offer an alternative to those parents who seek something else for their children. If this legitimate role is understood, it should be possible for public and religious school educators to develop more cooperative ties.

See also Private Schools.

—James G. Cibulka
University of Wisconsin-Milwaukee

References

Cibulka, J., O'Brien, T., & Zawe, D. (1982). *Inner-city private elementary schools: A study*. Milwaukee, WI: Marquette University Press.

Coleman, J., Hoffer, T., & Kilgore, S. (1982). *High school achievement: Public, Catholic, and private schools compared*. New York: Basic Books.

Levy, D.C. (Ed.). (1986). *Private education: Studies in choice and public policy*. New York: Oxford University Press.

RESEARCH ON ADMINISTRATION

The two dozen entries pertinent to educational administration in the most recent *Encyclopedia of Educational Research* and the thirty-three chapters in the more recent *Handbook of Research on Educational Administration* vividly document the highly specialized condition of inquiry that has emerged over several decades. The entries and chapters report not only sophisticated treatments of administrator and organizational behavior but also significant research activity in economics and finance, politics and policy, and specialized topics such as collective bargaining, the law, and comparative educational administration. Within the diverse and generally noncumulative character of prevailing inquiry, two significant trends have appeared. The first is emphasis on studying in detail the work lives of administrators. The second is emphasis on exploring the connections between administrator work and the technical core of instruction.

Direct Observation of Administrator Work

The 1970s and 1980s have witnessed a burgeoning of direct observation studies of administrators at work which drew heavily on ethnographic approaches and newly developed modes of studying work activities (e.g., structured observation). Several intensive interview studies of relatively small samples of principals and superintendents complemented the direct observations of administrator work and life. Research of this genre has generated increased knowledge and provided more detail about what administrators do and in what activities they primarily engage. The findings have ascertained that the school administrator's life, like counterparts in business and public administration, is characterized by fragmentation, variety, and brevity in the pattern of activities. The school data particularly suggest a discernible disconnection of management activity from the central technical core of instruction, a conclusion that is less firm when the subjects observed and interviewed are associated with schools and/or school systems that are judged effective. Other pertinent findings are (a) that principals enjoy considerably more opportunity to exercise discretion than has been fully understood, (b) that certain patterns of administrator behaviors become so routinized that they preoccupy administrators, and (c) that participation in evaluation activities has become increasingly more noticeable in response to both the political and professional press.

Research has, then, generated richer and more precise descriptions of administrator behavior. In addition, the concepts and methods employed by investigators have provided practitioners intellectual tools and perspectives for doing their own mapping and analyzing. For example, one continuing educational program for principals (Peer Assisted Leadership) trains administrators specifically to use the "shadowing" and "reflective interviewing" techniques that enabled a team of researchers to conduct a highly productive and enlightening set of field studies. Peer Assisted Leadership also trains participants to collect, analyze, and synthesize the data collected by shadowing and interviewing against an elaborated version of the general purpose model noted above.

The use of models has illustrated that many descriptive studies did not attend systematically to either the antecedents or the consequences of the administrator behavior. The studies have enlightened scholars and practitioners on what administrators actually do but have revealed less about why administrators do what they do. The inquiries have also offered limited support for the view that what administrators do really affects only minimally the technical core of education.

Effects and Consequences

A second discernible trend in inquiry in educational administration is interest in the outcomes or effects of what administrators do. The concern for outcomes is a longtime issue, set as a research agenda many years ago. The late 1970s and early 1980s, however, have seen the emergence of a self-conscious emphasis on identifying administrator effects, materially influenced by the literature on teacher, classroom, and school effects, and the effective schools movement.

In contrast to those descriptive studies that made no particular effort to select participants known or reputed to have had discernible effects on schools, other descriptive studies did make special efforts to identify administrators associated with effective schools, however variable or evanescent the criterion measure. Still other studies compared administrators reported to be effective with administrators reported to be ineffective. The literature from studies that made the special effort to identify effective performers, or performers associated with effective schools, offers a generally more positive view of administrator effects than the set of studies that used other criteria to select participants.

The concern for instrumental outcomes asks essentially for a mapping or charting of the territory lying between behavior and effects. Much of the current action in educational administration, among both researchers and practitioners, including most of the staff-development movement, focuses on how best to map that specific territory and to seek the salient connections. Administrative theory suggests the value of concentrating on what is manipulable, an emphasis that turns the administrator's attention directly to questions of what he or she can and cannot affect and what is most worth attempting to affect. The empirical literature reports that there is considerable discretionary latitude available to administrators in answering both questions. Administrators are much less prisoners of others' expectations and preferences and much more the captains of their own destiny than commonly thought.

The empirical literature not only enlightens the question of what can be affected but also the likely routes of effect. On the "input" side, educational administrators in the public sector can exercise, as indicated earlier, only limited influence on the composition of the student body. Research over more than 20 years reveals, however, that they can exercise and have exercised significant influence on the composition and performance of the teaching force (even in large districts that presumably enforce highly uniform personnel and supervisory policies) and the financial and physical resources available for education. One set of resources that appears to make a real difference and that is susceptible to administrator influence is the level and amount of parental involvement, with discernible differences in specifics related to the socioeconomic status of the school attendance unit or of the school district.

For the most part, however, it is the "throughput" side that recent research suggests is both the most crucial and the most manipulable dimension. Instead of accepting loose coupling between managerial activity and core technology as a constant and invariant condition of schools, a considerable body of inquiry has documented that the coupling between and among organizational levels in schools is a variable condition readily susceptible to manipulation. Direct observation and interview studies of schools that began with a choice of "effective schools" and looked at what administrators in those schools do and how they behave vis-à-vis the technical core of instructional activity (and control of pupil behavior) have reported direct administrator involvement in such activities as (a) taking the lead in goal setting, (b) securing group commitment to common goals, (c) performing rigorous but appropriate performance evaluation, and (d) vigorously sponsoring carefully elected staff development activities.

The particular value of studies that have revealed that organizational coupling is a variable rather than an invariant condition is that they have enriched the meaning and understanding of instructional leadership at all levels, not just the work of the site administrator. These studies say, simply and directly, that one of the ways in which administrators at the state, the district, and the site levels can contribute to the improvement of instruction is to tighten, intentionally, the coupling between managerial work and core technology. As of the late 1980s, however, much still remains to be learned about the most productive extent and forms of coupling across state level, district level, site level, and classroom level activities. Norms of local control and professional autonomy remain both strong and resilient. Also problematic is how much of what appears to apply to the administration of "effective" elementary schools fits the secondary school with its significantly different organizational structure and distinct societal and educational purposes.

In addition to concern over organizational coupling, recent research and analysis focused on instrumental outcomes have also stimulated renewed interest in school "culture" and climate. Like the explorations of and argumentation over coupling, discourse on school culture and climate draws on long standing and deep intellectual roots. As contemporary organizational analysts in both business and education have exalted excellence, efficiency, and productivity, the salience of organizational culture has reclaimed serious attention. The focus on school culture has emphasized the administrator's responsibility for and strategic location in contributing to the deliberate building of working goals, norms, and acceptable activities at both the adult and youth levels. The focus also urges the administrator to concentrate on building a social solidarity that supports the achievement of commonly established and accepted school goals.

Concluding Remarks

Editorial limits on length precluded detailed commentary on other significant trends in research on educational administration, including (a) increased diversification and specialization, (b) a related recognition of the depth of complexity of educational administration as an organizational, an economic, and a political activity, (c) a sharpening of interest in the philosophical and epistemological questions that shape practice and inquiry, and (d) a related increase in concern about the influences of values on administrator behavior and policy decisions. The interested reader will find more detail on the several trends identified above and on other relevant and provocative research in the references.

See also Administrative Theory; Bureaucracy; Organizations: Principles and Theory; Systems Theory.

—Norman Boyan
University of California, Santa Barbara

References

Boyan, N.J. (Ed.). (1988). *The handbook of research on educational administration.* White Plains, NY: Longman, Inc.

Hoy, W.K., & Miskel, C.G. (1987). *Educational administration: Theory, practice, and research* (3rd ed.). New York: Random House.

Mitzel, H., Abramowitz, W., & Best, J. (Eds.). (1982). *The encyclopedia of educational research* (5th ed.). New York: The Free Press.

RIGHTS: TEACHERS' AND STUDENTS'

In the landmark children's rights case, *In re Gault* (1967), the United States Supreme Court affirmed: "Whatever may be their precise impact, neither the Fourteenth Amendment nor the Bill of Rights is for adults alone." Again, in 1969, the Court declared: "It can hardly be argued that either students or teachers shed their constitutional rights to freedom of speech or expression at the schoolhouse gate."

Indeed, thousands of recent cases grounded on constitutional protection as well as contract law and civil rights legislation have alerted administrators to the need to protect the rights of those within the "schoolhouse gate." Given space limitations, this article highlights only a few of the complex issues surrounding teacher and student rights.

Teachers do not, by virtue of certification, have a right to a teaching position. Nevertheless, after being hired, a teacher's contractual rights are protected by Article 1, Section 10 of the Constitution. Similarly, citizens of the United States have no inherent right to a public education. Yet, when a state institutes an instructional system, all children have the right to a public education on an equal basis. This right extends to children of illegal aliens, the handicapped, and mentally retarded. As the courts have affirmed, the federal constitution confers basic rights on both teachers and students which administrators may not abridge without due process.

Freedom of Speech

The first amendment guarantee of freedom of speech applies to teachers' rights to academic freedom and their right to speak out on matters of public concern. Assuming that their actions will not negatively affect their ability to perform in the classroom or will not create a conflict of interest, teachers also have a right to a private life, to associate with whomever they wish, to engage in civil rights activities, and to support candidates for public office. Whether or not a teacher may actively participate in partisan politics or run for political office is not settled.

Students have rights to freedom of religion, speech, press and association. Thus, students have the right to attend a public school free of religious indoctrination by the state. Students have the right of free expression in print provided it is not harmful, obscene, libelous, or disruptive. Whether school-sponsored or not, student literature and publications must be free of arbitrary conditions; however a time and a place for distribution of student literature may be established where necessary to maintain order. Public school students do not enjoy the freedom of association accorded to teachers and other adults. Administrators may restrict student organizations if the group is likely to disrupt the school or substantially interfere with other students.

Right to Privacy

The Fourth Amendment guarantees the right of the people "to be secure in their persons, houses, papers, and effects against unreasonable searches and seizures." There are few legal precedents involving search of public school teachers. It is clear, however, that any intrusion into the private lives of teachers must be limited to conduct that may affect their ability to perform in school. Students' rights must be respected in situations involving searches of their persons, their lockers, and personal belongings. The 1974 Family Educational Rights and Privacy Act (20 U.S.C.A. 1232G) also delineates students' rights with respect to their school records.

In order to maintain orderly, healthy, and peaceful school environments, school administrators sometimes find it necessary to search student lockers and desks. The courts recognize that students have a diminished expectation of privacy in their lockers and desks since school authorities retain control of them. Administrators are generally held to the standard of reasonable suspicion, not probable cause, when search is deemed necessary. Ordinarily, where police are involved, a search warrant is necessary. Understandably, where search of a student's person is involved, greater efforts must be made to protect his or her rights. Drug testing and background checks of teachers are certain to occasion litigation in this area in the near future.

The Fifth Amendment ensures that no person "shall be compelled in any criminal case to be a witness against himself nor be deprived of life, liberty or property without due process." The right against self-incrimination is invoked in cases where administrators have questioned teachers or students about conduct outside the school. Thus, the Fifth Amendment also creates a right to privacy.

The Ninth Amendment provides that "the enumeration in the Constitution of certain rights shall not be construed to deny or disparage others retained by the people." Teachers and students have relied on this amendment to support their claim to certain so-called personal life-style rights such as privacy and grooming.

Equal Protection

The Fourteenth Amendment provides in part that no state shall "deny to any person within its jurisdiction the equal protection of the laws." This clause has been used in a variety of teacher and student rights cases as well as discrimination cases. This amendment specifically prohibits states from depriving citizens of life, liberty, or property without due process of law. For teachers, property rights may be at issue in such matters as tenure and contractual rights to employment. Liberty interests of teachers may be involved when, for example, a teacher having been stigmatized in the course of dismissal proceedings is unable to find employment. The property rights of students often relate to cases involving suspension and dismissal. Liberty rights of students may pertain in discipline cases.

Due Process

The courts have not defined due process of law in terms applicable to all situations. Rather, the judiciary has provided guidelines and flexible procedures. For example, in *Goss v. Lopez* (1975), the Court stated: "At the very minimum, therefore, students facing suspension and the consequent interference with a protected interest must be given *some* kind of notice and afforded *some* kind of hearing." When teachers have a property interest, for example, in a continuing contract, the school district may not suspend or dismiss that teacher without a) written notice of the charges, b) an impartial hearing, including an opportunity to present evidence and cross examine, and c) receipt of a transcript of the proceedings.

Conclusion

Perhaps more than any school-related case in recent history, *Goss v. Lopez* challenges administrators to address such critical questions as, How is an administrator to balance the rights of the individual with the important social need to conduct effective and efficient schools? Does the traditional, school-as-family image of the school where mother and father know best still work? How much discretionary power does an administrator need to develop a safe learning environment?

See also Due Process; Judicial Decisions; School Law.

—John J. Lane
De Paul University

References

Fischer, L., Schimmel, D., & Kelly, C. (1986). *Teachers and the law.* New York: Longman.

McCarthy, M.M., & Cambron, N.H. (1981). *Public school law, teachers' and students' rights.* Boston: Allyn & Bacon.

Reutter, E.E. (1985). *The law of public education* (3rd ed.). New York: Foundation Press.

RURAL SCHOOL DISTRICTS

The rural school district is an integral part of the educational system in America. Historically, schools in rural areas have served as the backbone of education for millions of citizens in every state. As recently as 1913, one-half of all school children in the country were enrolled in the more than 100,000 one-room schools. While these particular schools have dwindled rapidly along with the numbers of school children living in nonmetropolitan areas, larger rural schools continue to provide educational benefits to a substantial number of students in rural areas.

The U.S. census defines the rural population as comprising all persons living outside urbanized areas in the open country or in communities of fewer than 2,500 inhabitants. By this definition, some 30 percent of the population live in rural settings. Currently, over half of the nation's school districts are located in areas classifed as rural. Of this number, slightly more than 4,000 districts representing approximately 27 percent of all districts in the country have fewer than 300 students. Rural districts are similar to those of urban areas in organizational pattern and administrative characteristics. However, they are substantially different in terms of numbers of students, population density, and financial support. The situation in rural schools creates an avalanche of problems for the school administrator. The superintendent finds it difficult to obtain adequately trained teachers. Teachers sometimes must get along without support specialists; in-service training for teachers is lacking at times. Problems arise when the principal seeks to improve the curriculum and to maintain modern school facilities.

It is generally agreed among researchers and educators who are involved with rural schools that they are uniquely different from larger schools located in metropolitan areas. This distinction is important since in past decades public policy decisions have often been oriented to the improvement of school programs by emphasizing solutions to problems that occurred in urban schools. Size became a major criterion for good schooling during the decades of the 40s through the mid-70s. As a result, hundreds of small rural school districts were eliminated or changed radically (consolidated) as a means of improving the education of rural youth.

The assessment of educational change during the 1980s placed more restraint on the consolidation of rural school districts. Declining enrollments in many rural areas, increased transporation costs, and the continued isolation of a number of rural schools from larger populated areas have made it increasingly difficult to enlarge the enrollment of smaller schools. More importantly, changing attitudes about the values of a small school education and the importance of growing up in a nonmetropolitan area have made the traditional solution of school consolidation not as beneficial as once suggested. Since the 1970s, the migration of urban residents to rural areas has been substantial. These new country residents in many instances are seeking a slower-paced life-style, smaller pupil/teacher ratios in school, and more individual attention for their school-age youth. The values of smallness; the benefits of local control; and the closeness of administrators and teachers with parents, children, and community are perceived by many as preferable to bussing and attending larger schools.

Educators in rural schools are faced with a number of challenges in attempting to provide quality programs for their students. Factors of isolation, scarcity of population, lack of financial resources, and distances to major service centers greatly hinder educational improvement. Many rural educators at the national, state, and local levels believe that public policy toward schools must change from a generic approach to one that recognizes the values and unique problems of rural communities. A differentiated policy that will assist rural schools and communities to build on their strengths and improve weaknesses is needed.

A number of states have recognized school differences, and state legislatures have established funding formulas which give school districts extra financial support to operate small schools in sparsely populated regions. A handful of states have also created offices within the state departments of education to assist the rural districts to improve their educational programs.

More than thirty states have developed intermediate regional service units to provide needed services to rural school districts. The agencies working cooperatively with the schools provide services that the districts individually could not afford. Services vary from cooperative purchasing and media distribution to employment of school specialists and traveling teachers.

Fruitful school improvement has been noted when local school systems join together to deliver services to the schools collectively. These types of support groups are called *educational collaboratives*. They are voluntary and exist to exchange goods and services among the districts involved.

A few universities are realizing the needs of rural schools and are providing a broad range of services. Universities may help schools that need specialized classes with the use of an electronic blackboard system. With the electronic blackboard, the teacher uses the classroom as a studio while the presentation is transmitted to school districts who do not have a specialist in that subject area. Other support areas needed by rural schools are in the training of the teachers for rural areas, an internship program, and in-service programs specifically focused upon rural problems.

Despite the many obstacles to better education for students who attend schools in rural areas, small school districts are persistently improving their programs. Rural educators have found that being small has its problems, but it also means that schooling is more flexible and personalized. In the minds of many, the strength of the rural school is its smallness. The school administrators, teachers, parents, and community members know one another, respect each other's viewpoint, and are committed to keeping school and community as a traditional and invaluable way of life.

See also Computers, Administrative Uses; Consolidation of Schools; School Districts.

—Ivan D. Muse
Brigham Young University

References

Barker, B. (1985, Spring). A description of rural school districts in the United States. *The Rural Educator, 6*(3).

Nachitgal, P. (1980). *Improving rural schools.* Washington, DC: Institute of Education.

National Center for Education Statistics (1983-84). *Statistics of state school systems.* Washington, DC: U.S. Department of Education.

S

SCHEDULING, STUDENT

Scheduling demands the development of a detailed and timed plan for the utilization of a given set of resources and procedures. Instructional programming is similar to what is more traditionally called *scheduling*. Some argue that programming focuses on *sequencing*, whereas scheduling emphasizes *timing*. In its broadest definition, however, *scheduling* includes the *timing* and *sequencing* of learning resources to achieve programmed educational missions. The time frames in a schedule may vary from a module as brief as ten minutes to longer periods of 60 or 70 minutes or to a large blocked time unit of several hours.

The responsibility of the principal is to verify that the schedule is accurate, informative, relevant, and flexible. Computer scheduling does not eliminate the so-called "headache" of instructional programming; it raises the technique to a more sophisticated level, allowing better correlation of the intricacies of machines with the complex human being.

Factors Affecting Scheduling

Regardless of school size, scheduling is no easy task. A variety of factors influence how the instructional program is structured and operated. *Some* components are (a) the specific courses to be offered in a school program; (b) the effect of double extended school sessions, if these are in use; (c) school activities; and (d) negotiated agreements.

Policy decisions relating to class size are also dictated by certain conditions: (a) national, regional, or state recommendations; (b) the philosophy of the district and administration; (c) room and building capacity/special facilities; (d) negotiations; and (e) fiscal considerations.

Registration

Registration at the secondary level or in any school utilizing a *departmentalized* plan involves the integration of external requirements, student/subject selections, teacher qualifications, and time units into one comprehensive, workable operation. How registration is handled may well be the factor determining the efficiency with which a year or semester is begun and consequently the school year itself.

Closely associated with the registration of students is the concept of *preregistration*. The planning of registered students either the semester or year before enrollment has been a vital part of effective school operation. In some schools, students meet in homerooms or counseling groups, study the list of possible course offerings, and then complete the necessary forms. All selections are then tallied, and a schedule is constructed. In other schools, the schedule of offerings is constructed first, students then register for classes, necessary adjustments are made, and the final schedule is redistributed. Registration handbooks are strongly recommended.

Registration cards should be color coded by grade or level to assist in filing, locating, or analyzing cards and schedule placement.

Master Schedule

Once registration is complete, a *master schedule* needs to be constructed. The master schedule is the comprehensive schedule of the program offerings for a particular school. It is a record of all pertinent information needed by the principal to operate the curriculum in that school. It generally is maintained in the principal's office for reference purposes, while a *teaching* or *class* schedule is printed and distributed to faculty and students for their use.

Types of Schedules

Regardless of the technology involved, three basic types of schedules are used at this time: (a) *block* or *group*, (b) *mosaic*, and (c) *modular* (flexible).

1. *Block-time scheduling* is most common in small high schools generally offering limited numbers of sections per class and in the junior high or middle schools where students are usually grouped into their classes for blocks of time.

2. The *mosaic pattern* of scheduling is the most widely used type of scheduling practice. Basically, it is a "trial and error" technique using various devices to limit the chance factor. The success of this technique relies upon the use of a conflict-resolution sheet, particularly with the single-section courses, since two or more sections of courses can be maneuvered to fit within the schedule. The usual pattern is to begin with senior schedules and move down the grade-level pattern so as to be certain that graduation needs can be met.

3. *Modular (flexible) scheduling* uses periods of time (called *modules*), normally ranging between 10 to 30 or 40 minutes. *Units* are identified as a prescribed number of pupils. The *modular unit*, therefore, refers to a prescribed number of students meeting within a specified unit of time. Thus, when large group, small group, and independent instruction are utilized, the day-to-day flexibility of a schedule can be designed to meet various planned instructional needs. Computers are a requisite in large schools for this type of scheduling because of the numerous possibilities available.

See also Computers, Administrative Uses; Enrollment Projections.

—Anthony Saville
University of Nevada, Las Vegas

References

Dempsey, R., & Travers, P. (1982). *Scheduling the secondary school.* Reston, VA: National Association of Secondary Principals.

Hughes, L., & Ubben, G. (1984). *The elementary principal's handbook.* Boston: Allyn & Bacon.

Saville, A. (1973). *Instructional programming.* Columbus, OH: Charles E. Merrill.

SCHOLASTIC APTITUDE TESTS

Scholastic aptitude tests are used in education to predict students' success in school-related tasks. The best known aptitude test used in education today is The Scholastic Aptitude Test (SAT), developed by the College Entrance Examination Board and later administered by the Educational Testing Service (ETS). Other aptitude tests are the School and College Ability Test (SCAT) and the Graduate Record Examination (GRE). Since the SAT dominates the field of scholastic aptitude tests, this article focuses on that instrument. The comments can be generalized to other aptitude tests, however.

According to the Educational Testing Service, the SAT measures developed abilities of verbal and mathematical reasoning and comprehension that are acquired gradually over many years of experience and used both in school and nonschool settings. There are two other rationales for labeling the SAT an aptitude test: first, it is not tied to a particular course of study as are achievement tests; and second, it is designed to assist in predicting future academic performance. Achievement tests, on the other hand, measure a student's mastery of certain subjects.

Three principal arguments are generally advanced for the usefulness of the SAT in college admissions. It is considered to be an important *supplement* to high school grades. When test scores are consistent with high school grades, the grades are confirmed. When the scores are inconsistent, further study of the applicant's qualifications may be warranted. A second argument is that the SAT is an objective measure. It is not subject to the various grading standards of our nation's diverse secondary schools. The third major argument in support of the SAT is that high school students use their SAT scores to help them select colleges appropriate to their ability.

All of the arguments advanced in support of the SAT and the rationale behind labeling it an aptitude test should be carefully weighed. Recent research has raised some significant questions about the usefulness and applicability of the SAT for higher education. For example, the main purpose for the SAT in college admissions is that it helps predict students' academic success in college. This fact has been established through hundreds of validity studies conducted over several decades. However, recent research by James Crouse published in the *Harvard Educational Review* presents strong evidence that small increments in predictive effectiveness do not necessarily translate into improved admissions decisions. Most colleges make essentially the same acceptance decisions without the SAT as they make with it.

Similarly, the Educational Testing Service has never presented evidence which shows that the SAT is less tied to high school curricula than achievement tests. The limited available evidence suggests, quite to the contrary, that aptitude tests are no more curriculum-free than standardized achievement tests.

The argument that admissions officers need the test to control for grading standards also does not hold up under scrutiny. Schools such as Bowdoin and Bates receive more than 2,000 applications annually, but do not need the SAT to make admissions decisions. Many colleges in the United States receive fewer than 800 applications and have admissions officers who could evaluate candidates without the SAT.

Nor has the Educational Testing Service studied how students use their SAT scores to select colleges. No one knows to what extent students do this, and whether it is, on balance, a good thing. In fact, it may be true that colleges use the College Scholarship Service to purchase the names of SAT-takers far more than students use their SAT scores to select colleges.

In addition to the above-mentioned problems, there are two other abuses of the SAT that deserve mention. The SAT is frequently named as a measure of school quality. Small increases, for example, in national SAT averages are cited as evidence that educational reform is working. But even the Educational Testing Service does not argue that the SAT measures school quality. Powell and Steelman in a recent *Harvard Education Review* article also discuss many adjustments which should be made in state SAT averages before one should attempt any cautious comparisons.

The final caveat about using the SAT and tests like it is an obvious one, but one of the most important. The SAT should never be used as the single most important variable. It is designed to be a supplemental measure. The National Collegiate Athletic Association's ruling to institute a test score cutoff for freshmen athletic participation is an example of the pernicious effects of test misuse. The use of a single SAT cutoff score to determine athletic eligibility will penalize far more blacks than whites since blacks score about one standard deviation below whites on the SAT.

It is, of course, no secret that students, parents, guidance counselors, and high school teachers exhibit considerable concern over the SAT. Many people view it as the gatekeeper for higher education. But, in fact, most high school seniors are admitted to their first-choice college. The great majority of American colleges and universities are not at all selective. The average acceptance rate in American four-year colleges is about 80 percent. Probably not more than 40 private colleges in the United States admit fewer than 50 percent of their applicants, and perhaps only half a dozen or so have the luxury of admitting only 20 percent.

Certainly one reason the SAT has such a powerful hold is what might be termed a "bandwagon" effect. The College Board was organized in 1901 by some of the most influential and prestigious northeastern universities. The SAT was introduced in 1926 but did not become the Board's principal test until after World War II. As hundreds of schools decided to join the board after the war, it was logical for them to turn to the SAT. Institutions less prestigious than Harvard and Yale look to these influential schools for leadership.

But each institution should evaluate the usefulness of the SAT for its own purposes. Standardized tests may have some usefulness in higher education. However, they should be used carefully, and the traditional assumptions about their use should be challenged by individual colleges and those administrators responsible for the tests' use.

See also Test Score Reliability and Validity; Tests, Criterion- and Norm-Referenced.

—Dale W. Trusheim
University of Delaware

References

Crouse, J. (1985). "Does the SAT help colleges make better selection decisions?" *Harvard Educational Review, 55,* 195-219.

Donlon, T. (Ed.). (1984). *The college board technical handbook for the scholastic aptitude test and achievement test.* New York: College Entrance Examination Board.

Owen, D. (1985). *None of the above: Behind the myth of scholastic aptitude.* New York: Houghton-Mifflin.

SCHOOL BOARDS

School boards govern the public elementary and secondary schools in local communities throughout the United States as an integral part of our American institution of representative and participatory government. Their constituency is the people. More than 97 percent of the 97,000 school board members governing our nation's 15,350 public school districts are elected to office by the voters. The remainder are appointed by other locally elected officials. They oversee the expenditure of more than $125 billion in local, state, and federal funds.

The board of education, as a governmental entity (a) identifies the educational needs of the people in the local community within the societal context of not only the community but also the state and nation both today and into the foreseeable future; (b) determines the priorities of those needs; (c) adjusts those needs to local, state, and federally-provided financial resources available; (d) assures that educational programs offered are in compliance with law; and (e) evaluates program results and initiates changes as needed to assure a sound and equitable education for all students.

All of this is carried out by school boards within the overall framework of their own policies, state and federal law, the advice of the district's superintendent and other professional staff employed by the school board, and the school board's understanding of the political-social-economic environment in the local community in which its own credibility and legitimacy as a part of representative government are anchored.

Individually, school board members come from all walks of life. Through them, taxpayers and all citizens are assured of a direct channel to influence educational policymaking. Theirs is a tripartite function:

1. To serve as *governors* of the public schools in the local community. As a governing board, they employ a superintendent and, with his or her professional assistance, establish educational goals, set budgets, hire personnel, evaluate programs, provide for school facilities and equipment, approve contracts, and determine educational and managerial policy.

2. To serve as *advocates* for school children who are neither in a position nor possess the information necessary to champion the cause of education among the citizens of their own community.

3. To serve as *ambassadors* to the community. In this role, the school board explains the instructional program, presenting the facts in plain and understandable language. It keeps the public informed about public school operation and explains the curriculum. It imparts information about the students' accomplishments and the attainments of the teachers and school administrators. The school board points to the need for all citizens to support the public schools during the present time—a time when a good education is an essential safeguard in our technological and free society.

School board members have always been responsible for governance. In latter years, their other two functions of advocacy and ambassadorship have gained greatly in importance. This is due to various demographic facts of life. For example, declining student enrollments and the growing number of parents estranged from each other have combined to result in a decreasing proportion of adults who have youngsters in school or who are in a position to know personally what is going on in the schools.

Historically, caring parents have been the most vigorous supporters of the public schools. And they still are. But not only are their numbers diminishing; people are living longer. Thus, parents are becoming a smaller proportion of the population. School board members, working with parents, teachers, administrators, other school employees and older students, must ensure that public education is viewed not merely as a parental responsibility, but as the civic duty and the preeminent priority in state and local government in the United States—the duty and priority that Thomas Jefferson thought it should be.

See also State Boards of Education.

—Thomas A. Shannon, Executive Director
National School Boards Association

Reference

Knezevich, S.J. (1984). *Administration of public education: A sourcebook for the leadership and management of educational institutions* (4th ed.). New York: Harper & Row.

SCHOOL BUSINESS MANAGER

The nature of the business management function is such that it pervades every aspect of the educational enterprise. The conduct of the business affairs of schools and later school districts was originally the province of lay committees. As the size and complexity of school operations grew, this function became a part of the duties of the superintendent. Later, due to continued growth and increased complexity, these duties commonly were assigned to an individual other than the superintendent. The person who oversees the business management function may be called the school business manager, chief fiscal officer, or assistant superintendent for business or finance, depending on the location and size of the school system. In smaller districts throughout the United States, this function may be performed by a single staff person under the direction of the superintendent.

Roles and Responsibilities

The school business function is that of a combined educational generalist and technical specialist. As such it includes primary responsibility for traditional management functions such as planning and budgeting, organizing, staffing, controlling, directing, coordinating, and decision-making activities within the context of the wide number of support services undertaken by school districts.

A major function is the development and maintenance of the budget. The chief fiscal officer is responsible for coordinating the sources and amounts of revenues with the appropriate expenditure projections. The fiscal management of the school district is contingent upon the business manager's ability to develop long-range fiscal projections based on appropriate data about funding which must then be balanced against enrollment projections and facility, staffing, and faculty needs. This planning process is required in order that the superintendent and the board of education can make appropriate policy decisions which will result in a quality educational program provided in a cost effective manner. Additionally, the business manager is responsible for short term plans in response to immediate district needs requiring the disposition of resources.

Organizing and staffing functions require the school business manager to direct attention to the infrastructure of support services; for example, development of transportation plans includes determination of efficient bus routing, procurement of vehicles, and the training of bus drivers and maintenance personnel. Each district's food service, custodial, and maintenance functions require that the school business manager possess appropriate skills to organize an effective and efficient delivery of services.

In most school districts, the business function also includes the selection, recruitment, training, and evaluation of noninstructional staff. In larger districts, these duties are often performed by individuals who are charged with the day-to-day responsibility of the specific task area. These individuals, however, usually report to the chief fiscal officer.

Coordination of most noninstructional activities, in order that they complement instructional activities, is another major responsibility. The school business manager oversees the district's efforts to meet federal and state regulations concerning various title and grant programs. Additionally, he or she is responsible for the coordination of the various local, state, and federal codes and directives that ensure the health, safety, and welfare of students.

Decision-making duties are diverse, ranging from decisions affecting the daily operations of the school district to decisions of a much larger scale. The school business management function provides appropriate and adequate financial information upon which the superintendent and board of education can base their policy decisions. Inaccurate or inappropriate information can have severe ramifications for the successful operation of the entire school system. Evaluation of support services, in terms of personnel as well as programs, is another ongoing activity. Further, recommendations for efficient utilization of revenues is inherent within the business function.

Subsumed under these major roles are a wide variety of specific task areas. The extent to which these responsibilities are found in any one district will vary, depending on its specific organizational structure. Among the most common tasks are fiscal accountability and financial reporting; budgeting; legal control; resource management; transportation; purchasing and warehousing; plant maintenance, operations, and security; food service; support personnel services and supervision; risk management; data processing; and grantsmanship.

The nature of these tasks and the expertise required to perform them vary greatly and call for a broad knowledge base and a wide variety of skills. Certainly, the school business manager must fully understand the technical task-oriented skills. More importantly, however, as a member of the superintendent's administrative team, it is imperative that the school business manager envision these tasks as part of broad goals and be able to articulate connections between the tasks and the district's educational goals.

Relationship to Administration

The school business management function can best be described as one which (a) facilitates information for decision making by providing data to be utilized by other administrators and the board of education, (b) supervises fiscal solvence through the maintenance of the fiscal health of the school district on a short- and long-term basis, (c) advocates policies and procedures which lead to the efficient utilization of school revenues in order to enhance the overall educational process, and (d) provides a safe and sound learning environment by taking action which provides for the health, safety, and welfare of the students educated by the district.

Qualifications

Certification requirements vary from state to state for license as a school business manager, ranging from no requirements to specific business manager certificates to requirements for certification as a school superintendent. Regardless of the certification requirements of a specific state, school business managers should be trained as educators and in business practice. It is customary that school business managers have an advanced degree in educational administration with appropriate teaching experience. Continued professional development is provided by a number of national organizations, some of which have state level affiliates. These include the Association of School Business Officers, International; the Council of Educational Facility Planners, International (CEFPI); and the American Educational Finance Association (AEFA).

See also Budgeting; Financing of Schools; Funding Methods: State and Federal.

—W. Hal Knight
East Tennessee State University
—R. Craig Wood
Purdue University

Reference

Wood, R.C. (Ed.). (1986). *Contemporary school business management*. Reston, VA: Association of School Business Officials, International.

SCHOOL CLIMATE

Despite the similarity of structure and function of schools, visitors entering a particular school sense a unique set of internal characteristics—its *school climate*—which affects the lives of those in the building. This composite of qualities sets each school apart from others and has been described as its feel, tone, ambience, or atmosphere. Another climate metaphor is personality. Just as each individual has a personality, each school also has one.

Definition

School climate is a broad concept encompassing the total environmental quality of a school. It results from the interaction of four large material and social dimensions of school environment. *Ecology* consists of the material resources in the school. Components of this dimension include the physical facilities, materials, equipment, and financial incentives. *Milieu* arises from the background characteristics which adults and students bring with them. Components of this dimension include teacher education, experience, and satisfaction; also included are student socioeconomic status, self-concept, and morale. The *social system* consists of the formal and informal roles which pattern school operation and social interaction. Components of this dimension include administrative organization, instructional program structure, ability grouping, administrator-teacher interaction, teacher-teacher interaction, and teacher-student interaction and communication. The decision-making and participation patterns of teachers and students also are included.

Culture consists of the norms, belief systems, values, and patterns of meaning of persons within the school. Teacher and student commitment, student peer norms, and academic and pupil-control expectations are examples of cultural components; the cultural components also include emphasis, consensus, goal clarity, and rewards and sanctions. Thus, school climate is a broad concept. It summarizes the essence of interactions arising from elements of the four environmental dimensions: ecology, milieu, social system, and culture. Although difficult to explain precisely, climate is easily sensed and quickly grasped in the metaphors of feel, tone, and organizational personality.

Issues and Research

School administrators are interested in three major issues concerning school climate: How is climate related to faculty behavior and attitude? How is climate related to student outcomes, especially academic achievement and attitudes? Can climate be altered, and, if so, how can the administrator alter it in desired ways?

Because school is such an embracing concept and because examining it requires precise definitions and means of measurement, studies of school climate designed to answer questions about its effects have been completed by using different definitions and indicators, each of which is more restricted than the broader definition given above. Specifically, most research focused on climatic aspects arising from the social system and culture dimensions of the school's environment. Further, most studies have focused on relationships between climate and only one or two of the roles in a school, such as principal, teacher, and student. The number of climate studies completed with each of the more restricted definitions and measures ranges from hundreds to one. However, the accumulation of studies has produced a pattern of answers to the general questions of climate effects on faculty and students. An overview of major instruments and patterns of research results follows.

The most used school climate measure is the *Organizational Climate Description Questionnaire* developed for elementary school use but now available in revised form for both elementary (OCDQ-RE) and secondary (OCDQ-RS)

levels. The conception of climate underlying the questionnaire focuses on culture and social system aspects of the internal environment. It measures only the interactions between the principal and teachers and among teachers themselves. The original *Organizational Climate Description Questionnaire* measures eight distinct behavioral dimensions. However, these separate measures are typically combined into an overall description of school climate along a continuum from *open* to *closed*.

In an open climate, the behaviors of both principal and teachers are genuine. The principal leads through energetic example and emphasizes an appropriate mix of task orientation and consideration for individuals. Teachers work well together, are committed, enjoy a sense of both task accomplishment and social-need satisfaction and do not feel burdened by paper work, close supervision, or administrative regulation. In a closed climate, behaviors of both principal and teachers are phony and not at all genuine, each going through the motions with little commitment or satisfaction. The principal stresses routine trivia, unnecessary busywork, close supervision, and impersonal relations. Teachers exhibit minimum compliance behavior and feel frustrated and apathetic.

Teachers working in open climates tend to experience higher job satisfaction, be more innovative, express greater confidence in their own and their school's effectiveness, and have higher motivation. They are also more loyal to the principal. Open climate is associated with schools having higher student socioeconomic status, greater principal and teacher experience, smaller size, and elementary rather than secondary level.

Student outcomes are also related to a more open climate. It is associated with higher morale, lower alienation, and lower dropout rate. By contrast, climate, as measured by the *Organizational Climate Description Questionnaire*, has not shown a consistent relationship with student achievement. The instrument measures only principal and teacher interactions; effects of such interactions on student achievement are indirect. Results of adult interactions would have to filter into classrooms through individual teachers; they might then affect student learning.

The *Profile of a School* is a climate instrument which taps the school's managerial system (social system and culture indicators) by measuring relationships between the principal and teachers. Respondents are surveyed about leadership, communication, interaction-influence, decision making, and control processes. The survey also covers training, motivational forces, goal setting, and performance goals. All this is done in order to locate the school on an *exploitative-authoritative* to *participative* managerial continuum. Participative schools have been rated more effective and have higher teacher and student satisfaction.

Pupil Control Ideology is a restricted measure of student-control beliefs on a continuum from *custodial* to *humanistic*. It may be used with any professional role. Individuals at the custodial pole desire a highly controlled setting, do not trust students, desire unilateral downward power and communication, and do not attempt to understand misbehavior but take it as a personal affront. Adults at the humanistic pole desire the school to be a cooperative community, view behavior through sociological and psychological concepts, believe in student ability to solve their own problems, and support a democratic environment in which self-discipline is learned.

The *Pupil Control Ideology* may be used as a climate measure by averaging teacher scores. Humanistic climate is related to lower student alienation, resentment, and unrest.

Greater humanism is typically found at the elementary level and in schools with higher socioeconomic status students. Open climate is related to humanism. *Pupil Control Ideology* is related to affective student outcomes, but research shows no relationships with academic achievement.

Not all climate measures are oriented toward adults. The *Quality of School Life* scale may be completed by students as young as fourth grade. It taps three dimensions: satisfaction (milieu), reactions to teachers (social system), and commitment to classwork (culture). This scale was designed to measure nonachievement outcomes and can be used as a climate measure. *Quality of School Life* is related to student behavior, aspirations, and academic achievement.

McDill and Rigsby developed scales to measure high-school students' perceptions of academic climate (culture dimension). These climate indicators assess the press toward academic rigor, quality, and the centrality of academic performance in the peer-status system. These climate indicators are related to academic achievement and student aspirations.

Brookover employed climate scales (culture dimension) answered by students and teachers in his "effective schools" studies. Student climate scales include academic futility, present and future expectations and evaluations, academic norms, and expectations of teacher push and teacher norms. Teachers' measures include expectations for student completion of high school and college, teacher and student commitment to improvement, and academic futility. These measures are related to student academic achievement, self-concept, and self-reliance.

To summarize, school climate is a broad concept. No single measure or study has captured its totality. Each measure is oriented toward one or more selective climate dimensions and most assess climatic aspects arising from the social system and culture dimensions of environment. In general, measures of adult interactions are related to other adult attitudes and behaviors important for the satisfaction and effective functioning of educational professionals themselves; however, these climate measures show little relationship with student learning, though there are relationships with some student attitudes. On the other hand, measures which tap student and teacher perceptions of academic and expectational climate are related to student academic achievement and attitudes. Thus, climate is related to important behaviors and attitudes among both professional educators and students, although the relationships are complex.

Caution is advised against hasty use of these ideas and instruments. Those who wish to diagnose their schools should complete a serious study of school climate before beginning. References are provided at the end of the article. Uncritical use of these ideas and tools may result in outcomes similar to the blind men who each touched a different part of an elephant but could not put the whole of their perceptions together meaningfully.

Climate Improvement

Attempts to change school climate are even more difficult than defining and measuring the concept. There are few studies of attempts to change climate. Further, climate is generally stable because its components are anchored in the past as well as in the present. Human beings require predictability in their environments in order to function. The dimensions of ecology, milieu, social system, and culture all provide stability. To change them and their interactive results is a major and difficult task.

The physical condition of the building is often related to school effectiveness. Tidiness and obvious care send a message about the importance of the people who inhabit the building. Paint, bright murals, and graphic representation of important values may affect climate.

Climate may be affected, knowingly or unknowingly, by changes brought about for other reasons. Changing buildings, student attendance areas, or grade alignments within existing buildings because of declining or growing enrollment, desegregation, or other considerations affect both ecology and milieu dimensions. High faculty turnover may affect milieu. Decisions about what proportion of elementary and secondary teachers to put into a new middle school, whether to have a larger or smaller number of self-contained classrooms, and whether to organize the school by academic departments or interdisciplinary teams, or a decision whether to organize a large high school on the "house plan" will affect the milieu, social system, and culture bases of school climate.

Principal change is another way to change climate. The principal is the central figure in the school social system. A new principal may be able to bring about changes in climate through social system and culture adjustments. Principal change, however, does not guarantee desired climate change.

Attempting to change the climate of a school with a stable faculty and administrative leadership is the most typical case. Here, the support of the principal is absolutely necessary. Organization development is a sound strategy to pursue because it focuses on organizational rather than individual change. Although it is possible for the principal or other insiders to lead the change effort, serious consideration should be given to engaging a third-party consultant whose background has been checked carefully in regard to an ethical, effective, and flexible approach. The consultant should specialize in organization development or organizational training. Good consultants bring objectivity, skill, and breadth of perspective to insiders. Leadership support of consultants is crucial.

Typically, organization development involves two stages. During *diagnosis* data are gathered, problems are identified, and plans are developed. During *intervention* methods such as team building, intergroup problem-solving, conflict resolution, planning, training programs, survey feedback, and interpersonal process consultation are used. The exact program will depend on the particular setting, existing climate, and desired changes. To have a chance of success, organizational development must continue for two to three years. Climate change is difficult; it requires major time and financial investments and strong support from all administrative levels.

See also Social Learning in the Schools; Student Culture.

—Robert B. Kottkamp
Hofstra University

References

Anderson, C.S. (1982). "The search for school climate: A review of the research." *Review of Educational Research, 52,* 368-420.

Hoy, W.K., & Miskel, C.G. (1987). *Educational administration: Theory, research, and practice* (3rd ed., chapter 8). New York: Random House.

Schmuch, R.A., Runkel, P.J., Saturen, S.L., Martell, R.T., & Derr, C.B. (1972). *Handbook of organization development in schools.* National Press Books.

SCHOOL DISTRICT/UNIVERSITY PARTNERSHIPS

Partnerships between school districts and universities involve the sharing of resources in order to promote the interests of both institutions. Partnerships and collaboration imply mutual goals and mutual responsibility for the achievement of those goals.

Even without any formal partnership program, universities are inherently linked to school districts and, especially, the high schools. Universities are dependent on high schools for their entering students and for the quality of the students' academic preparation. High schools, on the other hand, are dependent on universities to set standards of quality. Substantial evidence indicates that high school standards and requirements are raised or lowered in response to the raising or lowering of university standards and requirements.

School districts and universities have also been closely linked through teacher education programs. Departments of education place student teachers in schools and rely on experienced teachers to assist in the training of prospective teachers. The university education faculty uses the schools as research sites and provides in-service education to teachers.

Beginning around 1980, school districts and universities have sought to move beyond traditional linkages and establish formal partnerships designed to improve the quality of education at both levels. Such efforts were a response to a variety of pressures, including a national concern about the quality of public education, a need of universities to enroll more minority students and more talented students generally, and an expectation that the resources of the university should be used to help solve serious societal problems. As a result, partnerships have been established to facilitate communication between high school teachers and their discipline colleagues in the university, to reduce transition problems for students moving from high school to college, to improve the preparation of prospective teachers and first-year teachers, to help schools deal with mandated school desegregation and for a host of other purposes.

Formal school district/university partnerships have been encouraged by third parties, especially foundations and educational associations. For example, the College Board's Project Equality has supported a number of model school district/university collaboratives. Individual partnerships have specific goals such as to develop curriculum units or to encourage eighth grade students to take more demanding high school courses; but the overall goal of the College Board project has been to increase the number of students who are well prepared to enter college.

As another example, in 1986, the Carnegie Forum's Task Force on Teaching as a Profession recommended the establishment of clinical schools where a significant portion of teacher education programs would be housed. University education faculty would teach some of their courses in the clinical schools, and the public school teachers would be given adjunct status at the university and cooperate in the training of teachers.

Substantial outside funding has also been available to enable school districts and universities to develop partnerships that help disadvantaged students prepare for and remain in college. Prominent among these programs are those that seek to identify and help prepare minority students for such careers as engineering and the medical professions.

While third party organizations have been helpful at getting partnerships established, most collaboration originates locally and is supported locally. These types of partnerships include the coordination of services such as recruitment and admission procedures, research consortia, and the teaching of college courses in high schools.

Programs that provide for the teaching of college courses in high schools are an important example of partnership and collaboration. Much duplication exists between the university curriculum and that of high schools, and the high school courses do not always challenge the more advanced students. Advanced-placement programs have been common for many years, but recently programs such as the Accelerated High School sponsored by the University of California at Berkeley and Project Advance at Syracuse University have extended opportunities for advanced coursework to more students and have helped establish close working relationships between high school teachers and university professors.

A number of obstacles get in the way of formal partnership programs that attempt to foster collaboration between school districts and universities. Seemingly trivial differences such as mismatched time schedules and bureaucratic procedures can make collaboration difficult. Of more significance, existing reward systems will often not adequately value work done in a partnership program. This is especially true in the case of the university. "Turf problems" arise as one institution or the other jealously tries to protect its own prerogatives and cherished ways of doing things. University faculty members sometimes treat teachers with disdain, while school people may distrust university researchers and regard their projects as irrelevant to school needs. This is particularly the case when a cooperative endeavor is presented as the pet project of the university. In these situations, politics can become intense, and cooperative ventures can become a series of meetings designed to address problems.

In order to overcome these obstacles and create effective partnerships, school districts and universities need to attend to a number of issues. First, partnerships should address common concerns and be based on shared perceptions of problems. Second, both the school district and the university should be involved in program planning; there should be shared control of the project, and participants should work with parity. Third, partnership goals should be sharply focused, rather than grandiose and general. Fourth, the institutions must provide meaningful recognition and rewards to individuals who work in the partnership project. Fifth, the support and active involvement of the chief executive officer of each institution is absolutely essential if collaborative programs are to have a good chance for success.

In order to secure needed resources to support a new partnership program, institutions frequently look for outside funding. Care must be taken to guard against the dissolution of the project as soon as the seed money is exhausted. It is also necessary to provide for explicit evaluation of partnership programs.

See also Advisory Committees; Business-School Partnership; Change Process.

—William Kritek
University of Wisconsin-Milwaukee

References

Maeroff, G. (1983). *School and college: Partnerships in education special report*. Princeton, NJ: Carnegie Foundation for the Advancement of Teaching.

Wilbur, F.P. (1984, October). "School-college partnerships: Building effective models for collaboration." *NASSP Bulletin, 68*(472-476), 34-49.

SCHOOL DISTRICTS

School districts are quasi-municipal and quasi-corporate entities which have been created by every state except Hawaii to establish and operate public schools within its district boundaries. (The entire state of Hawaii is one school district, governed by the state board of education and administered by the state superintendent). They are quasi-municipal in that they are a special type of local government entity and quasi-municipal in that they have the power to contract, sue and be sued, accept grants and gifts, and, in most cases, manage their own internal affairs. It is generally recognized that school districts possess only those powers which have been delegated to them by the state constitution or legislation, which are necessary to carry out the delegated powers, or which are implied by the delegated powers.

School districts are operated by citizen boards, which are known by a number of different titles, including school board, board of education, board of public instruction, and board of school directors. Members of the boards are elected by popular vote in most cases, although in some larger cities they may be appointed by the mayor. However selected, board members are state officers, charged with carrying out a state function, public education, in a defined area of the state.

School districts may be divided into fiscally dependent and fiscally independent districts. Fiscally dependent school districts generally must have their budgets and tax levies approved by another governmental body, usually a city council. Fiscally independent school districts may establish their own budgets and levy their own taxes, restrained only by appropriate state requirements.

With great variety from state to state, school districts have different classifications. Usually, a common district will operate only elementary schools, a union district will operate only high schools which serve a number of common school districts, and a unified or consolidated district will operate both elementary and secondary schools. City school districts are those that provide public education within cities, while county school districts have boundaries which are coterminous with the counties in which they are located.

School districts may be abolished, altered, consolidated, or created by the state, either by act of the legislature or, as necessary in a few cases, by state constitutional amendment. The state has the authority to mandate many of the activities of school districts, such as courses to be taught, taxes to be levied, financial records to be kept, reports to be submitted, number and terms of office of board members, and the method and time of the board members' election.

As quasi-municipal and quasi-corporate entities, school districts face a number of problems stemming from that mix of political and corporate attributes. They are governed by state statutes, constitution, and administrative regulations, while also under the same federal constitutional and legislative restraints as are their parents, the states. They discharge governmental functions, such as providing instruction, food services, and pupil transportation, but they also engage in proprietary activities, such as plays, concerts, and athletic events. Each of these types of activities is governed by separate bodies of law, whether constitutional, statutory, regulatory, or common or case law.

See also Funding Methods: State and Federal; Judicial Decisions; National School Boards Association; School Boards.

—Michael J. Stolee
University of Wisconsin-Milwaukee

References

Black, H.C. (1951). *Black's law dictionary* (pp. 1511-1512). St. Paul, MN: West.
Reutter, E.E., Jr. (1985). *The law of public education*, (chapters 3 and 4). Mineola, NY: The Foundation Press.Inc.
Valente, W.D. (1985). *Education law: Public and private, Vol. 1*. (pp. 39-50). St. Paul, MN: West.

SCHOOL IMPROVEMENT AND EFFECTIVENESS MOVEMENTS

In the last two decades a major shift in emphasis on the criteria of educational quality has occurred. The *Equality of Educational Opportunity* report (1966) marked a watershed in the concern for school quality and school improvement. The findings of that national study indicated that the kinds of input charateristics which had been the major focus in earlier years were not significantly associated with the basic academic outcomes in student achievement. School facilities and the paper qualifications of teachers were not significantly correlated with student achievement in reading, mathematics, and other academic skills. This finding that schools did not make any difference in student achievement led to a major shift in the criteria of educational quality from inputs to student outcomes.

Another finding of the *Equality of Educational Opportunity* report, as well as many others, was the discrepancy in student achievement between the children of the affluent social strata and the children of the poor and racial minorities. Early studies in the '40s demonstrated that differences in educational programs, particularly in secondary schools, were highly associated with differences in socioeconomic status of the families from which students came. Subsequent research has repeatedly demonstrated that the level of basic educational achievement is highly associated with the socioeconomic and racial or ethnic background of students. Furthermore differences between students from poor and/or minority families and those from more affluent families have generally increased as students move through the grade levels in most American school systems. The nature of the schools as identified by input characteristics made little or no difference in either the basic school achievement or later life achievement over and above the effect of family background.

The reaction of educators and educational researchers to the conclusion that schools made little difference in the achievement or the lives of students was the beginning of the contemporary school improvement movement. This movement is undergirded with an extensive expansion of research on school characteristics that affect outcomes for students and on the nature of effective teaching. We are now examining what happens in the school and in the classroom rather than examining the nature of the facilities and the expenditures for education. The nature of the student's family background and his or her presumed level of ability are still used as major explanations for failure to teach many students. Increasingly, however, we are asking how can we improve our teaching and how can we improve the nature of the school learning environment in order to provide high-level outcomes for all students, both children of the affluent and educated on one hand and the children of the poor and less educated on the other.

The finding that some schools can and do teach essentially all of their students, affluent or poor, to high levels of performance demonstrates that it is possible. Two shifts in school-learning theory have provided a basis for examining the conditions for learning. Benjamin Bloom has concluded from extensive research that all persons can learn the lessons which any person in the world has learned if provided the appropriate conditions for learning. Bloom's conclusion has resulted in educational researchers asking, "What are the conditions of schools that affect whether students learn the desired objectives?" Associated with this is the development of the sociology and social psychology of school learning which postulates that the nature of the school social system affects the learning of the students in the school. The improvement of schools has therefore increasingly shifted from an emphasis on identification of individual student differences and school input characteristics to an examination of the social conditions and processes involved in the teaching/learning process.

Political Implications

There are two parallel movements or aspects of the school improvement movement. The first of these arises from political action resulting from the nationwide concern about the quality of schools. Although some movement had been under way, the primary impetus for the political action to improve schools was from The National Commission on Excellence in Education report *The Nation at Risk.* This assessment of the condition of American education and the dangers associated with the failure to provide high-quality education stimulated much state legislative and executive action concerning education. School administrators are well aware that the state efforts to improve education take many forms. These include, among others, higher teacher salaries, merit pay for teachers, career ladder programs for teachers, higher or different requirements for teacher certification, teacher competency testing, and better teacher recruitment programs. All of these are oriented toward improving the quality of teachers. State programs also include longer school days, more hours to provide instruction, new graduation requirements, more courses or different courses, new educational services, new equipment (particularly technological equipment), higher graduation requirements, student basic competency testing programs, smaller classes (particularly in the primary grades), some provisions for choice of school, and numerous other changes.

In addition, the National Governor's Association has initiated the *Governor's Report on U.S. Education, 1991.* Seven task forces have been created with governors on the staff to recommend state policy options in a number of areas. These include (a) attracting and retaining good teachers; (b) improving young people's readiness for school; (c) expanding educational opportunity and choice; (d) encouraging results-oriented leadership; (e) making more efficient use of school buildings; (f) making effective educational use of advanced technology; and (g) assessing and improving the quality and standards of colleges. Actions and policy changes that may result from these governors' task forces are yet to be determined. They do however, represent the level of concern for the improvement of education through state government.

For the most part, the government legislative and executive programs have paid little attention to what happens in schools and classrooms, or the process of teaching and learning. Many of these programs have focused on doing more of the things previously done. However, a few states and the federal government are aware of the parallel school improvement movement generally identified as the effective schools movement. The National Institute of Education has identified and funded two centers for research on effective schools. The Center for Research on Effective Elementary and Middle Schools is located at The Johns Hopkins University and the one on high schools is located at the University of Wisconsin, Madison. Two states, Mississippi and South Carolina, have passed legislation which involves programs of school improvement based upon the findings of effective schools research. Connecticut, Ohio, New Jersey, and perhaps Departments of Education in other states have plans to enhance the quality and equity of education, also reflecting the effective schools research.

The New Jersey Department of Education is now involved in litigation over financing effective schools. This case, commonly known as *Abbott vs. Burke,* is probably the first test of the use of effective schools research as an argument against changing school financing to make it more equitable. The argument is that effective equitable education does not result from changes in financing. The programs of effective schools designed to bring about equitable education do not require additional financial support. Others argue that any effective school program requires major changes which cost money to provide the necessary in-service training, staff development, released time, and other needs. Court decisions in this and other cases will no doubt have significant impact on the effective schools movement as well as other state action.

These illustrations indicate that the effective schools research and effective schools movement have some impact on state and federal actions, but most states' legislative and executive actions have been relatively independent of the parallel effective schools movement.

Educational Implications

Although the effective schools movement involves some emphasis on input characteristics such as teacher preparation and educational technology, the primary focus is on the teaching which produces high and equitable outcomes for students. It also marks a shift in emphasis in school improvement from diagnosis of and sorting of children on the bases of presumed individual differences to emphasis on the school learning environment. Students' school achievement has previously been a function of family background and presumed differences of ability. The current emphasis on effective schools has shifted the focus to the nature of the school learning environment, the teaching-learning process, and teaching behavior in the classroom. The criteria of effective schools have become the level of the student achievement and the equity in student outcomes rather than the sorting and differentiating of students—a differentiating that produces increasingly wide gaps between the achievement of students from the more affluent families and the achievement of students from poor families. This school improvement movement focuses on the improvement in student outcomes rather than inputs into the school.

Although there is still inadequate knowledge of the nature of effective schools, the fact that there are some schools that are highly effective in teaching children of the poor and minorities as well as the affluent indicates that it can be done. A brief summary of the state of our knowledge regarding the characteristics of the effective schools and the processes of improving schools is appropriate.

Nature of Research

The research on school effects and effective schools has been predominantly on elementary schools; therefore, our knowledge is much greater for elementary schools than for middle schools and high schools. The recent research has been of two primary types. The first is the study of particular schools identified as exemplary, outliers, or other atypically effective schools. These studies have focused on identifying characteristics of the unusually effective schools which have been identified by various methods. In the second type of study, regression analysis has been used on a sample of schools to determine the degree to which characteristics of the school environment explain differences in student achievement.

Although some scholars have identified weaknesses in the various studies, it seems safe to conclude that research to date has provided two general findings. The first of these is that some schools are impressively effective in teaching students from all kinds of family backgrounds. Most American schools are reasonably effective in teaching the students from highly educated, affluent families, but relatively few have demonstrated their effectiveness in teaching the children of the poor—particularly black and Hispanic poor. Although the percentage of such effective schools is small, their existence does demonstrate that it is possible to teach essentially all students. The second major finding of the research to date is evidence that some characteristics of schools are significantly correlated with the level of student outcomes.

The correlates of effective schools have been variously identified, and their classification varies from study to study. Drawing on a wide variety of research, Brookover and his associates classified the characteristics of schools that are correlated with the level of student achievement in three categories. First is the *ideology* of the school, the characteristic beliefs, expectations, evaluations, and feelings about the students in the school. Second is the *organization* of the school, including teacher and student role definitions, student grouping patterns, principal's leadership, and related aspects of the organization. Third are the *instructional practices* of the school, including the identification of objectives, the type of instructional programs, and related instructional practices.

The late Ronald Edmonds identified the correlates of effective school outcomes in five general categories: first, principal's leadership and attention to the quality of instruction; second, pervasive and broadly understood instructional focus; third, an orderly and safe climate conducive to teaching and learning; fourth, teacher behaviors that convey the expectation that all students are expected to attain at least minimal mastery; and fifth, the use of measures of pupil achievement for program evaluation. Other research demonstrates that the patterns of grouping for instruction or stratification of the student body are associated with student outcomes. There is also an extensive body of research that indicates that actual time on task or time engaged in the teaching-learning process is highly associated with student learning.

It is important to recognize that, although there is extensive evidence from various studies that such school characteristics are associated with the school's effectiveness in teaching its students the basic skills, there is very little evidence which indicates that these or any other characteristics are actually causal in producing the desired achievement outcomes. Some of the characteristics identified may be the result of higher achievement, or higher achievement and the school characteristics may both be the result of other causal factors.

There have been many analyses and critiques of the effective schools research. Some critics seem to assume that effective schools are both impossible and undesirable. In any case, it is clear that more and better research is needed to provide a completely sound foundation for designing schools that are effective in teaching all children.

Completely controlled experiments over extended periods of time are extremely difficult, if not impossible, in school effectiveness research. However, longitudinal studies and natural experiments in schools that have undertaken programs to make them more effective are being designed to analyze both the characteristics of effective schools and the processes of change from less to more effective ones.

Although definitive knowledge of the characteristics of effective schools and methods of improving schools is not yet available, many schools and districts have undertaken to improve the quality of student outcomes in the last few years. Many of these programs have little or no relationship to the body of effective schools research, but numerous others are designed to change schools in the manner suggested by that research. The diversity of the programs provides an opportunity for longitudinal evaluative studies to determine the factors associated with both the nature of the school and the processes of improving schools.

Summary

The effective schools movement might be summarized by a few statements. First, it is characterized by the belief that schools can teach essentially all students, rich or poor, to high levels of performance. This is confirmed by the fact that some do. Second, it focuses reform attention on the schools as the basic unit for improvement. The emphasis is on the school learning-teaching environment rather than inputs into the school. Third, schools can change; some have already demonstrated that significant improvement in outcomes is possible. Fourth, a school administrator can make his or her school effective in teaching all students if he or she is willing to risk some objections by associates who insist that present schools are adequate or that other routes to improvement are better.

The relationship between the two parallel improvement movements that have been presented is not yet clear. As we have noted, some state legislators have drawn on the effective schools research in their school improvement legislation. A bill has been introduced in the U.S. Congress to do the same. Some attempts by states and local school districts to improve school outcomes are not likely to succeed. Some may interfere with the improvement of outcomes. It is important to evaluate carefully the effect of all such movements on student levels of performance in the areas of achievement deemed important. School administrators should therefore insure that all programs to improve student outcomes should be carefully and objectively evaluated to determine their effectiveness.

See also National Reports on Education; School Climate.

—W. B. Brookover
Michigan State University

References

Austin, G.R., & Garber, H., (Eds.). (1985). *Research on exemplary schools.* New York: Academic Press.

Brookover, W.B., Beamer, L., Efthim, H., Hathaway, D., Lezotte, L., Miller, S., Passalacqua, J. & Tornatsky, L. (1982). *Creating effective schools: An in-service program for enhancing school learning climate and school achievement.* Holmes Beach, FL: Learning Publication, Inc.

Kyle, R.M.J. (Ed.). (1985). *Reaching for excellence: An effective schools source book.* Washington, DC: Superintendent of Documents, U.S. Government Printing Office.

SCHOOL LAW

Schools are an integral part of American society. Hence school law has been shaped by the larger forces in the American legal system during the last two hundred years. The law, in turn, has influenced the school in this country much in the way it has influenced other public and private institutions. To understand the current trends in school law, therefore, it is important to look at developments in the larger historical and conceptual framework of the United States Constitution.

The constitution originally drafted and distributed to the states for ratification in the 1780's contained only seven articles which basically described the election and powers of officials of the federal government. It placed heavy emphasis on majority rule. The "tyranny of the majority" was viewed by many as an evil as great as the tyranny of the British Crown. Thus the Bill of Rights was adopted, containing the first ten amendments to the constitution. These amendments spelled out the freedom of speech, freedom of religion, the right to a trial by jury, the right to be free from self-incrimination, the right against cruel and unusual punishment, and a variety of other rights.

This created an interesting dynamic between the rights of the majority, as spelled out in the first seven articles, and the rights of individuals spelled out in the first ten amendments. Governmental officials, no matter how strong their majority, could not carry out policies and practices which abrogated the individual rights spelled out in the Bill of Rights. Individual rights described in the Bill of Rights and subsequent amendments to the constitution were ultimately extended as limitations upon the power of state and local governments as well. This tension between the rights of the majority on one hand and the rights of the individual on the other has been the touchstone for many of the great legal debates within the country in the past two hundred years.

Striking the balance between individual rights and majority rule is also at the heart of understanding school law. For most of our history, for example, it was thought that teachers gave up many of their individual rights when they became public employees. Likewise, students were said to relinquish constitutional freedoms when they entered the schoolhouse. These bedrock concepts of pre-World War II school law were dramatically altered between the mid-1950s and the mid-1970s.

These years marked a significant expansion of individual rights and the corresponding diminution of the rights of school officials. Whenever a new individual right for teachers or students was identified, the sphere of authority exercised by school officials was curtailed. In many instances, the policies or practices of the school officials were backed by solid majorities of people within the school districts. Yet those policies and practices had to yield to the individual rights guaranteed by the U.S. Constitution.

This trend is often said to have begun with the 1954 Supreme Court decision in *Brown* v. *Board of Education*. Racial segregation of students mandated by state law in four southern and border states was declared unconstitutional because it collided headlong with the rights of students under the equal protection clause of the Fourteenth Amendment. There can be no doubt that the segregation laws in those states enjoyed wide public support. Yet the U.S. Supreme Court held that those policies were superseded by the rights of individual school children.

Ten years later the United States Congress enacted the Civil Rights Act of 1964. Among other things, this act prohibited discrimination on the basis of race and religion by institutions, including schools, receiving federal financial assistance. While most people would agree that the Civil Rights Act represented appropriate public policy, it still must be recognized as a curtailment on the discretion of local school officials to hire teachers on the basis of whatever criteria they chose.

In 1968, the U.S. Supreme Court decided *Pickering* v. *Board of Education*, in which a public school teacher had been discharged for writing a letter to a local newspaper criticizing the way in which the school administration handled athletic budgets and a school bond issue. The Supreme Court held that public school teachers had the rights of any citizen to speak out on matters of public interest. Although the discharge of this teacher for writing the letter to the newspaper may have had wide public support in the community, his discharge violated his First Amendment rights of free expression. Again, in striking the delicate balance between the rights of public officials and the rights of individuals, the Supreme Court came down on the side of an individual. This had the impact of curtailing the discretion of local school officials to react to teachers and other employees who publicly criticize the operation of the schools or engage in open discussion on other matters of public interest.

The free expression rights of students were at issue in a 1969 decision of the Supreme Court in *Tinker* v. *Board of Education*. Students had worn black armbands to school to mourn the deaths caused by the war in Vietnam. The students were suspended from school until they were willing to return without wearing the armbands. The Supreme Court held that students were entitled to engage in nondisruptive free speech activities inside the schoolhouse. School officials could bar such expression in advance only if they could forecast material disruption of the educational process caused by the free expression. The expression could be stopped and later punished only if school officials could demonstrate that such material disruption had occurred. Again, when the rights of school officials to carry out policies they perceived to be in the best interest of the majority of their school district clashed with the constitutional rights of individuals, the U.S. Supreme Court favored the individual, thus curtailing the discretion of school officials when dealing with students arguably exercising free expression.

Beginning in 1972, the United States Congress enacted a series of laws which created and enforced new individual rights in education. In that year Title IX of the Education Amendments was enacted. This provision outlawed sex discrimination in education programs receiving federal funds. Congress also barred employment discrimination on the basis of race, color, creed, religion, and sex in the employment practices of public and private employers, including local school districts. In 1973, Congress enacted Section 504 of the Rehabilitation Act, which prohibited discrimination on the basis of handicap by institutions, including schools receiving federal funds. In 1974, Congress enacted the Family Educational Rights and Privacy Act (commonly known as the "Buckley Amendment") establishing a host of new individual rights with respect to the maintenance and disclosure of students' education records. Also in 1974, Congress enacted Public Law 94-142, which granted a multitude of substantive and procedural rights to students needing special educational services by the schools.

The U.S. Supreme Court in early 1975 decided two cases on 5-4 votes which probably represented the extreme in terms of the emphasis on individual rights in education. In *Goss v. Lopez* the Court held that public school students were entitled to procedural due process prior to even short-term suspensions, except in emergency situations. The Court also held in *Wood v. Strickland* that school board members could be sued for personal money damages if they knew or should have known that actions taken against students violated their constitutional rights. It is interesting that the court should decide that elected local school officials could be held accountable in money damages for constitutional violations when the court itself had difficulty agreeing on what represented a constitutional right for students.

Several years earlier, however, the Supreme Court had sent a signal that it might be shifting away from an emphasis on individual rights and towards a position more supportive of the right of elected officials to carry out policies and practices perceived to be in the best interest of the majority. In *San Antonio v. Rodriquez*, the Supreme Court held, again on a 5-4 vote, that it was not a violation of the Equal Protection Clause for the state of Texas to rely on the local property tax to finance schools, although this led to wide fluctuations in the dollars available per student among school districts. This case is important because, among other things, the Court held that education was not a "fundamental interest" under the equal protection clause. That holding made it much more difficult to use the clause as a basis to overturn the practices of state and local education officials and was an indication that the expansion of individual rights was coming to an end.

The unwillingness of the Supreme Court to identify new individual rights in education continued in 1977 in *Ingraham v. Wright*. The Court held that students were not entitled to a due process hearing prior to the administration of corporal punishment. The Court also held that corporal punishment was also not "cruel and unusual" under the Eighth Amendment to the constitution. A year later the Court held in *Horowitz v. University of Missouri* that students were not entitled to a due process hearing prior to an academic dismissal. *Ingraham* and *Horowitz* together suggested that the Supreme Court was not inclined to expand procedural rights along the narrow disciplinary area outlined in *Goss v. Lopez*.

In more recent years, the trend away from individual rights and towards the rights of school officials has continued. For example, in *Grove City College v. Bell*, the Supreme Court held in 1984 that Title IX—the federal law prohibiting sex discrimination in the schools—applied only to those specific aspects of a school or college that receives federal aid. This decision may mean that Title IX does not apply to the athletic programs of schools and colleges, one area where progress towards sex equity has been particularly strong. Later in 1984, the Court held in *Smith v. Robinson* that students pursuing successful cases under the special educa-

tion law are not entitled to reimbursement of attorneys' fees. Without the possibility of collecting attorneys' fees from a school board at the end of a successful lawsuit, students and their attorneys would be substantially less likely to pursue litigation as a remedy for perceived injustices. While the decision does not affect students' substantive rights under special education legislation, it will have a serious impact on the willingness of students to take legal action to secure those rights.

In early 1985, the United States Supreme Court in *New Jersey v. T.L.O.* held that school officials had the right to search students' belongings with a reasonable suspicion that the student was concealing evidence of a violation of school rules or criminal statutes. The test articulated by the Court in *T.L.O.* was that the validity of a student search ". . . should depend simply on the reasonableness, under all the circumstances, of the search." While the Court left many important issues relative to student searches unresolved, such as the right of school officials to search lockers, the decision was an important reaffirmation of the right of school officials to conduct searches of students' belongings without first obtaining a search warrant from a court.

In late 1985, in *University of Michigan v. Ewing*, the Court strongly supported the right of school officials to make academic decisions. The case involved a medical student who was dismissed for poor scholarly performance. The Court's decision left only a very narrow legal basis on which to challenge academic decisions by school or college officials.

Thus the trend since the mid-1970s has been distinctly away from the identification and enforcement of new individual rights and towards a re-emphasis on the rights of school officials to operate schools in a manner deemed most appropriate. While individual rights are still an important reality in the operation of the schools, more and more it is clear that these rights need to be balanced against the need for educators to operate schools efficiently. At some point the balance may swing back towards individual rights. But that is the genius of our system of laws. It is flexible enough to accommodate subtle changes in the attitudes of the majority of people while at the same time respecting the established rights of individuals. Following and even influencing this trend are the major challenges in the study of school law.

See also Due Process; Judicial Decisions; Rights: Teachers' and Students'.

—Thomas J. Flygare
Sheenan, Phinney, Bass & Green
Manchester, New Hampshire

References

Reutter, E.E., Jr. (1985). *The law of public education* (3rd ed.). Mineola, NY: The Foundation Press.
Valente, W.D. (1980). *Law in the schools*. Columbus, OH: Charles E. Merrill.

SCHOOL SECRETARY

The school secretary should really be given the title of executive secretary or school director because of the variety and scope of the secretary's roles and responsibilities. The secretary is a secretary, but he or she also functions as a receptionist and as director of operations or even as a first aid provider. Positions range from one secretary per school at the elementary level to as many as 12 to 18 in large high schools, not all of whom are classified as secretaries. A general description follows which may be covered by one or more persons.

The secretary's training is 85 percent on the job. Skills must include the basics of typing, filing, shorthand, letter writing, word processing, and preparation of memorandums. Other skills must go far beyond the basics and are rooted in human relations, communications, verbal skills, technical knowledge, and the use of resources. Personality traits must include poise, loyalty, cheerfulness, a sense of responsibility, discretion, neatness in work and dress, adaptability, and leadership.

The secretary must serve in many roles such as surrogate parent and nurse, receptionist, secretary, coordinator of activities, host(ess), moderator, facilitator, counselor, information provider, and classroom or playground supervisor, but the most important role is that of communicator. A person in this position must be able to listen to and comprehend information, store it and relate it with accuracy and appropriateness of time and place.

The duties of a school secretary include answering the phone and providing callers with answers; being aware of the basic policies of the state, the school board, the administration, and the school; keeping records as required by all policies governing the school; assisting school administrators in fulfilling their roles; assisting teachers in providing the best education possible for the youth they serve; assisting parents in understanding and accepting the role the school plays in their children's lives; preparing correspondence as needed; keeping abreast of new developments, new equipment, new ideas, and new resources; functioning as a buffer between people with conflicting views; acting as a communications link between the various segments of the school; and often handling several of these duties simultaneously.

The secretary often serves longer than any one administrator and frequently sees several come and go.

Some of the problems to be avoided by the school secretary are these:

1. Secretaries are often privy to information which is confidential in nature, and a breakdown of this confidentiality is to be avoided.

2. Another problem which will lead to difficulties for a secretary is to become clannish or to be exclusive in working with the staff.

3. Open criticism of others by a secretary can result in isolation and diminished effectiveness.

4. Many times, the public's first and only contact with the school is the school secretary. The image the public has is based on these contacts. It therefore follows that the role of receptionist takes on great significance. This is a role that must be handled with diplomacy and tact.

The school secretary's position is unique in the realm of such positions.

See also Delegating Authority; Job Descriptions.

—Fran Johnson
Sunnyside Unified School District
Tucson, Arizona

References

Bull, F.T. (1985, Fall). "What constitutes an effective school?" *The National Educational Secretary, 51*(1), 8-10.

Casanova, U. (1985-86). "Are you the office?" *The National Educational Secretary, 51*(2), 12-13; *51*(3), 20-22; *51*(4), 18-19.

Fortenberry, R. (1985, Winter). "The role of the educational office personnel in effective schools." *The National Educational Secretary, 51*(2), 14-15.

SCHOOL SECURITY

In its simplest form, *school security* is the educational community's response to unwanted behaviors. This response takes various forms, ranging from New York City School's $30 million budget and 1,200 commissioned law officers through Prince George's County, Maryland, School Security Department, with a $1.8 million budget and 35 commissioned investigator/counselors, to Arlington, Texas' Security Chief supported with a cadre of guards.

Not only has the response of school districts been different throughout our country, but also problems differ in school districts as a function of their size, location, and socioeconomic mix. Clearly, Burlington, Vermont, has problems much different in tone and character from those in Tuscon, Arizona, or Salem, Oregon. Regardless of size or perceived problems, all districts have faced the problem with the same basic requirement: to differentiate between students who violate laws and students who violate rules. The former are committing crimes, the latter are engaging in disciplinary violations. Districts that have made that differentiation have found themselves in a position to respond to specific types of events with specific types of responses. And these highly specific responses represent the first step towards controlling unwanted events in public schools.

Information: The Key to Control

One of the ways school security offices help school districts is by promoting an orderly understanding of the nature and extent of the problems posed by misbehaving students. This understanding usually flows from the method used by school security personnel to keep track of crimes that occur in and around schools. Incident reports, filed in the district's central office, are often computer-analyzed to produce composite "profiles" of the characteristics of unwanted incidents. Typically, these "profiles" picture what is happening; where is it happening (zone of school); when is it happening (by time of day and day of week); who thinks it is a problem (who referred it); how it was handled (dispositions); and who was involved (characteristics of victims and offender).

Once this information is in a useful form (computerized and accessible) and is actually used (interpreted routinely each week), the district as an entity and the individual schools as subunits are in a position to formulate plans and practices designed to control future events that follow patterns of disruption signaled by the data.

Based upon analysis of the collected data, the specific nature of a districts's problems becomes evident. From the data flow the responses. Responses may range from reassigning nighttime roving patrols to providing intensive covert surveillance, from increased playground supervision to forming "student security advisory councils." It is important to stress that, nationally, school security operations differ as school district problems differ. The common elements generally include concern for protecting people and property both while school is in session and after hours.

Organizational Considerations

Critical to the success of any security operation is its visibility within a school district's administrative hierarchy. It is particularly important that the school system recognize that the director of security is an integral part of the superintendent's staff. This direct access promotes uniform and consistent districtwide enforcement of policies and practices relating to the handling of youth who commit serious misdeeds on school grounds.

This access is also important as courts increasingly scrutinize a school district's handling of administrative dispositions that have heretofore been wholly governed by the discretion of school principals. That is, as courts increasingly inquire about the administrative management of such issues as search and seizure, district administrators are increasingly advised to prepare, adopt, implement, and monitor consistent and fair practices for handling miscreant youth. School security offices can fulfill that function.

Options for School Districts

School districts interested in evaluating existing operations or in upgrading or changing services have a variety of options.

1. Security Audit: A security audit involves a team of security specialists who explore a district's exposure to legal liability and building-level vulnerability. Audits may be narrow in scope (e.g., an audit of the quality of existing alarm equipment) or broad (e.g., examining districtwide policies and practices).

2. Staff Training: A wide variety of training seminars and workshops are available. Examples include training in peacemaking, forming student security advisory councils, assertive discipline, team training for security action-planning, crime prevention techniques, and incident profiling procedures.

3. Computerized Data Collection: Thanks to recent developmental work sponsored by the National Institute of Justice (U.S. Department of Justice), complete packages of instructional material are now available to help district administrators implement computerized profiling practices.

Additional information on school security may be obtained from the National Alliance for Safe Schools in Austin, Texas, or the National Institute of Justice, Washington, D.C.

See also School Climate; Student Alienation; Vandalism; Violence in Schools.

—Peter Blauvelt
Prince George's County School District
Upper Marlboro, Maryland

Reference

Blauvelt, P.D. (1981). *Effective strategies for school security.* Reston, VA: National Association of Secondary School Principals.

SCHOOL-BASED MANAGEMENT

School-based management is a generic term for a complex of decentralized school management practices that place primary authority and accountability for decision making at the school site level. Associated terms are decentralized management, responsible autonomy, school-based budgeting, site-based management, lump sum budgeting, and shared governance.

School-based management is a matter of degree in both breadth and depth. Breadth refers to the range of management functions that are decentralized. For example, all or portions of the functions of teacher recruitment, teacher selection, program development, teacher evaluation, and budgeting might be decentralized to the school-site level. Depth of school based management refers to the level of the hierarchy to which decisions are decentralized. That is, decentralization might stop with the principal, or it might be extended further to teachers, or perhaps to parents and other citizens at the site level.

Advocates of school-based management cite the advantages of decentralized administration: lodging decision-making power nearer the point of implementation; improving the capacity of each school to adapt to the unique needs of its clientele; increasing faculty motivation by providing teachers with a sense of ownership; shortening the lines of communication; and creating a stronger sense of accountability at the school-building level. Skeptics point out the disadvantages: the "looseness" that accompanies the loss of centralized control; the difficulty of enunciating and achieving districtwide goals; curriculum articulation problems; diseconomies of scale; and public relations problems that may result from pronounced variations in school program quality. In districts where school-based management practices are adopted, the advantages are simply regarded as more compelling than the disadvantages.

Preconditions

Certain conditions must exist in a school district for school-based management to be feasible. First of all, the school district must have the prerequisite authority before decisions can be delegated. While this may seem obvious, state school systems do vary in the degree of centralization. If most of the important decisions are made at the state level, the district can hardly decentralize in any meaningful way.

A second precondition is an absence of turbulence in the district and its community. Movement to a school-based management system requires the expenditure of considerable energy, and such energy is unlikely to be available in periods of high stress and discord.

The existence of a cadre of competent building-level administrators is the third precondition. While principals are important figures under any system of school management, their strengths and weaknesses are magnified when they acquire more decision-making authority. The success of school-based management may not require that the district have a "super principal" in every building, but the principals must be reasonably competent, be willing to assume more responsibility, and have a capacity for growth. If there are principals who do not have such qualifications, they should be replaced through reassignment or attrition before school-based management plans proceed.

The fourth precondition is the support of the board of education. Board members may become uncomfortable when administrative decisions are removed from their scrutiny and become dissatisfied with what they regard as an absence of control. Unless board members are committed to school-based management, they will soon force its demise. The task of convincing the board of education logically falls to the superintendent.

Planning and Implementing

It is difficult to overestimate the importance of planning in moving from a conventional centralized system to a school-based management plan. Planning should include the development of a document detailing the school-based management program and its purposes; design for the in-service of persons whose roles will be substantially affected; a time-line for implementation; a review of the proposed plan by personnel who will be most affected by the program; and construction of a data base for building level planning.

As the person responsible for the organization of the school district, the superintendent is logically the one who would be taking the initiative to develop a school-based management plan. The first planning step might be informal discussions with the school board and key administrators to test their receptivity to such a plan. These initial discussions could convince the superintendent either to move ahead, to delay while providing the board and administrators with more information, or to discard the idea altogether.

Once it is decided to proceed, a formal planning group should be established under the leadership of the superintendent. This group should consist of representatives from the groups directly affected by school-based management—central office administrators, principals, teachers, parents, and citizens. This ad-hoc group should serve as a steering committee throughout the planning, early implementation, and initial evaluation of the program.

The first task of the members of the planning group is to familiarize themselves with the varieties of school-based management. Then, they should begin developing a document outlining the district's proposed school-based management plan. One of the first considerations will be the degrees of latitude to be permitted at the building level with regard to three major areas: curriculum, personnel, and budget. Some constraints will necessarily be placed on the autonomy of individual schools. State and federal laws, state education agency rules, collective bargaining agreements, and student transportation requirements are examples of inherent constraints. School district goals, the superintendent's objectives, the district's testing program, curriculum and program organization guidelines, and budgetary limitations may also be used to impose limits on school autonomy. A management-by-objectives plan should be prescribed to provide the superintendent with a means of monitoring and influencing developments in each building.

The major elements in the plan should spell out the particulars of decision-making authority, roles, and relationships. Any school-based model of management will place more authority for decision making with the principal and will shift the roles of central office administrators away from control and toward facilitation. Changes in job definitions and organizational procedures will reveal just how much control is to be decentralized. Where authority is lodged for writing guides, selecting materials, and determining scope and sequence will indicate the degree to which curriculum development is decentralized. Similarly, the identification of the decisionmakers for recruitment, selection, and teacher evaluation will indicate the location of control over the personnel function.

The amount of budgetary authority to be delegated to the principal is a crucial decision in developing a school-based management program. Inasmuch as personnel costs, which account for most of the school budget, are largely determined by district salary schedules, little control over a large portion of the budget can be allocated to the site level. Excluding personnel costs, it would be feasible for principals to receive a lump sum which they may then allocate according to building-level priorities.

The plan must also address the role of teachers and community members in school-based management. The amount of teacher participation could be left to principal discretion, or structures and procedures for teacher involve-ment in school site decision making could be prescribed. Similarly, the decision regarding the nature of community participation could be left to the principal or prescribed by the plan. Except in small districts, some amount of prescription seems advisable.

In-service training should initially focus on central office administrators and principals whose roles and functions will be most affected. Subsequently, teachers should receive training concerning their role in school-based management and in participatory decision making. Similar training should be given to parent and community advisory councils if they are to be a part of the plan.

An implementation timeline should be constructed to detail the various events and when they are to occur. The implementation might require three to five years. One year should be devoted to the in-service and orientation of personnel. After that, the implementation might proceed by phases, with more decisions being delegated to principals the second year, teacher participation commencing the third year, and community participation beginning the fourth year.

Once the ad-hoc committee has developed the plan, it should be reviewed and discussed by the parties whom it will affect. It could be the focus of a series of faculty meetings in each building, and it might be presented in PTA and service club meetings. The ad-hoc committee should then revise the plan in light of the issues raised in these meetings. The superintendent should prepare the document for final approval by the board of trustees.

Prior to implementation of the plan a data bank should be constructed for the use of building-level planners. Among the kinds of data that should be made available, aggregated both by district and building level, are enrollment projections, personnel characteristics and qualifications, and achievement test scores.

See also Administrative Team, District Level; Delegating Authority.

—Ray Cross
Corpus Christi State University

References

Burton, N., Toews, E., & Birnbaum, D. (1981). *School based planning manual.* Seattle: Seattle Public Schools.

Decker, E.D., Liebermann, J., Powell, M., & Whitneck, W. (1977). *Site management: An analysis of the concepts and fundamental operational components associated with the delegation of decision making authority at the school site level in the California public school system.* Sacramento, CA: State Department of Education.

Lindelow, J. (1981). *School based management: School management series, #23.* Eugene, OR: ERIC Clearing House on Education Management (Eric Document Reproduction Services No. 208 452).

SCHOOL-COMMUNITY RELATIONS

Although most administrators have acknowledged, over the years, the importance of school-community relations, it now needs to be recognized that this relationship is undergoing challenge and change. The public school as a cherished institution of American democracy is, for the first time in modern history, in danger of losing its role as the primary means of educating the nation's young. Reasons for this are myriad. The economy plays an important role. The odious fallout of Watergate tarnished all public/governmental agencies. Test scores fell for a time. Prestigious reports viewed education with alarm. The highest executive office in the nation, by advocating changes in the church-state balance, cast doubt on the moral integrity of educators and their work. The now perennial thrust for vouchers and/or tuition tax credits further weakens the foundation of American public education.

In addition, the nature of the local community is changing. Parents may want to participate in school-community relations, but often there is only one resident parent per child, and that one must work during the usual school day. Often the parents who do participate in school programs are critical of personnel and seem to be hostile. More often, citizens are confused about their role in regard to schools and seem reluctant to speak out. Perhaps these are the last vestiges of years of conditioning by educators to suggest to others that the professional educators know best and should be left alone. For all these reasons and more, the administrator must establish a climate in which faculty and staff agree that community relations are an essential part of their educational positions and not merely necessary evils. Anything less than broad-based understanding, support, and participation by the entire family of educators will lead to mediocrity.

Recommended Approaches

The need to justify schools and secure/maintain their support is probably the most important objective of community relations. Other objectives are to report to the community about the school program and the progress of students, to determine the educational needs of the community, and to discover and make use of community resources.

A minimum program of community relations requires administrators and boards of education to determine policies for and to provide the usual procedures for activities such as parent organizations, open houses or other versions of school visits, handbooks of routine rules and procedures, and newsletters. These are, of course, in addition to routine student progress reports and regular public-relations releases to all available media. This minimal program includes only outgoing communication and thus can never be completely satisfactory. All of these usual practices must be done with care and skill if the message from the school is to find its audience.

Good practice in community relations is not always and everywhere good practice. It is good for a particular objective, but practices that are well-chosen to accomplish one objective may be useless in regard to other objectives. Therefore administrators cannot collect a bag of tricks for community relations and relax. The practice must be both appropriate to serve the purpose, and it must be properly executed. For example, advisory councils as a procedure to earn the support of the community can be effective. As a means of reporting student progress, they are nearly useless.

Incoming communication must go beyond the parent-initiated request for information; it must extend beyond the biennial survey, usually performed when the levy must be put on the ballot. (In this connection, note that the ballot is one pragmatic communication channel available to all citizens. The message is either one of support or rejection.) Administrators must now discover or invent ways of identifying the aspirations and fears of new publics, "new" in the sense of regular, planned involvement with schools, as well as traditional publics and the host of single-interest groups.

Administrators must also discover or invent ways of communicating before discontented individuals and groups seize the initiative by invoking an ever-increasing means of community-to-school communication: the law suit. Legal battles damage the fragile, implied psychological contract of home and school and are wasteful of precious time and resources. Many costly legal entanglements can be forestalled by prompt attention to legitimate concerns of parents and other citizens. This requires careful, organized listening to all community voices.

Among promising practices used by schools in relating to the community are advisory councils, school and business partnerships, and citizen participation as volunteer aides or guest resource persons. But all of these practices can be detrimental if the administrator does not involve others *in* the school, such as teachers, as well as others in the community.

Clear guidelines on involvement are essential at the beginning and throughout a program of community relations. By definition, school-community relations cannot be a solitary effort performed on others by administrators. Busy work to give the appearance of meaningful participation will invariably boomerang and, worse yet, may ruin opportunities for subsequent honest involvement, since a history of manipulation and tokenism is hard to overcome.

Concluding Observations

The administrator of a successful school or school district must now possess, or have direct access to, political understanding and skill in school-community relations in order to secure and maintain an essential base of support in competition with other agencies with their own agendas and their own need for support. The public school monopoly has been broken. Therefore, administrators must convince skeptical faculties and staff workers of the necessity for, as well as the benefits of, a new orientation to the client population. This leadership will require a philosophical commitment to the concept of honest and open participation by all parties to public education.

Finally, despite optimistic interpretations of research reports, it is premature to assume that a sound community relations program will cause effective schools or that parent participation will improve student achievement. This may well be the case, but it may also be the reverse: that effective schools create good community relations and improved student achievement encourages parent participation. At this point the association exists and that, for the time at least, should be reason enough to attend to both elements in the equations: effective schools and sound community relations. This association represents a compelling reason for educators to give a high priority to community relations.

See also Business-School Partnership; Communicating with the Community; Community School Involvement; Community School Programs; Public Relations.

—Richard W. Saxe
University of Toledo

References

Marburger, C., Henderson, A., & Ooms, T. (1986). *Beyond the bake sale.* Columbia, MD: National Committee for Citizens in Education.

Saxe, R. (1984). *School-community relations in transition.* Berkeley, CA: McCutchan.

Zerchykov, R. (1985). *A citizens notebook for effective schools.* Boston: Institute for Responsive Education.

SCIENCE EDUCATION

Science education is the study and teaching of facts, concepts, principles, and generalizations commonly associated with the "natural" sciences. Implied in the definition is the study of how science is taught, the ways in which science is learned, and processes used by scientists as they conduct inquiries of natural phenomena. One distinguishing trait of science and science education is the *method* of science—empiricism. The empirical method is *the* mechanism by which scientific discoveries may be verified or refuted. While there may be authorities in science, authoritarianism has no place in either scientific research or science education. The hallmark of science education is to construct experiments so that when using similar conditions, the results may be duplicated.

Why Science Education?

The impact of science and technology on the world's culture is so pervasive that schools must offer systematic science instruction at all levels of schooling to insure a scientifically literate society. While science education has its origins in the empirical or scientific method, it is critical for students and teachers to understand, integrate, and apply the processes of science in other fields of study.

The processes of science are usually listed as observing, inferring, communicating, measuring, using space/time relationships, using numbers, classifying, predicting, interpreting data, defining operationally, controlling variables, formulating hypotheses, experimenting, and reading about science. By carefully examining the list of science-teaching processes, one easily concludes that these processes may be used with virtually every topic taught in the school curriculum.

Issues

Several contemporary issues are related to science education; however, only a selected set will be discussed. The first critical issue for science education is to have science taught systematically and as a *basic* in grades 1 through 8. Few states or provinces in North America define science as a "basic" which requires instruction at all major school levels.

The second issue relates to science instruction. In the elementary grade levels, textbooks are substituted in lieu of a balanced educational approach with appropriate print materials and selected science experiences. The term "hands-on science" is used to describe the laboratory components of science education. It is with "hands-on" experiences that children actually learn about the empirical characteristics of science.

The third issue is related to the development of critical thinking. The application of the fourteen processes of science education will help students to think critically. Quite obviously, this often means that social issues must be evaluated and discussed in science classes—at the appropriate grade level. For example, the topic of evolution evokes a general hysteria from persons who confuse *revelation* with empiricism. In science classes, controversy will emerge, but the ultimate evaluative criterion must be the testable experiment. Science teachers must continually apply and clarify the concept of empiricism as scientific or value-laden controversies emerge.

The fourth issue is related to the appropriateness of the science content being taught. Science as a discipline is a knowledge-expanding field. It is impossible to teach all the relevant topics in grades K-12. Thus, a major issue among science educators is what should be taught, how much coverage should be provided, and when should the topics be introduced or expanded in the curriculum. The scope and sequence of the science curriculum must be matched with learning theories that are compatible with what is known about the intellectual development in children and adolescents.

The fifth issue relates to the appropriate integration of computer skills with science instruction. Science education offers a unique opportunity to use computers to display data, arrange data, and synthesize data from student-generated experiments or activities.

The final issue concerns teacher preparation at the preservice level and the offering of quality in-service programs to practicing teachers of science. Teaching science at the middle school, junior high school, or high school level is a life-long commitment to continued learning. States and school districts have a responsibility to offer relevant course work, workshops, and educational experiences that will enhance instruction and knowledge of teachers of science. At the elementary school level, the issue is exacerbated by anxiety over teaching science, per se. Appropriate staff development in science education at the K-6 level is a critical need in all schools.

Implementing Programs

Schools with successful science programs have six critical elements. First, there is a districtwide determination of science *goals and objectives* from kindergarten through grade 12. Included are the reasons for supporting science education and the concomitant skills and processes.

The second element is the *scope* of the program. As print materials usually form the basic structure of a science program, it is important to select the most representative materials to illustrate the scope of topics. A wide array of topics needs to be identified to provide scientific literacy to the children in grades K-12. Further, local units relating to science and technology must be developed in order that children may realize how science influences their own living environment.

The third element is to develop a science *sequence*. Again, textbooks often determine the order of teaching. However, the sequence of a well-designed science program illustrates (a) the logic of science; (b) topic relatedness; (c) incremental learning and articulation of concepts; (d) developmental considerations for the relative difficulty of science concepts; and (e) time allocations and schedules to insure that science is taught systematically, not intermittently, at every grade level.

The fourth element is the absolute necessity for all teachers to *develop and practice a wide repertoire of instructional strategies*. Modern science programs require teachers to (a) ask questions in a systematic and humane manner; (b) use inquiry strategies that illustrate inductive, deductive, and hypotheticodeductive logical systems; (c) manage individualized, small group and large group activities; and (d) encourage their students to engage in creative science experiences. Lecturing to students about science should be used sparingly, if at all!

Evaluation is the fifth element. Two phases are needed: the first to show how well students are learning, the second to indicate how smoothly the program is running in the school district. Such an evaluation plan improves programs. Parents are informed about their children's progress.

Staff development for teachers and administrators is the final element in creating and maintaining a science education program.

Conclusion

Adopting a science program is a demanding process. Planning and implementing a quality program requires time, effort, and financial support. By following and expanding suggestions set forth here, you can improve the odds of providing a good science program.

See also Curriculum Development; Staff Development.
—Donald C. Orlich
Washington State University

References

Orlich, D.C. (1980). *Science anxiety and the classroom teacher.* Washington, DC: National Education Association.
Peterson, R., Bowyer, J., Butts, D., & Bybee, R. (1984). *Science and society.* Columbus, OH: Charles E. Merrill.
Rowe, M.B. (Ed.). (1982). *Education in the 80's: Science.* Washington, DC: National Education Association.

SEX DISCRIMINATION

Stereotypes about groups of people exist. They may be based on the clothing people wear, or patterns of behavior in which they engage. Some stereotypes are based on gender; every culture socializes its members to assume certain stereotypical male and female roles. For a long time in our country, our educational systems and economic institutions treated males and females differently. That differentiation today, for the most part, is illegal. Once our political and legal systems began to take a serious look at the impact of sex discrimination in education and employment, the inequities were recognized and legal processes were set into motion to make corrections.

A lot of sex discrimination against women in education and in employment has been unintentional. It often has been the result of traditional practices that impact more negatively on women than on men, the judging of women and men by group characteristics that may not apply to a particular individual, the assumptions about the relative needs of women and men, or other beliefs and practices of long duration.

Several laws and regulations were designed to challenge or change these old traditions. One is Executive Order 11246 covering all federal contractors. The order embodies two concepts: nondiscrimination and affirmative action. Nondiscrimination requires the elimination of all existing discriminatory conditions of employment, whether purposeful or inadvertent. Affirmative action requires that the employer make additional efforts to recruit, employ, and promote qualified members of groups who were formerly excluded.

The first federal law prohibiting sex discrimination in education became effective in 1971. Titles VII and VIII of the Public Health Service Act were amended to prohibit sex discrimination in admissions to federally funded health-training programs. The second law prohibiting sex discrimination in federally assisted educational programs was Title IX of the Education Amendments of 1972. While discrimination against females was the major reason for the passage of Title IX, the law covers discrimination against either women or men on the basis of sex. Any educational institution which receives federal monies is required to comply with the requirements of Title IX. This includes all schools—preschools, kindergartens, elementary schools, secondary schools, vocational schools, junior colleges, community colleges, four-year colleges, universities, graduate schools, and professional schools.

Although Title IX covers both students and employees, the legislation has had the greatest impact upon opening educational program opportunities to women students. Policies, practices, and procedures that once perpetuated sex discrimination are finally being changed. As an example, it is now illegal to ask questions in a job interview about age, marriage, family planning, child care plans, and spouse's employment, because answers to these questions are often used to decide whether a woman should be admitted to certain educational programs or employed in positions of responsibility. Overt sex discrimination in recruitment, admissions, housing, financial aid, and athletic programs' health care has largely been eliminated. The remaining problems lie in the interpretation and application of the new policies and procedures, the understanding of the subtleties of sex discrimination in its covert forms, and the commitment and resolve to carry out the intent of the new policies by eliminating sexism and gender stereotypes.

An example of these problems can be found in our educational and vocational counseling services. Although counseling within the educational setting cannot take all the blame or credit for the career and personal choices students make, it typically mirrors the attitudes prevailing within the institution and the society. Fifteen years after the passage of Title IX, we find far fewer females as compared to males in mathematics, computer sciences, engineering and technology, and the physical sciences. Negative stereotypes about women's ability to succeed in these fields in spite of evidence to the contrary still prevail. This kind of stereotyping is called *sexism*.

The word "sexism," only recently defined by dictionaries, denotes discrimination based on gender. In its original sense, sexism referred to prejudice against the female sex. In a broader sense, the term indicates any arbitrary stereotyping of males and females on the basis of their gender. Sexism is also a manner of acting or a behavior of one person used in a disparaging way against another person because of his or her gender. We cannot deny that this kind of behavior exists in our society, nor can we deny that it is aimed more often at women than at men. How do we change the environment in which we educate our young in order that sexism can be eradicated?

To begin with, we must recognize that the manner in which teachers treat boys and girls in the classroom during their formative years profoundly affects their later lives. The types of criticism and support provided boys in the classroom may assist them in becoming more independent and autonomous learners. Research on classroom biases suggest that teacher-pupil interactions vary with the subject areas, with boys likely to receive more attention in stereotypically male areas than girls. Those who are examining classroom interaction report that boys are more salient to teachers than girls. This is true regardless of the subject area, but it is particularly true when the subject is mathematics or science.

Sexist treatment of women in the classroom encourages the formation of behavior patterns which give men more dominance and power than women in the world. Boys talk, on average, three times more than girls in classrooms at fourth-, sixth-, and eighth-grade levels. Teachers praise boys for academic success but girls for neat papers. They give boys more time to respond to questions and more cues which can assist them in thinking about a question than girls. When girls seek attention from the teacher, they are told to raise their hands before speaking; boys who call out in the same way, however, receive the teacher's immediate attention. Fortunately, classroom biases can be eliminated through teacher training and an understanding of the problem.

Second, we must recognize that administrators and supervisors play key roles in developing effective schools. They have the ability to orchestrate the variables leading to positive educational outcomes. Last, but surely not least, we need to increase the number of women in administrative positions. Their visibility in key positions will symbolically define the appropriateness of leadership roles for women as well as for men.

See also Judicial Decisions; Sex-Role Stereotyping; Women in Administration.

—Marian J. Swoboda
University of Wisconsin System

References

Fennema, E., & Peterson, P. (1985). "Autonomous learning behavior: A possible explanation of gender related differences in mathematics." In C. Marrett and L.C. Wilkinson (Eds.), *Gender influences in classroom interaction.* New York: Academic Press.

Lindgren, J.R., Ota, P.T., Zirkel, P.A., & Gieson, N.V. (1984). *Sex discrimination law in higher education: The lessons of the past decade.* (Association for the Study of Higher Education—ERIC Higher Education Research Report Serial No. 4). Washington, DC: Association for the Study of Higher Education.

Sadker, D., & Sadker, M. (1985, March). "Sexism in the schoolroom of the 80's." *Psychology Today, 19*(3), 54-57.

SEX EDUCATION

In recent years, much has been written on the topic of human sexuality education in the public school. Educators have advocated the inclusion of human sexuality education in the curriculum as a separate course, as a separate sequence of courses, as an entire integrated strand within the K-12 curriculum, or as a series of topics infused into already exiting courses. All major studies to date have shown overwhelming support by parents and the community for human sexuality education programs within the school structure, despite the objectives of a vocal minority.

It is most often the actual or perceived threat of negative community reaction which delays, prevents, or diminishes the program in quantity and quality. However, a considerable research base in the areas of program effectiveness, student achievement gains, teacher effectiveness, and program implementation has evolved. This research base, coupled with notable successes in program implementation experienced by dozens of school districts throughout North America, now allows us to construct a proposed model for program implementation which can accomplish the major goals of a quality human sexuality education program, while mini-mizing negative community reaction. This model has four main components, each containing sequential activities. These components are precursor activities, the advisory committee, the school district, and follow-up activities.

Precursor Activities

Advocating a comprehensive human sexuality education program is a tricky business for the educational community. While it is possible to develop a program totally within the confines of the educational community, experience has shown that it is better to begin with a community base which advocates its inclusion in the curriculum.

Experience with successful comprehensive programs which have avoided controversy suggest that a three-part approach is advisable before actually beginning a human sexuality education program. The first step is the formation of a community study group whose charge and function should be clearly defined. This group should examine the needs of youth in the community, speak with health workers, and read materials which present a balanced view of human sexuality education in the curriculum. The intent of the group should be to develop broad recommendations for the administration as to whether human sexuality education is necessary in the school system, a list of suggested areas to cover in the curriculum, and potential networking possibilities both within and outside the community. Given these recommendations, the next step is for the administration to issue a statement of support for the group's efforts and to appoint an advisory committee to make specific recommendations for program content, direction, and goals, including those aspects of teacher training which specifically relate to program content. It is important that the study group and advisory committee be separate, although they may contain a few members in common.

The Advisory Committee

It should be noted that the advisory committee is one of the most critical components in establishing a high quality, comprehensive program. The committee should function as curriculum advocates, a buffer between community pressure groups and educators, and as reviewers of curriculum materials. They should hold regular meetings with the community.

The committee would be ideally chaired by an influential member of the community, with experience in group process and mediation, since such a group may have internal disagreements over emotionally charged issues. The committee must be truly representative of the community, with a membership weighted in favor of parents, teachers, and health workers. Care should be exercised in keeping those with a religious/political agenda off the committee, while encouraging communications between the committee and such individuals. An upper level administrator should be on the committee, as well as one or more members from the original community study group. In general, the committee should be limited to fewer than twelve members and should have a clear agenda for each meeting. Once established, the committee should be a standing one, enabling the members to be proactive rather than reactive.

The School District

At the district level, personnel such as curriculum supervisors, teachers, and others should take the recommendations of the advisory committee and further develop the suggested materials or otherwise adapt them for use in the curriculum. Ideally, a good human sexuality education program is infused into existing curriculum areas, such as language arts, home economics, science, and social studies.

Teacher training must absorb a great deal of attention at the district level. A human sexuality education program should never be forced onto teachers. Provisions should be made for training newly arriving teachers in future years. Teachers are the delivery system and to ignore their training needs is to ask for trouble in later years.

Once implemented, logistical support should be provided for teachers. These might include centralized scheduling of guest speakers, rotation of teaching resources within the system, curriculum reviews, attendance at professional conferences, and dissemination of information related to *both* human sexuality and human sexuality education. The later point is too often overlooked. Teachers also need coursework and continuing information related to sexuality.

Finally, the district must make plans for program evaluation before implementation. These plans should include teachers, students, parents, and community members.

Follow-Up Activities

After the program evaluation is completed, the results should be used as a vehicle to communicate with the advisory committee and the curriculum developers. Strategies for revisions should be formulated and implemented.

Follow-up activities should also include strategies for extending the community network and for increasing community involvement and servicing. Plans should be drafted for parent training in areas such as human sexuality, parent/child communication in sexual areas, the sexual development of children, community resources available for sexually-related issues, and other topics. Community linkages should be broadened and information about the program's experiences disseminated to the educational community.

In all cases, the program should be open for scrutiny by community groups. The perception of a "hidden curriculum" should be avoided at all costs. Teachers and administrators should be ready for the infrequent opposition which may occur when this model is followed through training in group processes, conflict resolution, active listening skills, and public relations. Those opposed to human sexuality education on religious/political grounds usually have objectives which can be characterized and which lend themselves to open, thoughtful, and honest community responses. Human sexuality education should be a *community* response to student needs and not the school operating in isolation. If this latter perception can be avoided, the program will surely succeed.

See also Community-School Involvement; Curriculum Development; Staff Development.

—Les Picker, President
Pyramid Group
Elkton, Maryland

References

Kirby, D. (1980). "The effects of school sex education programs: A review of the literature." *Journal of School Health, 50,* 559-63.

Picker, L. (1984). "Human sexuality education: Implications for biology teaching." *The American Biology Teacher, 46,* 92-98.

Scales, P. (1981). "Sex education in the 70's and 80's: Accomplishments, obstacles and emerging issues." *Family Relations, 30,* 337-41.

SEX-ROLE STEREOTYPING

In *The Nature of Prejudice*, Gordon Allport asserts that both prejudice and normal information processing among human beings are based in stereotyping. In the information-receiving process, persons organize information by collapsing it into categories based on similarities. They thereby focus on generalities and ignore some unique aspects of the information being processed. Nevertheless, some aspects of stereotyping are negative because they cause unfair treatment of some groups of people. Sex-role stereotyping is a case in point. To the extent that either males or females in our society are limited in their opportunities or achievements, because of the views either they or others hold about their potential based strictly on their gender, sex-role stereotyping is negative.

In schools, there are several areas where sex-role stereotyping operates, including the curriculum, school policies, and personal relationships among faculty, staff, and students. For example, regarding curriculum, if boys are encouraged to study advanced mathematics and girls are not, sex-role stereotyping is probably at work. If girls are encouraged to participate in artistic projects in a school and boys are not, regardless of their levels of talent or interest, sex-role stereotyping is probably at work. To the extent that any course is taught using illustrations which are more familiar to one gender than the other, when the course itself does not require material which is more familiar to either boys or girls, there is probably some stereotyping about which gender will profit most from the course going on. At the policy level, if school policy provides more support for boys' athletic programs than for girls' athletic programs, then sex-role stereotyping is probably at work. If more of a school's budget is devoted to remedial reading programs (an area where boys are most likely to have problems) than to remedial mathematics programs (an area where girls are most likely to have problems) sex-role stereotyping may be at work. In policy determinations, the stereotyping takes the form of deciding whose interests or problems are most important based on general considerations of gender.

Regarding relationships among students, faculty, and staff, stereotyping can teach powerful lessons which are not an intended portion of the curriculum. If a classroom teacher notices and comments on the appearance of female students and the ideas and achievements of male students, then sex-role stereotyping is probably at work. What is being taught in this case is that women are valued for their appearances and men are valued for their minds. There is evidence that boys get more attention than girls in the classroom and in special services. What is being taught here is that boy's needs are more important than those of girls. If the students in a school treat all members of the opposite sex as potential romantic partners rather than recognizing the unique characteristics of their opposite-sex friends, then sex-role stereotyping is probably at work.

In all such situations, a great deal of potential is denied; the potential of the female who is talented in mathematics and the male who is talented in art; the general intellectual potential of the females who are noticed only for their appearance; the athletic abilities or interests of the girls whose athletic program is underfunded; and the unique personality and intellectual characteristics of the males and females who are seen by the opposite sex only in terms of their eligibility for romantic or sexual relationships. Potential which is denied is likely to be undeveloped. Undeveloped potential is a loss to both individuals and to society. Thus, it is worth spending some effort on counteracting the effects of sex-role stereotyping.

The school may have to face some issues before making attempts to counter the effects of sex-role stereotyping, however. For instance, while experts believe that there are far fewer gender differences than stereotypes usually imply, and that in many areas the similarities between men and women are far greater than the differences, the evidence is not all in. Neither is there conclusive evidence which would tell the school administrator exactly what results will accrue from attempts to reduce sex-role stereotyping or the schedule on which those results will appear. The timetable for social change is rarely available in advance. Thus, the administrator may be placed in the position of advocating an approach which is unpopular with some of the parents or voters in the school district. The principal or superintendent may be unable to point to unequivocal evidence that the proposed interventions have a desirable effect, such as increased success or satisfaction in the lives of the students when they reach adulthood.

For the school administrator who is committed to an attempt to reduce sex-role stereotyping and its negative effects in the school, the question of what strategies to use is crucial. One approach might be to discuss the known effects of sex-role stereotyping in the areas of employment, earnings, and self concept with parents, faculty, staff, and students in order to enlist their aid in developing programs designed to eliminate the aspects of sex-role stereotyping about which they are most concerned. This promotes a feeling of control rather than of being manipulated without consent or control and utilizes the creative potential of these groups. Title IX coordinators may act as resources in the implementation of these ideas. Plans which are made and implemented using this consultative strategy should clearly be accompanied by an evaluation plan which was developed using the same strategy. That is, students, faculty, staff, and parents should be involved in a discussion of the desired results (the goals of the program) and how and when those expected results will be assessed.

It is clear that social values as well as developmental stages (in the case of the students) are involved here. No administrator should undertake a program of change expecting easy results. A more reasonable expectation is heated controversy followed by slow change. Only the strong and the patient will persevere.

See also Sex Discrimination; Women in Administration.

—Lenore Harmon
University of Illinois

References

Maccoby, E.E., & Jacklin, C.N. (1974). *The psychology of sex differences.* Stanford, CA: Stanford University Press.

Sargent, A.G. (1985). *Beyond sex roles.* St. Paul, MN: West.

Tavris, C., & Offir, C. (1977). *The longest war: Sex differences in perspective.* New York: Harcourt Brace Jovanovich.

SINGLE-PARENT FAMILIES

A trend toward single-parent households is apparent in the demography of the United States and certain developed countries of Europe. It is possible that this is a growing phenomenon in all countries, but data for developing countries on this trend are not so readily available as in developed countries. The U. S. Census Bureau reported in 1984 that there were 50.1 million households with two parents, 9.9 million households headed by women, and 2 million headed by men. Another closely related datum reported the same year was that full-time working wives earned an average of more than $10,000 a year less than working husbands ($13,070 compared with $23,800 for men).

This phenomenon is one of several demographic trends to which schools must become accustomed. The great increase in Hispanic population, the rapidly decreasing proportion of white Anglo students in schools, and the increasing choice of religious schools by Protestant families all have consequences for the future of public and private schooling in the U. S. Projections for the future are that a much higher proportion of children will live for a little more than three years with only one parent. Teachers in urban schools have long been aware that large percentages of their students live with one parent, usually a mother. Even in small towns of Pennsylvania, teachers report as high as one-third of their students live with only one parent. Parochial school teachers are expecting a growing proportion of each classroom to include children of one-parent homes.

Children of one-parent homes most often live with the mother, visit the father, or have visits from him occasionally. By far the largest cause of one-parent homes is divorces, although there has been no increase since 1983 in the percentage of divorces of all marriages in the U. S. One-parent children live mainly with mothers who suffer from low, if not below-poverty-line, income. The lack of money in these households has consequences for the behavior of students.

A mother's education is the most important predictor of a child's achievement in school, followed by a father's occupation. The most important resource of parents for children really is time, followed by money. The amount of time the mother spends with the school child, especially in the preteen years is related to the child's school achievement, but important as that variable is, the quality of that time, or how it is spent, is also highly important.

The resource of time spent and how the time is spent is affected by the mother's work situation. The mother who must work all day, organize household activities, and find time to work with her children is a mother who is working under pressure. She must either sacrifice a social life with other adults or shorten her attention for her children's school activities.

"Two heads are better than one" is an apt phrase for family resources, including time spent with children—one parent does not have the time or energy to spend on children's school and homework activities that two adults do. Nor does one parent have the knowledge of the school calendar and community and school resources available to children and access to other adults who are interested in furthering their children's school careers. Parental advocacy of other children has a great pay-off for their children's academic performance, school activities, and knowledge about how to succeed academically from kindergarten through graduate school.

Does the performance of children of one-parent households differ from that of children of two-parent households? That depends; the easy early answers to that question are getting decidedly more complex and qualified. Brown in 1980 reported a survey of the behavior, including achievement, of children of one- and two-parent families. He found that in elementary schools, one-parent children were much less apt to be high achievers and more apt to be low achievers than two-parent children. However in high school these differences were much less marked, although still somewhat in favor of two-parent children. Among low-income secondary students there was little difference according to type of family structure.

Pupil conduct was far more related to the membership of the family (one parent or two parents) than was pupil achievement. Elementary school children from one-parent homes were much more frequently suspended, and were more apt to be truant than children of two-parent homes. However, absenteeism was not related to type of home structure. The data for secondary students was even more dramatic. In Brown's sample, there were no cases of expulsion of students from two-parent homes; all the students who were expelled were from one-parent homes. Again, absenteeism was unrelated to the number of parents in the home, but suspensions and tardiness were far more frequent among students of two-parent than one-parent homes. These behavioral data may be related to the fact that two parents are more powerful advocates for their children than one parent, especially in such severe disciplinary events as expulsion. One parent may ignore some warning signals sent by the school, and when the school authorities opt for the "final solution" of expulsion, the single parent has less knowledge, time, money, and friends to fight the matter through. Expulsion requires procedural due process steps which allow parental advocates of their children many possibilities to defend their children, but single parents, especially poor and nonwhite single parents, simply lack the know-how or resources to do battle for their children.

The findings concerning achievement of children of one- and two-parent households are less simply in favor of the latter, as variables are controlled. Simple survey methods such as those used by Frank Brown led to conclusions which had to be qualified, given the use of statistical controls. Moffitt's report in 1981 of a study of father-absent boys in Denmark indicated that, using WISC scores, high SES father-separated boys had significantly higher scores in vocabulary and arithmetic than low SES father-separated boys. High SES father-separated boys scored significantly higher than high SES boys with two parents. However, low SES boys with and without fathers present did not differ significantly on both measures.

Shilling in 1982 studied a large sample of students of one- and two-parent homes in Pennsylvania. He said:

> from the findings of the controlled analysis it can be inferred that single-parent children achieve at lower levels because of the adverse social conditions in which many single-parent families live. Single-parent families were poorer, lived in areas of greater population density, had lower levels of parental interest in school, and were disproportionally members of the black race. All of these factors point to adverse social conditions for single-parent children that relate to lower achievement levels rather than intrinsic failings of the family struc-

ture. Interestingly, when the effects of these variables were held constant, white single-parent children achieved at higher levels than white two-parent children. This surprising finding possibly suggests that many nuclear families today are not as facilitative of child's school-related development as they once were considered to be.

He found that family structure was an even poorer predictor of the achievement of black children than it was for white children.

The widespread impression that losing a parent causes achievement to drop is simplistic. Other, more powerful factors are at work. What should perhaps be of most concern to teachers and administrators is that the known data illustrate that schools may define children of single-parents as disciplinary problems when in fact those children have attendance patterns no different from children of two-parent homes. School organizational structures may be punishing the one-parent child or withholding its support in many subtle ways.

Legally, the school must cooperate with noncustodial parents in providing them with information on their children. The school is caught in a vicious dilemma, however, if the noncustodial parent attempts to take the child home after school without the custodial parent's permission. School policies must be prepared to deal with such contests between parents. More frequent, however, is the phenomenon of the neglect or disinterest shown by the noncustodial parent which is more devastating psychologically.

School psychologists suggest a variety of mechanisms for single parents and their children in order to provide more support in the competitive atmosphere of the school. Among these suggestions are support groups of single parents meeting at night to explore ways to help children at home with school tasks; providing after-school activities for latch-key children, many of whom are victimized while alone after school; providing group counseling support sessions for children, placing father-absent boys of elementary age in classrooms with male teachers; and coordinating with community groups which provide additional activities and adult role models for children.

What school personnel have to keep uppermost in mind in order to help children of single parents, as for all children, is to maintain high expectations for their achievement and conduct. Discipline interacts with achievement. Poor discipline is related to low achievement. A school climate in which all children are respected and expected to mature in conduct and achievement is the strongest kind of support for all children. Children of single parents should not be defined as special targets of disciplinary concern nor as easy targets for suspension or dismissal. Fairness is the most essential element of due process. There is no substitute for fairness. But fairness is only a base on which to build expectations. High expectations of children is a necessary condition for high achievement. The fairness inherent in high expectations for all students, along with reassuring support for all children, is a key element of the culture of an achieving school. Parents and school personnel have to work together to establish a success-driven system in which children are encouraged and helped by parents, teachers, and administrators at home and at school.

See also Counseling and Guidance; Student Culture.

—Patrick D. Lynch
Pennsylvania State University

References

Burns, C.W., & Brassard, M.R. (1982, October). "A look at the single-parent family: Implications for the school psychologist." *Psychology in the Schools, 19,* 487-493.

Moffitt, T.E. (1981). "Vocabulary and arithmetic performance of father-absent boys." *Child Study Journal, 10*(4), 233-41.

Shilling, F., & Lynch, P.D. (1985, Winter). "Father versus mother custody and academic achievement of eighth grade children." *Journal of Research and Development in Education, 18*(2), 7-11.

SOCIAL LEARNING IN THE SCHOOLS

Considerable social learning occurs in schools. One aspect of this is self-identity, which is constructed in the school and which is based partly on interactions with others. Students, for example, learn to see themselves as academically capable or incapable, likeable, creative, nice, trustworthy, repulsive, trouble-makers, or unimportant, a recognition based on feedback from teachers and other students. Similarly, teachers construct an identity of themselves as teachers based on feedback from students and colleagues. As people internalize a self identity, they act on it, giving others the expected behavior. For example, the student designated as a trouble-maker becomes good at making trouble.

A second aspect of social learning is systems for classifying and describing people. Such systems are somewhat arbitrary, reinforce stereotypes, and affect how we deal with others; nevertheless, because they provide a way of ordering our social world, we tend to take them for granted. Students develop fairly elaborate systems for classifying each other. For example, Grant and Sleeter found that junior high students distinguish among popular kids, out-of-its, big mouths, hard guys, teachers' pets, athletes, burn-outs, and handicapped kids. Students could name the others they thought belonged to each category, and characteristics they attributed to each. Teachers commonly classify their students, for example, as fast or bright, average, and slow. These designations often are made early in the year and often are based on little data collected by the teacher. Once made, they suggest stereotypes that often are freely applied to students. Students classify their teachers, commonly designating them as nice, mean, good, too easy, and so forth. Administrators distinguish between teachers, for example classifying some as "goers" and others as "the dregs."

A third aspect of social learning is social skills. To the extent that students interact with others in school, they learn social skills. All students do not necessarily, however, learn productive social skills automatically. Students who feel socially inadequate tend to avoid social interaction, and thus miss social practice. Others develop inappropriate social skills, such as kicking a peer to express disagreement. School is an excellent setting for teaching and encouraging the practice of social skills; some teachers are very skilled at doing this.

A fourth aspect of social learning is developing a sense of belonging to a social group. The extent to which this happens varies widely among members of a school, and affects academic learning. Some students and some teachers develop close ties of affiliation with others who feel valued by the school itself. These are people who feel good about school, like being there, and do what they believe the institution expects. Others are isolates who develop very little feeling of belonging, and have no close friends in the school. School can be an alienating experience for them, although some invest their energies in their work and on the surface may appear satisfied. Schools often contain a counterculture—a group of students with close ties to each other, but who feel alienated by the institution. Youth gangs are an example. School authorities often perceive such students as poorly adjusted or antisocial, which in a sense is partly inaccurate since group members may relate very effectively with each other.

Academic Learning

One implication for academic learning is that teachers and students respond to each other as people. For example, a teacher who feels uncomfortable around speakers of Black English may communicate that discomfort by maintaining physical distance from Black English-speaking children, failing to smile at them, and correcting their speech without acknowledging that it is a dialect and without acknowledging what the speakers are trying to say. Students, too, can sabotage instruction on the basis of their feelings for a teacher. Students who normally behave well can destroy a mathematics teacher's attempt to teach because they think he or she is strange. Just as teachers often communicate dislike for certain students, students sometimes refuse to learn for a teacher they feel does not like them.

A second implication is that people usually invest themselves in their work when they feel they are a part of the institution, and when social relationships are supportive. For example, students who feel important to the school are more likely to invest time and effort in schoolwork than are those who do not. In desegregated schools, bused-in students sometimes feel like visitors in someone else's school and feel hesitant or tentative about involving themselves actively in the school's demands.

A third implication is that peer groups themselves establish norms concerning what individuals should do in school. Some student peer groups support intense studying; others do not. Some teacher peer groups support working hard to develop creative and interesting lessons, while others support getting by. Individuals tend to conform to peer-group expectations in order to belong and have friends.

Social Learning

One factor is the structure of classroom work. Classroom work can be competitive, individualistic, or cooperative. Competitively structured classrooms often have permanent ability groups (such as reading groups); they have whole-class teaching with students called on to recite orally, which lets everyone in the classroom know who knows the material and who does not; and the teacher applies grading practices which compare students against each other and reward a limited number with high grades. In such classrooms, students categorize and associate with each other on a basis of perceived academic ability, and they internalize self-identities commensurate with their standing in the classroom's academic hierarchy. For example, the most successful students develop the strongest self-images, associate mainly with each other, and act as if they are superior to their peers. Teachers often teach students differently in accordance with this system of categorizing, giving the best students the most and the best instruction, while often ignoring slow students.

Classrooms with an individualistic task structure typically feature individualized, one-on-one work, and independent projects. These classrooms tend not to foster the stereotypes and social divisions of the competitive classrooms. More often they foster individualism and a tendency to ignore others, since students may spend relatively little time associating with others, especially those they do not already know.

Classrooms with a cooperative task structure tend to foster the least stereotyping and the most egalitarian mixing on the part of students. In such classrooms, students complete much of their work in structured groups, talking and working with their peers. As long as the teacher periodically rearranges who is in the groups, students have an opportunity to associate with many different peers. If the teacher structures the work so that everyone is able to participate productively, students develop positive perceptions of most of their peers. Some teachers deliberately use cooperative groups in which students are mixed on the basis of race, sex, or handicap, because this effectively builds better relationships among students and reduces stereotyping.

A second factor affecting social learning is whether standards for success are unidimensional or multidimensional. A unidimensional standard means that classroom success is based primarily on one or two areas (often reading). Since students are rarely all equally good in one area, a hierarchy soon develops in which some students consistently rank high, some average, and some low. When combined with a competitive task structure, this produces a classroom with distinct winners and losers. A multidimensional standard means that several different abilities are rewarded regularly. If one is not good in one area, one is likely to be good at something else. Differences among individuals are recognized but not necessarily ranked hierarchically, and stereotyping is discouraged because students discover a variety of talents and abilities in each other.

A third factor that strongly affects the social structure in the school is how the school divides students for instruction. Divisions that are relatively permanent, allocate students to different kinds of instruction, and suggest some students to be better than others become an important part of the way people in a school perceive and act toward others, as well as themselves. The most common divisions of this nature include tracking in secondary schools, ability grouping in elementary schools, special education and other remedial programs, other pull-out programs such as gifted education, and vocational electives such as industrial arts and home economics. When relatively permanent divisions are used, members of the school learn to see these as reflecting different kinds of people, such as "bright people" and "slow kids," and the occupants of each group as possessing whatever characteristics one associates with that group. Thus, for example, students in an honors class are all perceived as being capable learners and as good and valuable people. Considerable research shows that members of permanent divisions internalize the stereotypes that characterize that division. For example, lower track students see themselves as unimportant to the school and as incapable of doing school work very well; this perception leads many to stop trying and to lose interest in school.

The factors just discussed—task structure, evaluation standards, and how students are divided for instruction—all affect how members of a school categorize, perceive, and interact with each other. If these are changed, social relationships also change. But social relationships in a school are also formed in the wider society and local community; often these are further reinforced in the school. Of particular concern here are social relationships among racial groups, social class groups, and between the sexes.

Teachers, students, administrators, aides, and so forth all bring into the school personal identities and background experiences that depend in part on their membership in race/class/gender groups. They also bring with them perceptions of other groups, which they apply to people they encounter in the school. For example, teachers often expect less of lower class and minority students than of white middle-class students, and often expect white male students to be more analytical and mathematical than other students. Male and female students usually perceive each other stereotypically, and during adolescence become skilled at acting out stereotypic and unequal gender relationships in the process of learning to date. White students learn to view race as a problem caused by minorities, while minority students learn to distinguish among open-minded and bigotted whites. All these affect the social as well as academic dynamics of the school.

Often school staff members believe they can do little to change a school's race/class/gender dynamics. Actually, they can do quite a bit. First, the task structure, evaluation standards, and division of students for instruction can either reinforce or reduce these social stereotypes and divisions. Second, staff members themselves can control how they perceive and treat their students, examining, for example, whether they expect more of middle-class than lower-class students. Third, the curriculum usually reinforces the status quo by concentrating on contributions, perspectives, and experiences of white wealthy males, giving only cursory attention to other groups. In addition, teachers are often uncomfortable discussing openly with their students what they actually think about their own and other groups. For example, while most secondary students are preoccupied with constructing a personal gender identity and learning how to relate to the opposite sex, few teachers discuss how gender identities and boy-girl relationships relate to sexism and male dominance in society.

Conclusion

All schools operate as social systems, and the social system in a school affects, and is affected by, many other areas of school life. As educators increasingly understand how the social system operates and how the school helps create it, we can make more deliberate and thought-out attempts to improve the quality of life of all members of a school experience.

See also Classroom Management; Cooperative Learning; Group Processes; Student Culture.

—Christine Sleeter
University of Wisconsin-Parkside

References

Boocock, S.S. (1980). *Sociology of education* (2nd ed.). Boston: Houghton Mifflin.

Grant, C.A., & Sleeter, C.E. (1986). *After the school bell rings*. Barcombe, England: Falmer Press.

Slavin, R.E. (1983). *Cooperative learning*. New York: Longman.

SOCIAL STUDIES EDUCATION

Social studies, a discipline distinct from other fields, arose in the 1920s as a response to persistent social, political, and economic crises. In contrast to its cognate fields, social studies is new to the school curriculum and continues to evolve in definition, goals, and objectives, therefore remaining for many a puzzling subject.

Of the many proposed definitions of social studies, one widely accepted was that of Edgar Bruce Wesley, who believed in the early 1930s that social studies could be defined as the social sciences simplified for instructional purposes. Some forty years later there evolved this definition: Social studies is the integration of social sciences and humanities for the purpose of instruction in citizenship education. In 1984, seventy years after the founding of the field, one authoritative definition is that offered by the National Council for the Social Studies: Social studies is a basic subject of the K-12 curriculum that (a) derives its goals from the nature of citizenship in a democratic society that is closely linked to other nations and peoples of the world; (b) draws its content primarily from history, the social sciences and, in some respects, from the humanities and sciences, and (c) is taught in ways that reflect an awareness of the personal, social, and cultural experiences and developmental levels of learners.

What is significant about the evolving definitions is that they emphasize the integration of the humanities and social sciences and citizenship education as the goal of instruction. Consensus on the goal and definition provides a rationale for scope and sequence that envisions social studies in terms of a developmental, concept-oriented, problem-solving citizenship-education curriculum, K-12. But despite the apparent consensus, there is disagreement on what these terms mean and what they imply for classroom instruction. Thus, teachers have different interpretations of how schools should promote good citizenship. The National Council for the Social Studies in an attempt to bring consensus to the field has published a set of curriculum guidelines which translate the goal of citizenship education into the following four objectives: (a) gain knowledge about the human condition, including past, present, and future; (b) acquire skills necessary to process information; (c) develop skills to examine values and beliefs; and (d) apply knowledge through active participation in society.

The guidelines offer a set of objectives that govern the design of curriculum activities and materials for each grade level, K-12, thus guaranteeing an integrated, developmental, and relevant curriculum with the ultimate goal of graduating a student who has developed the skills necessary for effective citizenship in a democratic society. In short, citizenship is not so much a definition as it is a set of four objectives stated as skills which if learned would prepare students to function as good citizens in a crisis society. If substantial, though by no means complete, agreement may exist in social studies on definition, goal, and objectives, then where exactly is the disagreement? What is it that fuels the sense of some that social studies is not an organized, coherent curriculum? Undoubtedly disagreement is at the level of meaning and application, for though it is relatively easy to reach agreement on terms such as integration, citizenship, gaining knowledge, processing, valuing, and participating, it is extremely difficult to reach agreement on the concrete meaning of these undefined, and imprecise terms as applied in everyday classroom practice.

One interpretation of how classroom teachers have conceived the meaning of goals, objectives, and definition suggests that three distinctly different traditions of teaching have evolved: social studies taught as citizenship transmission, social studies taught as social science, and social studies taught as reflective inquiry. The tradition of citizenship transmission is largely an effort to pass on to students an uncritical loyalty to what are taken as the dominant values, beliefs, and practices of a particular society. The social science tradition teaches the processes of various social sciences, believing that citizenship is best practiced when citizens think about the world and make decisions as would a social scientist. The reflective inquiry tradition assumes that citizenship is best taught when students identify social/personal problems based on their needs and interests and process those problems through a rational system of reflective inquiry.

In summary, social studies as a curriculum in the schools has been relatively brief in comparison to other fields, with much of its seventy year existence marked by attempts to reach consensus on goals, objectives, and definition. Consensus has begun to emerge on the goal of social studies as citizenship education, a definition that includes integration of the social sciences and humanities for the purpose of decision making in a democracy, and four objectives which emphasize gaining knowledge, processing, valuing, and participating throughout the K-12 curriculum. Disagreement continues to exist on the level of classroom practice where teachers tend to interpret the meaning of social studies in at least one or a combination of the three traditional ways. Social studies was created as a field in recognition that training in the skills of self-governing and decision making in a democracy required a formal curriculum that prepared the nation's youth for citizenship responsibilities.

See also Curriculum Development; Social Learning in the Schools; Values Education.

—James L. Barth
Purdue University

References

Barr, R.D., Barth, J.L., & Shermis, S.S. (1977). *Defining the social studies*, Bulletin 51. Washington, DC: National Council for the Social Studies.

Barr, R.D., Barth, J.L., & Shermis, S.S. (1978). *The nature of the social studies*. Palm Springs, CA: ETC Publications.

"In search of a scope and sequence for social studies, Report of the National Council for the social studies task force on scope and sequence, November 1, 1983." (1984). *Social Education, 48*, 249-62.

SPLIT-BRAIN CONTROVERSY

A large body of evidence indicates that the left and right cerebral hemispheres have somewhat different information processing abilities and propensities. Evidence comes from a variety of sources, including the study of patients with unilateral brain injury and of patients with surgical disconnection of the two halves of the cortex (the so-called split-brain patients); there have also been clever investigations of neurologically normal adults and children. While certain asymmetries are now well-established, the study of hemispheric asymmetry continues to be one of the most active areas in cognitive neuropsychology where many of the most important issues are debated. Thus, it should not be surprising that implications for education are speculative. Furthermore, a variety of inaccurate characterizations of hemispheric asymmetry have found their way into educational publications, making it all the more critical to separate what is well-established from what is, at best, highly speculative.

What is generally accepted at the present time is that for 90 to 99 percent of right-handed humans, particular regions of the left hemisphere have a special role to play in the production and understanding of language. Given the importance of language to human thought and communication, it is not surprising that for many years the left hemisphere was referred to as the "dominant" hemisphere, with the right hemisphere thought to play a "minor" role in cognitive processing. More recently, it has been discovered that the right hemisphere contributes to some language processing and is dominant for some nonlanguage functions. Although the view of right hemisphere specialization is still developing, the right hemisphere seems particularly adept at processing spatial relationships. For example, performance on the block design subtest of the Wechsler Adult Intelligence Scale is more impaired after right hemisphere injury than after left hemisphere injury and is performed much better by the disconnected right hemisphere than by the disconnected left hemisphere in split-brain patients. The right hemisphere is also thought to play a dominant role in the perception of human faces (especially unfamiliar faces) and in the production and recognition of emotion.

It is important to realize that hemispheric differences are relative rather than absolute (with the likely exception of speech production). That is, for most functions both hemispheres have some role to play, but they may differ in their relative ability and/or in the precise way in which the function is carried out. There is little support for the popularized view that many complex psychological functions are the *exclusive* property of only one hemisphere. Instead, when tasks become at all complex both hemispheres are likely to make contributions, and the optimal level of performance demands efficient cooperation between the two hemispheres. As an illustration of this, consider some of the processes involved in a rather common task: reading.

Reading and understanding a paragraph involve the extraction of meaning from a set of visual symbols. The task involves reasonably complex visuospatial processing as well as the lexical analysis of individual words, processing the grammatical relationships within a sentence, and having the ability to place the meaning of each sentence in a larger context. Thus, while reading is generally thought of as a "language" activity and the left hemisphere is often thought of as the "language" hemisphere, it is likely that both hemispheres play a role in normal reading. For example, the right hemisphere almost certainly contributes to the visuospatial analysis of the material, and recent evidence suggests that the right hemisphere plays the dominant role in using contextual cues to understanding. In contrast, the left hemisphere plays the dominant role in processing individual words and the grammatical cues to language. Consequently, it would be inappropriate to consider "reading" the exclusive property of only one hemisphere. Instead, it is best performed by integrating information from both hemispheres—a situation that is likely to be the rule for many cognitive processes. Some suggestions about the relevance of hemispheric asymmetry for education will be considered with this in mind.

As early as the first third of this century it was suggested that various learning disabilities are a result of a failure to establish left-hemisphere dominance for language. During the last twenty years or so noninvasive measures of hemispheric asymmetry have been refined to the point of permitting empirical tests of this theory. On the whole, the data do not provide any strong indication that the magnitude of hemispheric specialization per se is related to learning abilities. This is not to say that there are no neuropsychological correlates of specific learning disabilities. What is emerging is the finding that specific cognitive deficits are correlated with inferior performance by those regions of the cortex that are normally most involved in the specific cognitive processes. For example, at least some subgroups of dyslexics seem to have problems with certain left-hemisphere language processes, whereas others may have problems with right-hemisphere processes or with integrating information across the two hemispheres. Thus, contemporary neurophysiological research is illuminating the neurological bases of specific learning disabilities, an exciting prospect for neuroscientists.

Do the neuropsychological findings to date have practical implications for education? Probably not. This research is still in its beginning stages and many of the major findings need to be replicated before applications are considered. Even after such replication, it is not obvious that knowing the neurological region correlated with a student's deficit will help the teacher to formulate a more effective program of remediation. Of considerably more use in constructing a remediation will be a thorough knowledge of the individual student's psychological and cognitive strengths and weaknesses which can be determined without knowing the neurological underpinings.

In recent years the claim has been made that our educational system has educated primarily the left hemisphere and ignored the right hemisphere. As a result, various changes in curriculum have been suggested. While there may be many good reasons to introduce changes into our school programs, the reasons are not by and large to be found in the research on hemispheric asymmetry. What might be called the "right hemisphere education movement" has been based on speculations about hemispheric asymmetry that go far beyond the scientific data, speculations that fail to appreciate that hemispheric assymetries are typically relative rather than absolute so that both hemispheres are almost always involved in our cognitive activity. While suggested curriculum changes appear to take on new importance when couched in neuropsychological terms, there is the danger that worthwhile changes will be inappropriately reversed when it is discovered that they were based more on neuroscience fiction than on neuroscience fact.

The next few years will be exciting times in cognitive neuropsychology, but it will continue to be difficult to separate well-founded facts from overly popularized fantasy. It is important that educators take the time to know the difference.

See also Cognitive Development; Intelligence and Intelligence Testing; Learning Styles.

—Joseph B. Hellige
University of Southern California

References

Best, C.T. (Ed.) (1985). *Hemispheric function and collaboration in the child.* New York: Academic Press.

Bradshaw, J.L., & Nettleton, N.C. (1983). *Human cerebral asymmetry.* New York: Prentice-Hall.

Hellige, J.B. (Ed.) (1983). *Cerebral hemisphere asymmetry: Method, theory and application.* New York: Praeger.

STAFF DEVELOPMENT

The need for staff development extends from first-year teachers and provisional teachers needing help with basic classroom management strategies to veteran teachers needing revitalization. Certified teachers being rehired after several years of being out of the profession also can benefit from staff development. The returning teachers are often assigned to teach in grade levels and in subject areas for which they were never prepared. They need to catch up with developments in technology, curriculum content, instructional strategies, district goals, and evaluation procedures.

A Differentiated Plan

School officials should recognize that all teachers do not need the same staff development plan. Because the needs for staff development differ for different groups of teachers, the menu for staff development should be varied, specific, and well balanced so that all participants can thrive. Administrators and supervisors should attempt to find out what may be needed by different segments of the faculty and organize groups with common needs such as first-year teachers, provisional teachers, returning teachers, and veteran teachers. Each group of teachers should define their long- and short-term goals for the year. Goals should complement district goals, be specific and measurable with clear criteria for reaching the goal; then, a different staff development program should be selected or developed to meet the goals of different groups of teachers.

Time for a Change

The length of time in terms of hours and months required to change teacher and student behavior is in direct relationship to the complexity of the behavior and the proximity of the change to the existing behavior. Learning to take roll and pass materials efficiently might require a two-hour workshop which includes modeling and practice with followup in the classroom. Learning to provide interactive instruction which develops higher-order thinking skills is likely to require an excellent teacher ten two-hour workshops spaced over an entire school year.

When and Where

The findings of most studies on the effects of staff development agree that workshops held for two or three days at the beginning of the school year have little chance of changing teacher behavior. Teachers are eager to be in their rooms preparing for the first day of school. Being required to attend workshops or lectures at this time is likely to be frustrating and a waste of time and money. More useful would be a one-day welcome back to school with time for groups of teachers to share ideas, set goals for the year, and plan appropriate staff development sessions. For every rule there is an exception: In this case it is the first-year teachers who would most likely benefit from a workshop on procedures for setting up the classroom before school starts.

During the remainder of the school year, staff development can be scheduled during school hours, after school, or on weekends. The activities can last two hours or all day. A continual program consisting of two-hour workshops spread over several weeks has several advantages. First, the teachers can receive information in a sufficiently small conceptual unit to think actively about it and consider it in terms of their own context and value system. Second, teachers have a chance to try the idea between sessions and report their success or failure. They can receive suggestions and assistance from other teachers and try again. The two-hour workshops can be conducted in release time during school, after school, or on Saturday morning.

How to Teach Teachers

Under what conditions are teachers most likely to learn new ideas and continue to use the ideas in their classrooms? Teachers can "go through" expensive staff development programs and never change their behavior. Sitting through lectures and taking notes does not insure that ideas will be used in classrooms the next day. How teachers are taught is as important as what is being taught.

The process must be respectful. Teachers are professionals with specific training and experience. Start where they are. Expose them to a set of ideas and ask, How would that work with the children you teach? How might you change that strategy so that it would work in your classroom? The idea is to get teachers to think about teaching, not just give them formulas or jargon to repeat.

Teachers learn by doing. Information can be presented via television, lecture, modeling, readings, role playing, discussion, small group problem-solving episodes, vivid examples using classroom situations that teachers can understand, or all of the above. The trick is to get the teacher interested enough in a new idea to commit to trying it in the classroom the next day and to connect the new learning to the teacher's prior knowledge.

Workshops should be interactive. All participants should take part in their own learning every time. In order for this to occur, the number of participants must be limited so that all can take part. Six to eight participants is a good size for easy participation. Larger groups can be broken down to this size for group work. Teachers need to discuss freely the applicability of the workshop idea for their classroom space, their students, and their school.

A problem-solving approach should be taken. Teachers should not be given all the answers. Allow them to figure some things out for themselves, and it will work better for them. Make time for teachers to share good ideas. Let them define problems, generate solutions, foresee consequences, execute a plan, and evaluate the results. The best teachers are good learners.

A supportive environment is needed. People are most willing to take risks and try something new when they feel safe and supported. When people feel threatened, they are rigid and defensive, and it is hard for new information to get through the learning channels. Teachers need to know that principals and colleagues support their efforts to improve.

Teachers as Teachers

Use the talent within the school district. Ask teachers known to have excellent classroom management skills to share practical ideas with first-year teachers and teach them effective strategies. Returning teachers needing an update on curriculum and technology could also be taught by experienced teachers in the district. Teachers assigned to teach at a new grade level or subject area could be assigned a "buddy" teacher at the new assignment to assist in this transition.

The veteran teachers who need rejuvenation may require a staff development program emanating from outside the district. Most districts hire a consultant to provide a one- or two-day staff development program. The carry-over into classroom practice from this type of program may not be noticeable. A more effective method of staff development is to send one or two faculty members to become certified trainers in a desirable program. As certified trainers, they are a resource and can provide in-depth training to faculty throughout the district.

Peer observation is yet another effective and inexpensive method to develop awareness of classroom processes and promote self-development. Teachers taking part in peer observation give two reasons for liking it. The first is "I get a chance to see how other teachers work, how they organize and manage their classroom space, and how they interact with students I also teach." The second reason given is that "Objective observation data of my classroom is given to me for me to analyze. I can learn about my classroom and my behavior, and I can make some decisions about how to improve."

Several rules must be followed to make sure peer observation will be a positive experience. Confidentiality must be assured and preserved. Teachers must feel that nothing seen or heard in their classroom will hurt them or their students. This is a self-improvement process, not an evaluation. It helps to give this assurance if teachers sign an oath of confidentiality that nothing seen or heard in the classroom observed will be spoken of outside that classroom.

The observation system used must be objective and should focus on one set of behaviors at a time. For example, recording the children the teacher speaks to on a seating chart for one class period can help a teacher identify patterns of interaction and identify students who are never called upon. Such observations serve to raise teachers' level of awareness and encourage them to distribute interactions more evenly among the students.

Administrators must make time available for teachers to conduct peer observations. In some schools, administrators teach a class for several teachers, allowing them to observe each other. Other principals hire a substitute teacher who teaches the first period for teacher A, the second period for teacher B, the third for teacher C, etc. This rotation of the substitute could allow six teachers to observe in another teacher's classroom. Where teachers have preparation periods they can observe other teachers during this prep time. One secondary school system in New York finds peer observation so valuable that teachers are required by contract to observe in one classroom a month for the entire school year.

To make the best use of the peer observations, time must be made available for the teachers to analyze their own data and discuss it with their peers. This is not a coaching situation where one person tells the other person what he/she did right or wrong. A group facilitator may guide the teachers' analyses of their own data by asking such questions as "Where were the children sitting to whom you spoke most often? To whom did you not speak? Why might that be?" The analysis meetings should be kept small (6-8) in order that each participant has ample opportunity to discuss problems and solutions.

Evaluation of Staff Development

It is essential to have a method of evaluating what happened to teachers and students as a result of the staff development intervention. Administrators need to know if the time, effort, and money expended were worth it. This question can be answered if teachers and students are observed or tested on measures related to the program before the intervention and after the intervention. If first-year teachers want to become more efficient organizers, the time spent getting started should be measured before the staff development program and several times after the intervention has occurred to see if management time has been reduced. If veteran teachers want to increase the number of higher-order questions asked, then they should be observed for the frequency of this type of question before and after the intervention.

Administrators also want to know the impact of staff development upon students. If all of the teachers go through a staff-development program on lesson design, will the lessons be improved? Will the students be more on task and achieve more? To answer these questions, administrators need pretest and posttest student-engaged rate data as well as gains on achievement tests. Also crucial to this question is the frequency teachers use the new lesson design and how well it fits their own mode of teaching. Teachers will not continue to use strategies which feel uncomfortable to them or make teaching more difficult.

Staff development should make teaching more fun and a little easier! Reward your teachers for their efforts. Give them gold stars, pictures in the paper, recognition at staff meetings, opportunities to report what they have learned. A few positive strokes go a long way in helping teachers be the best that they can be.

See also Faculty Workshops; Supervision, Clinical; Teacher Professionalism; Teachers, Beginning.

—Jane Stallings
University of Houston

References

Griffin, G. (1986). "Thinking about teaching." In *Association for Supervision and Curriculum Development Yearbook, 1986* (pp. 101-13). Alexandria, VA: ASCD.

Heath, D.H. (1986). "Developing teachers, not just techniques." In *Association for Supervision and Curriculum Development Yearbook, 1986* (pp. 1-14). Alexandria, VA: ASCD.

Stallings, J. (1986). "Using time effectively: A self-analytic approach." In *Association for Supervision and Curriculum Development Yearbook, 1986* (pp. 15-27). Alexandria, VA: ASCD.

STAFF EVALUATION

In an era in which the nation seems committed to improving education, an effective program of staff evaluation would appear to be essential. An effective program of staff evaluation should be comprehensive in scope, should provide a school district with the information needed to provide focused supervision and valid personnel decisions, and should instill in both the evaluators and the evaluatees a sense of ownership, usefulness, and fairness about the entire evaluation program. In the following sections these characteristics will be discussed in more detail.

Philosophy, Goals, and Objectives

A comprehensive program of staff evaluation would include the school district's philosophy of staff evaluation, evaluation goals, and specific evaluation objectives. The main purpose of providing this information is to make clear to all concerned why the school district believes staff evaluation is important and what the district is attempting to achieve. A short excerpt of one school district's philosophy, goals, and objectives of staff evaluation is presented for illustration.

Philosophical Statement: "Evaluation is a process which is done *with* people, not to them."

Goal Statement: "The ultimate purpose of staff evaluation is to improve the quality of students' learning experiences."

Objective Statement: One of the objectives of the staff evaluation program is to provide staff members with valid, useful feedback on their performance which will aid their self-improvement.

It should be emphasized that a school district should try to involve the staff in the development and/or revision of the philosophy, goals, and objectives of staff evaluation (as well as many other aspects of the evaluation program). Philosophy, goals, and objectives are not elements of a staff evaluation program which should be unilaterally developed by administrators and school board members of a district and then imposed on staff members. While the final responsibility for approving the different elements of a staff evaluation program rests with the school board, staff members' involvement during the process of developing and revising the program will be important if they are to develop a sense of fairness and ownership about the program. In addition, staff members potentially can contribute valuable ideas which can result in a more effective staff evaluation program than if they were not involved.

Staff Evaluation Criteria

The selection of criteria to be used in the evaluation of staff is probably the most important decision that a school district can make in designing a staff evaluation program. The criteria are the standards against which staff members are to be evaluated and are usually expressed in a school district's rating form or evaluation instrument. If the criteria or standards are not valid, then the evaluation is not likely to be fair, useful, or even defensible in the face of challenge.

While many readers may believe that their district's staff evaluation criteria are valid, the author's examination of many school districts' evaluation instruments raises considerable doubt about the legitimacy of that belief. The criteria in all too many school districts' evaluation instruments seem to be primarily based on personal preference or educational philosophy. Although the educational philosophy of a school district can certainly be considered in selecting the specific standards by which staff performance will be judged, the main basis for developing staff evaluation criteria should be theory and research on staff effectiveness and student learning.

In recent years theorists and researchers have made great strides in identifying the kinds of personal qualities, teaching behaviors, and instructional conditions that seem to be associated with staff effectiveness. While it is not the purpose of this article to discuss these findings, references are provided at the conclusion for further investigation.

Also, the reader is encouraged to stay current with educational journals such as the *American Educational Research Journal* and *Elementary School Journal*, where theory and research on staff effectiveness are frequently presented.

In addition to valid standards for judging staff effectiveness, it is important that the standards or criteria be reliable. Reliable criteria are those criteria which more than one evaluator of an individual would apply in the same manner. If, for example, a school district believes that it is important to evaluate teachers on the degree to which they possess enthusiasm, but two evaluators who observe the same teacher at the same time give the teacher a different rating on enthusiasm, then the criterion statement the school district is using may be permitting inter-rater unreliability. In order to achieve reliable criteria, a school district should try to avoid using high inference criteria, such as "enthusiastic" (or should define more specifically the behavioral components of teacher enthusiasm), and should include in its staff evaluation standards only those criteria which can be observed and rated with little inference as to whether the attitude or behavior is being manifested. An example of the latter would be, "The teacher informs the class of the objectives for the lesson."

Staff Evaluation Process

The process of staff evaluation should begin with a meeting in the early fall between those who are to be evaluated during the year and the evaluator(s)—in most cases, the principal. At that meeting topics for presentation and/or discussion should include the criteria for evaluating staff members, the evaluation procedures that will be used, the timetable for evaluations, and the role of both the evaluator and the evaluatee. The purpose of the meeting is to provide an orientation about the upcoming evaluation to staff members and to provide an opportunity for questions and clarification.

Following the orientation meeting, the evaluator(s) will either begin classroom observations of staff members or will schedule individual conferences with staff members before conducting observations in the classroom. Although scheduling a preobservation conference with every staff member may not be necessary, such a conference should be held with those teachers whose lesson planning will constitute part of the basis for the evaluation and for those teachers whose objectives, techniques, and curriculum may not be familiar to the evaluator. During the preobservation conference the discussion can focus on the nature of the teacher's planning for the lesson to be observed, special classroom circumstances that the evaluator needs to be aware of, and any other topics that seem relevant to the evaluation. Also, during the preobservation conference, the dates and times for the observation can be scheduled, as well as a follow-up conference.

The classroom observations represent the most important phase of the staff evaluation process. Although data on staff performance can be gathered from sources other than the classroom—such as student test scores, student interviews, or follow-up studies of student achievement—the most typically utilized source for generating evaluative data about the staff has been and is likely to continue to be the classroom. Staff members carry out their most important responsibility in the classroom; therefore, the classroom offers the greatest opportunity to evaluate teacher effectiveness.

While research has not indicated the optimum number of observations for each teacher nor, for that matter, an optimum length for each observation, there seems to be agreement among authorities that a teacher should receive more than one observation (especially if weaknesses are to be identified and diagnosed), and an observation should be sufficiently long to obtain a representative sample of a teacher's behavior. In addition, if initial observations reveal significant teacher weakness which, if not corrected, could lead to nonrenewal or dismissal, then more than one evaluator should be involved in conducting the classroom observations.

Since the main goal of the observations should be to collect data which can be used to suggest improvements and, if sufficient improvement is not forthcoming, to provide an adequate basis for a recommendation for nonrenewal or dismissal, the evaluator(s) should take careful notes during and/or shortly after observations. These notes should form the basis for planning a conference with the teacher to share the results of the observations and recommendations for improvement or other personnel action.

The post observation conference phase of the evaluation process is important and needs to be thoughtfully and carefully planned. If classroom observations revealed certain areas of teacher performance in need of improvement, then the evaluator should be able to offer specific and helpful suggestions. These might include intraschool or interschool visitations, videotaped analysis, special workshops, or other approaches.

Staff Nonrenewal or Dismissal

Thus far the emphasis in the discussion has been on formative evaluation or evaluation which has as its objective the improvement of an individual. However, after a number of observations and conferences it may be concluded by the evaluator that a teacher is incapable of further needed improvement. Before this conclusion is communicated to the staff member, the evaluator should attempt to solicit the assistance and judgment of other evaluators who have expertise in the area under consideration, and the evaluator's supervisors should be apprised of the situation.

For many administrators the mere thought of recommending a teacher for nonrenewal or dismissal, especially if that teacher has tenure, causes anxiety. Furthermore, it is acknowledged that "getting rid of a teacher" is not easy, nor should it be, since someone's career may be at stake. If nonrenewal or dismissal is being considered, administrators and the school board members will need to adhere to certain elements of due process. Nevertheless, if a teacher is performing unsatisfactorily, according to the school district's standards, has received adequate supervision, and does not appear capable of sufficient improvement, then the administrator needs to accept the responsibility—including the frustration and hard work—of recommending nonrenewal or dismissal. If a school district's evaluation program is an effective one, the identification and removal of such teachers should not be an overwhelming, nor legally impossible, task.

Trained Evaluators

A well-designed evaluation program may still not achieve its goals if the individuals who are assigned responsibility for conducting personnel evaluations are not adequately trained. Although many, if not most administrators, may believe that they are competent to conduct personnel evaluations, teachers' feedback and reports of evaluation practices suggest that this belief may not be well founded. Many administrators have received no in-depth university training in personnel evaluation and, since leaving the university, their training typically has consisted of little more than attending a one-day workshop and/or reading an occasional article on the topic.

While many administrators seem to think that by becoming knowledgeable in school law they have achieved competency in conducting personnel evaluations, a background in school law—important as it may be—is only one of the areas of knowledge and skills necessary for conducting competent personnel evaluation. Many administrators also need training in how to conduct classroom observations and evaluation conferences and how to analyze, synthesize, and make judgments about contextual and personal data. They also need additional training—or at least refresher training—in supervision which is aimed at helping staff members to improve their performance.

School districts have the primary responsibility for providing the kinds of training previously described for their administrators, although a cooperative venture between a school district and a nearby university would be desirable in that both entities have complementary resources to contribute. The training should be presented in a practicum format that includes case studies, simulations, and videotape critiques of evaluators' performance. Through this type of in-service education a school district should, over time, be able to develop a cadre of well-trained evaluators who are producing fair, valid, and useful evaluations.

Program Assessment

A program of staff evaluation is no different from any other program in education in that it needs to be periodically assessed if it is to improve or maintain its standards of excellence.

The assessment should have as its main objective the identification of the strengths and weaknesses of the school district's staff evaluation program. Data on these aspects could be collected, for example, through the use of perception surveys, structured interviews, follow-up studies, and analyses of test data. Although ideally an attempt would be made each year to collect assessment data on the success of the program, there should be an effort to assess the staff evaluation program at least every three years. This effort should include the solicitation of feedback from those staff members who have been evaluated. While it is possible that staff members who did not receive a good evaluation will express negative attitudes about the program, some useful information can be generated even from negative feedback.

School board members and administrators need to follow up on the results of any assessment of the staff-evaluation program. The absence of or a limited follow-up is likely to destroy the credibility of assessment efforts and increase the dissatisfaction of staff members. Organizational follow-up does not have to mean implementing every recommended change, but it should consist, at a minimum, of a full report of the assessment results (disseminated to those who participated in the assessment), accompanied by a discussion of the changes that will and will not be made, and an explanation for those changes.

Conclusion

Staff evaluation potentially represents an excellent means for improving the professional resources of a school or school district. The key to realizing that potential, however, lies in the development of an effective program which includes the various elements discussed in this article.

See also Due Process; Supervision, Clinical; Teacher Dismissal; Teacher Effectiveness.

—Richard A. Gorton
University of Wisconsin-Milwaukee

References

Bridges, E. (1986). *The incompetent teacher: The challenge and the response.* Philadelphia: Taylor & Francis.

Harris, B. (1986). *Developmental teacher evaluation.* Rockleigh, NJ: Allyn & Bacon.

Milman, J. (Ed.). (1981). *Handbook of teacher evaluation.* Beverly Hills, CA: Sage.

STAFF ORIENTATION

School climates shape new staff. In turn, a climate is shaped by new teachers who become the tradition bearers. New teachers usually acquire a school's norms through informal dialogue with peers. Each person filters information according to preconceived ideas of what a "good teacher does." Teachers join a school and instantaneously assume full responsibility with little guided adult-adult contact. The "sink or swim" approach decreases the impact of supervisors. The proposed staff orientation model addresses these realities.

A new staff-orientation program includes "pre-in-service days," in-service day(s), the first week, and the first semester. Informal contact during the months before school begins reduces the "first day" stress. For example, you can introduce the person to future colleagues. Select a "buddy" to help the new person. The "buddy" needs to know that frequent personal contact is important. The administrator needs to schedule a common planning period or lunch period for the pair in order to facilitate interaction.

A copy of the current staff directory should be provided as support for the new staff member during the crucial first weeks. Also, the administrator should provide a building tour, including survival locations such as the washrooms, cafeteria, mailroom, office equipment, etc.

The in-service day for new staff should include time with the department head or teaching team, presentations by central office personnel, and introductions of each of the new teachers. Something personal during the introductions— a hobby, a holiday trip, children, last employment, or university degree—helps people establish common ground. The administrator should lead a tour of key offices, extending the awareness of the physical environment. For a high school, this could include the deans', guidance, attendance, and assistant principals' offices. For an elementary school, the locations might include the nurse's, attendance, and custodial offices. In each office, the occupant should briefly describe the services to teachers and students, including explaining all the forms. Finally, the administrator should host a luncheon for the new staff and key personnel, providing an opportunity to build social relationships.

At the end of the first week, the administrator should schedule a brief meeting, with refreshments, to answer questions. Key service people, or administrators, should "drop in." The administrator should explain the "peer observation program" outlined in the next section.

During the next several months, the department head (high school) or principal (elementary or secondary school) should schedule at least three observations of selected peers for each new staff member. Access to "models" can increase the rate of understanding of the attractive elements of a unique school culture. Rather than discover from the students or by random contact with colleagues how "everybody is doing it," the new staff member will have direct experience with how model teachers handle attendance, late papers, unmet expectations, student conflicts, or questioning strategies.

The relevant supervisor should schedule a discussion time after each observation. Criteria for selecting model teachers should include teaching skill and the ability to explain decisions made in the classroom. The administrator needs to meet with the buddies and with the new staff after a few months. Two questions could be used to start the session: "What helped you most in your transition to our school?" and "What did you most need to know that you did not know?" The responses can be used to modify the new staff orientation program. Thus, the school will have a adaptive program which is in itself an excellent model and epitomizes quality.

See also Staff Development; Teachers, Beginning; Teachers, Sources of Help for.

—Ed DeYoung
Barrington High School
Barrington, Illinois

References

Lortie, D.C. (1975). *Schoolteacher* (chapters 2 & 3). Chicago, IL: The University of Chicago Press.

Peters, T.J., & Waterman, R.H., Jr. (1982). *In search of excellence* (chapter 3). New York: Harper & Row.

STATE BOARDS OF EDUCATION

State boards of education, sometimes called state boards of public instruction or regents, are found in 49 of the 50 states. All state boards are charged with the general control over public elementary and secondary education in their state. Their authority is statutory and not constitutional. State boards are composed of lay members who are appointed or elected for terms of about 6 years. The boards are served by the professional staff of the state department of education and by a chief state school officer, called a commissioner of education or state superintendent of public instruction, who is either appointed by the state board or governor or elected by popular vote. The state board of education, chief state school officer, and state department of education constitute the state educational agency.

Historical Background

By the time of the American Revolution, the idea was generally accepted that (a) society should resort to legal means to compel parents to educate their children; (b) education was necessary for good government; (c) education was a state function; and (d) church and state were separate in matters of education. Indeed, the new congress required all states to make provision for a state system of public education as a condition of statehood.

Early educational leaders such as Horace Mann, Henry Barnard, Caleb Mills, John D. Pierce, John Swett, and Calvin H. Wiley were all chief state school officers in their respective states. They used their positions to promote public education; marshal public support; collect data; secure financial resources; improve teacher training; recommend courses of study and textbooks; encourage professional leadership for the schools; and recommend new direction, goals, and policies—functions that continue substantially unchanged today. When these early leaders had finished their work, and with the advent of compulsory attendance laws, state boards and chief officers became respected and necessary institutions for the governance of education at the state level. In 1837, only three states had state boards of education; 38 of the 48 states had a state board in 1945; and 48 of the 50 states had one by 1964.

The Progressive "good government" movement of the first half of the twentieth century affected education in three ways. First, this movement worked to insulate and separate education from the mainstream of American politics. Second, Progressive reform efforts also accelerated the professionalization of education. Finally, the separation of education from the political mainstream and professionalization of education consolidated education as a special purpose government at both the state and local level. The result was a boon for a wider and more important role for a nonpartisan, professionally staffed state board of education.

A Profile of State Boards

State boards have anywhere from 3 to 27 members. Thirty-five states have 7–12 members with 9 members being the most frequent. In six states, the chief state school officer is a voting member of the state board. A few states have students, educators, legislators, representatives of higher education, and other state officials as members. In 36 states, the governor appoints the board; in 10 states, the board is popularly elected. Local school boards elect the board in Washington, and the state legislature elects the state board in South Carolina and New York. In Wisconsin, which has no state board of education, the authority customarily residing in the state board is held by a popularly elected chief state school officer.

State boards have only those governance, policy making, and supervisory responsibilities that are delegated to them by the legislature. Indeed, while they are established by both tradition and law, they are ultimately creatures of the state and can, therefore, be abolished by the state. Hence, their roles and functions can be modified by the state legislature.

All state boards of education have general responsibility for public elementary and secondary education. However, other areas of jurisdiction vary among the states. For example, in 44 states, the state boards have jurisdiction over vocational education, and in 18 states over vocational rehabilitation. In 42 states, state boards govern adult education. In 25 states, they have responsibility for some form of textbook selection, and in 23 states, they are responsible for some aspects of educational television. In 10 states, these boards have jurisdiction over public libraries. State boards in 21 states have absolutely no involvement with nonpublic schools; most other states have some involvement, but only North Dakota and West Virginia have comprehensive ju-

risdiction over nonpublic schools. Finally, four boards have governance functions for 4-year postsecondary institutions with 13 having jurisdiction over 2-year postsecondary institutions, including vocational-technical schools.

Future Dilemmas

The principal, ongoing debate concerns the supervisory-regulatory versus the consultation-leadership roles of the state board. On the one hand, boards must promulgate rules, interpret statutes, enforce regulations, and ensure minimum standards in fulfilling their regulatory role. On the other hand, there is greater expectation that state boards should provide leadership in school improvement, evaluation, long-range planning, and political coalition building.

Another dilemma confronts state boards of education. They are expected to ensure equity in the distribution of state aids and equal educational opportunity for individual pupils while simultaneously promoting educational excellence beyond minimum standards and optimizing personal choice. This dilemma is compounded by the political demand for efficiency in an environment of scarce financial resources. Leadership is expected; yet, the boards must function as proxies for federal programs and priorities in an environment of heightened partisanship where political leaders frequently seize the educational policy initiative and where litigation frustrates negotiation and coalition building. Morever, the traditional apolitical, special government status, and low-profile role of state boards does not augur well in such a complex, politicized environment where dramatic leadership, strategic planning, and access to financial resources and political power are requirements for the year 2000.

See also State Departments of Education.

—B. Dean Bowles
University of Wisconsin-Madison

References

Campbell, R.F., & Mazzoni, T.L., Jr. (1976). *State policy making for the public schools.* Berkeley, CA: McCutchan.
Fuhrman, S., Huddle, E., & Armstrong, J. (1986, April). "Improving schools: The state role." *Kappan, 68* 594–96.
Wiley, D. (1983). *State boards of education: Quality leadership.* Alexandria, VA: National Association of State Boards of Education, Inc.

STATE DEPARTMENTS OF EDUCATION

State departments of education, sometimes called state departments of public instruction, function in all 50 states as the professional education arm of the state board of education and the chief state school officer. The state department is under the general policy control of the state board of education and under the administrative control of the chief state school officer with authority derived from state laws, state board policies, and chief officer directives. The sizes of state departments range from less than 50 professional employees to over 3,000. The state department has general responsibility for public elementary and secondary education and other policy areas unique to the several states.

The Chief State School Officer

Each state has a Chief State School Officer (CSSO) who may have any of a variety of titles including commissioner, director, secretary, or state superintendent of schools, education, or public instruction. Sixteen states elect the chief school officer. They are appointed by the state boards in 27 states and by the governor in 7 states. The term of office ranges from 1 to 5 years; 25 states have 4-year terms. However, in 18 states they serve "at the pleasure of" the appointing authority and are, therefore, without an assured term of office. The legal qualifications require some educational license or experience in 22 states; 18 states require a university degree, and 16 states have no requirements except state citizenship. Salaries are low when compared with other areas of education, the scope of responsibility, and comparable positions in the public and private sectors. In all states, the Chief State School Officer is the executive secretary to the state board and, in 6 states, is a voting member of the board. The Chief State School Officer recommends policies and the budget to the state board; is the chief executive officer for implementing the laws and regulations emanating from the state constitution, statutes, or board policies; and is the administrator of the state department of education.

Historical Background

By the middle of the nineteenth century, both the chief officer and state board were established, respected, and necessary insitutions for the governance of education at the state level. However, the development of state departments proceeded gradually over approximately the next 150 years in five historical stages.

The "Statistical and Accounting" stage lasted from the early nineteenth century to around 1900. During this period, the function of the state department was to collect and report data about the status of public education and to disburse monies in the state school fund. In 1900, there were only 130 state department employees in all the 50 states, or less than three per state.

During the "Regulation" era, from 1900 to around 1930, emphasis was placed on the adoption of minimum school standards and their enforcement by supervisors. By 1930, the median number of employees increased to 28 per state, but much of that increase can be attributed to federal activity in promoting vocational education and vocational rehabilitation programs.

The "Leadership" period, from 1930–1965, focused less on regulation and more on technical assistance, school improvement, and consultation services to local schools. By 1950, the median number of employees increased to 126 per state.

In 1965, Congress passed Title V of the Elementary and Secondary Education Act to "strengthen state departments of education" both to administer new federal programs and to enhance leadership capability in planning, evaluation, and public support functions. This "Enhancement" period lasted from 1965 until 1982 when Title V was eliminated and state department funds were cut.

The "Retrenchment" period, which began in 1982, restricted the federal role in strengthening state departments of education in two ways. First, state departments have tended to use federal funds to administer federal programs. Second, they have cut back on leadership functions and have virtually abandoned planning, evaluation, and public support efforts.

The Future of State Departments of Education

The future of state departments will evolve from current roles and functions in five specific areas. First, in the area of "Operations," they will continue to operate specialized schools and programs such as those for the handicapped, vocational education, and gifted and talented. They may also take a greater role in providing direct services to pupils and families outside the traditional school as they work more closely with at-risk pupils.

Second, in the area of "Regulation," state departments will continue to interpret and enforce statutory and regulation-based program standards and approve or sanction local districts not in compliance.

Third, the "Technical Assistance" function will most likely expand into more areas of the school program, including testing and curriculum development, as the demands for accountability grow and as schools attempt to address the program needs of at-risk pupils and prepare pupils for the world of work.

Fourth, the "Planning and Evaluation" function will be a relatively new area. State departments will require state discretionary dollars in an era of retrenchment for long-range planning incorporating data from statewide databases, testing and assessment programs, and employing older financial accounting systems as well as newly developed pupil accounting systems. They will need a capability to plan, and to evaluate current, projected, and simulated programs for the improvement of education. The new planning and evaluation functions may stress the development of model programs and the implementation of proven programs through a strong state emphasis on and investment in staff development.

Finally, the "Public Support" function will be critical as education becomes more market-oriented. The chief state school officer will find it increasingly necessary to use the "bully pulpit" to promote public education in much the same manner as Horace Mann did in the early nineteenth century. The public support function will evolve so that public education can effectively compete in the political marketplace for resources and in the community marketplace for students. The market orientation will require state departments of education to communicate missions and programs and build political coalitions effectively. The success of state departments will depend on the vision and political acumen of the chief officer and the capability of the department to plan, evaluate, and build political support.

See also State Boards of Education.

—B. Dean Bowles
University of Wisconsin-Madison

References

Campbell, R.F., Cunningham, L.L., Nystrand, R.O., & Usdan, M.D. (Eds.) (1980). *The organization and control of American schools* (4th ed., chap. 3). Columbus, OH: Merrill.

Council of Chief State School Officers. (1983). *Educational governance in the states.* Washington, DC: U.S. Department of Education.

Dentler, R.A. (1984, February). "Ambiguities in state-local relations." *Education and Urban Society, 16,* 145-64.

STUDENT ABSENTEEISM AND TRUANCY

Student absenteeism and truancy continue to be lingering problems for school administrators; this has been the case since the enactment of compulsory school attendance laws in this country. One of the primary reasons for instituting these laws, in all fifty states and the District of Columbia, was to counter, reduce, and (ideally) eradicate chronic student absenteeism and truancy. Over the years, school officials, along with teachers, state and community leaders, legislators, politicians, parents and others have devised numerous inventive ways to enforce these laws. For the greater part of this century, states, cities, and school districts have searched for effective ways to contain the problems of chronic school absenteeism and truancy. Without a doubt, there have been some successes. However, all reliable indices suggest that these problems continue in spite of the efforts to eliminate them. Evidence further points out that in some cases the problems are more extensive, entrenched, and growing than frequently reported.

Truancy

In order to address the problem of truancy, a working, acceptable definition is needed. Chronic absenteeism and truancy mean absence from school, or an educational facility, by a school-age person, with or without parental consent and without a valid reason. These terms are often used interchangeably. There are, however, some subtle distinctions in usage application. Chronic absenteeism describes the act of a school-age person not attending school and implies a more sporadic school attendance pattern than that of a truant. It tends to be used to describe younger (under 12 years old) nonschool attendees. Truancy, on the other hand, tends to be used to describe more sytematic, deliberate and oftentimes prolonged school absenteeism for young people in a higher age bracket than those who are labeled chronic absenters.

Too often a student who does not attend school might be labeled a chronic absenter in one school district, but be considered a "school phobic" in another. Each is given different labels and therefore different treatment for absenting himself or herself from school. Or a student might be permitted to take time away from school if he or she indicates that time is needed to "regroup." Another school district might view that as outright truancy.

Therefore, agreeing upon a definition, the types of extenuating circumstances acceptable, and the number of days involved before one is declared to be a chronically absent or truant student is most important. There needs to be a common understanding and acceptance of a definition for chronic absenteeism and truancy. Language and terms used with a commonly held meaning are critical to understanding and addressing any problem related thereto.

Causes

According to available data, causes of chronic absenteeism and truancy can be placed into two broad categories: external-related causes and school-related causes. External-related causes include financial and economic problems, familial obligations, peer-group pressures, legal and judicial involvement of students, and sociocultural and environmental influences. School-related causes include irrelevant curriculum and/or poor instructional methods; inflexible school schedules; insensitive, uncaring teachers, administrators and/or other school personnel; listlessness and disinterest in school; poor academic and/or social skills; and sloppy school accounting procedures.

These causes are based on the most often cited causes given by truants themselves. The most frequently cited causes, when placed in ascending or descending order often may differ from one school district to another, reflecting the socioeconomic, political, traditional and historical factors in the family- and community-value systems within specific locales. But the same causes consistently appear.

Solutions

Some successful programs for solving the truancy problem have been modeled on the following practices:

1. Creating and instituting several diverse educational designs and modes which appeal to and accomodate the varied educational needs, styles, and abilities of the student populations.

2. Making incentives available to students who exhibit good, improved, or perfect school attendance records.

3. Providing appropriate alternative educational and vocational programs for students who appear to have trouble adjusting to the regular school offerings.

4. Telephoning, visiting, and writing on a regular basis parents of chronically absent or truant students to inform them of their children's school absences.

5. Developing cooperative and supportive working relations among school personnel (i.e., counselors, teachers, attendance officers, security persons, administrators, social workers, and others) in a team effort to work more effectively with students displaying truancy patterns and potential truancy patterns.

6. Counseling parents of truants and truants themselves to develop coping skills and to combat negative school feelings.

7. Educating and training personnel to work more creatively and successfully with students who are chronically absent or truant.

8. Hiring more personnel to work with students who have poor school attendance records.

9. Highlighting and discussing in both school and community the myriad problems associated with truancy and absenteeism.

10. Seeking community and citywide solutions to truancy and conditions that cause truancy.

11. Implementing police sweeps or pickups of truants on the street during school hours.

12. Fining and jailing parents and/or truants for violations of the compulsory school attendance laws.

13. Involving all segments of the community in reducing truancy and conducting programs and activities toward that end.

Programs designed around the above practices have shown various degrees of success throughout the nation. The strongest impact on reducing truancy rates while concurrently increasing school attendance has been the result of combining several of the above program elements for implementation at the same time.

Summary

It is clear that there is a problem with reducing school absenteeism and truancy among the school population. As a nation, we have struggled with ways to address successfully the problems which are directly as well as indirectly related. There have been some successes, but not nearly enough to claim that the problems are inconsequential. Too often the schools have been expected to carry the brunt of the effort.

Two overarching concerns for school administrators in successfully meeting the challenge for reducing school absences and truancy are

1. Having an accurate and systematic student accounting system which provides correct input data, conversion process, output information, and relevant feedback.

2. Having programs and personnel within the school setting who are able to articulate and demonstrate for the public that school absenteeism and truancy must be addressed by the school working in conjunction with all of the public institutions outside of the school.

See also Dropouts; Student Alienation; Student Culture; Student Discipline.

—Betty W. Nyangoni
District of Columbia Public Schools

References

Children Out of School in America: A Report. (1974). Washington, DC: Washington Research Project. Children's Defense Fund.

READ, Resource Handbook for School Administrators. All About Student Attendance, Legal Aspects, Policy Procedures, Current Practices. (1984). Pontiac, MI: Department of Pupil Personnel, Oakland Public Schools.

School Safety: National School Safety Center Newsjournal. (1985). Sacramento, CA: National School Safety Center.

STUDENT ALIENATION

Student alienation is a perplexing problem that negatively influences the attitudes, values, and behaviors that large cohorts of youth exhibit toward the school and the wider society. When students feel separated and cut off from their families, friends, school, or work, alienation occurs. Researchers have provided insight into this phenomenon by developing clear definitions, identifying probable causes, and determining the extent to which it is manifested in specific behaviors. School administrators can help to ameliorate student alienation by initiating the development of innovative programs and recommending changes in existing programs.

There are two aspects of student alienation: social structural and personal psychological. Student alienation is an inherent aspect of the social structures (e.g., the shared rules, behavioral uniformities, roles, and functions) that help to coordinate stable interactions of individuals within social systems, e.g., families, communities, or schools. These social structures are alienating to the extent that they cause the fragmentation of experience. For example, the roots of alienation can be found in a trend in which increasing numbers of families are living in disarray. Data suggest that in 1984 25.7 percent of the U.S. families with children under age 18 were headed by single parents; by 1990 it is expected that between 30 percent to 50 percent of all families will be headed by single parents. The increase in single-parent households is associated with the number of children reared in poverty. In 1983, more than 50 percent of single-parent families were living below the poverty line, compared with 18 percent for all families with children. In addition, more than 50 percent of married women and 69 percent of single women with school-age children work outside the home. In

the school environment, student alienation can be produced from the structured curriculum, the short periods, the constant flow of students from one classroom and subject to another, and the disciplined and regimented aspects of the school.

The combined effects of fragmented family structures and regimented structures in schools have created a culture in which young people are left to fashion their own fragmented and idiosyncratic values out of the contradictory and incoherent images of meaningful living they collect from peers, parents, television, teachers and relatives. In this way, social structural phenomena contribute to the personal psychological dimension of student alienation. This dimension is characterized by five interrelated categories of personal perceptions by individual students: (a) *powerlessness*, the sense of low control of mastery over events; (b) *meaninglessness*, the sense of incomprehensibility of personal and social affairs; (c) *normlessness*, the sense that the social ideals to which most people profess are continually violated in practice; (d) *self-estrangement*, the student's engagement in activities that are not intrinsically rewarding; and (e) *isolation*, the student's placement of low reward value to goals or beliefs that are typically highly valued in society.

Both the structural and psychological aspects of student alienation are manifested in several antisocial behaviors that appear to be increasing among youth. Researchers estimate that 15 percent (i.e., about 2.4 million) of all American teenagers between the ages of 16 and 19 are unlikely to become productive adults because they are already alienated from society as a result of drug abuse, delinquency, pregnancy, unemployment, and dropping out of school. About 1,250,000 white, 750,000 black and 375,000 Hispanic 16 to 19 year olds are among this growing population. Among the findings: drug and alcohol abuse among young people are up sixty-fold since 1960; the dropout rate is about 23 percent overall, 35 percent for blacks and 45 percent for Hispanics; about 25 percent of persons arrested are under age 18; teenage pregnancy is up 109 percent among whites and 10 percent among minorities since 1960—a million teens become pregnant each year; teenage homicide is up 232 percent for whites and 16 percent for minorities since 1950, where suicide is up more than 150 percent since 1950.

Administrators can contribute to the amelioration of student alienation by developing innovative programs which focus on increasing student's involvement, engagement, and integration in both the school and the community. One approach administrators could use to initiate the amelioration of student alienation is the Amplified Project Team. The team could be employed to study the extent to which student alienation is present within the school, and recommend specific programs which would lead to the increased involvement, engagement, and integration of alienated students.

Several important steps should be taken to organize the Amplified Project Team. First, *specify the goals* (e.g., a plan to reduce the dropout rate) for which the project is being organized. The goals of the project will be different for each individual school and should be based upon a realistic assessment of the extent to which the school is currently affected by student alienation. This assessment can be conducted by determining the extent to which the "manifestations" of student alienation, (e.g., student absenteeism, dropout, drug and alcohol abuse, teenage pregnancy, etc.) exist in the school. Even if clear evidence of the existence of student alienation is not found, the administrator may want to implement a team to target the needs of high-risk students, e.g., minority, poor, etc., with the goal of preventing the future occurrence of such manifestations in the school. The goals of the team should have high priority and the Amplified Project Team should have the support of the top administrators involved with the school. The team should be delegated the responsibility, authority, and resources needed to accomplish its goals.

Second, *appoint a core group* to see the project through from start to finish. Instead of hiring supplementary personnel, the administrator should select high-status influential members of the staff, e.g., teachers, counselors, supervisors, to serve on the core group. Other core group members should include influential students, parents (especially those of high-risk students, e.g., poor, single-parent, working parents, etc.), community members, and members of the board of education. Third, *designate a target* completion date. Fourth, *relieve the core group* staff members from a portion of their other responsibilities. Fifth, *communicate with all* those likely to be affected by or interested in the project or its mission.

The amplification of the core group involves adding staff as different phases of the project are undertaken. The administrator should attempt to involve top administrators, staff, students, parents, and community leaders in substantial ways at appropriate times as the project evolves. The selection of amplification staff should be based on the members' competence and knowledge in a particular area. The plans submitted by the team should be given a high priority for implementation.

See also Dropouts; Student Absenteeism and Truancy; Student Culture; Student Discipline.

—Larry G. Martin
University of Wisconsin-Milwaukee

References

Bronfenbrenner, U. (1986, February). "Alienation: And the four worlds of childhood." *Kappan, 68*, 430-36.
Harris, B.M. (1985). *Supervisory behavior in education*, (chapter 6). Englewood Cliffs, NJ: Prentice-Hall.
Newmann, F.M. (1981, November). "Reducing student alienation in high schools: Implications of theory." *Harvard Educational Review, 51*(4), 546-64.

STUDENT CULTURE

Culture is defined in terms of communication, often as the shared communication tools of a group of people. This includes language, tools and weapons, religious patterns, types of food, ways of learning—in sum, a culture is the shared perspectives which enable members of a cultural group to communicate with one another. The depth of the cultural influence can be measured by the lack of conflict in communication. In the perfect culture, people might argue and fight, but they would never misunderstand each other or misunderstand each other's words, tools, non-verbal communications, etc.

Student Culture

Edward T. Hall presents one of the more practical models for analyzing cultures in *The Silent Language*. Hall's original task was to develop a training model for the Peace Corps which would allow volunteers to assess quickly the major cultural patterns of their host countries. Hall's model is easy to learn and apply and has been used to analyze the conflicts between the two primary cultures of the school, namely, the student and adult cultures.

The Three Reaction Patterns

Hall begins with three reaction patterns: formal, informal, and technical. Formal patterns are those behaviors performed for traditional reasons. We do not think about them; we just do them. An example would be that most of us do not work on the weekends. We do not think about that; we just do not show up for work on weekends. In reality, the weekend is not even the weekend at all. Most calendars list Sunday as the first day of the week and Saturday as the last day of the week. It does not have to make any sense because, "We've always done it that way." Formal patterns are the most resistant to change because they have the weight of custom behind them. If you do not believe that, find a calendar which begins the week with Monday (in many ways a more rational approach), and see how long it takes you to get used to it.

Informal patterns are also usually out of awareness. However, they do not have the weight of custom behind them, and they are relatively easy to change once they are pointed out to us. We learn most of our cultural patterns informally. No one really sits down to teach us how to speak or interact with others. Rather, we learn these most important skills through imitation.

Technical patterns are distinguishable from both formal and informal patterns in that the individual practicing the patterns is fully aware of how it was learned and its purpose. For example, while weekends are a formal pattern, the number of days in the year is a technical pattern, including such things as leap year. We know that the year is a measure based on the rotation of the earth around the sun. The first day of the season is also a technical pattern. The names and number of days in each month are a formal pattern.

Technical patterns change much more rapidly than either formal or informal patterns. They often change when a new technical pattern arises. Further, technical patterns change more rapidly because they do not have the force of custom to maintain them.

The Primary Message Systems

Hall lists ten primary message systems: interaction, association, subsistence, bisexuality, territoriality, temporality, learning, play, defense, and exploitation. In the process of understanding a foreign culture, we must learn that culture's reaction pattern (formal, informal, or technical) and how our culture's reaction pattern differs.

We will discuss only the two most critical primary message systems, but those who are interested in the effect of cultural differences in the school should read either of the references listed at the end of this article.

Interaction. Interaction is the way that we communicate and relate to other individuals.

Students tend to be informal in their interaction patterns. They are neither particularly tradition- nor rule-oriented. When they are with their friends, they often have no specific discussion topics or agenda items. They just get together to talk or play. This is their basic method of interaction. The school, however, expects them to use much more formal and technical interaction patterns. For example, only one person should talk at a time in class, there would be no "horsing around," and when the teacher speaks, everyone else should be quiet and listen. While some of these may appear to be technical patterns of interaction ("If everyone speaks at the same time, no one will hear anything that anyone else is saying and we will not learn"), in actuality, there is no particular reason to assume that the students are not learning when they are talking to each other in informal groups. There is also no reason to assume that occasional horsing around will hinder learning. However, we, as teachers, tend to believe that that is the case.

Students often do react formally in their social interactions with each other. There are a whole set of formal rules about how they should act and dress and generally how they should behave. Ostracism is a continual threat for those who violate these formal taboos. However, these are largely nonclassroom behaviors and therefore are not central to this article. In the in-school situation, the critical point is that the difference in the interaction-reaction pattern (formal and technical for the teachers and informal for the students) often leads to conflict. Because we view the student as the cause of the conflict, we often call the conflict a "discipline problem." In reality, it is a difference in the way students and teachers deal with interaction.

Association. Association is the way that we interact with institutions or the way that we are viewed and view ourselves because we are members of a particular institution. Students react to association informally and technically. They tend to have few rules and those that they do have are technical; that is, they make them up as they need them and discard them when they are no longer needed. Teachers, on the other hand, enforce a series of rules which have a tradition and history; that is, they are formal in nature. Students may say, "Why do we have to follow all those dumb rules?" Teachers, on the other hand, will use either technical or formal arguments, "If we do not obey the rules, we have anarchy" (technical) or "I am the teacher in this class and you will do as I say" (formal). Again, the reaction to the pattern is different and the result is a cultural conflict.

Cultural Ignorance

Many of the problems facing schools can be attributed to cultural ignorance; that is, neither the students nor the adult staff are aware of the cultural patterns of the other. It is not reasonable to expect students to understand the cultural patterns of the teachers since students are, by definition, not sufficiently learned to have that level of sophistication. However, teachers are rarely trained to recognize cultural differences. This means that many problems facing the school will continue to be unresolved not because they are unresolvable but because they are being viewed from the perspective of the supposed necessity of the more powerful participant enforcing a supposedly justifiable set of cultural patterns on the weaker participant. The weaker participant will often rebel and neither learning nor peaceful behavior will result.

Schools for entirely too long have allowed themselves to live in a monocultural world. We believe that what we teach and what we expect behaviorally is sound and necessary. While many of our cultural and societal biases are positive and/or necessary, others may interfere with the educative process. Closer analysis might lead us to question some of our cultural expectations. At present, there is very little cultural and institutional self-analysis. In any event, we should at least learn our own school cultural and institutional biases and determine if those are indeed the ones we wish to maintain.

See also Multicultural Education; Social Learning in the Schools; Student Alienation.

—Frank Besag
University of Wisconsin-Milwaukee

References

Besag, F., & Nelson, J. (1984). *Foundations of education: Stasis and change* (chapter 7). New York: Random House.
Hall, E.T. (1959). *The silent language.* Greenwich, CN: Fawcett.

STUDENT DISCIPLINE

Student behavior problems are as old as formal education. They can be effectively handled by applying a few basic principles: (a) Know the facts relative to the infraction, (b) know the rules which apply, legal and otherwise, and (c) do not take action while angry, under emotional stress, or while suffering from fractured dignity.

All behavior, constructive as well as destructive, has underlying causes. Though an educator may not have the background or the time to engage in a detailed psychological analysis of each behavior problem, skills can be developed for recognizing boredom, frustration, insecurity, and other factors which frequently lead to discipline problems.

In fulfilling the complex roles of helper, enforcer, and referee, the administrator can implement a successful discipline program by working closely with teachers in a unified team effort. But caution must be exercised. The time when an administrator could function as prosecuting attorney, judge, jury, and executioner is gone. Such terms as "due process" are part of the vocabulary of many students. Though a detailed knowledge of the legal aspects of school discipline is not required of the administrator, especially since this area is constantly changing, it is important for educators to understand that the rights of students are being "protected" as never before. The logical move is to ask for help before taking any action that might be questionable or unlawful.

Reasons for Problems

In any social system, people are unsure as to the restraints under which they are functioning until they test them. Appropriate behavior patterns then emerge. Students will test teachers, not only because they feel it is their obligation to do so, but also because they need recognition as a person. This personal need for attention from others can often be satisfied in the school environment by periodic recognition of the student's accomplishments.

Some problems have an academic base. The educator may be dealing with students who are bored or frustrated. Often such students will use misconduct as a means of voicing their dissatisfaction with the situation.

Many students are born conformists. They fear being different, and even the best students will sometimes engage in questionable activities, yielding to the call of conformity and peer pressure.

Since school is only one of the many influences to which students are subjected, often they may harbor resentments stemming from urbanization, family changes, or unemployment within the family. Such conditions may negatively affect their attitudes and behavior. Also, to many youngsters, rebellion is simply a part of growth and development. The change from childhood to adulthood is a confusing time when all sorts of strange phenomena bombard their bodies and minds, and many teens deal with the stress by rebelling.

Avoiding Discipline Problems

Many discipline problems referred to principals or assistant principals are actually teacher-generated. Administrators should insist that certain classroom criteria be met by the teacher. Classroom organization should be maintained and assignments spelled out so that students know what they are to do. Also, evidence of teacher indecision can serve as the point of entry for misbehavior.

Relationships with students must be natural and sincere. Even small children can detect insincerity, and any attempt to fool them usually creates problems. Students expect adults to act their age. The administrator-pupil relationship is not a peer relationship, but rather adult-student. As part of the adult maturity, administrators, in the eyes of the students, should be consistent and fair in dealing with behavioral problems. This often means developing a thick skin against criticism and strong self-discipline to control one's temper, thereby avoiding arguments and verbal exchanges with the student.

Administrators should approach the punishment of students with control, being careful to avoid threatening or humiliating remarks. Actions or remarks which humiliate do not promote learning, and threats are unnecessary if students know the standard of conduct they are expected to maintain. If violation of that standard deserves punishment, then appropriate punishment should be meted out. According to the stimulus-response ideas of training, rewards or punishments should follow immediately after the act involved. This is not necessarily true in the discipline arena. If the cycle of infraction-judgment-punishment moves too rapidly, the offender can come out of it feeling that he now has a "clean slate." A case that is in the pending category can give rise to a great deal of introspection and self-examination.

Strategies for Improvement

The administrator must know the law as it applies to disciplinary matters. Laws vary from one state to another in terms of what the administrator can do and what students can do. Being aware of local customs and conditions regarding discipline can also guide the administrator in dealing with behavioral problems. All comments concerning a problem situation should be withheld until the source of the problem has been localized and dealt with.

Working on a constructive basis with student leaders has a big advantage in solving discipline problems. A wise administrator works to maintain good rapport with student leaders.

Administrators should encourage teachers to keep referrals to a minimum, seeking administrative support only when the problem is clearly too big to be handled in the classroom. When problems are referred, the administrator should learn as much as possible about the student, gathering background information from school records and teacher or counselor input. The meeting with the student should be in a private setting if at all possible. Many educators have been surprised at the sort of person they encounter when they deal with students privately.

Some behavioral problems are best dealt with when parents and school officials are involved in a joint effort. Administrators must be willing to work with parents as appropriate to establish lines of communication which are vital to solving discipline problems.

This article discussed problems of student discipline in schools and touched upon preventive approaches for the administrators. Ideas presented here have merit for all educators as they deal with growing and lingering discipline problems in schools.

See also Disruptive Students; Due Process; Student Absenteeism and Truancy; Student Alienation.

—William A. Kritsonis, Editor-in-Chief
National Forum of Educational Administration and
Supervision Journal

References

DeBruyn, R.L., & Larson, J.L. (1984). *You can handle them all*. Manhattan, KS: The Master Teacher.

Kritsonis, W.A., & Adams, S. (1986-87). *School discipline: The art of survival*. Baton Rouge, LA: Land & Land.

Snyder, K.J., & Anderson, R.B. (1986). *Managing productive schools: Toward an ecology*. Orlando, FL: Academic Press.

STUDENT NEWSPAPERS

Student publications in the school program are in a state of flux, but their inclusion can be justified on solid grounds educationally. Problems and issues derived from both new and familiar factors such as administration, faculty, adviser, student staff, demographics, and cultural milieu affect student publications.

A constant turnover of advisers and members of the student newspaper staff contributes to and results from some of the problems noted here. The trend to increased graduation requirements and the conservative thrust for abolition of all but the "solid" subjects have militated against finding time in the schedule for journalism. Declining finances and populations, combined with an increasingly pluralistic and litigious society, have necessitated re-evaluation of dollar and teacher allocations to journalism as an academic program. Faculty apathy or antipathy, inept advisers, immoderate student staffs, and local activities have reinforced fearful administrators' negative effect on student publications.

No other subject in the secondary curriculum is more basic than journalism because it requires and stresses such a wide range of skills. For language arts and social studies it is a laboratory which provides a "lifetime-benefits" activity focusing on growth in analysis and creativity, investigative and academic skills, leadership, and self-realization. Participation in publication activities provides career education and assists a student to progress toward productive citizenship and informed consumership. Student publications experiences facilitate liberal education and a "hands on" learning of democracy.

The Student Newspaper's Purpose

As a result of the decision of the U.S. Supreme Court in a Missouri case involving a high school student newspaper, it is essential that school officials define the basic purpose of the student newspaper and communicate this purpose frequently to all affected parties.

In *Hazelwood School District v. Kuhlmeier* (Case #86-836) Justice White, writing for the Court, stated that "A school may in its capacity as publisher of a school newspaper or producer of a school play 'disassociate itself' not only from speech that would 'substantially interfere with its work ... or impinge upon the rights of other students' but also from speech that is, for example, ungrammatical, poorly written, inadequately researched, baised or prejudiced, vulgar or profane, or unsuitable for immature audiences."

The Missouri decision would appear to give school officials considerable latitude in approving suitable content for the student newspaper. However, this latitude also gives school administrators an implicit responsibility to guard against the suppression of student views merely because they differ from the *personal* views of the administrators. A continuing challenge for school officials will be how best to define the purpose and role of the student newspaper in such a way that they are educationally defensible *and* responsive to diverse views on issues and concerns that are important to students.

Recommendations

The recommendations set forth here are based on the literature and the experience of the authors as journalists, educators, school administrators, and school media advisers. The recommendations also are based on various surveys of advisers, principals, and distinguished journalism educators. The suggestions are aimed at student newspapers but apply largely to other student media.

In-Service Education. As a means of avoiding or alleviating problems, in-service education is urged for administrators, faculty, and advisers on the topics discussed below, particularly on the objectives and functions of the student newspaper. The authors have found that principals do not understand First Amendment rights or choose to risk violation rather than local consequences.

Academic and Vocational Roles. These roles of the journalism program should be clearly delineated through study groups or workshops involving students, faculty, local and central school authorities, local media representatives, and lay citizens. The status of the student newspaper must be defined as to whether it is a part of or a product of a journalism class or a reduced, noncredit, or cocurricular activity to be pursued during or out of school hours. The journalism class should not be a dumping ground for misfits. Counselors should be made aware of the activity's vocational contributions, and the language arts faculty should be aware of the opportunities for implementing "sorting across the curriculum." Principals report that fewer controversies arise when journalism is first required of the student newspaper staff one or more semesters as a credit subject in which ethics and responsible exercise of First Amendment rights can be included. To reduce student staff turnover, participation on the newspaper should be built into the rewards system (points toward a school letter, recognition day, participation in interscholastic meetings and competitions).

Advisers. Recruitment and selection of advisers is crucial to the school newspaper's quality, management, and freedom from controversy. Principals encounter fewer controversies when advisers have had professional preparation and experience, certification in journalism, and an activities salary supplement. The dignity and value of the position should be signaled by the time, funding, and facilities provided.

Finance. Advisers and students should be provided necessary funds, supplies, facilities, and modern equipment. Careful policies should be established regarding support through subsidy, student subscriptions, sale of ads, or a combination of these. Membership and some travel expenses should be provided for the adviser and staff to encourage participation in interscholastic journalism events and competitions.

Publications Advisory Board. A board should be created to develop school policy concerning student publications. Rather than censor, the board could serve as a review body to recommend and advise when staff and principal or adviser reach an impasse on an article or practice. The board makeup could vary widely for local reasons but should include the principal, advisor, editor, a student government official, a local media representative, an attorney, and a parent. Principals who were members of such boards reported either fewer or no controversies.

Information and Support. Organizations concerned with student newspapers include Association for Education in Journalism and Mass Communications; Journalism Education Association (*Communications: Journalism Education Today*); Quill and Scroll Society (*Quill and Scroll*); Student Press Law Center (Kennedy Foundation); and National Association of Secondary School Principals (annual advisory list on activities and contests).

See also Extracurricular Activities; News Media; Rights, Teachers' and Students'.

—E. Joseph Broussard
University of Southwestern Louisiana
—C. Robert Blackmon
Louisiana State University

References

Benedict, M. (1982). *Principal's guide to high school journalism.* Iowa City, IA: Quill and Scroll Foundation.

Long, R., Buser, R., & Jackson, M. (1977). *Student activities in the seventies: A survey report.* Reston, VA: National Association of Secondary School Principals.

Sybouts, W., & Krepel, W.J. (1984). *Student activities in the secondary schools: A handbook and guide* (chapter 9). Westport, CT: Greenwood Press.

STUDENT PREGNANCY

One million adolescents become pregnant annually in the United States (one in ten girls). While Title IX of the 1972 Education Amendments prohibits schools which receive federal funds from excluding any student on the basis of pregnancy or parenthood, pregnancy is the major known cause of school dropouts among females. Among mothers under age 15, the situation is even more extreme as four in ten never complete eighth grade.

Not only is the age at which a mother first gives birth the strongest influence on the level of education she will attain, but the young mother is also more likely to live part of her life on public assistance. Because early childbearing may result in the mother leaving school, many adolescent mothers do not acquire the skills or qualifications which would enable them to become self-supporting. A disproportionate number of women on welfare are teen mothers or women who first went on welfare as teen mothers.

To compound the problem of unemployment and underemployment further, studies indicate that the younger a woman is at the birth of her first child, the more likely she is to have more pregnancies and to have them in closer succession.

Although the *rate* of pregnancy among adolescents has decreased since the 1950s, the *number* of teenagers giving birth has increased because of the larger number of adolescents in the total population. Sixty percent of the pregnant teens who give birth are more likely to be from the lower socioeconomic groups and minority families. In the 1950s, the probabilities were higher that pregnant adolescents were more likely to have abortions (if they come from the upper socioeconomic classes) than to become single parents.

Title IX mandates that pregnant students, regardless of marital status, have the right to participate in any program, course or extracurricular activity offered by schools which receive federal funds. Schools may offer separate, voluntary programs and courses, but these must be comparable to the regular curriculum.

Teachers and social workers who have worked with pregnant teens recommend programs which have a dual purpose. First, the schools and community should consider ways to prevent teenage pregnancy; and second, schools and community agencies need to help the pregnant teen and the adolescent mother to secure a high school diploma and acquire vocational skills which would enable her to succeed in further training or in higher education.

Studies suggest that teenagers who have fairly well-defined aspirations or career goals are more motivated to avoid pregnancy. To avoid engaging in early sex, adolescents also need support from home, school, and peers. Programs which build interpersonal communication skills and promote self-esteem prompt teenage girls to delay sexual activity; the same is true of the programs which foster career planning and high aspirations.

In spite of the fact that television programming in several European countries permits more explicit displays of sexual behavior than is allowed in the United States, the teenage pregnancy rates in these countries are lower than they are in the United States. These European countries provide comprehensive school programs of sex education which include information on birth-control methods. Their government clinics, in addition, provide free or low-cost contraceptives to adolescents.

The sporadic and spontaneous nature of adolescent sexual behavior will continue to result in unplanned pregnancies. For those teenagers who do not choose abortion (about 60 percent), schools should develop programs which assist and encourage young mothers to secure resources which would enable them to continue in school. These resources include prenatal care, parent education, financial assistance, counseling, and child care following the delivery.

Programs which have had the best success rate for keeping teenage mothers in school are those which are staffed by sensitive teachers, administrators; and counselors. Three types of programs are most commonly found in the United States. One type of program is hospital-based and provides primarily health services. School-based programs are of two types. One is the alternative school or program which may be comprehensive in nature, providing prenatal care, counseling, social services, parent education, and a comprehensive academic program. While alternative school programs are the most costly because the teacher/student ratio is usually lower than in the regular setting, alternative programs usually have the flexibility to use available community services for the health, counseling, and day-care components.

The second type of school-based program is located in the regular high school. The St. Paul, Minnesota, Maternal and Infant Care Project is nationally recognized for reducing adolescent pregnancy. Health clinics are operated in four high schools where comprehensive services, including family planning, are offered by a team. Locating a pregnancy prevention program and a program for teenage mothers in the regular school facilitates easy access to the regular academic and vocational courses not normally found in the alternative school.

See also Community-School Involvement; Demographic Trends; Judicial Decisions; Sex Education.

—Carol Payne Smith
Western Michigan University

References

Dryfoos, J. (1983). *Review of interventions in the field of prevention of adolescent pregnancy*. New York: Rockefeller Foundation (ERIC Document Reproduction Service No. ED 250 409).

Sung, K. (1981). "The role of day care for teenage mothers in a public school." *Child Care Quarterly, 10*(2), 113-24.

Teen parents and their children: Issues and programs. (1983). Washington, DC: Hearing before the Select Committee on Children, Youth and Families. House of Representatives, Ninety-Eighth Congress, First Session (ERIC Document Reproduction Service No. ED 245 146).

STUDENT RESPONSIBILITY

One of the major goals of schools is to prepare students for democratic citizenship. A key element in this function is the development of student responsibility. While the family usually *begins* the task of teaching students self-discipline and responsibility, it is the school that has been held increasingly accountable for successfully *completing* this task. This expectation to prepare responsible citizens is problematic for schools. It is problematic in large part because schools have limited resources, while students place varying demands on the school based on factors such as race, ethnicity, gender, and social class. For example, the most frequent response to students demonstrating a lack of responsibility (e.g., engaging in misconduct, truancy, or a failure to complete assignments) is to strengthen the disciplinary code to deal more harshly with the "offenders." Yet research suggests that such a get-tough approach is counter-productive to the development of self-discipline and responsibility.

We must acknowledge two facts about student responsibility. First, student responsibility is in part developmental and therefore dependent on the capacity or readiness of students to assume increasing responsibility for their intellectual, physical, and emotional selves: Simply stated, students in the same grade frequently differ quite markedly in their ability to act responsibly. Second, student responsibility is in part experiential and therefore dependent on the opportunities each student has to exercise responsibility. Thus, in order to maximize the development of student responsibility schools should attend to the following six areas.

First, teachers should offer well-planned instruction. This involves using appropriately leveled instructional strategies and materials to maximize successful learning experiences for all students, using a variety of positive motivational devices rather than threats to facilitate classroom management, and planning classroom activities and the transitions between activities to minimize the time in which students can act irresponsibly. Well planned instruction provides repeated opportunities for students to take responsibility for their own learning.

Second, teachers should model a caring respect for others and use rewards and praise rather than negative sanctions as the basis for an incentive structure. Such teacher behavior contributes to the development of positive interpersonal relationships both in and out of the classroom which, in turn, help bind students to the school. Student responsibility is enhanced when teachers treat all students and adults equitably, and focus on the student as a person rather than on the students' behavior. When we acknowledge that the school years become progressively more difficult for students as they seek individual identity, then we can recognize the importance of teachers and building leaders modeling appropriate behavior.

Third, all of the school's staff should contribute to creating a positive learning environment which maximizes a student's sense of belonging, competence, and worth. Student responsibility is enhanced when a student derives (a) a sense of belonging from identification with the school, (b) a sense of competence from success in and status from activities sponsored by the school, and (c) a sense of personal worth from interactions with students and adults in the school. By contrast, the development of student responsibility is likely to be retarded when students experience attacks on their senses of belonging, competence, and worth from adults and other students. Thus, school personnel at each school should create a learning environment that permits *each student* to develop a sense of belonging, competence, and worth.

Fourth, the disciplinary code of the school should be developed with the involvement of students; it should be printed and distributed to all students, parents, and school personnel; it should be discussed by teachers and students; and it should be administered firmly, fairly, and consistently. When students act responsibly, good discipline is maintained. Discipline, however, must be taught. Teachers should teach students the value of having rules and of following the rules; they should discuss the consequences of violating the particular rules that are operational in the school. Teachers help students to act responsibly by setting limits for acceptable behavior and holding students accountable when they exceed those limits.

Fifth, student responsibility is enhanced by providing a variety of opportunities for students to practice responsible behavior not only in the classroom but also in cocurricular and extracurricular areas. Such activities could range from classroom tasks such as collecting pencils in the elementary grades to writing and producing a television show on teenage employment to out-of-classroom activities such as playing in a seventh grade string quartet or leading the debate team in a multistate tournament. Teachers should design comparable experiences for all students that challenge them to be successful in accepting escalating responsibility.

Sixth, and finally, teachers should develop a curricular focus on the importance of responsibility in a democratic society. Such a focus would engage students in the crucial exploration of the values, norms, and beliefs of the American society, as well as develop the students' capacity for critical thinking. In carrying this curricular theme across subject areas (e.g., English, science, and social studies), *all* students would experience both problem solving and higher-order thinking activities.

To facilitate these six important activities at the school level, teachers and building leaders should work with the appropriate central office personnel to (a) design a school-specific plan to enhance student responsibility for democratic citizenship, (b) survey their building to assess the current levels of implementation of the six activities outlined above, (c) develop an ongoing and sequenced series of staff-development activities for teachers *and* building leaders that focus on those factors found from the survey to be missing or ineffective, (d) provide both coaching and feedback experiences for teachers and building leaders as they practice new behaviors in the targeted activities, and (e) develop a mechanism to monitor systematically the effectiveness of these new behaviors and use these formative data to fine tune the program designed to enhance the development of student responsibility.

Finally, we should note that the development of student responsibility is a function of sound instructional and management practices, and that such programs have a greater likelihood of success if they are designed and implemented by the staff of individual schools, rather than mandated by the district or the state.

See also Character Education; Cooperative Learning; Social Learning in the Schools; Values Education.

—William T. Pink
National College of Education

References

Newman, F. (1981). "Reducing student alienation in high schools: Implications of theory." *Harvard Educational Review, 51*, 545-64.

Pink, W.T. (1986). "In search of exemplary junior high schools: A case study." In W.T. Pink and G.W. Noblit (Eds.), *Schooling in social context: Qualitative studies* (pp. 218-49). Norwood, NJ: Ablex.

Wehlege, G. (1983). "The marginal high school student: Defining the problem and searching for policy." *Children and Youth Services Review, 5*, 321-42.

STUDENT-CENTERED CURRICULUM

A student-centered curriculum is based on the perception that education is not primarily a program of training students in particular preidentified skills, but is a matter of providing opportunity for students to discover what they would like to learn and how to learn the subject which interests them. Through the student's imagination, cognitive and effective domains of learning are brought together into a synergistic whole. As the result, students gain a greater mastery of their thought and feelings and discover new ways to relate to their world.

Basic components of a student-centered learning program were originally identified in a Ford Foundation study reported by Weinstein and Fantini. First, the students and their particular interests and concerns are identified and the basis for those concerns understood. The students are active participants in the process by which their interests and concerns are articulated and explored.

Second, the interests and concerns of the students are related by faculty and students working cooperatively to the content of a specific course. Course outcomes are thus dependent both upon course content and the focus provided by the students. When student interest and course content are effectively merged, student motivation to learn is high.

Third, strategies for learning are chosen by faculty and students in a continuation of this process. Vehicles for learning are chosen on the basis of the students' experience and preference. The student who asks, "What do I need to learn in order to reach my goals?" will select both the content and the vehicle for learning needed to meet those goals. The aim of these vehicles for learning is the development of reading comprehension; computational skills; oral and written communication; skills in description, critical analysis, and conceptualization; and self-awareness and self-presentation skills on the part of the learner.

Valuing learners and their concerns and including them in the process by which curricular foci are developed and vehicles for learning are chosen are the fundamental components of a student-centered curriculum.

See also Cooperative Learning.

—Glenn E. Whitlock, Clinical Director
Christian Counseling Center
Redlands, California

References

Jones, R.M. (1986). *Fantasy and feeling in education.* New York: New York University Press.

Weinstein, G., & Fantini, M.D. (Eds.). (1970). *Towards humanistic education, a curriculum of affect.* New York: Ford Foundation, Praeger Publishers.

Whitlock, G.E. (1984). *Person-centered learning: Confluent learning processes.* Lahnam, NY: University Press of America.

SUBJECT-CENTERED CURRICULUM

Most authorities who have studied and written about curriculum theory and planning identify three sources for the curriculum: the individual as learner, the values and institutions of the society, and the discipline or organized fields of knowledge. There has been a question of how to give recognition to these three sources. Some authorities have contended that they can and should be treated with equal emphasis. Others have contended that one source can be given priority while the other two may be taken into account in some way.

Traditionally, the priority has been given to the discipline; thus, a subject-centered curriculum. This is particularly evident at the high school and junior high school or middle school levels. Schools at these levels are generally organized by departments and scheduled by subject areas.

The subjects which are taught in the elementary and secondary schools are basically derived from the disciplines which are taught at the colleges and universities. Indeed, this is the way colleges and universities are organized.

One of the issues that educators face is how to translate the disciplines which make up the colleges and universities to the curriculum of elementary and secondary schools.

There are too many to include all of them, and many may not be suitable for elementary or secondary school students. For example, history, geography, political science, economics, sociology, and anthropology are commonly taught as separate disciplines at the college and university levels but are often combined as "social studies" at the elementary and secondary level.

The most basic issues concerning the subject curriculum are scope and sequence. What generalizations, concepts, processes, and facts should be included at a particular level and what should be the sequence or order of presentation and study? The study of a subject presupposes the presentation of the subject matter in a sequential and organized order—generally from the simple to the complex or chronological. The subject curriculum results in the use of textbooks which present the subject in an organized fashion as the major instructional resource, teaching as exposition of subject matter, and an age/grade structure with appropriate student grouping practices.

Another issue concerning the subject curriculum is that of fragmentation and correlation. Generally, students in a subject curriculum are not confronted with how the various subjects are related. Also the subject-centered curriculum as presented in textbooks tends to focus on the past rather than the present and the future. It is left to the teacher to relate the subject to the present, the future, and to other subjects. There have been and undoubtedly will be new "subjects" identified such as career education, environmental education, and survival skills. But given the history of the curriculum, they eventually disappear or are subsumed in the more traditional subjects.

There is also the issue of which subjects are to be required and which elective. This raises a related issue of how many subjects it is reasonable to expect students to study at any particular time. The Carnegie Unit was invented in the early 1900s as a way of quantifying a high school program so that the colleges and universities might assess a student's school experiences. The expectation was that a high school graduate would present 16 units for admission to the college or university. During the 1980s, the requirement for graduation has increased to as many as 24 units in many school districts.

Perhaps the most basic reason for the priority given to the subjects or disciplines as the primary source for the curriculum is that it is how most people have experienced elementary and secondary schooling. It is not only how the colleges and universities are organized and how teachers are prepared to teach, it is how most of us have "gone to school." Thus, the subject-centered curriculum is both a practical and political reality.

See also Curriculum Development; Mastery Learning.

—Rolland Callaway
University of Wisconsin-Milwaukee

References

English, F.W. (Ed.). (1983). *Fundamental curriculum decisions.* Alexandria, VA: Association for Supervision and Curriculum Development.

Lux, D.D., & Ray, W.E. (1970). "Towards a knowledge base for practical arts and vocational education." *Theory Into Practice, IX*(5), 301-08.

Tyler, R. (1949). *Basic principles of curriculum and instruction.* Chicago: The Chicago Press.

SUBSTITUTE TEACHERS

A substitute teacher is a stand-in for the regular teacher when he or she is absent. Instruction is to be continued, discipline maintained, and students' welfare protected. It is estimated that a student will have a substitute teacher seven to ten times a year. This increase in the use of substitutes is a result of liberal use of sick leave and increased availability of personal and professional leave for teachers. School districts must identify the role of substitute teacher through articulated expectations and practice. Some want a baby-sitter, emphasizing discipline and maintaining order. Others want a resource person who is prepared to teach special topics and/or who has specific talents to offer for enrichment. A third role is expecting the substitute to deliver a prepared lesson in order that student learning and the sequence of the lessons continue.

Substitutes are recruited from former teachers, unemployed new college graduates, or aides trained to be substitutes. Potential substitutes are offered jobs through colleges, newspaper advertisements, the professional staff, parent-teacher organizations, area education agencies, and memorandums sent home with elementary students.

The hiring process for substitutes includes application, letters of recommendation, evidence of teacher certification, college transcript, birth certificate verifying American citizenship, physical examination, and evidence of having worked with students. An interview provides further screening. Sometimes observing applicants in a teaching situation and requiring their attendance at in-service workshops are additional requirements.

Schools recognize the importance in providing orientation for substitutes. This often saves considerable time solving problems or responding to hundreds of questions. In small districts, orientation may be combined with orientation for new teachers. In larger districts, the orientation ranges from a workshop of several hours to full-day meetings.

A handbook should be developed for substitute orientation. A handbook explains the philosophy of the district regarding substitute teachers. It sets forth certification requirements and application procedures. The handbook also explains payroll deductions and how salaries are paid. There are references in the handbooks to professional expectations, orientation procedures, and workshop expectations. Responsibilities and how assignments are made are covered in the handbook. Details such as school addresses, time schedules, and the names of principals and their secretaries are given. Such a book also contains a district map showing the location of schools; bus and subway routes to various schools are explained. A calendar of events is included. A handbook usually contains evaluation forms for substitute experience. There also is a reference to appropriate dress.

Some workshops focus on the development of lesson plans, reinforcement techniques, effective discipline practices, handling emergencies, instruction, typical problems, and tricks-of-the trade. Substitutes may be required to observe regular teachers before being assigned. A tour of the district is often included.

Building-level orientation may include a tour of the building and information about district policy, discipline procedures, emergency drills, playground rules, lunch, lunch money, reporting in on arrival, bell system, attendance-keeping, and end-of-the-day procedures.

Principals often have a folder compiled by each teacher for substitutes containing a welcome from the principal, specific suggestions from the teacher, general instructions, location of teacher's mailbox and lesson plans, special assignments, and a request for a written statement from the substitute regarding work covered and performance of students. Other information in folders includes procedures for checking out at the end-of-the-day; emergency and attendance procedures; schedule of teacher's classes; bell schedule; building map; class rolls with indication of students needing special help; seating charts; location of books, materials, keys, equipment; class rules; location of workroom (copying machines), lunchroom, lounge; where coats may be hung; names of helpful students; and evaluation forms for the day.

The principal can provide support to substitutes by extending simple courtesies, such as reserved parking and establishing a buddy system. The "buddy" can be a nearby teacher, department chairperson, or any helpful adult. This network can be established at the first of the year; therefore, when teacher "x" is absent, teacher "y" automatically becomes a buddy to teacher "x's" substitute.

Principals should expect the regular staff to be well prepared for substitutes. Visiting the substitute's room to see how things are progressing and to offer encouragement and appreciation are additional indications of support.

The regular teacher provides assistance by setting high expectations of students in advance of his or her absence. Student aides can provide additional assistance. Detailed lesson plans are a tremendous support.

An evaluation of the substitute experience is conducted by the substitute teacher and the regular teacher. Both evaluations may be submitted directly to the principal.

It is to the substitute's advantage to develop materials to be used during unstructured time or in the event the regular teacher left nothing to do.

The average pay of the substitute teacher is $30 to $40 per day with the range being from $21 to $93 per day without fringe benefits. They are paid once or twice a month.

Districts are experimenting with new terms to describe substitutes such as "relief teacher," "temporary teacher," "guest teacher," "reserve teacher," "resource teacher," or "supply teacher."

See also Classroom Management; Lesson Plans.

—James E. Ferguson
Community School District
Iowa City, Iowa

Reference

Pronin, Barbara (1983). *Substitute teaching: A handbook for hassle-free subbing.* New York: St. Martin's Press.

SUICIDE

Suicide rates among adolescent age groups have increased dramatically in the last thirty years. Further, there has been a marked increase in suicide attempts, many of which are unreported. Mental health professionals are busy trying to disseminate information and develop programs in an attempt to remedy this situation. References at the end of this entry will give the practitioner greater insight into the causes and trends of this problem.

Several states have written legislation aimed at public awareness and school involvement in the issue of teenage suicide. There are many, however, who fear that state-mandated programs will be inadequate, insufficient, or simply disregarded by the target audience. The school itself can do a great deal to address the problem of adolescent depression and suicide.

Intervention

Model suicide intervention programs currently exist in various schools. The thrust of these programs is to use regularly appointed staff personnel such as teachers, counselors, and nurses and to train them in the skills and techniques of suicide intervention and prevention. School psychologists and/or social workers can serve as consultants to the intervention unit. The objective of such an intervention unit is to make an initial assessment of those students who appear to be extremely withdrawn, depressed, or in crisis. Those students who are identified as having a particular need are referred to the proper agency for services.

What Can Be Done

The school administrator can lead his or her staff through a number of important steps in developing such a team. Staff members must consider their personal commitment and willingness to serve on such a unit. Each must know his or her personality, temperament, and character. The administrator can assist and guide in these matters.

With the help of the librarian, the administrator can establish a reading list of literature relevant to adolescent depression and suicide. The administrator must evaluate the student body and its needs, look for model programs which are adaptable to the school in question, and plan and design an appropriate training program.

The administrator must evaluate local and county mental-health resources, contact parent and community support groups, and develop procedures which govern the actions of team members. All of this can be done with help from team members and their trained consultants. A flow chart delineating positions and responsibilities is a valuable tool.

Operational Considerations

Properly selected volunteers and recruits from the regular staff must be trained in the signs and symptoms of adolescent depression and suicide. Frequent follow-up workshops are an asset. A brochure given to students and parents which is also available in school offices can help publicize the team's existence. A school bulletin board may be used to display pictures of team members and to post the times members of the team can be seen. Posting of a flow chart showing membership and how referrals are made is necessary for clear communications.

Debriefing meetings for all intervention team members should be held at least once a month. Business and organizational matters should be part of these meetings. More important, individual cases should be discussed at length. Constructive feedback on the handling and referral of each case should be the goal of the debriefing sessions.

Peer counseling is an option available to the advanced intervention unit. Peer counselors should be trained in the signs and symptoms of the problem. Their role should be that of the reflective listener. Their objective is to refer students in need to adult members of the team for further evaluation.

Final Concerns

Networking is a vital concept of suicide intervention in the school. Staff members find consolation in the fact that fellow members of the staff trained in the signs of the problem are easily accessible. Comfort is taken since help is available next door or right down the hallway.

There are some specific matters that must be addressed:

1. Be patient. Conduct a needs assessment, know your student body, and encourage your most able staff members to be part of the team. Realize that members of the team will demand shared decision making and an equal voice in all matters.

2. Plan and organize carefully, with your goals being to educate the staff and gain credibility among the students. One poorly handled case can cause you to lose student support for some time.

3. Develop parental and community support. Hold information programs and open the lines of communication. Develop a network which is viable not only in the school building but throughout the community at large. Remember, if the suicide intervention unit saves only one youngster in a year, the rewards and benefits are of enduring value.

See also Community School Involvement; Counseling and Guidance; Student Alienation.

—Richard J. Konet
Westfield Senior High School
Westfield, New Jersey

References

Hoff, L.A. (1984). *People in crisis: Understanding and helping* (chapter 5). Menlo Park, CA: Addison-Wesley.
Slaiken, K.A. (1984). *Crisis intervention* (chapter 16). Newton, MA: Albyn and Born.
Wekstein, L. (1979). *Handbook of suicidology: Principles, problems, and practice.* New York: Brunner-Mazel.

SUPERINTENDENT OF SCHOOLS

The superintendent of schools functions as chief executive officer of the local school system. He or she is responsible to the board of education. The precise role of the superintendent has been redefined over time, and current professional discussion and research center on how the role should be conceptualized to meet present and future challenges. Following are primary responsibilities for which the superintendent is accountable:

Professional Leadership: Providing professional advice to the school board through presentation of recommendations on all problems and issues and development of appropriate policies; providing instructional leadership for all educational programs to reflect cultural and socioeconomic diversity; and interpreting needs of the school system through short- and long-range planning.

School-Community Relations: Leading in the development and operation of programs incorporating participation by all segments of the community; utilizing the contributions of all concerned in the development of policy; establishing liaison with all appropriate community agencies; and fostering relations with news media and political officials.

Managing Human Resources: Recommending all appointments, promotions, and suspensions; providing for supervision, evaluation, and planning of staff utilization and professional improvement; and providing a climate of high morale and organizational effectiveness.

Managing Fiscal Resources: Developing and implementing a budget which serves the needs of the system; proposing short- and long-range planning related to physical plant, equipment, and supplies; and advising on problems of school finance at the local, state, and federal levels.

Mediation: Recommending policy to the board or mediating the terms under which legislative mandates or court dictates are applied in the school system.

Negotiation: Guiding the board in establishing objectives for all negotiations in the collective bargaining process; suggesting policies and coordinating the gathering of data; making proposals and answering counterproposals; orchestrating the values, information, resources, and policies which create a total school program.

Instruction: Furnishing instructional leadership to the board, employees, and community through realistic and challenging objectives; and providing vision, a commitment to change, utilization of new approaches, persistence, and otherwise "showing the way."

The superintendent pursues these responsibilities in an ever-changing environment, marked especially by the following problem areas:

Change: The setting in which the superintendent functions cannot be viewed apart from the social issues and trends of the day. There is an array of forces pressing for changes and threatening conflict in public education. A superintendent must be aware, informed, insightful, and vigilant.

Decisions and Evaluation: Superintendents face the problem of dealing with the local autonomy of the school district within the context of federal and state law, citizen expectations, and frequent indifference or irresponsibility toward the schools. The superintendent must define and seek implementation of decisions which result in educational quality, and must lead an evaluation program which provides proof of such quality.

Planning: Coordination of planning is a persistent problem for superintendents. Legislation, regulations, and mandates from the state and federal levels establish standards but seldom provide funding to meet such expectations. Changing intergovernmental relationships also pose planning difficulties, and coordination among city, county, and school agencies is crucial.

Finances: Primary funding for school districts comes from the local level, and superintendents necessarily must spend much time seeking fiscal support from the community. Decisions must be made about whether to operate an educational program based on previous patterns of fiscal support or to seek to educate the board and the citizenry to ways in which quality can be increased with additional resources.

Instruction: A key problem for superintendents is the recruitment of a quality staff of teachers and administrators, giving appropriate consideration to issues of racial balance and affirmative action. Lack of reciprocity and consistency among certification standards and retirement programs presents additional difficulties. The relationship between salary schedules and the quality of performance is also often a concern. Superintendents must develop definitions of quality teaching procedures for such evaluation and work out programs of effective staff improvement.

Curriculum: A major concern of superintendents is the development of a curriculum that meets the diverse needs of students in their communities. What strategies should be used in bringing about educational advancement for minority students? For the culturally deprived? For the handicapped? For the gifted?

Values: Diverse structures in relation to values as prescribed by school, church, family, and other segments of the community raise questions about educational goals, curricula, faculty, and resources. The superintendent must wrestle with issues of defining quality education, determining who best can set such criteria, and deciding on how quality is ultimately to be measured.

Board, Superintendent, and Staff Relations: For many superintendents, clarifying the respective roles and responsibilities of their offices in contrast to the school board is a significant problem. Closely related is the crucial question of developing a harmonious and effective working relationship with all segments of the district staff.

Communication: Keeping all necessary communication lines open and effective is an ongoing problem for superintendents. Communication within the school district organization must reach all parties in a timely manner, and the superintendent must also be able to identify the diverse interest groups in the community which have a need for information as well as feedback to offer.

Credibility: It is essential that the school superintendent maintain the respect and support of all parties, most particularly the school board which employs him or her. The credibility of superintendents rests to a great extent on their courage to champion actively decisions based on the best professional judgment rather than submitting multiple options and making decisions solely on the basis of political considerations.

The overall challenge facing the superintendent of schools is that of determining the manner in which time, talents, energy, and professional knowledge and insight can best be devoted to managing the schools and at the same time providing leadership for desirable change.

See also Central Office Personnel; School Boards: Superintendent Selection.

—Richard Gousha
Indiana University

References

Blumberg, A., & Blumberg, P. (1985). *The school superintendent: Living with conflict.* New York: Teachers College Press.

Rubin, L. (Ed.). (1980). *Critical issues in educational policy: An administrator's overview.* Boston: Allyn & Bacon.

Sergiovanni, T.J., & Carver, F.D. (1980). *The new school executive: A theory of administration* (2nd ed.). New York: Harper & Row.

SUPERINTENDENT SELECTION

The most important decision made by a school board is the selection of its superintendent of schools. It is a choice which should be made with great care and careful planning. Employing the right superintendent will make the difference between an effective school district and one in which many problems exist. When a superintendent is needed, boards of education have steps to follow—and, if properly followed, they will make a wise choice.

The first step is to decide if the selection of a superintendent will involve a search or if an individual has already been identified to succeed the superintendent who is retiring or leaving the school district. If a successor has been identified, then the board of education should employ the person as soon as possible, announce its decision, and work to establish support for the new superintendent. Here, as in all cases of new leadership, the previous superintendent is appreciated; but the new superintendent should receive the immediate loyalty and support of the board of education.

If a search is to be conducted, the board should first decide whether it wishes to conduct a local search or a national search. A national search would require more time and expense, but usually results in a larger number of qualified candidates from which to choose. It also provides an opportunity to give national visibility to the school district. A local or area search, however, generally provides an adequate number of qualified candidates.

When a national search is to be conducted, the board needs to decide if the search will be conducted by the district personnel, by a consulting search firm, or by the district personnel office in cooperation with a consulting search firm. There is no one best way to conduct the search, except that using a consultant may save time and provide a larger pool of candidates. Because consultants typically have directed other searches, they can usually provide valuable experience in carrying out a search. A consultant may also be helpful in conducting a comprehensive background check of the candidates.

Whether a search firm is employed, or whether the search is conducted by the district, the following steps should be followed:

1. Determine the qualifications desired in the new superintendent.

2. Produce a brochure which describes the position, the community, the school system, the process for applying, and the deadline to be observed.

3. Inform appropriate individuals, agencies, and educational institutions about the position. Send them a copy of the brochure.

4. Accumulate an appropriate file for each candidate.

5. Screen the candidates down to 5 to 8 for personal interviews.

6. Reduce the candidates to 2 or 3 and visit the city in which each currently works.

7. Have a second interview with the final two or three candidates.

8. Make a selection.

9. Announce the selection.

10. Hold a reception for the new superintendent.

Issues

Boards of education who decide to conduct the search themselves should do whatever is necessary to provide confidentiality during the initial phases of the search. Individuals often do not wish to have their current employer know about their interest in a new position, unless and until they are likely to be hired for the new position. Confidentiality cannot be guaranteed for the final 5 to 8 candidates, and finalists should be told that inquiries will be made in their home communities.

A second issue for boards who conduct their own search is the extent to which background examinations will be conducted. Will a credit check be made? Will a police check be made? Will a check be made of organizations to which the individual belongs? Will the candidates' background be examined prior to the current position? It is in this area that consulting service may be helpful—if the board wishes to conduct an in-depth, extensive background search.

Participation

A final issue to be examined is the extent to which all board members participate in the search. Do *all* members read files of *all* applicants? Does a board committee screen the applications to a smaller number? How will background examinations of the candidates be conducted and who will make them? Who will visit the communities where the finalists now work? Unless these questions are carefully examined and settled, the board can find itself in a divisive process of finding a new superintendent of schools.

Selecting a new superintendent can be a unifying and satisfying process for boards of education. It is also one which requires time, preparation, knowledge, and sensitivity to the needs of the district and candidates; it needs to be carried out in a consistent, orderly fashion. If done well, everyone will profit—board of education, community, and students, as well as the candidate selected. If done poorly, the district will not obtain the best possible candidate. What is most important is that the board of education know the kind of person it wants, communicate these qualifications, establish a clear process for obtaining applicants, and conduct adequate background examinations. Then it can be confident that an able person will be selected as its new superintendent of schools.

See also Superintendent of Schools.

—Harold V. Webb, President
Harold Webb Associates
Winnetka, Illinois

References

Thomas, M.D. (1976). *Board-superintendent partnership.* Salt Lake City, UT: SMSG.

Tyack, D. (1974). *The one best system.* Cambridge, MA: Harvard University Press.

Wirt, F., & Kirst, M. (1982). *The politics of education: Schools in conflict.* Berkeley, CA: McCutcheon.

SUPERVISION, CLINICAL

Clinical supervision has emerged over the past several decades as a useful management and supervisory tool for observing teaching. A five-stage observation cycle, the heart of the clinical supervision process, had its beginning at Harvard during the 1950s when the practice of team teaching was being developed. The observation cycle evolved as a useful mechanism for teachers to observe and give feedback to each other in developing team-teaching behaviors. Since those early days, clinical supervision has evolved into an observation system which supervisors and principals use in gathering data on teaching performance.

Two differing views of clinical supervision have emerged, each making use of observation cycle methodology. One approach emphasizes helping teachers to develop more effective teaching behaviors. The other approach emphasizes evaluating the extent to which teachers demonstrate effective teaching behaviors.

The inspection (evaluation) approach to supervision, once predominant, began to lose its influence in the American work place in the 1940s as knowledge accumulated about ideal conditions for adult performance. The intent of this article is to establish a rationale and identify behaviors for the helping, or coaching, approach to clinical supervision, which is now more accepted. Research studies and various scholarly analyses provide strong evidence that work conditions either nurture or hinder productive work performance.

We know, for example, that when teachers are involved in making decisions about school goals, there is a traceable link to gains in student performance. Further, when teachers participate in designing the school's in-service programs, are trained in observation methodology, and coach each other, effective changes in classroom behavior result. When teachers have the opportunity to innovate, are recognized for their achievements, and are encouraged to give structure to undeveloped dimensions of the schooling process, teachers contribute significantly to the school's development. Also known is that reinforcement and recognition by management tends to function as an additional stimulator to staff performance.

Consequently, the school's capacity to foster growth increases when teachers are viewed as partners, rather than as problems. The successful transformation of schooling to a more productive enterprise may well depend on the ways in which teachers are viewed, and clinical supervision in practice is a symptom of healthy management assumptions and expectations.

Effective Teaching Behaviors

The power of coaching increases when coaching technology is linked with existing knowledge about teaching and learning. Research indicates, for example, that when learning objectives guide instructional planning, there is a positive effect on achievement. Also, when readiness is diagnosed and used by teachers for assigning levels of difficulty, students are more able to succeed in learning tasks. Classrooms that are managed by learning-task systems which focus on learning goals, high expectations, and student self monitoring successfully alter achievement patterns. Most students succeed when assigned to appropriate tasks, when teacher expectations are clear, when high levels of task engagement exist, when productive behaviors are reinforced, and when timely feedback and correctives are provided. When students work together, participate in setting and monitoring learning goals, and are involved in an array of learning arrangements, achievement levels tend to increase and remain high.

In successful schools, the knowledge mentioned above drives teacher goal setting and coaching activities. It provides a standard toward which teachers strive over time.

Clinical Supervision

The research-generated knowledge base for clinical supervision is slight, due to the recent development of its methodology. However, findings from effective schools research provide help in understanding the powerful dynamics of coaching. For example, we know that in effective schools principals conduct frequent formal and informal observations to coach teachers in their development of instructional skills. "Effective teaching behaviors" guide the supervisory activity as principals and teachers seek to improve teaching and to influence the norms of student achievement. Coaching is successful in helping teachers to transfer new skills to classroom use when peers, supervisors, and principals are trained in observation and feedback skills and use them regularly.

Observation Cycle

The five stages of the observation cycle have been a focus for numerous workshops in recent years. The observation cycle and its basic functions are viewed in this section as central to a coaching approach to clinical supervision.

A supervisory coaching approach is presented below to guide the development of sound supervisory practice, using the observation cycle as its central coaching methodology. The objective is to develop and operationalize a peer and supervisory coaching program for all teachers in which feedback on performance is provided regularly and systematically.

Four guiding principles to supervisory practice are likely to foster a nurturing coaching climate: (1) build and maintain self-esteem; (2) provide behavioral feedback; (3) seek cooperation; and (4) coach for learning.

Preconference. An agreement is reached about the focus for the particular observation and the types of feedback that are sought. The observer(s) seeks to understand the teacher's plans for the time to be observed. Questions are asked about the context (third grade mathematics: multiplication); learning outcomes (master the 4's multiplication table); and instructional strategies (group contest). A decision is made about the focus for the coaching cycle (peer learning). The observer(s) then plans how to collect data that will inform the teacher about the appropriateness of objectives, diagnostic and placement decisions, program plans, and the observed teaching and learning patterns.

Observation and Data Collection. Data are collected as they relate to agreed upon questions and problems. Observable behaviors are recorded as they relate to a combination of factors: (a) the agreed upon coaching focus (cooperative learning activity); (b) feedback requests (teaching behaviors that facilitate mastering the 4's times table); and, (c) annual teacher goals (develop a system for peer learning). An entire lesson is rarely observed, but rather, a sample is observed and analyzed to understand teaching decisions and their impact on student performance.

Analysis and Strategy Session. The observer(s) reviews the collected data and analyzes the relation to teaching expectations and the current knowledge base. High-level intellectual inquiry is necessary as observers examine patterns and come to understand their meaning. First, all data are reported, without commentary to establish a "photograph" of classroom happenings. Themes are identified and interpreted, making use of emerging knowledge about teaching and learning as well as collective professional experience. The observer(s) seeks to identify the key professional issue to be addressed in the feedback conference (teaching cooperative-learning groups to plan and monitor their own learning). After a feedback focus has been identified, the observer(s) develops a strategic plan for conducting the conference. Central to the success of the conference is building and maintaining the self-esteem of the teacher being coached.

Feedback Conference. The observer(s) provides feedback and interpretation relating to the agreement, and involves the teacher in discussion and planning. The first task is to establish a climate in which the teacher feels secure and ready for feedback. It must be evident that the teacher and observers are partners in both the examination and the development of better teaching practice. As the conference proceeds, data are reported, interpretations are shared, and teacher reactions are encouraged. Productive teaching behaviors need to be recognized and reinforced, and alternative promising behaviors are identified for exploration and consideration. A desirable outcome is for a plan to emerge that reflects ways to stretch teaching practices in directions that will be helpful to learners.

Postobservation Critique. The observer(s) and teacher observed (or a process observer) review the first four stages. Behavior patterns are cited for each stage, reinforcing those which functioned well, while alternative promising behaviors are discussed for other areas. The intent is for the coaching process itself to become the focus for examination so that those who coach have the opportunity to learn about the dynamics, the technology, and skills of coaching.

Conclusion

A culture of high expectations for teacher development combined with the use of coaching behaviors within the five-stage observation cycle provides a context within which teachers are likely to develop in productive ways. In addition, when teachers are partners in developing the school's capacity to stimulate learning, nurturing work conditions are likely to alter both teaching and learning norms in desirable ways.

See also Staff Development; Supervision, Teacher Views; Supervisory Personnel; Teachers, Sources of Help for.
—Karolyn J. Snyder
University of South Florida

References

Cogan, M. (1973). *Clinical Supervision*. Boston: Houghton Mifflin.

Goldhammer, R., Anderson, R.H., & Krajewski, R.J. (1980). *Clinical supervision: Special methods for the supervision of teachers*. Boston: Holt, Rinehart & Winston.

Snyder, K.J., & Anderson, R.H. (1986). *Managing productive schools toward an ecology* (chapters 10 & 13). Orlando, FL: Academic Press.

SUPERVISION, TEACHER VIEWS

Since the inception of organized education in America, teachers have been perceived by school boards as employees who need to be supervised. In most school systems, the principal is assigned the responsibility for teacher supervision; in large school districts, general and/or subject-matter supervisors assist the principal in carrying out this assignment. The intent of supervision varies, but the primary focus has been and continues to be on the improvement of teaching effectiveness.

Because teacher supervision has become an established practice in American education, most teachers probably accept or at least resign themselves to the fact that it will occur. However, in recent years increasing numbers of teachers have developed mixed feelings about teacher supervision. Although it is difficult to determine the extent to which their views are becoming characteristic of most teachers, the questions that these views raise may pose a direct challenge to the practice of teacher supervision as it has evolved over the years.

For example, many teachers question whether they need to be supervised. They take the position that, when they were hired, the school district apparently thought they were good teachers, and since then, they have continued to improve themselves to the point that they no longer need to be supervised. Besides, they argue, whatever limited improvement may still be needed can be accomplished on their own without supervision by a principal or supervisor, especially since most principals lack the expertise for supervision.

The view that most principals lack the expertise for supervising teachers seems to be widespread among teachers. Generally, when this view is expressed, teachers assert that the typical principal possesses limited knowledge and skill in most areas of the curriculum and teaching methodology. Comments also are made about how long it has been since the principal was a teacher and how unaware the principal is of the current realities of the classroom. In addition, questions are raised about whether a principal or a supervisor really has the time, given all the other administrative responsibilities, to do an adequate job of supervising teachers. As a result, teachers conclude, they see very little follow-through and value to teacher supervision. If they are going to be supervised, they recommend that it be done by someone who has the time, instructional expertise, and human relations skills needed to help them improve as professionals. The "master teacher" approach seems to appeal to these teacher critics of traditional teacher supervision.

Exacerbating the ambivalence felt by many teachers about supervision is their perception that all too often teacher supervision is no more than teacher evaluation. These teachers report that, under the rubric of supervision, their classrooms are visited (often without any preobservational conference), and some type of rating form on their performance is filled out by the principal and discussed with them. However, usually little specific assistance of a constructive nature is provided, and almost no supervisory follow-up occurs unless a teacher's performance is so bad that dismissal must be considered. Although teachers who are critical of supervision feel that teacher supervision ideally should be a cooperative venture in which the teacher can be open and candid to the principal about the teacher's limitations and need for improvement, they believe that the association of teacher supervision with teacher evaluation tends to make teachers defensive and negative about teacher supervision.

These negative views, although perhaps not characteristic of most teachers, need to be taken seriously, if for no other reason than the apparent paucity of strong, favorable teacher views of supervision. Perhaps more important, these negative teacher views of supervision are in direct conflict with the view of many administrators and administrator organizations who see the principal as an instructional leader and are contrary to the perception of the public that teaching quality has deteriorated in recent years so that teacher supervision is needed now more than ever. Whether any of these views about teacher supervision is valid can be debated. However, unless the issues raised by teachers expressed in this article are adequately addressed, it is likely that teacher resistance to supervision will grow, and teacher supervision will fail to make any major contribution to the improvement of American education.

See also Supervision, Clinical; Teachers, Sources of Help for.

—Richard A. Gorton
University of Wisconsin-Milwaukee

References

Blumberg, A. (1980). *Supervision and teachers: A private cold war*. Berkeley, CA: McCutchan.

Cooper, J.A. (1982). "Supervision of teachers." In H.E. Mitzel (Ed.), *Encyclopedia of educational research* (pp. 1824-1834). New York: The Free Press.

Oliva, P.F. (1984). *Supervision for today's schools* (chapter 2). New York: Longman.

SUPERVISORY PERSONNEL

The education profession and educational systems have been plagued by difficulty in identifying supervisory personnel and in defining their roles. Consistency in titles or role labels is nonexistent. This problem leads some to believe that the only supervisory personnel are those with the title "supervisor." That leads others to believe that some school systems have no supervisors. Obviously, both perceptions are incorrect, since any organization of people established for delivering an instructional program requires that at least someone in that organization must assume responsibility for that instructional program.

Need for Supervisory Personnel

The declared need for supervisory personnel in a school system depends upon one's perspectives about supervision. Those who view supervisors as meddlesome people who interfere by acting as police agents may perceive supervisory personnel as unnecessary or even undesirable. Those who view supervisory personnel as facilitators who assist with and support the efforts of others may perceive supervisory personnel as essential to the organization.

A generally held perspective is that the purpose of supervision is to bring about improvement in the instructional program. If the instructional program is perceived to be the purpose for which schools exist, a reasonable perception is that supervision is necessary. If supervision is perceived to be necessary, then it would seem that supervisory personnel are needed in school systems.

Types of Supervisory Personnel

The types of supervisory personnel found in a school system will depend upon such factors as size of the organization, financial resources, and perceived needs of the instructional program. The variety of position titles that can be found for supervisory personnel reflects, at least in part, the organizational structure of the school system and the expectations for the position. For example, some positions may carry responsibilities for only the elementary or secondary programs. Some may have basic responsibilities for the instructional process, while others have sole responsibilities for curricular matters. Others may have K-12 responsibilities, and some may have responsibilities for teaching strategies only. Others may focus on only one curricular or programmatic area. Some may have responsibilities that are similar to administrative tasks, and others may be more of a consultative nature. Seldom do administrators at any level have positions that do not include responsibilities related to the instructional program. Sometimes supervisory personnel are placed in decision-making roles, and other times they are structured to be advisory. Although teachers are not identified as supervisory personnel, their involvement in activities pertaining to supervision of the instructional program cannot be denied.

Using Supervisory Personnel

As expectations for school systems increase, a tendency exists to rearrange the additional tasks among existing personnel. It is quite possible that tasks are added without subtracting any of the existing responsibilities. The result often is a reduction in effort and time available for supervisory tasks. While it is vital to assign tasks to persons qualified to accomplish them, it also is essential to define each person's expectations, making it reasonably possible to meet those expectations without weakening the emphasis on the instructional program.

One consideration in making appropriate use of supervisory personnel is that of numbers. If an expectation exists for considerable contact time with individual teachers, this expectation must be realistic in terms of the number of teachers for whom the overseer has responsibilities. While no specific ratio of supervisor-to-teachers has been defined with any consistency, it is obvious that in the case mentioned the number would be, of necessity, a small one. In cases where the position expectations refer to working with groups, the size of the groups involved needs to be adjusted to the specific responsibilities.

An observation should be made here that a supervisor need not do everything, but rather organizes and coordinates the efforts of others who have contributions to make to the instructional program. Also to be noted here is the need for delegation of tasks to those who have the expertise required.

Supervisory personnel should be involved in influencing, planning, evaluating, and managing the instructional staff and the instructional program. This involvement will result in providing leadership for the long- and short-range goals and should be focused on selected expectations for those in supervisory positions.

Two of the most commonly recognized expectations of supervising personnel focus on determinations regarding the curriculum and on effective instruction. These expectations represent a need for clarification of what is to be included in the instructional program and how that curriculum is to be delivered to the students. This requires management of human, physical, and financial resources in order that the curriculum established for the school system can be appropriately implemented.

Supervisory personnel also are involved in achieving other expectations for the instructional program. Those who have responsibilities for instructional improvement must be concerned with the professional development of the instructional staff. This requires the identification of needs and planning for meeting those needs. Assistance is needed in helping the staff develop expertise and grow professionally for the benefit of the school system.

The leadership of supervisory personnel also must focus on achieving responsiveness of the school to its identified community as well as responsiveness of the community to its school system. Someone in the school system also must study the social horizon through research, self-study, and exposure to the broader educational community. This will assist in keeping the instructional program current as well as in helping to plan for instructional expectations for the future.

The district administrator has the responsibility to secure the clarification of role expectations for supervisory personnel in order that best use is made of their talents. Other expectations should be assigned to persons who have different responsibilities for the school system.

See also Assistant/Associate Superintendent; Association for Supervision and Curriculum Development; Central Office Personnel.

—Robert Krey
University of Wisconsin-Superior

References

Eye, G.G., Netzer, L.A., & Krey, R.D. (1971). *Supervision of instruction.* New York: Harper & Row.

Netzer, LA., Eye, G.C., Stevens, D.M., & Benson, W.W. (1979). *Strategies for instructional management.* Boston: Allyn & Bacon.

Wiles, J., & Bondi, J. (1980). *Supervision: A guide to practice.* Columbus, OH: Charles E. Merrill.

SUPPORT STAFF, PROFESSIONAL

Professional support staff refers to "special services" personnel who function individually and as members of an interdisciplinary team. This article focuses on the school psychologist, school social worker, school nurse, and learning disabilities specialist. Public Law 94-142, "The Education for All Handicapped Children Act," defines these as "related services" and adds guidance counselors, occupational and physical therapists, speech pathologists, recreation therapists, and allied-health professionals to the list of professional support staff personnel. Since the passage of the Act in 1975, members of the support staff have become increasingly involved in the daily activities of elementary and secondary schools.

School Psychologist

School psychologists plan educational and mental-health programs for children. They administer individual diagnostic tests to assess intellectual potential, personality dynamics, social behavior, and adaptive behavior. They determine causes of learning or adjustment problems. School psychologists are particularly concerned with identification of "exceptional children." Exceptionality includes a wide range of handicaps such as mental retardation, emotional disturbance, or learning disability and also encompasses pupils who are gifted and talented. School psychologists are a resource for parents who seek advice in child-rearing practices, family problems, or academic concerns. Administrators, cognizant of psychologists' strict adherence to confidentiality, utilize them as good listeners or as problem-solvers. Trained in group dynamics, the school psychologist can facilitate collaborative efforts among a teacher, parent, and administrator in the search for solutions to a child's problems. School psychologists assist principals in the interpretation of group aptitude or achievement test data. Also, they may assist an administrator in unraveling the complexities of special education regulations.

School Social Worker

School social workers serve as liaisons between the school, child-study team, and home. The social worker's assessment of the family environment and developmental history places the child's problems in perspective. School social workers maintain awareness of referral resources in the community. These resources include individual practitioners in counseling, family-counseling agencies, state departments of human services, and child-protective agencies. School social workers are often the most knowledgeable staff members regarding post-school placement of mentally retarded, emotionally disturbed, or physically disabled adolescents.

School Nurse

As the health services representative on the child-study team, the school nurse interprets findings of the physical assessment. The nurse's other responsibilities include maintaining health and immunization records; conducting height, weight, vision, hearing, and, in many states, scoliosis screening; assisting the school physician in physical exams; administering medication and treatment; and serving as liaison with the state health agency. School nurses are resource persons for those on the staff who teach the family life/health curriculum. Administrators can seek the assistance of the nurse in conducting school-safety inspections and identifying health hazards.

Learning Disabilities Specialist

Learning disabilities specialists administer tests and diagnose learning problems in academic areas (reading, language arts, mathematics, study skills), visual and auditory perception, learning style, and other factors related to success in a classroom environment. They provide relevant and specific recommendations to classroom teachers. Learning disabilities specialists can assist principals in grouping pupils for instruction or deciding upon appropriate class placement.

Referral

When a teacher or parent requests help from the special services team, consultation usually precedes testing or intervention. The support staff works with the teacher, principal, and parent to analyze the problem and suggest solutions. If these solutions are not successful, standardized testing, interviewing, and classroom observation are utilized. The team may recommend instructional strategies and/or counseling by the psychologist or social worker. For pupils diagnosed as handicapped, an Individualized Education Program (I.E.P.) is prepared.

Support Team

The principal confers individually with the psychologist, social worker, nurse, or learning disabilities specialist with regard to a specific pupil. The principal may invite one member of the support staff to be a resource person during a parent conference.

Some administrators utilize support personnel effectively by scheduling meetings at regular intervals. Participating in meetings, in addition to the administrator, may be the school psychologist, social worker, learning disabilities specialist, nurse, counselor, director of student-personnel services, program supervisors, and speech pathologist. Members of this advisory group review a pupil's status in the time period since the last meeting. An action plan, designating responsibilities, is developed with a target date for review. Maintaining minutes helps to record progress and to remind members of their assignments.

It may be to the principal's advantage to view the support team collectively as a building resource—discussing broad issues (e.g., school climate, discipline, attendance, staff morale) or assisting in goal-setting, program evaluation, and in-service training. Support staff, when utilized to the fullest extent by the building administrator, can contribute significantly to the total instructional program offered by the school.

See also Handicapped Students; Health Problems and Health Services; Pupil Personnel Program.

—Roger D. Zeeman
Bridgewater, New Jersey

References

Thomas, A. & Grimes, J. (1985). *Best practices in school psychology*. Kent, OH: National Association of School Psychologists.

U. S. Department of Health, Education, and Welfare: Office of Education (1977). "Education of handicapped children." *Federal Register, 42*, 42474-42518.

Wold, S.J. (1981). *School nursing, a framework for practice* (pp. 20-29). St. Louis: C. V. Moseby.

SYSTEMS THEORY

Thoughtful educators will find that a knowledge of systems theory will help them understand the dynamics of the organizational settings in which they work.

Systems theory is derived from concepts developed in the biological sciences about the ways complex organisms known as *open systems* function internally and in response to their environments. Some of these functions include the intake of energy from the environment to fuel internal processes, the continued interaction and interdependence of internal components, and the alteration of patterns of internal interaction to cope with changes in the environment.

Some social theorists have developed *open social systems theory* and strongly assert the applicability of organic systems concepts to the description and explanation of how complex social organizations (such as schools) function. These theorists declare that there are compelling similarities between the ways that organisms and organizations operate internally and in response to their environments.

From the open social systems perspective, schools are seen as purposive groupings of human and nonhuman technical resources (teachers and computers, for example) which are formed and reformed to achieve socially approved educational goals. The human technical resources within schools are assigned specialized functions such as teaching, pupil guidance, and system management. The interactions of these (and other) elements are prescribed in ways considered to have a potential for achieving desired outcomes. However, prescribed patterns are subject to review and evaluation and may be temporarily or permanently altered by administrators in response to perceived ineffectiveness or accommodation to new or modified goals. (It should be noted that the term "closed system" as used by some education commentators generally refers to obstructions in channels of communication into and out of some schools. Truly *closed* i.e., totally independent, *social systems* have not been identified.)

A significant concept of open social systems theory is that the addition to, deletion from, or alteration of a system's goals is viewed as occurring primarily in response to pressures resulting from significant changes in the environment. For example, some external conditions which are considered likely to induce such changes in schools are (a) long- or short-term adjustments in the economy affecting the ability of communities to support school operations; (b) changes in the socioeconomic, ethnic, and racial composition of surrounding communities which send children to schools; (c) the existence and degree of influence of ideological and other kinds of special-interest groups; (d) the existence and strength of organizations representing teachers and other school employees; (e) the extent to which national, state, and local political groups and individual politicians express satisfaction or dissatisfaction with the processes and products of schooling; (f) the opinions of private-sector employers regarding the adequacy of preparation of pupils for needed occupational roles; and (g) the number and kinds of employment opportunities available to members of the work force.

Continuing this line of reasoning, changes in goals are seen by open systems theorists as predictive of changes in skill requirements and the structure of relationships of human resources. Thus, significant developments in industrial and service technology rapidly or gradually lead to reconsideration of many factors in schools. A partial listing of such reconsiderations by administrators and policy makers might include (a) the kinds of subject matter in which teachers in various levels of schooling should have competence; (b) the levels to which competence needs to be achieved by teachers and pupils in selected knowledge and skill areas; (c) the extent to which resources should be allocated or reallocated to enable emphasis or de-emphasis of selected cognitive or attitudinal aspects of school programming; (e) the extent to which instructional decision-making prerogatives should be redistributed among professional school personnel; (f) the extent to which (and whether) the structure of the occupation of teaching should be stratified to reflect varying degrees of estimated competence; (g) to whom and for what should accountability be assigned; and (h) the extent to which economic incentives should be adjusted to attract and hold persons with high potential for success as teachers.

Turning from the effects of external forces on decisions and relations within the school, social systems theorists assert that the internal system's diverse elements, which are in constant interaction, are strongly influenced as well by intrinsically generated pressures. They declare that the quantity and intensity of both conflict and cooperation between and among various system elements is highly variable. For example, the instability of the nature of interaction within and between such formal system groups as teachers, administrators, ancillary services personnel, support personnel, and pupil personnel is, in major part, attributable to differences in objectives and goals of each of the groups. In addition, formal group differences are augmented and complicated by informal group and individual personality differences and perceived needs. Extremely complex combinations of sociological, psychological, economic, political, and cultural motivational forces are seen as underlying the persistent ebb and flow of conflict and cooperation within a system, thus affecting goal achievement.

Several further concepts of importance and with considerable operational significance to administrators should be noted here. The first is that, like complex living organisms, organizations (including schools) tend to acquire and store more energy (resources) than are required for current functioning. They do so to provide a margin of safety against the possibility of unforeseen shortages which might weaken or even shut down a system. The second is that open systems (such as schools) are likely to promote and support continually increased specialization of roles and functions of persons in the system. The phenomenon is thought to occur primarily in response to environmental changes which impose new goals on the system. The third is

that as organizations become increasingly specialized internally they become concurrently less flexible and hence less able to consider and implement different paths to the achievement of objectives.

See also Administrative Theory; Bureaucracy; Organizations: Principles and Theory.

—Lawrence Barnett
University of Wisconsin-Milwaukee

References

Boulding, K.E. (1978). "General systems theory: The skeleton of science." In J.M. Shafritz and P. Whitbeck (Eds.), *Classics of organization theory*. Oak Park, IL: Moore.

Huse, E.F., & Bowditch, J.L. (1973). *Behavior in organizations: A systems approach to managing*. Reading, MA: Addison-Wesley.

Katz, D. & Kahn, R.L. (1978). *The social psychology of organizations*. New York: John Wiley.

T

TEACHER ABSENTEEISM

The most effective programs for reducing teacher absenteeism are positive in their approach. They focus on the improvement of attendance rather than the reduction of abuse. These successful programs also have one other element in common—they are progressive in nature. That is, the severity of the district's response to a teacher's abuse of leave policy escalates as the seriousness and/or frequency of abuse increases.

Implementation of a district attendance-improvement program should begin with an anlysis of teacher attendance patterns for the two previous years. The analysis should show the number, reasons given, duration, and dates of absences of individual teachers with summaries by building and by district. This information establishes a base line of data with which to compare the effectiveness of the program and highlights patterns of abuse (Fridays, hunting season, etc).

The second step in implementing an effective attendance-improvement program requires action by the board of education. To emphasize the importance it gives to excellent attendance, the board should adopt a policy stating that excellent attendance is essential for excellent schools and is not only valued but expected. Then, in conjunction with a task force of principals and other unit administrators, the superintendent should develop procedures to implement the board's policy. These procedures should include the appropriate process for applying for leave, guidelines for approving leave applications (in some states these are spelled out in the negotiated contract), responsibilities of administrators in monitoring and enforcing leave policies, and guidelines for graduated penalties for violation of leave policies.

The superintendent's task force should also develop a program for orienting teachers and their leaders to the absence problem (days lost, cost of substitutes, lower teacher morale, weakened instructional program, etc.). It may be desirable to include teacher leaders on the superintendent's task force from the very beginning to obtain their support and ideas. In any event, it is important these leaders realize the district's only concern is to increase teacher attendance, not to discourage the legitimate use of leave days.

Once these processes are complete, the district is ready to put its plan into action. Through announcements, individual conversations, and other means the district must communicate to every teacher the board's concern for excellent attendance. In addition, every teacher must routinely receive a report of his or her own attendance record—for the current period as well as the cumulative totals for the year. In many cases, providing this information alone will correct abuses of leave policies. Teachers with exemplary attendance records should be recognized within the building and perhaps should be given district-wide recognition.

Teachers are also less likely to take an unwarranted leave day when they know other teachers are depending on them. Principals can foster this feeling of interdependence by providing a work format that encourages faculty to work together. Not only will teacher attendance increase, but so will morale and productivity.

Teachers requesting leave should be required to call or speak directly to the principal. Virtually every study of teacher absences cites this as being the single most effective deterrent to abuse. This is especially true for early morning call-ins for sick leave. Teachers are much less likely to call their principals than they are a secretary or answering service when the legitimacy of the requested absence is questionable.

Once it has been determined that there is reasonable cause for suspicion of abuse, the principal should confer with the teacher in question. This may require special training of the principal. Awkward handling of this conference or precipitious action by the principal can result in serious morale and/or labor problems.

When there is strong suspicion of malingering, the district should require the teacher to be examined by medical specialists selected and paid by the school. If medical or other evidence warrants, the teacher should be reprimanded. If an oral reprimand is not effective, a written one should be given to the teacher and a copy placed in his or her file. Subsequent steps are reduction in pay, suspension with pay, suspension without pay, and dismissal. The process for following these final steps should have the approval of district legal counsel.

It should be noted that an effective means of increasing attendance utilized by some schools is to pay teachers at the end of the year (or upon retirement) for unused leave days. Careful consideration should be given before implementing this policy, however, because it connotes that leave days are the property of the teacher to be used or sold back to the district as he or she chooses. This definition is inconsistent with that of leave as a form of insurance and it nullifies the concept of abuse.

In summary, the level of teacher abuse of leave policies does not appear to be related to job satisfaction. The evidence does indicate, however, a strong positive correlation between the value and attention accorded excellent attendance by the district and the actual level of teacher attendance. In essence, the most effective way to achieve and sustain a high level of teacher attendance is by letting teachers know that their attendance is necessary and valued, focusing attention on the problem of abuse, and responding in relation to the severity of abuse.

See also Teacher Accountability; Teacher Professionalism; Teacher Satisfaction; Teacher Stress and Burnout.

—Robert Thompson
Lamar University

References

Bridges, E.M. (1980, Spring). "Job satisfaction and teacher absenteeism." *Educational Administration Quarterly, 16*(2), 41-56.

Educational Research Service, (1980). *Employee absenteeism: A summary of research.* Arlington, VA: Author.

Pennsylvania School Boards Association, Inc. (1978). *Teacher absenteeism: Professional staff absence study.* Harrisburg, PA: Author.

TEACHER ACCOUNTABILITY

Although the term "accountability" first appeared in educational literature in the late sixties, many of the concerns expressed in the concept had been present in American public education almost from its beginnings. As early as the mid-nineteenth century, Horace Mann raised serious questions about the quality of education in Boston's schools and proposed the use of uniform tests for measuring educational outcomes. The accreditation movement, begun in 1872, which established standards to distinguish between good and poor schools, was another early manifestation of the concerns embodied later in educational accountability. The National Assessment is a more recent precursor of accountability. Essentially, the demand for teacher accountability is an expression of the public's concern over the quality of learning in public schools.

Definition

During the early seventies many government officials and professional educators attempted to define educational accountability. Although their definitions varied, each definition included as a central theme the idea that those directly involved in the teaching/learning process are those who should be responsible for the results. Pupil responsibility was not excluded from the definitions, but, in general, educators placed greater emphasis on the responsibility of teachers and principals for pupil achievement.

Issues

The major issue in teacher accountability is to what extent the teacher should be held accountable for student outcomes. Is there any guarantee that the patients of physicians will not die? Is there any guarantee that the clients of attorneys will not have to pay judgments or spend time in prison? No, of course not. Why, then, should teachers be held entirely responsible for educational outcomes? Like physicians and attorneys, teachers should be expected to provide services to the best of their abilities. In several studies that elicited the opinions of teachers regarding accountability, the teachers voiced no major opposition to the concept, although many questioned the advisability of some of the approaches. For example, a majority of teachers did not support merit pay as a viable means of achieving accountability. Neither were they willing to have their teaching evaluated by persons outside the field of education.

Teachers were willing to accept responsibility for curriculum decisions, for individualizing instruction, for providing scope and sequence in instruction, for classroom management, and for professional interaction with parents. They were not willing to accept responsibility for the intellectual abilities and prior educational accomplishments of their pupils. The former are tasks expected of any well-trained professional educator, while the latter conditions are beyond the teacher's control and yet are major determinants of educational outcomes.

A second major issue concerns the kinds of procedures that will be employed in determining teacher effectiveness. Of equal importance to many teachers is the question: Who will conduct the evaluations?

Approaches

One early method of implementing teaching accountability required teachers to write behavioral objectives for each course. In this approach, teachers identified and prescribed what should be learned; they specified the anticipated behaviors and performance levels of their pupils. Although theoretically sound, behavioral objectives often had a limiting effect on the instructional process because many teachers tended to become too specific. Performance-based objectives, a recent adaptation of behavioral objectives, were introduced to allow for greater flexibility in assessing student performance while retaining the ability to measure the effectiveness of the learning process.

Soon after the advent of the accountability movement, testing was perceived by many school administrators as the logical beginning point for measuring teacher performance. By this time, testing was well established, and it seemed reasonable that achievement test scores should reflect the quality of instruction provided by teachers in the schools. Student evaluation of teacher performance is a recent adaptation of the use of tests to measure educational outcomes.

Performance evaluations, made by the principal, have been the primary method of assessing teacher performance for at least fifty years, but much criticism has been leveled against this method: the principal is not qualified to make judgments about classroom performance; the evaluation is entirely subjective; actual observation time is minimal; and teachers perceive the process as negative. Recent innovations in teacher evaluation sanction greater flexibility, increased objectivity, and improved communication.

Peer or collegial evaluation has been suggested as an alternative method of performance evaluation. Advocates contend that peers are familiar with classroom activities, that they do not threaten the teacher being evaluated, and that they have more opportunities for observation and conferences than the principal. Whether these and other contentions are factual remains to be seen. Many of the new merit-pay plans and career-ladder plans do incorporate peer evaluation in the process.

The presentation of approaches to teacher accountability has not been exhaustive nor have the approaches been entirely disassociated. Other viable approaches can be found in the literature and should be examined for possible application in schools or districts.

Implications

Accountability, although a relatively new concept in education, gives definition to the public's awareness of the need for more effective schools. Obviously accountability is a complex process that will require both time and resources for effective implementation. With accountability, teachers must assume a great deal of responsibility for educational outcomes, although they cannot be held totally responsible. That responsibility must be shared by students, parents, supervisors, and administrators. In the final analysis, great care must be exercised in the implementation of teacher accountability. With judicious application it can improve the quality of American public education.

See also Supervision, Clinical; Supervision, Teacher Views; Teacher Professionalism.

—Mary Louise Mickler
University of Alabama

References

Allen, S.V. (Ed.). (1970). "Accountability '70." *Compact, 4*(5).

Lieberman, M. (Guest Ed.). (1970). Eight articles on accountability. *Phi Delta Kappan, 52*(4).

Mickler, M.L. (1984). "Accountability: Perceptual changes over a decade." *Educational Horizons, 62*, 90-93.

TEACHER CERTIFICATION

According to the federal constitution, each state has the responsibility for education and for ensuring the public that only properly prepared people are allowed to instruct children and youth in schools. States vary in how they assume this responsibility. Each state has the legal authority to license or certify an individual to teach in the public schools. Certification verifies that an individual has satisfactorily completed the requirements for a given certificate. Completion of the courses and/or experiences specified in certification requirements is assumed to be sufficient evidence of ability to teach.

There is much change and controversy today in state requirements for teacher certification. On the one hand, several states have made it more difficult than ever before to obtain a teaching license by upgrading program entry and exit standards, by requiring the passing of examinations, by mandating increased field experiences and internships, by making certificate renewal more difficult, and by designing other measures to improve the quality of those entering into and exiting from teacher preparation programs. These more rigorous requirements were the result of criticism of schools and teachers which peaked in 1983 with several national reports pointing out the shortcomings of our educational system.

On the other hand, the mid-1980s has developed into a period of serious teacher shortage in many academic areas, including science, mathematics, bilingual education, elementary education, and other areas depending, to some extent at least, on geography. Many urban areas have severe teacher shortages. These shortages were brought about by several factors; among the factors are relatively low teacher pay, poor working conditions, a teacher surplus in the 1970s with few jobs available, retirements by a growing percentage of teachers, and little encouragement of high school students to choose teaching as a career. Given this situation, many states began experimenting in the early 1980s with alternative teacher certification requirements. Some states have made it easier than ever before to become a teacher. New Jersey is one such state.

Issues

There are several critical issues involved in teacher certification. One issue is the rapidly expanding use of paper-and-pencil tests to measure everything from basic skills and subject matter competence to pedagogical and in-service skills. State- and nationally-normed tests of the sit-down and timed variety are being used in most states for an increasing number of purposes. An overreliance upon such tests appears to be developing. Teacher effectiveness is not easily measured, but most experts in the area agree that it has to be measured by a variety of different procedures, many of which should involve actual performance in a classroom and evaluation by peers. Improving classroom teaching and teacher effectiveness is being simplistically reduced when one assumes that because of passing some standardized test (where one marks on a sheet from alternative responses provided) one is able to respond spontaneously and appropriately in an effective manner with real students.

Another serious and related issue surrounding teacher certification is that fewer and fewer minority candidates are graduating with teaching certificates; they are finding it difficult to cope with standardized testing and increased academic standards, which are generally defined in traditional ways. The situation is particularly problematic in states such as California, where minority populations already comprise the majority in many urban schools. The population of minority teachers is decreasing at precisely the same time that minority school populations are increasing dramatically. This is a serious problem which cannot and will not be resolved by traditional measures.

A third major issue is the serious question of whether professional education courses and teacher preparation programs are needed at all. New Jersey, Virginia, California, and other states have put into place alternative routes to certify teachers. These routes allow "teachers" to avoid courses and programs associated with formal teacher preparation. At a time when national accreditation and state approval procedures are being strengthened to help assure that only competent teachers will be in schools, alternative means of entering teaching have developed to cope with the severe teacher shortages in some areas where not enough fully-qualified teachers are available.

Trends

Two major trends in teacher certification include the expansion of internship programs and a change in the basic process of recertifying teacher licenses. Internships are expanding to provide support for new teachers in their initial year(s) in order to ensure a smooth transition into full-time practice, to provide opportunities for professional development, and to assess the skill level of beginning teachers. Sometimes called induction or beginning teacher programs, internships usually involve a regular full-time assignment with salaries at the first-year level. Interns are provided support and are assessed by other teachers or a team such as an administrator, teacher, and university representative.

Another trend in teacher certification is for states to move away from permanent certification toward periodic renewals and even optional ways to renew certificates. Some states—Minnesota, for example—allow alternatives to graduate credits for renewal. In-service education of teachers has been undergoing a radical shift in recent years away from university programs to state and local programs for teacher recertification. Life licenses have been eliminated, and local school districts are assuming a more major role in recertification efforts and in teacher professional development.

Future Directions

What is likely to happen in the future?

1. States will continue to exert more control of teacher certification. More governors and legislators will become involved in the important political issue of the quality of schooling and teaching in America.

2. The use of standardized, paper-and-pencil tests will grow in popularity to measure at least a teacher's basic skills and subject-matter competency.

3. In general, teaching certificates will become more difficult to obtain and to retain as academic standards, field-experience requirements, professional development, and in-service expectations become more uniformly rigorous.

4. Teaching as a profession will regain some of its lost status as the quality of teachers, relative pay, and working conditions improve.

5. The teacher shortage will taper off, and supply and demand will equalize.

See also Competency Testing, Teachers; Teachers, Beginning.

—John P. Sikula
California State University, Long Beach

References

Haberman, M. (1984). *An evaluation of the rationale for required teacher education: Beginning teachers with and without teacher preparation* (prepared for the National Commission on Excellence in Teacher Education). Milwaukee: University of Wisconsin-Milwaukee, Division of Urban Outreach.

Sikula, J.P. (1984). *Teacher preparation and certification: The call for reform.* Bloomington, IN: Phi Delta Kappa Educational Foundation.

Sikula, J.P. (1985, Fall). "Today's good news about teacher education." *The Professional Educator, 8,* 1-4.

TEACHER DISMISSAL

Dismissal occurs when a board of education decides to terminate the employment of a teacher and records this action in its official minutes. As a result of this decision, the teacher is involuntarily removed from the district's payroll and is denied all other benefits, rights, and privileges of employment. Dismissal is not to be confused with a forced resignation. Although the teacher leaves the organization against his or her will in both instances, the forced resignation provides the teacher with an opportunity to save face because the district records the departure as a voluntary exit. Teachers, especially those who have tenure, are far more likely to be eased out than to be dismissed.

Irrespective of the mode of termination, administrators need to understand the legal aspects of dismissal because forced resignations seldom occur unless the administrator

also builds a case for dismissal. This article focuses on three of these aspects, namely, the legal rights of teachers prior to dismissal, the reasons or causes for dismissal, and the conditions under which a teacher is entitled to these rights.

Legal Rights

Before teachers are dismissed for any reason or combination of reasons, it is important for school officials to be aware of the teacher's legal rights and to ensure that the teacher receives each of these entitlements. Dismissal is a legal minefield, and trivial procedural errors may lead to a reversal of the decision if it is contested in the courts. Because administrators rarely possess the legal expertise to navigate this minefield successfully, they should seek the advice of legal counsel when they first suspect that a teacher is "at risk," i.e., a possible candidate for dismissal. This attorney should be a specialist in teacher dismissal cases.

The substance and scope of a teacher's legal rights relative to dismissal depend upon the teacher's legal rights relative to employment and contractual status. In most states probationary and temporary teachers possess few legal protections when they are dismissed at the expiration of their contract. These protections are usually specified in the local collective bargaining agreement and the policies of the board of education. When probationary and temporary teachers are dismissed in the middle of their contract, they are entitled to the same rights as tenured teachers. An employment contract, like tenure, constitutes a property right under the Fourteenth Amendment of the United States Constitution. The contract can be broken and tenure can be taken away only if the school administration proves that there is cause for dismissal and provides the teacher with procedural due process. Since the vast majority of teachers have tenure and/or work under contracts which are in effect for at least one year, it is essential for administrators to understand how cause and due process figure in teacher dismissal.

Dismissal for Cause

Dismissal for cause means that the teacher can be terminated only for those causes stipulated in the state's education code. Moreover, the burden of proof rests on school officials to demonstrate by a preponderance of the evidence that there is cause for dismissal (i.e., the teacher is incompetent, insubordinate, or guilty of immorality or unprofessional conduct). The teacher is assumed to be innocent of wrongdoing until the evidence convincingly shows otherwise.

Proving that there is cause for dismissal is rarely straightforward. Most state education codes list the causes for dismissal but do not define them. This definitional ambiguity, coupled with the lack of clearcut standards for deciding whether cause exists, creates an extremely problematic situation for administrators. Rarely will administrators know in advance whether they will be able to persuade a court judge or a hearing officer that there is cause for dismissal.

Teachers can be dismissed for a variety of reasons or causes. These are generally enumerated in the state education code and include causes such as incompetence, immoral conduct, insubordination, unprofessional conduct, neglect of duty, and alcohol or drug abuse which makes the teacher unfit to instruct or associate with children. Incompetence is seldom offered as the sole cause for dismissal. Because incompetence is so difficult to prove, incompetent teachers are often charged with unprofessional conduct, insubordination, or neglect of duty as well.

Satisfying the burden of proof is time consuming as well as problematic. Unless the cause for dismissal involves a single egregious act by the teacher (e.g., molesting a student), administrators must accumulate numerous specific instances of the teacher's failings and use these concrete examples to demonstrate that a pattern of inappropriate behavior exists over an extended period of time. For example, in seeking to prove that a teacher is incompetent, administrators must show that a teacher persistently fails to meet one or more of the district's criteria for evaluating teachers. It may take administrators one to two years to assemble this information. Since conclusions about the incompetence of a teacher must be based mainly on the observations of administrators and supervisors, school officials will need to make frequent observations and evaluations of the teacher. Ideally, these evaluations should reflect the judgments of at least two supervisors; moreover, one of these administrators should have expertise and experience in the subject and grade levels taught by the teacher "at risk." Conducting these observations and preparing written reports of what transpired in the classroom requires a major investment of administrative time and effort.

Procedural Due Process

Prior to dismissing a tenured teacher or a probationary teacher in the middle of his or her contract, administrators are legally obligated to provide the teacher with procedural due process. The due process rights of teachers are usually spelled out in the state education code and must be strictly adhered to; otherwise, the courts are likely to overturn the decision to dismiss the teacher. The essence of due process is fairness; some common elements of due process are as follows:

Adequate notice. Teachers have the right to know in advance what the district's rules and expectations are for a teacher's conduct and performance. Districts can provide adequate notice by preparing job descriptions and adopting criteria for evaluating teachers. In addition, teachers should be provided with copies of these policies, and principals should be held accountable for reviewing these policies with teachers at the beginning of each school year and for implementing these policies uniformly throughout the district.

If a teacher fails to follow the rules or to meet the district's expectations, administrators are obligated to let the teacher know that his or her behavior is unsatisfactory. In communicating this negative information, administrators need to inform teachers about the specific ways in which their conduct is deficient. For example, merely stating that the teacher has poor discipline is not enough; the administrator must also specify in what respects the teacher's discipline is inadequate (e.g., failure to establish rules for the students' behavior or failure to enforce rules that have been established).

Opportunity to improve. Given the harshness of the penalty, teachers are entitled to a reasonable period of time to correct their behavior or improve their performance. What is reasonable depends on the facts and circumstances surrounding the case. Some of the relevant facts are total years of teaching service, the length of service in the district, and the teacher's record of conduct and performance during this time period. For example, if a teacher has been teaching

in a district for twenty years and has received positive evaluations during this period, it seems harsh and unreasonable to allow the teacher only eight weeks to remedy twenty years of teaching practice.

If the cause for dismissal is incompetence, administrators are also obligated to assist the teacher in overcoming his or her deficiencies in the classroom. Before supervisors choose the types of remediation to be used in improving a teacher's poor performance, they need to ascertain whether his or her difficulties stem from (1) managerial and/or organizational shortcomings, (2) limitations of the employee (e.g., lack of effort or ability), or (3) outside or nonjob-related influences (e.g., marital or financial difficulties). Once the underlying causes of the teacher's difficulties have been pinpointed, it is important for administrators to prescribe remediation that is targeted to the perceived cause(s). Supervisors need to be especially sensitive to difficulties stemming from managerial or organizational shortcomings (e.g., inadequate supervision, too many preparations, and an excessive number of "difficult" students). Teachers may not be dismissed if their problems stem in part from these sources.

Final warning. Prior to issuing a notice of the intent to dismiss, administrators are obligated to provide teachers with a written warning that specifies the consequences of a failure to improve. Ordinarily, this final warning contains the following: (a) copies of previous observations, evaluations, and warnings; (b) a specification of the areas in which the teacher must improve; (c) details about the length of time in which improvement must occur and the assistance, if any, to be given; and (d) a statement that the teacher will be dismissed if he or she does not bring his or her performance up to the required level by the date specified in (c).

Formal hearing. A fundamental aspect of due process is the right of an employee to a fair hearing before a dismissal decision is reached. This basic right of teachers conveys a number of ancillary rights such as (a) a statement of charges and access to the materials upon which they are based; (b) an opportunity to be represented by counsel; (c) an opportunity to call witnesses on one's own behalf; (d) an opportunity to cross-examine witnesses; and (e) an opportunity to appeal an adverse decision. It is highly important for the board of education to maintain as much distance from the district administration as possible during the dismissal proceeding. This means that the board of education should not seek advice from the superintendent or anyone else who has been involved in presenting the case against the teacher. Such consultation violates the teacher's right to a fair hearing whether it occurs during the hearing or during the deliberations following the hearing. In preparation for the hearing, administrators should rely on an attorney to explain the entire dismissal proceeding, to assess the strengths and weaknesses of the case, and to advise them of potential pitfalls.

Conclusion

Teacher dismissal poses a formidable, but surmountable, challenge for school districts. Principals and supervisors view dismissal as an unpleasant and unwelcome responsibility; moreover, they often feel ill-prepared to handle the emotional and legal problems inherent in dismissing a teacher. Under these conditions, the dismissal of a teacher is likely to be attempted and to succeed only if the superintendent is fully committed to the need for dismissal and coordinates the efforts of the relevant participants—board members, the personnel director, the principal, and the attorney. When administrators recognize that a teacher is "at risk," a concerted team effort is an absolute necessity.

See also Due Process; Rights: Teachers' and Students'; Teacher Accountability.

—Edwin M. Bridges
Stanford University

References

Beckham, J. (1981). *Legal aspects of teacher evaluation*. Topeka, KS: National Organization on Legal Problems of Education.

Bridges, E. (1986). *The incompetent teacher: The challenge and the response*. Philadelphia, PA: Falmer.

Phay, R. (1982). *Legal issues in public school administrative hearings*. Topeka, KS: National Organization on Legal Problems of Education.

TEACHER EFFECTIVENESS

Arriving at a consensus on the meaning of teacher effectiveness and on devising ways to measure it has defied resolution for the better part of a century. Research on teacher effectiveness has expanded dramatically since 1965. Powell and Beard, in reviewing research on teacher effectiveness during 1965-1980, report more than 3000 studies. It was during this period that a major shift took place in the conceptualization of teacher effectiveness, especially in identifying, defining, and redefining relevant variables, and in focusing attention upon relationships which exist between and among the variables.

A useful model identifying nine variables which can be employed to analyze teacher effectiveness more objectively has been proposed by Medley. Five variables—preexisting teacher characteristics, teacher competencies, teacher performance, pupil learning experiences, and pupil learning outcomes—are viewed as criteria for evaluating teachers. Four variables—teacher training, external context, internal context, and individual pupil characteristics—are not controlled by the teacher. The external context variable refers to characteristics of the school (environment) in which the teaching is done; among these conditions are funds, facilities, administrative actions, supervisory actions, and community support. The internal context variable includes pupil characteristics such as learning potential, motivation, values, and family concern for pupil growth.

From a research standpoint, this model provides a basis for increasing knowledge about pupil learning outcomes through achieving a better understanding of the interrelationships among the five variables used as criteria for evaluating teachers. From an administrative standpoint, the model is useful in that it identifies variables to be included in gathering information and making decisions about teacher effectiveness.

While research continues to examine the contribution of each of the variables to pupil learning, the school administrator can utilize the model in ways such as (a) using the framework for staff development purposes, such as acquainting administrators, supervisors, and teachers with the variables which comprise the anatomy of teacher effectiveness; (b) establishing a teacher effectiveness information system designed to gather, store, retrieve, and analyze data on each of the variables; (c) utilizing the teacher effectiveness information system to link desired and actual learning outcomes to curriculum and supervisory processes; and (d) making concentrated efforts to learn more about those variables which tend to be useful in identifying more and less effective teachers within the school system.

Impediments

The reviews of teacher effectiveness suggest that while there are controlled efforts to differentiate between more and less effective teachers which take into account evidence showing an individual's ability to produce changes in learners, impediments to achieving this goal are formidable. They include

1. *Administrative Irrationality.* In the context of teacher effectiveness, administrative irrationality refers to the failure of administrators to make use of the best methods for improving organizations. It means, with regard to teacher effectiveness, using current concepts and generalizations to influence results people achieve in work they perform and activities they engage in to cause those effects. Absence of a comprehensive set of plans to improve teacher effectiveness is an illustration of administrative irrationality. Adherence to false premises—that performance appraisal is unnecessary; that performance should not be tied to results; that administrators should not be involved in performance appraisal; that performance appraisal does not involve confrontation; that appraisal has no connection with individual, group, or system objectives—is an example of administrative irrationality. The states of mind—the beliefs as well as the vested interests of boards of education and professional educators—have to a considerable extent helped to shape the century-long lag in an improvement in teacher effectiveness. It is conceivable that, in part, the lag has been due not to the absence of relevant information but to the plethora of irrelevant information and its irrational application.

2. *Technical Irrationality.* Technical irrationality refers to injudicious use of the extensive array of techniques, operations, materials, growing fund of knowledge, and know-how that can be utilized in a design to improve teacher effectiveness. Failure to develop an appropriate information system to carry out the design; dropping formal evaluation plans and relying on seniority as a basis for personnel actions; appraisal oversystematization; use of achievement tests as the sole criterion of teacher effectiveness; and inadequate, incomplete, and irrelevant information employed in decisions about personnel effectiveness are examples of technical irrationality. Absence of position guides and unit objectives, failure to train appraisers to carry out the appraisal design properly, and refusal to disclose appraisal information to appraisees add to the list of illustrations that point to instances wherein absence or abuse of available technology can impede progress toward improving learning outcomes.

3. *Measurement Complexity.* Theories concerning teacher effectiveness and its measurement are numerous, sometimes confusing, and often contradictory. While this state of affairs reflects the complexity of the issues involved in assessing teacher effectiveness, the search to become more knowledgeable about how to improve the education of teachers and to judge their effectiveness continues. When one considers that measurement of effectiveness is confounded by a number of factors (what is measured, who does the measuring, reliability of instrument application, idiosyncratic behavior of pupils and teachers, the difficulty of linking specific behaviors to effectiveness), the challenge of teacher effectiveness analysis becomes apparent.

4. *Environmental Impediments.* Although the central administration of a school system is primarily responsible for developing and implementing plans conducive to attainment of its goals and objectives, it does not have unilateral control of this function. The system is subject to environmental influences such as unions, courts, boards of education, political organizations, and other power groups. Of the influences just mentioned, unions have been most prominent and most reactionary in efforts to develop better systems of assessing learning outcomes.

5. *Excessive State Regulation.* One of the negative outcomes of recent state-generated educational legislation is the mandatory application of numerical rating systems to assess personnel performance. Critics of this approach suggest that (a) ratings are primarily trait-oriented and focus more on evaluation as a major purpose to be served rather than on learning outcomes; and (b) performance appraisal systems are usually counterproductive when personnel affected are not involved in determining performance standards by which they are to be judged.

6. *Faulty Research Designs.* It has been observed in the literature on teacher effectiveness that faulty research designs represent a major impediment to establishing useful indicators which are outcome rather than process based. When measures of teacher effectiveness are based on criteria which are not outcome based (personal attributes, verbal classroom behavior, instructional strategies), results often tend to be confusing, misleading, and counterproductive. Moreover, some investigations report findings which minimize the linkage between teacher behavior and student outcomes, the implication being that teachers affect student behavior minimally. In essence, many research designs ignore the totality of variables involved in the teacher effectiveness structure model depicted by Medley.

7. *Evaluation Models.* Five contemporary models for appraising teacher effectiveness have been identified in the literature. These are referred to as (a) common-law models (rating); (b) goal-setting models; (c) product models; (d) clinical-supervision models; and (e) artistic models. The chief criticism of models (a), (d), and (e) is that they are not concerned primarily with pupil outcomes. The point is frequently made in the literature that the practice of assessing teacher effectiveness without having valid data regarding his or her ability to effect changes in pupils seems wanting. The traditional rating system, for example, which relies heavily on (a) rating scales to evaluate teacher characteristics, and (b) the belief structure of the raters, violates most of the knowledge that has been developed relative to improving personnel effectiveness.

Administrative Strategies

Any list of administrative strategies for improving teacher effectiveness is arbitrary, but there are several which merit special attention. These include the following:

1. *Organizational Culture.* Culture includes accepted regularities that tend to appear in each of the significant areas of organizational life. One of the ways to enhance organizational culture of educational institutions is to stress effectiveness as a value of cardinal importance. By making teaching excellence the centerpiece of its aims, translating this value into plans that create better teacher understanding of what is to be done, developing helpful approaches to getting it done, and establishing clean criteria for its evaluation, the gap between cultural values and cultural reality can be narrowed.

2. *Teacher Effectiveness Planning Model.* A model such as that described earlier which depicts key elements in teacher effectiveness represents a useful administrative tool. It can serve as (a) a means of increasing staff members' awareness of factors considered to be important in effectiveness planning and decision making; (b) a way of integrating the concept of pupil learning experiences and pupil outcomes into the instructional culture; (c) a device for bringing into focus the importance of teaching strategies in relation to learning experiences and outcomes; (d) a reminder of desired teacher competencies and their significance in the performance of desired teaching strategies; (e) a guide when assessing teacher characteristics in the recruitment and selection processes; (f) a basis for a teacher effectiveness information system; and (g) a visual aid for reviewing and linking methods, techniques, and management of teaching in terms of the totality of the concept of teacher effectiveness. Such a review could include the efficiency and effectiveness of (a) conventional forms of instruction; (b) variants of conventional forms; (c) programmed instruction; and (d) variants of programmed instruction.

3. *Management Models.* For a period of time longer than befits the profession, the divisive and counterproductive assumption that a clear line of demarcation should prevail between administration and supervision has impeded resolution of these important and frequently conflicting tasks. This conflict is referred to in the literature as the two-model dichotomy: the bureaucratic and the professional. The former model stresses central authority, planning, and decision making. The professional model, by contrast, emphasizes teachers' autonomy in planning, organizing, and conducting their work. Research on effective schools has begun to challenge the dichotomy assumption on the grounds that a convergence of the models is both possible and urgently needed. The view that the teacher should have absolute autonomy in any teacher-related activity is not rational; the view that stringent control of teachers and teaching is an administrative obligation is not rational. Efforts to maximize coordination of teaching and increase the discretion of teachers in teaching-related activities must be a part of any strategy for improving teacher effectiveness.

Summary

The previous text has identified in a general way some of the issues relating to teacher effectiveness that are ready for more debate, dialogue, theory building, research, and experimentation. There is no doubt that there are critical teaching problems to be resolved, the total number depending on investigations into what is taught, the learning levels at which it is taught, and the quality of administrative leadership and instructional support provided for improving learning outcomes.

See also Staff Evaluation; Supervision, Clinical; Supervisory Personnel; Teacher Accountability.

—William B. Castetter
University of Pennsylvania

References

Ellson, D. (1986, October). "Improving productivity in teaching." *Phi Delta Kappan, 68*(2), 111-25.

Medley, D.M. (1982). "Teacher effectiveness." In H. E. Mitzell (Ed.), *Encyclopedia of educational research* (Vol. 4). New York: Free Press.

Powell, M., & Beard, J. W. (1984). *Teacher effectiveness: An annotated bibliography and guide to research.* New York: Garland.

TEACHER GRIEVANCE PROCEDURE

Grievance procedures are included in virtually all collective bargaining agreements because there is little intrinsic incentive for an employer to comply with agreements which create benefits flowing from the employer to the employee, thus increasing the costs of operation and limiting the employers' discretion to manage the enterprise. Without some formal enforcement mechanism, the only way employees could compel compliance would be to litigate under the common law of contracts or exert the traditional marketplace pressures of strikes, slowdowns, boycotts, and the like.

In the 1940s, due to the wartime necessity of avoiding strikes in the defense industries, the grievance procedure was developed and implemented as a means of providing for the execution of collective bargaining agreements. With the assistance of legal requirements and administrative enforcement procedures, it has become so successful that a grievance procedure is currently a virtual *quid pro quo* of collective bargaining, especially in the public sector where the right to strike is either withheld entirely or severely limited.

The following elements are common to most grievance procedures: (a) definition of grievable matters; (b) format and timelines for filing and disposition of complaints; (c) in-house appeal processes; and (d) conditions for external appeal. These typically establish strict standards of form (oral, written description of violation, citation of provisions allegedly violated, relief sought, etc.); timelines (how long after the event can a request for review be filed?); and topic (not all dissatisfactions with the workplace are subject to resolution by the grievance procedure). Supervisors and managers at every level, from building administrators to personnel officers, to district administrators, and even to the school board itself, should carefully assess every grievance received on each standard to insure that it complies with all requirements of form, timeliness, and topic. Failure of a grievance to meet any one of these standards renders it procedurally defective, making it unnecessary for the employer to respond to its substance. Though the substance of such a grievance should never be acted upon, employers cannot make grievances go away simply by challenging each one on procedural grounds. Disputes over whether one of the standards was or was not met are, themselves, grievable and ultimately subject to formal litigation.

Key Considerations

The oral discussion step in most grievance procedures reflects a fundamental labor relations belief that disputes regarding the workplace should be resolved at the lowest possible level. Nevertheless, there is great pressure not to solve them there. Employers are always reluctant to grant the relief sought in grievances because by doing so they may modify the language of the agreement to increase an employee benefit. Employees are likewise reluctant to accept denials of their grievances: to concede that the employer's denial of the benefit is justified means that it will have to be bargained. Hence, most grievances go through several appeal steps before they are resolved or abandoned. Not every grievance need be appealed through all available steps; however, teachers' organizations are permitted discretion in deciding which appeals have sufficient merit to pursue to the highest levels of adjudication.

Compliance with the filing steps and other procedural requirements listed in the grievance procedure is crucial. Any departure, no matter how slight, can terminate a review of the merits of the dispute. An employee's failure to file a grievance in a timely fashion is tacit accession that the action which prompted the complaint did not violate the agreement; likewise, employer failure to respond to a valid grievance in a timely fashion is tacit accession to the complaint and remedy.

If a complaint must initially be made orally, an employer is not required to accept a written complaint that has not been preceded by an effort to solve the matter through discussion. If a complaint must be in a stipulated format, i.e., citation of specific articles, and remedy sought, responses to incomplete filings need not be made. If the agreement requires the aggrieved employee to file the complaint, the association may not do it on his or her behalf. Employers generally prefer language requiring the complaint to be made by individuals, and employee associations prefer to have the discretion to file in behalf of the entire group regardless of whether the individual desires to pursue the matter.

Only matters which can be referred to provisions of the agreement may be brought up in a grievance; consequently, grievance procedures define those which are subject to it. The definition preferred by employee associations is broad in scope: "A grievance shall be any complaint arising out of the employment relationship." This permits employees to complain about anything that happens to them in the workplace whether or not it can be referred to a provision in the collective bargaining agreement. Grievances over matters as trivial as seating arrangements in the employees' lunchroom can result. The definition preferred by employers is narrow in scope: "A grievance shall be an issue or dispute regarding the interpretation or application of a specific term of this collective bargaining agreement." Here, if the matter of employee interest is not referable to specific contract language, it cannot be a part of a grievance, no matter how important it seems at the time. From time to time specific topics will be explicitly excluded from part or all of the grievance procedure.

The employer may not ignore employee concerns simply because they are not unequivocally described in the collective bargaining agreement. Grievance arbitrators and courts consistently hold that a grievance may properly be drawn from "the essence" of the agreement. Also, a narrow scope definition of a grievance is not sufficient to permit the employer to impose unilateral changes in wages, hours, and conditions of employment when the contract is silent regarding a disputed matter. If a grievance concerns a mandatory topic of bargaining, bargaining regarding it probably will be required, even midterm in a current agreement. Where the grievance and the relief sought strike directly at the employer's duty to establish policy and manage the enterprise, however, there will be no duty to consider it. Whether a topic can be brought up in a grievance is a proper dispute for submission to arbitration and adjudication.

Deciding the Merits

Only after a grievance is determined to meet form, time, and topic requirements, can its merits be considered. Both sides of the dispute must be thoroughly investigated and discussed to determine exactly what occurred because the formally filed grievance is usually a biased version of the events that prompted it. After the investigation, a review of past grievances on similar matters should be conducted to determine whether past practice on the matter exists.

Restraint must be exercised in making a decision. Though solving personnel problems at the lowest possible level is a strong tradition in labor relations, it is quite possible that the problem presented is beyond the authority of the immediate supervisor or would create new contract obligations. If so, there is no choice but to deny the grievance. Restraint must also control denial of a grievance. It is better simply to reply, "grievance denied—no violation on the collective bargaining agreement," than to provide the explicit rationale for the decision. Upon appeal, the argument could be limited to the reasons initially stated, thus precluding the presentation of creative and persuasive rationale developed with the assistance of legal counsel.

External Review

The terms of a local collective bargaining agreement may place limits on how far appeals may be taken. Thus, some topics may not be appealable beyond the superintendent, or the board of education. Any limits included in the agreement will be honored upon review except that employees may not surrender their right to litigate for vindication of constitutional or statutory rights.

The general pattern of external review is for disputes to be submitted first to binding arbitration, although advisory arbitration is sometimes a preliminary step. The arbitrator's function will be sharply limited by common law principles of arbitral practice. First, an arbitrator must use existing contract language to resolve the dispute (new language of responsibilities not contemplated by the terms of the agreement may not be created). Second, the words in a collective bargaining agreement carry their common and ordinary meaning unless expressly modified by terms of the agreement. Where the terms of a contract are clear, an arbitrator is not free to force his or her sense of justice or equity into the agreement. Third, clear and unambiguous language must be enforced even though the results differ substantially from the intention of the parties. An award, however, no matter how closely drawn from the terms of the agreement, may not result in practices that would be in violation of labor relations or general statutes. Fourth, where the issue is a matter of law rather than interpretation of the terms of the agreement, the arbitrator may not make a determination; only a court can determine matters of law. Fifth, arbitrators may not impose punitive damages; remedies are limited to restoring the aggrieved party to the conditions that would have occurred had the collective bargaining agreement not been violated. Depending on the collective bargaining agreement or the state law, an arbitrator may not be permitted to fashion a remedy of his or her own, but may be limited to selection of one or the other of the disputants' positions.

An appeal of an arbitrator's award is almost always first to the state's public employment relations board, although if the issue clearly is a matter of law, initial judicial review may be granted. Nevertheless, the judicial preference is to require exhaustion of all administrative remedies prior to granting a court hearing. Deference to the arbitrator's determination pervades judicial review because the principle followed is that by having agreed to arbitration in a grievance procedure, the parties also agreed to accept the arbitrator's determination, for good or for ill. Consequently, appellate reviewers will not examine whether an award is wise or unwise, only whether it could have been made within the terms of the agreement. Absent egregious and perverse misconstruction that a court finds repugnant and shocking to its sensibilities, the award will be upheld.

See also Collective Bargaining.

—Delbert K. Clear
University of Wisconsin-Milwaukee

References

Clear, D. (1983, 1984, 1985). "Collective bargaining." In P. Piele, & S. Thomas (Eds.), *Yearbook of school law.* Topeka, KS: National Organization on Legal Problems in Education.

Ostrander, K.J. (1981). *A grievance arbitration guide for educators.* Boston: Allyn & Bacon.

Weld, S. (1979). "Complaints, grievances, and grievance arbitration: The key to effective personnel relations." In C. Mulcahy (Ed.), *Municipal labor relations in Wisconsin.* Madison, WI: State Bar of Wisconsin.

TEACHER LAYOFF

For the first time in the history of American education, school districts have been faced with negative growth patterns ensuing from birth control, two-income families, high costs due to inflation, and a mobile, unstable population. These factors, coupled with declining state and federal funds, have resulted in school boards' reducing instructional and, in some instances, administrative staff in order to maintain fiscal solvency.

Reduction-in-force (RIF) or teacher layoff was unheard of until the mid-1970s. Today it is so commonplace that nearly every school board has a policy governing the implementation of such a plan. Since reduction-in-force is both commonplace and devastating, school boards have sought policies and procedures that are fair and impartial to the staff member being laid off or terminated.

The most common reduction-in-force procedure employs the time-honored industrial model of reducing the staff on the basis of seniority. That is, the last hired are the first fired or laid off. But education is a unique entity, and layoffs done by seniority are not always, it has been found, the fairest and most impartial method of reducing the staff. Other factors such as state certification in the area taught, additional training, teacher evaluation, and past performance are now beginning to appear in board policies governing layoff and recall procedures.

Reduction-in-force by seniority is positive in one sense and regressive in another. There is merit to maintaining experienced teachers, as long as they are competent. But it is regressive to dismiss young, talented teachers with fewer years of service, especially those minority teachers hired under affirmative action plans who are just beginning to bring about proportionate representation in the field of education. By and large, younger teachers are more enthusiastic, better trained, and are more willing to participate in the total school program than are their more experienced counterparts. Administrators and school board members are now finding that reduction plans using seniority as the only criterion will not work effectively if comprehensive schools providing both curricular and extracurricular offerings are desired. Therefore, the additional criteria of certification, past performance, teacher evaluation, and willingness to be involved in extracurricular activities are now being considered as part of reduction policies in many districts. Prior to the time when such reductions became commonplace, the private-sector seniority model seemed appropriate. Today experience has shown that education must handle this problem differently from industry.

Reduction-in-Force Policies

There are as many different reduction-in-force policies as there are school corporations. The following board policy which comprises the criterion determinants of certification and seniority incorporates many of the guidelines found in such policies throughout the United States:

1. In the event of a reduction-in-force, or recall after layoff, the following criteria shall be the sole determinants: (a) certification, (b) seniority.

2. Seniority is defined as the teacher's length of continuous service from his or her date of last employment in the school district and is not interrupted by approved leaves of absences.

3. When two or more teachers have the same length of service, the teacher who signed his or her individual contract with the school corporation on the earliest date shall be considered senior. If two or more teachers signed their individual contracts on the same date, then the teacher with the earliest birthdate shall be considered senior.

4. One districtwide seniority list, based on service with the district as of June 30, 19—, shall be established. This list shall contain the names and dates of signed initial contracts and all areas of certification for all teachers, including teachers on official leaves of absences. The initial seniority list, based on service with the district as of June 30, 19—, shall be posted in each faculty lounge and available to each teacher who requests a copy thereof. Teachers shall have a period of 45 days to file exceptions to their placement on the seniority list with the assistant superintendent of instruction. No exceptions shall be entertained which have not been filed within this time period. This list shall be kept updated and posted annually.

5. A teacher whose current assignment is not available due to a reduction in staff shall be allowed to displace the teacher in another teaching assignment in accordance with the criteria specified in Paragraph 1.

6. Teachers who have been laid off will be recalled on the basis of seniority with the teacher with the most seniority on layoff being called back first using the criteria specified in Paragraph 1.

7. Seniority shall be broken when a teacher (a) resigns, (b) is discharged for just cause, or (c) fails to report for work within 30 days after receipt of a written notice of recall to work after a layoff given by the board, by registered or certified mail addressed to the teacher at his or her last address appearing on the records of the Board; a teacher who is employed in another school district at the time of recall shall be allowed to complete his or her contractual obligation before returning. In the unforeseen event that a teacher is unable to return within the 30 day time limit because of illness of physical incapacity, such teacher shall return as soon as he or she is released from his or her doctor's care.

8. A teacher on layoff shall remain on the recall list as long as he or she expresses his or her desire to do so to the board at least once per year in writing.

It is imperative that school districts maintain community credibility in the face of cutbacks. Any district suffering from declining pupil enrollment cannot afford to be burdened with incompetent and unsatisfactory teachers. The school district faced with decreasing numbers of pupils must adopt aggressive evaluation procedures for the removal of teachers who do not provide adequate instruction or related services associated with the comprehensive school. Reduction-in-force policies must be designed to address the problems of declining enrollment and to maintain the highest quality of teaching performance.

See also Teacher Tenure.

—James K. Walter
Kokomo, Indiana

References

Carfield, R.D., & Walter, J.K. (1984, November). "Teacher evaluation and RIF—Can there be peaceful coexistence?" *NASSP Bulletin, 68*(475), 48-53.
Mamchak, P.S., & Mamchak, S.R. (1982). *School administrators' encyclopedia*. West Nyack, NY: Parker.
Thomas, D. (1977, March). "Strategies for closing a school, reducing staff." *NASSP Bulletin, 61*(407), 8-19.

TEACHER PROFESSIONALISM

Several lines of research have revealed the unintended consequences of viewing teachers as bureaucratic functionaries whose work needed to be closely regulated and supervised. The regulatory approach to improving teaching resulted in standardized curricula, bureaucratic reporting requirements, hierarchical evaluation systems, and overemphasis on standardized tests. These bureaucratic accountability mechanisms generally led not to more effective teaching but to more standardized teaching.

As teachers were compelled to comply with bureaucratic accountability requirements, they found it more difficult to teach their students in ways that were academically sound. They were being forced to teach narrower, less intellectually honest, less practical curricula that failed to meet the needs of a growing number of students. Paradoxically, the more teachers conformed to bureaucratic requirements, the lower the quality of education became. As teachers violated their own standards of good teaching, their frustration increased and their job satisfaction declined. Equally important, their students, the next generation of potential teachers, observed their teachers' growing disaffection with teaching.

Fortunately, professional accountability—an alternative to bureaucratic accountability—shows some promise of taking hold. While bureaucratic accountability demands conformity to prescribed routines, professional accountability demands performance in accord with standards of good teaching. Practicing teachers would be held accountable for teaching academic subjects with intellectual honesty and practical foresight and for making appropriate instructional decisions on behalf of their students and classes. To bring about professional accountability in teaching, the public must be assured that teachers have been adequately prepared to discharge their responsibilities. This would require rigorous teacher preparation, intensive supervised induction, meaningful certification requirements, and discriminating evaluation prior to tenure. These changes—which will occur only with the active participation of teachers—would make teaching a profession.

A number of recent developments signal what may become the era of teacher professionalism: (a) the Holmes Group (a group of school of education deans) issued its long-awaited report, *Tomorrow's Teachers*, calling for a major restructuring of teacher education in order to prepare teachers who can teach professionally; (b) the Carnegie Forum (a group of leading citizens and educators) issued its widely heralded call for the creation of a National Board for Professional Teaching Standards; (c) the National Education Association and the American Federation of Teachers pledged support for the National Board; (d) the National Education Association renewed its longstanding commitment to the creation of state boards for professional teaching standards; and (e) the American Federation of Teachers called for experiments along a wide variety of fronts to expand the role of teachers in decisions regarding personnel and policy.

The major impetus for professionalization lies outside the control of individual school districts. The drive toward professionalization has begun with proposed changes in teacher education and licensing. These changes would result in teachers in whom the public and policymakers would have confidence. However, professionalization requires changes in the way that states, school systems, and educational personnel make decisions and operate. Only as these changes occur will students and the public reap the benefits of professionalization.

The professionalization of teaching will require changes in control over licensing and licensing procedures. Changes in preparation, selection, and instructional practice will be necessary. Professionalization also will call for changes in evaluation and development.

As in other professions, teachers will need to control the boards which regulate entry to their ranks. With the granting of legislative authority given to other professions, boards, composed primarily of teachers, will determine the qualifications or standards for entry to teaching and will enforce those standards. Only those who meet these standards will be allowed to practice the profession of teaching. The professional standards boards will need to develop or adopt licensing procedures which have credibility. These licensing procedures—unlike simple multiple-choice tests of knowledge or simplistic rating sheets of teaching behavior—will demonstrate reliably and validly that prospective teachers are competent to practice. These licensing procedures will need to mirror the educational and professional preparation of teachers.

Teachers, like other professionals, must be—and must be seen as—liberally educated members of society. The academic currency associated with a person's being liberally educated is a bachelor's degree in the liberal arts. That degree signals, as well as U.S. higher education has ever been able to signal, that a person is generally educated in the main branches of knowledge and more educated in a single field. With respect to the latter, it also signals that the person has mastered a field at a level sufficient to teach a particular subject in high school.

A profession of teaching will require that a teacher master the professional and pedagogical knowledge base underlying teaching. Teachers cannot operate professionally unless they know the philosophical, social, political, and economic context of schooling. That knowledge enables and empowers teachers to participate responsibly in educational decision making. Teachers cannot teach as effectively as they might until they master the available and growing pedagogical knowledge base. Increasingly, preparation for all professions occurs at the graduate level.

Entry to teaching, like entry to other professions, can best occur under a supervised induction or internship. Here seasoned professionals help novices to learn how to translate theory into practice and to learn those instructional practices which can be learned only on the job. The intern would have to complete satisfactorily the internship in order to take the state board's licensing examination.

Teachers, like other professionals who work in bureaucratic settings, should participate in the selection of their peers. The success of individual teachers depends upon the quality of their peers. The identification of teaching quality is best pursued within a framework that involves a number of teachers and other educational personnel in the assessment of additions to a school staff. Furthermore, the success of a school depends upon coordination among the members of the staff. A major means for that coordination is the articulation of a school's instructional goals and the search for and selection of staff members who share those goals.

Professional instructional practice requires that teachers know their subjects, their students, their school's goals, and pedagogical practices. With knowledge of these, they plan, deliver, and evaluate instruction, making appropriate instructional decisions in behalf of their students. Control over instructional practice in a school is the collective responsibility of all members of the professional staff in the school. In this way, teachers participate in setting the conditions under which they work. They coordinate the curriculum of the school.

In a profession of teaching, the role of evaluation changes. Extensive teacher preparation and intensive licensing procedures mean that most teachers will not require the continuous oversight implied by the conventional approach to teacher evaluation. Nothing is gained by an annual visit by the principal to complete an evaluation checklist. Instead, seasoned professionals can help each other improve their performances through classroom visits, consultations, and seminars. Occasionally, of course, instances of instructional practice which constitute malpractice will be found. For these instances, exceptional procedures must exist and be brought to bear to remove teachers who cannot or do not teach in a professionally responsible manner.

When teachers teach professionally, students benefit, for then their educational needs become the predominant concern. No longer will teachers experience the ethical conflict which exists when bureaucratic requirements and standardized tests drive the curriculum and force them to teach in ways which contradict their professional judgment.

The professionalization of teaching implies the restructuring of schooling. That restructuring means a redefinition of the roles and responsibilities of teachers and administrators. Administrators must be prepared to share their planning and decision-making responsibilities; teachers must be prepared to assume these responsibilities. To some extent, the professionalization of teaching will decrease the need for middle-level administrators in the central offices and schools. The jobs of many middle-level administrators exist because school districts now believe that they must closely direct and supervise curriculum and teachers. A professional teaching force will not require close supervision. Moreover, senior teachers can, in extra-classroom time, perform the instructional leadership functions previously performed by middle-level administrators. Through savings effected by a reduced administrative hierarchy, school districts will be able to pay teachers salaries commensurate with their responsibilities.

See also American Federation of Teachers; Career Ladders; National Education Association; Teacher Accountability.

—Arthur Wise
The RAND Corporation

References

Darling-Hammond, L. (1984). *Beyond the commission reports: The coming crisis in teaching.* Santa Monica, CA: The RAND Corporation (No. R-3177-RC).

The Holmes Group, Inc. (1986). *Tomorrow's teachers: A report of the Holmes Group.* East Lansing, MI: Author.

Wise, A. E., Darling-Hammond, L., & Berry, B. (1987). *Effective teacher selection: From recruitment to retention.* Santa Monica, CA: The RAND Corporation (R-3462-NIE/CSTP).

TEACHER SALARIES

The prominent pay plan for classroom teachers is the single-salary schedule. This plan provides for equivalent salaries for equivalent preparation and experience. The assumptions underlying this type of structure include the following: (a) Salaries for teachers are scheduled and paid solely on the basis of professional preparation and experience; (b) teacher effectiveness increases with experience and preparation; and (c) all positions are equal in importance and responsibility.

The single-salary schedule is deeply rooted in American education. It is easy to understand, administer, and utilize in school budget preparation. In practically all school districts, a teacher is placed on a salary scale reflecting the qualifications met; he or she progresses up that scale by a series of periodic increments until the teacher eventually reaches a maximum beyond which he or she cannot progress further. The single-salary schedule may have an index or ratio applied to it, a technique by which a system of multipliers is used to establish incremental steps; it may have preparation differentials in relation to a base salary. Generally teachers' salary scales are relatively flat. Usually, the ending salary at the time of retirement is only about twice the beginning salary.

Individual Bargaining

In the absence of a single-salary schedule, teachers would have to bargain individually for their pay. Because it is impossible to measure the merits of the individual teacher accurately and objectively and because personal and psychological factors cannot easily be eliminated, individual bargaining tends to give the advantage to the aggressive, the politically powerful, and the personally influential. It favors individuals who can exert pressure in one way or another. The single-salary schedule, on the other hand, is impersonal and objective. It eliminates many psychological conflicts.

Criterion

In many school districts, seniority is generally the sole criterion for incremental advancement. In the great majority of cases, increments are granted annually. Increments do not have to be the same every year, or be given every year, or be given during the probationary period, or be the same for all positions; they do not have to be automatic, and they may be conditioned upon satisfactory service.

Factors Determining Salaries

There are a number of factors which determine the salaries paid in a public school system: earnings in other occupations, living standards and the cost of living, the cost of the preparation for teaching, the supply and demand for teachers, public opinion, taxable resources and the tax base, federal and state aid, public expenditures for other purposes, the size of the community, the type of community, and the bargaining strength of the teachers' organizations.

Pay Based on Performance

A matter of major interest in the United States today is the movement to base teacher-pay decisions on classroom performance. There are appropriate methods of rewarding teacher competence. Many states and communities are currently examining various approaches.

Many teachers object to having pay related to performance since there can be real problems in trying to quantify the teaching art for measurement purposes. One of the findings that comes from research on incentive systems is that such plans work best when teachers trust the administration. Since representatives of the administration make the individual pay decisions, a critical matter is the attitude of the teachers toward the administration along with their attitudes toward the concept of using pay as a motivator. Otherwise, any merit pay plan can be undermined by members of the educational staff.

Data suggest that individual preferences on merit-based pay are influenced by teachers' needs and by the situation in which they find themselves. Employees high in achievement needs seemed to prefer merit systems. Those with strong security needs do not. Teachers, as a group, tend to have strong security needs.

The evidence suggests that the history of merit pay in education has a poor record. Merit pay for teachers has been debated for three-quarters of a century. The issue is a controversial one and has been the subject of numerous studies. To be successful, a merit pay system must be based upon a performance evaluation structure that teachers believe has a direct and meaningful relationship between the performance evaluation process and actual performance. Since there are so few valid and reliable measures, pay for performance will remain controversial.

Teachers desire to be compensated at levels compatible with like kinds of professions. As the debate persists over education in American society, teachers will continue to make their pay a part of the discussion. But teachers must also be willing to have some pay at risk if they wish to attain comparability.

As educational reform continues, compensation for teachers will be an integral part of the reform movement.

See also Merit Pay; Teacher Accountability; Teacher Professionalism; Teacher Strikes.

—R. Warren Eisenhower
Fairfax County, Virginia, Public Schools

References

Alexander, A.J. (1974). *Teachers, salaries, and school district expenditures.* Santa Monica, CA: Rand.

Bell, M. (1978). *Teachers' pay.* Geneva: International Labour Office.

Rebore, R.W. (1982). *Personnel administration in education* (chap. 8). Englewood Cliffs, NJ: Prentice-Hall.

TEACHER SATISFACTION

Teaching has been always a demanding profession. Some administrators may believe survival in the profession is a function of stamina, and they advise their staff, "If you can't stand the heat, get out of the kitchen." Effective educational leaders realize that they must organize their schools in such a manner as to promote a positive sense of satisfaction among those teachers who respond effectively to the challenges of their profession.

Teacher satisfaction is a function of the extent to which the school fosters the fulfillment of a hierarchy of needs among its staff. This hierarchy consists of both lower- and higher-order needs. Most schools foster the fulfillment of the lower-order security and social needs of teachers. By virtue of obtaining a teaching position, teachers earn a salary which allows them to assume an adequate standard of living. Also, most teachers pursue their responsibilities in a relatively safe and orderly school environment. Through their everyday interactions with colleagues, these teachers fulfill their need for affiliation.

While most schools foster the lower-order security and social needs of teachers, it is important to note that this is not always the case. In some settings, student violence is a major problem, and teachers are required to spend most of the day in their own classrooms. The anxiety and isolation resulting from such conditions prevent teachers from fulfilling their lower-order needs and limits their level of satisfaction. This lower level of satisfaction accounts for the higher teacher turnover in problem schools.

Once lower-level teacher needs are met adequately, schools must face the challenge of fulfilling their teachers' higher-level esteem, autonomy, and self-actualization needs. To fulfill their esteem needs, teachers must believe personally that they are doing a good job and develop the sense that their colleagues believe they are doing a good job, too. At the autonomy level, teachers believe they can exercise authority and control in the educational program planning process. They can use their discretion to make program adjustments and modifications without seeking permission from administrators or their supervisors. Self-actualization goes beyond autonomy, such that teachers perceive themselves as pursuing their responsibilities in a personally creative and innovative manner. They believe they are achieving their goals and working at full potential.

Teacher satisfaction increases to the extent that schools can foster the fulfillment of these higher-level needs. Since these needs are arranged in a hierarchy, the failure of the school to make provisions for the fulfillment of the next higher-level need can result in reduced levels of teacher satisfaction. For example, some schools foster the fulfillment of teacher needs up through the esteem level, but make few provisions for the attainment of autonomy and self-actualization needs by requiring their teachers to adhere to a prescribed instructional plan as specified in systemwide curriculum guides. Such policies, which limit the professional discretion of teachers, inhibit the fulfillment of their higher-level autonomy and self-actualization needs, resulting in lower levels of satisfaction.

Viewing teacher satisfaction as simply the fulfillment of a hierarchy of needs raises many questions. What happens if schools foster the fulfillment of some needs, but not others? If schools alleviate those factors associated with teacher dissatisfaction, will teachers become more satisfied? How important is pay as a satisfier? The literature has shown that satisfaction and dissatisfaction are not on a continuum. There are particular factors that account for teacher dissatisfaction.

These factors tend to be associated with the lower-order security and esteem needs of teachers. They include factors related to the conditions of work such as job status, salary, job security, working conditions, and interpersonal relations with superiors, peer teachers, and students. On the other hand, there are factors which account for teacher satisfaction. These factors tend to be associated with the higher-order esteem, autonomy, and self-actualization needs of teachers. They include factors related to the nature of the work itself—factors such as achievement, recognition, responsibility, and the potential for growth and advancement. As the school is organized to foster higher levels of satisfaction among teachers, strategies must be planned to minimize the effects of those dissatisfiers associated with the conditions of work and to maximize the effects of those sources of satisfaction derived through the work itself.

Too often school systems address the issue of teacher satisfaction by only minimizing the dissatisfiers associated with the conditions of work. Some of these school systems have attractive facilities, ample instructional materials and resources, attractive salary and benefit packages, and positive interpersonal relations among administrators, teachers, and students. With all these positive conditions, some find it perplexing that teachers in such settings are not highly satisfied.

To achieve higher levels of teacher satisfaction, efforts must be made to go beyond attractive working conditions and to foster among teachers the fulfillment of those needs associated with the work itself, such as recognition, responsibility, and achievement. Teachers must be involved professionally in planning the educational process in their school. They must be recognized for their contributions to the improvement of the instructional program and rewarded for the achievements of their students. Without adequate attention to such consideration, the level of satisfaction among teachers will not reach its full potential.

Studies of the extent to which schools are meeting the lower- and higher-order needs of teachers provide some interesting insights. Teachers perceive their lower-order security and social needs to be met to a greater extent than their higher-level esteem, autonomy, and self-actualization needs. The analyses of teacher need deficiencies with respect to background variables indicate that higher-order need deficiencies tend to be greater for secondary-school teachers than for elementary-school teachers. Security and esteem need deficiencies tend to be greater among younger, less experienced teachers than for older teachers. This finding raises the interesting question of why older, more experienced teachers perceive their needs to be met better. Is it because they have become better adjusted to the realities of their profession, or do only those teachers who perceive their needs to be met continue in the profession? Male and female teachers did not tend to differ significantly in their perceptions of the extent to which their needs are being met.

This brief summary of the research supports the observation that while schools are meeting those lower-level needs of teachers associated with the conditions of work, more attention must be devoted to meeting those higher-level needs associated with the work itself as schools address the issue of teacher satisfaction.

Recently, pay has received considerable attention in the literature on teacher satisfaction. Some advocate that all we need to do is to pay teachers more and they will become more satisfied. In this context, pay is a dissatisfier associated with the conditions of work.

To raise the salaries of all teachers will reduce the level of dissatisfaction, but will not result in increased satisfaction. Pay can be used to increase teacher satisfaction, if it is linked to recognition, responsibility, or achievement through well-designed career ladder or merit pay programs. While such programs vary considerably in scope and complexity, some examples follow to show how pay can be used to fulfill those higher-order needs of teachers associated with their work itself.

In some career ladder programs, select teachers work a longer school year to become involved in curriculum-revision efforts. Thus, they are compensated for this additional time. Here pay serves as a form of recognition for these teachers' contributions to the educational program. Some other career ladder programs include differentiated staffing arrangements where particular teachers assume a higher level of responsibility for the educational program (i.e., key teachers, team leaders, resource teachers). Thus, these teachers are compensated for their additional responsibility. In such situations, pay is a satisfier, since it is a function of the responsibility assumed by the teachers. Some merit pay programs include specific criteria for relating level of compensation to the accomplishments of the classroom teachers. When such programs are based on fair and equitable criteria, pay is a satisfier, since it is a function of the teachers' achievements.

It is best to view teacher satisfaction as a continuing challenge for the administrators who lead our schools. We must not lose sight of the fact that schools exist for developing the potential of the students they serve as well as for developing the potential of the teaching staff. Efforts to organize schools to meet the lower- and higher-order needs of teachers are worth the time; it is time well spent. The satisfaction teachers derive through their work is manifest in the positive learning environment they create for their students as well as in the subsequent achievements of these students.

See also Career Ladders; Teacher Professionalism; Teacher Salaries; Teacher Stress and Burnout.

—Edward F. Iwanicki
University of Connecticut

References

Brandt, R.S. (1985, November). "Making teaching more rewarding." *Educational Leadership, 43*(3), 5.

Lawler, E.E. (1981). *Pay and organization development.* Reading, MA: Addison-Wesley.

Sergiovanni, T.J., & Starratt, R.J. (1983). "Teacher motivation and supervisory effectiveness." (chap. 8). In *Supervision: Human perspectives* (3rd ed.). New York: McGraw Hill.

TEACHER SELECTION

The process used to select teachers varies considerably from school district to school district. While the majority of school districts have not established policy to guide the teacher-selection process, a number of larger districts have highly sophisticated selection procedures that rely on as many as ten or more selection criteria. For example, the Dallas Independent School District uses application forms, state certification credentials, college transcripts, principal preemployment interviews, cooperating teachers' perceptions, college professors' (practice teaching supervisors') perceptions, personal and professional references, recommendations by a tri-ethnic committee, formally-scored interviews, an essay exercise, and a test of verbal and quantitative ability. This process can be contrasted with teacher selections that are based on "gut feelings" or political considerations in less sophisticated districts.

Despite the difficulties associated with selecting the best teachers from the total available universe of teacher applicants, agreement exists that making the right staffing decisions is absolutely critical to the welfare of the schools. Recognizing the serious limitations that exist, the following eight-step process should increase the likelihood of the right person's selection for the job. This process is ultimately designed to enable the person in the decision-making role to make an informed estimate about which candidates have the best chance of being successful in a particular teaching situation.

Teacher Selection Process

The process to fill any vacancy should always begin with a job analysis. The purpose of a job analysis is to determine what the job entails. What are the most important tasks to be performed by the job incumbent? What special assignments or requirements such as club sponsorships, coaching assignments, or committee responsibilities will be attached to the position? What must a person know in order to do a particular job and what special skills must he or she possess? Are there certain personal characteristics required by the job? Is it important, for example, that a particular position be filled by a minority, a woman, or a person with excellent social skills?

The second step in the selection process is establishing criteria for selection. Exactly what knowledge, skills, or characteristics must a candidate possess in order to be considered for the available position? While generic openings that can be filled by generic teachers do not exist, several broad generalizations of what a teacher must know and be able to do apply in nearly every instance.

In addition to a prospective teacher's knowledge of the content appropriate to his or her field, the basic tenets of teaching, and the pedagogy, there must also be some evidence of commitment to the teaching profession and to students. Teaching is mentally and physically demanding and requires a person who is willing to put in long, hard hours while enduring endless frustrations for a rather modest salary. With this in mind, it is not surprising that the last general requirement for all teachers is that they enjoy reasonably satisfactory mental and physical health.

Each teaching situation is unique with its own set of opportunities and constraints. Every child, every group of children, and every school, for that matter, has unique needs that must be matched to the talents and abilities of a particular applicant. Every teaching vacancy should be viewed as a unique opportunity to improve the school and the school system. It is therefore necessary to decide which selection criteria will help to achieve this aim.

The next step in the selection process is the generation of a pool of applicants for the available position. In larger districts, the recruitment may be handled centrally, while in smaller districts the administrator with the opening may have this responsibility. In any event, a job-vacancy announcement must be prepared and widely circulated in locations where applicants are likely to be found. An administrator gets in touch with applicants through newspaper advertisements, bulletin-board postings, professional journals, and colleges of education. The most important consideration in recruitment is to take those actions that will generate the largest potential pool of teacher candidates who are likely to meet the selection criteria. This will enhance the possibility of securing an excellent teacher.

The fourth step in the process is to gather as much data as possible about the candidate pool relative to the selection criteria. As a general rule of thumb, the more information generated the better as long as it relates to the selection criteria. Generally, each candidate should complete a simple application form that serves to collect such job-related data as educational background, work experience, certification information, standardized test scores, references, and a writing sample. You may collect other information on the application form, but be certain it is job-related data. Other minimal data usually required of all applicants include college transcripts and letters of recommendation. Many districts are now requiring sample lesson plans, and some prefer videotaped teaching demonstrations.

The data gathered in step four are used to screen the total pool of candidates. "Gross paper screening" is the term that is used to describe the elimination of those candidates who clearly do not meet the minimal qualifications for employment. For example, those who are not certified, do not hold a college degree, hold a degree in an inappropriate field, or simply do not meet any one of a number of essential selection criteria established in step two can be eliminated at this point. The credentials of the remaining candidates are then compared in what is termed "fine paper screening" on each of the selection criteria, so far as the available data allow, in order to arrive at a list of candidates who will be invited for a personal interview. A profile sheet that includes a means to estimate the extent to which a candidate meets each of the selection criteria should be used to complete this phase of the screening process for each candidate. The field of candidates for a teaching position can thereby be reduced to a manageable number, perhaps three to five, to be interviewed in step six.

The personal interview is the most preferred, and possibly the most abused, tool for teacher selection. The numerous liabilities inherent in the use of personal interviews can be considerably reduced by following several suggestions. Always use a structured format to interview candidates and devise a system to record responses in order that answers of candidates can be compared and scored. Avoid commercially prepared instruments, since they may not meet the needs of unique situations and have generally received unfavorable reviews in the research literature.

Be certain the questions you ask are job related and do not infringe on the rights or privacy of job seekers. Design the questionnaire in such a way that applicants are forced to respond to questions that will give you insight into their knowledge of subject-matter content, their use of appropriate methodology, and their relations with students and colleagues. Ask questions that are unique to the school situation, such as the willingness of the applicant to teach certain groups of children, perform extra duties, or sponsor programs or events.

Employ group interview techniques and reach consensus on how well candidates performed in the interview. This will help reduce the bias that frequently creeps into interviews conducted by one person. Teachers have much to contribute in group-interview situations and have repeatedly expressed satisfaction in being consulted in employment decisions.

In step seven, all the data are weighed, and a hiring decision is made. It may not be possible to make a completely objective decision at this point. Such is the state of the art. However, through a comparison of the profile sheets and interview records of all the candidates, a thorough check of references, and the thoughtful consideration of the opinions of other respected colleagues, a sound decision generally results.

Step eight consists of notifying all the candidates of the results of the process. It is a good practice to notify by telephone all those who are interviewed. They are usually eager to know the outcome, and a personal call is appreciated whether or not an offer is extended. If you have done a good job during the preliminary screening, very often there will be more than one excellent candidate who participated in the interview phase of the selection process. A little common courtesy extended to unsuccessful candidates may be rewarded when a good candidate is needed to fill a future vacancy.

If unsuccessful candidates ask why they were not offered the position, it is usually good practice to reply in general terms, "Although you were a very strong candidate, we found someone who was more qualified." Dealing with specifics such as, "Your references were poor or your grade point ratio was a little low," can cause difficulty. Individual candidate profile sheets should be kept on file to be used in the event someone raises a question regarding an employment decision, to serve as a data base for future hiring or to evaluate the total selection process.

Teacher selection is a continuing series of decisions rather than a single decision. Information about candidates is gathered and screened through a set of criteria until only those most likely to be successful on the job emerge at the end of the process. Clearly, subjective judgment must play some part in teacher selection, but an approach in which subjective judgment plays no more than a minor supporting role should be employed.

See also Competency Testing, Teachers; Principal Selection; Teacher Certification.

—Leonard O. Pellicer
University of South Carolina

References

Bredeson, P.V. (1985). "The teacher screening and selection process: A decision making model for school administrators." *Journal of Research and Development in Education, 18*(3), 8-15.

Kahl, S.R. (1980). *The selection of teachers and school administrators: A synthesis of the literature.* Unpublished manuscript. (ERIC Document Reproduction Service No. 221 917).

Shields, J.J. & Daniels, R. (1982). *Teacher selection and retention: A review of the literature.* Unpublished manuscript. (ERIC Document Reproduction Service, No. ED 219 340.).

TEACHER SHORTAGES

This nation is facing a shortage of classroom teachers that could become our biggest crisis ever in teaching. The National Center for Educational Statistics (1985) forecast that between 1983 and 1992, approximately 1.7 million new teachers would be needed to staff our elementary and secondary schools. This article outlines the factors contributing to the shortage and examines some possible solutions to alleviate the problem.

Why a Shortage?

Two factors contributing to an increased demand for teachers are changes in student enrollment patterns and teacher turnover. Recent student population projections estimated the nation's school-age population would grow from 44.6 million in 1984 to 50 million in the year 2000, resulting in an accelerated demand for new instructors.

A large number of the teachers who entered the profession during the "Baby Boom" of the 1950s and '60s are now reaching retirement age. In addition, several recent studies reveal that a growing number of teachers are dissatisfied with teaching and are leaving the profession, resulting in a heavy turnover rate.

The projected supply of new teachers is down from previous years, based on the percentage of students receiving bachelor's degrees in preparation for teaching. In 1971, 37 percent of the bachelor's degree candidates throughout the country had prepared themselves to teach. That figure dropped to 15 percent in 1982. The number of persons preparing to teach will likely be low in the foreseeable future for a number of reasons including (a) the changing attitude of prospective teachers, (b) a variety of career options available for women, and (c) inadequate rewards for teaching.

Changing attitudes of college students are indicated by an annual survey of current college freshmen conducted by the American Council of Education. The most recent survey revealed that only 5.5 percent of the respondents are planning careers in teaching as compared to 23 percent in 1968. The current freshmen class also stated that "being well off financially" was a "very important" goal for 71 percent of the respondents compared to 39 percent in 1970. Such a shift in attitude may help explain one of the major reasons why a number of college students are not choosing teaching, a career noted for its below-average salaries.

As their career options continue to grow, fewer women are becoming teachers. Traditionally, teaching has been one of the few professional occupations available to females. Today, more women are choosing jobs in business, law, and other professions.

Inadequate rewards, both extrinsic and intrinsic, for teaching also are contributing to the diminishing teacher supply. The beginning salary for teachers is near the bottom of all professions requiring a bachelor's degree. In addition, recent research shows a number of negative factors influence the way teachers perceive their work. These negative factors include lack of respect and confidence by the public, a lack of automony and control, the absence of some system of career advancement, and inadequate teaching facilities and materials. These changes pose problems for teacher retention, and, as they become better known, they inhibit the recruitment of new teachers as well.

Possible Solutions

Fortunately, some positive efforts are already under way to make teaching a more attractive profession and thus help meet the demand for new teachers. Improvements are being made, but more are needed in four areas: (a) increasing public confidence and support for the nation's schools, (b) improving compensation for teachers, (c) gaining better working conditions for teachers, and (d) developing a vigorous recruitment program to attract qualified individuals to the teaching profession.

Increased public confidence and support are two important elements to improving the attractiveness of the teaching profession. Some evidence of growing confidence in the nation's education system is beginning to show after several years of steady decline. National attention has been focused on improving schooling by various national commissions and organizations. As schools implement recommended reforms, public confidence will likely continue to increase, accompanied by financial support.

At least three approaches can be utilized to improve teacher-compensation systems: (a) increasing salaries across the board, (b) increasing starting salaries, and (c) providing some type of career ladder for teachers. The California Commission on the Teaching Profession reveals that over the past decade, teachers' purchasing power has declined 15 percent. The commission, therefore, recommends restoring some of this lost purchasing power for career teachers by "catch-up" salary increases. The commission also recommends increasing beginning salaries to $25,000.

Several states have instituted mentor or master teacher programs. Such plans provide for a form of career ladder that permits teachers to receive additional compensation for performing different levels of responsibility, such as curriculum planning, staff development, and peer coaching. Such efforts not only help to improve salaries but involve teachers in important aspects of the educational enterprise.

Improved working conditions also will help to make teaching a more attractive career. Attention needs to focus not only on providing adequate facilities and supplies but school governance as well. Teachers should be involved in making decisions affecting their work place and profession.

Finally, a vigorous recruitment program must be initiated to attract outstanding individuals to teaching. Programs must be established to promote the opportunity and importance of a teaching career and emphasize the future demand for teachers.

In summary, America is headed for a critical teaching shortage. The demand for new teacher candidates is up because of increased student enrollments and a high rate of teacher turnover. The supply of new teachers is down because fewer college graduates are choosing teaching as a career. In order to alleviate the problem, teaching must be made a more attractive profession. This can be accomplished, in part, by increased public confidence and support, an improved teacher-compensation system, better working conditions, and a vigorous teacher-recruitment program. Unless more is done in these areas, the nation will face its most severe crisis ever in staffing our schools.

See also Teacher Certification; Teacher Professionalism; Teacher Selection.

—Donald W. Empey
Glendale, California, Unified School District

References

California Commission on the Teaching Profession (1985). *Who will teach our children?* Sacramento, CA: Author.

Empey, D.W. (1984). "The greatest risk: Who will teach? *Elementary School Journal, 85*(2), 167-176.

National Center for Educational Statistics (1985). *Projections of educational statistics to 1992–93.* Washington, DC: U.S. Printing Office.

TEACHER STRESS AND BURNOUT

The 1970s was a period of introspection when people began to look inward to assess how they were being affected by outside forces, including the pressures associated with their occupations. Teachers soon found that the stress associated with their jobs was having a profound effect on their lives. While teaching has always been a stressful occupation, educators perceived the stress in teaching to be increasing and having a detrimental effect on their personal well-being. Insufficient instructional resources, large class sizes, student discipline problems, the lack of public and parental support, and the need to serve a more diverse student population were cited as factors contributing to the increased stress associated with teaching.

As qualified teachers began to leave the profession, it became evident that this was not because they "could not stand the heat of the kitchen," but rather, because the stress associated with teaching had increased beyond the point which could be tolerated by many dedicated individuals. Rather than serving as a motivational force, the stress associated with teaching was having a debilitating effect on teachers. This debilitating effect of stress became commonly known as "teacher burnout."

Reactions to the focus on stress and burnout in the teaching profession were varied. Some failed to accept the reality of this phenomenon and alleged that burnout was really a copout, the failure of teachers to meet the demands of their profession. Teachers' associations provided the counterargument that, unless the issue of stress in teaching is addressed adequately, teachers will begin to leave the profession in epidemic proportions. Analyses of such arguments pointed to the need for research to provide insights regarding the burnout syndrome among teachers. In response to this need, studies were initiated at a number of universities in the late 1970s to address the following issues: (a) What is burnout? (b) What are the sources of stress which account for burnout? (c) Who is affected by burnout? (d) What can we do about burnout? Subsequent discussions are based on these studies.

Exhaustion and Depersonalization

The definition of burnout developed by Maslach and Jackson through their research in the helping professions is most appropriate for the study of teacher burnout. They have identified three aspects of burnout—emotional exhaustion, depersonalization, and reduced personal accomplishment. Emotional exhaustion is characterized by the depletion of a teacher's emotional resources and the feeling that one has nothing left to give to others. Depersonalization consists of developing negative, cynical, and sometimes callous attitudes toward students and colleagues. Finally, reduced personal accomplishment is the feeling of no longer being effective in fulfilling one's responsibilities. The level of burnout experienced by a teacher is a function of the frequency and intensity of one's feelings with respect to these three aspects. In applying this definition, teachers are not classified as burned out or not, but rather placed on a continuum from more to less burned out.

Sources of Stress

Burnout can be accounted for by the stress resulting from three major sources: societal, organizational, and role-related. Societal sources of stress result from the pressures placed upon schools by social and political forces in the community. The poor public image of schools and teaching in the late 1970s was a major source of teacher stress. Organizational sources of stress result from the failure of schools to organize properly to meet the needs of students and teachers. Stress increases when teachers are directed to implement programs which they believe are not appropriate to the needs of their students, or when they are provided with insufficient resources to achieve the desired educational outcomes. Role-related sources of stress are those associated with the particular role the teacher assumes in the school. Sources of such stress include discipline problems, difficulty in developing appropriate instructional programs for special needs students, and poor relations with administrators and/or peer teachers.

These societal, organizational, and role-related sources of stress are interrelated and cumulative. For example, the poor public image of schools can result in lower funding levels. Lower funding levels make it necessary to reduce the number of teaching positions and to increase class sizes. Increased class sizes require teachers to meet the educational needs of a more diverse group of students. Each step in this chain of events makes teaching more stressful.

Levels of Stress

The results of our studies utilizing the *Maslach Burnout Inventory* indicated that on the average teachers experienced only low to moderate levels of burnout. Since averages can be deceiving, participants' responses were analyzed further to identify those teachers for whom stress was more of a problem. The following trends emerged: (a) Male teachers perceived teaching to be more stressful than female teachers; (b) secondary teachers perceived teaching as more stressful than elementary teachers; and (c) beginning, less experienced teachers perceived teaching as more stressful than veteran teachers. Less stress was experienced by teachers in healthy school organizations as well as by those in school settings where role conflict was minimized and teachers' needs for esteem and self-actualization were satisfied.

Coping with Stress

Efforts to alleviate teacher burnout must be directed toward particular sources of stress. Societal sources of stress are difficult to combat. Educators are fortunate that recently the public has adopted a more positive and supportive attitude toward education, thus reducing some teacher stress. As additional resources are provided to improve the quality of education, consideration must be given to alleviating sources of teacher stress when making changes in the organization of a school and its programs. Despite such efforts, teaching will continue to be a stressful occupation and attention also must be devoted to reducing role-related sources of stress. A broad range of strategies is available for dealing with role-related stress, including meditation, physical exercise, and time management, to name only a few. The key in reducing role-related stress is for the teacher to identify the technique which is most effective for alleviating a specific type of stress. While some may benefit from exercise, others may benefit from time management. Also, while exercise may be effective in alleviating the tension resulting from discipline problems, time management may be more appropriate in dealing with the stress of completing end-of-year reports. For these reasons, effective stress management programs must expose teachers to a variety of stress reduction techniques.

See also Teacher Professionalism; Teacher Satisfaction; Time Management.

—Edward F. Iwanicki
University of Connecticut

References

Anderson, H.B.G., & Iwanicki, E.F. (1984). "Teacher motivation and its relationship to burnout." *Educational Administration Quarterly, 20*(2), 109-32.

Gmelch, W.H. (Ed.). (1983). "Coping with stress" [Special issue]. *Theory into Practice, 22*(1).

Maslach, C., & Jackson, S. (1981). *Maslach burnout inventory manual* (Research ed.). Palo Alto, CA: Consulting Psychologists Press.

TEACHER STRIKES

For maximum effectiveness a strike management plan must be developed and instituted before the strike begins. This plan should consist of effective prevention strategies as well as methods for coping with work interruptions. The first step toward prevention is understanding why teachers strike.

While most school officials probably would not like to think that their actions or inactions could contribute to a decision by teachers to strike, the following factors if present could contribute, over time, to the development of an atmosphere in which teachers may feel that a strike is necessary: (a) failure to hear employee concerns; (b) insufficient or inconsistent documentation of teacher misbehavior when moving to reprimand or dismiss a teacher; (c) disparaging or reacting negatively to union representatives or teachers; (d) withholding or resisting requests by teachers for information in their personnel files; (e) flaunting authority or power; (f) leaving the impression of secretive, unfair, or arbitrary decision making (g) failure to compromise or settle legitimate teacher grievances at the earliest possible stage; or (h) stalemate in negotiations.

To prevent teacher unrest that could lead to a strike, administrators must first work diligently to solve legitimate grievances and/or problems affecting teachers. This means the district must make a conscientious effort to work with teachers and the union throughout the year, not just during negotiations. Regular meetings of the principal and teachers can be an effective technique to diffuse problems before they become major issues.

Second, the district must negate union solidarity efforts by satisfying teachers' safety and esteem needs before they can be exploited. It is rare to find an effective school at the epicenter of a strike. If a job action does occur, the satisfied teachers will be late in joining and halfhearted in their support; some may not even honor the strike. To achieve this teacher loyalty, the principal must be highly visible and must have earned teacher confidence and respect. The principal must also create a "students first" climate by establishing that "negotiations are taking place elsewhere between the union and the district, but in our building we are going to have school and let the negotiators argue the issues."

Third, the district must give teachers information that will prevent rumors; a district may want to use both formal and informal systems to provide teachers with accurate information. The formal system, to be used only after negotiations cease to be effective, includes in-district memoranda from the superintendent to teachers detailing the status of negotiations; television and newspaper reporters are given information at a press conference. The informal system is one of "leaks" and behind-the-scenes conversations between district administrators trusted by teachers and teacher leaders not involved in negotiations. These avenues, to be effective, must provide scrupulously accurate inside information.

If all fails and a strike is in the offing, administrators must remember that normally calm, considerate teachers may, in the heat of a strike, become recalcitrant and demanding. Consequently, the first rule in developing a strike-management plan is to prepare for the worst but respond only as severely as the situation demands.

When developing a plan, the district must first and foremost retain a law firm that has successful experience in resolving school-district labor disputes; administrators should follow the lawyers' advice. This is important because the local school attorney is usually not prepared to cope with the dynamics of these potentially highly volatile situations.

Second, with the assistance of legal counsel, a written discription of the responsibilities of every administrator and board member should be prepared. This description should include a list of the most important do's and don'ts. Once the description has been completed, it should be reviewed with the administrators and members of the board of education.

Third, implement the plan at the first sign of an organized job action. Do not get behind in the game!

Fourth, keep the schools open. For strike-related reasons as well as to maintain state aid, the schools should continue to operate. This will require hiring substitutes and getting them safely in and out of school buildings.

Fifth, continue to negotiate in good faith to resolve the strike. Even-handed, professional conduct by the administration will do much to reassure the community and break teacher solidarity.

Sixth, prepare to address problems resulting from the strike. There are likely to be teacher-to-teacher, teacher-to-administration, and other after-strike hostilities that must be defused as quickly as possible. This takes special training and sensivity on the part of the principal.

In summary, a school climate where administrators value teachers as professional colleagues is the best available defense against strikes. However, there are times when factors outside the control of the school board and administrative team will override all preventive measures and allow or cause a strike to occur. In such cases, the advice of competent legal counsel, a good strike-management plan, and continued good-faith discussions to resolve disputed issues are the best weapons for achieving resolution.

See also Collective Bargaining; Conflict Resolution; Human Relations; Problem Identification.

—Robert Thompson
Lamar University

Reference

Fletcher, M.R., Herring, J.D., & Pole, A.D. (1979, June). *Management procedure and anticipated work stoppages.* (ERIC Reproduction Service No. ED 176 422).

TEACHER TENURE

The concepts of teacher tenure and continuing contracts have been a part of the education legal landscape since the early years of the twentieth century. However, like school finance, discipline, desegregation, and many other educational issues, tenure has been a source of controversy for many years.

The public currently believes that the majority of public school problems relates to poor teaching and that tenure laws protect incompetent teachers and inhibit improvement. At the same time, the professional teachers' associations (NEA and AFT) defend the need for contractual tenure provisions on the basis of (a) job security, (b) employment stability, and (c) academic freedom.

Definition of Tenure

Webster's New Collegiate Dictionary defines tenure as "a status granted after a trial period to a teacher protecting him from summary dismissal." As defined in this article, tenure pertains only to the elementary and secondary public school classroom teachers of America.

Teacher tenure has developed a technical meaning in school law that refers to indefinite or permanent employment from year-to-year under certain conditions. There is no common law involved. The tenure status of a teacher, therefore, depends upon the provisions of the particular state tenure law under which he or she is employed.

There are two types of tenure: by law or contract. A definite tenure law will include, among other things, provisions regarding permanent status, dismissal, and due process provisions. Generally, teacher tenure laws accomplish three goals. They (a) specify that a teacher is entitled to permanent employment status after the successful completion of a probationary period (two to five years, depending on the state); (b) list specific reasons for which tenured teachers can be dismissed; and (c) outline procedures which are designed to protect the tenured teachers' rights.

History of Tenure

The first tenure law was passed in New Jersey in 1909, some twenty-three years after the establishment of the Federal Civil Service Commission.

By 1918, seven states, plus the District of Columbia, had teacher tenure laws and by 1944, 44 states had tenure laws. In the remaining four states, a continuing contract required teachers to be informed in writing by a specified date (normally April 1) that their contracts would not be renewed. If they were not so notified, they were hired automatically for another year.

By the early 1960s, only four states—Mississippi, South Carolina, Utah, and Vermont—were without tenure laws.

In the 1970s, teacher tenure came under heavy attack. Its opponents tried, in about half the states, to repeal or weaken tenure laws. However, none was rescinded, and very little change has occurred in state tenure laws in the past decade.

The Tenure Debate

The tenure debate usually intensifies during times of teacher surplus. Tenure laws are criticized for a number of reasons: (a) They give teachers greater job security than other groups of employees possess; (b) once adopted, they are very difficult to change; and (c) they make it nearly impossible to weed out incompetent teachers. Proponents of tenure recoil with horror at the thought of schools without teacher tenure. They conjecture several scenarios to illustrate their concerns: (a) A return to the "spoils" systems where the actions of even the most well-intentioned administrators could breed timidity of thought and action among many classroom teachers whose basic need is for job security; (b) adversarial and divisive relationships fostered among professionals as collective bargaining, in the absence of state tenure statutes, intervenes to ensure due process and protection; (c) morale problems and factionalism which will inhibit cooperative efforts and shared responsibilities; (d) the loss of a stable, yet flexible, mechanism for attracting and retaining qualified teachers; (e) high teacher turnover which will in turn be a deterrent and disruptive force to planned change and curriculum development; and (f) the greatly decreased motivation of a teaching staff to participate in professional growth activities in an institutional setting that ignores their basic need for job security.

Emergence of Contract Tenure

A number of large teachers' organizations have negotiated tenure clauses into their collective bargaining agreements in the last ten years. This has led some opponents of statutory tenure to conclude that the trend toward contract tenure precludes the need for the statutory variety. They point to protections for teachers that the courts have drawn from constitutional amendments.

However, the proponents of state tenure statutes point out that in many areas of the country strong bargaining units do not exist and that the gaps in protection of teachers would be very significant if left to local unions.

Concluding Remarks

Teacher tenure is not an unconditional guarantee of employment; rather it is a statement grounded in law that protects the employee against termination where there are no substantial grounds for dismissal. The courts have ruled that there is no vested right to public employment as long as the termination of a contract is not in violation of the exercise of one's constitutional rights.

Tenured teachers may be terminated, but the procedures for such termination are specified in state statutes and in most cases are explicit. These statutes require due process considerations for the employee, including a written statement of the cause or causes for termination, advisement of the witnesses against him or her, opportunity to be heard, an impartial hearing board, a written statement of the findings, conclusions and recommendations, and advice concerning the teacher's right to further appeal.

Many administrators claim that tenure procedures are so legalistic and cumbersome that virtually nothing can be done with incompetent teachers. Other experts agree that tenure causes the most trouble when coupled with poor evaluation and supervision procedures.

See also Collective Bargaining; Rights: Teachers' and Students'; Teacher Dismissal; Teacher Professionalism.

—Kenneth McKinley
Oklahoma State University

References

Cambron-McCabe, N.H. (1983). "Procedural due process." In *Legal issues in public school employment*. Paper presented at the meeting of the National School Boards Association, Miami Beach, FL.

Chenoweth, R.L. (1979, April). *Will your due process procedure keep you out of court*. Paper presented at the meeting of the National school Boards Association, Miami Beach, FL.

Palker, P. (1980). "Tenure: Do we need it." *Teacher, 97*(8), 36-40.

TEACHERS, BEGINNING

The term "beginning teacher" generally applies to graduates of four-year teacher preparation institutions who are certified by the appropriate licensing agency and employed by school systems, private schools, day care, or other educational institutions.

Profile of Beginning Teachers

Major issues concerning beginning teachers include the recruitment of qualified education majors by colleges and universities, especially in the areas of science and mathematics; the provision of adequate compensation for beginning teachers; the recruitment and retention of qualified minorities by school systems; and the provision of career opportunities for classroom teachers as they advance beyond the beginning stages.

A beginning teacher can offer enthusiasm, new ideas, and professional competence to a school faculty, especially when offered administrative and peer support during the initial years of employment.

As a group, however, recent education majors have performed poorly on standardized tests of academic achievement and have had low class rank. The most competent beginning teachers are those most likely to leave the profession within five years of employment. College graduates trained to teach science and mathematics are taking higher paying jobs in business and industry, causing a shortage in the classroom of certified teachers in these areas. Competent women and minority students, formerly a large part of the teacher pool, are finding greater employment opportunities in nonteaching fields than ever before. A large number of World War II era teachers are reaching retirement age, and with enrollments in schools of education having declined due to the low pay and status afforded to teachers, a teacher shortage is predicted. Additionally, in many areas, demographics indicate a "baby boomlet." These combined facts have caused many state legislatures and local school districts to seek new ways to attract more and better quality teaching candidates for their school systems. Perceived remedies to teacher shortages, such as higher salaries and better working conditions, including lower class sizes and opportunities for advancement within the teaching profession, have spawned ideas ranging from merit pay, career ladders, and extended employment to lateral entry plans.

Common Problems

Beginning teachers sometimes find themselves ill-prepared for their teaching assignments. It is postulated that problems may occur because beginning teachers are undertrained for the demands of their work; they have not been selected for employment on the basis of skill in teaching and have received general training which may not apply to their specific teaching assignments. Beginning teachers may have difficulty in applying generalized training to concrete situations. Some beginning teachers receive little or no on-the-job supervision and receive the least desired student and extra-duty assignments. Trauma experienced in the first year can affect the level of effectiveness which that teacher is able to achieve and sustain over the years and can influence a decision whether to continue in the teaching profession.

Research summarizing fifteen studies done over a fifteen-year period reported that beginning teachers expressed concerns and anxieties in the five following areas: (a) their ability to maintain discipline in the classroom; (b) students' liking of them; (c) their knowledge of subject matter; (d) what to do in the case they make mistakes or run out of material; and (e) how to relate personally to other faculty members, the system, and parents.

Helping the Beginning Teacher

Helping the beginning teacher achieve success is a combined responsibility involving university and school system personnel. An ongoing support network involving college professors, principals, supervisors and master teachers must be crafted to offer assistance while, at the same time, not overwhelming the beginning teacher with additional burdens. In-service programs involving teacher mentors, reduced classloads, extra-duty assignments, favorable class schedules, and constant feedback involving a nonevaluative counseling environment can all serve to assist a beginning teacher.

Whatever process is adopted, it is clear that beginning teachers are in a critical phase of their careers. Nurturing and support as well as ongoing training are needed. Success or failure of a beginning teacher can greatly affect the quality of service delivered in our schools. A teacher's success means that another high-level professional is in the classroom.

Boards of education, school administrators, teachers and college-level personnel should all participate in setting standards for the recruitment and selection of education majors, for the supervision and support of beginning teachers, and for the implementation of programs necessary for insuring a quality workforce for future generations of school children.

See also Staff Development; Teacher Selection; Teachers, Sources of Help for.

—Howard L. Sosne
Wayne County, North Carolina, Schools

References

Ryan, K. (1979). "Toward understanding the problem: At the threshold of the profession." In K. R. Howey and R. H. Bents (Eds.), *Toward meeting the needs of the beginning teacher* (pp. 35-52). Minneapolis: Midwest Teacher Corps Network.

TEACHERS, SOURCES OF HELP FOR

Teachers can be helped in many ways, through many sources. Perhaps the major reason why in-service training programs are often rated low on effectiveness by teachers is the tendency of planners to depend on too few sources, especially those known to have little appeal or impact on participants. Several sources of help for teachers will be presented and briefly discussed here.

Sources of Help

Fellow Teachers. Several recent studies have indicated that teachers value the contributions that other teachers can make to their professional growth. These benefits can come about in many ways, ranging from informal discussions in the teachers' lounge to highly organized and orchestrated arrangements for intervisitations, team teaching, and departmental or grade-level cooperative efforts.

The importance of the terms "organized" and "orchestrated" must be recognized; for example, intervisitation is much more likely to be productive if the visitor is assisted beforehand in developing observation skills and using reliable instruments. The process of developing such observation skills is, in itself, a source of help to teachers.

Team teaching, team research, and other cooperative arrangements can be mutually helpful to the participants, provided that the teams or cooperatives are carefully planned, organized, and supported, and not just "turned loose to do their thing." Even the best teachers can benefit from the stimulation, challenge, and novelty of working together, assisted by administrative and supervisory personnel.

Campus-Level Administrators. Although the question of whether a school principal can be both a manager and an instructional leader is still being debated, the evidence clearly indicates that many principals *do* work effectively in both roles. In most schools, where the principal has no assistant and there are no supervisors available at the district level, the principal has no alternative to serving as both manager and instructional leader, if both types of responsibility are to be met.

Assuming that principals—as well as assistant principals, if they are available—can handle management as well as instructional leadership tasks, this source of help to teachers is potentially an important one. Although teachers have revealed in several studies that, in general, they do not expect their principals to provide supervisory assistance, they *do* value the help principals can give by such means as reducing interruptions and paper work to a minimum, supporting the teachers in conflict situations, and "running a smooth school."

In addition to expecting their principals to be good managers, however, teachers also value more direct instructional assistance, *if it is truly helpful.* Although intrusive or nonhelpful interventions by principals are not welcomed by teachers, the efforts of principals who are skilled in instructional assistance are appreciated. These skills include observing instruction; working with teachers in analyzing and interpreting both observation data and teacher self-appraisal data; joint planning of growth activities; and monitoring, providing feedback, and evaluating growth activities.

District-Level Supervisors. Much of what was said above, concerning principals, could be repeated here. In addition, supervisors (or coordinators) working out of the central office have an added advantage of being in a somewhat less threatening role than the principal occupies as the chief evaluator of teacher performance. Although the line/staff distinction between principals and supervisors is not quite as clear as is often assumed, district-level supervisors do usually benefit from not being directly tied to the summative evaluation of teacher behavior. To the extent that this separation from summative evaluation exists, supervisors are free to provide helpful assistance. Although supervisory staffs are usually unrealistically small, they can specialize in supervision without being responsible for administering schools, as principals are.

Intermediate Unit Personnel. Most states now have organizational units between the local school districts and the state educational agency with a wide range of responsibilities that include the provision of in-service training for teachers. Such programs vary greatly, even within states, but one valuable contribution that such intermediate units can make to teacher growth is the offering of services that many small local school districts cannot afford. Even the teachers in large and wealthy districts often benefit from the variety of programs and services made available to them.

Teachers' Organizations. National, state, and local organizations for teachers also provide programs that can be useful to teachers. As with the intermediate units, the teachers' organizations can tap a wide range of resources not ordinarily available at the school or school district level. Although many associations' programs consist largely of speeches and discussions, other methods can also be employed and sometimes are.

Reading. The value of reading—as with every other potential source of help—depends on its quality and appropriateness. If these conditions are met, reading has certain advantages as a source of help for teachers: it is adaptable to individual needs, it is economical, and it is plentiful. Hence, although professional literature is not always highly stimulating, and the reader usually has no opportunity to interact with the reading material, the method can be valuable. It can be especially helpful as an introduction to, or as a supplement to, other growth activities.

University Programs. Most universities (and colleges) are, of course, in the business of providing in-service as well as pre-service education for teachers. Although the quality of courses and other offering varies greatly, even within institutions, this source of help for teachers can be an important one. A good course, for example, can contain a suitable mix of activities ranging from traditional methods such as reading, lecturing, and discussing to the use of cases, scenarios, individualized instructional packages, tutorials, research, laboratory exercises, simulation, human relations training, and many other possibilities. Each method has its own strengths and weaknesses, but a judicious combination can result in an exceedingly helpful experience for teachers or teachers-to-be. These same methods are available to other individuals and organizations that provide programs for teachers, including several discussed above.

Visits to Other Campuses. What was said previously about utilizing fellow teachers would apply here as well. By extending the range of possibilities to exemplary practices elsewhere, teachers can get additional help, and can also interact in a way that can make the experience mutually helpful. First-hand exposure to different practices in the context in which they occur can be more convincing than merely hearing or reading about them.

Planning with Care

Whatever the *sources* of help for teachers are in a given situation, some crucial aspects of their use must be considered. In addition to the matter of quality, which was stated previously, users should plan growth programs in logical, sequential, and purposeful ways. For example, logical steps might be the determination of (a) needs (knowledge, understanding, skill, attitudes, values); (b) the most appropriate delivery system for meeting the specified needs (reading, lecture, clinical supervision, etc.); (c) the most appropriate organizational arrangement for the selected methods (school district or service center workshop, university course, departmental study group, etc.); and (d) the best methods of evaluating effectiveness of the program (classroom observation, student test performance, teacher self-appraisal, etc.). Merely selecting activities on a basis of ready availability or convenience, without regard to the considerations stated above, is not likely to produce the desired results.

Relationships should also be considered. Interpersonal contacts are important to most people which suggests that companionship, collaboration, reinforcement, and support are essential ingredients in improvement programs. The favor with which teachers tend to regard help that they get from other teachers is probably due in part to the human relationships that enter into the interaction.

The complexities that permeate the process of effecting change in human beings are well known, but deliberate on-the-job growth can and does occur if the complexities are recognized and dealt with properly. Whatever the sources of help that are available or produced, the teacher should be heavily involved in the entire process.

See also Supervision, Clinical; Supervisory Personnel; Teachers, Beginning.

—Ken McIntyre
University of Texas

References

Glickman, C.D. (1985). *Supervision of instruction* (chaps. 14 & 15). Boston: Allyn & Bacon.

Harris, Ben M. (1980). *Improving staff performance through in-service education* (chaps. 6, 7, & 8). Boston: Allyn & Bacon.

McCleary, L.E., & McIntyre, K.E. (1972). "Competency development and university methodology." *Bulletin of the National Association of Secondary School Principals, 56*(362), 53-68.

TEACHING APPROACHES, FUTURE

A century-long look at classroom instruction reveals barely detectable shifts in teaching practices. In blueprinting the classroom as a workplace, one is reminded of Roger Barker's contention that settings seemingly have "plans for their inhabitants." Historically, it would appear that the physical properties of our nation's schools, together with society's demand for mass, compulsory education, have essentially circumscribed what has occurred in classroom settings.

In designing classroom practices to fit the physical surroundings of the classroom, teachers have sought out those tools and practices which have met their tests of efficiency: simple, versatile, reliable, and durable. Additionally, they have sought out technologies which have held the greatest promise for solving problems defined by teachers. Two-way interactive TV is an example of a technology which is likely to be incorporated into routine teacher practice. It is an efficient, uncomplicated methodology for transmitting knowledge, while preserving teacher dominance and enhancing teacher-pupil interaction. Moreover, two-way interactive TV is likely to be perceived by educators as an accessible tool for addressing the twin goals of education in a democratic society: equity and excellence. Specifically, in isolated areas such as Little Fork-Big Falls, Minnesota, the issues of academic equity and excellence in rural America forge a compelling concern in search of technologically-creative solutions.

Today, educators are being reminded that if learners are to acquire and nourish the skills and competencies needed to satisfy the demands of tomorrow's corporate culture, they will require classrooms which provide opportunities for cognitive and psychological growth. Peer evaluation of student writing, for example, offers learners rich opportunities for observing how their writing produces certain effects in others. Additionally, collaborative problem-solving activities engender a sense of group inclusion, acceptance, support, trust, and reality testing. Because learning is so heavily social, initiating and sustaining student skills related to working with others, in explaining, hearing, and trusting, is likely to become the key to developing a successful learning environment during a period of social and technological transition.

In contrast, teaching practices—such as computer-assisted instruction—which displace, interrupt, or minimize relationships are likely to be de-emphasized. Data related to the low completion rates for distance learning via computer, for example, pinpoint the difficulty of sustaining student motivation and participation in the absence of a teacher, learning group, and social structure. In essence, while information-related technologies are likely to reroute historical patterns of access to knowledge, "learning without being taught" is unlikely to emerge as a dominant theme in tomorrow's wired classrooms.

Despite their current political attractiveness in suburban schools, personal computers are as likely to displace the teacher as a primary agent of instruction as the telescope was to displace the astronomer. When Thomas Edison argued in 1913 that "books will soon be obsolete in schools," he failed to draw the issues related to the accessibility and cost-effectiveness of textbooks versus films. Pointedly, educators who decry the "dreadful state of current instructional software" often anticipate that developers will risk substantial capital outlays to fill curricular niches at pedestrian prices. That this did not happen with film is perhaps the best predictor that it will not occur with software.

In contrast, there is an abundance of exemplary applications software: word processors, data bases, telecommunications, statistical-analysis, spreadsheets, graphics-design, and laboratory-instrumentation programs. Using these available tools, personal computers may be viewed less as an extension of the teacher and more as an intellectual companion for the student. As a result, classroom applications are endless in their diversity and inventiveness. Moreover, because generic software tools appeal to a variety of markets within the broader culture, their developmental costs are spread widely enough to make them potentially cost-effective for schools.

Teaching for tomorrow will likely require that educators develop rich opportunities for youth to confront and cope with the demands of global awareness by immersing students in a diversity of thought, values, beliefs, and cultures. Classroom discussions of international events provide poignant opportunities for promoting moral growth and preventing global catastrophe by focusing upon such issues as national versus individual sovereignty. Additionally, cultivating multilingual talents as well as multicultural understandings will engender a vibrant sense of community and global interdependence.

As society evolves toward an electronic world market, the political and economic destiny of nations will likely hinge on a redefinition of time, space, and scale. Multinational corporations, with worldwide communications systems, may well reshape the nation-state mode of government. Relatedly, through their power to create a world system of labor, they may well insist upon universally-required information-literacy experiences in the world's classrooms. Just as the invention of the printing press in the fifteenth century precipitated demands for universal literacy, contemporary technological innovations appear destined to extend the literacy metaphor.

In the classrooms of tomorrow, teachers are likely to nurture problem-finding and problem-solving behaviors which are anchored in a series of familiar search skills: the ability to read and follow directions; frame questions as part of a presearch strategy; spell and/or estimate using wildcard characters; understand sets, subsets, and relationships; differentiate between general and specific; understand the appropriate use of a controlled language such as Library of Congress subject headings; differentiate alphanumeric characters; employ synonyms and antonyms; and enter electronic data efficiently. In the context of a worldwide economy, however, information-literacy skills will need to be embedded in an idealized perspective: the belief that a humane society must provide for competing ways of life.

Max Weber has contended that authority can be fractured into three components: traditional, rational-legal, and charismatic. Historically, tradition has functioned as the taproot of teacher authority in the classroom. In recent years, school policy and classroom practice have been shaped by legal principles. Predictably, the curricular chimes in the classroom of tomorrow are likely to sound a gentle charismatic call to teachers to be in charge: physically, intellectually, and spiritually. Rather than relying on rules and aggressive displays of manipulative control, tomorrow's teachers are likely to manage their classes through charisma. Moreover, tomorrow's charismatic teachers will likely rediscover an ancient truth: Self-discipline is rooted in relevant tasks, not in seductive praise, homicidal glances, or ossified discipline codes.

In essence, the overarching mission of life in the classroom is learning how to learn. Instructionally, teachers are confronted with a recurring refrain: Which methods advance which educational goals? Alfred North Whitehead contended that the "best education is to be found in gaining the utmost information from the simplest apparatus." Martin Buber countered that in the ultimate sense it is relationship which educates!

See also Computer-Assisted Instruction; Multicultural Education; Technology Education; Television in Instruction.

—Richard F. Bowman, Jr.
Moorhead State University

References

Bowman, R.F. (1985). "Teaching in tomorrow's classrooms." *The Educational Forum, 49*, 241-48.

Cuban, L. (1986). *Teaching and machines* (chap. 3). New York: Teachers College Press.

TEAM TEACHING

A definition of team teaching should not be a rigid definition since team teaching is not a rigid program. A team teaching program is and must be an evolving program; that is, methods and procedures will change from time to time. Therefore, team teaching exists when two or more teachers regularly, purposefully, and deliberately work together in planning, instructing, and evaluating learning experiences.

Teaming can be achieved through large-group presentations, small-group instruction, and/or through programs of individual study. Perhaps the greatest gain from using this eclectic teaching approach results when the student has the opportunity to imagine, to contemplate, to analyze, to synthesize, to judge, and to create ideas.

Although there are almost as many variations as there are teams, all team teaching is based on the premise that teachers can accomplish more working together than working alone. Despite the many variations, team teaching can be classified as either hierarchic or synergetic. The hierarchic team can be likened to a pyramid with the team leader at the apex and master teachers just below, with regular teachers at the base assisted by student interns and teacher aides. The synergetic team is formed by two or more teachers willing to cooperate as professional equals. This would include (a) an associate type of arrangement, wherein there is no designated leader, but leadership emerges as a result of interactions among individuals and given situations, or (b) the coordinated team type, wherein there is not joint responsibility for a common group of students, but which includes joint planning by two or more teachers who are teaching the same curriculum to different groups of students. Synergetic teams may be developed to work within conventional facilities and schedules.

Team teaching developed as a means of correcting faults that prevailed in instructional arrangements in our nation's schools. The need to develop a team of teachers with differentiated status and talent was evident. A more efficient use of human and material resources and the need to free teachers from restricted classroom situations by offering them a chance for meaningful interaction with peers spearheaded the team teaching movement.

Team teaching provides teachers with the vehicle to be more aware of student needs, especially since there is more than one teacher observing and teaching the individual student. Thus, the student can associate with several teachers. As a result, these teachers can objectively and subjectively use the holistic approach in the assessment of each student. The emphasis upon the team reinforces the concept that more and better planning for students would occur.

There is a certain degree of accountability for which each teacher is responsible, and, therefore, teaming can succeed for all. With better planning, curricular needs of each student can be more fully met; slower learners can work at their highest potential, and the accelerated learner can be stimulated and challenged to new heights. Opportunities for teachers to concentrate upon their academic expertise (teacher specialization) as well as to expand other areas of broad knowledge in related fields abound when teaming is initiated. Exposure to varying types of teacher personalities, teaching styles, teaching techniques, and a plethora of multisensory materials can be invaluable for the neophyte team member as well as for the experienced educator.

Certain individuals outside the team are important in making a team successful. The support of school administrators is especially critical in scheduling common preparation periods, helping with organizational problems, explaining the new team approach to parents and district personnel, and, most importantly, maintaining an open and supportive atmosphere where teachers feel free to take chances. Administrators should be involved in planning the team approach from its inception.

The greatest obstacle with team teaching is getting teachers to cooperate with one another. Conflicts arise when people with different teaching methods and personalities are working together. Another roadblock which may delay the teaming is the insecurity of teachers. They do not understand the team teaching concept and would rather the way they are teaching because they are comfortable with it. Admittedly, team teaching is not for everyone.

Teaming is not merely a label to be used interchangeably. It is a concept that embodies an action approach, group psychology, and a variety of methods. It is a concept that allows teachers and students to share their talents and demonstrates that teaching are two sides of the same coin. "Be not the first by whom the new are tried, nor yet the last to lay the old aside." Education refers to the continual process whereby new things produce advancements in learning. The same can be said for technology.

—Robert Di Sibio
D'Youville College

The preparation of team teaching, Washington, for inter-

cassette recorder's counter to find a specific point directors do not have the advantage of being able to large-group viewing. This advantage of the development of such systems that project television room wall. Systems also primary computer screen displays project computer screen displays capability is useful for computer

The VHS system is entrenched in come from developments in 8 mm, which is more compact and technology is also advancing. Videodiscs store images and project them more have the disadvantage of being expensive to

development is videotex, which is a for broadcasting text and graphics. useful for distance education and for information that needs frequent updating.

Preparing for the Future

The two major influences on implementation of "information age" technology in schools are its vocational possibilities and educational possibilities. Concurrent trends to viewing the computer as a subject of study and as a tool for study raise the question of what kinds of preparation for students and staff are most useful.

A consensus exists among economists and the business community that no great increase is likely in the number of people directly employed by the high technology industry in the coming decade. This category includes engineers, programmers, and some scientists. Many jobs, however, will demand the use of technology for work-related tasks. Other jobs, too, are expected to be restructured because of advances in technological tools. Students thus need to be prepared in ways that anticipate changes in career structures.

Another activity being restructured because of advances in computer applications is learning itself. The electronic technologies have novel, powerful ways of making information available to students. For example, machines can emulate human reasoning in certain domains. They can be designed to formulate and present problems, analyze the strategies of someone solving the problems, and adjust their feedback in an instructive fashion.

Employers and educators have concluded that instruction in general problem-solving and critical-thinking skills as opposed to merely "basic" skills and machine familiarity is vital in preparing students for future workforce requirements. At the same time, the rapid rate of change in the new computer technologies has meant that educational programs for teachers and students must be designed to be flexible enough to accommodate new technological developments.

There are few tested models for such programs. Those that are being introduced into schools and school systems are basically experimental and very diverse. Some features of successful programs for both students and teachers are beginning to be identified, but no one program can serve as a complete model. In fact, research suggests that local experimentation in program design is a useful avenue for administrators to pursue.

Classroom Issues

Equity. Analysts thus far agree that equity of access and of use of technology among students is important for career preparation, for utilizing the technology investment in the best way, and for the future of the educational system. To insure that all students experience the full range of technology available, the present trend in schools is to move from "computer literacy" courses and from the use of computers to reinforce basic skills towards broader program goals. Good programs that emphasize tool functions of computers, for example, as writing aids, data organizers, and spreadsheets, and the motivational features of technology are most likely to integrate technology into a range of subjects, to provide access for all students, and to offer greater support of comprehensive reasoning skills.

Organization. Integrating technology in classes of science, social studies, and mathematics demands an analysis of classroom organization patterns. Computers are found most often in lab settings. Using tool software in content areas means that communication between computer coordinators and classroom teachers must be facilitated. Computers are also often used on movable carts and in classrooms, but in fewer numbers than are found in a laboratory. Low numbers of computers in classrooms encourage small group learning and schedules of rotating use. Teachers need assistance and support in planning schedules.

Assessment. How best to assess the use of technology in schools is not known at present. Nonetheless, pressures of accountability develop when technology programs are justified to communities. Some steps an administrator can take to ensure meaningful evaluation of programs are to become personally acquainted with the program aims so that useful support for the program is facilitated; arrange parent education or participation in technology use so that realistic expectations can be established; develop program goals in conjunction with parents, teachers, and staff developers; and, develop goals that are deemed feasible and that are reviewed for appropriateness.

Teacher Preparation

Although states vary in their requirements of teachers concerning technology education, teachers across the country have demonstrated their willingness to learn technological skills. Resources for teacher training, however, have been less available than resources for equipment. Training most often depends on local district or state allocations. It is important that administrators and school board members insist on adequate resources for this component of a school technology program.

Surveys show that successful teacher-training programs are organized to be voluntary, relevant to classroom needs, and distributed over extended periods of time. Training may be made available at a variety of sites, including the school, the district or regional office, or local higher education institutions.

Incentives for training are important to provide. Often, salary credit or credentialling incentives can be arranged. Release time and course credit may also be provided. One critical incentive and ingredient of success for the adoption and maintenance of technology lies in encouraging teachers' professionalism in this domain. This may be accomplished by insuring joint teacher/administrator participation in the design of training, in courseware design, and in courseware selection.

Teachers need support from administrators, colleagues, and experts for implementation of technology programs. Adequate support means being provided time and resources necessary for training, for preparing materials, and for reworking curriculum objectives.

Support from local industry for a school educational technology program may be possible as well. Local businesses may provide hardware and training directly or indirectly; technical firms may also be induced to create summer apprenticeships for school staff and students.

Decision Making

Although districts are trying to prepare teachers and students quickly for new developments in technology, top-down, large-scale decisions about programs are a risk since they can quickly result in unadaptive implementation. A five-year district implementation plan, for example, is likely to need changing. In order to insure flexible, equitable use of technology in education, administrators need to encourage collaboration at all levels of the school system, with attention to describing the particular needs of the student population and the particular adaptations that district teachers have envisioned for technology.

See also Career Education; Computer Literacy; Educational Goals and Objectives; Support Staff, Professional.

—Laura M. W. Martin
Bank Street College of Education

References

Bennett, R.E. (Ed.). (in press). *Planning and evaluating computer education programs.* Columbus, OH: Merrill.

Shavelson, R.J., Winkler, J.D., Stasz, C., Feibel, W., Robyn, A.E., & Shaha, S. (1984). *"Successful" teachers' patterns of microcomputer-based mathematics and science instruction* (N-2170-NIE/RC). Report prepared for the National Institute of Education. Santa Monica, CA: Rand.

Sheingold, K., Martin, L.M.W., & Endreweit, M.E. (1985). *Preparing urban teachers for the technological future* (Technical Report No. 36). New York: Bank Street College of Education, Center for Children and Technology.

TELEVISION IN INSTRUCTION

The development of the portable videocassette recorder other equipment has created exciting new opportunit the use of television in instruction. Effective use equipment, however, requires understanding techr options, types of video curriculum materials, an priate instructional applications. Each of these to cussed in this article.

Television Technology

Videocassette recorders have several ad 16 millimeter film projectors as devices to images. They are easier to operate and main used to record as well as play back vir Recordings can be made from off-th (assuming copyright is not violated) or by production. A camera is necessary to d videocassette recorder does not have a c be inexpensively installed. Affordable t low professional-looking tapes to be cr students.

The teacher can use a videoca and fast forward/backward controls in a video production. Film pro capacity, but they do have the a project onto a big screen for lar vantage is disappearing wi videocassette recorder and tel onto large screens or an ordin have been developed that pr onto large screens. This ca education.

Although the half-inc schools, competition may millimeter video technolc portable. Videodisc techr store many more vide sharply, but have the produce.

Another recent television technology Videotex may prov transmission of inf

Since video technology is constantly changing, educators considering purchase of video equipment should get expert advice. They also should establish a maintenance program to preserve their equipment and tapes. Otherwise, oxide from videotapes can build up on a VCR's components and damage tapes played on it. The maintenance program also should include training of teachers and students in the proper use of video systems.

Video Curriculum Materials

There is a wealth of instructional videotapes for most curriculum subjects, especially the physical and social sciences, the arts, physical education, and foreign language study. They range from brief productions of 15 minutes or less to entire courses of instruction. In addition, video productions originally developed for other purposes, such as theatrical films and documentaries, are available for school use. School librarians have catalogs such as *PBS Video: The Best of Public Television* for accessing the entire range of video materials available for purchase, rental, or loan. Teachers also can make their own video productions, or videotapes of trips related to the subject they teach, for example.

Some developers are using new video technology to create innovative instructional materials. One such innovation is a videodisc simulation that plays musical pieces with one instrument missing so that students can tune their instrument and play along with world-class orchestras. Another is inquiry-type simulations on video that enable students to "perform" science experiments that would be too dangerous, expensive, or time-consuming to perform in a classroom.

Instructional Applications

Television sets and videocassette recorders are becoming increasingly compact and portable. Therefore, they can be used in a wide variety of settings, including classrooms, media centers, and homes.

Sesame Street, probably the most widely used instructional video production, was designed for broadcasting into the homes of low-income preschool children. Similarly, many universities have "campus of the air" programs in which students earn advanced degree-credit by watching video classes at home. Some professors assign students the task of viewing video productions at a media center on a self-scheduled basis.

Television has already proven its value in distance education. Students who live in remote areas, such as parts of Alaska and Australia, routinely view instructional video productions on videotape or from closed-circuit and satellite broadcasts.

Most elementary and secondary educators do not make instructional use of television outside the classroom, even though students spend many hours watching television. (By the end of high school, students spend more hours each week watching television than they spend attending school.) Educators can take advantage of students' attraction to television by lending instructionally-relevant video productions to students to view on a home or library videocassette recorder.

According to one survey, television is used by more than one half of the school teachers in this country. Elementary teachers, who are the heaviest users, tend to rely on public television productions. Secondary teachers rely predominantly on instructional videotapes. Educators find that television is an especially helpful learning tool for handicapped students who have difficulty comprehending text and lecture presentations.

Television is being used increasingly to train teachers and other education personnel. For example, many colleges of education train preservice teachers by having them conduct practice lessons that are videotaped and replayed to provide feedback. This process, sometimes called microteaching, is of proven value in helping teachers learn new teaching skills.

Television also is becoming an important tool in inservice education. Many professional organizations in education make videotapes of new techniques and trends available to their members. Also, school districts should consider making a library of tapes of its teachers conducting different types of lessons. The library would give teachers a convenient way to "visit" each other's classrooms and share ideas.

Instructional Functions

Contemporary instructional theorists believe that students' learning is facilitated if instruction follows a sequence of steps. Teachers should plan carefully how to fit television into such sequences.

The first step typically is to create an anticipatory set, which has the purpose of focusing the student's attention on the learning that is to take place. Showing a relevant, stimulating video production is an excellent way to create such a set.

Subsequent steps involve providing the learning objectives, informational input, and modeling. Objectives and information can be provided by the teacher or by a textbook, but television is an unparalleled medium for modeling, which means presenting a visual representation of the concept or skill to be learned. Much of the curriculum involves things that exist outside of the classroom and that are inherently visual (e.g., the culture of another country, historical events, the laws of physics and behavior). Video productions can bring these things directly into the classroom.

Television has limited application to the next steps of checking students' understanding and providing guided practice. An exception is the learning of physical and expressive skills, such as those involved in acting or playing a sport. In these instances the instructor can make a videotape of the learner and replay it in order that the learner can observe his or her performance.

Television also has limited application to the final steps of instruction, namely, providing independent practice and closure. The most relevant application is to situations in which students are being encouraged to develop their creative expression. Teachers can assign students to develop video productions (e.g., enactments of historical events or episodes in a novel, or "video posters" to advertise upcoming events) that stimulate them to develop higher levels of thinking and creativity.

Conclusion

Television was first used in schools to show complete network or closed-circuit lessons. This application did not work well because many teachers resented being replaced by a television monitor, and the broadcasts often were at inconvenient times. Recent advances in instructional theory show that television is best used as one element in a total instructional plan under teacher control. Today's teacher, drawing on the distinctive capabilities of video technology, can provide more powerful learning experiences for students than ever before.

See also Instructional Objectives; Staff Development; Teaching Approaches, Future.

—Meredith D. Gall
University of Oregon
—Barrie B. Bennett
Center for Education,
Edmonton, Alberta

References

Clark, R.E., & Salmon, G. (1986). Media in teaching. In M. C. Wittrock (Ed.), *Handbook of research on teaching* (3rd ed., pp. 464-78). New York: Macmillan.

Fuller, F.F., & Manning. B. (1973). "Self-conceptualization reviewed: A conceptualization for video playback in teacher education." *Review of Educational Research, 43,* 469-528.

Gagne, R.M., & Briggs, L.J. (1979). *Principles of instructional design* (2nd ed., chap. 10). New York: Holt, Rinehart & Winston.

TEST SCORE RELIABILITY AND VALIDITY

Educational decisions are made daily on the basis of test scores. In order to assure that these decisions are appropriate and based on accurate data, educators need to attend to the issues of test score reliability and validity.

Reliability

Reliability is a measure of the stability of test scores. Suppose a test is administered to the same group of examinees on successive days at the same hour with no intervening instruction in the area tested. If the test scores are highly stable (or reliable), each examinee will get the same or close to the same score on both administrations. The closer the pairs of scores are, the more stable or reliable they are over time, twenty-four hours in this case.

Now consider two different tests constructed by drawing items randomly from a large pool of items all covering the same topic or area of instruction. If these are administered to the same group, one immediately after the other, the score difference for an examinee from one test to the other will be partly due to differing test content. Then the closer the pairs of scores are, the more stable or reliable they are with respect to random selection from the item pool.

Of course, differing test content or the passage of time are not the only reasons or even the main reasons that examinees' scores differ from one administration to another. Transitory examinee characteristics, such as feeling better or worse than usual, have their effect, as do administration conditions, such as noise level, temperature, lighting, and ventilation. Evaluation of reliability takes all effects into account, and it is usually not possible to know the relative contribution of each factor separately.

A reliability coefficient is a Pearson product-moment correlation coefficient between two sets of scores. Correlation coefficients range from -1 through 0 to +1, but negative values are not meaningful with respect to reliability. A coefficient of 0 means that there is no relationship between the two sets of scores. A coefficient of 1 would occur if all examinees got the same score on both administrations. Reliability coefficients (signified r_{xx}) may be evaluated (roughly) as follows:

r_{xx} = .90 or higher	Good reliability. Suitable for making decisions based on test scores about individual examinees.
r_{xx} = .80 to .89	Moderate reliability. Suitable for use in evaluating individual examinees along with other information.
r_{xx} = .60 to .79	Modest reliability. Suitable for evaluating a group based on the group's average score.
r_{xx} = .40 to .59	Doubtful reliability. May be satisfactory for tentative conclusions based on average score over a large number of examinees.

If a reliablity coefficient arises from two sets of scores on the same identical test, it is called a *test-retest coefficient*. When arising from two different tests drawn from the same item pool, it is called an *alternate-form reliability coefficient*.

In practice, more often than not, it is not feasible to administer a test twice to evaluate reliability. In this case, reliability coefficients can be estimated from responses to a single administration, provided nearly all examinees have time to finish the test. If the test items are scored either 0 or 1, the Kuder-Richardson formulas 20 and 21 (KR20 and KR21) may be used. KR21 is easier to calculate but is less accurate than KR20 if the items vary in difficulty. Coefficient alpha (Cronbach's alpha) is similar to KR20 but allows for varying numbers of points to be assigned for answers. Split-half reliability estimates are obtained by correlating scores from two halves of a test and adjusting the resulting coefficient upward to allow for the fact that it came from alternate forms only half as long as the actual test. Estimates from this method are subject to fluctuation, depending on which items happen to be in each half.

Note that in all of the above discussion, only scores were described as being more or less reliable. Tests *per se*, that is the instruments themselves, cannot be described in this way. A test may yield highly reliable scores under one set of circumstances and scores of low reliability under another. Factors to be considered in this regard are administration conditions, appropriateness of the test for the examinees, and examinee motivation and attitude. When these factors are unfavorable, the scores are likely to be less reliable than otherwise.

Validity

Validity like reliability is a characteristic of test scores, not of tests themselves. A set of scores is valid to the extent that correct inferences about the examinees may be made based on their scores. Such inferences are mainly of two types. The first type of inference is about how the examinee performs (or will perform) on some task such as another test, in school generally (e.g., grade-point average), or in some "real-life" situation. The second type of inference is about how much the examinee knows over a well-defined domain of knowledge. For either type of inference to be at least approximately correct, it is first necessary that the scores be sufficiently reliable. Obviously, if examinees' scores fluctuate wildly from one administration of a test to the next, inferences based on these scores are highly likely to be erroneous. On the other hand, high reliability does not guarantee validity. For example, highly reliable general vocabulary scores may be of little use for predicting reading comprehension scores in a specialized area.

The first approach to validity requires another set of scores or outcome measures on the same examinees who took the test for which score validity is to be evaluated. This is done by computing the Pearson product-moment correlation coefficient between the two sets of scores, which is then called a *validity coefficient*. The outcome measure is usually called the *criterion*. The test having scores which are being evaluated for validity is called the *predictor*. When two tests are used for the same purpose, for example, to evaluate achievement in high school social studies, this correlation should be relatively high. In contrast, if one set of scores represents academic ability, e.g., the verbal scores from the Scholastic Aptitude Tests, and the other set of scores is grade-point average in college, the correlation will be somewhat smaller.

Scores from a test may be more valid for one criterion than another. For example, IQ scores correlate more strongly with measures of academic achievement than with measures of mechanical aptitude. Nevertheless, some of the abilities measured by an IQ test do contribute to mechanical problem solving. Therefore, the correlation between scores on an IQ test and a mechanical-aptitude test should not be negligible if scores from both tests are reasonably valid. Validity coefficients (signified r_{xy}) may be evaluated (roughly) as follows:

r_{xy} = .90 or higher	Very high validity. The predictor could probably be substituted for the criterion for many purposes.
r_{xy} = .70 to .89	High validity. The predictor gives substantial information about likely criterion performance.
r_{xy} = .50 to .69	Moderate validity. The predictor gives some information about likely criterion performance.
r_{xy} = .30 to .49	Modest validity. Used in combination with other predictors, the predictor should increase prediction accuracy.
r_{xy} = less than .30	Negligible to slight validity. Nevertheless, such results may be meaningful for research outcomes or theory development.

The second type of inferences (about how much the examinees know in a given area) is usually evaluated by analysis of the content of the test. Hence, this kind of evidence is said to establish the degree of *content validity*. This approach to validity is appropriate for most criterion-referenced tests and for norm-referenced tests developed to measure specific domains of knowledge, such as mathematical computation, vocabulary, U.S. government, etc. The content validity approach is less conclusive or definitive for tests covering broader content areas, e.g., a test to measure high school social studies achievement. Evaluation of content validity does not yield a validity coefficient as described above. Instead, content validity is usually evaluated by experts, who deliver quality judgments, such as adequate/inadequate or poor/fair/good/excellent. In reaching this judgment, the experts may observe and interview examinees to check on whether they are actually using the knowledge to be tested to answer the test questions. The scores will be consistent with the experts' judgments if they were competent, if the scores are sufficiently reliable, and if the examinees were well motivated and had backgrounds appropriate for the test.

Occasionally, the term *construct validity* appears in the literature. The main ideas underlying this approach to evaluating validity have been covered above. Basically, construct validity is evaluated by an accumulation of evidence, mainly correlations between the scores being evaluated for validity and a large variety of other measures. In addition, the effect of treatments designed to change the characteristic being measured may be taken into consideration along with judgmental evidence such as that used to evaluate content validity.

See also Competency Testing, Teachers; Tests, Criterion- and Norm-Referenced.

—Robert B. Frary
Virginia Polytechnic Institute and State University

Reference

Ebel, R.L., & Frisbie, D.A. (1986). *Essentials of educational measurement* (4th ed., chaps. 5 & 6). Englewood Cliffs, NJ: Prentice-Hall.

TESTS, CRITERION- AND NORM-REFERENCED

Testing has been transformed into a powerful judge of the quality of education. Tests administered within schools are generally either criterion- or norm-referenced. Educators need to know the distinctions and differences which exist between the two types of tests in order to understand their appropriate applications and interpretations.

Definitions

Criterion-referenced tests are deliberately constructed to yield measurements that are directly interpretable in terms of specified performance standards. Test performance in relation to objective standards tells what a student can do or cannot do. In contrast, *norm-referenced tests* compare a student's performance to a norm or average of performance by other similar students. They tell where a student stands compared with other students and help to determine a student's place or rank in class.

Use and Interpretation

Criterion-Referenced Tests. Opponents of criterion-referenced tests suggest that their importance has been exaggerated. Often without factual basis, critics have expressed the concern that creative drive will be shackled to a trite, though basic, curriculum. As a result, student involvement in exploratory classes for those who are not academically inclined may be severely limited.

On a political level, some fear the state will gain too much control and teachers and students may be unfairly tested with devices invalid for them. The strict standards of mastery may cause many late-bloomers to leave school early, putting an extra burden on the unemployment rolls. Critics also claim the tests are designed as a racist plot, potentially explosive in our society. They may give teachers the opportunity to weed out their problem students and move them to other programs.

The question of ethics also arises. Is it right to test students, then offer them no recourse for remediation when they fail? Or, will early graduation, offered as a mastery bonus, deny some youngsters the fun and maturing period they should experience during their last years of school? Coaching for higher grades presents another problem. The rich, who can afford coaching, have an unfair advantage on tests designed to ascertain achievement. The tests will no longer discriminate for skill but could instead discriminate for wealth.

For teachers, the added burden of management systems and additional teaching time necessary for mastery attainment will mean more work for already overloaded teachers. In addition, teachers feel uneasy using a grading system which has the potential to administer all As when its goal is reached. Teachers seem hesitant to admit that this grade inflation could mean they are really competent to teach.

Many proponents of criterion-referenced tests on the other hand see great value in their usage. Competency is guaranteed for all, students and teachers alike, since students will not be promoted until they achieve mastery at their present level. All who graduate will be good readers and speedy calculators. Students will go out into the world ready to face life and employment requirements in a responsible way. As a result, the high school diploma will regain its former high value.

In addition, criterion-referenced tests, with their definitive objectives, would draw the support of the citizenry. Curricula with a new list of sequenced goals would reflect articulation of content within and across grade levels.

Norm-Referenced Tests. A major concern of critics of norm-referenced tests is that poor readers are at a gross disadvantage since the tests are often more a gauge of reading ability than of the student's achievement in the particular area. In addition, due to the wide variation in programs, normed tests frequently do not measure content that corresponds to the content of the school's curriculum. No matter how diligently a test author may attempt to construct an instrument that will conform to the central tendencies of curriculum practice, the instrument is certain to contain items of information that students in a particular school never had an opportunity to learn. Furthermore, the absence of a national standardized curriculum points up a severe limitation of the practical value, for most schools, of the nationally standardized norm-referenced tests.

Critics also contend that makers of standardized tests fail to achieve their aim of measuring broad understanding related to widely accepted objectives fully or convincingly. They try to avoid details that are likely to be products of rote learning. However, understanding does not exist in a vacuum. Consider the question, "How does climate make a difference in the way people dress?", is too simple, and too easy, and the question reveals little about a student's understanding of how climate affects how people live. So, test makers have concluded that it is better to ask questions about particular climates and particular peoples. They might ask, "In what way does a Laplander in the Arctic Circle live differently from a Congolese living at the Equator?" Immediately, there is difficulty. Some curricula provide a study of Laplanders and Congolese, while others will sample other peoples to illustrate the same understanding. Thus, norm-referenced tests focus on facts instead of broad understanding.

Proponents stress that norm-referenced tests are (a) indispensable for learning whether a student made greater progress last year than this year; (b) useful for learning if the student made any progress at all; (c) useful for learning whether, in relation to other students of his age, the student is well informed and well equipped, or poorly informed and poorly equipped; (d) useful in making diagnostic decisions; (e) most appropriate for selection, placement, counseling and guidance, program or curriculum evaluation, and administrative policy decisions; and (f) worthwhile for making general comparative decisions based on grade-equivalent scores, and a variety of other scores obtained from the tests.

Suggested Applications

Criterion-Referenced Tests. Criterion-referenced tests provide an equitable method for assessing student progress. The need for unhealthy competition will be eliminated as these tests are used for diagnosing weaknesses and prescribing remediation on an individualized basis. Used in this manner, criterion-referenced tests become a learning device, providing the student a goal and teaching the student how to learn. They define and document the degree of objective competence for each individual. Applying the feedback and correction policy to classroom learning can produce a high level of mastery. In addition, criterion-referenced tests are useful in identifying gifted students, those with specific abilities.

Teachers can find many ways to use the test scores. As a diagnostic device, they can be used for evaluation of any reteaching that needs to be done. Making decisions concerning grouping will be easier using the scores for promotion, and failure decisions can also be simplified. Most importantly, teachers can use the test objectives to set up their instructional objectives. After all, the objectives have been selected by large numbers of people. Teaching the objectives before assessing achievement is a must.

Applications for criterion-referenced test scores by boards of education are numerous. Budget decisions which are documented by test scores are much easier to make. The scores also show exactly where weak areas are located. Needed materials and resources can be allocated in an effort to strengthen the program. In-service training may be scheduled. Federal grants may be sought, backed by score documentation. In the future, criterion-referenced test scores for students may be used to decide teacher effectiveness.

A final but excellent use for these tests is to keep parents informed regarding the progress of their child. This may help them to assume part of the heavy responsibility now delegated to the school.

Norm-Referenced Tests. Norm-referenced tests have been standardized by administration to thousands of students, whose scores become the basis of "norms." By referring to a table of appropriate norms, furnished by the test publisher, the teacher may convert a student's raw score to a figure that tells how that student compares in relation to the performance of others. The conversion may be in terms of percentile ranks (if a student has a percentile score of 70, that student's performance is better than 70 percent of those upon whom the test was standardized) or in terms of grade-equivalent scores (if a student has a grade-equivalent score of 5.2, that student's performance is equal to that of the average child who is in the second month of grade 5). These data are useful in reporting student progress and rank to parents.

Closing Statements

Test data, fallible as they may be, are more objective when used properly than any of the alternatives. Educators realize that they must make decisions and that properly used test data can enhance their ability to make sound decisions. Increasing demands for accountability are also being made by the general public. By and large, the public tends to respect and accept data to judge accountability. The accountability movement grew in reaction to the public's increasing disenchantment with education. Since the public's disenchantment with current education is not likely to subside quickly, strong demands for accountability and testing in the future are likely to prevail.

See also Test Score Reliability and Validity.

—Mary Oellerich Dalnoki Miklos
Georgia Southwestern College

Reference

Borich, G., & Kubiszyn, T. (1984). *Educational testing and measurement.* Glenview, IL: Scott Foresman.

TEXTBOOK SELECTION

Textbook adoption is the process through which a state, school district or classroom teacher reviews and selects a particular textbook or textbook series. The United States is almost equally divided between states that conduct state-level adoption of textbooks and those that do not. In a few states, state-level textbook adoptions are conducted only at the elementary level. In general, however, states that adopt textbooks at the state level do so at both the elementary and secondary levels. In the twenty-two "adoption" states, school districts select textbooks from a list of textbooks approved by the state. In the twenty-eight "nonadoption" or "open" states, local school districts, schools, and classroom teachers usually select textbooks from all available published programs, with little or no state guidance.

The major difference, therefore, between adoption and nonadoption states is the two-stage review process in the adoption states. Textbooks are first reviewed at the state level, where the total list of available texts is pared to a predetermined number. Or, rather than a specific number, the final list may include all those books that are acceptable to state reviewers. In the nonadoption states there is only one review conducted at the school district or school-building level.

At the school district level, in both adoption and nonadoption states, policies may establish a multistage textbook selection process. A school district may approve a specific list of texts from which each school and/or each teacher may select, or district policies may dictate a particular textbook series to be used throughout the district. It is not certain which of these is the most prominent practice. However, the trend is presently toward the adoption of a single textbook series throughout a district. At the other extreme, few districts in the country allow individual teachers complete freedom to select textbooks for use in their classrooms.

Purposes for Textbook Adoption

The three most prominently mentioned reasons for selecting textbooks on a state, district, or schoolwide basis are (a) Textbook costs are reduced through volume purchases; (b) textbooks of a "higher quality" are selected when there is a broad review of available textbooks; and (c) a uniform curriculum can be achieved only if common textbooks are used. In addition to these primary reasons, two additional reasons for conducting textbook adoptions are sometimes mentioned: (d) textbook adoptions ensure that there will be a periodic review and purchase of textbooks; and (e) the textbook review process provides an opportunity for public participation in an important aspect of education.

Issues and Concerns

One of the major issues in textbook adoption is whether the advantages of textbook adoption can be achieved just through local school district adoptions or whether there is a need for state-level adoptions. This debate has been continuing for a number of years, and it seems that the question will not be easily resolved, since there are strong proponents on each side of the issue.

There is also a continuing debate about the effect of textbook adoption on the overall quality of textbooks. Some educators argue that textbook adoption committees conduct such poor evaluations of textbooks that publishers tend to invest more resources in marketing than in improving the quality of the textbooks.

The major problems of textbook selection and adoption are well known. Textbook adoption is a highly bureaucratized and political process. Some of the common problems of textbook selection/adoption committees include the lack of time to conduct an adequate evaluation, the lack of clearly stated criteria that can be used to evaluate the textbooks, and the use of poorly described and often confusing procedures. Little attention has been paid to improving the textbook adoption process. If we are to improve textbook adoption, we must improve the review processes of each individual reviewer. That is, we must understand and help to improve the procedures that both individuals and committees utilize when they review textbooks. The most important phase of the textbook evaluation process takes place when a textbook is in the hands of a reviewer. To improve that process, the following eight suggestions are made:

1. The criteria for evaluating a textbook must be understood by everyone involved in the process, starting from understanding what a textbook can do and what it cannot do as an adjunct to an instructional program. We need to understand that textbooks are not total programs: they are instructional aids to be used as part of a program.

2. Evaluation techniques for reviewing books should be developed, tried and revised. Textbook review committees should have practice in using these procedures prior to the time that the books are actually reviewed.

3. Textbook reviewers must receive a significant amount of training in proper review procedures. This kind of training is almost never provided as part of an undergraduate or graduate teacher education program. The review and evaluation of a textbook is a process that involves specific skills. It is not a task that one should learn "while engaged in the process;" those who learn how to review textbooks, who take the time to study the textbooks thoroughly, are those who should be given the responsibility to make recommendations regarding the books to be used.

4. Local schools should adopt the criteria to review textbooks. State legislatures and state boards of education should set the broad goals of education, and school boards should be responsible for implementing those goals. One of the most important implementation functions is the selection of textbooks.

5. Committee members need adequate time to study the textbooks thoroughly. Textbook evaluation is an important professional activity. Teachers should be provided with ample release time to carry out their reviews. In almost all of the reported studies, lack of adequate review time was a major limitation reported by reviewers.

6. Sampling techniques must be developed in order that a smaller number of specific items can be reviewed in greater depth. There is no way to review all books about a particular topic thoroughly. Random selection procedures

have been demonstrated to have adequate validity in research. These techniques can help textbook evaluation committees perform a more thorough evaluation.

7. Textbook reviewers must be trained to provide specific information regarding each factor they review. It is not enough to say that something is good or bad or to provide general summaries. The evaluation evidence must be specific to each point that is reviewed.

8. Feedback to publishers from the results of textbook reviews must be specific and thorough. Publishers must learn what reviewers like and dislike. Publishers generally believe that their books fail to be adopted because they did not adequately market the texts. They need to be told why their textbooks are not acceptable.

See also Curriculum Development; Staff Development; State Departments of Education.

—Roger Farr
Indiana University

References

Farr, R., & Tulley, M. A. (1985). "Do adoption committees perpetuate mediocre textbooks?" *Phi Delta Kappan, 66,* 467-71.

Tulley, M.A. (1985). "A descriptive study of the intents of selected state level textbook adoption processes." *Educational Evaluation and Policy Analysis, 7,* 289-308.

Tulley, M.A., & Farr, R. (1985). "The purpose of state level textbook adoption: What does the legislation reveal?" *Journal of Research and Development in Education, 18,* 1-6.

THEORY X, THEORY Y

Of primary interest to public education is the performance of teachers and support personnel in the conduct of instruction and related activities associated with quality education. Teachers, particularly, need to show enthusiasm and initiative, take responsibility for their own work and their own improvement, and share in efforts to improve their schools. These qualities in a teacher, as in any worker, are increased when the work and the relationships of colleagues provide satisfaction, stimulation, and support. This is particularly important in schools since schools are humanizing and educating institutions and should be characterized by growth and development in every phase of activity. Therefore, administrators of schools need the understandings and skills to increase motivation toward individual and group work satisfaction and self-fulfillment. Theory X-Y is one means of explaining how leadership affects motivation.

Basic to an understanding of Theory X-Y are three conditions which are present in every organizational setting, such as a school. These are the following: (a) The individual (in this case the teacher) has personal interests, attitudes, and needs which must be harmonized with the purposes and requirements of the organization (school); (b) individuals within each organization join in informal ways to share information relating to their interests associated with the organization and form attitudes about the organization and its work, about its worth, and about how they will come to terms with organization requirements and activities; and (c) organizational leadership attempts to manage individual and group participation in order to get the work of the organization done. Should individual and group purposes not be compatible with those of the organization, serious problems can result. These include bickering and conflict, lack of cooperation, and reduced effort which can lead to more explicit actions, such as teacher unionization. On the other hand, leadership which can unite individuals and the influence of informal groupings behind an organized effort for quality performance and improvement can produce the highest levels of achievement of which the organization is capable.

Douglas McGregor, who proposed Theory X-Y, expressed what he termed to be a self-fulfilling prophecy that individuals respond to the expectations that important others hold for their behavior. He labeled traditional approaches to management as Theory X and stated that this traditional approach, or leadership style, was based upon certain assumptions. These are the following: (a) The average person (teacher) is by nature indolent—will work as little as possible and seeks to minimize effort unless closely supervised; (b) the average person (teacher) lacks ambition, dislikes responsibility, and prefers to be told what to do; (c) the average person (teacher) is inherently self-centered and resistant to organizational needs; (d) the average person (teacher) will resist change; and (e) the average person (teacher) is gullible and can be easily influenced by the demagogue.

School administrators having beliefs exemplified by McGregor's Theory X would assume a leadership style compatible with this view in working with teachers. Such administrators would exhibit a low level of trust and would likely not have high expectations for performance. They probably would not attempt major changes in curriculum and instruction and would rely upon detailed staff assignments and prescriptions for lesson plans, reporting, and discipline. The means of carrying out administrative actions would either be a tough, prescriptive approach or a paternal, manipulative "human relations" approach. The self-fulfilling prophecy occurs when staff respond in a half-hearted, or even resistant fashion confirming for the administration that people are indeed as he or she believes them to be. Thus, the prophecy is fulfilled and a cycle is established in which the administrator pursues these assumptions in further administrative actions.

As a counter to Theory X, McGregor proposed Theory Y which basically states that people desire responsibility, seek and find satisfaction in the work they do, wish to identify with and support organizational goals, want to develop and increase their potential, and respond when permitted to participate in a genuine fashion. As in the self-fulfilling prophecy, when administrators believe these assumptions about human nature and act upon them, a cycle of actions characterized by trust and mutual support develops. Administrators need to examine their own beliefs carefully and to put Theory Y assumptions to the test in order to confirm that people do respond to positive expectations.

Since the advent of Theory X-Y many techniques have been developed and tested in order to initiate Theory Y based administration. These include self-studies of school climates, participative management and organizational problem-solving teams, organizational development approaches, and a variety of specific in-service and project-oriented activities.

See also Theory Z.

—Lloyd E. McCleary
University of Utah

References

McGregor, D. (1958). *The human side of enterprise.* New York: McGraw-Hill.

McGregor, D. (1967). *The professional manager.* New York: McGraw-Hill.

Pugh, D.S., Hickson, D.J., & Hinings, C.R. (1985). *Writers on organizations* (chap. 5). Beverly Hills, CA: Sage.

THEORY Z

The findings are clear: a common sense of purpose and a broad-based commitment to goals are critical factors that separate the most effective from the least effective schools. Successful schools have administrators who possess a vision of what is possible, share decision-making authority with teachers, and develop long-range plans for improvement. For some schools to become effective, however, it may be necessary for administrators to modify their views of leadership and learn new interpersonal and decision-making skills. One of the best ways for school administrators to begin altering their leadership behavior is to study Theory Z, a management approach that combines the best of Japanese and American practices.

The term "Theory Z" took on meaning in 1981 with the publication of a book of the same name by William Ouchi. Ouchi studied successful Japanese companies (Theory J) and contrasted them with American companies (Theory A). Theory J companies were characterized by lifetime employment, consensual decision making, and collective responsibility, among other traits. Theory A companies, on the other hand, had short-term employment, individual decision making, and individualized responsibility. Theory Z leadership occurs in companies that have successfully adapted Japanese practices to the realities of American culture.

Theory Z companies have a number of things in common. First, they are built around a corporate philosophy against which all policies and practices can be compared. Second, these companies nurture high quality relationships among employees; trust and openness among individuals are valued. Third, clear, accurate communication is sought among workers of the same job description and across roles. Consequently, a cooperative team approach is used in the completion of tasks. Taken together, these characteristics result in an organization that is dynamic and self renewing.

It is important to remember, though, that Theory Z is more than a mere set of gimmicks. It is an organizational way of life that includes a leader's belief system as well as his or her actions. The dignity of each person is respected, and concern for employees pervades the organization.

What are the benefits of Theory Z management? The trust and high-quality communication that exists in Theory Z organizations improve the job satisfaction of employees. This, in turn, leads to greater productivity. Workers become more creative and take a more positive approach to problems. As a result, companies become more profitable. In schools governed by a Theory Z approach, teacher morale improves and staff members display more enthusiasm for their jobs. Energy is liberated for problem solving in a wide range of areas; the solutions to these problems are likely to lead to greater student learning and more positive attitudes about school.

Implications for Administrators

Many school administrators will find little that is new in Theory Z. These administrators have fostered a climate of mutual respect and involved their subordinates in decision making. They have worked collaboratively with others to develop a district or school philosophy and to establish long-range plans.

Unfortunately, Theory Z type approaches are not applied in schools to the extent they could be. Studies have shown that many of the best and brightest teachers are leaving the profession. While teacher job satisfaction varies from school to school, it is highest in schools with good communication and shared decision making between teachers and administrators. Other research has shown that teachers want to develop closer collegial relationships and assume more responsibility for their own goals.

Where should an administrator begin who would like to become more Z-like? A logical place to start is with the development of a district or school philosophy. Professional staff, the business community, parents, and students could examine existing documents (e.g., school board goals and policy statements, the findings of needs assessments, etc.) to develop a base for their work. From their discussions they could list beliefs that are unique to their district or schools and write a mission statement. While this process is time consuming and may prove frustrating, a philosophy that is jointly established provides a basis against which future activities can be judged.

Another starting point is to initiate a cooperative team approach to planning and problem solving in the district or school. In most instances, teachers and administrators will need to learn new skills (e.g., consensus decision making) and participate in team building activities to establish trust and rapport. Team members must come to know each other as human beings as well as professionals. It is critical that these teams be involved in identifying problems as well as solving problems. Quality circles, groups in which six to ten teachers and administrators study problems (e.g., communicating with parents) and propose well-thought-out solutions to management, are one form of such collaborative approaches.

Change toward more Z-like schools must begin at the top. Superintendents establish the tone for their districts just as principals set the tone for their schools. Authoritarian superintendents cannot expect their subordinates to become more Z-like without first altering some of their own attitudes and behaviors. Principals must become collaborative in their approach to the staff if they expect a cooperative ethos to pervade their schools. It will take time for administrators to modify their attitudes and learn new skills, just as it will take time for work teams to establish trust and rapport. Theory Z is obviously not a quick fix to the complicated problems schools face.

Administrators can learn about Theory Z in study groups or through the use of outside consultants. Teacher leaders in the district should attend these sessions whenever possible. In the long run, however, Theory Z approaches cannot be successfully implemented without a well-designed staff development program. Administrators and teachers must acquire or hone their interpersonal skills and must learn the processes required for collaborative decision making and problem solving.

A number of benefits await Z-like administrators. They are likely to be more satisfied with their work because competitive, adversarial relationships have been minimized. They will feel more productive because important problems are being solved. These administrators will enjoy watching the teachers they have empowered take on challenges that result in better teaching and learning. Most importantly, Z-like administrators will know that when teachers and administrators work together, students are the primary beneficiaries.

See also Decision Making; Quality Circles; Theory X, Theory Y.

—Dennis Sparks, Executive Director
National Staff Development Council

References

Miller, W., & Sparks, D. (1984). "Theory Z: The promise for U.S. schools." *Educational Forum, 49,* 47-54.

Ouchi, W. (1981). *Theory Z: How American business can meet the Japanese challenge.* Reading, PA: Addison-Wesley.

TIME MANAGEMENT

Educators, because of the very nature of their jobs, have time management problems. All lose and waste time every day. Since school administrators and supervisors are responsible for scheduling, disciplining, observing staff, supervising, conferencing, and evaluating, time is a valuable commodity that must be properly managed.

The following suggestions may be useful to busy administrators:

1. Discourage and discontinue unnecessary meetings. Ask if the meeting is really necessary.

2. Try to make decisions without meetings. Never use a committee if a decision should be made unilaterally. Administrators and supervisors are busy people, and one more meeting pushed into an already over-crowded day is an extra burden.

3. Use secretarial support services wisely. With training and experience, secretaries can perform many of the time-consuming jobs and free administrators for matters which need their attention or expertise.

4. Eliminate unnecessary paperwork. Realistically, paperwork will need to be done, but through planning, the burden may be minimized. Frequently, a phone call may be a more expedient means of responding to an inquiry than a written response. Secretaries can help in this area as well; allow them to attend to your correspondence and some of that (dreaded) paperwork. Obviously, administrators must do some paperwork themselves, but they should pass along the routine matters to their secretaries.

5. Screen reading materials and question their purpose and continued existence. If the materials have "outlived" their usefulness—throw them away.

6. Set priorities. Every day should be planned and that planning should include stating priorities and writing them down. Take charge of your calendar and put first things first. Distinguish between the urgent and the important. The "best laid plans" can often go awry—things come up that need to be dealt with immediately, but that still should not prevent planning or setting priorities from occurring. If a classroom is to be observed, do not accept telephone calls or visits from people who do not have appointments, etc.

7. Focus on one thing at a time. Many "irons may be in the fire," but completion can only come with one thing at a time.

8. Establish a quiet time during which to accept calls and return calls or just "get it together." A quiet time might be right after lunch when students are "replete" from lunch and back in class. It is a time, also, to think about the morning and what still needs to be done to complete the day. After being on the job, other appropriate quiet times may be determined.

9. Delegate responsibility and avoid the tendency to "do it yourself." The talents and expertise of staff members should be used. Not only does it build confidence among the staff but it alleviates some burdensome tasks. Input from staff builds unity and, when well done, can enhance the administrator's image.

10. Focus your attention on critical issues and activities. How much time is spent on trivial matters? Eighty percent of the value is accounted for by 20 percent of the items/people, while only 20 percent of the value is accounted for by 80 percent of the items. Learn to concentrate on your valuable 20 percent activities.

No plan for time management is "foolproof," but administrators and supervisors can learn to manage their time if they really work at developing good time management skills. Remember, everyone has the same hours to work with each day. Make the most of them by careful planning and time management skills.

See also School Secretary.

—Janet Varejcka, Principal
Bennett County High School
Martin, South Dakota

References

Hart, L.B. (1980). *Moving up: Women and leadership* (chap. 7). New York: Amacom.

Neal, R.G. (1983). *Managing time: An administrator's guide.* Manassas, VA: Public Employees Relations Service.

TRANSPORTATION MANAGEMENT

State departments of education estimate that one-half of all students enrolled in public schools ride to and from school on school buses. It is estimated that almost five percent of public school budgets may be allocated to transportation service. Therefore, administrators must consider pupil transportation as a high-priority item with a high degree of responsibility.

The two major goals of school bus transportation are safety and efficiency. To achieve these goals it will be necessary for school board members and administrators to accept the primary responsibility for transportation. A school board must adopt general policies for the administrator to implement. Policy matters such as eligibility criteria, level of service, acceptable conduct rules, approved disciplinary action, maximum riding time, walk to stop distance, and safety standards must be well defined and adopted.

Once a school board has adopted these policies, the administrator will be able to develop procedures that will lead to the attainment of the two goals: safety and efficiency. Also, the administrator is in a position to make decisions which are supported by the adopted board policy.

The administrator serves as the focal point in the daily operation of the pupil transportation network. In order to operate an effective program, the administrator must consider pupil transportation when planning class schedules, assigning duties, developing community-relations programs, and organizing all other activities involved in the day-to-day operation of the school.

It is strongly suggested that the administrator accept the concept that the school bus ride is an extension of the school day. This concept will enable the administrator to relate events and experiences that take place in the school bus environment to the school environment. This concept must be conveyed by the administrator to the school staff. Too often a school staff will hold the belief that what happens on the school bus is not a school problem. Basically, the school day begins for a rider when the rider boards the bus and ends when the rider leaves the bus at the designated drop-off location.

Transportation supervision at each school site is the legal responsibility of the administrator. When a school has a complex transportation network, the administrator should consider identifying one staff member to facilitate the transportation service for the school.

A close and harmonious working relationship must be developed and nurtured between the administrator and the drivers. The administrator must work to make drivers feel an integral part of the school family.

To expedite a safe operation, the administrator, in cooperation with the drivers, needs to identify safe loading areas. In most urban school districts the schools were built without considering the need for transportation. Designating a loading area at a school may involve traffic officials, police representatives, and other safety agencies. The administrator must be sure to involve the school engineer in this matter. It is the school engineer who assumes the responsibility of keeping the loading area clear for the buses and the riders.

As the administrator has the authority to suspend a pupil from school, the administrator has the authority to suspend a rider from a bus. At no time is a driver to have the power to suspend a rider from the bus.

A program for rider management should be developed cooperatively by the administrator, staff members, transportation representatives (managers, safety directors, drivers) and parents. Any program that is designed must ensure the safety and welfare of *all* school bus riders. A rider management program should include the following: (a) the driver's responsibility for riders while traveling to and from school, (b) accepted standards of rider behavior, (c) the rider's right to due process, (d) the process to resolve problems when a driver needs help, (e) the conditions under which a rider can be suspended from a bus, and (f) the responsibility of parents for damage to a bus by their children. An administrator may wish to expand this list as a need develops. However, the list of regulations and procedures should be printed for general distribution. Proper rider behavior is important to ensure a safe ride.

Rider education cannot be limited to a "one time a school year" experience. The administrator must convey to the school staff the need to bring the bus riding experiences into the classroom. A curriculum guide could be developed for use at each grade level. The National Highway Traffic Safety Administration's *Highway Safety Program Standard 17, Pupil Transportation Safety* requires rider instruction at least twice a school year for all school bus riders. In addition most states require two school bus evacuation drills each school year.

In developing a rider education program, the instructional approach should not be limited to telling riders what to do. Using the school bus as a classroom, visiting bus garages, demonstrating behavior (acceptable/not acceptable), videotaping riders on the bus, videotaping riders at bus stops (boarding/leaving), or other creative approaches will make the learning process more meaningful as well as enjoyable. It may be necessary to initiate some type of remedial instruction as the result of a problem or an accident. The administrator must be willing to repeat the instruction as often as rider conduct requires it.

Incentive programs will lead to rider interest and improved behavior. Consideration may be given to recognizing good riders, the bus of the month, the driver of the month, or the most improved bus. In any case, an incentive program should be developed by the ridership team: drivers, riders, teachers, parents, and administrators.

Records for transportation are necessary because of potential legal involvement. Daily performance records must be kept for each route. These records might include items such as arrival times, departure times, driver attendance (regular/substitute), efficiency data, and accident details. The administrator may sometime find the need to remove a driver from a route. Documentation of the driver's performance will be accepted as evidence; general statements that cannot be verified will be considered as heresay and not accepted.

Documented ridership problems should be maintained for each rider. These records should be made part of the student's cumulative folder for future reference. Riders who may be well behaved in the home and in the classroom may be troublemakers on the bus. Documented problems will assist the administrator in deciding the type of action to take in regard to the rider.

Transportation matters can be controversial, emotional, and political; they must be taken seriously. The administrator must be prepared to respond in a knowledgeable manner if litigation should occur.

The school bus is a highly visible public-relations tool for an administrator. It is often said that the public bases its opinion of a school on the performance of a school bus: (a) If the riders behave on the bus, they behave in school; (b) if the riders misbehave on the bus, they misbehave in school; (c) if the bus runs on schedule, the school runs on schedule; and (d) if the bus is neat and clean, the school is neat and clean; "as the bus goes, so goes the school."

Transportation service cannot be ignored. It is a complex and time-consuming responsibility for an administrator. It can be a positive force for an administrator who is willing to accept its many facets. It is governed by statutes, it is vulnerable to weather conditions, and it is potentially highly emotional.

Oftentimes the administrator must be willing to view transportation through the eyes of a bus terminal manager, a parent, a rider, a driver, or a teacher, as well as an administrator. Transportation is never boring, for there is something new happening each day on each trip. Flexibility and a sense of humor will assist an administrator in maintaining a successful transportation network. In any case, the administrator must remember that a school bus is still the safest form of transportation.

See also Administrative Tasks; Desegregation Plans; Pupil Personnel Program.

—Richard F. Wenzel
Milwaukee Public Schools

Sources of Information

American Automobile Association Foundation for Traffic Safety, 8111 Gatehouse Road, Falls Church, VA 22042

National Highway Traffic Safety Administration, NIS-14, United States Department of Transportation, Washington, DC 20590

National Safety Council, Motor Transportation Department, 444 N. Michigan Avenue, Chicago, IL 60611

U

UNIVERSITY COUNCIL FOR EDUCATIONAL ADMINISTRATION

The University Council for Educational Administration (UCEA) is a nonprofit corporation with a membership consisting of major universities in the United States and Canada offering the doctorate in school administration. A number of school districts are also affiliated through its partnership program. The purpose of the consortium is to improve school administrator preparation through the cooperative efforts of its member universities. The council was founded following an exploratory conference held at Teachers College, Columbia University in 1956. Initially, thirty universities from North America were invited to join. The consortium remained at Columbia University under the direction of Daniel R. Davies, the first Executive Director, until 1959. The offices were then moved to The Ohio State University at which time Jack Culbertson became executive director. It continued to be housed at Ohio State until 1984, when it moved to the campus of Arizona State University, in Tempe.

Currently there are fifty university members and ten affiliated school districts. They engage in a variety of activities and produce a number of publications and instructional materials. These activities and publications proceed from a basic set of goals sufficiently stable to give the council an identity, yet flexible enough to respond to changing conditions in educational administration. Briefly stated, the goals of the University Council for Educational Administration are (a) to advance understanding in all areas relating to educational administration and to enhance the research capabilities of participating institutions; (b) to develop methods of instruction, new materials, and other approaches to bring about effective preservice and staff development programs for all professionals in educational administration; and (c) to create effective pathways and networks for exchanging new understandings and methods.

The council publishes three major journals related to educational administration in cooperation with Sage Publications and a host university. They are *Educational Administration Quarterly*, a journal containing conceptual and theoretical articles, research analysis, and reviews of books; *Educational Administration Abstracts*, a journal containing summaries of articles from approximately 140 professional journals; and finally, *The Journal of Educational Equity and Leadership*, a periodical devoted to consideration of equity-related educational needs of Hispanics, blacks, American Indians, Asian Americans, and women. It also publishes a quarterly newsletter, the *UCEA Review*, which informs professors of educational administration of the activities and work of their colleagues and the projects of the consortium.

Periodically, the council has undertaken sponsorship of commissions and study groups to examine areas important to the profession and make recommendations for the future preparation of school administrators. In 1986, it undertook sponsorship of the National Commission on Excellence in Educational Administration. This National Commission, consisting of prominent educators and private citizens, published its findings in 1987. It is the intention of the leaders of the consortium that selected recommendations of the National Commission become an agenda for change within universities belonging to the University Council for Educational Administration.

Since its beginnings, the council has been actively involved in the professional development of professors of educational administration. For example, career development seminars are held nearly every year. A second avenue of professional growth, aimed specifically at graduate students was begun in 1966. Graduate student seminars are planned and organized by students, cosponsored by a member university, and typically include prominent scholars in the field and a regional group of graduate students.

Other ways it affects the profession and professional preparation include the sponsorship of a monograph series, resource documents, and occasional papers, all concerned with issues of importance to school administration. There are ten program centers hosted by member universities addressing questions of particular interest to our profession. The council sponsors a partnership program that seeks to discover and foster ways member universities and interested school districts can cooperate to their mutual benefit. Historically, it has produced instructional materials, particularly simulations, for various educational administrative roles. Also important in the framework of the organization is the fostering of interuniversity cooperation. Through the *UCEA Review*, social gatherings, computer networking, and assorted meetings, it brings together professors of educational administration from North America's leading universities.

The council is governed by its legislative body, the plenary session, which meets each year to set the expectations about improvement of preparation and to oversee the operations of the consortium. The plenary session, which consists of a representative from each member university, is guided in its decisions by the executive committee and executive director.

The University Council for Educational Administration began as an elite consortium of major universities. It continues to have as its members the major research universities in North America. Membership is restricted to universities which award doctoral degrees in educational administration, have a highly regarded faculty, and express a willingness to engage in cooperative work to improve the profession.

—Patrick B. Forsyth, Executive Director
University Council for Educational Administration

URBAN SCHOOL DISTRICTS

Demographic changes have largely shaped the contemporary American central city, its financial and social conditions, and its schools. According to the 1980 federal census, the term *central city* applies to (a) any city with a population of at least 250,000 persons, (b) any city in which at least 100,000 persons are employed within the city limits, (c) any city of at least 25,000 persons where at least 40 percent of resident workers do not commute to work outside city limits and, in addition, hold at least 75 percent of jobs available within the city and, (d) any city with a population ranging between 15,000 and 25,000 that meets the two resident and job holding requirements mentioned in (e) and additionally has at least one-third the population of the metropolitan area's largest city.

The larger unit, composed of the central city and its suburban fringe-communities, is known as the Standard Metropolitan Statistical Area. This unit was developed by the Bureau of the Budget (now the Office of Management and Budget) to define areas of daily interdependency using commuting as a criterion. The term "Standard Consolidated Statistical Area," a relatively new unit, denotes a much larger geographical area.

Three major trends involve shifts in population that define important social welfare dimensions of cities and metropolitan areas as a whole. The three social dimensions are (a) shifting patterns of population density; (b) changing rates of urban settlement by populations varying in race, age, income, housing, crime, and social attitudes; and (c) altered patterns of migration.

Over the last two decades, there has been tremendous movement of populations away from the central city. Since 1970, the nation's Standard Metropolitan Statistical Areas (cities and suburbs combined) have been losing population to nonmetropolitan territory. The most remote areas of New England, the Southwest, the Appalachian region, and other fringe areas have gained migrants at the expense of cities and suburbs. This shift reverses a trend toward centralization that dates back to the early nineteenth century and has resulted in the growth of population corridors linking two or more Standard Metropolitan Statistical Areas. There are 13 of these corridors nationally.

The 1980 President's National Urban Policy Report noted, "Central city poverty tends to be concentrated in specific neighborhoods. This is particularly true for minority and female-headed households. This pattern of concentration of poverty appears to have increased during the 1970s. One indication of this comes from trends in the poverty rate for census tracts where more than 20 percent of the residents were poor in 1970. From 1969 to 1976 the rate of poverty in these low income areas in large central cities increased from 31 percent to 39 percent, and the proportion of female-headed and minority households in such areas also grew."

Central cities provide a wide range of services (e.g., sanitation, public transit, parks and recreation, police and fire services, health and hospitals, welfare, libraries, and education). The U.S. Department of Housing and Urban Development views education as the most problematic among these services: "In terms of the nation's future, urban public education is clearly the number one problem in the urban services area. The ratio of high school graduates to all 18-year-olds has fallen since 1969. Dropout rates have risen particularly among minorities . . . test scores are lower than ever in many urban schools. For many pupils, schools are merely custodians. Many schools accept truancy as a fact of life. School crime and vandalism are at alarming levels."

Despite decreasing numbers of students in urban school districts, costs continue to rise as the result of growth in expenditures per pupil and with increasing teacher salaries and related benefits. For the most part, cities have been unable to increase their tax base. In addition to the fiscal problems, urban schools have faced social and political constraints. Federal legislation and local legal battles have forced urban schools to provide equal access to educational facilities for all students. This, more specifically, has meant accessibility to all system schools by minority groups, particularly black students. Since black residents are often least able to provide tax-paying support by virtue of past economic discrimination and current economic stagnation, the school system is heavily dependent upon more affluent (generally white) taxpayers. For many large urban school districts, policy emerged as a set of coping strategies designed to (a) provide "quality amenities" (attractive public schools), "uncontaminated by the presence of undesirable groups"; (b) ensure fiscal responsibility unthreatened by default; and (c) maintain social order unblemished by institutional chaos and disciplinary disruption.

Policy has continued largely unchanged in the 1980s. The administrative staff of urban school systems shapes and affects the policies established by boards of education and local elites. These administrative staffs came under attack in the late 1960s and 1970s for being insulated from community pressures, isolated from the real world of the schools, and trapped by rule-oriented behavior. By the 1980s attempts were made to correct these problems through public accountability and administrative decentralization.

See also Demographic Trends; Inner City Schools; Minorities and the School System.

—Francesco Cordasco
Montclair State College

References

Borman, K.M., & Spring, J.H. (1984). *Schools in central cities.* New York: Longman.
Hillson, M., & Cordasco, F. (1982). *Education and the urban community.* Washington, DC: University Press of America.
U.S. Department of Housing and Urban Development. *The 1980 President's National Urban Policy Report.* (1980). Washington, DC: Author.

VALUES EDUCATION

Paideia from antiquity has oriented youth to become, in Homer's terms, "speakers of words and doers of deeds." As the normative groundwork for all other values required for the full realization of human nature and its potential, this understanding of education by the ancient Greeks forms the basis for the classical virtues of wisdom, courage, temperance, and justice. Illustrating such character strengths are the acquired capacities, respectively, to distinguish good from bad, endure hardship, control appetite, and give to each his or her due.

Ancient philosophy also asks, however, "Can virtue be taught?" Unquestionably it can, but must start with habit-formation in the young who cannot as yet theorize about virtue. Thus the capacities cited above must first be exemplified by parents, teachers, and others who possess them in good measure. For example, youth unaffected by those around them who wisely and courageously decide to defer sexual gratification will not be disposed later to reflect how control of such instincts is essential to the cultivation of maturer values such as lasting friendship and love.

As good role models for the young, adults must express their own wisdom by not intemperately or unjustly wielding their authority. For such irrational behavior may only make youth aimlessly rebellious or dumbly submissive, rarely imaginatively creative in defiant response. Inappropriate role modeling by family, peer, and media figures means that schools cannot always remedy the harm done to youth elsewhere. Arbitrary and willful teachers, counselors, and administrators, however, can only make things worse.

Even in modern societies and their public schools, *paideia* can never be value-free. Denominational values such as Protestant, Catholic, Jewish or Moslem piety cannot be taught. Without such teaching, can hegemony be allowed in a religiously pluralistic society? But pedagogical modeling of the classical virtues is a nonsectarian and universal human good upon which can also be based contemporary instructional and normative goals. Among these is the education of youth eventually to think and act for themselves so as not to remain uncritical and compliant proteges of their significant others. The aim is not to make of them ethical egoists, but to help free them from prejudice so that they will in time work for greater democracy at home and peace abroad.

In Dewey's and Kohlberg's terms, this marks the vital transition from preconventional and conventional levels of moral development to the postconventional. Such growth is from impulsive self-centeredness in childhood to habitual concern for significant others in adolescence to intellectual dedication to the general welfare and human rights as an adult. The same process, in Piaget's terms, is from the sensorimotor gestural and concrete operational to the formal operational stages of cognitive and moral growth. Illustrated, these are the student's initial sense of wrong when disobeying parents, subsequent guilt when breaking the rules of play or work with others, and, finally, dismay when he or she is an agent or observer of injustice done to oneself, familiars, or even strangers.

Paideia according to the classical teaching of social virtue and *paideia* according to the contemporary teaching of individual worth are therefore both essential to values education. It is the training of the student's mental faculties in such a way that he or she acquires a mature outlook along with a maximum cultural development. But should schools do more than provide good role models of virtue for youth? Should the curriculum empower the youth for more than the abstract reasoning necessary to deal with both numerical equations and equal rights? In short, is a special values education curriculum called for?

For Dewey it sufficed to make the schools community centers wherein cognitive learning was engendered by real and not just textbook tasks, and the aim, accordingly, was to help the young to become good problem-solvers—whether it was laboratory discovery of the mathematics and physics of aerodynamics, say, or the value of cooperative individualism while doing so. Knowledge consisted of hypotheses directed at practical difficulties, scientific, technical, aesthetic, or social, all of ethical value in skill building.

Kohlberg, however, favors more explicit values education. He would introduce young students to moral dilemmas in the classroom that typically relate stealing, for instance, to saving life. Values of property, loyalty, altruism, justice, indeed life itself, and others, are thereby examined against one another with increasing objectivity. Kohlberg would also make students responsible for dealing with the antisocial behavior of their fellow students—antisocial behavior ranging from stealing and drug-use to violence. Such curriculum attention to moralization does not seem inconsistent with Dewey's vision of schooling as an experimental apprenticeship in improving decision making by free men and women in the making, or students in school.

Inasmuch as school itself is already a society in which youthful egos or selves develop through interaction, active role-play affords further pedagogical opportunity in values education. Learning to take the roles both of "wrong-doer" and "victim" even for the young, under careful teacher guidance and direction, leads to mastery of the Golden Rule or the Kantian principle of generalizing rules to see if "the shoe fits" everyone. Lying, for example, loses its attraction when a student rehearses the parts of those he or she lies to, i.e., practices reciprocity.

Role playing stimulates both cognitive understanding and moral development this way via imagination. Imagination is natural to the young as seen by their love of storytelling. Perhaps, as Bettelheim argues, greater use should be made of fairy tales early on in values education. The Brothers Grimm, for example, deal with fundamental questions of good and bad, right and wrong, justice and injustice in images and settings fetching to children. They also depict the importance of the classical virtues of taking responsibility for one's own life. And they help the young to develop emotionally by resolving their conflicting attitudes towards parents, teachers, and others in authority, thus to reaffirm their trust in life and establish their sexual identity.

Such psychological strengths are as crucial to self-growth and social responsibility as the classical virtues. A programmatic values education cannot therefore disregard them. All such proposals, however, depend on one prime desideratum bearing on the preparedness of teachers, counselors, and administrators, if not also parents, school board members, and other taxpayers. This is that they know themselves by measuring their actions against the criteria of the social virtues, of respect for the worth of the individual, of pedagogical imagination and versatility, and of their own psychological or emotional maturity. Anyone seriously deficient in these respects is hardly to be entrusted with *paideia*.

See also Character Education; Social Studies Education; Student Responsibility; Teaching Approaches, Future.

—Erling Skorpen
University of Maine at Orono

References

Dewey, J, (1909). *Moral principles in education.* Boston: Houghton-Mifflin.

Kohlberg, L. (1976). Moral stages and moralization. In T. Lickona (Ed.), *Moral development and behavior* (pp. 31-53). New York: Holt, Rinehart & Winston.

Bettelheim, L. (1976). *The uses of enchantment.* New York: Knopf.

VANDALISM

Vandalism is a topic which has received extensive attention in the past several years because of its enormous impact upon society. Within schools it has taken a financial toll and has contributed to declining morale. The people who have had to face vandalism have been frustrated by trying to put an end to it; they have been puzzled by the sort of personality that it must take to be destructive. Dismay has been felt as people see the variety of ways in which the destruction can be done. Surprise has been expressed over the huge sums of money which have been and are being spent in attempting to control the problem.

Dealing with the Problem

In response to the problem, large school districts have employed expansive security forces. Other school systems have resorted to electrical equipment which will mechanically stand guard over its buildings. Some districts have put the responsibility directly on the building administrator. All sorts of combinations of the above methods are used along with sensitive efforts to include the students in the campaign to do away with vandalism.

Focal Points

Since the principal must establish the method for controlling vandalism within the school building, it would be appropriate for attention to be directed toward eight major focal points which can be addressed independently, but experience suggests that the greatest impact is gained by interrelating as many of them at one time as possible.

Student Role. Setting a tone is extremely important. Students need to be taught to take pride in the school and in its achievements; the principal and staff must focus attention upon the positive activities and successes of students.

Teacher Involvement. The teaching staff needs to have a sense of being needed in the process of protecting a building. Teachers must feel that the principal is there in the building with them, and that, if they catch a youngster doing something wrong, they will be backed up. Of course, members of the staff will have to help lock up the building; they will need to patrol the restrooms, and they will need to feel that everyone is doing his or her part. Paraprofessionals will have to be even more widely used.

Administrative Commitment. It is not enough that building administrators want things to go well; they must give a great deal of themselves. They may have to get firm agreements from the school board and superintendent in order that support will be there when it is needed. If discipline cases are taken to a hearing officer, that person must develop the on-going feeling that the cases are solid. Finally, it is essential that building administrators be out in the halls, especially when students are moving from one place to another.

Custodians. By spreading the custodians' hours around the clock seven days a week, one gains certain benefits and forfeits others. The custodians are not supervised. A great many pluses occur when the custodians are there all night. One, they lock the building. Two, they can open and close the building for special meetings. Three, anyone who is watching the premises with bad intent will know that someone is there twenty-four hours per day.

Parents' Roles. Parents can be a solid source of support. At the beginning of the year, the rules must be clearly stated to them. Having regular discussions adds to their sense of participation; they can ask questions and make suggestions in the discussion sessions. It is only by having the building administrator dealing with the parents fairly, consistently, and openly, that he or she gains support of the vast majority of the parents.

Neighbors. A principal or administrator would find it helpful to visit people who have homes adjoining the school property. The neighbors should be asked to call the principal if they see any problem around the school during school hours or the police if it is after school time. Arrange with the police for anonymity for callers. The schools will gain many more eyes and minds working on the problem of vandalism by enlisting the help of neighbors.

Police. The police officer in his security function at an extracurricular event or stationed in the school can be a great force for good or can bring about problems. School officials would be well-advised to screen the people they use and advise them as to how the problems are to be handled.

Professional Security. If the situation that exists is bad, one may have to turn to professional patrols. They are expensive, but they clearly give everyone the notion that the school system means business. Involvement by local police can be much more valuable in the long run and far less expensive! Praise by the school officials for the voluntary attention by on-duty patrolling officers is necessary.

Since school officials seldom have been trained in antivandalism techniques, it can be helpful to use outside consultants who have worked on the problem. Sometimes we make assumptions based on the knowledge of a given setting. A consultant can look at what is often an emotional problem and bring to it new insights.

See also Student Alienation; Violence in Schools.

—Karl Hertz
Mequon-Thiensville (Wisconsin) School District

References

Hertz, K.V. (1984, May). "Vandalism and school security." *National Association of Secondary School Principals' Bulletin, 69,* 1-2.

Zwier, G., & Vaughan, G.M. (1984, Summer). "Three ideological orientations in school vandalism research." *Review of Educational Research, 54,* 263-92.

VIOLENCE IN SCHOOLS

"Society prepares the crime; the criminal commits it." So said Count Alfieri almost two hundred years ago. School violence, in a real sense, mirrors the violence of the society which shapes the schools. The courts are beginning to mandate that school districts enforce the inalienable right of students and staff to a safe, secure, and peaceful school environment. This responsibility, however, must be shared by parents, students, educators, and community leaders.

Public schools have been invaded by crime and violence in recent years. Landmark research in the *Violent Schools-Safe Schools* study disclosed that during a one-month period (a) approximately 282,000 secondary students reported being attacked; (b) almost 8 percent of urban junior and senior high school students missed at least one day of school a month because they were afraid to attend; (c) approximately 5,200 secondary teachers were physically attacked, 1,000 of whom were injured seriously enough to require medical attention; and (d) approximately 525,000 attacks, shakedowns, and robberies occurred in public secondary schools in one month. The report concluded that the risk of violence to teen-agers was greater in school than anywhere else. Since the *Violent Schools-Safe Schools* study, these tragic trends have continued.

In a 1984 report on school violence and discipline submitted to President Reagan, his advisory panel concluded: An orderly school environment was essential to learning; disorder in some American schools was significant enough to pose obstacles to positive educational experiences; and, no amount of money, teacher raises, or improved facilities, materials, or curricula will encourage students to learn if they are distracted by fear.

Some students growing up in a violent society tend to perceive violence as a legitimate vehicle for conflict resolution. Because of the prevalence of crime and violence in and around many schools across America, an atmosphere of anxiety and apprehension of being criminally victimized often exists. This may result in bringing weapons to school, joining gangs for protection, truancy, or dropping out.

Clearly schools cannot improve until communities improve. This change requires a committed partnership effort. What can schools, parents, students and community leaders do to make school safe? (a) Hold community discussion forums to establish meaningful student, parent, and community participation that deals with specific school safety issues and potential solutions. (b) Track trends of school violence through effective incident reporting procedures. Evaluate when, where, who and why incidents occur. (c) Develop fair discipline codes and consistently enforce them with the assistance of all those affected, particularly students. (d) Develop positive discipline alternatives for violators including restitution and remediation strategies. (e) Provide support to students and staff who are victims of violence. (f) Develop high expectations of behavior and classroom performance for students. (g) Return character education and citizenship training to the school curriculum.

The issue is not the degree of school crime and violence, but rather the impact it has on the quality of our children's education. Students are missing school because they fear for their personal safety. Teachers are leaving the profession because they are tired of dealing with discipline problems. Educational quality is diminished in a climate of violence and fear. Students and staff are unsafe while we accept the conditions as a reflection of the community and society. The freedom of education and safety are two of the most prized rights in our democratic society. Reducing crime and violence in schools does not solve all our educational problems, but it is a major step towards that end.

See also Character Education; Community-School Involvement; School Security; Student Alienation.

—Ronald D. Stephens, Executive Director
National School Safety Center

References

Baker, K., & Rubel, R. (1980). *Violence and crime in the school.* Lexington, MA: D.C. Heath.

National School Board Association. (1984). *Toward better and safer schools.* Washington, DC: Author.

Rapp, J., Carrington, F., & Nicholson, G. (1986). *School crime and violence: victim's rights.* Malibu, CA: Pepperdine University Press.

VOCATIONAL EDUCATION

In many ways vocational education is unique within the secondary curriculum. Substantively it represents a strong competing focus—preparation for work—to the predominant academic curriculum. Administratively, vocational education programs are part of a complex arrangement of state and local advisory councils, local school districts, and federal and state funding patterns. While vocational teachers are part of the school organization in which they work, they are also responsive, and responsible to, state occupational area supervisors and local vocational program administrators.

Federal legislation authorizing expenditures for vocational education programs date from the 1917 Smith-Hughes Act. The need for this legislation grew out of seemingly contradictory desires to provide equal educational opportunities for all students by providing an education based on student background and socioeconomic class. Motivated by the increasing numbers of working class students enrolling in public schools, proponents of vocational education saw a practical, occupational education as most appropriate to their background and status. Today there are multiple purposes for vocational education. During the early 1980s, vocational education was touted as a key component in economic development activities. Vocational education could supply trained workers in areas for which there were critical shortages and lure firms into depressed areas. Now, in the mid-1980s, vocational education is coping with academic excellence, basic academic skills, and retention of potential dropouts in school.

The various amendments to the 1963 Vocational Education Act have emphasized different needs for vocational education, but two complementary purposes seem to have held fairly constant over the years as central to federal support for vocational education. A primary purpose is to meet local and regional needs for trained workers, especially in areas in certain skill shortages. A secondary and related purpose is to provide equal labor-market advantages for youth and adults in special groups—disadvantaged, gender minority, handicapped, displaced workers, limited-English proficiency, to name but a few.

Studies of the outcomes associated with participation in vocational education show that vocational program graduates who obtain employment in the area for which they were trained receive significant wage and employment benefits over comparable students without vocational education. Employers are generally positive toward vocational education as a provider of specific occupational skills. The majority of vocational graduates work in occupations related to those for which vocational education programs provide training—sales, clerical, crafts, and operatives occupations. Compared to similar students with no vocational education who go to work directly from high school, vocational program graduates have a clear advantage—if they seek and find work in the area for which they were trained.

Academically, vocational education is attracting groups of students in need of reinforcement and remediation in basic skills and is providing little instruction to meet that need. The reason why vocational education attracts students less proficient in basic academic skills is a mix of perceptions of vocational education as being "easy" and nonacademic, as simply fulfilling student expectations for their career and life roles, and as an organizational system within the schools that sorts students by background and ability into curriculum areas.

The current press for academic excellence and achievement has led some to question the utility of vocational education at the secondary level. National study commissions have asserted that the best preparation for work is a good general education, and that America's economic problems would be improved if high school students concentrated more on proficiency in basic academic skills, especially science and mathematics. The implication is that vocational education should be left for postsecondary programs at two- and four-year colleges and technical institutes. However, others worry that removing vocational education from the high school will deprive students moving directly into the labor market from high school of needed opportunities to learn entry-level job skills and to obtain the economic advantages associated with high school vocational education. Potentially, vocational education could provide a relevant and applied curriculum for potential dropouts and aid a college-bound youth in real life problem solving and applications of theoretical constructs.

The currency of the skills taught in vocational classes has been a perennial source of debate. On the one hand, there is a strong press to update the occupational content, to keep pace or even predate emerging technologies and their applications. Now, however, attention to academic achievement and the retention of dropouts has forced vocational education to consider the time and attention given to instruction and reinforcement of basic academic skills. To some, if vocational education is to survive in the high school, it must upgrade and diversify the content of what is taught.

Strategies for school administrators in working with vocational education programs and personnel must emphasize coordinating and integrating the vocational program with the rest of the instructional program. For example, scheduling can effectively separate vocational program students from their peers. Due to laboratory periods or even scheduling part-time periods in area vocational skills centers, vocational students frequently are cut off from interaction with nonvocational students. Effort needs to be made to integrate those students with their nonvocational peers in common courses.

Success for vocational education may require developing and articulating more effective relationships with other employment and training systems. As alluded to above, the relationship of secondary vocational education to the rest of the secondary curriculum is being called into question. Vocational education at the secondary level must strive to integrate programs and students more closely with the rest of the high school. Similarly, vocational education must differentiate and relate its programs to those offered by and under the Job Training Partnership Act (JTPA), two-year postsecondary colleges and technical institutes, and a variety of other employment-training deliveries.

Vertical coordination can be improved by developing coordinated programs with local two- and four-year postsecondary schools. Such programs insure that vocational students are able to maximize high-school training especially in technological areas. Such programs might provide the basics in a given field during students' junior year and senior year of high school. Specific occupational skills are then taught at the postsecondary level, utilizing the core concepts and skills developed in high school.

See also Business Education; Industrial Arts Education.

—Linda Lotto
University of Illinois

References

National Commission on Secondary Vocational Education (1984). *The unfinished agenda.* Columbus, OH: The National Center for Research in Vocational Education, Ohio State University.

Silberman, H.F. (1982). *Education and work. Eighty-first yearbook of the National Society for the Study of Education, Part II.* Chicago, IL: The University of Chicago Press.

WOMEN IN ADMINISTRATION

While women dominate the teaching field, they remain an underrepresented group in the administrative ranks of the nation's schools. This is particularly true in secondary school principalships and superintendencies. The reasons women are underrepresented are complex and are directly related to their roles in society. Although women have emerged as a major component in the entire work force, their career aspirations are often limited. The realities of family responsibilities and the lack of early career orientation during the educational years continue to limit the career futures for many women. All too often females realize too late that their male counterparts do have more experience and preparation and have demonstrated an earlier, more continuous commitment to career.

Although statistical reports often appear bleak, there is evidence that increasing numbers of women are in entry-level positions such as dean, assistant principal, director, coordinator, or department chairperson. This, in itself, is encouraging since it is from this pool that principals and superintendents will emerge.

The problems in obtaining administrative positions for women are similar to those of many males, but they are often magnified. The reality of dual career families places constraints on the mobility of many prospective potential administrators. Furthermore, while not as unusual as it was ten years ago, it remains less likely that families will relocate due to a female spouse's upward mobility and career advancement. It also is a reality that, in general, females, more than males, will interrupt their employment, defer their educational plans, or subordinate their career aspirations due to child-bearing/child-rearing responsibilities. Even as women in today's society develop increasing degrees of comfort with their dual roles and develop higher expectations, their problems in obtaining positions are magnified.

Given the low number of women in administrative positions, few appropriate role models exist. This creates a problem not only for women in applying for positions but for those charged with interviewing and hiring. The typical or "expected" image of the administrator for most hiring bodies remains that of a male. Thus, just as women do not have the benefit of observing many successful women in the roles to which they aspire, employers suffer from a similar lack of experience and are part of a society accustomed to seeing males in administrative positions. Faced with a female candidate, employers see the unique rather than the ordinary. This very basic problem of being "unusual" or "different" will diminish only gradually. Women need time

to continue what has been for many slow but steady progress and to become more visible in entry-level administrative or quasi-administrative positions. Only by occupying more administrative positions will women be able to demonstrate leadership and management skills seen as essential preliminary qualifications by prospective employers of administrators.

For any new administrator, male or female, the first year in an administrative position is a challenge and offers new pressures. For the most part, these pressures are not gender-based. By virtue of the new position, all new administrators become, to some degree, public figures who serve as representatives of their schools. All administrators, as an example, find their communication skills are quickly tested. They encounter, on a daily basis, situations which require them to exhibit excellent oral and written skills with pupils, parents, faculty, and fellow administrators in both large and small group settings.

It is likely that women, in these situations, will be a particularly visible minority, and this visibility can create additional problems and pressures. Not only is it likely that these women may be subjected to closer scrutiny because their numbers are few, but they may experience more isolation than men. Most new administrators, while experiencing increased responsibility and authority in their new roles, also experience feelings of deprivation due to the missing reinforcements which came to them through close and continuous daily interactions with students. No matter how helpful or supportive male colleagues are or try to be, females in new roles still do not have the benefit of observing female colleagues in the same numbers as do men.

Dealing with conflict, longer days, and more evening activity is a major adjustment which needs to be made by the new administrator and also her family. Establishing priorities, as well as determining trade offs, is the response required of any administrator in the first year; these adjustments, however, are often more difficult for women than for men due to the expectations held for women by families, colleagues and, indeed, themselves.

Observers and writers over the years have been quick to attribute certain weaknesses to females in administrative roles and to create a number of stereotypes. Recently many of these observations have been labeled as myths, and researchers have generated evidence that women administrators are as, if not more, effective than men.

Women ordinarily bring more years of experience in classrooms to their first year as administrators; thus, they come to their positions with a rich background of strategies which can be helpful to teachers in improving instruction. Women emerge in various studies and surveys as particularly strong in areas such as working with their staffs and using collaborative techniques in problem solving. Coupled with some of the gender-based, positive characteristics such as compassion, understanding, and nurturing attributed to women as a group, it is easy to see why women in administration receive high marks for their performance in evaluating the school staff and providing instructional leadership for the school. The school staff is often traditional and may be reluctant initially to accept the female administrator. Despite this, faculty members do respond favorably to the interest women show in student learning and the professional performance of teachers. Furthermore, women are judged to gain more satisfaction than men from supervising the instructional aspects of their schools.

See also Affirmative Action; Sex Discrimination; Sex Role Stereotyping.

—Mary Ann Lynn
Illinois State University

References

Biklen, S.K., & Brannigan, M.B. (Eds.). (1980). *Women and educational leadership*. Lexington, MA: D.C. Heath.

Gross, N., & Trask, A.E. (1976). *The sex factor and the management of schools* (chaps. 7 & 15). New York: John Wiley.

Shakeshaft, C. (1986). *Women in educational administration*. Beverly Hills, CA: Sage.

Index

by Linda Webster